Architects

of

Self-Destruction

Architects

of

Self-Destruction

The Oral History of Leftöver Crack

by Brad Logan
and
John Gentile

Rare Bird
Los Angeles, Calif.

THIS IS A GENUINE RARE BIRD BOOK

Rare Bird Books
453 South Spring Street, Suite 302
Los Angeles, CA 90013
rarebirdlit.com

Set in Dante
Printed in the United States

Grim Reaper Cover Image by Nick Gomez © 2021 / @nickgomezprints

10 9 8 7 6 5 4 3 2 1

Publisher's Cataloging-in-Publication Data available upon request.

For Alec, Nick, Brandon, and Jack.

"It is certain that we can't escape anguish, for we are anguish"
—Sartre

Foreword
by Damian Abraham

By the time Choking Victim showed up on my radar, ska was well into its third wave. All the vibrancy of the original Jamaican first wave and the uniqueness of the cultural cross-pollinating second wave UK Two-Tone scene was gone in my eyes. This time ska was grafted onto the sunny SoCal EpiFat punk that was the predominant punk sound of the time. Seemingly spurned on by the commercial breakthroughs of bands like No Doubt and Goldfinger, the ska bands of this new era seemed to be increasingly poppy and generic. By the late nineties, "ska-punk" had become a pejorative and an almost shorthand for disingenuous white suburban careerists that saw the path to rock stardom paved with syncopation and Warped Tour skank pits.

Released in the heady days of the summer of 1997, "Give Them the Boot" was a cheapo CD sampler to herald the arrival of Rancid's Tim Armstrong's Hellcat Records. With a fantastic mix of songs and a price point under five dollars, it became a staple in the CD collection of seemingly every kid I knew. At the time, I was helping out on a popular local punk radio show and we played the shit out of that thing! Of all the songs we played off it, the band that people responded to most was Choking Victim.

The band's breakneck speed and the lyrical rawness hit differently than most of the other ska-punk making waves at the time. This wasn't a pop song about good times or love, it was a punk song about having scabies. Much in the same way that Operation Ivy was a punk band that happened to love ska music, Choking Victims' approach to music never seemed to be a genre exercise. The realness of it all seemed to bleed out of the speakers. And sure enough, as stories about them began to spread through the pre-internet punk network, it was clear very quickly that this was not a band doing any sort of cosplay.

And then it was over. Leaving behind a handful of singles and a posthumous LP, they seemed destined to follow in the footsteps of Operation Ivy and become a band whose legend would only grow with time. But in the same way Op Ivy was just prologue for what was to come, the demise of Choking Victim merely set the stage for what Sturgeon had planned for the next act.

As someone that can attest to the power of a visceral band name, few are as jarring as Leftover Crack and given the, by then, well-known relationship with drugs that certain band members had, it felt particularly blunt. At the same time, the name reflects the honesty that this band embodies. What Leftover Crack has to say might not always be pretty or even be something I personally agree with, but it is always their truth. The same can be said for this book, which is honest even when very ugly.

Leftover Crack seems very much like the last of a certain type of New York band—pre-Giuliani—from a time when squats not condos went up in derelict buildings. The changing face of New York itself becomes a secondary character as this under acknowledged part of New York's punk history is told in the background of this story: from Squat or Rot to Coney Island High to 9/11 and beyond.

This book has been absolutely essential for helping my understanding of, in my mind, one of punk's most interesting bands. Tales of onstage blowups, getting banned from all manner of venues, and the general chaos that seemed to engulf the band are in endless supply. Touring in Fucked Up, we would hear stories from former roadies and promoters about how it became too much for them. Choking Victim is a band so storied that at times the myths can obscure the reality.

This book pulls back the lore enough to expose the actualities of things. As much as it is about one of punk's wildest bands, it's also a story steeped in tragedy and triumph. It's the tale of a band whose sonic innovations have had world-wide reverberations all while remaining brutally uncompromising artistic.

A couple of years ago, we got the chance to play with Leftover Crack at the Bouncing Souls 30th Anniversary show. I had known Brad Logan for a few years by that point but hadn't ever had a chance to see them live. The show was fantastic! Sturgeon was on another level as a front person. After the show, I heard stories of an inter-band parking lot fight. No matter how much you try and separate the band's creative output from the strife, one has to understand how it informs the music. That is the reason why their music has always stood out. Leftover Crack's music is inseparable from the lives they lived. It is political and also intensely personal.

Great artists bring you into their world. They live in their art to the point that they become indivisible from it. They allow viewers to journey inside. Few punk bands have lived their art more than Leftover Crack and showed the world a more orthodox version of the punk experience.

Damian Abraham
of Fucked Up, *Turned Out a Punk*
May 2021

Prelude

Brad Logan (Hellcat Employee; Guitar—Leftover Crack, F-Minus): Sturgeon is curled up on a bench in Tompkins Square Park and his face is covered in blood. He has a black eye. Drugs are spilling out of his pockets. I'm supposed to be Hellcat Record's "A&R" guy, and I'm supposed to be helping record Choking Victim's album, which we just started.

Sturgeon looks up at me and mumbles, "I'm not recording today, I quit! I walked over to Skwert's house and he punched me! That's it! It's over!"

I am supposed to fly back to California and tell Tim Armstrong that we recorded the Choking Victim album and it was amazing and everyone would love it. Instead, the band had gotten into a fistfight, the singer had gotten his ass kicked, and they were breaking up on the second day of recording.

"So much for being an A&R guy," I thought. How could anyone be in a band with these guys? How did I get in this situation? How could things get any worse?

1
Hellcat

Brad Logan: I was an errand boy for Hellcat Records, which was Tim Armstrong's label. That's Tim from Rancid. I had been a roadie for Rancid for the past three years. I tuned guitars and set up band gear onstage. We were on tour continuously starting September 1995 with the *Out Come the Wolves* tour. Tim and I became pretty good friends and we got really close. One day Tim tells me, "I'm going to start a record label and I'm calling it Hellcat. I got this girl named The Wix who's gonna run it, and if you want, you can work there too, between tours." I didn't think twice. I said, "Sounds like a great idea, count me in!"

The Wix (Hellcat Employee #2): Tim Armstrong was renegotiating a new record deal with Brett Gurewitz and had said he'd stay with Epitaph if he could have his own label. He knew I worked for Moon/Ska Records and Vic Ruggerio had spoken highly of me. Tim had gotten to know me a little bit so he asked if I would be interested in running a label.

I asked Tim if I could sign bands that I liked and he said "well… yeah!" Tim is a really gracious guy and he's really open. What I saw and learned a lot from him was a lot of humility and respect to everyone. He believed in me. Tim and I discussed it. We wanted the bands to have full artistic control, but we wanted to get them out there, and Epitaph had Sony distribution across the world.

Charlie Ackerman (Hellcat Employee #3): At Epitaph records, I did publicity, I did marketing, I did a magazine. Then, when I worked at Hellcat Records, I was the number three employee and The Wix was number two, before Chris LaSalle. Everyone at Hellcat was really tight knit. I was fourteen years old when I started there, and I was sixteen when I met Brad Logan. I literally grew up at Epitaph records. It was my high school and college.

Christina White (Epitaph Records—Radio and Publicity Department): I think that Charlie Ackerman was one of the first people to have inside knowledge at the label. Charlie was a teenager—he was Brett's cousin or nephew or some shit and that motherfucker was like fifteen or sixteen years old, rolling around with adult degenerate record label executives…if you could call us executives. "Executives." I don't think a lot of people had a lot of outside proper music industry experience. Most of us were kids out of the scene who were like, "Oh, I have a brain, and they saw something in us and thought we could do this." And we thought, "oh, we *could* do this!" We were all making pretty good money and we were living in Hollywood and there was a bar scene.

One day, it was like, "Oh, hey, so Brett's doing a label with Tim. It's called Hellcat and this is Chris and The Wix…" I don't remember their titles except that The Wix was seeing one of the guys from the Slackers and Chris used to hang out with Run-DMC. That's what I remember. I think that's as far as it went.

Charlie Ackerman: So, I was talking to Brett and Brett told me that they had this thing going on with Tim. Brett was always very vague—he was also high as a kite at the time, which didn't help. He said Tim was going to have his own label and it was described to me as the "punk rock Dr. Dre and Death Row." That didn't end well... neither one...one ended better than the other...

Then, one day, this crazy broad called "The Wix" shows up. I say crazy only in the most positive way, but...she was a *crazy* fuckin' broad. And it was a whirlwind from there. Then we put out the fuckin' *Give 'em the Boot* compilation that had Rancid, the Slackers, F-Minus on it. I compiled that. Tim would listen to everything a million times and overanalyze it and ask everyone's opinion a million times. Wix made the cover in one night with Jesse Fisher—there was *this* version, there was *that* version—they did some ghetto Photoshop, made it look like a photocopy when it wasn't a fuckin' photocopy, and they banged it out in one night.

The Wix was stressed out all the time, but I don't know about what. She was the closest friend I had at the time, but I have no idea why she was stressed out.

Brad Logan: I think the Wix had a lot of pressure on her as the manager of the newly formed Epitaph offshoot. I could be wrong, but I don't remember her powers as being specifically defined. It must have been fucking anxiety inducing. As for me, my job description was rather ambiguous too, but I didn't really give a shit. I was having fun. I was on the payroll but I'm not sure if Brett Gurewitz even knew who I was.

Seth Olenick (Photographer; Hellcat Records Intern): At the time at Epitaph, Brett Guerewitz wasn't around. I never met him. Andy Kaulkin was running everything. Chris LaSalle was really good to me. And he's good to you as long as you're useful to him, and then, when you're not... It's funny, I was there a lot when it was, "Hey, Chris, this call is for you," and he was like, "Yeah, tell them I'm in a meeting," "Tell them I'm busy." He was good to me...for a time...

The Wix: We didn't really have employees so much. We used the infrastructure of Epitaph that was already there. They had a "bullpen." They had a marketing team. They had an art department. Brett Gurewitz is a genius. It was a very cool atmosphere. There was a cactus garden and he encouraged people to take breaks. There were video games and there were massages every Friday. He would bring someone in to do the massages. It was the nineties. It was how I imagine Microsoft is like today. It was very relaxed.

Brad Logan: With Hellcat, I was always "on-call." I didn't have set hours. I wasn't sure if I really had a job there, but I got a check every two weeks, so I guess I did?

We even had pagers! But it was more like a crew than a job. We were all friends off the clock. Me, Tim, Wix, Charlie, and Chris LaSalle. We would roll together to go see bands or to taco stands, movies, all over. It was one of the best times of my life. I guess what I did for Hellcat was a little bit of everything. I say I "swept the floors" and "cleaned the toilets," but really it was more like clerical things—help with ad artwork, running masters to the pressing plant, picking up finished orders, stuffing envelopes. And in some cases, like with Agnostic Front and Choking Victim, I was the go-between for band and label. At least initially. I didn't have the power to sign anyone or discuss "business." But I would just be sent out to meet bands, hang out with them, and get a feel for who they were as people, and convince them to sign to this label that I thought was totally great.

I think that's why Tim wanted me out there—either that or he couldn't find anything else for me to do. Most of the heavy lifting, business and production-wise, was done by the Epitaph staff.

Charlie Ackerman: I'm not even sure what Brad did. But I had a bullshit job, too. I guess I was there for youthful exuberance. It almost felt like when some band would come to look at the office, we were there as the "flash cash on the drug deal" that was the record transaction.

Tim was cool. He was a very unique individual. I think that Tim is a lovely man but I fancied him the Howard Hughes of punk rock. Very reclusive, very secretive, very mysterious. He still lives in a big house up on the hill. He was a really sweet dude and totally took care of me and looked out for me. But he was always very strange.

Normally, if you're having a conversation—just two guys talking—maybe we want to do something, so we establish what to do without thinking that there may be an alternative plan…but not so with Tim. He always holds something back or is thinking that there is something else at work. But it's gotta be hard for a dude. He was the biggest punk rock star at the time and everyone was trying to finagle something out of him, so I suppose you get a little suspicious. I lived at his house forever and was there constantly. He was always great to me. He was always kind. But he always seemed strange.

Brad Logan: Tim hears and sees things that most people miss. He can see potential in other people that I'm not sure that they can see in themselves. I think with some of the artists signed to Hellcat, he could see value in them when very few others could.

2

Victim Comes Alive

Brad Logan: Hellcat received a demo cassette. It had "Choking Victim" written on the face of the tape and nothing else. Maybe it came with a note. Charlie said to me, "You gotta hear this shit! It's amazing!" I think Tim had given it to him. The first thing I thought was, "Cool name!"

I was blown away immediately. Tim already knew about them and had met Sturgeon before. I remember Tim saying to me, "They're the only punk-ska band around that reminds me of what we were doing in Operation Ivy." Well, I didn't know shit about Operation Ivy, but I knew there were about a million crappy "ska-punk" bands at the time. And they all worshipped Op Ivy, so that was a heavy endorsement. On the demo was "500 Channels" and maybe a few more. Tim asked me if I would go to New York and contact the singer to get the ball rolling on making a Choking Victim record with Hellcat.

After that, I have no idea how I found Sturgeon. These were the days of landlines and pagers. No computers, no cell phones. Tim had handed me a crumpled piece of paper with a phone number scrawled on it. It turned out to be Sturgeons mom's number. I phoned and left a message with her. A week later Sturgeon called me back. When I got to NYC, we arranged to meet in front of Coney Island High, which was a punk club on St. Marks between Second and Third Avenues. I walked down St. Marks and noticed a guy sitting on the ground in front the club. He looked like a young, dirty, homeless guy—dreadlocked and dressed in all black. "This has gotta be my guy," I thought. It was!

As we walked down the street chit-chatting, the first thing I noticed was that his speaking voice sounded just like his singing voice. He seemed highly intelligent, and possessed a warped sense of humor, just like mine. He was also one of the more politically conscious people I had met at the time. I think that was the first thing we connected on. We talked music, books, small talk mostly. He was well-read and had pretty good taste in music—eighties new wave, classic rock, weird shit for a young punk. You can tell a lot about a person by what they listen to, read, and watch on TV.

Sturgeon (Singer/Guitar—No Commercial Value, Choking Victim, Leftover Crack, Star Fucking Hipsters): Brad and I have a chemistry. We're good-humored people. In general, we're not ill-natured or nasty mean people. When we are in conversation, we like to make people laugh. He's quick-witted. That's not something you can practice.

Brad is a really honest person. He comes from Southern California and that is where people won't tell you the truth to your face. Or they will act nice to you even if they don't like you. In New York, you tell them to cut the shit because that's not how things operate.

Brad goes off quickly like a powder keg. He can be very short tempered—especially if he hasn't gotten enough sleep. If he's angered, he'll get upset over things that he probably shouldn't get upset over. We usually yell for a minute or two and then usually, within a few minutes, we drop our anger and talk about it without remaining angry and work it out. I can't remember arguing with Brad and it not being resolved quickly.

Brad Logan: I'm probably the only guy in the band that has never physically attacked Sturgeon.

He and I would get into arguments and shouting matches. "Fuck you!" "No, fuck you!" "No, fuck *you!*" "No, fuck YOU!" "No, FUCK YOU!!!"

But we would always resolve it. The bottom line is that we are friends and we always work it out. Sturgeon *always* needs to be right...but *so do I...*

I think on the inside Sturgeon is a pretty sensitive guy. And the roots of these songs are based in a longing for a better world, one where people aren't so shitty to one another. I mean, that's what I see at least.

Ara Babajian (Drummer—Leftover Crack, Star Fucking Hipsters, the Slackers): Scott is the most lovable narcissist/sociopath you'll ever meet. You'd die for him, but he wouldn't die for anybody. I'll give a couple examples of who he might really be, because honestly, I'm not sure who he really is. I remember a picture of him at his mom's house that I always used to see—just a sweet eighth-grade boy. He could have been class president, staring back at me with all the hope in the world.

I remember him coming to my apartment one time, using up all the ice in the ice trays, and refilling them only about halfway, as if to say, "Yeah, I understand your conventions. But I'm not going to follow them *completely.*" I remember when I worked in a bookstore in the East Village in the early nineties and he would come in and just sit on the floor for hours because C-Squat was freezing and he just wanted to be somewhere warm that had free water where he could read the latest issue of *Eightball.*

Greg Daly (Tour manager—Leftover Crack, Choking Victim, Napalm Death, many others): Sturgeon's really smart. He can be crazy. But you can look back lyrically at what he's been singing for two or three decades, and he's not wrong about a lot of things. You wish he was for our sake, but he's not.

Jack Terricloth (Singer—World/Inferno Friendship Society): Sturgeon is a singer and he's playing a character that is unhappy with himself. But don't all singers? Sturgeon is coming from a place of angst. I think Sturgeon is just expressing himself. In actuality, I don't think he is actually unhappy. I think he is very happy with himself in real life. I've had this conversation with other members of World/Inferno while Leftover Crack was on stage. Sturgeon's a performer. He's like a Ziggy Stardust as opposed to a David Bowie.

Alice Hour (Singer—In Evil Hour): Sturgeon is an incredibly intelligent, talented individual, and he's a fucking great songwriter. He also has the ability to distill a topic in a way that is accessible to people with a layer of offense that is absolutely delightful to people. The man is pure unrestrained id. He just does without thinking. He is impulsive, reactionary, unpredictable, and that's what we like him for. He definitely does not always get it right, but that's what we like him for, too.

Mikey Erg (Drummer—Star Fucking Hipsters, The Ergs, Direct Hit!, Worriers, 7,419 other bands): Sturgeon's so well-rounded, musically. That made so much sense as to why I was drawn to his bands in the first place. He likes everything. He can take in a lot of musical information and can put it out so it doesn't sound like the same old punk rock stuff.

Pete Steinkopf (Guitar—Bouncing Souls; Producer): Leftover Crack are not afraid to talk about the darker side of life—but they always keep some sort of positivity in their message. That's something that people miss. They balance concepts and musical ideas that no one else could.

Joe Jack Talcum (Vocals / Guitar—Dead Milkmen, Low Budgets): Leftover Crack and Choking Victim always seemed like normal people to me. I think Sturgeon's normal. Maybe what's normal to me isn't normal to other people? I've played shows with Leftover Crack and Sturgeon. It always went well and nothing happened. I think Sturgeon is an amazing songwriter. He writes catchy songs that are easy to sing along to. He has a lot of humor in his songs, like Dead Milkemen do, sometimes—dark humor. That's one of the reasons I like his music.

Jesse Cannon (Producer/Engineer): Between Choking Victim and Leftover Crack, you never get that many people that have that much vision in one band that are also stubborn as fuck about achieving that vision—so it's no wonder the people in those bands can never get along with each other.

Skwert (Drummer—Choking Victim): When I first heard about Scott, I didn't really care about what people thought of him, because...people maybe thought I was a jerk, too. One of my friends, who is now dead, was not cool with him. He was like, "Man, fuck that guy!" And I was like, "Why?" But I never really could get to the bottom of it. When I met Sturgeon, we just clicked musically and that was it. Jon Dolan, the Choking Victim drummer before me, gave me the sticks. He said, "Alright, I'm out," he didn't say why, and I was in. We were more musical collaborators than we were friends.

When we first had contact with Hellcat records, Hellcat had reservations because we were some young little shits. They didn't know us, and they didn't know what they were getting into. We were less a solid bet than the Pietasters or Slackers. Those are bands that were working, or professional. We were just…just a ball of energy, if you will.

Sturgeon: The first time I met Skwert he was in a band called the Foul-Mouthed Elves from Boston. The only thing that I remember about them is that they played a cover of Dead Kennedy's "Moon Over Marin" and it sounded really good. I feel like I never paid attention to that song before. I used to go to C-Squat after school and jam with people. I didn't know that C-Squat had only been there for about a year.

I had no idea that the muddiness of the basement was due to the building only being open for a year. Popeye would be down there and maybe Webbie, and whoever else was a musician. I didn't actually play with Skwert for a while.

Denise Vertucci (Head of Fistolo Records; Mischief Brew contributor): Whenever Choking Victim would play in Baltimore, Sturgeon would end up staying at my dorm in Loyola. I remember him looking at my wall, which had Rancid posters on it, or maybe just a magazine article with Tim Armstrong, and Sturgeon thought it was so funny that he was signed to the label of the guy that was on my wall.

It was always fun when Sturgeon came down because he and my roommate wouldn't get along. She's awesome, but she was definitely not a punk and she's very opinionated and he's very opinionated so they always clashed. It was actually comical. What set her over the edge was she, Sturgeon, and I were coming back from the movies in suburban Baltimore and maybe she was speeding and…we got pulled over. I saw the cop walking up to the car and he was looking at Sturgeon and I was like, *"Oooh nooo…"* The cop said to Sturgeon, "Is that a real tattoo?" and Sturgeon said, "Is that a real gun?"

I was like, "Oh, my God, we are all going to jail." She wasn't really happy with him after that.

Brad Logan: Choking Victim got on the *Give 'em the Boot* compilation, which was put together by Tim, the Wix, and Charlie. It had bands on the Hellcat roster and a few others.

Charlie Ackerman: Then, just after *Give 'em the Boot* came out, all of the Choking Victim dudes just showed up at Hellcat! It was Sturgeon, Skwert, and Shayne plus Skwert's girlfriend and two giant fuckin' dogs—they all just showed up uninvited…I think Tim had talked to Sturgeon by saying "you should come out" with no actual invitation intended and they just posted up. They came out and it was like…*what?*

Sturgeon: Hellcat was dragging its feet and we had nothing to do with our lives. We went out there uninvited and showed up.

Charlie Ackerman: They had fuckin' nowhere to go. I was like sixteen living at my mom's house in the valley. I was like, "You can crash at my mom's house, I guess." I had all of fucking Choking Victim living in my mom's poolroom for the better part of…it was a minute. They actually lived in the poolroom in the backyard.

Seth Olenick: The first time I met Sturgeon was 1998. I was an intern at Hellcat at the time. He was staying at Charlie's place and Charlie was my boss even though Charlie was younger than me. Sturgeon would come in every now and then.

I had to drive him around at one point. He stunk. He smelled like rotten ass. Over the years, I would go to C-Squat. Eventually, you do get used to the squatter smells.

He never changed his clothes when I saw him. As far as I know, he stayed in those clothes. I shot a lot of the early Leftover Crack shows. Looking back at the pictures, his clothes were *always* the same.

Mike Trujillo (Producer): With Sturgeon, there are immediate aromatic aspects. He was a little crusty, a little stinky. That's certainly something. At the time, he was probably using drugs more. So when I first met him, he just seemed enthusiastic and was basically squatting in LA—he may have been popping pills—that might have impacted his presence. When you're scavenging and you're a squatter you're always trying to figure out where you're going to stay or eat or get a ride somewhere—so that sort of energy was around him.

Charlie Ackerman: Sturgeon was always just Sturgeon—pilled out of his fuckin' mind constantly. On Klonopins all the time. I *did not like* Sturgeon when I met him. It felt like he was always trying to get one over on me, take advantage of something. And the culture at Epitaph was that "you take care of your bands, you take care of your artists, and you do whatever you can do." I tried to do that and it always felt like he was reaching into my pocket. "Can I get one more thing? Can I get one *more* thing?"

I remember Skwert was pissed because he thought they were coming out to do something, and they were not in fact doing *anything*. I liked Skwert. Shayne was sweet. Sturgeon just fucked up the whole thing. A crackly ass junked-out mess of a giant Klonopin.

I think they ended up at The Wix's place. Then, they moved to Brad's garage.

Sturgeon: We eventually ended up living in Brad Logan's garage when we were waiting. Living in Brad's garage was not a party. It wasn't a garage attached to a house. There was no toilet or running water. There wasn't even a normal door. We had to manually hoist up the rusty garage door and slam it down to get in and out. We would go and panhandle across the street at 7-Eleven and then we would walk the mile plus in the oppressive LA heat in our all black, long sleeve, long pants, dirty squatter clothes to the Epitpah offices and hang out there all day, stinking up their offices.

So, the Wix paid for us to stay at the Olive motel, a crack motel across from Hellcat. It was probably the last one of two crack motels on Sunset. It's a now a boutique hotel, which is just a shitty motel with carpet and paint. We each had our own room. It was twenty-five bucks a night, but if you stayed a week it was twenty bucks a night. There was a fancier hotel that was like ten bucks more a night, so I never stayed there. I was like, "Fuck this! I'm gonna stay at the twenty-five-bucks-a-night hotel." Then, I was like, "Damn, that's a lot of money!" Now, you can't get a thirty-dollar hotel anywhere.

Once, we heard shots. We're musicians and we're not getting up before noon. But somebody drove behind the Olive Motel and got in a standoff with the LAPD. It sounded like fireworks. Gunshots just started. Somebody got shot like fifty times. It didn't even make the news because those things didn't make the news then.

I got up and went to Skwert's room and there was a bullet hole in the window. I think the parking lot from behind the hotel room was a little higher than the hotel, so the cops didn't mind spraying the wall. So, if you were eight feet tall…or getting an airplane ride from your daddy…you'd have gotten shot.

3

Epitaph Records

Mike Trujillo: I ran into Sturgeon and he said, "I really want to record some songs right now," and I had just purchased my first digital sixteen-track recorder to start recording bands. I asked if he wanted to come record for free in my garage.

We did a cover of "Money Changes Everything," "Fucked Reality," and "Hate Yer State." Two of the songs were released as the *Victim Comes Alive* seven-inch.

Charlie Ackerman: When they finally got the record contract together, they're over at Mike Trujillo's place in Highland Park. I lived in Highland Park, too. Sturgeon had nowhere to go and they didn't give him enough money in his contract—they left the homeless guy to be homeless and roam around. "Here's money to record your record and that's it." So, I was like, "Alright, dude, you can stay at my pad."

I had Sturgeon come over to the house. I have my roommate there, so I jokingly said to him, "You can take a shower three times a week and stay inside or you can sleep on the patio." Motherfucker spent two months on the patio! After he leaves, there are piss buckets and piss bottles and I'm like, "Motherfucker, the bathroom was right *THERE*, dude!" Ya know?

Sturgeon: I only stayed at Charlie's place for a week. We might have stayed at his mother's a couple of times. I don't remember whom he lived with, but Charlie did not understand where we came from or why we were homeless.

A sixteen-year-old, he's going to be, "I'm going to use strong language when it comes to Sturgeon's smell." I remember the first time I was in an enclosed space with a squatter. I followed a friend into the hallways in an apartment above San Loco and the stench was potent.

I didn't like it at first, but as time went on, I grew to not notice and then embrace it. If someone is going to piss themselves or shit their pants, that's a different level. But if you are keeping it clean and wiping your ass with toilet paper and not neglecting anything, the odor is not that bad. Something about human stench—it somehow equalizes when you don't shower for a while. Your body gets to know that it's not showering and dampens down and turns into a different animal that really is not that unpleasant.

Charlie Ackerman: He'd come inside to hang out. He was there for two months and was just pilled-out the whole time. You could always tell because his voice would just go to crap: "Krrrkkrkrkrkrkrr!" "Jesus Christ, he's fucked up again, bro!" But, I've had worse houseguests. I don't think he stole anything.

Brad Logan: Sturgeon's not a thief. He might steal from a chain store, but he's not a thief.

Christina White: My office was upstairs at Epitaph, in the balcony. It was big open sky windows, lots of light. It was me, Kim-Chi, and Charlie. We had these big desks and this big, beautiful, gorgeous down-couch. Sturgeon's ass rolls up and wants to take a nap.

Sturgeon starts to lay on my big, beautiful couch and I say, "Nuh-uh, buddy, no way. You can get your stinky ass off the couch…

so, no way." Sturgeon's like, "Yeah fine, well, fuck you, whatever," and he goes downstairs to the mailroom. He picks out a cardboard box and then flattens out the cardboard box and brings it upstairs and lays it on the couch and then lies down. I was so impressed with his tenacity. That's pretty ingenious, you know? "This bitch doesn't want me to dirty up her couch, so I'll lie down on this cardboard!"

And then it got around the office, "Oh, did you hear what Trashy said to Sturgeon?" and it sort of made me look prissy, which I am.

To be really fucking honest, I had never engaged in any of that kind of behavior, like squatting. I wasn't a crust punk or a train punk, so I just knew that they were staying with The Wix, or sleeping in the cactus garden, and when they got some money they'd stay at the Olive.

Sturgeon: Pennywise was on a skateboard video game where you would stand on the skateboard and jump around, sweating your ass off. They had that in the Epitaph boardroom and we would sit there and play on that all day. We would make long-distance calls and use their computers. We would make copies. We treated it like a drop-in center. We probably annoyed most people working there. But at the time we didn't care.

I might have sold some copies of *The Gang's All Here* and the *Suffer* to a record store on Hollywood Boulevard. They had to have known I was doing that. I think they had an informant at the store because whenever an intern did that, they would get fired. But I guess they couldn't fire me.

At some point, I noticed that food would be in the fridge for days, a whole week, and then it would disappear because the cleaning people would throw it out on Friday. I would try to eat all the leftovers at the end of the week. But I got so used to that, that the last time we visited Epitaph and were playing a show, I was like, "this could be a leftover," and I ate it, and someone walked past, looking like a sad puppy dog, and I was like, "I crossed the line...I think I just ate someone's lunch..."

Mike Trujillo: Sturgeon was sleeping at Epitaph. People at Epitaph weren't ready for that level of punk rock. It was polished southern California punk bands that were relatively well-off and here comes this scavenging, off-putting guy and who didn't give a shit, and who was probably a little more punk rock, or a *lot more*, than the other bands. He got a reputation quickly. He had a little camping setup that you need to survive, which sort of weirded people out. People would see him with his utensils and see him washing up in the bathroom. People couldn't handle it. People couldn't handle him washing up outside. It was like having a homeless person around.

Sturgeon: We didn't have the internet at the Olive Motel. We'd go over to Epitaph and say, "Oh, I'm gonna go to a website," and type in the website. It's loading. Go into the bathroom and shoot up. Come out fifteen minutes later...still loading! Everyone probably knew I was doing a bunch of heroin at Epitaph because Mr. Brett was doing heroin, too! It has a stinky smell! It's a stinky drug!

Mike Trujillo: As liberal as punk rockers think they are, this quickly challenged aspects of their identity that they hadn't confronted before. Sturgeon kind of didn't give a shit. Tim Armstrong wanted to produce the record, and Sturgeon didn't give a shit. You're supposed to be punk rock, but you can't escape the social capital of people who have a certain esteem—Brett Gurewitz and Tim Armstrong—but he didn't give a fuck about either of them or being near them, or gaining that social capital for esteem. He didn't need to perform in certain ways.

Charlie Ackerman: Sturgeons a fuckin' dick. But it's been twenty years. I was listening to his records recently. He hits some solid points. The message stands.

4

Crack Rock Steady

Sturgeon: In Choking Victim, the term "Crack Rock Steady" came up and that has stuck with my bands. I don't dislike it. It's something that I made up. It's not like I thought about it that much. It became a thing and a Choking Victim song. I never was like, "I should have called it *this*." It was silly at the time and it's still a silly thing. It's not supposed to be serious. It's reggae and ska music on crack. It wasn't supposed to relate to anybody's drug use. It was just something that was made up to be funny and clever—I don't know *if* it *is* clever.

I probably listened to Jamaican music before two-tone music, but I was a fan of two-tone before I recognized the difference between Jamaican rocksteady and two-tone. I listened to old Bob Marley and the Wailing Wailers. I didn't know it was called rocksteady.

During that time, when that crack rock steady phrase came to be, I was best friends with Jungle John. He's not alive anymore. He died in the late nineties and I don't even know his last name. He was called Jungle John because he liked jungle music. He went out to the West Coast and I heard that he died.

I don't know that much about him, but he was my best friend for four months. Four months is a lifetime when you are in your early twenties. We were walking down Avenue B between Eighth and Seventh street and I looked up and said, "Leftover Crack—that's a really good oxymoron!" He agreed. For all I know, he said it, but it doesn't matter. Already, I was pretty sure that my next band was going to be called Leftover Crack. I wasn't sure how it would go down.

We had hung out all winter. It was winter '96-'97, I think. We were drug buddies. We would panhandle and make money to buy drugs. We would do that and spend the rest of the day hanging out. We would spend a lot of time playing pool.

We were doing heroin. But I don't feel like we did a lot. We would get our money together, we did it, and then we hung out. I don't remember it being on our mind all day. We just hung out all day.

At the time, it was a really cold winter and no one had heat and we were both in different squats, and heroin is very warming. You wake up in the morning, cold as hell, and you'd do drugs and feel good all day. You'd get warm in the bars and you wouldn't worry about the cold that most people worry about. We had a food supply or we'd go around looking in the garbage. My friend, she let John stay on the floor, and she'd bring back sandwiches every day from her job at a bank. Lunch was catered and the uneaten food was thrown in the trash. She'd grab them and we'd go back and eat the sandwiches. Then we would split up and that would be the end of the evening for us.

Skwert: The music of Choking Victim wasn't calculated. It really was just a reaction of people getting together and wailing on something. It was "here's one riff, here's another riff."

I always thought the satanic thing in Choking Victim was parody. It was the most outrageous thing we could think of. The three elements—satanic, crack smoking, cop killing—they just seemed so ridiculous to me. You're punk rock and you're doing things to be outrageous. I'm not a Satanist. If you believe that stuff, well, hey. I don't personally believe in that stuff. It was tongue-in-cheek, at least for me. The ska part only magnifies that.

I've been into the ska scene since I was thirteen or fourteen. I had a lot of skinhead friends and grew up listening to dancehall and reggae. A lot of the ska sound from Choking Victim had to do with me. I wasn't just playing a punk beat on ska. I was trying to fuse a rock sound with a ska drumbeat.

When we first started playing, Sturgeon had a serious quality of depth. The songs were right from the heart and everybody could gravitate to them. If a little kid can bop up and down, which is my test, then you've got a good song. That was the majority of our songs.

Sturgeon: Around that time, I met Ezra, who was also living at C-Squat. He was a nice guy. I must have heard him play guitar. He was really good. That's how I hired everyone for Choking Victim. If they could play and they seemed like they had nothing to do, and ended up at C-Squat, that worked.

He was probably a lot more reliable than other candidates to be in our band. We also realized that we had similar tastes in music. It was always a plus if someone lived in C-Squat. Choking Victim didn't really have people that didn't live in C-Squat or live at a squat within a block of C-Squat.

One of our mutual friends said that Ezra was interested if we were doing anything. I ran into him in the hall one day. I said, "We're practicing tomorrow, do you want to listen to this stuff and try playing guitar on it?" I think the first thing he said to me was, "I'll come as long as you don't mind having a balding band member." He was very concerned about being bald. This was over twenty years ago and he never really balded. Up through today, he hasn't balded as far as I know.

Ara Babajian: When I first met Ezra, he was always wearing a hoodie and came across as kind of spooky. He would lock and unlock his rehearsal space for us to use late at night on Twenty-Third Street. He would kind of appear out of the mist and then retreat back into it.

Skwert: Ezra joined Choking Victim about six months before the end of the band. The funny part about Ezra, he was the first guy in the scene that I knew that did his taxes. He was deep thinking and I'm just not sure where his head was at. I don't know if I ever met the "real" Ezra.

5
"Artistic Differences"

Mike Trujillo: I got a call from Choking Victim and Tim Armstrong was pushing to produce their album. They didn't want to work with him. They called me and asked me if I wanted to come to New York to record their album.

Brad Logan: One day Sturgeon calls me up and says, "Hey, Choking Victim is playing a show in York, Pennsylvania. Do you want to come with us?" It was me, Sturgeon, Skwert, Shayne, and Mike Dreg —he drove. We piled into Mike's pickup truck and drove four hours, *four fucking* hours. I couldn't believe we were driving four hours from New York City for one gig only to turn around and drive four hours back.

When we got there, we found out that the opener was Kiss It Goodbye, a Revelation Records metalcore band. The bill couldn't have been more mismatched. It was the era of the earnest, deadly serious hardcore guy and Choking Victim were a bunch of stumblefuck ska-punkers.

There were maybe twenty people there. As we were watching Kiss It Goodbye, Sturgeon kept shouting "play some ska!" between the songs. They were visibly annoyed, but didn't respond...or play any ska. The drummer played the entire set with his back to the crowd with the drum set facing the back wall. What the fuck is the drummer thinking? Where I come from, that means someone is going to lob a beer can at your head for sure.

Mike Trujillo: I remember for the Choking Victim record, somehow Brad came along and I remember not being sure why—it was almost like they wanted a label representative to just be there. He just came out to New York and he didn't really do anything. Here's this nice guy who wants to be involved, but the actual purpose of it wasn't clear.

Sturgeon: We were all set to record the Choking Victim album at the squat around the corner where Skwert lived, called Serenity.

Pezent Shayne (Bass—Choking Victim): We had to record at Serenity because that's where Skwert had all the stuff. If we had recorded at C-Squat, there would be cats and homeless kids just crawling all over the wiring. It would have been a mess.

Skwert: Serenity was lower east side hippies and artists and activists. They were people that had their shit together. They knew how to fight eviction and all that. With C-Squat, the squat itself was peripheral. You might not have a window, no electricity or water. You were living in a godforsaken building. By '93, C-Squat might have had running water. There were times where it was just cut off and you weren't getting it for a while.

C-Squat was run by people that were into punk, but weren't just "punks." It was train-hopping, hobo-ey, art kind of people. There was a contrast between serenity and C-Squat. Serenity had its shit together and C-Squat was everybody just getting fucked up and everybody just doing whatever they wanted.

Serenity, initially, was kind of a hippie...or yippie...scene. This is one thing you have to remember before Choking Victim and all these other bands—punks weren't allowed into the real squats.

Serenity was one of those squats where there were no punk rockers for a while. Bat from Public Nuisance was the first punk that they let live at Serenity. A guy called Horsehead might have been there before Bat. He was more in line with that scene. Serenity was more of a real squat in that it had running water and electricity. My wife and I had a kid and so we moved into that place.

Because of the way it was set up, we decided to record *No Gods/No Managers* at Serenity.

Sturgeon: I wasn't living at C-Squat at the time. I was living at my friend's house in the Bronx. That was Eugenio from 2000 Dirty Squatters. It was a long commute…maybe an hour and a half. I got there on time and nobody else was there and the other two members lived at C-Squat, just down the block. I said to Skwert, "I'm outta here!" which meant that I was going to go walk around the block. He thought it meant "I quit," which wasn't the case.

Then, he sucker punched me and I fell down. He hit me or kicked me a few more times and I was pretty beat up. I stumbled out of there and down the block and lay in the street.

I was lying on Ninth Street between Avenue C and Avenue D. Then, Mike Trujillo came up to me. I had a bloody nose and was lying there. I was like, "Skwert beat me up!" He continued on to the squat. I realized that if I lay there, people from the band were going to keep coming up to me all day. So, I walked up to Tompkins Square Park toward Avenue A and Ninth Street, which was not an area that is commonly walked through by the crusties of that era. I went up there and lay on a bench.

Brad Logan: Choking Victim broke up the second day into recording *No Gods/No Managers*. We had arranged to go out and record the band in Skwert's room at Serenity. It was across the street from C-Squat. I flew out to NYC with Mike Trujillo from Epitaph the day before. He had a rack of out-board recording gear about the size of a large suitcase. I was also there to film "raw footage" for a possible Hellcat video. I was filming them setting up, rolling joints, talkin' shit, walking to the store. Everyday things. The band started in on their first day of recording. I was staying somewhere else in the city, so after they tracked for a bit, I took off. The next day around noon I went down to C-Squat to see what was up for the day. When I got there the other three guys from the band were standing in front, kind of looking at the ground, bummed out. I was like, "What's up? Where's Sturgeon? Aren't you guys excited to do this? This is going to be great!"

Someone mumbled, "Sturgeon and Skwert got in a fight. Then Skwert punched out Sturgeon. We don't know where he went. We think he went to Tompkins Square Park."

I was like, "You're fucking kidding me."

So, I go to Tompkins Square Park, walk through all the trails, and I come up on Sturgeon. He's lying on one of the benches there with a black eye and dried blood on his face. Syringes and drugs were spilling out his pockets in broad daylight. I was like, "Dude, what the fuck?"

He goes, "I'm not recording today, I quit! I walked over to Skwert's house and he punched me! That's it! It's over!"

I remember thinking, "It's over before it even began." Then, I'm thinking, "Shit, this isn't good. What kind of band does this the second fucking day of recording?" Then I thought, "What the hell am I gonna tell Hellcat?!" So, I go back to the stoop at C-Squat and tell the rest of the band, "I think Sturgeon's quitting, I'm going to go get some lunch." So much for being an A&R guy.

Mike Trujillo: We were only recording Choking Victim for two days. Skwert and Scott got in a fight. I showed up the second day of recording. Sturgeon was sitting out front the door. Sturgeon had been waiting out front and was pissed and grumpy. Skwert and

Sturgeon had antagonism already. Skwert is intense and Sturgeon is a grumpy dude.

When Sturgeon got to C-Squat, I was going to run to the store and Sturgeon was going up to call up to Skwert. And I hear Skwert's dog barking. Three minutes later, Sturgeon comes stumbling out the door with blood pouring out of his face. He hobbles away and I'm like, "Fuck!"

I think what happened was Sturgeon was up there and there was some antagonism, and at some point, Sturgeon said to Skwert, "Fuck this record!" It was something they had argued about and Skwert just started beating the shit out of Sturgeon. Sturgeon said that he was on the ground and was like, "Okay, this beating should stop at some moment," and it just didn't stop. It was this insane violent response from Skwert. I think Skwert was tired of Sturgeon complaining about stuff and he just lost it. They had enough back-and-forth over this thing and that just set Skwert off. But I'm guessing that there was more to the conversation.

Sturgeon: When people that you invest heavily in your life… there's a trust lost when someone is violent. I knew Skwert was a violent person, but he had never turned on me. The second he did, I lost a lot of trust in him and I think he knew that. I think he knew that once he laid a finger on me, things were over, and I think he knew there was nothing he could do to make it better. Back then getting punched was a new and terrifying thing to me. Now, it's just another Tuesday night.

Skwert: We had a…"fundamental disagreement." It was over a lot of things. It pertained to arrangements of recordings and who was going to be where during the recording. It was about things that were inconvenient. We got into a fistfight. I was just seeing red. It was over…"artistic differences."

Sturgeon: Eventually, I went out to California to finish recording the record. It took us a long time to complete it. I would call Epitaph collect from wherever the fuck I was in America and have them dial a long-distance number for me and have them connect me to that call. I'd call from Philly collect, have them connect me to Montana, and then talk to someone in Montana for two hours. It must have been, like, the most expensive phone calls in the history of phone calls.

Brad Logan: After the fight, I was on to other things already. I didn't want to be in the middle of a band breakup or whatever it was. Sturgeon said he didn't ever want to see Skwert again, so the band was basically done.

Tim told them he would put the record out anyway, even though they had broken up. I figured things might cool off at some point, but they never did. I think it's one of the greatest sounding punk records I've ever heard. Mike Trujillo was just starting out as a recording engineer, and the band was pretty green. I think a lot of its greatness came about by accident—because nobody knew what they were doing. I loved how abrasive it was. It was brutal and visceral, especially next to what was coming out on Epitaph at the time. If they had been best buddies, it wouldn't have come out the same.

Pezent Shayne: After the fight, we all kind of recorded separately. We did the whole thing and did the lyrics later. We never played shows after that. That was it.

6

Mix of the Gods

Brad Logan: It was 1998. I was living with Tim and Brody at Tim's house in LA, just coming off a long run of Rancid tours. I was feeling pretty optimistic about things. That year F-Minus recorded our first seven-inch in Tim's home studio.

Sturgeon: After I finished the Choking Victim record, I went to the Bay Area for a while. I had some money from an advance on songwriting royalties. The reason I had a large advance is that we were given $5,000 as an advance on our publishing, which is a really shitty deal, because basically we are giving them our songwriting royalties for nothing because they are going to recoup that money from record sales. I knew it was a terrible deal even though I was broke and homeless, but I had to fight with Skwert on the phone over it because he wanted to take it. I don't know how he won that argument.

I got most of it because I wrote most of the songs, but Skwert claimed amounts by other bandmembers that weren't there, which was fucked up. It was fucked up that Epitaph gave Skwert John Dolan's royalties, and maybe Sasha's—any royalties that weren't mine ended up with Skwert, except I made sure Shayne got paid for "Crack Rock Steady" because I like Shayne.

I didn't want to sell the songwriting to the record label, but Skwert insisted on it. I had a couple of grand and I left a thousand with Mike in LA. I knew I was going to spend it on drugs and I wanted to use it to spend on musical equipment to keep doing musical stuff.

After that, I moved around and hopped trains. I mainly went to San Francisco. I went to the Tenderloin and was sleeping at south of Market, under the highway 101. I traveled up and down the West Coast a little. I didn't have a place at C-Squat at the time and I moved out of the squat I was living at in Philadelphia. I didn't have anywhere to go.

When I was living in San Francisco, because I didn't have any money, I could stay under the 101 overpass on Sixth and Harrison and I'd sign up for general assistance and get money, but they would always want to put me in housing.

At the SRO—that's a single room occupancy, which is where homeless people go in San Francisco—I wasn't sleeping much. I was starting to auditory-hallucinate. Staying in an SRO is basically like being in a prison cell. I was cut off from a world that I knew and all my friends.

I stayed at one a little bit, but I was paranoid and I felt safer staying on the street than staying where I didn't know anybody. It's not like I could have gotten a job. If people offered me a place to stay, I would go stay with them. But I only stayed a few days at people's houses. Also, if you stay with someone, you are away from your friends that are staying under the overpass. You want to hang out with your friends, not with someone whom you like less but is offering you a place to stay. You're missing the social life of what your friends are doing.

So, it was either live under the bridge, or stay all by myself. When we were under the bridge, the police mainly left us alone.

There were places that were off-limits and the police would let you know that. Even to this day, San Francisco is more forgiving. They are more open to homeless than other cities. You are more likely to be left alone than other cities. You can't get away with that shit in Manhattan. I feel like it still is that way.

You'd sleep until there was some reason to get up. Maybe there was free food somewhere or you wanted to panhandle to get food or drugs or booze. Normally, you wouldn't get up much earlier than ten or eleven. It really depends on where you were at the time. If I was at a squat, I'd sleep in much later. If I was outdoors, I might get up at seven or eight because you know you might get told to move on by the cops.

At the time, I didn't have access to instruments, so I didn't really play or write anything. I would panhandle. I would go and beg for money and meet up with my friends and we would drink and do whatever. I was using, but not a lot because I didn't have any money. I was doing heroin, smoking crack, and taking benzos—pills like Klonopin and Xanax. I was smoking crack and shooting heroin.

I first smoked crack in New York out of a bong at C-Squat. That's '94 or '95. A friend of mine had some and said, "Let's figure this out." We went up to my room and Skwert left his bong there.

When I was staying under the bridge, we would smoke crack once every day or two. I did at least. I wasn't that bad yet. I was getting bad. I might have been smoking it every day. It's a pretty mentally addictive drug. It's not something that you get sick if you don't have, like heroin. You definitely think about doing it again after you've done it.

Eventually, I decided to move to Montana. I had a girlfriend there...or maybe a girl that was a friend... She was on probation and was stuck living up there. She told me I could move to Montana and stay with her for free. She told me I didn't have to work or anything and she'd take care of me. So, before I left, I told Mike Trujillo that I wanted to get a four-track.

When I first went to Montana, I was trying to get clean. I was pretty sick for a while. When I got there, I ate a ton of food. I could not stop eating food. I was eating to fill the void. I was not ingesting drugs, so I wanted to get something inside me. I ate a lot of pasta and I gained a lot of weight.

I got the four-track in the mail and I borrowed a drum set from a friend of ours. I borrowed a bass and I basically tracked five or six songs that I made up of songs that I had already written. I did the drums during the day for a week or two. I would spend all night until four a.m. doing guitar and doing the vocals.

I finished a demo tape. It had a four-track version of "Rock the 40 Oz," "Soon We'll be Dead," "Stop the Insanity," "Nazi White Trash," and "The Good, the Bad, and the Leftover Crack." I recorded some parts with my friend in Montana and his band Disgruntled Nation. We recorded in the bass player's trailer. It was abandoned, but it was on his property. They practiced there. I'd come there to hang out. Sometimes the practice would be a show. There would be twenty or thirty people there in that little mobile home. It was nicer than some places that I've practiced in—like squats in New York without windows and it's so cold that you can't feel your hands. When you were playing the guitar, the strings would slice your hands, and that hurts so much worse in the cold. We would play really fast because the guitar player that finished first could hold the bare lightbulb with his hands for a tiny bit of warmth until the next song started.

Then, on the flipside of the cassette were songs that I was considering covering. I sent a copy to Brad, Alec, and Mike Trujillo. "Under Pressure" was on the tape and so was "Open Letter to a Landlord" by Living Color. I used to like making mixtapes a lot.

Brad Logan: While Sturgeon was in Montana, he was pretty much off my radar. Choking Victim was over, and I didn't hear from him, really. I did see him once when Rancid came through Montana on the Warped Tour. He seemed happy and told me he had been working on music. I was working at Hellcat and touring with Rancid again. And in between all that, F-Minus was doing shows and making records.

After a while, I was hanging out at out Tim Armstrong's so much, he suggested I just rent a room in his house for cheap. So, I did. It was either a really small room or a "walk–in" closet, I wasn't sure. But it had a bathroom attached to it, too.

I didn't hear from Sturgeon for a long time, then one day I got a cassette in the mail. It said "Leftover Crack" on one side and "Mix of the Gods" on the other side. The MOTG side was a mix of influences, and possible covers. It had songs like "Under Pressure" by Queen. On the flip were some "Leftover Crack" songs that he had recorded by himself. He played all the instruments. In the letter that came with it, he asked if I would be interested in joining the new band he was putting together called Leftover Crack.

Seth Olenick: Sturgeon had come back from Montana with a tape that had just said "Leftover Crack" on it. It was awesome. It had "Nazi White Trash," "Soon We'll be Dead," and some other songs. He had done it on a four-track. He told me he was going to form a band with Alec. They came over to my parents house in LA, and as far as I know, that was the first time Sturgeon showed Leftover Crack songs to Alec.

I can't remember what Alec's reaction was...I suppose I can make something up… "Alec was blown away! He *knew* something *special* was about to happen."

Brad Logan: Alec probably didn't give a fuck.

Sturgeon: Alec liked the songs. A couple of them were from our earlier band No Commercial Value. He had been in a sober cult when we were doing the Choking Victim album and they wouldn't let him see me or play music with us. He was excited to be available again and playing songs he could…hum in the shower?

Seth Olenick: The songs were amazing. Sturgeon knew what he wanted. He was very determined to get that. Just watching him in a band, you can see what he likes and he knows how to make it happen.

Brad Logan: When I first heard the new songs, I was hooked. Most of it ended up becoming the first Leftover Crack record. I remember there was also a song called "Where I'm From" about a straight-edge kid who "breaks edge" and starts smoking weed. To this day, it's still one of my favorites.

Sturgeon: For "Where I'm From," Jon Dolan played guitar and I played drums and we both took acid and we recorded what we considered to be credible as a straight-edge song as any.

Brad Logan: The songs were very crudely recorded.

Sturgeon: I picked Brad Logan because we hit it off. He shared a lot of my interests. To the day, he's down to do whatever. If people want to make a band happen, and need a guitar player or a bass player, he'll volunteer. A lot of people are like, "I'll do it," but he is the guy I trusted to make the time to come and do it.

In Choking Victim, Skwert vetoed a lot of songs I wanted to record. The *Give 'em the Boot* compilation had come out and Choking Victim had broken up. So I already knew that Leftover Crack was going to be a thing, even though it wasn't a thing yet. I even slipped "the good Leftover Crizack" into the vocals on the opening track of *No Gods/No Managers*, on "500 Channels." I knew that no matter what it was going to be a band and that these songs were going to be recorded. I wasn't fucking around. I knew I was going to make music and was going to do this with my life.

7
First Recordings

Sturgeon: At the time, I didn't have an ID, or I didn't have a driver's license or a non-driver's license. If I had to make an appointment, I would take a Greyhound because you don't need an ID. You could book seventy-two hours in advance and freeze the price, and then pay later, so that would give you enough time to get the money to pay for the ticket.

I went down to LA to record our first Leftover Crack recordings. We recorded in Mike Trujillo's garage. It was me, Mike Trujillo, Alec, Brad, and there was another drummer that was around for a minute. He wasn't bad. He was a great drummer. He might have been Mike's drummer in Blindside. What ended up happening, we went to record and Brad had his friend Amery Smith, who played with the Beastie Boys for their punk songs, record with us. If you get anything by the Beastie Boys in the late nineties that has punk, that's Amery. He was the first drummer in Suicidal Tendencies. He was the only obviously white dude hanging upside down. They were part of the Venice 13 gang or something. They were skate punks from Venice. Amery was an amazing drummer. That first Suicidal record blazes and the drums might have been the fastest played at that time.

But when we first started working with Amery, I wasn't aware that he was in other bands. Somewhere in there we found out whom Amery had been playing with. It wasn't a big deal where I was nervous or intimidated or starstruck. What was a big deal was later, when I was back in Montana and HBO put the Tibetan Freedom Concert on TV—there he was playing with the Beastie Boys and he was wearing the *same clothes* that he was wearing the next day when he came to practice with Leftover Crack! He literally played a giant concert in a stadium and then flew to California and the next day he was practicing with us! He didn't even stop at home.

Brad Logan: Amery Smith was the original drummer of F-Minus. He recorded a couple of compilation tracks and the track we did on the *Give 'em the Boot* compilation. He played all our early gigs, too.

We were both roadies for bands. That's how we met. Amery worked for Beastie Boys and Rancid and the Beastie Boys did quite a few shows together in the nineties. They had the same manager. At the time, I had given up the idea of ever playing music again. I was happy to just travel and string guitars for a living. When we first met, I was like, "Oh, shit, you played on the first Suicidal record!" He was a fucking humble legend. A great guy, a great drummer, and super down-to-earth, too. When I finally got around to putting a band together, I knew he was the guy to play drums.

Amery Smith (Drummer—Leftover Crack, F-Minus, Beastie Boys, Suicidal Tendencies): So much happened in such a short period of time. I had quit F-Minus just before a show, before they played with At the Drive In. I got in Sarah Lee's face about how she booked a show with a band that sounded like fucking Pearl Jam. "How could you book us with this? This isn't punk at all!" F-Minus didn't play because I left. Sarah and I did what Sarah and I do, which is have a knock-down, drag-out fight.

Months later, Brad gave me a demo tape and asked if I would come down to play. I said sure. I came to a practice and it was Scott, Bradley, and Alec. When it came time to record, Brad, Sturgeon, Alec, and I went to a place called "The Shack" in Playa del Rey. I had some gear, some DAT tape decks. We set to record the original material that was part of the set list. We got some drum tracks there. Sturgeon didn't like the guitar or the amp and he couldn't get the tone that he liked. He didn't have any gear, just some things lying around. He really liked the location, it had windows and natural light and it really affected his mood and I never thought of that… "Oh, yeah, natural light can make you have a positive mood."

But, since Michael Trujillo had also converted a garage into a recording studio, we just took the tapes and started all over in Mike Trujillo's house. It was one room— no isolation booths. Mike Trujillo didn't come to the first practice as a musician. When he showed up, we were running through the songs and Mike walked in skeptically. He said, "Yeah, that's kind of it, but it needs to be faster." And I was like, "Fuck, man, faster?!"

Brad Logan: We recorded *Rock the 40 Oz.* in Mike Trujillo's garage studio. We went over and banged 'em out in a couple days. The songs were already written so, we just played them accordingly.

Amery played drums, Alec played bass, Mike T and I played guitar. I don't remember us all being there and recording at the same time though. I came in and did my guitar parts after the drums and bass had already been recorded.

Sturgeon: Recording Leftover Crack was a lot different than recording Choking Victim. We used to argue a lot in Choking Victim because it was unproven whether I was good songwriter or not. After doing a record for Hellcat and getting that far, even though we weren't well known, it was sort of known I was a decent songwriter. One of the things that I laid out was that it was my band and that I didn't want to argue about stuff. If people had an idea, let me know, but in general I had everything written and everyone knew beforehand that it was all written, including the drums, and I just wanted better musicians to play the stuff that I had written.

I don't think that's definitively the best way to make good music. There are all different ways to do it. If you know what you want, it is a great way to work and cut through a bunch of crap. At that time, I definitely knew what I wanted a song to be and how long I wanted them to be—things that take me years to figure out at this point.

I really wanted to have a band that could play live and record. Choking Victim had fallen apart. The amount of times that Choking Victim played concerts are in the low dozens. Under thirty, probably. So, I really wanted to play the new songs live.

Amery Smith: I never realized that I was actually in the band. A lot had happened in a short period of time, and before we knew it, we booked three shows. The first show was at Headline Records, Thursday, June 17, 1999—that's the first Leftover Crack show. We played with nobody inside Headline records at nighttime. Maybe there were fifteen people there. There might have been shoppers. Sturgeon was pretending to shop while singing. If that constitutes being in the band, that would have been it for me.

Brad Logan: The show was at like four in the afternoon. There were about ten people there shopping for records and standing around. They didn't seem to mind a band playing, but they could have easily gone without it.

Seth Olenick: I was at the first show. Sturgeon didn't pace himself and lost his voice on the first song. There were maybe fifteen people there. I was pretty sure there was a rack right down the center so you couldn't have a proper crowd anyway. But the band played it like it was Madison Square Garden.

I also went to the third Leftover Crack show. It was in La Cañada. It looked like an elementary school talent show. They were on a stage that was maybe four or five feet off the ground. There were streamers for curtains. That show was also very lightly attended. Again, they played like it was Madison Square Garden.

8

Rock the 40 Oz.

Sturgeon: Once we got everything recorded, I wanted to put out the recordings as a 7-inch. The Choking Victim LP still hadn't come out and I was anxious. Adam Greenwald was friends with Mike Trujillo. He was putting out Mike's band or a band that Mike recorded. Adam said he would pay for pressing the 7-inch and put it out. At the time, I didn't have money to put out a 7-inch. I didn't have an address for mailorder. I was still traveling a lot and was basically homeless. So, Adam Greenwald put it out.

The cover is a collage. I had a friend of mine wearing a black trench coat. He's holding a 40 oz. and a gun. It's the same person on both sides of the cover. He's wearing the same Circle Jerks shirt and you can see that. And then, I put the Columbine kids' face over his.

Brad Logan: I thought the cover of *Rock the 40 Oz.* was pretty funny, and shooting bullies was definitely a fantasy I could relate to. If you've ever been on the receiving end of an ass-beating by school-bully-shitheads, you know what I mean.

Columbine was a horrible tragedy. But I was capable of having more than one emotion simultaneously. Elementary and high school were great for me on one hand, but really fucked up on the other. I had friends and my grades were okay, but kids and teachers can be totally shitty. You got picked on for being different, for being too smart, or not smart enough, or for not having the right clothes, or for being too fat or too skinny. The only way to rise above was to fight, or withdraw into your own world, or both.

Shoot the kids at school / All in a bloody pool / I'll show the teachers too /
'Cause they can't tell me what to do

—Excerpt from "Rock the 40 Oz."

Sturgeon: I had actually written "Rock the 40 Oz.," including the line "shoot the kids at school," and recorded it, before Columbine. I think the four-track recording was a few weeks before Columbine. Up until then, there hadn't been that many school shootings. There were some, but they weren't as notable with as many casualties and the national attention.

One of the things was that the shooters were outcasts. They were definitely on the fringes of social life at their school. Something that I thought about a lot was the community—there was one black student and he got shot and killed. There was much to do about Eric Harris and Dylan Klebold being racists. It made me think about the community they lived in where there would only be one black student in the school. What type of town was Columbine where it was almost entirely white families and there was one black student?

It was brought up later by Michael Moore. He talks about how the town was supported by an arms manufacturer, so the community supported arms manufacturers and weapons and munitions makers, and on top of that it's a racist town. If there's one black family, you assume that black families don't feel comfortable living there or can't afford to move. It's indicative of that community and what type of people come out of that community. I'm sure that helped shaped the shooters. Is there a deeper institutional racism that is in effect that can easily influence oppressed kids that are always outcasts at the same time? Maybe it's bullshit, but I think it is worth looking into.

Brad Logan: I think a lot of people missed the humor and irony with Leftover Crack. Songs that addressed topics like depression, suicide, and drug addiction were not accepted like they are now. Neither was being outspoken about anti-racism, anti-sexism, anti-transphobia, and anti-homophobia on a mainstream level. So, the band has always had enemies. I liked the way Sturgeon was able to write seriously about these things while peppering in humor. It's not easy to pull off and I think it made the songs more relatable. A lot of "political punk" can be pretty dry and textbook-y. Not that I don't like that stuff. But who the fuck wants to get lectured?

9

Three Sixes, Baby

Brad Logan: During the period of *Rock the 40 Oz.* and before *Medicore Generica*, the band wasn't really a band yet. It was basically a one-man band—Sturg and an assemblage of different personalities. That's what Sturgeon did, and does. He put together a band of people he interacted with and got along with.

When the *Rock the 40 Oz.* seven-inch came out, the reception was pretty good. But I didn't commit to the band until much later. I was still busy with all my shit, and honestly wasn't sure it would materialize into a real band.

In the liner notes of the first press of *Rock the 40 Oz.* was "keep an eye out for the Leftover Crack full-length, *Shoot the Kids at School*, out on Hellcat records Summer 2000." As to both the time frame and the title, that was a rather optimistic declaration. I don't know if Sturgeon ran that past Hellcat or not. I assumed that Sturgeon had already made some kind of a deal with Hellcat. But I was in the dark about all of it.

Sturgeon: Choking Victim was on Hellcat. We had signed a three-record deal, but we knew that we were breaking up. I had new songs, and I had written songs for Choking Victim that didn't get used for some reason or another.

Once *Rock the 40 Oz.* was put out, Hellcat saw that we had music and people were interested. Also, we were on Hellcat's compilation CD *Give 'em the Boot II*. Hellcat approached me and I probably could have asked for more money, but I think I said, "I don't care, just give me the same deal." They gave me the same amount of money and I gave them another album. Brad was always our spy for Hellcat that defected. At that time, Brad wasn't officially in the band.

At the time, Ezra was doing INDK. He's always been of the mind that he can only do one band at a time, which is ridiculous. That's not how a "professional" thinks. There was a practice room with Leftover Crack, INDK, Ambulance Limited, and that band with the Hot Topic-y dance music. I've never heard them to this day…oh, it was Mindless Self Indulgence.

INDK's album *Kill Whitey!* had come out just after that. The sequence on that record was terrible. They ended the record with "Start It Up." That's dumb as shit! They start each show with that song. They're trying to be clever. No. Put it in a good order. I really like that record, but the song order is terrible.

Ara Babajian: In 1999, I start getting calls from Alec inquiring about royalties from the Agent 99 compilation we had put out that year. I think he wanted to sue me or something! Incidentally, once we straightened that out, he asked me if I wanted to join this new band he was starting with Sturgeon called Leftover Crack. The two of them had been living on the West Coast, Alec at some safe house in Newport Beach and Sturgeon washing dishes in Kalispell, Montana. Their plan was to move back to the East Coast, to New York City, and make a go of it with this new band, Leftover Crack.

I expressed a wary interest in at least hearing what they were up to. A couple days later I received a cassette tape with four-track demos of most of the songs that would wind up on *Mediocre Generica* and a note from Scott telling me how much he'd love to play with me, how perfect I'd be for the band and signed "three sixes, baby" with a drawing of a little sturgeon fish. I listened to the tape and was literally haunted by how good the songs were, particularly "Rock the 40 Oz." I literally could not get to sleep for several weeks because that song would be swimming around in my head.

Anyway, I took that as a good sign and agreed to join the band on the condition that they pay me fifty dollars per gig. I liked them and was happy to see them again, but I didn't trust them! So, I was protecting myself against any further fuckery by these two scamps. Fifty dollars worth of insurance against one of these drug addicts stealing my drum kit or stiffing me on a show payment. But I wound up falling in love with both of them all over again and becoming a full band member once I realized the significance of what we were doing and how much joy it was giving me. Ultimately, those two guys gave me my confidence back, my mojo, and made me realize my inner badass. I will always be indebted to them for that.

That's when I first met Brad. He showed up at Funkadelic studios in New York City during one of the very first Leftover Crack practices on a little Schwinn bike. I knew of him and F-Minus from the *Give 'em the Boot* compilation that Hellcat put out in 1997. I thought F-Minus was one of the greatest and funniest band names I'd ever heard and once I got to know Brad, perfectly in keeping with his personality and sense of humor. And they were a great fucking band. So, Brad was like the cool older kid.

Brad had already been through the worst parts of addiction and was able to counsel the rest of the band through their addictions and hard times. He was such a steadying influence and fantastic buffer between Sturgeon and the rest of us because he had the ability to add levity to the darkest situations. I can't tell you how important it is when you're somewhere in remotest England in the middle of a six-week tour pulling one of your bandmates out of the gutter, literally, and Brad just looks over and says, "Hey, Darby Crash! Wipe the heroin off your shoulder and get in the fucking van!"

Eventually, Sturgeon persuaded Ezra to join Leftover Crack after a trial period of rehearsals. I'd understood that Ezra had done some secret work on the Choking Victim record and he seemed kind of wary about getting himself back into any sort of musical situation with Sturgeon. The thing about Sturgeon is that if you're not strong enough mentally, he will consume you. His vision and will are so strong that you kind of need to know what you're all about if you're going to hang out with him, lest you wind up getting carried away by his ambitions, interests.

Sturgeon's a very persuasive guy, ultimately always gets what he wants, gets to where he needs to go. The four of us playing together—Sturgeon, Ezra, Alec, and me—felt so undeniably right that it would have been insane for Ezra to say no. And at that time, during the rehearsals that would lead up to the recording of *Mediocre Generica* and the tours to follow, Ezra was one of the most solid, righteous, sober, earnest, dependable, and talented people I'd ever met. He would write entire symphonies on his four-track and build a fucking bathroom for himself at C-Squat in a matter of hours. He's just pure genius and will…much like Sturgeon.

Brad Logan: Around that time, I was touring with Rancid. Through touring with Rancid, I stated picking up tours with other bands from the same circuit—guitar tech, drum tech, tour manager. That's how it worked. You didn't apply for those jobs, it was all word of mouth. Between tours I would work at clubs in Los Angeles and New York. It was the same thing, word of mouth. I had been lucky. Through music I was able to avoid having to get a "real job" for quite some time. Just as well, the real world sucked.

Plus, I had zero skills in anything but dead-end stuff—customer service, truck unloader, shelf stacker, janitor. What I had learned at those jobs, plus the spending of my formative years in shithole clubs around sketchy people, perfectly prepared me to work in the music industry on all levels.

Being road-crew for Rancid every night was complete chaos. Bodies would be flying, adrenaline was maxed, people would climb on stage and try to steal shit, and gear would be falling apart. I was in a constant state of alert. I don't know if the band enjoyed it, but I sure as fuck did. However, if something broke it was my job to fix it. It was a different perspective for me, because as a lover of chaos and unpredictability, I was used to letting the chips fall where they may, so to speak. It was all fun, what I liked about punk shows. Plus, I really liked the band, so it was an easy gig for me.

Sturgeon: When Brad was living with Tim Armstrong, I think I stayed there once or twice over the course of a month. Tim lives at the top of a steep hill that is at least a mile plus to the nearest store.

Those guys would not give me fucking food. I had to dumpster dive Tim and Brody's garbage. They would never offer me food, which was weird. But maybe I should have just taken it? I felt that wasn't appropriate somehow. I didn't get the vibe that I could just eat anything in the fridge. It was never offered to me.

I was there for a day or two and I was starving. When they would go do something, I looked in the garbage and they had all this stuff that had just "expired" like a day or two ago—cooked salmon, sausage…so I cooked it all and ate it. It was delicious. Then there was the time we played Risk for like eight hours and they ordered like twenty Domino's Pizzas and didn't offer me any pizza. And I was like, "Uh…can I have any pizza?" and they were like, "…*Yeah*…" But they weren't particularly friendly about it.

There was some sort of communication breakdown. Who orders like twenty pizzas for two or three people? And what rich person orders Domino's Pizzas? You kind of have to be a fucking idiot if you're ordering Domino's Pizza if you have any money because you can have any pizza in LA. That and Little Caesars are the two worst pizzas on earth. Even dumpster diving and eating pizza from Little Caesars or Domino's is gross. I'd rather pass.

Like, who doesn't offer a guest food? I did not feel like I was welcome to eat that food. You know, I'm not stupid. So, what's wrong with *me?!* What's wrong with Tim Armstrong that I had trouble asking him for food and they couldn't offer it?

Tim also insisted that I take his copy of *Chopper*—his Australian copy of the book by Mark Read. I proceeded to argue with him about how I didn't want to be responsible for his book and I didn't really care about reading it and I was about to be riding a freight train and there was no way I'd be able to account for it. But he insisted that I take it. I feel like the trap was set.

10

𝔐𝔢𝔡𝔦𝔬𝔠𝔯𝔢 𝔊𝔢𝔫𝔢𝔯𝔦𝔠𝔞

Ara Babajian: We rehearsed the songs that would become *Mediocre Generica* for several months in a practice space on the east side of Manhattan every Monday night from 9:00 p.m. to midnight. Sturgeon brought all of the material and the rest of us would add parts and arrangement ideas accordingly. Sturgeon's idea was really just to get the first five great songs together and have them lead off the album, with the idea that everything after that was probably not going to be listened to anyway and was mostly filler.

We recorded *Mediocre Generica* over the course of a few days in a studio in Koreatown. The session was engineered by a classic New York/Long Island/Queens type character named Kenny who was infinitely patient with us bringing all our friends in to basically squat the place and get drunk for a week. I believe Kenny was suggested as an engineer by Mike Trujillo.

Sturgeon: We recorded the bass and drums with Kenny in New York and in addition we had Jerica from the Scofflaws record some keyboards. She discovered that Kenny's keyboard was tuned down half a step, which is why *Mediocre Generica* is half in standard tune and half a step down. She was like, "This sounds wrong." We were like what do you mean? She flips the keyboard over and she sees some switch that is like flipped up or down or whatever. At the time, it was hilarious to me to tune a guitar.

Ara Babajian: We did pretty much first and second takes of everything because the material was so well rehearsed and we'd played a handful of shows by this point. Sturgeon knew exactly what he wanted the concept of the record to be, how the songs should be sequenced, what parts should be played where, what the cover art should look like, everything. He has an amazing ability to follow the logic of his concepts, to see the big picture of a project and move toward it in a very inspiring, willful way.

So, we'd finish whatever bullshit jobs we'd been working during the day, then go to the recording studio at night and bash out the record. I don't remember a ton of what went on there, because it was a long time ago, but I do remember hearing a playback of "Stop the Insanity." There's a moment in the chorus after Sturgeon sings the lyric "stop the insanity!" and there's a massive drum fill on the floor time and right before he sings the next lyric "let's end humanity!" In that split second between those two parts you could actually feel a massive wave of physical sound hit you, it was actually hardcore that swung!...like you're at the beach and you get knocked down by one wave only to stand up and get leveled by another...you could really feel all of these songs on a very visceral level. And that's when I knew we had something special, that we were making a great record that we could at least be proud of regardless of whatever was going to happen to it in the marketplace.

Sturgeon: Ara and Alec are probably the best musicians I could have hired. They are like workers. They are very professional. They always were. Their methods of working on music are blue collar if you will. It's less creative and more efficiency and performance. They can play anything you throw them.

Ara Babajian: By the time the songs were recorded, we all had a part in arranging them and recording them. We all added our own styles. There was that investment. And then, financially, we had an investment as well. We were all paying into the cost of a rehearsal space. It felt like we had a stake in it. Sturgeon had the 80 or 90 percent stake in it, where it was his life on the line if it didn't work out. The rest of us were like, "Well, if it doesn't work out, we'll go back to what we are doing." For Sturgeon, it was all or nothing—it was this is going to work or else. I always respected that. The early songs were great songs. I loved supporting the songs even if I had little to do with them because they were such great songs. It's not hard as a drummer to get behind a great song.

I knew that we were a force to be reckoned with. The only real question regarding the record at the time was its length. It clocked in at something like twenty-five minutes. So that's why you hear all of those little spoken parts and that other version of "Gay Rude Boys Unite" on there, as well as some other stuff. It was really to flesh out the record, the concept, at a time when everyone else was making these seventy-minute CDs.

Sturgeon: Literally no one was there for all of the recordings except for me. I wrote the songs on a four-track. It's a point of contention. Alec and Ara ganged up on me later and neither of them remember that I paid them money to record the songs. They learned the songs in a week, we recorded in a week, and then I spent like year on the record and then they were like, "We don't remember what we signed, but we signed a contract and you owe us a bunch of money."

Epitaph and Hellcat didn't trust me ever. Like ever. When they had me sign the contract, they didn't want me to sign it alone, because I was already always calling them for money for drugs, calling from Philadelphia, "I need money!" They'd wire me two hundred bucks and I'd go to North Philly to buy dope. I was sick, sad, and living in a squat. It's freezing in winter. You're desperate.

They wanted to have more responsible people sign the contract, as well. So, having Alec and Ara sign it made it more official. Maybe they thought that I would just shoot it all up. I don't know that, but that's what I imagine. That's why Brad was there to investigate us to begin with. I'm surprised that they signed us after they sent Brad out. I guess what it was is that Brad didn't snitch on us! We definitely weren't trying to wine and dine Brad. We were just, "Please dude, help us! Our lives are dying! We need to record this shit! We don't have forever to sit around! We don't have day jobs! We need to get you to convince people to let us record these tracks!" At the time, Brad was the closest to an A&R person that we ever met. Grease the wheels!

I feel like we did more time doing backup vocals than bass and drums. Alec and Ara were focused. We went in and banged it out. We only did like four or five two-hour rehearsals.

After tracking, at Mike Trujillo's house, he had like a thirty-two-track board. This was before automation. When we were mixing a song, Mike would be on the left side of the board and I would be on the right. Each of us have about ten moves or things we have to do over the course of a song. So, at like ten seconds on the song, Mike has to pan a guitar to the left, on second twelve I have to turn vocals down because it's too loud, and to get the song mixed exactly what we wanted it to sound like. And then we'd listen to it in Mike's car in his driveway. We had heard like a hundred records going to and from his work at Epitaph. We would listen to at least one or two records a day, so we knew what we wanted our record to sound like. That shit is painstaking, you know? When you have like a four-minute song and Mike is in move nine and I'm in move sixteen with twenty seconds left in the song, and you make a wrong move or mess something up, that's heartbreaking. Just that alone can make a song take days to mix.

The great thing is that Mike Trujillo loved what we were doing enough to stick around. He'd get up at whatever time, punch in at Epitaph doing whatever all day, and then he would come back and meet me and work for six or seven hours doing some shit and he had no complaints. He gave more than anybody else in the band to make those records good.

In my opinion, most of *Mediocre Generica* is not a record. It's a bunch of filler *sounds*, not filler *songs* that I put together because I didn't have a full record of music. I don't know where I was at with that. We have like a thirty-minute record with like four minutes of classical piano; Pachelbel's canon; we have me playing an organ as an interlude; we have me, Ara, and Alec playing a dub reggae song; we have me fucking with a broken guitar string…and then you have a bunch of space at the end of the record before a "secret song," because I didn't have enough content to make a full record. It seems like an EP if anything.

But people like that. We have skits on it. Me and Mike Trujillo do a Prince Paul type skit. If I have one regret, I should have never put a skit on any album. Maybe somebody loves them, but I cringe every time I hear them. Arrg! Why? Under what circumstances did I think this was a good idea! I feel like I still do it.

11

𝔖hoot the 𝔎ids at 𝔖chool

Sturgeon: I wanted to call the first album *Shoot the Kids at School*. I don't have fond memories of grade school. All my schools were public schools and there weren't a lot of white kids in the public schools in New York City. But we didn't get picked on for being white so much. There was this girl Belinda on the bus who was very dark skinned and they all made fun of her because she had dark skin, and I thought that was fucked up. I don't know if I could really grasp the meaning of why she was bullied, but I knew it was fucked. So, I didn't get bullied because I was white or because everyone else has been oppressed by white people. But I *did* get bullied plenty, but it was more random and I feel like I got bullied by white kids more than anyone else.

In school, I got pretty good grades. It was hit or miss. I got on the honor roll and the advanced programs through junior high. Then, in high school, I got into Bronx Science, which is one of the hardest schools to get into. I wanted to go to Stuyvesant, which was four blocks from where I lived, and Bronx Science was an hour and a half both ways from where I lived and you had to take a bunch of trains.

I tried out for the School of Performing Arts, which is the *Fame* high school. Of course, I didn't get in. I felt like it was a popularity contest. To this day I would never pass one of those. I'm not outgoing in the ways popularity contests are run. Are popularity contests things in reality? I'm not sure. But anyway, I'm not winning them.

I think it was all ready to go with the title *Shoot the Kids at School*—cover art and everything. BJ Papas took pictures for the cover art. To be fair, the picture for the cover art was really offensive and I could not find stock footage of a school. I did have mixed feelings about it. I didn't want it to be "Leftover Crack, the white power band that shoots non-white kids at school." People have never brought that up to me, but I still have a guilty conscience about it.

Seth Olenick: I was at the shoot that BJ Papas did that was supposed to be the cover of *Shoot the Kids at School*. It was Sturgeon with a gun and it was edited to place him in front of a school with kids running out.

Sturgeon: It was all ready to go and Chris LaSalle at Hellcat did what a lot of people do. Instead of saying why it was being censored, he said, "I don't feel comfortable, I have a child." This and that.

Chris is like oddly convinced that I prophesized Columbine. He was like, *"Ooohhh!"* I was like, "There have been school shootings for ages." Police have been killing people forever. The World Trade Center was bombed in 1993.

Brad Logan: Chris LaSalle had little kids in school. But he came from a hip-hop background and was used to motherfuckers talking about "capping people"—this and that. So, I'm not sure he really even cared. Although I don't think it was his place to make the call on a title change.

Christina White: We had already been dealing with the fallout from Columbine. There were rumors circulating that one of the shooters had a Bad Religion T-shirt on. Epitaph was already on crisis publicity alert. There were also a lot of songs getting banned at that point, like "Let the Bodies Hit the Floor." I think a Pennywise song was being circulated in that conversation nationally. As far as the temperature at the label, we were already on guard.

And then, Leftover Crack rolls in with *Shoot the Kids at School* to be provocative, which they excelled at. They really did. It was a very punk way to be. I feel like there's still a conversation in the greater punk community—"Oh, fuck you, you were offended? Well, then, you're not punk." But do we have to be offensive to be punk? And it seems to me that the Leftover Crack answer was a resounding "yes."

If I remember correctly, there was a marketing meeting and we were in the conference room sitting around a table. It was like, "Here's the records coming out...and then there's this one...and they want to call it...uh...*Shoot the Kids at School*..." and there was a silence.

Eventually, there was a big discussion about freedom of speech, artist integrity, and how do we handle this, and how do we deal with this, and where's the line. I feel like Epitaph has always prided themselves on being a career-driven label for musicians. You're going to come in and do what you do and we're gonna try and sell it without compromising your integrity or your artistic vision. That was something we tried to do as punks and not be sellouts. How do I take the Bouncing Souls from the streets of New Jersey and sell them to the masses without getting them to sell out?

We took it very seriously. This is what the artist wants. So... how do we say "no?" Because "saying no" is not what we do. We say "yes" all the time. I think that as far as politically, as far as the label, and realistically, we weren't going to be able to get those records in stores, the press wasn't gonna cover it, with that title. It was going to be a shit show. Not that we were afraid of a shit show, but it felt insensitive as well.

Seth Olenick: At Hellcat, everyone was talking about how no one would print that title. That was when Columbine happened. Everybody was really uneasy about it and they asked me for some photos that I had taken and that ended up being the cover. Some contact sheets were inside and my portrait of the band ended up being the back cover.

I took photos of Sturgeon after BJ Papas was done with her original shoot. He was supposed to be the subject for one of my classes. And every week I was supposed to bring in progress of my work. And each week Sturgeon would have to push it back, so I'd have to tell my teacher. And my teacher was like, "It's okay, it's okay!"…and then later on I found out my teacher was giving me an F every week and I got the worst grade I ever got in college. I got a C-minus in that class and that was the difference of me graduating with honors. So, Sturgeon was central to my not graduating with honors. I was .03 GPA away from honors!

Sturgeon: If we look back at the history of school shootings in America, there are more school shootings than just Columbine and one happened a year or two before Columbine. It wasn't like the concept of school shootings popped into my head out of nowhere. It popped in my head because it had happened. It was happening more frequently when I came up with the title. Columbine was way bigger and more people were getting hurt and killed than any other school shooting. That there were two people made it more "unique." The point is that when Epitaph censors your record and art, they really go to town on that shit.

Christina White: I do think *Shoot the Kids at School* is a great title. But I kind of feel like the offensive punk shit is low-hanging fruit. Try to dig a little deeper. You can still be clever and you can stick it to the man, you can still engage with people on that level without just throwing a piece of shit in their face. The vulgarity doesn't have to win.

Ara Babajian: I thought it was extremely disheartening and cowardly of Epitaph and Hellcat to make us change what was a really amazing social comment and concept. I didn't have kids at the time, otherwise I might have felt differently. But, back then, I just thought that particular record label was purely satisfied to risk nothing with a bunch of bands that really didn't have much to say. They gave us an opportunity when no one else did, but they didn't really understand us or have our backs. It was a big fight with them to change the cover and title.

I remember Sturgeon having screaming matches with Chris LaSalle, the Hellcat general manager in my apartment, on my phone, because Sturgeon had no phone at C-Squat. Me, my wife, Sturgeon, and Alec, would all be there just kind of yelling at LaSalle in the background. We felt totally helpless. We were ready to quit our jobs, get this band off the ground, get the record out and introduce Leftover Crack to the world. Instead, we had these cowardly corporate authority figures telling us what we couldn't do, just like in school.

So, Sturgeon said, "Fine, you want to indulge in mediocrity, you mediocre motherfuckers? We'll call the record *Mediocre Generica* and you can make your 99 percent royalty rate off of your own mediocre, bankrupt ideas."

Brad Logan: When I heard it was changed to *Mediocre Generica*, I was like, "Wow, great title!" I thought it was done on purpose by Sturgeon.

That was my motherfucking state of the union anyway! Mediocrity was what F-Minus stood against. Punk rock in California had become one trendy, happy, shitty, board-shorts-wearing, fuckin' fun in the sun, fuckin' pop punk, fuckin' mutation of punk rock after another. Warped-tour culture. Everybody wanted to sound like "California punk, maaaan," and it was all just *Mediocre*.

Personally, I think *Mediocre Genrica* is a better title than *Shoot the Kids at School*. It was such a better statement of the times—or was at least as good. *Medicore Generica* could represent the criticism of a lot of things that were going on at any given time, in the music industry, or the art world, or society.

Sturgeon: I *didn't* want to change the title of *Shoot the Kids at School*. There was a time that it wasn't going to be released as anything, after I told them the title I wanted. They agreed to let me change the title. I had to give them new art and a new name. I really thought it was overkill. I had to give them all new art? I had, like, one offensive picture associated with the title. The other art didn't have anything to do with anything. Behind my back they even changed the titles to some songs. They changed one song to the title "NC." "NC!" To this day, I have no clue what that means…Wait…Wait…NC…"No clue?!" Is that what it stands for? That song was called "mercy me, shoot the kids." I get it. They were like, "We can't use 'mercy me.'"

I think that the title change of the record mattered a lot. It was one of many small sabotages to my band's career. It started with the fact that Choking Victim couldn't play ska shows or punk shows because it would be, "Oh, you're a ska band," or, "Oh, you're a punk band." We could only play ABC No-Rio, C-Squat, and any other squat that just happened to be having a show. But playing CBGB was pretty arbitrary. You come to audition night and if you bring in like ten people, they'll book you.

A lot of people don't notice this, but every Leftover Crack album has an essay in it. The *Mediocre Generica* essay is about Columbine… or did I put it in *Fuck World Trade* because they wouldn't let me…

Ara Babajian: I remember Sturgeon crying at rehearsal one night after Hellcat had refused to release the album as *Shoot the Kids at School*. He was crying like somebody had stabbed him in the fucking heart. I was so moved. I understood so well in that moment what his art meant to him that I fell in love with his heart and his purity. His band literally was his life.

Sturgeon: I was at the end of my rope and I needed some content. I didn't want it to be good anymore because I spent so much time and energy trying to make the art be as good as I could. The album art and the cover art, and the fonts and shit, everything I put into that was worthwhile and good. When they told me I needed to change it, it seemed someone decided that I needed to be punished because there was no reason to make me change *everything*. One of the reasons I was told that they couldn't do *Shoot the Kids at School* was because they couldn't get it printed.

Brad Logan: You could say they had Sturgeon over a barrel. They were saying, "If you don't want to change the name then we're not putting it out," and that sucks. I can understand how Sturg felt like he was being censored. But another way to look at it is to just change the goddamn title and move on.

Sturgeon: I wish it was titled *Shoot the Kids at School* and I've always thought Hellcat's censorship was unnecessary. Except for the censorship of the Choking Victim art—which was great because Skwert made the art for *No Gods* and I did not love it. His cover was that he just cut some shit out from magazines. I'm not saying Skwert is a bad artist, I just didn't like *that* art. I thought I could make better art. It wasn't up for debate, but because it got shut down, I sort of recreated a version of his art. It was kind of generic to me for no reason. I feel like one of the reasons that Leftover Crack and Choking Victim did well is that it goes beyond the music and the lyrics. A band can be derailed by having a poor taste in art or poor taste in band name.

Ara Babajian: As Sturgeon, it's not always easy to be a "nice guy." He was the one making all the decisions for the band. He was the one risking his neck the most. It was his vision that was on the line, more so than any of us. We were all essentially supporting his vision. So, if things didn't work out, that all fell on him. Sometimes there just is not a nice way to put your art across or push your will forward. When you're your own booking agent, your own manager, no one is doing that for you, and you just want to create— but first if you're going to get your art out there, you have to be a mercenary, a pirate, and a businessman. I think that's the position that he found himself in, initially. That's just how it goes. If you want to do good in music, you have to be a bit of a pirate—some people can accept that with him, but most people can't.

12

Gay Rude Boys Unite

Sturgeon: One of the times I was staying at Tim's house, Buju Banton's manager was there. Tim was trying really hard to sign Buju Banton. Buju Banton was, at the time, and still is, notoriously homophobic—like famously homophobic... When I was alone with his white manager, who spoke with full-on patois, I was already aware of a song on US Bombs' album *War Birth,* which was on Hellcat, called "Don't Need You." It's just the most homophobic song I've ever heard! It's just so shocking to me that it was part of a culture of the label that we had signed to.

Here's the line so stay on your side / You're so sensitive, go play the Smiths / I like girls and you like all the boys / I can tell you got that kind of lisp / Don't need you

—Excerpt from US Bombs' "Don't Need You"

World is in trouble anytime Buju Banton come / Batty boy [Patois equivalent of the slur "f*ggot"] *get up an run at gunshot me head back / Hear I tell him now crew / Boom bye bye inna batty boy head / Rude boy no promote no nasty man / Dem haffi dead*

—Excerpt from Buju Banton's "Boom Bye Bye"

Sturgeon: I knew that Jamaican rude boy culture was traditionally homophobic…and that was very much reinforced by Buju Banton's manager.

I said, straight up to the manager, "Hey, so what's up with Buju Banton and the homophobia thing?"

She acts like I'm in on the secret because it's Tim's house. She's like, "Shabba Ranks, he apologized for being homophobic!" But then, she's all excited and giddy. "Buju Banton *never* apologized for being homophobic! Isn't that great?!"

I didn't know what to say. I think I was literally speechless. I was like, in my brain, "This is batshit crazy!" I was like piecing together that Buju Banton was going to be on Hellcat, and US Bombs are on Hellcat…I'm really out of my element! I'm an anarcho-punk. I'm anti-homophobic, anti-sexist, anti-racist, and these people are celebrating "unity" because they're anti-racist…but *just* anti-racist.

It felt gross. I'm in this room with these people that are the total opposite of my politics. I had to get out of there. I had to clear my mind and cleanse my palette. I went back to the Olive Motel. I had some crack to smoke and some shit to think about. The first few lines of "Gay Rude Boys Unite" formed in my head before I passed out.

I had a guitar that was given to me by Mr. Brett. He was having drug problems at the time and I think he had recently gotten clean. It was a Telecaster. Someone talked me into asking him for it, and he gave it to me. For as much as I like being a squatter punk or whatever, I didn't like to be the guy who was running to the record label for a guitar. But he gave it to me and it helped.

I wrote the rest of "Gay Rude Boys Unite" at the Olive on that guitar. That song was pretty easy to write lyrics to. The best songs are the ones that don't even seem to come from you, but through you. "Infested," "Gay Rude Boys Unite," "One Dead Cop," and

"The Lie of Luck" were all written by a Jesus Angel…on the fourth of July…in the year of the dragon…

I'm no Weird Al and I'm not a jingle writer, but I feel like "Crack Rock Steady" is a good approximation of "Ranking Full Stop," "Too Much Pressure," and those songs. I feel like "Gay Rude Boys Unite" is a pretty good approximation of Operation Ivy. It's not necessarily traceable, but when I tried to learn "Yelling in My Ear" and "Healthy Body," I could mimic it. And to Lars and Tim's credit, eight months later, it registered in their brains that "this song is about us." But I feel like they may have taken more offense then was necessary.

I like to give that gift of offense to people and let them do with it whatever they like. They can let it slide off their back or they can be butt-hurt for an hour, or you can take this offense all the way to your fucking grave, and I feel like they might be doing that. Which is fine. A little goes a long way sometimes.

Jesse Michaels (Vocals—Operation Ivy, Common Rider, Classics of Love): When I first heard *Mediocre Generica* and Leftover Crack, I liked them immediately. But, at first, I thought "Gay Rude Boys Unite" was an anti-Op Ivy. I wasn't sure if they were taking a shot at Op Ivy or if it was a tribute. That's okay. Every generation takes a shot at the earlier generation.

Sturgeon: Maybe Tim and I were like two magnets that could only repel each other. I don't feel like there was any way that either of us could relate to the other.

Jesse Michaels: I knew that Tim and Sturgeon had a beef at some point. I don't really know the nature of it. I think Sturgeon described it to me once. It sounded like something that should not last forever because it didn't seem to be that serious. It seemed to be more of a misunderstanding than anything else.

13

Chopper

Sturgeon: So, I'm working at Wetlands and Lars and the Bastards are playing there. The new Leftover Crack record is done but it's not out yet.

I met Lars a couple of times before and he told me that he loved "Fucked Reality," which surprised me because I wouldn't say it's the worst Choking Victim song…but let's just say that it has the least amount of effort put into it.

It seems to be the favorite song of a lot of people. I don't dislike it. There are some songs like "Crack Rock Steady" and "Fucked Reality" that are just somehow a little too simple for me. I feel like a song should have two parts, maybe. But all the best Choking Victim songs had one part. "Fucked Reality" doesn't change. "Crack Rock Steady" doesn't change. Maybe Leftover Crack songs change too much. Maybe people change too much.

So anyway, Lars is playing Wetlands and the new Leftover Crack was supposed to come out in May 2001 and we had to wait until September 11, or whatever, some arbitrary date. I can't count—but I can count on that being a long time to wait, especially when you're like twenty-four. Time moves really slow at that age. It sucks.

Well, Lars and Tim were at the Wetlands. I think Lars seemed nervous because the Bastards were new and he was playing New York City. If you can make it in New York City, you can make it anywhere. If you break in New York City, you just break. Dropkick Murphys are there. King Django is there. John John from Nausea is there.

Lars is weird to me. At the show, he kind of blows me off and pretends he doesn't know who I am. I thought that Tim was the "masked bastard" in Lars Frederiksen and the Bastards, but later I learned that he wasn't. I was like, "Hey, what's up?" I have a case of beer in my hand—I'm working that night. I'm working class, unlike those guys…I'm "classy" and working. I was like, "Hey, what's up?" I may have even been like, "Hey, what's going on with the record?" because Tim said, "Call me anytime there's a problem." And every time there was a problem, I'd call and he'd never call me back.

So, Tim is like, "Hey, what's up, man?" Tim up to this point had made a very unconvincing case that he's my friend. "I'm your buddy, call me anytime!" But he doesn't answer the phone *ever*. And then, when I'm like three fucking feet from him, he is still acting like he doesn't know who I am. It was weird.

Maybe I'm being unkind. It seemed fucked up to me. Tim was like, "Uuuhhhh…where's my book—my first press of my *Chopper* book?" That's the first thing out of his mouth.

I was like, "Ohhh…well…it's at my ex's house in Montana. I'll probably never see it again." I think that was that and he just walked away. I thought that was a weird way to treat bands on your label. I followed him into the dressing room with a case of beer. He probably thought that I was just following him or was there at my leisure. He probably didn't understand that I had a job that I was working and he was in my way. I wasn't that fazed because I never felt like those people were my friends and we didn't come from the same world. I felt that they weren't sincere with me.

14
9/11

Seth Olenick: *Mediocre Generica* came out on...September 11, 2001. That might be the only reason it didn't go platinum or double platinum.

Ara Babajian: I had worked at the World Trade Center throughout the recording of *Mediocre Generica* on the eighty-second floor of Tower Two. I'd work for The Man during the day then go play drums for Leftover Crack at night. I worked right up until September 7, 2001, when I gave notice that I would be leaving for tour on September 11 and would not be coming back.

Alec Baillie: On September 11, I was in my apartment in Greenpoint, Brooklyn, with my now ex-girlfriend Leah Pollard and my good friend David. Dave woke me up after the first plane had crashed into the tower. I was like, "Oh, shit, that's crazy! I'm going to go back to sleep."

The second plane crashed and Dave woke me up again and I was like, "Oh, shit, this is crazy!" The three of us walked down to Woodhull Hospital in Bushwick to try to donate blood. Because no buses were working and no cell phones were working, no one could communicate. By the time we got there, they told us that they weren't accepting any blood because they had received no patients from the World Trade Center and we were like, "Oh, that's not good."

Sturgeon: On 9/11, I worked a few blocks from the World Trade Center at the Wetlands until about five in the morning and then biked home and went to sleep at C-Squat. The person I was a guest of at C-Squat was knocking at my door at nine a.m. saying, "The World Trade Center is on fire." I was like, "Cool, I don't care!" He said, "Put on the TV!" So, I saw the hole in the building and went up to the roof because we were only a mile and a half away and then I saw the second plane hit. It was a pretty crazy day. We were just up there acting crazy and then the towers fell.

Brad Logan: I had flown into New York on the ninth or the tenth to start a tour with F-Minus that was starting there. I was staying on my friend Genice's couch in Brooklyn. She woke me up at about nine in the morning saying, "Dude, you have to look at what's on the TV!" Both the towers had been struck and there was smoke billowing out of them. I was waking up and trying to make sense out of it—what the fuck has happened? At that point, it looked like some bizarre airplane accident. I walked down to the corner of her block to the bodega and grabbed a cup of coffee. She was on Metropolitan Avenue and at the end of the street, you had a direct view of the towers. I'm sitting there drinking coffee, pondering the event, and the first tower dissolved in front of my eyes.

I thought it was a hallucination. It was surreal. The building just melted in front of me. My first thought was, "This can't be happening! It's too big to fall down! And then my second thought was, "Oh, my God, there are thousands of people dying in front of me right now!" There were no words. It was just shocking. Nothing short of traumatizing.

A half an hour later, all cell phones were out, there was no reception. After both towers fell, I went to Kellogg's Diner to get something to eat, and Kellogg's was packed. In typical New York fashion, people were downplaying it. But, as the day unfolded, it became clear that this was not just some weird sort of airplane disaster. There was some real sinister shit going on.

There were people coming over the bridge, covered in soot. We spent the night on the street, hanging out, walking around like it was doomsday. It was really creepy.

Ara Babajian: So, instead of waking up that morning and leaving for tour, I awoke to the catastrophe of that day and frantic phone calls from family and friends who thought I still worked in the towers. I got a call from Sturgeon saying, "Hey, uh, Ara, just checking to see if you're okay and all and just letting you know that the tour is still on,"…which I thought was pretty funny and indicative of Sturgeon's willpower. Nothing, not even 9/11, was gonna stop the tour from happening!

Sturgeon: Ara is one of the success stories of 9/11. He worked in a bank in one of the World Trade towers. His last day of work was the Friday before the eleventh. We played a couple of shows with Stiff Little Fingers that weekend and our first tour started on Thursday, the thirteenth, two days after our record came out. He quit and the person that replaced him died. The guy got there early and died. It was a new job, and it was his second day of work. That was one of the floors that a plane hit. That's crazy.

Alec Baillie: Ara was working for some bank. His job was terrible anyways. He told me they had this seating system with these rows, where the more senior you are, the further back you are. So, if you're new, there are hundreds of people looking at your back.

The first show of our tour was scheduled for September 13 because our record was scheduled to be released on September 11. Ara had quit his job on the Friday prior to September 11, which was in the World Trade Center. He quit his job to go on tour with us. I like to credit myself with saving his life.

In fact, ska saved Ara Babajian's life, literally.

Sturgeon: *Leftover Crack* saved Ara's life.

Ara Babajian: Personally, 9/11 represented a second chance at life. I felt like I had been given a reprieve. I narrowly missed something—a death—who knows? Maybe I would have shown up that day and saw the buildings on fire. It kind of lit a fire under me, no pun intended, to do something with my life that was meaningful. It made me sad for New York City. It felt like your heart and the city's heart were stabbed by this horrible thing. I didn't need to know, or understand, the political ramifications. I just knew that the heart of my city had been stabbed and was hurt. I knew it was never going to be the same and it never was the same again. Everything changed in the city and the country that day and it still is a hard thing to talk about. Everything changed for the worse.

Sturgeon: When the buildings fell, that was kind of the first indication that there was something that the official story wasn't correct. That planes hit the buildings, they caught on fire, and then they fell. Controlled demolitions…? It doesn't make sense.

Alec Baillie: I don't think there's a conspiracy, but I think it was an inside job. I think it was by the people who benefitted from it. The people that had insurance policies that benefitted from the damage, the people that benefitted from the resulting war that made it easy to win over the American people because they were angry. It's a false flag where you attack your own people to get them riled and attack your real target.

No one really knows exactly what happened but you can't fucking tell me that the US would allow two planes to hit two of the tallest buildings in the world in Manhattan, but then, a few blocks away, buildings that were not hit by planes collapsed and caught fire. Give me a fucking break.

Brad Logan: All the fatalities, all the casualties, I don't care what the causes were or if it was an inside job, or the political ramifications, I don't give a fuck about any of that. What I saw was a bunch of people dying right in front of my eyes and it was horrible. I never want to see anything like that ever again.

Sturgeon: Our first tour was with The Unseen and F-Minus. Ron Martinez, our booker, would book us with street punks and questionable skin-headed type bands, and I was very vocal about what was going on with 9/11 at those shows. But I think that polarization has a lot to do with the success of this band as well. A lot of people wouldn't and still won't talk about 9/11 as frankly as I will.

Brad Logan: The tour was started with F-Minus. I had left Leftover Crack to tour with F-Minus. We did maybe three shows. We were meeting Leftover Crack in Chicago. So, we met up with them in Chicago and the show was chaos. Leftover Crack had an upside-down American flag backdrop. People were throwing shit and the whole vibe was pretty intense. F-Minus started getting calls from promoters that shows were getting canceled, so we abandoned the tour. Leftover Crack kept going.

I got dropped off at an airport in Columbus, Ohio, and flew to see my then girlfriend, now wife, in Lawrence, Kansas. There were two people on the plane.

Alec Baillie: A lot of people after September 11 in the United States got caught up in the anti-Islamic feeling. Even people in the punk scene who should know better were becoming a lot more patriotic. Obviously, Leftover Crack's politics are…you know…a lot of them are…not so…*patriotic*. So, we took a lot of shit on that tour. We would get shit from the audience. People would boo us. There was always the threat of getting attacked.

Sturgeon: We did at least thirty-five shows. We went south, we went west, we went all the way through Montana and played everywhere we could. We got back to New York and had a few days off and then we had a week and half in Canada. Then we had a week or two off and then we went to Europe for a month and half. I had never toured before even though I wanted to. I can look back on those tours and would be miserable now, but I had a great time. I never really got to do that. It's the reason why we play music. It's not because we want money or fame, it's because we have a drive to do it. It's fucking fun.

15
First Tours

Alec Baillie: We were playing at the Opera House in Toronto. We were opening up for AFI. It was probably the biggest show that we had played to date. When we all got onstage, we just kind of froze. I had never played to that many people. We hadn't had a chance to sound check so the sound was super weird. We just kind of failed miserably. After the fourth or fifth song, Sturgeon said something about the World Trade Center and Ara just walked off. It had already been a long tour. We only had a few days left on the tour, and that's when he quit. I think we only played five songs.

Ara Babajian: I walked off stage during a show after Sturgeon introduced *"Osama Bin Baillie* on bass!" in front of a couple thousand people opening up for AFI. I was just not in a good place, mentally. It's laughable in retrospect that such a thing should have set me off, but anyway, that's where my mind was at. I had a narrow escape from the World Trade Center attacks. I knew a lot of people who died. I had a lot of emotions I was dealing with at the time. So, a little joke like that could set me off.

I was really suffering from some kind of PTSD. I'd known a lot of people who died at the World Trade Center and I just couldn't square that with some of the things that Sturgeon was saying every night about it being a good thing that the towers had fallen. He did his best to protect my feelings and get his point across, but there was really no perfect way to do that.

So, despite some amazing shows on that first tour, I really just existed in my own little bubble with my wife doing merch and the two of us trying to tour manage and handle the finances of the band, while the guys, Ezra, Scott, and Alec, were enjoying a lot of camaraderie each night on the road.

I just had too much shit to deal with. I had to go. And once the tour was over, I was done. I just could not wrap my head around my near death and the death I had experienced

Sturgeon: I believe Ara quitting the band had very little to do with 9/11. I think it had to do at that point that Ara wasn't into touring in a punk band for months and months. Ara and his wife were on tour and I think they wanted to settle down a little bit, even if it was just his wife and not him. I don't know if they realized that themselves.

Ara Babajian: Touring is difficult for me—having to leave my family and being on other's people time. After the show, you always try to find the place where you'll get the best night's sleep. Sturgeon and I would always battle for the best room. We would race through the house instinctively trying to find a dark and quiet place. But a lot of the time, you're just in someone's living room and there's a party going on next door, and you just have to put in earplugs and do your best dealing with people walking over you to go take a piss. Sometimes they are taking a piss over your body literally because the bathroom is the only place you can sleep.

Whenever I quit the band, Sturgeon always made a point of giving me a hug and saying words to the effect of, "Well, I hate to see you go. But we both know you'll be back." And he'd give me a mischievous smile and I'd smile back and say, "Yeah, probably."

Alec Baillie: After Ara quit, JP Otto of Stockyard Stoics took over for drums and played on the subsequent tour, which was eight weeks.

Sturgeon: JP was in the Stockyard Stoics and The Readymen, a ska-punk band from back in the day. We played with the Stockyard Stoics a bunch. We got them on the Stiff Little Fingers show, which was really exciting for them. They were friends of ours that were politically minded.

JP Otto (Drummer—Leftover Crack, Morning Glory, Stockyard Stoics): When I was playing in the Stockyard Stoics, we had played with Leftover Crack at C-Squat and maybe the Wetlands. I remember watching them thinking, "Oh, I could play drums for these guys."

My first impressions of Sturgeon were that I underestimated him quite a bit in terms of his musicianship and creativity. Maybe it's the situation where everybody is the same age, so it's, "Oh, yeah, there's another that guy plays guitar and screams into the mic." But he writes *goooood* songs. When Sturgeon is in a good mood, there is no one more fun to hang out with. But when that guy is in a rotten mood, there is no one you want to get way from more. That's just kind of how he is.

I think Sturgeon called me on a Wednesday. It was their first US tour and they were in Canada and Ara had quit. Sturgeon asked me, "What are you doing next week?" I said I had no plans. He said, "Okay! You're going to Europe with us!" He told me to go buy the Choking Victim album and the Leftover Crack album and learn all these songs in two days. They were back in the city on a Saturday and we rehearsed all day that day and all day Sunday and flew out Monday and then played our first show in England on Monday night.

Dale Tomlinson (UK Tour manager): My first experience was picking them up at the airport. I picked them up and I'd never met any of them before. Soon, we pulled over because they wanted some food. Stza was in the bins—rattling around in the bins eating all these kind of old chicken nuggets, and I was like "What ya doin'?" and he's going, "Well, no one's eating them!"…so that was my first meeting.

JP Otto: The shows were pretty hit or miss, like all the early tours… but it was more hits than misses. The thing about Europe is they always want these super long sets. But we had like twelve songs. Sometimes, we played the set twice and hoped nobody noticed. Sometimes, someone in the crowd would be like, "Oh, yeah! I've heard this one before!" and they didn't realize that we just played it thirty minutes earlier.

Brad Logan: We would get attacked by the audience all the time. In France, we got assaulted by the audience at every show. Literally *every one* of the five shows we played in France on that tour. I don't know if they had something personally against us or if they were showing their love by spitting on us and punching us onstage. I remember at one of the shows in France, Alec had to do the Sid Vicious thing and use his bass as a club to hit people and fend them off.

Dale Tomlinson: I was a ska fan when I was a kid. I loved Two-Tone and stuff like that. I wasn't too hip on the American ska stuff, ya know, like ska-punk. I mean, everybody liked Operation Ivy and I like the Bosstones because I liked his gravelly voice. Most of the other stuff I didn't really like. But Leftover Crack had something, I don't know what it was…like his voice…there was something really dark about Leftover Crack that I really liked. It was really nasty sounding, and I'd never heard a nasty-sounding ska band before. There was something about Stza's gritty voice, almost like a little rabid dog or something attacking ya.

The lyric content was really serious and very honest and very political and very brutal when a lot of the stuff at the time was pop punk—ya know, nursery rhyme pop punk, which I didn't like. And then the next time they came over, they were just fucking huge. And the kids just went mental and the audiences were fucking great. When I was with them I thought, this is the best band in Europe right now!

So when I'd grab the people and as soon as I said the word "ska" they'd be mad and say, "Oh, fuck that!" And I'd say, "No, come check the shows out!" The kids just went mental for it. All the kids who were into the nice ska stuff, well, they just turned overnight.

JP Otto: There were parts of Europe that were not so good. Maybe people hadn't heard the band yet. Eastern Europe was rough. Playing out in Poland, I think that was the first time I ever played in a band that actively got booed. We were playing with the old-school US band Iron Cross.

Those Polish guys weren't too hip to what we were putting down. We were just up there playing punky ska reggae stuff and they were just like, "Booooooo" and we were like, "Wow, this isn't working out so well?"

16

It's Okay...We're Americans

Joe Porter (Leftover Crack van driver, merch person, fan): The first tour that I drove the van on was the first US one after Ara left. It was Sturgeon, Ezra, JP, Alec, and me. Bill Cashman asked me to drive the van. He was like, "Leftover Crack needs someone to drive and I can't do it and I told them that you might want to do it and you don't drink so you'd be good for driving on this tour." I hated my job at the time, so I agreed to do it.

I was like, "I'm on tour for two months so I need all this stuff." Anything I could ever need I brought. Leftover Crack was my favorite band and I was going on tour with them. I brought the two Case Logic CD cases with me from my car. I was like, "We'll be on tour and I'll never get sick of it. These guys will like all of these bands from New Jersey that they've never heard!"

The first moment I showed up I was like, "*What* am I doing?" Immediately, Sturgeon starts yelling that I had all of this stuff that I didn't need and that I had way too much stuff. Then he started going through my CDs. He was like, "This sucks. This is crap. This is no good. You are *not* bringing these CDs with you." It was like, "Great, the first five minutes of a two-month tour and the band hates me. This is going to be fun."

The first show of the US tour, we got there, and we played, and afterward there was a party. Ezra didn't really know me, and he was like, "Joe, there's a party that we're going to go to, and we're gonna get this bottle of rum. Do you want anything?" and I said, "Oh, thanks, man, but I don't really drink." He paused then, and was like, "Oh, we can get some coke." I was like, "Yeah! Coke sounds great!" I didn't realize until half an hour later that he meant blow and not a soda! I was like, "This is going to be a weird tour."

I felt like a square who was a fan of the band who didn't fit in. At one point, Sturgeon bought me a pair of black pants. I was wearing like khaki-colored Dickies. He was like, "You can't…you can't keep wearing those. I'm going to buy you some black pants and you gotta wear these now."

We listened to the Hives and System of a Down non-stop. I would never have expected that band to listen to *that*. At that time, I didn't get along with Ezra because he was being such a "boss" to me the whole time. He would get mad because I didn't know what I was doing driving. I had never driven outside of New Jersey. I had never driven a van with a trailer.

Since I had never driven outside of New Jersey, I didn't know that you had to pump your own gas in other places. We drive into Pennsylvania and we stop to get gas and I was like, "I think I can figure this out." But…I forgot to put the cap on and close it.

JP saw that and he basically gave me a stern talking to. And I was like, "God, these guys hate me! I can't believe I'm about to do two months with them!" Driving through the Rockies, Ezra kept giving me shit because I didn't know anything about switching gears and it was snowing like crazy. The transmission turned over one time and Ezra was like, "How many times do I have to tell you to switch into second gear!" I was like, "Well, I've never done this before!" Then, Ezra was like, "It doesn't matter! You're a professional!" And,

I was like, "Well, actually, I'm *not a* professional!" And Ezra was like, "If you're getting paid to do something it means you *are* a professional!"

Sturgeon: Joe Porter would *only* eat chicken sandwiches. Like a fried, fake chicken filet on bread with no condiments. It was the only thing he would eat. That seemed strange to me.

Alec Baillie: We were in a little twelve-person van that we bought for $1100 at the police auction at the Brooklyn Navy Yard. That van lasted us for a few tours. We would almost always pick up hitchhikers.

JP Otto: Sturgeon wanted to pick up every hitchhiker. We picked up some Mormon kid in like Utah or wherever and the Mormon kid was like, "Do you know about boys...that dress like girls?" and asked all these weird questions. We left him at a rest stop.

We would be late for a show and Sturgeon would be like, "Pick up those people! I don't care if we're late, if you don't pick them up I'm not playing tonight!...why are you still driving?!"

I'd say, "I didn't see anybody, dude!"

Alec Baillie: One day, we picked up these guys and they had three dogs. JP was not a fan of picking them up. And so, one of the dogs shit on JP's sleeping bag.

JP Otto: Squatter kids with the dogs...and the dogs always shit in the van! Goddammit! *Goddammit!* This is where we live! This is why we don't have dogs in the van!

Alec Baillie: After that, for picking up people, there was a three-dog minimum.

Brad Logan: F-Minus had been touring on our first album. We were relentless. It was constant Europe and US touring. One time during a break in tours, I went to see Leftover Crack at the Showcase

Theatre in Corona. They were so good. I couldn't believe it was the same band I had been in a year ago. After the gig, I said to Sturgeon, "If you ever wanna add another guitar player, I'd love to play with you guys again." Sturgeon says, "Yeah, lemme think about it." A month or so later, I got a call from him and it was on. I went out to New York City and started rehearsing with them. When I joined the second time, I think JP Otto was on the drums.

Then started the countless USA and Europe tours with Leftover Crack, too. At that point between the two bands, I pretty much lived in a van. I don't know how I did it without going insane. Maybe I did go insane and I'm too insane to know it.

Van touring is kinda like jail. You have to reduce your personal space down to the size of a coffin. If you're lucky, you'd have a whole bench seat to yourself. You're playing shows all over the world, but your personal space and time become very small. Tuning people out, picking your battles, learning to get by with the bare essentials, these become important skills to learn. You do everything together as a group. Alone time becomes gold. If you've ever found a band person sitting behind a club alone, looking like shit and trying to appear invisible, that's why.

You barely get any sleep because you have to drive to the next gig and it's eight hours away so you drive right after the show. You set up. You break down. The next night you're staying at someone's house and there's a party going on around you while you try and burrow into your sleeping bag. Or you're all staying together in someone's one-bedroom apartment. Or you're sleeping in an abandoned building in the dead of winter.

You have to be in the mental and physical shape to do it or you will just crack. You're fatigued, you're irritable, you're lonely. It can break you. I've seen it happen. I've been broken a couple times, too.

I've had staph infections from not showering and weeks of playing the dirtiest clubs in the world, wearing the same clothes every night because after a while you become comfortable in your own filth. I came home from one tour with a boil on my back the size of an orange. I had to have a doctor lance it and take antibiotics for weeks. You could look through the hole it left and see my ribs. I still have the scar. That was after a long summer tour. The van was knee high with trash. Beer cans, food wrappers, magazines, coffee cups, clothes, anything you can imagine. I loved showering as much as the next person, but sometimes it would be days before we played anywhere or stayed anywhere where that was an option.

I remember we were on tour in France one summer and pulled into a roadside rest-stop to use the toilets. It was ninety-degree sweltering French summer heat. As we opened the sliding door on the side of the Sprinter, a tidal wave of trash spilled out onto the ground next to the van. I looked out and noticed a family outside their car a couple parking stalls away; Dad, Mom, and the kids just staring at us in *horror* as six grimy shitbags all dressed in black climbed out of a van following a massive pile of garbage. We were so tour-burned by that point none of us even stopped to pick anything up. "It's okay, we're Americans," Sturgeon said to the family, then walked off to take a piss.

Joe Jack Talcum: One time, Leftover Crack was supposed to play a show in Philadelphia, but it was canceled the day of the show. I'm not sure why. Maybe it was their lyrics? They were trying to find a show, and someone asked us if we could throw the show in the basement of the Town Managers' house. So, we did. They showed up and it was a great show. It was a lot of fun. Nothing unusual happened except that it was a show in a basement, which isn't that unusual. They were very professional and normal to me.

Joe Porter: We were in Pittsburgh, and we stayed at this completely disgusting house. Brad, me, and Alec played darts for like a half hour. It was an electric dartboard and it kept making this noise, "Mer ma mant." That house was so awful, so that sound became the soundtrack to anything that went bad. "So-and-so is fighting with So-and-so?" "Mer ma mant!" "The promoter doesn't want to pay us?" "Mer ma mant!" That noise could get you through anything.

At that house, the bathroom was so disgusting. Brad said he needed to take a shower. I said, "You could take a shower in there," and Brad looked in and said, "If I took a shower in there I would have to have all my skin burned off with acid after." In the morning, I just wanted to get out of there. It was so nasty. We had the tour itinerary in a binder and I saw it and I was like, "Oh, I don't want to forget that!" It had all these crumbs on it and I just brushed the crumbs off, and they went into the floorboards.

As we are leaving, the guy comes running out. "Who took that binder!" I said, "Oh I did…" He yells, "What did you do with all the crack I had on it?!" So, I had brushed all of crack into the floorboards.

I was at the end of my rope. We had been on tour for a month and I was like, "I'm drained. *This* guy hasn't taken a shower the entire time. *This* guy is being a jerk the entire time. We got to Reno and I just went behind the building and called my dad. I was like, "What am I gonna do, I cannot stay with these guys!" My dad was like, "You can always come home, but maybe it will turn around." And it did. I love Ezra now, but he was being military dad the entire time.

Sturgeon: You gotta love the fact that Joe held his own. He made it through the tour. The constitution of most people would have crumbled by the time JP Otto is giving him a stern talking. They would be crying and on a bus back to New Jersey and Joe stuck it out for two months and that says a lot about Joe.

Brad Logan: A common occurrence would be walking into a gas station shop while the van was getting gassed up. I'd look around at Joe Porter and the other guys, and I'd see the shifty looks on their faces. I knew what was up. They were just stuffed to the brim with shoplifted shit. Snacks, magazines, tools, whatever they could get their hands on.

Joe Porter: That was so pointless. That continued for many bands I went on tour with after that. A lot of people weren't used to what we did in Leftover Crack. One time, I was so black-out drunk from a drive from Minneapolis to Milwaukee—I fell out of a van at a gas station and somehow made it to the bathroom. I had to hold myself up at a urinal to pee. Then, I went in and thought I was being like really slick, and shoplifted some candy and got away with it. Everyone in that band was like, *"What* are you doing!?"

Brad Logan: Everyone would come back to the van and just empty their jackets and pockets, then go back for round two.

Joe Porter: The craziest show around that time was in LA at the Showcase. The merch area was like up on a balcony and I remember just being completely overwhelmed. A common thing doing merch for the band is that everything needs to be duct-taped down at all times. I was mobbed with people trying to buy merch. Every person, they are all so curious about the lifestyle of the band and squatting and New York City and you become their question-and-answer man. You become the info desk.

And you are also being completely swamped with people trying to buy merch and you are hit with the same stupid questions and eventually you're like, "I don't know. I live with my parents in the suburbs."

And stuff was just flying off the table. Every time you turn around stuff was getting stolen. Someone jumped off the balcony at the show and it was just way too out of control.

Renée Berol (Fan): We used to have shows at the American Legion Hall on Sixty-Ninth street in Upper Darby, near Philadelphia. Because it was the American Legion hall, there were American flags hanging on the walls. I don't know who decided to book Leftover Crack there. Three quarters of the way through the set, people started pulling the flags off the wall. Someone passed Stza a flag or he just grabbed one, but he held it up and lit it on fire and that started a chain reaction. Kids started lighting every flag in the hall on fire. I think almost all of them got burned. I think we weren't allowed to have shows there for a little while. We definitely ruined that.

17

Baby Jesus

Sturgeon: We were being held hostage by Epitaph. *Mediocre Generica* had been out for a long time and Epitaph / Hellcat obviously did not want to do another record with us. I would call Chris LaSalle every day to ask to get out of our contract.

We just wanted to get dropped. So, until we could get out of our contract, nobody would talk to us about releasing anything. So, we called ourselves the Crack Rock Steady 7, which really was just Leftover Crack.

The name the Crack Rock Steady 7 comes from a time that Choking Victim played a show with the Slackers. Dave Hillyard of the Slackers had a project called the David Hillyard Rocksteady 7. So, just to annoy him, I told him I wanted to call my future project the Crack Rock Steady 7.

Brad Logan: The split record wasn't a slag on Hellcat at all. We were approached by this guy Joe Oz, who had this record label outta New York called Hell-Bent. He asked if F-Minus wanted to do a split with LoC and we were down. I just didn't know we weren't contractually allowed to do things like that. Maybe Sturgeon did, hence the name change. I didn't know anything about the record business. I was like, "Someone wants to record us and put a record out? Fucking great, let's go!"

I just mentioned it to Tim Armstrong in passing and he hit the ceiling. I said, "What did we do wrong?" and he was like, "You can't put records out with other labels, you're a Hellcat artist!" I was like "Oops," and he's like, "It's already done so just go for it."

I think initially he thought I was trying to do something behind his back. But, when I explained it to him, it was apparent that I didn't know how record contracts worked at all. I never even read ours. None of us did. I learned a lot about the record business in that period.

We covered the Middle Class on that record. The Atta brothers from Middle Class had a vintage furniture and guitar store in Fullerton. I walked in and said, "You guys don't know me, you don't know my band, but you guys were a big influence on me. We did a cover of 'Love Is Just a Tool.' Sorry we didn't ask for your permission. Here's a copy." They were really cool about it.

Sturgeon: I continued using the satanic imagery in Leftover Crack, which I had been using in Choking Victim. Initially, the satanic theme was an appreciation of the iconography. I could never, to this day, figure out a good Leftover Crack logo. Choking Victim was easy. We took the CV out of the No Commercial Value logo and put the squatter symbol on it and it made itself.

For Leftover Crack, I tried for a while, scribbling and asked people, but the L-O-C never fit together as a way that was pleasing as a logo. Throwing the pentagram on it was kind of a logo.

I've been an atheist since I was a preteen. I was bar mitzvahed. I didn't care. Around my thirteenth birthday, my stepfather committed suicide. He was a musician—a drummer. I liked drumming. I wanted him to teach me drumming and he would not. He died and my mom was distraught. It was brought to me as, "Would you have a bar mitzvah because our family needs something positive right now because our stepdad killed himself?" They had been married for maybe eight years. He had been around since I was little. I knew I was atheist, but some of the family members would still give you money. "You'll have several hundred dollars." I was like, "Ooohh, money! I'll do that!" We did a bar mitzvah after my thirteenth year—maybe half a year later.

Kristen Kay Ferrell (Artist—Leftover Crack, F-Minus): The Crack Rock Steady 7/F-Minus split was the first time Leftover Crack used my art. They've used my artwork on a lot of their releases since then.

My artwork, and my artwork for Leftover Crack, has satanic themes, or anti-Christian themes. But that also comes from the fact that I was raised by evangelicals. I was put in an evangelical, Southern Baptist cult when I was fourteen for two years in the woods, in Branson, Missouri, because the church told my parents that I was possessed by the devil. I was a victim of the satanic panic when everyone thought satanic cults were killing babies. That was heavy in the Midwest and that's what got me sent away. They pushed me to study the Bible and I understood how batshit crazy it is and I became dedicated to logic and science.

Now, I have zero spirituality. Nature is just atoms in the cosmos. Our brains are just electrons bouncing around in a lump of matter in our skull. It is our responsibility to be held completely accountable for our own behavior so everyone can have a good life.

So, I joined the Satanic Temple, who fight weaponized theology. Weaponized Theology is what evangelical Christians are. They've weaponized their God. The Satanic Temple, which was only founded a few years ago, is very different from the Church of Satan. Now, I'm not a spokesperson for The Satanic Temple, and these are only my opinions about why I was drawn to be a member. The Satanic Temple was formed as a community with likeminded beliefs against Christian tyranny. It's a very political movement that has an atheistic theology. They don't believe in God or Satan.

They are governed by science, they are governed by ethics, they are governed by empathy. That is how we as a community progress through our political movements. It is now a recognized religion so they can sue in the same of religious freedom when Christianity oversteps the separation of church and state.

So, that's why a lot of my work is very anti-Christian and pro-demonology imagery. It's kind of a "fuck you" to Christians. Plus, it's just more fun to paint dark things than it is to paint bowls of fruit and landscapes.

I'm not coming from a place of making creepy, spooky art to be like Hot Topic. It's not just that this will piss off your parents. With my art, there's a history behind it, there's a reasoning for it. It's not flippant. I think that's why it matches.

Leftover Crack's music doesn't come from just a "I'm here to piss off parents" knee-jerk rebellion. It's not "fuck you, that's why!" The lyrics are well thought out, they come from a place of experience. They come from a place of pointing out injustices and pointing out people that have been harmed by our society— pointing out how things have broken people. It's not "I'm gonna say fuck you and here's a fuck you." It's "there's a very good reason for this fuck you, here's why, and fuck you."

My musical tastes do not align with Leftover Crack. I'm not a ska-punk girl. I'm more inclined to listen to the Paper Chase. I respect it, because it's not *just* ska-punk, it's not just rebellion for the sake of rebellion. There's a little more to it. I like to think that's similar to my work. Each piece is just more than "I like spooky art!" I think they complement each other in that way.

At art school, you have to take lots of art history. When you look at classical works, when you look at a portrait of a stodgy, rich, old couple, there is so much more going on than you realize at first. The fruit that is used, if an apple is used instead of a pear, that means something. If a bird is used, what kind of bird? Especially in old religious art, every single element of that painting, to the colors that are used, means something. It is its own symbolic language, and if you know the symbolic language, you understand what they are saying. Because the population was mostly illiterate, this is how they told Bible stories. This is how they told the stories of history and their monarchs. The symbolic images told the story. I found that beautiful.

That kind of sent me down this path. I'm going to take all of these symbols and I'm going to make them mine. Okay, if you see a swan, it means marital union. If you cut that swan's head off, it means the union is severed. Every finger has a meaning, so if you cut them off and sew them onto a different part of the body, that means something else. You can take the puzzle pieces of these symbols and rearrange them to make your own picture.

People don't know the specific story behind my work because most people aren't versed in this classical key. I know what my paintings mean, that's what's important for me. But I like people to get their own meaning from it. I just love the classical puzzle.

Ara Babajian: To be honest, I thought the over-the-top Satanism was really juvenile and I really just wanted to be a great fucking band playing great fucking music. I couldn't understand why we had to do all this provocative smart-ass shit in order to get attention. Let the music get the attention!

But in retrospect, I was wrong. I think that the mythologizing of the band that Sturgeon did via this imagery and some of the writing about himself that he did with songs like "Crack City Rockers" and "Heroin or Suicide" are unbelievable works of art, real documents of a real life. And the name Leftover Crack, although it made me wince at the time, has endured as a fucking great band name and genius existential druggy conundrum: There's no such thing as Leftover Crack, that is, we're not really here. If you have a problem with us, with any of this, then it's your problem, not ours! It's Situationism, Dadaism, which are the art movements that were the very foundations of punk.

Sturgeon: I am an atheist. I was brought up Jewish in New York City, which is a very atheistic place. We went to Israel when I was eleven and we saw all the holy sites. These places, the Muslims, the Christians, the Jews, it's all holy to them. Ehhh…it's stupid. I mean, it's obvious that none of them are right. How could one prove they are right over the other? And how could you do that if you were brought up one way over another?

But I was never really taught in Sunday school that God was a thing. Judaism, especially reformed Judaism, isn't so much a theistic religion as Christianity and Islam. I think it's a little more like, "we're better than everybody because of our bloodline" by saying we're God's chosen people. It's a way of saying we are better than everyone. I don't think too many Jews are picturing God looking down and saying, "Yeah, you and me, we're buddies!" Nah, that's a very Christian way of looking at things. "Yes! Thumbs up, Jesus!"

Brad Logan: I'm not an atheist. I've always been attracted to occult sciences and spiritual quests. I think everybody should be entitled to their own beliefs, or lack thereof. It's a very personal thing. I wasn't raised in churches or temples, but I've been to them, usually on holidays. My dad was Jewish and my mother was Greek orthodox. But neither were forced on us. We were free to find our own way. I was thankful for that. I did, however, inherit the guilt of existing from them.

18
Drummer Wanted

Sturgeon: JP played with us for a month and then I kicked him out. He pissed me off on tour. He only lasted like the Canadian tour. It was stupid. It was his personality—plus, one of the last nights in Canada I was trying to sleep in a loft in Canada. He's like hanging out, talking to the one other person that was there and I was like, "Yo, what the fuck? Can you like shut up or whatever? Do you even care? Do you want to play in this band?" And he was like, "I don't know." I was like, "Cool, you're fired!" and that was that.

JP Otto: We did like fifty shows in sixty days. We did two months around the US and then up to Canada. It was the second or third to last day of the tour and we were hanging out at someone's house. Sturgeon claimed the only mattress. The rest of us were hanging out in the kitchen telling jokes and drinking beer and just having a good time.

Next thing you know, Sturgeon just appears in the door and says, "Are…are you…are you gonna be laughing like that…all night?"

I said, "I don't know, probably…I'm a pretty funny guy!" and everybody starts cracking up.

And he looks at me and says, "You know what, I don't want you to go to Europe with us!" And I was like, "Well, I guess that's settled." He huffed and went back to his mattress and we all looked at each other and were like, "Well, that's that."

I finished out the last three shows and it was a little awkward. I think we had a week or two off and it was supposed to be back to Europe for a month. I think Sturgeon called me and apologized and was like, "You know, we really want you to play Europe with us," and I was like, "Yeah, I don't think so. Nah, I'm done."

Quite honestly, I just don't think our personalities at that point were compatible. Either it was going to be a miserable month for me or I could say "fuck it" and stay home. So, I stayed home.

Sturgeon: After we fired JP, he played with us on and off a lot. He played with us more than almost any other drummer. It's funny. I like JP and he's a great drummer. But I think there's something in his personality that doesn't mesh with us. But, other that, I think he's good people.

After that, it was Coach from Two Man Advantage on drums. We played the Knitting Factory a year after 9/11. I made papier-maâché World Trade Centers and put smoke bombs in them and flew little planes into them during "Born to Die." I didn't know it at the time, but apparently Coach was horrified and wanted to quit the band. I think his take on it was different than ours. He knew people that died that were firefighters that went into the fray. He can be upset at us all he wants, but he should really be upset at the United States government and the people that let firefighters go into a building that was being demolished in a controlled demolition. People knew that was happening and they still let people go in there—*that* was pretty fucked up.

So, after the Knitting Factory show, we were going to play "Holidays in the Sun" in Asbury Park. We were billed pretty highly up and it was the first time we were kind of getting credit for being a band that drew people in. But, after the Knitting Factory show,

Coach didn't quit, like, right away…he waited like a week to tell us he was quitting.

One of the reasons that Coach quit was because one of his friends was a fireman that died in the World Trade Center. But, he was also in the band the Bullies. We had played with them at Nightingale's a few years earlier and that night they were fucking assholes. They were like douchebags. I think they were missing a band member and weren't ready to play. They wanted a specific set time so they sat on the stage and held the stage for a time, and blocked us, and waited for their friend to show up and that whole band was dicks, that's all I remember. It makes sense they were firemen. Maybe they weren't necessarily punks.

So, we had like five days before the Asbury show to get a drummer. Most people didn't want to be involved with us because they were afraid of our politics at the time. So, we had some trouble getting a drummer. We got a drummer suggested by John Dolan from Choking Victim.

At the Festival, Two Man Advantage was also playing. There's this pipe thing coming out from the back of the stage. Ezra sees it and, seemingly in slow motion, jumps up, does this gymnastic thing, swings from the pole, and dropkicks Coach in the chest and knocks him down. Coach is like 6' 4", so he's hard to knock down. But I feel like those guys remained friends after all of that.

It turned out that our new drummer could not play drums. So, all the way up to right before the set, I wrote a thing about 9/11. I had a whole year to do it, but I wrote it in about ten minutes leading up to the set.

We were playing for the crowd on the main stage outside the Stone Pony and we're just playing fucking terribly. So, instead of playing all our shitty songs that sounded terrible, I read this thing that I wrote. But there were a lot of skinheads and street punks and a lot of mixed opinions and I kind of said exactly what was on my mind about what I knew a year later. I definitely wasn't apologetic about anything.

The second we were done playing, I got off the stage and walked around the crowd because I definitely didn't want to get jumped at some point after the show. I'm not gonna hide. I'm just gonna walk around the whole crowd. So, if someone's gonna come at me, *now* is their chance. I have my ideas in my head and my ideals and if you're mad at me, you're mad now, so you better come at me. And nobody came at me. I was surprised. Nobody gave me dirty looks or anything. It was weird.

To this day, I hear people talk about how much they loved that show. Yeah...but we were *terrible*. Most people can't remember what I said, but they liked it. Maybe that was it. Regardless of what was said, maybe no one was talking about 9/11 a year later. Maybe it meant different things to different people. It's the only thing I can imagine. I don't know. *I* don't even remember what I said.

Interlude
Squat or Rot

John John Jesse (Bass—Nausea; Guitar—Morning Glory): How are you gonna change the world with a bunch of anarchist squatters that can't even get along in the same room?

Eden Brower (C-Squat and Fetus Resident): The first squat I ever stayed in was C-Squat. I was finishing high school in Queens. I hated my mom and I hated where I lived and I kept running away and then the police kept bringing me back. So I started staying at C-Squat in 1990. I think the building just opened and had their first meeting. They were talking about all the plans for the building and how they were going to build it up.

I watched Dave Lawrence's room when he wasn't there. He was really good at hooking up electricity. Later on, when I got to know people and wasn't intimidated anymore, people called me "ghost" because I would wear hippie stuff and just go down the halls and not talk to anyone and kept my head down. It's just because I was intimidated!

Dave Lawrence told me later, when he got back, it looked like a hippie exploded in his room. And people were like, "That's ghost, she doesn't talk to anyone." There were like sheets hanging and you had to watch where you were walking. There was plywood put down on top of joists that were burnt down. There were ladders that went to the higher levels. You had to use a flashlight to walk around at night. There were no real doors, just sheets hanging down.

Sturgeon: I moved in to C-Squat in 1993. The squat scene seemed to be lot of musicians. The squatter punk world was a lot smaller then. There were a lot of squats then. It was like a microcosm. It was outlaw-ish, but self-sufficient. We kind of had power against the police because there were so many squats. We were always in fear of being evicted, but we had the power of numbers and the network of squats, which was prepared to mobilize quickly, which was known as an eviction watch.

C-Squat was dirty. *It was really dirty.* It was always under some phase of construction. It was also dirty because it had never been swept or mopped. It wasn't trashed like a regular abandoned building. People would hang out in the hall and leave their beers. People would smoke cigarettes and leave their butts all over. People didn't want to store their useless dumpster shit or their renovation materials in their rooms, so they would leave stuff outside of their rooms, cluttering the hallways.

There was never really a set way that C-Squat worked. There technically would be a vote. There were sixteen votes and if someone left or moved out, or if for some reason an apartment was empty, people would vote if they wanted someone to live there. If someone moved out of the building, usually someone that had already been living there a long time would say, "I want to move into the vacant room." After that, there still would be an empty room. Then there are five people up for an open room and there would be a secret vote or people would raise their hands and vote yay or nay.

But it wasn't always like that. Sometimes people would evict, or force out, other people. Someone may have just been living in someone else's room for so long and that person wasn't there and they just inherited it. I saw some shitty *Lord of the Flies*–style room grabs, and I was even attacked by C-Squat's more ruthless and violent houseguests who decided to "evict" me early one morning. Skwert helped me thwart their plans and Alec helped me get to Beth Israel, where I was a guest for the better part of a week.

Pezent Shayne: I got to C-Squat the day after New Year's 1994. There were a few people that lived in C-Squat that said they lived here, but I didn't realize that "living here" didn't actually mean that you lived here. It just meant that you were sneaking in, or were someone's guest, or were just a big fat liar.

I moved in with Cisco. Cisco had moved into someone's room that was in limbo because someone had left and they had to decide at the next meeting what to do with it so we sub-squatted the squat. Cisco was like, "You can stay with me, I've got a room!" He didn't really. So they kicked us both out and somebody took us in.

C-Squat looked like a coal mine. There were timbers all over. There were extensions cords all over and water would run all over the extension cords. In the winter, when it got really bad, we had a competent person sit by a wood stove. You can't let the smoke be seen, so the wind in an open corner would blow the smoke away. If people would see there was smoke, they'd call it as an abandoned building and say it was on fire. So you needed someone who wouldn't pass out when the stove was lit. Webbie was that person and so when it got really bad, everyone would go sleep in Webbie's room. All the dogs and cats were there, too. You would just bundle up in shitloads of blankets. Then, you'd wake up with cat shit on you.

When I first met Skwert, he showed me how to hammer copper pipes flat so they look like a fuse. But it's not really a fuse. It's a horrible thing to do. If something happens, they'll melt and light the entire box on fire. The purpose of a fuse is to stop something like that! We'd fake fuses and hammer them into four-inches-flat strips and stick them into the things. It would get our power going, but you had to make sure that you didn't short anything out—fire always starts in the middle of the wall, so you don't see the fire starting until it's too late. I've been electrocuted a lot of times.

I know how to do a gravity flush. Pooping on a toilet that never stops flushing is also really weird. It's like a windy type of atmosphere. I know how to divert water, if that's to be called plumbing. That's what's important—diverting water into a catch basin so it's not going onto your bed. I'd drain the water off into the tank and you'd have a big hole in the roof. You'd use tarps and run it to the toilet. It's like shitting on a cloud.

Caroline Bowden (C-Squat and Serenity Resident): When I moved into C-Squat, I first stayed in Webbie's room, and there wasn't any plumbing or anything like that. I think there could have been old plumbing where they would have to bucket flush, but we'd have to save buckets of water up to be able to throw down these pipes. I remember where Skwert's first space was—it was in the crumbled chimney. I went in his room one evening and I didn't see anything and it was pitch black. There was no electricity. He was like, "There's only a plank here, so you gotta be careful walking."

There were literally gaping holes below us. But at the end of this plank there was this cone where he would piss. So, I think there was a pipe that went into the ground at the end of that. But, in that apartment, I think we did have to do a lot of piss bottles. There wasn't a bathroom per se. We had a bucket we put water in to utilize it, but in the main area there was a bucket-flushing toilet. Sometimes I would come into the space and Skwert would be sitting on a milk crate with an actual toilet seat on it and a bag in it and that's the way he would go to the bathroom. It was kind of surreal. I would walk in and be like, "Oh, he's just taking a dump right there in the middle of the room."

Sturgeon: For the better part of a year, all of the stairs in C-Squat were removed from the second floor all the way up to the roof. I called it chutes and ladders. If you lived above the second floor, you had to climb up a series of ladders and finally when you got up to the fifth floor, which I lived on, you had to walk across the naked joists, which weren't even cemented into the walls—so they were wobbly.

I had zero construction experience up to that point in my life, so my room was built out of series of pieces of wall and doors that I found on the street that I crudely nailed together, kind of resembling an igloo. When I had to piss, if not in a bottle, I would go in front of my igloo, walk across five naked joists, and go into an upside-down traffic cone that was connected to the toilet pipe for that part of the floor.

The whole time that there were no floors, we were all smoking a lot of angel dust, which is very disorientating in of itself, plus drinking innumerable forty ounces and liquor. Surprisingly, no one ever got seriously injured from a fall.

We also used to practice on the fifth floor in Popeye's room, which was adjacent to where my igloo was, so whenever our band had a show, if it was Choking Victim or the Dregs, we had to take all of the gear and tie it to a rope that was attached to a pulley that was hanging from the roof. We would carefully lower each piece of equipment to the second-floor landing, and then place it into a rubble cart, which is one of those carts the post office has for sorting mail.

Our hallway, which is now our actual front hallway to get into the apartment part of our building, was lined with those carts. We would fill each one up of them up with the rubble we were removing from our rooms while we were constructing the building, until garbage day. We would all have to get up at 7:00 a.m. and be prepared to push the rubble carts out the front door and dump them into the garbage truck because the city wasn't paying them to pick up squatters' garbage.

By the time Choking Victim was playing shows, no one had a vehicle, so whenever we were playing a show, we would load up a rubble cart and push it down the street. I think Pezent Shayne might have painted a Choking Victim logo on the side.

Pezent Shayne: We also spray-painted headlights and put a grill on it. For a Coney Island High show, we just put all the gear in the cart and rolled it down there and chained it up right next to the Dropkick Murphys tour bus. The Beastie Boys, the Slackers, and F-Minus were all hanging out. "What's up, dudes?!"

Eden Brower: Everything everyone was doing was totally illegal. Stealing sheetrock, stealing electricity, stealing joists. You'd go to a building that was being worked on and steal something and bring it back to your squat. Some squats, like Pest House, collapsed, and there was stuff in there that people could use. When me and Shayne were dating, everyone went over to Pest House after it collapsed. "You should go get stuff that you can use—like BX cable. It should be used by someone." We were there and the building was falling around us and I was like, "We should get out of here." The building collapsed the next day.

Caroline Bowden: I had no power. Eventually, there was a super who lived there and everyone wanted him to run their electric. He was the guy that got the electric to the building. But he would go into the sewer and pull the conduit, and everyone would buy their own BX cable to get this connected so we had power. But we'd only be able to run it during the day so it couldn't be seen. But at night we'd have to close our heavy curtains so nobody could see the electric running through inside the building. I remember the first person who put a doorbell downstairs at Serenity. It was a really monumental moment.

John John Jesse: The squats we had when I first started squatting were real rag-tag. We'd break into a place and that place would last as long as it could, and that could be anywhere from one hour to three days, usually. But there were so many abandoned buildings back then. You could just jack into any place. And we were young, so you could just climb in through a second-floor window. But there would be like, no stairway, no floors in the apartments, completely uninhabitable. You could get electricity going if you could run a power cord from the phone lines. But we had no money for power cords. We didn't even have one dollar, and if we did we would go buy a quart of beer and split it, a pack of Marlboros and split it, or grub change and get, like, the cheapest generic Wonder Bread type bread, and some Bon-Ton potato chips, and then you take the bread and smash the potato chips in there and make this potato-chip sandwich and it wasn't so bad, believe it or not. But most of our nutrients came from hops and barley.

Caroline Bowden: We would go stay at different squats, like Umbrella House, and there were a couple of them that had spaces open that we heard of. But they want to make sure you're the right fit for the building and that you're gonna pull your weight. That's the point—they didn't want anyone who was just going to be this fly-by-night and show up for a month and leave. Our bid to get into Serenity was an initiation and we had to tar the roof. Our space was on the fifth floor, there were no windows, it was a raw space, and the roof had been fire damaged. There was a big gaping hole. So we had to fix the roof and then tar the roof. We had one man helping us, but really, I have visions of me in the dead hot summer and I'd have my daughter, Rosie, in a baby stroller up on the roof and me just tarring in the dead heat. We'd leave to go get a snack and we would walk to the park and water fountains. We had no electricity or water, so Rosie would bathe in the fire hydrant, or we'd go to the sprinklers. Sometimes we did the dishes in the fire hydrant. But then, once we got into Serenity, and we stole our electricity, we'd have a couple of plugs running.

So I'd have a coffee pot, and that's the thing we did everything in. We'd boil water in it, and I'd make hot water to give Rosie a bird bath...the coffee pot was the everything piece of machinery. But even on the fifth floor, we had no bath. It was this raw space we had to work on in order to live there. So we tarred the roof and got all that done, but we didn't have windows for a whole winter. We had made a loft, and we had put a blanket over the opening of it, but you climbed up into it. We called it the time machine because you'd get in there and lose track because the winter was freezing down in the space. We had a video machine, and we would watch movies up in this loft and close it off. It was a weird experience.

But that was another thing—getting building materials. You'd end up finding them, or wandering the streets looking for them. Sometimes we'd get a shipment of sheetrock, but most other stuff was just found at different construction sites. Things would get liberated in order to fix up the property.

Eden Brower: There were always shows. I saw Nausea a bunch.

John John Jesse: Every show back then was a crazy show. Some stupid shit would always happen.

I've seen fights. I've seen people get their ear bit off—like, who does that? But the madness of our life and environment, and what we chose to live in, was just like...every day was kind of unbelievable.

Henry Rollins called us to open for him. He called us personally after hearing our demo. He was very nice, even though I don't think they liked sharing a dressing room with us. I don't think any of those guys drank, but we did and we brought a huge entourage with us—all of these fucking characters from New York City... playing an all-ages club with no alcohol allowed! And I think he heard our music, but didn't know we were so punked-out, y'know?

Sturgeon: Maybe one of the reasons that clubs treated us shitty was the result of Nausea wearing out the welcome of crusties before we ever got there.

Caroline Bowden: You kind of felt like you could take on the world, and you put yourself in a position where, like, I would go down to the East River with a shopping cart with my kid in a backpack carrier and collect firewood, and I would go into the garden and start a fire and I would make a pot of curry. And people from neighboring buildings would smell it and come over. It was just this camaraderie, a community of people who are like-minded and you all work toward this one goal. All that's great. And a lot of those people left and bought land and took whatever they learned and applied it to their own. You're in this collective with people you might not have necessarily chosen, so you learn a bunch of crap from it and take that and go somewhere. I just loved it. It really was awesome in the beginning. But after a while you really wanted to get out. You got the politics involved, being around the same people all the time, the drama, there was a lot of drugs.

Eden Brower: I remember when the Daniel Rakowitz thing happened. He sold weed and carried a bag. He'd be talking and you'd realize that he was talking to the bag and he'd be like, "Shut the fuck up!" and then he'd open the bag and there would be a live chicken in a bag... But then he killed his girlfriend and he's still in jail for it. He used to sell food in the park and there's a rumor that he put her in the food.

There was a band called Bloodsister and I made friends with them and they had keys to the room where the murder happened. I saw the crime scene. They thought it would be cool or punk rock to wear Rakowitz's girlfriend's clothes on stage—which now I think is fucked up. But at the time, there was so much craziness going on and they were like, "We have access to the room," and that was that!

John John Jesse: The Lower East Side was always an artist neighborhood. You had hippies there in the sixties. Artists and punks move into places that are kinda like the ghetto. They move in there and then it becomes an "artistic community" and after that is when gentrification happens, y'know? Punks move into the cheapest place and then the artists see, "Oh, look, punks are here already!" so they stay there. Then eventually musicians move in, and then it becomes this "hip place to be." Shortly after that gentrification starts, no punk or artist can ever afford to live there ever again.

Eden Brower: The first squat that I got a room at was Fetus. It was a lot of artsy people. It wasn't all punk rock kids. Fetus mysteriously burned down when everyone was out of the city and were over at the "Beer Olympics." People say they paid neighborhood kids to burn it down.

I didn't go to the Beer Olympics, though. I was dating this guy Jody and we finished working on our room. We cut carpet that we found in the garbage and we finished the wall and we went to buy a disposable camera to take pictures of our room. When we got back, it was gone. So, I took pictures of that. I had cats. I don't know what happened to them.

I remember it burning for a while. It's just burning and there's no point in going in. We were like, "That's all of our stuff." We were digging through the rubble later to find our stuff. The Red Cross showed up with cots and blankets. People had a sense of humor because it's just a squat. It's not meant to last forever. People said to the Red Cross, "Help us, we're homeless!" People put their cots where they thought their room might be and people were laughing and drinking.

After Fetus burned, people at C-Squat were really good about taking us in. I stayed at my friend Eric Jenkins' room in C-Squat. I think there was a lot of heroin around—well, now I know there was—and I was naïve about it then.

I did heroin once at Fetus. I was like, "I see why people like this!" even though I spent half the night puking. I was so thirsty, so I was like, "I'll drink a gallon of orange juice," and then I just puked forever. A week or two later, my friend Dave died in front of me, at La Plaza. The EMTs came and just stood around doing nothing. The guy who tried to bring him back with CPR couldn't and then Dave OD'd later. Watching that, I was, like, terrified and I never did it again.

I think that's why they put the kibosh on La Plaza. We fuckin' trashed that place. You had to go take a shit? You just walked to the corner of La Plaza and took a shit. Since it was between all these different squats, it was just like a hangout spot. It was a place to hang out outside and drink. Everywhere you went you would see your friends. It was crazy and it was a free-for-fall. I think someone OD-ing in there is what caused them to clean it up.

In 1992, during the riots…that was insane. People were just, like, fighting with cops in the street. That's the first time I met Popeye. He was just running down the street completely naked. People were like, "It's a riot!" That was about Tompkins Square Park being closed.

I was there when they evicted Glasshouse on Avenue D. That was really scary. People know it's a lost cause once the police are there. They have guns, they have batons, they have the law on their side. You're not gonna win. We all went over there and held hands in front of the building and they were barricading inside. There was a cop there and I guess we looked really scary to him—people with tattoos on their faces! Now, like, Miley Cyrus has a tattoo on her face, you know?!

But this cop was like really scared when we showed up and were holding hands in front of the building and he pulled out his gun and pointed it at us! And someone, maybe it was Amy of Nausea, was like, "Hey, we're not doing anything, we're just standing here!" It was scary. His hand was shaking. He must have been a rookie or a young cop and didn't know what to do. The other cops were just looking bored and jaded. "These kids look smelly and we're going to have to touch them and they have lice." The young cop was like, "Nobody come close!" the other cops were like, "Hey…that's not necessary…" I was like, "Holy shit, is this going to escalate!"

It was to just like, make a stand, but you're going to lose, which we did.

Sturgeon: There was a constant fear of being evicted. C-Squat was the hard-partying squat. We were the fuckups. We were not just the left-wing anarchist punks, but we were the ones also doing drugs and everybody knew that. It's kind of miraculous that we got to keep our building. The cops knew that, but they kind of let it go. Then Giuliani ended up making a deal and giving us one of the last buildings in the neighborhood and now we own it.

In the early days, police would just find their way into the building somehow, and come up the stairs with an old warrant looking for someone, or they'd come into the basement while we were throwing a show. It would be an undercover cop. "Are you a cop? Yes? You have to go." They'd be terrified. Or they would wait outside and arrest kids there.

John John Jesse: There were very few times that cops could catch us. Because they were so fat, and we were scrawny and fast as hell. And we knew the neighborhood; none of those cops were from that neighborhood.

If they did catch you, cops would give you an ultimatum. No one carried IDs back then, and it wasn't a law to carry ID in New York City. That wasn't a law 'til somewhere in the nineties. So, a cop would say, "Either I arrest you, or you get a fuckin' beating." We always took the beating. I got 'em all, and they ranged from anything like getting punched in the gut or the head to just getting pushed on the ground. Either, like, not so great, or just something to make them feel better. But they would give you the option.

Eden Brower: When Thirteenth Street was getting evicted, they brought in tanks. At the time, MTV really wanted to be in on the squatter scene. They wanted to be hip. They hired these DJs like Jessie Camp. Jessie used to jog around a track, but with, like, all his punk gear on. They wanted weird people, but they were kind of, like, taking advantage. MTV was just trying to milk the scene for punk points. So no one really warmed up to them. Someone took a camera from MTV and took it into the punk house to film it, but I think someone stole the camera. MTV was just really wanting to be a part of this.

In the squatter world, things move, like, really fast. I moved in with Shayne and we went train hopping for like a month. That's very intense. You really get to know someone quickly with that lifestyle.

Eventually, they had a meeting about me not being there. And it was the time C-Squat was becoming a co-op and you're supposed to be living in the space at least six months out of the year, otherwise you're just warehousing your space. And they were right. So I moved out and moved in with John Heneghan, who would become my husband.

A few days later, I came to hang out, and they were shocked, I wasn't mad at anyone. I just wanted to hang out.

19

Fuck World Trade

Sturgeon: With the Epitaph contract, I learned the lesson that it was our money that was advanced to us, so they were just getting something for free. So, we financed the next record ourselves to get a better deal. We recorded and mixed *Fuck World Trade* before we even had a deal.

F-Minus recorded with Steve Albini, so we got in contact with Albini through Brad. He was real easy to work with. Occasionally, I had heard about bands having a bad time with him like Black Francis—but not Kim Deal—of the Pixies. After talking with him, it became evident that bands having a bad time with him were ones that weren't down to earth and had their heads in the clouds. I could see that—especially from the bands that don't get along with him. It makes sense that those bands wouldn't get along with him, because he's down to earth. He's not into mincing words, treating things as "too important." It's art. It's music. It is what it is. Let's get it done or whatever.

Steve Albini said to me, "If there's ever any recording that you like that I've done that you want to sound like, let me know." Two of my favorite recordings that he produced were of Pixies and Neurosis.

He told me that Neurosis was coming in and asked if we minded if they practiced while we recorded the next day.

I told him that and somehow we ended up at Electrical Audio on the last night or two of recording, and Neurosis was coming in. I met Dave Ed of Neurosis, whom I have mutual friends with, and I met Neurosis for the first time—mainly Dave Ed, because he was nice to me and he's still my friend. That's one of my favorite bands of all time.

Brad Logan: Electrical Audio had two rooms. One was all brick with wood floor, and the other is all metal with concrete floor and a control room behind thick glass that looked like a prison guard tower. They're sonic opposites. We used the brick and wood room for no reason that I knew of but it sounded really good. I remember thinking the metal and concrete room had a real institutional vibe, but I also remember thinking that the room would sound insane.

Steve Albini: They wanted to make an energetic, confrontational, powerful record, but they wanted it to sound good. They didn't want a messy haphazard record. So there was quite a bit of attention paid to the equipment they wanted to use. Mistakes were corrected as they went along, so there weren't mistakes left on for no reason. They were diligent. They wanted a good sounding record that portrayed their aesthetic. For a band that has an image that portrays a certain sense of disorder or lack of care, it's worth noting that they were careful and were very specific about how they wanted the record to sound.

Sturgeon: Steve wanted us to write out all the song lyric, so he could follow along and reference where he was in the song. That's the *only* task that I got Alec to agree to do aside from recording the bass in the studio.

Brad Logan: For *Fuck World Trade*, I was only there to do my parts and that's the way it's been with every Leftover Crack record. It's easier and less confusing that way, I guess.

Steve Albini is mesmerizing to watch work. It's like watching a master chef. He records everything analog direct-to-tape, and he edits and splices by hand, with scissors!

Sturgeon: When we were mixing "Operation M.O.V.E.," I would tell him that I wanted it to sound like a Neurosis song sonically. Our drummer had "cheated" the double kick and we were going to place a digital delay on it to make it sound like a double kick. Steve said, "Hold on a second." He grabs a razor blade and within twenty seconds, he hacks up the two-inch tape, splices it, and puts in back in the machine, and there was a double kick. I have no idea how he did that. It does prove analog is better than digital...if you're Steve Albini.

I'm manic, so I get worked up working on a song and I want to get a million things done at once, which caused Albini to take more breaks than usual. He would say, "I need to cook on this." He always used cooking metaphor for thinking. I noticed his TiVo upstairs was completely full of cooking shows. I assume Steve Albini really likes to cook. People say he never eats, but I think that's because he likes to eat really good food and cook really good food. That's just my guess. Between his cooking metaphor, his TiVo, and that he has a really fancy coffee machine and converted the whole band over to using it instead of going to Starbucks the first day. He's definitely a gourmet. I think he has standards, just like he does for recording music.

Brad Logan: Albini would work non-stop twelve-hour days like it wasn't shit, and seemingly never slept. I think I only saw him eat food once the whole time.

Sturgeon: We recorded a new version of "Gang Control," which was originally done by Morning Glory. I think for Ezra, he was horrified when I was cutting the parts. I probably cut sixty seconds out of four and half minutes of "Gang Control." That's not much. He was not happy. But, at the end of the day, because it's my band, I got to do it that way. To this day, I feel like he bristles about it. But he also gets the benefit of saying that the song he wrote is *the* favorite Leftover Crack song. "Gang Control," hands down, voted by fans is the favorite Leftover Crack song. That's why we close the shows to this day with that song, with or without Ezra.

I always thought that Ezra was an amazing songwriter and was one of the best technical musicians I ever played with. The main flaw in his work is that he doesn't know what he likes 100 percent as much as he should. But I think he loses confidence in things he knows are good and the reason he loses confidence is because someone talks shit about it and he loses confidence and that's the thing. You gotta know what you like and what is good and not falter when people stand up or combat you. If this is the way you want it to be heard, you shouldn't compromise.

Steve Albini: Sturgeon has a very specific routine that he wanted to use. He wanted to use an SM57 microphone, plugged into his guitar amplifier, and then recorded with another SM57 and he wanted that SM57 to be put through the bottom of a plastic Dixie cup. He clearly had developed this set up and had used it before, and having your own specific set up is completely normal. But it did result in a particularly shrill vocal sound. I recall the bass player reacting pretty negatively to it. On playback, he described it as being an "auditory hallucination from shooting cocaine." Apparently that is called a "ringer." Everyone else but me seemed to know what he is was talking about.

Sturgeon: I learned that vocal thing from Nico. We only did it once before, but I thought it came out pretty good. Steve refused to offer an opinion about anything we were recording. If you think, "Oh, how refreshing, he's not offering an opinion," you're probably naïve. Steve was absolutely deadpan. It was quite difficult to tell if he liked something or didn't like something, or if he found something funny or annoying.

Brad Logan: We would be like, "Whaddaya think?" And he would be like, "What do *you* think?"

Steve Albini: When you are working on a record, you have an obligation to do as good as a job as you can to translate their ideas. If you're working on a record, it's a bad idea to even contemplate if you like the band or not. That's not a helpful mechanism. If I'm sitting in a control room passing judgment rather than paying attention to the technical details, you're not doing the proper job from a technical standpoint. You're not taking it seriously enough. So, I don't have an opinion about the music that I recorded, unless I encounter it in the wild much later on.

Brad Logan: Recording for *Fuck World Trade* was done in multiple sessions. We started at Albini's then followed up with more stuff at Jesse Cannon's studio in New Jersey. The whole thing wasn't recorded in one shot in Chicago. Standard operating procedure was multiple sessions over a long period of time. Not really the way that I prefer to do things. I'm a fan of blasting everything out in a day or two, to capture the moment.

Sturgeon: After we did all this stuff with Steve Albini, I still had a lot of vocals to record. A few years before, Brad and I recorded a track for a benefit comp that I put as Osama St'z Laden and the Crack City Crew, which was the original version of "Super Tuesday," and my voice was just shot when I recorded the vocals. I sent it to Jesse Cannon to see what he could do. He took it and somehow made it amazing. So, we hired him to finish *Fuck World Trade*.

Jesse Cannon (Producer/Engineer): I get the tapes and Albini is very conventional, but he aligns to different things in certain matters. So, I call him up like, "So, this one thing is coming up funny," and I get that very famous Albini condescension: "Oh... *Leftover Crack*..." He's got that thing of being an asshole while also being helpful and professional at the same time. We recorded at Coyote studios and in my parents basement. My parents actually found Sturgeon and Ezra to be really nice and delightful. However, my girlfriend, who also lived at my parents house, could not take the smell...she said she was going to move out. I was like, "What are you going to do, move out and *not* pay rent somewhere else?"

Jack Terricloth: They had some members of World/Inferno record with them on "Soon We'll be Dead" at Jesse Cannon's. It sounds like the Pogues doing goth, which is why I assume he asked me to do it.

It was a very beneficial experience. Sturgeon was like, "It's a very serious song, Jack." He also freaked out the jazz squares that were there.

The lyrics were definitely his lyrics and he was definitely particular about that. He was not happy about changing even one line. I did get one minor change in there. I'm a much more positive person than those songs. I remember Peter Hess walking out for the lyrics "our brains in our heads." He said to me, "Where else would your brain be?"

Bill Cashman: I drove to Jesse Cannon's house with Sturgeon. At some point before then, Sturgeon and Alec and Ezra had a falling out. Sturgeon said he wanted someone to go in the studio with him because there was no one else there or maybe he wanted a second opinion or maybe he just needed a ride and was telling me that to get a ride.

One time I dropped Sturgeon off and was going to pick him up, like, way later. But a few minutes after I dropped him off, I get a call to come pick him up "right away." I say "okay" and I get back to

Jesse's house. Sturgeon is literally kicked to the curb with a box in his hand. He had been kicked out of Jesse's house and Jesse was no longer going to be working with Sturgeon. I don't remember what the fight was about and Sturgeon got back in the car and was very quiet and we drove back to C-Squat.

Jesse Cannon: Sturgeon and I fought a lot. At that point, I'm at a real ascendant point in my career. I'm doing a Cure record, I'm doing a Dillinger Escape Plan record at the same time, I have a song on MTV—at one point while making that record, I had an entire hour of songs I had worked on, on MTV straight. So, I had a pretty big ego at that point.

Sturgeon and I are really clashing. I do have the deference that the artist always wins, though.

During the mixing it got tense. So I was talking to him on the phone and I had a flip phone and I accidentally left it on, and didn't hang up, and I hear Sturgeon saying rude shit about me—I don't even remember what it was! I was like, "Oh, you're not grateful for my time? Fuck you, see ya later!" I'm out on the road with the Cure. I'm working with Dillinger Escape Plan. I don't need this!

Sturgeon: I don't know what it is about me, but I need to mix a record over several months, as opposed to several days. Me and Jesse are in a room alone together a lot. I feel like I need more guitar in a song and he *pretends* to turn the knobs and says it's there. He doesn't want to turn the guitar up.

Jesse Cannon: A lot of the battle was vocal clarity. He was like, "Add more guitars!" But people should hear these important, intelligent lyrics. At one point, he conceded that the tattoo on his ear may affect his ability to hear treble.

Sturgeon: Bill Cashman is driving me around from Joe Porter's house to Jesse Cannon's. So, we arrive at Jesse Cannon's house and all of his files for *Fuck World Trade* are on his steps in a box and it's drizzling out.

I guess that Jesse got sick of working on the record. I call every recording studio in New York and nobody has the format that he has the files on. Somehow, it only fits Jesse Cannon's hardware. At this point, we end up at Coyote and we record "Clear Channel Fuck Off" and "Soon We'll Be Dead." We always liked Coyote.

Basically, after a month or two of not being able to finish the record because of the problems that we had, Jesse Cannon took me back and helped me finish the record after all. He promised that he would also help us master the recordings in a week or so. He never answered my calls again, so I purposefully misspelled his name in the liner notes.

20

𝔅randon 𝔓ossible

Alec Baillie: We started having Brandon Chevalier-Kolling, or as we called him, Brandon Possible, drum for us. He was the drummer for the X-Possibles, a punk band from New York City. We watched him play at one of the Tompkins Square Park shows and were impressed, so when a spot opened up in Leftover Crack, we asked him to join the band. He was really a one-of-a-kind, overall sweet guy.

Brad Logan: At the time, we had about two drummers that we would use whenever one was available. But Brandon was the first guy that everybody liked, that had nothing but time, and that was down to do anything, anytime, anywhere, so all the boxes were checked.

He was super enthusiastic, innocent, motivated, and not embittered by being in a band for x number of years at our level, with all the crap that came our way. He was just a breath of fresh air.

Ron Martinez (Booking Agent—Leftover Crack; Vocals—Final Conflict): Leftover Crack was Brandon's favorite band. I went, "Wow! They finally got the drummer that fits with them." He was so happy to be in the band.

Sturgeon: I didn't know Brandon too long, but I looked up to him. He was an amazing drummer. He seemed like he knew the secrets to being happy. I don't meet a lot of people that I am in awe of and respect and look up to. He was a person that I was prepared to follow.

This was a person that I saw as a way out—a way out of being unhappy in playing music and being wasted all the time. He seemed like a person that I could get healthy with. I had known a lot of punks, and by punks I mean people that dressed like punks, but I hadn't met a lot that were as politically aware as he was. He seemed like he was just meant to play music and to do things for the right reasons.

He quickly became a friend of mine and was the best friend I've ever had in a band. We were tour buddies. We would stay in the same room.

We were gonna start our own band. We weren't going to necessarily stop Leftover Crack, but I wanted a band where we could go on tour, do a show on Friday and Saturday, and use the rest of the week to fuck around. I was really sick of touring, but not having a chance to enjoy where we were, and hang out with people, and relax. The idea behind the new band was something where we could actually really enjoy playing music again. That was the original band called Star Fucking Hipsters.

21

𝔄lternative 𝔗entacles

Two towers falling down, I'll be at zero ground / We're "flying friendly skies" until the city dies / And you don't wanna see through human history / Empires will always fall, this is the final call

—Excerpt from "Super Tuesday"

Sturgeon: *Fuck World Trade* was my reaction to 9/11 and skepticism as to the official story. I think 9/11 reeks of having the cooperation of the US government on the most basic of levels. No matter what, even if it was hijackers, it's still a conspiracy in the sense of the word. I don't think we really know what happened and the government knows and they definitely lied about it. I am sure that they are implicated on some level, whether it's just that they didn't warn people when they knew it was going to happen, but I think it goes deeper than that.

My initial protests and reasons for being outspoken were because of American citizen hypocrisy, even anarchist punks, who were seemingly so much more upset by the quote unquote "9/11 attacks" than what our government goes around the world doing every day—murdering people and perpetuating genocide and destroying the earth, culture, and ancient lands of indigenous people and murdering them in the name of making money for the Empire, gaining resources in an exploitative manner.

It is disgustingly indicative of our Eurocentric megalomania of our country's basic foreign policies, not to mention the disregard of the lives of non-white people around the world.

The fact that people don't bat an eye when this happens all the time and are thrown into despair when it happens in my hometown—most of the people that acted like that didn't grow up like I did, a stone's throw from the building. I'm not saying people that didn't grow up there didn't feel that way. I'm not trying to discount anybody's tragedy. I'm trying to say that tragedy is fucking tragedy and to place one tragedy higher than another is…"inhumane" is not the right word, but it's insensitive in and of itself. That's what my protest was about. People's insensitivity to the attacks perpetrated on people around the world.

When I think about the war on terror, I think about people living in terror because this so-called war has been declared. If that isn't terrorism, then I don't know what is—because it's officially sanctioned by the US government, it doesn't take on a sinister agency? It's about the difference between terrorism and war. The difference between terrorism and an army attack is efficiency. It's the government controlling a bunch of people at once under a corporate blanket, or whatever, where they have everybody in their niche, whereas a rag-tag group of terrorists is somehow more terrifying? I disagree. I think it's the other way around.

At first, my protest was due to our overall insensitivity about our sanctioned attacks on innocent civilians throughout the world. But when it became clear that 9/11 was a reason to go out and take away people's rights and spread out the blanket of the army around the world—that's when I became less proud about my initial protest and realized that the hands at work were far too insidious to even imagine.

The fact that our government wanted it to look like a foreign attack—the spin that they put on the thing that they did... Well, "putting a spin" on something implies that you didn't put it out there in the first place, usually. When a newspaper puts a spin on something, they don't usually perpetuate the injustice that they are trying to justify or scapegoat. I think there needs to be a new word when a government or a corporation goes out there perpetrates, an atrocity, and then steers the description of it. "Spin" is a little too lighthearted.

But then, when the government is the government *and* the journalists, and they're blacking out the media, it's horrifying. I do think that when we are old it will all come out. There's no reason why it won't. There's been no false flag attack like this that hasn't come out eventually.

Dale Tomlinson: When the World Trade Center actually happened, Leftover Crack were the only band, the *only* band, who sang about it, talked about it, out of *all* the punk rock bands on the planet. They were the only band, especially from America, who said anything about it. And that's what blew me away as well. Like, why is nobody else talking about it and they had the balls to have a T-shirt with it on and all that kind of crap? And nobody else had done that. And I was like, *this* is punk rock. Because all the punks should be talking about it and singing about it and nobody said shit except Leftover Crack. So, I'll give them that as well.

Sturgeon: We knew we had a good record, but, at the time, we were still being held hostage by Epitaph and that contract. No label would talk to us because they had, like, a building full of lawyers. I've never been in the building, but I just know that the lawyer that we spoke to that put the contract together was in a building with a bunch of other lawyers not far from the Epitaph compound. Fat Wreck Chords should have signed with us then. Brad said a lot of people there liked us. We were a little too anarcho punk during *Rock Against Bush*. A little too strong-willed with our politics.

We had sent out demos to all the labels that we were interested in and I don't even know if that's how Alternative Tentacles heard about it. I don't even know how we got in touch with them. They hadn't even heard the record.

The Dead Kennedys are hands down one of my biggest inspirations for being a political punk. There is no band that I had heard as early as them that said all the stuff that was important to me with some tongue-in-cheek humor. Nobody ever doubted that they had a sense of humor.

A-F records was the only one that had heard it, but they didn't offer us any terms that were worthwhile for any band that was worthwhile. I told Anti-Flag, "You guys would never sign this contract, why would you give it to me?" They were like, "Uh..." They didn't really say anything. But it was good—A.T. was now suddenly showing an intense interest, which had them battling with A-F for our next album.

Bill Cashman (Tour Manager): Around that time, Sturgeon was really deciding between A.T. and A-F records. We went to meet Anti-Flag at one of their shows. I remember them really pitching it. They really wanted to sign Leftover Crack. Sturgeon asked Pat from Anti-Flag, "Do you care if we call the new album *Shoot the Kids at School* or *Fuck World Trade*?" Pat said, "I don't care what you call it. We love your band and want to support it." I remember telling Sturgeon that A.T. was better, but A-F can take you on tour.

Jesse Luscious (Alternative Tentacles General Manager, Lookout Records General Manager, Fat Wreck Chords Production Manager; Singer—Blatz, The Criminals, The Pathogens): Sturgeon either emailed or called me because he knew me and he knew I worked at Alternative Tentacles and they were looking for a new label after Hellcat. He was like, "We're looking for a label. We're really pissed off about Hellcat not letting us use the title and cover we wanted for *Mediocre Genrica* blah blah blah." Then, he said that he really wanted to be on A.T. Like any label, the staff who work at A.T. are always trying to get the people who sign bands to sign different bands. It happens at Fat Wreck Chords, it happens at Alternative Tentacles, it happened at Lookout—usually the people who sign the bands are like, "Yeah, yeah...*no.*"

At A.T., the person who signs bands happens to be Jello Biafra. I went to Jello and was like, "Look, Jello, this band is very popular, their fans are our people, they're revolutionary, they'll start a lot of shit, they'll sell a lot of records, and they want to be on A.T. really, really badly." But Jello won't sign a band unless he likes the music personally. So, the promise of good songs wasn't enough. Leftover Crack had to deliver the songs...and they did.

Brad Logan: I loved the Dead Kennedys' first record, *Fresh Fruit for Rotting Vegetables. In God We Trust Inc.* was great, too. "Nazi Punks Fuck Off," brilliant! They were one of the first international touring, US hardcore bands that I can remember. I feel that, along with Circle Jerks, D.O.A., Youth Brigade, and Black Flag, they paved the way for DIY touring.

I *was* pretty nervous but also excited to meet Jello. To me, he was like the history of California punk personified. Generally, I don't like meeting people I admire. I've had some bad experiences. But Jello was great. He was really friendly and down to earth, and what also struck me was that he was very candid. You could ask him anything and he would talk to you about it and he wouldn't get all weird. But, once you ask him, you better have some time to kill because he won't stop...which is cool because he's a fuckin' treasure trove of tidbits. Punk history, record collecting, politics, conspiracy theories, current events, and useless knowledge, I could listen to the dude for hours...and *have.*

He'd come out to our shows and be standing right there in the front of the stage, too. That really impressed me.

Sturgeon: When I first got into punk, The Ramones were a constant—I grew up in New York. Dead Boys and Ramones, Ramones and Dead Boys! It never struck me that it was "punk," but when I first started learning music, I learned from that music because it was easy, but I wasn't inspired by them.

I was inspired by the East Bay and the whole Bay Area—especially Dead Kennedys. It was something I couldn't do on guitar, but I wanted to strive for it. It's interesting that Op Ivy, Neurosis, and Crimpshrine all shared a practice space because they were the three most influential bands on me, hands down, that exist. If you had to take Choking Victim or Leftover Crack and boil them down to three bands, you could probably take Op Ivy, Crimpshrine, and Neurosis and get almost every part of every song I ever wrote out of it. Maybe you could say Jawbreaker, but you can get Jawbreaker from Crimpshrine easily because they are very similar—very similar musical styles, very similar vocals.

But then on top of it, the Dead Kennedys lyrics! That's all you need. You can get away with mediocre lyrics if you have great music…but why not have great lyrics, too? I think a lot of bands get away with mediocre lyrics. A lot of the Lookout bands got away with shitty music, but good lyrics.

There's one point where I feel like I loved every band on Lookout records. Green Day I didn't like, but I don't know why—they weren't popular yet. I did like Pinhead Gunpowder. I think it has something to do with the lyrics that Aaron Cometbus writes.

The Bay Area scene inspired me lyrically, then I went over to anarcho-punk to get that more militant stuff—Nausea and Reagan Youth. When I got into punk, Reagan Youth meant the world to me.

I'd go to Pyramid and it would be industrial punk alternative night. You'd hear the Cure, the Dead Kennedys, you'd hear the Specials, you'd hear Siouxsie Sioux and Skinny Puppy. It was like almost every week they played the same songs even though they didn't play the same songs. So I listened to all of that at once. Before I started squatting I was more of a "goth." Not that I dressed fancy. I just dyed my hair black and wore all black.

Ara Babajian: I met Jello a couple of times, briefly. With each new Leftover Crack drummer he would always say, "It's so good to hear the band with a good drummer! You're so much better than the last drummer." I think he said this to me twice!...And I *was* the last drummer!

Sturgeon: The first time I ever spoke to Jello Biafra on the phone was when I was in Guatamala on one of those international call booths. He wanted me to call the record *Free World Trade*. I said, "No." We wanted to call it *Fuck World Trade*, and that was important to us.

Bill Cashman: The first time I met Jello I was stage-managing a show in Asbury Park. I was told to meet him on the side of the road where he would be holding two bananas. I found him on the side of the road and there he was, holding two bananas.

I snuck him into the festival while he ate both bananas. He was already over an hour late. He had a sold-out auditorium of people waiting for him. Jello was nervous, so he goes out to me and asks me to go out to the stage and move the water bottle precisely one inch to the left. I said, "Are you serious?" He says, "Deadly."

So, I go out and everyone starts clapping, but they realized that I wasn't Jello. Then, I moved the water bottle precisely one inch to left and then Jello comes out and starts the show...

Years later I'm doing merch for Leftover Crack in San Francisco and Jello comes over to me. He puts his chin on his palms so his fingers are cupping his cheeks, kind of to look cute. He says,

"I hear you're friends with World/Inferno Friendship Society. I'll do anything to put their album out! Pretty please with a cherry on top!" So I say, "Okay…you can tell me why you made me move a water bottle to the left one inch at the Asubry Park show a while ago." He says to me, "Well, it sounds like someone was an hour late for a show and needed to use you as an icebreaker."

Dick Lucas (Singer—Citizen Fish, Subhumans, Culture Shock): Jello is a very, very clever man. He's got a blueprint-style memory. He knows everything. He's a very good talker. He can construct entire paragraphs in his head as he is talking. All things that are amazing—especially good for a singer, a lyricist, he's someone who not only knows his politics, but he knows them inside and out with all the facts.

Curiously enough, this gift of the gab is also the curse of the gab. Once you're in a conversation with Jello, it's hard to get much content in because there is a lot of content coming out! Fair enough, because the man talks for the world. He's a strange and wonderful man.

Sturgeon: Jello Biafra has just a terrible taste in music. He doesn't know what's good. So, he just goes for whatever is weird or has a gimmick and he signs that. It took him a while to realize what our gimmick was—we're crusties and we made it out of squats and we ride freight trains but we're in studios and recording. That was good enough for him but he also became businessman-y. He saw we were popular with some of his friends and he saw our shirts and merch and patches all over the place, so he signed us on the strength of that. He signed us because a lot of people like us. That's not a great way to gauge a band—there's a lot of really terrible stuff that a lot of people wear patches and shirts of. But it's not the worst way either.

Alec and I had lunch with Jello across from Coyote studios where we were rehearsing with Brandon. The lunch was one where we got a lot of food and then we got a lot more food and then we got Jello to pick up the check. I think we had two lunches each.

I had asked Brandon earlier, "Would it be weird if Jello came by?" I didn't think he actually would come by to our first rehearsal with this lineup and then Jello *did* come by and he watched us practice for an hour. It was our first practice with Brandon so it was kind of weird but it also made us look kind of cool to Brandon and it also showed that Brandon wouldn't crack under pressure.

I mean, how many people have the chance to have Jello Biafra show up to their practice? Probably not many! But, as I later learned, Jello will show up to anything. If Jello says he *might* show up to something, he probably will—even if it's like a show in an abandoned bike shop in the middle of West Oakland attended by eight people. That's definitely one of the enviable things about his personality.

Brad Logan: I was never in the loop for any band decisions like leaving or switching labels. It was Sturg's band and he was just enlisting my "talents" for whatever was needed. I had always been a hired gun in a sense, even though I had been there since show one. Leftover Crack were never like a unified band that made decisions together. We were never Minor Threat or whoever.

My priorities were with F-Minus. I was okay with it being Sturgeon's band. I would have liked to have been in on some of the decisions. But I was of the mind, at the time, "If they didn't need me, they didn't need me." And I think that's hurt the band in some ways. I don't think some of the decisions made have been what was best for the situation, which is why it's good to have the whole band weigh in sometimes.

Sturgeon: With A.T., we got all the terms that we wanted. But Anti-Flag wouldn't promise to take us on tour, which would have been good for us. We looked at the catalogues and A.T. has been around a lot longer, they've got a track record, they've put out some really great bands, even though a lot of them left the label, so we went with that.

Brad Logan: Sturgeon and Alec ended up meeting with Jello and decided to go with Alternative Tentacles. I thought, "Well, at least it's a cool punk label." I had already left Hellcat because I had moved out of town to New York City. I never had any problems working at Hellcat or doing the jobs there, but I had a grudge against my hometowns—Los Angeles and Orange County. Southern California is everyone's paradise, but it's not my paradise. I grew up here.

Sturgeon: Jesse Townley was the general manager at A.T. at the time. He's great. He's really diplomatic. Even if he doesn't like your band, he'll treat you like the other bands for better or for worse. I told Jesse once that the first time that I ran away from home and went to the Bay Area that I went to Gilman Street. I remember going to punk rock kickball and he was the only person that I recognized that was in a band that I listened to and I was like, "That's cool. He hangs out. He's *the people's punk*."

Jesse Luscious: Jello made the final decision. We knew they had a really bad falling out with Hellcat. We're friends with all those people, all the Rancid people. Jello goes back to Operation Ivy days with them. They are some of my closest friends. We chose to call up Hellcat and talked to Tim. I said, "Look, Tim, we're talking about signing Leftover Crack. Jello and I want you to know that this is about putting out the record—this is in no way a statement on what happened between the craziness of you and the band. We don't have any part in that. We do want to make sure this is cool with you." Basically, Tim was like, "Pffft...go for it."

Hellcat obviously wasn't going to put out anything else by them. It wasn't like we were stealing the band. I do think Tim appreciated that we were making it clear that we didn't have a part in stirring up the drama. Then, it went from there. When it comes to band's art and expression, Jello is very hands off—within reason. If a band who is small wants to put out a really complex package—a triple gatefold with silver foil—he'll say no.

In terms of the substance and the art, he might say, "That song needs some work." He'll work with an artist to make things presentable. But, in terms of cover art, he's not going to censor them. "I sign them because I trust them to do meaningful things."

Chris Ryan (Guitar/Vocals—Team Spider; Filmmaker): I did the original album cover for *Fuck World Trade*. It's not anything like you see. It was a shot of the World Trade Center from a low angle. It didn't have fire or explosions or anything. It was just crazy to say "fuck world trade" and have any association with the World Trade Center because it was still smoldering. It was a work of art.

But it got rejected by Jello and A.T. because it was political, but they demanded some accountability in that it doesn't really say anything. I guess that wasn't Jello's speed. So Sturgeon, again, goes back to his playbook—he just didn't want it to look good and what we did was not good art, but it was funny in a certain respect. So, to make it political, he made it Giuliani with a remote control flying the planes and there's Dick Cheney dumping the fuel, and George Bush is lighting the match and all this stuff.

I'm like two of the bodies in that picture. We just cut out their heads from some *Newsweek* article. We ended up walking to a gas station, had to get pictures standing next to the gas pump, holding the nozzles and not having a car…and one of the guys with us had giant dreadlocks and Sturgeon looking like Sturgeon…

So, we had to do it on the stealth before we got shut down. We're posing in suits and holding out matches. So we scuttle out of there. Sturgeon wanted to have Giuliani remote controlling the

Brad Logan and Tim Armstrong at Westbeach studios, Hollywood, 1996

WHAT I DO....

Brad Logan. Hellcat offices, 1997. Photo by Travis Keller

Choking Victim at ABC No Rio, June 1995. Photo by Chris Boarts Larson

Leftover Crack. L to R: Ezra, Alec, Ara, Sturgeon. 2000. Photo by Seth Olenick

Scott Sturgeon, Choking Victim. 1995. Photo by Chris Boarts Larson

Leftover Crack recording Rock The 40oz *in Mike Trujillos garage, 1999.
L to R: Brad, Sturgeon, Mike T., Alec, Amery. Photo by Seth Olenick*

Leftover Crack, 2000. Photo by Seth Olenick

SUNDAY!! SUNDAY!! SUNDAY!!

JUNE 20ᵀᴴ In this the year of the Beast 1999

Presenting ... Straight Outta' Lo-Cash...

The Good

Leftöver Crack

(w/people from F-Minus, Blindsided, & Choking Victim)

The Distillers
78 Rpms
& More

Hangin' Tuff
In The Triple-Nine

 ## @ The Epicenter in San Diego
8450 Mira Mesa Blvd 4:00pm

Flyer for second Leftover Crack Show, 1999

Scott Sturgeon. 2000. Photo by Seth Olenick

F-minus. L to R: Sturgeon, Sarah Lee, Jen Johnson, Brad Logan.
Sturgeon was a photo stand-in after Amery quit unexpectedly. 1997. Photo by Jesse Fisher

F-minus. L to R: Brad Logan, Erica Daking, Jen Johnson, Adam Zuckert. 2001. Photo by BJ Papas

Leftover Crack at C squat basement. 2000. Photo by Seth Olenick

Nausea. L to R: John John, Roy, Amy, Vic. 1990. Photo by Chris Boarts Larson.

Nausea. L to R: Amy, John John. Tompkins Square Park, Lower East Side. Photo by Chris Boarts Larson

Glasshouse Doom Room. Lower East Side, 1993. Photo by Chris Boarts Larson

Fifth Street squat anarchy car. Lower East Side, 1990. Photo by Chris Boarts Larson

Bulletspace squat. Lower East Side, 1991. Photo by Chris Boarts Larson

Fetus squat rooftop closet. Lower East Side, 1991. Photo by Chris Boarts Larson

Thirteenth Street squat.
Lower East Side, 1990.
Photo by Chris Boarts Larson

C-squat.
Lower East Side, 2020.
Photo by Bill Cashman

Dos Blockos veiw from Serenity squat.
Ninth Sttreet, Lower East Side, 1993.
Photo by Chris Boarts Larson

Pest squat.
Lower East Side, 1990.
Photo: Chris Boarts Larson

Josiah Steinbrek, F-minus.
Chicago, 2004. Photo by Brian Santostefano

Alec Baillie. Chicago, 2004.
Photo by Brian Santostefano

Ezra Kire. Chicago, 2004. Photo by Brian Santostefano

Brad Logan. Chicago, 2004. Photo by Brian Santostefano

Sturgeon. Chicago, 2004. Photo by Brian Santostefano

Leftover Crack. L to R: Alec, Brad, Sturgeon, Brandon, Ezra. Seattle, 2005.

Leftover Crack. L to R: Sturgeon, Brad. Tompkins Square Park, 2004. Photo by Konstantin Sergeyev

Tompkins Square Park chaos. Brad and Ezra. 2004. Photo by Konstantin Sergeyev

Recording at BBC studios. L to R: Brad, Ara, Sturgeon, Alec, Ezra. 2005. Photo by Angela Baillie

Tour burn in the hallways of the BBC. Ezra. 2005. Photo by Brad Logan

Dick Lucas and Sturgeon.
Lower East Side, NYC, 2006.
Photo by Brad Logan

Sturgeon, somewhere in Europe.
Date unknown.
Photo by Brad Logan

L to R: Franz Nicolay, April, Sturgeon, Jack Terricloth. Tompkins Square Park, NYC, 2006. Photo: Konstantin Sergeyev

L to R: Ezra, Brad, Alec, Jello, Sturgeon, Brandon. Knitting Factory. Hollywood, 2004. Photo by Angela Baillie

Alec, Ezra, Brad, Sturgeon. B.B. Kings, NYC, 2005. Photo by Angela Baillie

Funtimes in Scotland. Sturgeon. 2006. Photo by Brad Logan

L to R: Nick Phillips, Bill Cashman, Brad, Gregg Armen, Ezra, Alec, Sturgeon, Ara, unidentified fans. Kansas City, 2006. Photo by Angela Baillie

Sturgeon and Ezra. Tompkins Square Park, 2008. Photo by Konstantin Sergeyev

Sturgeon. Santos Party House, NYC, 2011. Photo by Konstantin Sergeyev

Leftover Crack Constructs of the State. L to R: Alec, Donny Morris, Sturgeon, Brad, Kate Coysh, Chris Mann. 2015. Photo by Alan Snodgrass

plane. I had this big muff distortion pedal and jammed an antenna into it like it was a remote control. It could have been so much better, compositionally—the people are not very big, the World Trade Center is the most generic picture. I think it was because it was a picture that no one could ever claim copyright for—A.T. couldn't survive any lawsuits after the lawsuits from the nineties. It's just this generic concept art and we sent it off to A.T. and they say, "Not political enough! Can you add a Haliburton the gas pump?" It felt like we were dealing with the ratings board for movies! Somehow that final thing cut the mustard as "being a political enough statement." Again, it was a little bit of a watered-down missed opportunity. Maybe I'm ruining the mystique of it.

Jesse Luscious: So, *Fuck World Trade* is a bit of an incendiary title, and the cover is…it has politicians guiding planes into the Twin towers…of course…the kids loved it.

With the cover, Jello would be like, "There are consequences to speech, but we'll do it, if that's what you really want to do." Sure. It's not going to be carried in Walmart or wherever. But that's not even a goal of bands like Leftover Crack even though, at this point, a sale is a sale for a lot of bands.

Steve Albini: I don't have an opinion on the title of it being good or bad—I just don't get it. They were about to put a record out for international distribution, which by definition is "world trade." They want people in other countries to be able to hear their music, they are putting their music into a production stream which is part of the world trade network. So it didn't seem to have a literal meaning to me, it seemed like it was just intended to be an open-ended statement.

I remember the album cover had an image of George Bush holding a gasoline pump on the twin towers. There are implications to that, that are ludicrous—that George Bush intentionally caused this thing as a pretext to assert dominance over the world oil supply or something. That might have been what it was meant to convey, but that is preposterous on its face, so that's probably not what it was meant to convey. It was probably meant to convey that George Bush was making matters worse in international terrorism and the fact that it was a gas pump was just meant to mean he was adding to the problem—I dunno. It didn't seem to warrant me paying enough attention to it to try to figure out what they were saying. It seemed inflammatory in a prankish way, and that's certainly not a problem for me.

22
Clear Channel (Fuck Off!)

Brad Logan: Sturgeon addressed the corporate takeover of the music industry on *Fuck World Trade*, which was inevitable. You can cry about it all you want, but that's the way things go. We thought the internet would level the playing field, but we were wrong.

Now major record labels are gone, but there's still bazillions to be made off of music, art, and suffering, and no shortage of people willing to sacrifice artists to do it. It creates a competitive atmosphere among artists, which is ultimately destructive in my opinion. It's artistically destructive at least.

The sovereign insincerity, the monopoly of greed / Nickelback, POD, Rancid, Brittney, and Creed / The bureaucrats they leech upon to mediocre trends / Your song in heavy rotation from the cash your label spends / From the products you promote for the ones who foot the bill / A prefabricated goose-step for the pockets that you fill / The monotony of censored products shine in the display / The same old song of compromise went platinum today

—Excerpt from "Clear Channel (Fuck Off!)"

Sturgeon: The first time we went on tour ever, we played the Shelter in Detroit and that was run by Clear Channel. It was packed, like 700 people. We hadn't heard of Clear Channel yet. It was like 2001, and they gave us $400 and a massive list of expenses. It was a long list with people's names on it and their tedious job titles. It might have been fifty cents a person or something. But Clear Channel's corporate headquarters decided that "expenses" at our Leftover Crack show should pay *every* employee in Clear Channel corporate...from the money *we* made, not the money *they* made! It's like what the fuck! We found out what Clear Channel was and how they syndicated music and made it terrible. We also started to notice that every single billboard we passed on tour had a Clear Channel logo at the bottom...even the creepy, anti-abortion ones.

By then, with Rancid, we had already had a falling out. I included Rancid in the lyrics because I felt like they were part of this machine of mediocre music that was homogenized and then syndicated and shoved down people's throats as "alternative music." "This is punk. This is metal. This is pop." These are also the days after 9/11 when every other band, like Rage Against the Machine, were being banned from the radio altogether. So the bands that leaked through tended to not have any type of strong message, if it was criticizing the government or family values.

It was obvious to me that Rancid would be a part of the Clear Channel world because they didn't seem to have any strong politics to me. So, I liked lumping them in there. I knew it was the best diss. You're in a popular punk song.

Brad Logan: "Clear Channel (Fuck Off)" is my least favorite Leftover Crack track. I don't like the composition, the resulting trouble that the lyrical content caused me—problems in my personal life, problems in my music life. I felt deeply hurt by it all.

I was on tour with Lars and the Bastards as a roadie, and we came through New York City to play a show. While I'm in town

I drop by C-Squat to visit. I get there and Bill Cashman says, "Do you know *Fuck World Trade* is out? Here, I have a copy for you."

I was like, "Whoa, that's great news!" I hadn't heard it yet. Then, Cashman says, "Yeah man, that's really fucked up about what he says about Rancid."

I was like, *"What. Are. You. Talking. About?"*

Sure enough, the first line, of the first verse, of the first song, of the first record after leaving Hellcat was slagging off Rancid and throwing them in the shit-pot with Nickelback, Creed, and whoever the fuck else. I was bummed out.

Being as how I wasn't there during the vocal sessions, and since it was never shared with me beforehand, I had zero knowledge of the lyrics that were bashing those guys. But I could already see how this was going to play out.

I was still friends with Rancid...if it was gonna come back on anyone in Leftover Crack, it was gonna come back on me. Which it did. And it put me in a pretty fucked-up spot. Tim took it as a personal stab in the back. I looked like a dumbass, and I felt taken advantage of by Leftover Crack.

Ara Babajian: We were all upset by this censorship of *Medicore Generica,* but no one more so than Sturgeon. To him it was an outrage. His art had been squashed. And I don't blame him. So, he wanted to tell Hellcat and everyone associated with it to go fuck themselves, in song! That's what "Clear Channel (Fuck Off)" is about. And Hellcat was not happy about this. Brad got shit for it for years, I got shit for it, Sturgeon...basically every band or promoter or booking agent that had anything to do with Rancid or Hellcat or Epitaph came down hard on us and either threatened to kick our ass or refused to work with us. It was ridiculous. But Leftover Crack won in the end simply by staying together and continuing to kick the shit out of lesser bands with nothing to say.

Brad Logan: So, I was on tour when the record came out and I didn't know what to do. I felt sick. I put time and energy into this record and was super psyched and now it was going to be a fuckin' albatross for me. It wasn't going to affect anybody else in the band the same way. I was the guy that had the personal relationship with Tim and with Hellcat. And now, I was like, "Wow, I'm just really not excited about this record. Fuck this record." I knew Lars and Tim wouldn't take it well. They would take it as a slag and take it personally—and after all, it was personal. But it wasn't my war.

I loved playing in Leftover Crack, but this had changed my attitude about everything. I hoped that when Tim did find out about it, he and Sturgeon would be able to settle their differences and work it out.

To Sturgeon, it was like, "Oh, it's a hip hop diss track." He didn't view it in the same way that I did. To him it was no big thing, you know? Sturgeon and I never talked about it. He and the rest of Leftover Crack never really understood the depth of it or never said anything to me if they did.

Soon, Tim called me. He was pretty pissed off. I didn't understand what he wanted me to do about *Sturgeon's* conflict with *him*. He said he wanted me to quit the band. The conversation ended badly.

I hated myself for staying. I felt boxed in. But I wasn't going to let someone push me out. Looking back, I should have told them *all* to go get fucked. Rancid probably thought I was lying. And I couldn't blame them. So, once that happened, it drove a wedge between me and Tim.

Sturgeon: I've seen Lars several times since then. He either doesn't recognize me or doesn't care about it anymore. One time, we were playing Rebellion Fest right before or right after GBH, and I saw the singer of GBH talking to Lars. I knew Rancid were picking on Brad and giving him a hard time. I wrote a note that said something like, "It's not really Brad's fault that I've talked shit on you guys." I signed my name on it. I went up to them with a fake British accent, *"Oi, ay've gaught a note f' ya, mate!"* He didn't recognize me, and I gave him the note and walked away. By the time he read it, I was gone in the crowd.

Brad Logan: I didn't see Lars again until about ten years later. I was his guitar tech for a lot of years but it was still awkward to run into him. I remember Lars mentioning to me that he wanted to kick Sturgeon's ass. I didn't know how to answer. I said, "Do it. You'll probably be doing him a favor."

23

The Sunshine State

Brad Logan: At some point during the *Fuck World Trade* tours, we developed a beef with a punk gang down in Florida. We started getting anonymous threats through the grapevine.

We were warned that the next time we came to town, some shit was gonna go down. One night we were playing this place in West Palm Beach. I didn't see anything sketchy going on before or during the bands before us. It was a strip mall show. It might even have been a coffeehouse, but it was packed with a few hundred people.

At some point during the middle of our set, this kid runs up to the stage and yells, "They're smashing your van outside!" The van was parked in the alley behind the venue. So, we get on the mic, "We hear that someone is smashing our van up, so we're going to go check it out." The crowd parts like the Red Sea and the backdoor flies open. We go running outside and there's a gang of goons smashing our windows. They're trying to slash the tires. They throw smoke bombs inside and were trying to torch the van. We immediately charged at them, and they all started running off in opposite directions. I'm chasing after one guy and he goes one way and Alec is chasing after another guy and he goes another way. So we're running after all these guys and punches are being thrown.

We come back to our van and every window had been smashed out except the front ones. Also, while I ran out, someone else grabbed my guitar offstage and ran out the front door. But when I was walking back into the club a kid comes up to me and hands me my guitar, "Here you go! I grabbed this from someone who was running down the street with it."

Sturgeon: The reason that I got out of them that they attacked our van was, when I saw Brad running toward the van and I turned to the last people that were there and said, "Why are you doing this?!" The guy starts *crying* and says, "Because you're called Leftover Crack and my brother smokes crack!" That's the most that *I* could get out of them.

Brad Logan: It was a love message to the band: "Fuck you, don't come back!" We taped up the windows with gaffer tape and plastic trash bags, and did the rest of the Florida tour. We had rented the van from a van rental place in Brooklyn. At the end of the tour, Ezra just drove it back to the rental place, cigarette dangling from his lips, trash bags flapping in the wind. With a straight face, he went up to the counter, dropped off the keys, and said, "Alright, thanks guys…" and left.

The following week we got another message from Florida. "The next time you guys come down here, you're *fuckin' dead!*" So we took that as an open invitation to come down.

At the time, in the early to mid-2000s it wasn't so popular for a cisgender band to be singing songs that championed gay rights, and it was equally less popular to be singing anti-fascist anthems in the Deep South. It sounds ridiculous now, but things were different then.

So, on the next tour, on our way down to Florida, right after we crossed the state lines, we stopped at a Home Depot. We bought five or six garden machetes to take to the clubs with us—the thinking being, "If we're gonna get rat-packed, I'm gonna at least have a machete in my hand."

Sturgeon: The machetes were...just in case. I always thought machetes were a great idea. You just jump over to Home Depot and get 'em for six bucks a piece. Ara's not going to sport one, but me and Nick would. They're not really that dangerous because they're not that sharp, so you can swing them around without really cutting yourself or someone else. Plus, they look dangerous.

Brad Logan: We were expecting trouble, but I didn't even think about it. I just went about my business. "If it's gonna happen, it's gonna happen." It's the same way I approached shows as a kid in LA. There wasn't security everywhere. It wasn't a nice, safe environment. People did get stabbed and shot and had the shit knocked out of them. It was dangerous, but that never stopped us from going to shows.

In Tampa, the leader of the gang that wanted our asses showed up to the gig with a bunch of his boys. We thought for sure that shit was going to go down. We had our machetes on us. I remember things getting tense while we were playing.

But then, the next thing I know, the leader guy is onstage and him and Sturg are hugging it out. He said something like, "You guys have heart, you have guts, we're squashin' the beef, everything's cool." Or some shit like that. Meaning they weren't going to try to attack us and kill us next time we went to Florida...I guess? At least there wasn't an open death threat against us anymore...at least in Central Florida.

Then, the crowd started cheering. The next thing I know, the dude stage dives back into the crowd and we just start playing again.

Sturgeon: The machetes did the job.

24
The Phoenix Riot

Brad Logan: We were playing a show in Phoenix on Halloween night. We're all dressed as cops.

Sturgeon: Before we played, I had a toy gun and I pointed it at someone that worked at the club and they kicked me out of the show, and they thought I was just someone there for the show. They kicked me out and said, "That guy can't get back in the show!" So that didn't help the situation. The guy that kicked me out realized that I was the singer of the band. So they had to walk me back into the club.

Ron Martinez: What I heard was that Sturgeon was dressed as a cop and he had a toy gun, and he walks up to this guy and puts the toy gun in his back and says, "Stick 'em up!" Sturgeon didn't know the guy was the owner and the owner didn't know Sturgeon was who he was, and he flipped out because according to the promoter, that same person had been held up at gunpoint recently, and the guy freaked out and had Sturgeon thrown out of the show. Sturgeon is saying the whole time, "I'm playing the show! You can't throw me out!" That set Sturgeon off in a bad mood before they even played. I guess that's why he went onstage in a combative mood.

Sturgeon: So, the show was going really late. A couple people in Leftover Crack thought it was a great idea to book their flight back to New York at 3:00 a.m., but the show was supposed to end at like midnight. But the show was going later and later. And the bar was one of those bars that's penned in and they wouldn't give me booze outside of there. So they kept bringing me to the drinking area and I kept drinking more and more and I was almost blacked out.

Brad Logan: Sturgeon and Ezra had been bickering all day and they took their bickering onto the stage. They were going back and forth with the insults. It was lame. It felt like it went on forever, but in reality, it was probably only like five minutes. It seems like an hour though when you have 500 kids staring at you waiting for you to shut the fuck up and start playing again.

The next thing I know, Ezra unplugs his guitar and walks offstage. So the rest of us say, "Fuck this, we're out," and leave the stage. But for some reason Sturgeon stays up there.

Sturgeon: It took me a little longer to come to the stage because I was at the bar or something and a couple of our band members left and we couldn't play. So I was like, "Fuck those guys! Let's riot!"

Ron Martinez: I get a phone call well after ten o'clock. I can hear sirens and police radios in the background very loudly. It's the promoter. He's like, "Can you hear that?!" and he's holding the phone out. I was like, "Yeah?" He says, "That's the riot that your fucking band just started at my show!"

Brad Logan: We're outside the back door and Ezra says, "Fuck that, there's no way I'm going back onstage." We can hear the audience starting to get very vocal about their displeasure. They're yelling shit and throwing things at the stage—beer bottles, loose change, food, anything.

Sturgeon was trying to talk the crowd down, probably thinking the gig would resume, but after a bit it just starts getting louder inside. Then, at some point, somebody walks onstage and tells the crowd the show's over, and it just turns into a full-scale riot.

People start throwing and smashing up barstools, smashing everything around. It was a sports bar, like a 500 or 600 capacity, cheesy dance and cocaine bar. The whole crowd inside spills out into the back lot where we were standing and it gets completely out of control. People are just trashing everything.

I remember a guy saying to Sturgeon, "I fucking love you! You're my favorite singer!" Then he punches Sturg in the face.

The venue was located next to an overpass on the I-10 freeway, which is a main roadway that travels through downtown Phoenix. There was probably a hundred or so metal chairs stacked up behind the club that they removed for the show. Then maybe fifty kids start grabbing the chairs and start throwing them off the overpass onto the passing traffic. People that were driving their car into the tunnel or out of the tunnel were having chairs raining down upon them.

I see Tyler King, the guy who put the show on, trying to push people back. He looks over at me and we both just shrug like, "Oh well, whaddaya gonna do?"

Police helicopters and cars showed up and you know how it ends from there. We were banned from Phoenix for at least five years. Every time we would try to book a show, the clubs would say, "No, thanks, we heard about you," On top of that, Tyler was pretty bummed. He lost a lot of money having to pay for all the damages, and made it clear if we ever somehow managed to play in town again he and his crew would show up and take it out of our asses. He held a grudge for a while.

We never got paid a dime for the show, but it was worth it. It was worth forfeiting the money and time, because you can't put a price on golden memories like that.

Sturgeon: That kind of got blamed on me. But that wasn't totally my fault. A lot of shit went wrong. I did get scapegoated a lot for the riot and things going bad. I'll take responsibility for it, but it wasn't all my fault. We made it seem like the club's fault, but at the end of the day it was because our bass player and guitar player left the show, not thinking about what might happen after they didn't play. They were worried about missing their flights.

I didn't buy a plane ticket for 3:00 a.m. after Halloween. I knew that was a stupid plan.

I knew I was going to kick it in town. It was Halloween. It's a fun night. I booked it for the next night or maybe even the day after that.

I woke up in a hotel room by myself. I didn't know where my band was. I didn't know anybody in town. I intended to kick it, but I was by myself and spent the day in a motel room and flew back. We're still banned from Phoenix city limits, I think.

Ron Martinez: Usually the riot is started by the police or the fans, but here the band started their own riot.

JP Otto: I think the city tried to bill the venue for the police helicopter time.

Brad Logan: The next tour was business as usual and the riot wasn't even mentioned. That's how we did it. Shut the fuck up. Get in the van and let's go.

25

Van Trouble

Joe Porter: The last tour I did was a European tour. I was on many tours with the band and every tour has low points. But, on the European tour, it was really low. It was stretched out and people were miserable most of the time. If it was going to be like that, I was like, "I don't want to do the next tour," which was a Southern US tour. I don't even know what the misery was from. It was a lot of things.

Dale Tomlinson: I was driving and was very tired and Ezra came up to me and said, "Hey, Dale, I'm a good driver. I can drive if you want me to. I'll take over." I don't really like doing things like that because I'm insured on the bus and that kind of thing. But I'm so tired that it's dangerous and Ezra totally reassured me. He kept saying, "Yeah, ya know, I'll drive." So he took over and I sat and watched him for a little while and it was through the night and he seemed to be doing the job so I was like, "Yeah, cool."

So I get in my little coffin and thinking I'll get a little bit of sleep. So basically we're driving along and I'm getting to sleep. I'm starting to relax and the next minute I just hear this massive screeching noise and I can just feel the bus rocking—but when you're in your coffin you can't see shit so you think you might be at the end of a fucking cliff, "Where am I, the bus is fucking tipping, I'm dead! Cliff Burton, here we go!"

It's the weirdest feeling when the bus is crashing, but you're in the coffin and you don't know where the hell you're going. There's a terrible sound and then silence.

It turns out that the bus is on its side, like fully on its side. So, I'm like, "WHAT THE FUCK?" ya know what I mean? But I'm all, "I left Ezra in charge! It's all my fault." So I climb out of the coffin in my bunk and everybody's freaking out and I get there and I'm like, "EZRA, WHAT THE FUCK? WHAT'S GOING ON?" And he was like, "Ahh, it's like a snow blizzard," or something. So we opened the passenger door of the bus because it was completely on its side, and we climbed out of it—the side door was actually the top, so we climbed out of it like a tank. And I thought, "Oh, my life is over! The bus is wrecked. Game over." But no one's dead, so that's alright. So, I get out and we're actually in a massive snow blizzard. There's snow everywhere. And I said, "Ezra, why the fuck didn't you stop? Why didn't you pull over?" and he's all stressed out and freaked out and we're really stressed like "fuuuuck!"

We're not going to make it to Berlin. It's peak middle of the night and these German cops came along. A big tow truck came along, too. I couldn't really be in a bad mood with Ezra, he was freaked out and it wasn't his fault really…*but he really should have just pulled over* to be honest with you. So anyway, the tow truck pulled the bus back up, and…I'm not joking…it had a fine scratch on it… and that's it. I couldn't fucking believe it. I thought the whole thing was going to be mangled and cost my insurance everything and I'd lose it all, ya know?

Anyway, they pulled it over and the German cops turned around to me and said, "You owe us 400 Euros." And I said, "*WE* owe *YOU* four hundred Euros?" They said, "Well, you scratched the crash barrier on the side of the motorway." And I'm like, "WHAT?!" So we had to pay for the barrier that we'd crushed. It was only 400 Euros, but still we had to pay it there and then. But I got in the bus and remarkably, unbelievably, it ran normal and we got to the gig. When we pulled up to the gig there was just a scratch on the side of the van that was pretty much it. It was amazing. But we couldn't get the back door open, we couldn't get Ezra's guitar out of it, but apart from that we came away pretty fucking unscathed.

JP Otto: When we got to the Czech Republic, we load in and are in the show. Dale is in the bus, but he drove through the night to get us there. He's asleep in the bunk. At some point he comes into the club and says, "Hey, someone broke into the bus. I was asleep in my bunk and heard someone rifling around. I yelled out 'hey!' and he ran away, but you all should go check to see if anything is missing."

Dale Tomlinson: My van got broken into and the ignition had been busted open, so I had to ring the AA people. They couldn't fix my ignition so I had to put a screwdriver in it to start the van.

Joe Porter: The only thing was missing were the keys to the minibus. So we had to wait for the dealership to mail the keys to where we were. We missed Amsterdam, France, and other shows. We were supposed to be in the Czech Republic for one day but we were there for like three.

There was a lot of fighting going on—mostly between Alec and Sturgeon—and it was making everyone bummed. There was this weird tension in the bus and it was sleeting most of the time. Then, Alec and Sturgeon got in a huge fistfight in the back of the bus.

Renee Louise (Singer—Skarp): I was quote, unquote roadie-ing. Really, I was just drinking and hanging out. I was sitting in the bus next to Alec and Sturgeon. Sturgeon gets drunk and runs his mouth and apparently Alec had had his fill of Sturgeon and just socked him in the face

Joe Porter: They were tackling each other and they were fighting each other and slamming each other into the table!

Renee Louise: Alec fuckin' knocked Sturgeon out. I was like, "Oh, no. There's blood." I don't even really remember what the fight was about, but I didn't want any blood on me. I think Sturgeon was just being a drunk guy and being irritating. Alec is not tolerant of that.

Joe Porter: When they finished fighting, Sturgeon's face was all bloody. Alec calmed down and he was trying to mend the damage with Sturgeon. But Sturgeon just *would not* wash his face for the next few days. I think he did it so Alec would have to see the blood on his face.

Renee Louise: The van didn't even stop driving during the fight. It just kept rolling along the Alps.

26

Take Me to Heathrow

Dale Tomlinson: So, I've lost my voice, and we're heading back from Germany, we travel all the way home, the band are all wasted, we get back to Heathrow, of course we're all filthy and dirty, stinking even more than the start. So, I pull up to Heathrow, drop the band off, and I say, "See ya," and I'm just driving off, and Nick, the merch guy, ran up and said, "Oh, Dale, Dale, you dropped us off at the wrong terminal!" And I said, "What?!" so I turned 'round, picked them all up.

Now, the next terminal, they're going to miss the plane if I don't get there in time so I'm fricking driving like a madman. So I drive and I kind of do an illegal maneuver and I pull up to the front to let the guys out. I say, "See you again!" The guys all run into the airport, and I think they catch the plane.

I'm just about to drive off and the next minute, I get surrounded by four massive military police cars and all these guys jump out with machine guns, right? And it's just me on my own. This is scary shit. And they're going, "What are you doing? What are you doing *here?*" but of course my voice is gone, right? So I can barely talk and I'm *whispering*, "Yeah I've just dropped this band off, right?" and I sound like this fucked-up gnarly Lemmy or something like that, and I look like shit because I've been up for twenty-four hours driving, and I'm stinking just horrendous.

So the guy, he's in the van with a fucking machine gun, and we don't have machine guns in England, so it's scary because it's just after the Twin Towers, so it's on fucking red alert. So, he's looking to the window and he's seeing the screwdriver hanging out and it looks like I've fucking hot-rodded the fucking van and he goes, "Get out of the vehicle!"

I'm like, "Oh, shit!" The guy pulls me out, slams me against the fucking van, and I'm trying to talk but I can't talk because my voice is gone and I'm like, "Ahh huuh aauuu," and I sound like a fucking moron, right? So they go, "Open the van!" and I say, "Okay" and open the side door. As soon as I open the side door two bottles of whisky roll out and smash on the floor, a porno mag falls out, the fucking whole place is filth. Fucking disgusting. Like some tramps have been living in there for a year, right?

So, I stood there like, "Awww, God, this looks fucking awful," and he goes "Right! Open the back up!" By now there are twenty fucking police around me with machine guns pulled on me! I'm thinking, "Oh, shit!"…and the band has left me, right, with two boxes of T-shirts to take back, right? Now, one of these T-shirts has the *fucking Twin Towers* on it, and the other T-shirt has fucking *"kill cops"* on it. So I'm shitting my pants, right?

So, I go to the back door and I open the back door, which for some reason loads of punks had wrote loads of fucking swastikas in the dirt on the back of the van, and like, "Punk rock! Fuck off all Americans!" and everything. So, that looks *great*. The cops start peering in with machine guns, and they're like "What's in those boxes there?" And I'm like, "Uhhh…just some…T-shirts…" But my voice is like, "Uuuhghu juusuust sooome tshuurts," ya know what I mean? So the guy's pulling out this box of T-shirts and I'm like,

"Oh, God, I'm gonna fucking die! One has Twin Towers, one's got 'kill cops' on it!"

So, he opens one of them and it's the Twin Towers one, and he goes, "What's this!?" I go, "Uuughhg it's the Twin Towers... they're from New York..." And he goes, "Leftover Crack? What's that mean?!" and I was like, "Ohhh, uuuh...it's an Irish thing...like leftover job, it just means a job, leftover job like leftover crack." So the guy bought that. So then he says "What's with the fucking towers?!" and I said, "Oh it's like a...*memorial* T-shirt 'cause my friends died in it." Then he said, "What's in the other box?!" And I told them just more T-shirts. So the cops went in and dragged it out, and they were just about to open the box full of shirts that said "kill cops," and the two cops just looked at me and said, "Fucking hell, this guy is just a waste of space. Just get the fuck out of here!"

The one cop has the box with "kill cops" in it, half opened, but he doesn't look down...then, he closes it and tells me to get out of there. And I'm not joking man—I shit my pants, literally.

27

The Death of Brandon

Alec Baillie: We were toward the end of a multiple-leg four-month tour in December of 2004 in support of *Fuck World Trade*. Everyone in our band and crew was pretty cracked at that point, especially Brandon, who was dealing with a severe case of heartbreak. During what I remember to be our third-to-last show of the year in Dallas at the Red Blood Club, he wasn't playing right. He seemed confused and was mixing up parts or just not playing well. Brandon was a fucking excellent drummer, so everyone was concerned.

Sturgeon: For the first time ever, Brandon was fucking up the drums a little bit. I asked him and he was like, "Yeah, I took these pills." I was like, "What did you get?" He said he had Valium and I said, "Can you save me one...and maybe don't do them before you play anymore?"

Brad Logan: After the Dallas gig, I saw Brandon at the bar drinking. He had mentioned that he had some Xanax and the last thing I said to him was, "Brandon, you really gotta be careful, don't drink on those things." And the last thing he said to me was, "Yeah, yeah, don't worry, I will." And I was like, "Okay..." And then I went down the street to Trees, and saw that band the Paper Chase.

Sturgeon: Later that night, Brandon and a friend of mine, and of his, had gone off to get drugs, hard drugs, in Dallas. I didn't see Brandon for the rest of the night.

Normally Brandon and I would share hotel rooms and it's getting really late and I don't even know where Brandon is. I call him and apparently he was in the hotel, but somewhere else. I get him to swing by the room. He's pretty fucked up. But, at that time, I guess he knew that other drugs are coming back to the hotel, too.

The point was that I asked him for Valium that he had and he didn't have any, which meant he took them. He had at least three earlier and that's a lot for anybody unless, like, you're taking that many regularly, and I know those guys weren't.

I hate to admit it, but I turned into kind of a dick. Part of it was that I was mad that he didn't save me a pill—but more so, I was upset that he was being irresponsible about his intake of substances. It seemed kind of dangerous. It didn't help that the person he was hanging out with seemed kind of dumb.

So, those guys go back to the room at the same time. It was five or six in the morning. We had a show in Austin the next day. I was arguing with him about that and I think I was dead sober the whole time.

I don't think Brandon was an intravenous drug user, but it seemed like he wanted to shoot up. I told our other friend to not let him do that. I lectured Brandon for not being honest with me about what he had been taking that night. I spent like a half hour lecturing him about being safe about drugs, oddly enough.

So, after that, I guess that he had snorted some heroin. I didn't see him do that, but I think he snorted it instead of shooting it.

We had a show the next day, so I was telling everyone, "Go to sleep, go to sleep." I was trying to be a responsible parent or some shit. I took Brandon's shoes off for him and he had his arms behind his head, like when you're lying on the lawn and looking up at the stars.

When I woke up several hours later, he was in that exact same position and I knew something was wrong. I jumped up and I went over and was jolting him and slapping him. He was still warm.

Brad Logan: Ezra and I had shared a room and we were walking out of the room looking for coffee or something to eat and we walked by Sturgeon's room. Sturgeon threw open the door. He yelled, "Brandon's not breathing! Come in here quick!" We ran into the room and Brandon was lying on the bed in clothes on top of the covers. He hadn't even climbed under the blanket. He was lying peacefully like he was taking a nap, except that he was as blue as an iceberg.

Immediately, Ezra, who had CPR training, pulled him off the bed and threw him on the floor and started administering CPR and pushing his chest and giving mouth-to-mouth resuscitation. Ezra tried that for ten minutes before it became apparent that he was gone.

Sturgeon: We called an ambulance right away and told all the guys to take any drugs or anything illegal and go away. The paramedics came, the police came, and I guess he was already dead.

Alec Baillie: Nick Phillips and I had gone out to eat breakfast in Deep Ellum when Nick got a call. Brandon wasn't breathing. We ran back to the hotel just in time to watch the paramedics roll him into the elevator while performing chest compressions.

Sturgeon: We were in the hallway, Ezra is there, Brad's there, a cop is there, and the cop says, "Does anyone know what this is?" and he held up a pill. Someone said it was a muscle relaxer. As I learned later, muscle relaxers are super dangerous. Years later, I was going through my own withdrawals, and I was at my friend's house and my friend had given me a muscle relaxer, and I was on the floor, and I had to pee, and I couldn't get up. I couldn't walk. I had to drag myself to the bathroom. I could barely breathe. That made sense about Brandon taking muscles relaxers with Valium and alcohol and heroin—it's a lot.

Alec Baillie: We followed them to the hospital and they put us all in a small room near the emergency room. Shortly after, someone came in to tell us he had died. I fucking sobbed. I remember Ezra trying to console me. Once I got my shit together, I called his mom Judith to give her the news. How do you tell someone's mother that her son was dead? I'll never forget that…it was surreal.

Ron Martinez: I remember getting the phone calls. My phone kept ringing at like seven a.m. and it was a Saturday. I ignored it and my phone rings again. I'm like, "Fuck this!" When the phone rings a third time, I go to pick it up and the first thing I can hear is police radios in the background and I instantly knew it was not good. It was Alec on the phone. Alec's voice was really shaky, and he was like, "Brandon's dead."

Brad Logan: The rest of the day entailed the non-glamorous situations that you don't see in the movies—the hours to kill while you wait outside the coroner's building, gathering Brandon's belongings, and then the long drive home, trying to process what had just happened. It was gnarly, it was pretty fuckin' gnarly, you know?

Alec Baillie: We canceled the tour and agreed among us to help Brandon's family with part of the funeral costs. The next week I traveled back to New York to grieve with Brandon's friends and family and attend the funeral in Asbury Park, New Jersey, where he was from. It was an open casket and his family had decided to dress him in his typical attire, which included his leather jacket.

Ron Martinez: Booking shows, I've had misfortunes—bands rolling vans and people getting hurt. But this was heartbreaking. This guy joins his favorite band and the band gets a guy that fits with them on multiple levels. And he's dead. Of course, this is what would happen to Leftover Crack.

Sturgeon: I feel like if I knew any better, if I knew then what I know now, I wouldn't have necessarily objected to him shooting up because he probably would have OD'd right then and we very likely could have saved his life. We could have called an ambulance right then and he could have been revived. But he didn't have that chance. If he had shot the drugs instead of snorting them, he very well could have been alive right now.

Brad Logan: Sturgeon was devastated. I don't think he was ever the same afterward. He and Brandon were really close, and I think Brandon's death really screwed up Sturgeon's head. I think in some ways he felt responsible. But as somebody who has known countless ODs, and as someone who *has* OD'd and then went right back to using, that's not the truth of the matter. It was Brandon's decision and none of us could stop it from happening. There was nothing any of us could have done.

28

The End of F-Minus

Brad Logan: Around 2004, F-Minus came to an end. We were influenced by classic era hardcore punk. Early 1980's Negative Approach, Agnostic Front, Circle Jerks, Middle Class, Wire, Discharge. We loved all those bands. But we were a bastardization. The idea was to strip it down, tear it down, get rid of all the bullshit. And not dragging things out too long was also a part of that.

Jen Johnson (Bass/Vocals—F-Minus): Before the band started, in 1995, I was living in Huntington Beach. Brad wrote a note on my door that said, "Do you want to start a band? Let's start a band." Brad didn't ask me. He told me.

Brad Logan: I knew Jen was the guy from day one. She was the best guy for the job. We had known each other from around town. I liked her attitude.

Jen Johnson: I really was into my band at the time. But Brad and I were writing songs and Brad said, "Well, here, you can use this song for *your* band."

Brad Logan: It was like I thought I was Prince or something. "Here, you *may have this song.*"

Jen Johnson: Well, except the song was only two chords. I think Prince might have more than two chords in his songs. Anyway, that is how F-Minus started.

But the bummer was, once we would get started, all three of the other band members would leave for tour. So, it took like two years to really get that shit started, so it was the longest start of a band ever.

But Brad finally got smart and said, "We really gotta do this, we can't have people touring all the time." We wanted Amery—also known as AWOL—in the band and we really wanted Sarah Lee. We met her at a place we used to practice at, where a bunch of bands did. We walked in on her one day, bleeding fingers from playing so hard, with the shittiest gear ever, chain-smoking, blood everywhere, and just *shredding* these emo songs in a room by herself. We thought, *"This* is our girl."

Brad Logan: She had a really bad attitude, which was perfect.

Jen Johnson: She just frowned.

Brad Logan: Sarah named the band, just threw it out at practice one night. We knew it was the right name the minute we heard it.

We started playing local shows wherever we could get them, LA, OC, and Inland Empire. Our very first show was a biker rally in the mountains of LA, with a Steppenwolf cover band. It was just a gnarly crowd of Harley riding badasses. But they liked us and let us hang around after our set to eat their food and drink their beer.

Jen Johnson: Me and Amery were loading gear after a show. He wasn't saying a word to me. Sarah Lee and Amery had a huge fight. They had a deep friendship that we weren't privy to. He said to me cryptically, "I want you to know that it was really great being in a band with you." He took to his special way of loading his drums in his perfect drum way, which always took a little bit longer than normal. Then, he drove away and I never saw him again.

I was like, "I guess this is why they call him AWOL."

Brad Logan: He was very professional about it. He packed up his drums in a calm, very orderly fashion, and said, "I'm sorry, but I'm quitting," and drove off into the moonlight. But I had no idea why he was quitting at the time.

After that, Lumpy started playing drums with us. He was the loudest drummer I have ever played with. He was louder than the rest of the band at full blast. We had to keep telling him to turn down.

Jen Johnson: We had our first official "meeting" at Epitaph because we were getting ready to go on our first tour. Toby Morse of H20 was also there, because we were opening for H20. Sarah Lee had gotten there a little early and went to the conference room and decided to pierce between her eyes. But she hit a vein and started to bleed...a lot. Toby Morse comes outside and he's like, "Bro-dude-bro-dude-bro-dude your fucking girl, she's bleeding, like she put a hole into her face! She's bleeding into a bowl!"

Brad Logan: She just sat there for an hour or so bleeding into a bowl. She was turning white. She didn't want help or a Band-Aid or anything. People at Epitaph were walking by, bumming. Then, not too long after, Sarah left F-Minus. I didn't know what we were gonna do. We had maybe a month before we were going to record our first record for Hellcat, maybe less. We could have done it as a three-piece, but I always hated a three-piece lineup. I felt it lacked symmetry. I wanted to preserve the integrity of the four-piece band, but Sarah left some big shoes to fill. She was the best musician in the band. Oh, and we also didn't have a drummer because Amery had just quit too.

I was in Tokyo on tour with Rancid and talking about the upcoming F-Minus record with Tim. He asked me if I could think of anybody who might be a good fit. I told him I had a gut feeling about this girl from NYC, whom I hadn't seen play guitar, but she told me she played guitar, and she had the most hateful, piercing, eyes I had ever seen. Tim said, "You're calling that girl right fuckin' now and seeing if she can join your band because we're not turning back!" He gave me his phone to call and I was like, "Uhhhh, Erika, I know you don't know me that well…"

Erica Daking (Guitar—F-Minus): I was in Boston, in college, and I got a random phone call one day to join Brad's band. Shortly after, I got a package of records, and a plane ticket in the mail. I was seventeen, this guy never had seen me play guitar, yet he flew me to California to play on this record.

At the time, I would have been a senior in high school, but I skipped my junior year. My whole life I was the youngest kid in my family. And everyone I hung out with was always older than me, so it wasn't weird for me to hang out with older people. But to fly to LA and join a band with a bunch of people who were all ten or twelve years older than me, whom I didn't really know, and was meeting for the first time? It was a pretty surreal experience…but also totally normal.

Jen Johnson: I met Erika for the first time when we were in the studio teaching her the songs to record.

Brad Logan: We toured endlessly and would take any show or tour we got offered. It didn't matter where, or if anyone showed up to see us.

Once we were booked to play a huge hall in Cologne, Germany, for some reason in the dead of winter. We played to zero people. There was another band and the doorman and that's it. Our set was only fifteen minutes long, so we played it three times.

Jen Johnson: We got put on a lot of big shows because we were on Hellcat. Mostly we played in front of hostile crowds that didn't know what to make of us. We played some huge arena in Riverside with The Offspring and TSOL at the height of Offspring's radio days. I got hit in the head with a full bottle and it fuckin' hurt, but I couldn't show that it hurt. I walked offstage and Jack Grisham of TSOL was there and he was like, "Show me who did it." It was during the time that he wore long skirts with no underwear. During the TSOL set, he went out there and got right on top of the kid and put his skirt over the kid's head and put his junk right in the kid's face.

Adam Zukcert (Drums—F-Minus): Chris Lagerborg, that's Lumpy, was the drummer just before the first album recording sessions. But Chris had the opportunity to go on tour as a drum tech for Slayer and there wasn't any time to postpone the recording. The band kinda knew what the deal was, and Chris kinda knew what the deal was, so Brad called me and was like, "Hey, would you be available to do this? We'll just rehearse for two or three days and just go in and do it." I was like, "Fuck yeah! We can even rehearse in my basement." Which we did. So, Brad came over and taught me the songs, then we went into Crystal Studios and banged it out in three days with Tim Armstrong.

Jen Johnson: Brody was there, we were all there just hanging out, and Tim wanted my bass to sound a certain way. For me, even though I didn't know shit about anything, I was always very opinionated on how I wanted things to sound, and I remember not sharing the same opinion with Tim often in the beginning. We would just butt heads.

I remember getting in a big screaming match with him. I don't remember what it was over. Brad and Brody called me in and told me to apologize. But I refused to. And later, that's why Tim and I became so close. He respected me for standing my ground.

Erica Daking: I learned all the songs a couple days before we recorded. We recorded everything live, and I remember Tim being in the control room and me not understanding what a producer was. He was producing the record, but it was more like him just sitting there being cool with everything we were doing. I thought it was the coolest thing ever at the time. One day in the middle of recording, we ordered Del Taco and I got food poisoning. It was the first time I ever got food poisoning and I was horribly sick. I've only ever gotten food poisoning twice in my life and both times it was from Del Taco. But I'll still eat there.

Brad Logan: Crystal was a really nice recording studio in a decaying section of Hollywood. People like the Doors, Jimi Hendrix, and Miles Davis made records there. Tim was there to make sure we didn't try to get arty or fuck it up by overproducing it. He wanted us to keep it pure. I learned a lot from him about how to harness raw power.

Adam Zuckert: One time, we played at Chain Reaction and Joe Sib from SideOneDummy was there doing this punk rock TV show thing. He had never seen us. So, before our set he was like, "Hey, man, let's do an interview after the show, we'll video it and everything and put you guys on our show!" We're like, "Great, no problem, sounds cool!"

So, we play and after the last song we're packing up, and we see Joe walk by and say, "So, hey, Joe, how about that interview?" And Joe goes, "Um...hey...you know what...? Yeah...we should get some coffee sometime! Yeah! That would be really awesome, cool, good to see you guys!" He said this while he was like waving and walking backward out the door.

Brad Logan: Jennifer had a full-time job, and every time she went on tour she would have to pay for her life in credit cards. It was becoming hard for her. So, she had to leave for her own sake. I mean, there was absolutely no money in this band, and we toured a lot. I understood, but it was hard for me. She was my rock.

Josiah Steinbrick (Bass—F-Minus): When Jen didn't want to do the band anymore it was pretty natural for me to come in and play bass. I think I learned all the songs in a day. Then we played a fucking gig in San Francisco, at the Maritime Hall, for like 3,000 people. Mike Dirnt was there, Lars was there, all these people. I mean, I came from a big East Coast punk scene, but these were people that were on MTV and shit. It was such a trip. I filled in for the tour for two weeks until Jen rejoined, then I think I helped sell merch or something after. A bit later I went to Europe with them for the *Suburban Blight* tour in Spring 2002 and eventually Jen didn't come back.

Erica Daking: One day, my dad was like, you guys should record a record with Steve Albini. And I said, "How would you even do that?" My dad says, "All you need to do is call him."

So, we did and that was that. I remember Steve being a man of very few words, but I seem to remember all of them. It was so fucking cold there too.

He hadn't heard any of us sing yet, and I was first up in the vocal booth. After I screamed the song out, I remember him pushing a button, and saying over the studio intercom, "You have a voice like a bird."

Josiah Steinbrick: The experience with Steve Albini was such a strange thing because it just felt so totally natural. He was really easy to work with and just so down to talk about old punk and hardcore. For him, he was obviously talking about an older part of his life, but he was still deeply connected to it. We were just chatting about records and music a lot, and he's still opinionated, and cranky as any teenager.

I remember being in the studio and we'd be talking about these sort of, like, obscure, first wave, 77, punky, pub-rock records, and nasty, angular, post-punk that we were getting stoked on. Then he'd pull out a guitar, and he and I would jam together in the studio. And he would ask me, "Oh, do you know this Ruts song?" Or PIL's "Death Disco," or something like that.

And we'd be jamming and I remember thinking, "this dude is the *worst* guitar player I've ever played with in my life." I was so fucking blown-away at how rudimentary his shit was.

I remember thinking it was really incredible to know that Big Black, and Shellac, and all that stuff sounded that way because that was his level of skill. That he never broke past just shredding-out like that. I thought it was radical that he was able to take it to such a wild level, but also that when you're in Electrical Audio he's still wearing a Stooges T-shirt, and he had a copy of "Funhouse" in the hallway, and that the primitive rock and roll spirit is still such a deep part of him that I understand now why he'd rather work with a Neurosis, or some shitty punk band instead of like…Bush or something. He was totally right, though.

Adam Zuckert: I think I was notoriously bad about doing song takes. I would be like, "Ah, I know I can do better, let's try it again." I remember toward the end of the day the band would be like, "No, dude, it's fine, we're not doing it again." And I even remember Steve Albini drew a little hangman picture with me hanging from the rope because I was starting to kill him with all the multiple takes.

Josiah Steinbrick: Albini did not eat food. He would not eat a fuckin thing till like 11:00 p.m. Then he would have an Eggplant parm or something, and then eat a ream of Nutter Butters 'til like 4:00 a.m., which is when we would wrap recording. Then he would go up to his zone upstairs and fuck around with his records, which he wouldn't let me look at. I remember being like, "Hey, can I check out your record collection?" and he was like, "NO."

Brad Logan: After the third album, the band came to an end. Erika and Joe wanted to start their own band and move on. And really, they did the band a favor. We had done what we set out to do, and we were quitting while we were ahead. I didn't want to continue with a revolving door of people playing. What held the band together all those years was the personalities of the people involved. Anyone can play an instrument, but you can't really replace character. It was everything.

Our last show was supporting Leftover Crack at the Knitting Factory. We did it as a five-piece with Joe playing guitar, Jennifer, myself, Erika, and Adam. We played everything we knew and that was that.

29

Tour Burn

Jesse Luscious: Back when we signed Leftover Crack, they were touring the country, and this was when they were really, really rough and out of control. They had played the First Unitarian Church in Philadelphia and it was a big fuckin' deal and they almost got the place shut down. The First Unitarian Church, it's like the Che Cafe in San Diego or Gilman in Berkeley. It's a DIY space—it's not the Live Nation or Bill Grahams of the world. All the other DIY spaces at the time in the US saw this happening. I think people bum-rushed the door and overloaded the space. I don't remember exactly what it was, but it was enough to give me, as a former booker at Gilman, heart palpitations. There was no concern voiced about the fact that it was a DIY space. It's not "the enemy." It's not a for-profit Live Nation corporate setting. You're basically shitting where you sleep.

Greg Daly (Employee—R5 Productions; Tour Manager—Leftover Crack, Choking Victim, Napalm Death, many others): The band was not to blame for the incident at the First Unitarian Church, but from the perspective of certain people at the show, they certainly didn't help the situation like we would have liked them to. The show was a really big show, too big for the space.

Subhumans, Leftover Crack, From Ashes Rise, that's a killer show. So, it sold out in advance. It was a huge gig and a lot of people showed up—people who didn't buy tickets that didn't think that the people that actually did buy tickets had more of a right to be there than them...and they *were* not cool about it. People were trying to sneak in, people were fighting, pissing on the floor. It was the general shithead-ness of a punk show, but it was overwhelming. People were trying to fight their way in, punch us at the door when we said it was sold out, and being really disrespectful.

Some dude punched me because he couldn't come in, but then, someone from Leftover Crack was like, "Oh, no, he's my friend, he's on the guest list, he's gotta come in!" I'm like, "No, he can't come in! He just tried to punch me! I'm not gonna let him in! I don't care if he's your friend!"

The band was not really supportive of us trying to run the show without people getting hurt, but I wouldn't say it was their fault. It was the fault of people showing up thinking that they were entitled to everything in the world and then throwing hissy fits when they couldn't have it.

From the perspective of people throwing the show, we just wished they said something like, "Sorry, it's sold out, we'll be back soon," or something like that, instead of the situation getting inflamed. At the time it was fucking annoying, but if I was them, I might have done the same thing.

Brad Logan: Some windows had gotten smashed out at the Church by quote, unquote "somebody wearing a Leftover Crack shirt" while we were playing. I was talking with Andy Nelson of R5 Productions, the promoter, outside of the show, and he was telling me that we were banned from there because our fans were rowdy and were smashing up the place. But he didn't know us as people. We never advocated destruction of venues—especially

DIY spaces or independent clubs. We went to shows at these same spots. We weren't into policing people, though, and when you come to a show, it's on you to know how to act in the situation. It's a personal responsibility.

We were pretty bummed about it. We always had a good relationship with the Church and R5. At the time, they were a small collective that put on shows. We were bummed because we loved that club, we loved Philly, we loved the Subhumans, and certainly, it wasn't anyone we knew that did the damage. But damage and riots seemed to follow us wherever we went for a few years. Nevertheless, I thought that we were unfairly pissed on and it followed us for a while.

Greg Daly: For the record, it wasn't R5 that banned Leftover Crack. It was the First Unitarian Church that banned them. They asked us to not book shows that did things like that. I'll add that 99.9 percent of the bands don't have this issue.

Jesse Townley: Word of the First Unitarian Church thing got back to Gilman. So, it got brought up at one of the meetings. Leftover Crack was coming around on tour. There was a proposal to not have Leftover Crack play because there was a concern of them not respecting the space and them endangering the space because they were so outta fucking control. I voted for that. "Yeah, fuck that." If they can't handle that, if they can't distinguish between Gilman or First Unitarian and Live Nation, then I don't want to risk Gilman. So, we voted to pass on the tour.

I told Sturgeon that. I remember we were talking on the phone because he was calling Alternative Tentacles about the record. I was like, "Yeah, just so you know, this is what happened, there was a vote at Gilman, and you're not playing Gilman, and I voted for it, just so it's one hundred percent clear." And he was like, "Oh. Okay."

I'm sure he had choice words when he hung up on me, but I feel that illustrates my balancing act with Sturgeon. I'm happy to work with him to get his art and music out. But, at the same point in time, when that band is in a really fucked-up place, they need to be called on it…and we did. And when I say we, I mean the larger punk community.

Within a short period of time, I mean months or a few years, they were much, much better in terms of not being completely out of control. I'm not being flippant, but by then, they didn't have anyone in their band die on tour, okay? They had their shit together and they played Gilman and they played Gilman a bunch of times since then. It wasn't like a "forever ban." It was like, your actions and your attitudes in Philadelphia were enough for us to say, "Yeah, we don't need that, we don't want to risk this space."

JP Otto: On one tour, somebody stole a box of merch at a show in LA, and I think Alec ended up catching him and punching him and taking the merch back. He popped him one and whatever, but Sturgeon had a fit and wanted to penalize him somehow by making him sit out the next few shows or kick him off the tour…something just really bizarre. So one of the guys from Intro5pect played like one show at the Showcase and, really, that just punished the rest of us.

Brad Logan: It was a sold-out show, and it was a total shit show.

JP Otto: Those kinds of things started happening and me and Ezra were like, "What is going on?" I felt like that wasn't the way we wanted to play music. That weird kind of animosity between band members and drama.

For instance, at Flagstaff, Arizona, I was outside waiting for us to play and Ezra said, "I'm gonna go inside and warm up." I'm outside for like twenty minutes wondering where everybody is and some kid comes outside and says, "Hey, you guys are playing right now, they've played two songs already and they're waiting for you." I was like, "What are you talking about?" And he was like, "Leftover Crack is playing and they're looking for you." Then, some lady cop came and grabbed me and said, "I'm gonna walk you inside because they need you to play and we don't want a riot!"

Later, a helicopter was called. It just circled the show, but nothing happened. I have no idea why they felt they needed a police helicopter to just circle the venue before we played.

Brad Logan: We were at the underworld in London. It was broad daylight and Alec and I decided to go get something to eat. We circle back to our van and we see this pair of legs sticking out of the passenger side of the van. We were like, "What the fuck?"

This guy pops out with this surprised looked on his face. The guy had a crowbar in his hand. Alec grabs the crowbar while smiling, "Hey buddy what are you doing?" and then starts *beating the guy* with his *own* crowbar. The guy runs down the street with Alec beating him.

Then, we opened the van to check out stuff and we see that the van had *already* been burglarized by *someone else* before the current burglar.

Greg Daly: I was at Rebellion Fest with World/Inferno Friendship Society. Jack Terricloth, Lucky Strano, and I wanted to go check out Leftover Crack. Inferno was on the weird upstairs stage where the Bay City Rollers and an ABBA tribute band played. But Leftover Crack was on the main stage and it was fucking packed. It was jammed to the wall.

Thousands and thousands of people are there and we're hanging on the side of the stage talking to Sturgeon and Alec and Brad and are just chatting, "Good to see you in wherever-the-fuck we are England." Lucky and I dipped off to the side.

At some point, Sturgeon started to disrobe. He'd kind of go on some rant—the lights were blinding him, I think—and I just remember, he had this case of beer and was rolling the beers like bowling balls across the stage into the crowd and the crowd was stoked. They were slamming the beers and throwing them around. Then, more of Sturgeon's clothes came off, and he was standing there naked.

I could see Brad very calmly unplug his guitar, very calmly wrap up his cables, very calmly pack up his guitar, and very calmly walk off the stage. It was amazing.

Brad Logan: Rebellion is always hot as hell. The festival happens in the hottest month of the year in England. Sturgeon just started doing a striptease where he took off an article of clothing one by one until he just got down to his socks and underwear. Then, nothing at all.

He probably played two or three songs totally naked. At one point, he took off his sock and put it over his junk, Anthony Keidis style. I was laughing my ass off. It was so ridiculous that we just kept playing.

There are rumors that I walked off stage. I don't remember that at all. *That* alone is not enough to get me to leave the stage.

Around that time, we played North Six, this club in Williamsburg. It was a couple of months after the fire that happened at the Great White show in New England where pyrotechnics set the club on fire and people were killed. It wasn't us, but someone put flyers all around town. It said, "featuring a spectacularly dangerous pyrotechnics display!"

Sturgeon: The flyer was put together by Nico. The "featuring a spectacularly dangerous pyrotechnics display" was added by me. It seemed ridiculous enough to me to obviously be satire, but some fucko cop sent it to the chief of fire department, who sent five engines. They waited through four other bands, but then they shut us down after we played one note.

Brad Logan: Getting our shows shut down by the police was commonplace. To me, that's a win.

Interlude
Drug Life

Brad Logan: Alcohol was the first drug that I ever took. It was around eighth grade. It was Boone's Farm Strawberry Hill wine. It was cheap and tasted like Kool-Aid, which made it deceptively easy to down a whole bottle and then completely lose your ability to think and function on any level, which is exactly what happened that first time. I got hammered and tried to swim in a community swimming pool and almost drowned, then ended up puking all over myself and waking up with a terrible hangover.

It sucked and I couldn't figure out why other people seemed to enjoy it so much. What was I missing? I figured I had just done it wrong and decided to press onward. The next time I tried it the results were much better. So much so, that I worked it into a regular ritual I did during the week. Even on school nights.

When I hit fifteen, I started going to keg parties on the weekends—drinking beer, smoking weed, watching bands. During the week, I was taking cheap speed pills at school with intriguing names like "cross tops" and "black beauties." Acid and mushrooms, and weed too, were mixed with malt liquors like Olde English 800, Colt 45, or Mickeys Big Mouth. And there were harder drugs, everywhere—coke, heroin, PCP, and quaaludes. Aside from these commercial drugs, people would do all kinds of crazy mad scientist shit, like making speed from Vicks inhalers. But I wasn't doing anything like that. All of those things scared me. I stuck with the kid stuff.

I got along with my parents until I started high school. They were awesome. They weren't super strict, but they weren't "hippie parents" that would let you smoke weed in the house or have your friends over to get wasted and listen to records. In fact, they didn't know I drank or smoked, or so I thought. But, actually, I have no idea of what they knew. I had a curfew, too. I loved them, but things were getting dark on my end. I never felt like I had a place in this world or fit in anywhere. I began spending lots of time alone and depressed. I would find the saddest music I could get my hands on and listen to it endlessly—often the same song on repeat until it emptied my head of any self-awareness.

I started getting into the drugs known as "downers," specifically hypnotics and painkillers. I was mixing them all with booze. Blackouts were a common result. Dangerous situations were frequent. Cartoonish, tragic-comic dramas played out in the incandescent haze of streetlights in parking lots and late-night schoolyards. There were good times, too.

The punk scene had exploded, and I was at small club gigs at least a couple of nights a week, minimum. Everybody, everywhere, came through LA, and spilled down into Orange County. All the shows and new bands opened my eyes and mind to a new existence and escape. I met the most unique individuals, an endless cast of characters that would forever alter my views on life.

But there were lots of mornings I couldn't believe I didn't wake up dead, and by the time I was out of high school, being wasted had become my full-time job. I wasn't interested in conventional social trappings. My parents and I ended up having a falling out that lasted into adulthood.

I didn't really have any problems with authority or even police per se. They would show up to parties or gigs, and sometimes shit would get outta hand. Kids would get hauled off just for "looking punk." I got pretty good at staying out of their way and avoiding confrontation. If you couldn't be seen, you couldn't be fucked with. So, my style was to become invisible and live the way I wanted to live.

My first punk band was The Oziehares. It was Mark Alva on vocals, Layne Oosthuizen on bass, Emil McKown from Twisted Roots and Black Flag on drums, Dez from Black Flag on guitar, and me on guitar. They were already a band for a year or two when they asked me to join. Mark and my friend Potato were my best friends and when the band needed another guitarist, I had gear and nothing to do, so it made sense.

We started practicing using Black Flag's gear in their practice space at SST records, when it was on Santa Monica Boulevard. Henry Rollins, Chuck Dukwoski, and Greg Ginn were there all the time, and they were the hardest-working, most dedicated musicians I had ever met. They were also totally cool as humans, and were a big influence on me. We'd watch them rehearse and it was no different than a gig. They were not fucking around and put 110 percent into it. It was like sitting in front of a jet engine full blast! It was during the era of their "Damaged" release, and they had just become a five-piece with Dez on guitar. SST operated out of an office building that they rented, and they also lived and rehearsed there, too. There was no warehouse for product. There would just be stacks of SST records all over, everywhere. Black Flag, Minutemen, Meat Puppets, and Saccharine Trust were basically the whole SST catalogue at the time.

My first gig with the Oziehares was at the Whisky a Go Go opening for UXA. I had never played there or anywhere before and was pretty nervous. To take the edge off, I ate a half-ounce of psilocybin mushrooms and washed them down with an Olde English 800 tall boy. It was the exact opposite of the right thing to do before playing the show. About five minutes into the set, the psilocybin kicked in, and I was blasted into some kinda dimension that wasn't earth. The combination of the lights in my face, stage-fright, psychedelics, and the crowd on the dance floor staring at me was too much. As soon as the last note of the last song was plucked, I bolted out the stage door of the Whisky, ran across the street, puked my guts out behind the Licorice Pizza, then hung out with a dumpster till the show was over. In my absence, somebody relieved me of my guitar and amplifier, which I left plugged in onstage. I never saw them again.

There was a guy in my neighborhood who was a couple years older than me and was in a motorcycle accident. He got addicted to painkillers. When the painkillers ran out, he copped heroin off the street and he was the first guy that turned me on to heroin.

The first time I tried heroin I got sick and vomited everywhere. I was sick the whole night. I couldn't believe it was the same drug that had been mythologized by my literary and musical heroes. It was fucked up. Had I been lied to? Again, there was that feeling I was missing something and had perhaps done it wrong.

Eventually I got reintroduced sometime later, and this time it took. It then became the antidote to the serious drinking and living problem I had developed by the time I was out of high school. No more blackouts and no more DUIs. I finally found a way to insulate my insecure and sensitive self from the cruel world.

Once I got my first habit, though, I became an official employee of the drug. I worked for it now, not the other way around. Copping dope to ward off the physical withdrawal and violent mental anxiety became the only thing that mattered. Everything else in life went on the back burner—bands, friends, family, jobs, fun. I existed in a parallel universe of dope streets, methadone clinics, strip motels, and jails.

The thought of leaving town to get clean never even occurred to me. My life started to spiral inward on itself until my world got very small. I had nowhere to go anyway.

This was my life from the mid-eighties to the early nineties. I had completely withdrawn from the punk scene. There was no time for shows anymore—the clock was always working against me. I was living on what writer William S. Burroughs called "junk time." My days were planned around not getting dope sick, and that was a full-time job. I was completely unemployable and therefore unable to pay rent to keep a roof over my head. I would "couch tour," or on a good night stay in one of the cheap, dilapidated, former-tourist-trap theme motels around Disneyland or Harbor Boulevard close by—places with names like The Tahiti Inn. It had an "island-get-away" motif that was a fitting punch line to the misery it housed—the dope dealers, prostitutes, absconding convicts, and families down on their luck. My people.

When times weren't as good, I lived in cars, the riverbed, parks, fast food bathroom pay toilets—you'd pay a quarter for an outside "heartbreak hotel" restroom to sleep in until you heard the blowers from the street cleaners in the morning. Then you knew it was time to move. There weren't any squats, or anything organized at least, and pretty much every abandoned anything was occupied with other parallel universe regulars. The only places that weren't were the places nobody wanted. And that's where I was.

Shoplifting became my hustle to support my habit, or "commercial burglary" as it was known in court. I wasn't into and never used violence or weapons. But it was a circuit, and it could be quite lucrative—return scams, straight-fencing, or "Kamikazes."

A Kamikaze consisted of two or more people and a car. We'd pull up outside a department store and the driver would sit with the car running, another poor bastard would run in—usually with a request per the dopeman—"grab me size thirty-four," and we'd grab an arm full of Levi's, bolt out the door, throw the goods in the car, and blaze off into the night, tires screeching through the parking lot.

A "return-scam" also took two people. My girlfriend and I would work as a team.

Back in the day you could return stuff to department stores without a receipt, as long as it had a store price tag. They would give you the cash back at face value. I would go in first and boost something small and simple like a $200 leather wallet or something like that. Then I'd walk out to the parking lot and hand it to my girlfriend, who would then walk straight back in and return it for $200 cash.

Southern California is big. There were a lot of stores and a lot of malls. We made a full time "career" out of boosting—strictly nickel-and-dime from a criminal standpoint, but as I saw it, small-time enough to keep from doing years in prison if I got caught. But even still, I knew it was only a matter of time before I went down for all this shit.

On the streets, in the dope neighborhoods, it was a war zone. It was hide-and-go-seek between you and the cops, or between you and the people looking to beat junkies out of their hard-earned cash. There were undercovers and detectives out there, and you could look at them and you would never tell the difference between them and any other dope fiend or dealer or homeless person on the street.

I got popped a lot of the time for just looking like a shitbag in the wrong part of town. Back then the cops could pull anyone over, run a background for warrants, rummage through your pockets, and go through all your shit. You were stopped and pulled out of the car and sitting handcuffed on the curb with all your possessions in the world on top of your car for everyone to see. What the fuck were you going to do about it? Out there it was just you and them.

I was always guilty anyway. Sometimes they would arrest me, or sometimes they would kick my ass, then arrest me, or sometimes they would let me go, knowing full well they could bust me. We were like employees of the same company who worked in different departments. My job was to steal and take drugs. Theirs was to arrest people like me. In the end, we were just doing our jobs, and in the big picture, we knew we were both fucked. It was all pointless.

I didn't mind going to jail all that much; after all, once you got settled it was pretty easy. Plus, I had nothing better to do. Doing time also taught me a lot about patience and making the best use of one's time. But what I really couldn't stand was the withdrawal kick after you first get busted. Running away from the kick the entire time "out there" only to be finally caught. That was the worst part of getting caught. Being separated from the dope. The freezing holding cells, the stench of Pine-Sol, and the hopelessness of returning to the world of the living. The despair of the drug leaving my system tortured me through the sleepless first weeks. All of the world's complications had been distilled down to one single problem, one that twenty-five dollars and five minutes could fix. It was my best friend and now my best friend was leaving me.

The last time I had withdrawals it lasted a month. I had leg cramps for a year afterward. But getting arrested that time saved my life. I couldn't stop on my own.

The last time I got busted, I was boosting compact discs from some chain store. I had a war jacket on and maybe five CDs under each arm, which wasn't winning the lottery but it was enough to get me through the night. It was dusk and I walked out of the store and I walked right into a police cruiser that happened to be driving by the front. I had gotten away with it and had walked right out in front of the cop. Of course, anybody that knew what to look for, knew that I was stocked with merchandise hidden in my jacket.

The cop says, "Hey, come here for a minute." I didn't even think of running. I was tired. I was a twenty-eight-year-old in the body of an eighty-year-old man and I fuckin' gave up. He knew what was going on and I opened my jacket and handed him the stuff and he took me away for shoplifting one more time. But I already had a bunch of priors, so this time I knew I was going to be in there a good long time.

I was so dopesick that time and was in jail for a couple of months that and I was able to take a real hard look at my life and decided that I didn't want to live like that anymore.

But, weirdly, after a little while, I got bailed out and I *never* got bailed out. No one ever cared if I was busted. I called an old girlfriend and I don't know why I called her. She managed to arrange bail for me from a biker bail bond. You didn't put up your car or your house—you paid them 10 percent and if you didn't show up to court, the bikers would hunt you down and curbstomp you. I knew the people she dealt with and I knew they were for real.

When I got bail, I was still fighting the case, and by fighting the case I mean trying to get the best possible plea deal. Eventually, I threw myself on the mercy of the court. I've been clean ever since.

30

Star Fucking Hipsters Forms

Frank Piegaro (Guitar—Star Fucking Hipsters, The Degenerics): I was looking to do something more serious. I was playing in a bunch of local New Jersey bands but we weren't doing anything. I reached out to my friend Bill Cashman. First, he asked if I wanted to play drums in Morning Glory. But I am a very novice drummer, so I passed. A couple of days later he said Sturgeon was looking to do a side band. A week later Leftover Crack was on tour, and I think…something…happened, which was the start of Star Fucking Hipsters…and we started jamming…

Bill Cashman: Actually, Star Fucking Hipsters was a band before the second incarnation that most people know. The first incarnation was Sturgeon, Brad, Jamie of Old Skull, Ara, and the singer from Help Me, Help Me, I Can't Breathe. That never really materialized.

As for the second incarnation, I was doing merch for Leftover Crack and the band was playing in Lexington. We had two vehicles. I was in the car by myself driving across town to go hang out with friends and I got a call from Brad. It was a gravely dead serious call. It was, "Bill, you have to come back now."

I drove back to the coordinates he gave me, which was somewhere in Lexington on an empty street. Nothing is going on. I pull up and the Leftover Crack van is halfway up a curb and everyone is standing outside and the doors are open.

So I pull up and get out of the car. Immediately, Brad, Erza, Alec, and everybody gets into the car and doesn't tell me what happened. Brad tells me there "was a party." They take my car and drive off. So, I go into the van with the door open and find Sturgeon curled up into a ball hiding under the seat of the van. I realize that somebody beat him up really badly.

We get in the van and we go back to the hotel. As we get to the hotel, the rest of the band is in the parking lot and then, in the parking lot, Sturgeon and Ezra get into a fistfight. Then, like it's a pro-wrestling match, Sturgeon yells, "It's Choking Victim versus Morning Glory! Who's going to win?!" But then, he follows that up by yelling, "Highly successful band…or band that's never toured?!"

I tried to get between them, but Sturgeon punched me in the face. So I was like, "I'm done with him for the night!" I get Ezra in the van and we go to a diner. Then, we're driving back to the parking lot. Me and Ezra see something, but it's dark and we're both squinting… It was Sturgeon and it looked like a scene from *Braveheart*! He was charging at the van. He had an orange parking cone on his head and he got as close to the van as he could and he chucked it at the van. And the cone just bounced off the van, which was hilarious.

As I'm driving Sturgeon back later, he looks in the mirror of the van and he looks at the massive bruise on his face. He says to me, "Did you do this to me?" In a moment, he thinks that I beat the shit out of him because he has no memory! I still don't know who kicked him in the face

The next day, the band takes the van and drives to the next gig. I'm left at the hotel waiting for Sturgeon to wake up. It's past call time and the cleaning lady is furious at me. I'm like, "I'm sorry my friend is a jerk." Eventually he comes out. He has a massive black eye and half of his face looks really bad...his orbital is, like, *fucked up*.

We get in the car and he's mostly quiet on the ride. He starts talking about wanting to break up the band.

Sturgeon: Starting Star Fucking Hipsters didn't have that much to do with not seeing eye-to-eye with Alec and Ezra. I was feeling very stagnant with Leftover Crack. We had all these songs out there, and I didn't want to keep making Leftover Crack record after Leftover Crack record and have all these extra songs that we couldn't fit into our set. I didn't want to be a band that diluted their concept. There's something about putting out that many records. It reeks of making it a day job or trying to make it or trying to make a hit. You don't need to keep throwing a record out every two years. People will come around.

I wanted a little less pressure. I felt a little less pressure to be political in Star Fucking Hipsters, even though I was political. I wanted to be able to be more silly. I wanted to do something different and I felt I had enough creativity to spread out to another band.

Leftover Crack is productive and we tour a lot. But we don't put out as much music as I'd like. People are busy doing different things. I wanted something where hungrier musicians were involved. I wanted to do something quicker. There's something about stepping back from Leftover Crack. If you play with a band like Leftover Crack for too long, it's easy to expect good things that shouldn't be expected or expect bad things that you shouldn't expect. It's easy to get trapped into strange ways of thinking. I think it's really beneficial for everyone to see how much work is involved in starting a band.

Bill Cashman: I think Star Fucking Hipsters was meant as a little bit of a "fuck you" to Leftover Crack. Leftover Crack was always fighting at the time. Star Fucking Hipsters was a rebound... Well, not a rebound, because Sturgeon was choosing to stop Leftover Crack with something fresh and people that weren't fighting.

Brad Logan: I wasn't fighting with anyone that I knew of. I just wanted to play music. It was Alec and Sturgeon. And Ezra and Sturgeon. And Alec and Ezra. And Alec and Alec...

Bill Cashman: Sturgeon asked me if I knew anyone he could start a band with. I immediately recommend Frank Piegaro of the Degenerics who, in my opinion, were the best hardcore band growing up and he was the best guitarist. He was the only person I recommended. I said, "He is *the dude*." Sturgeon asked me to call him.

When I called Frank, it was between Shelbyville and Springfield in Kentucky, which was an amusing *Simpsons* reference. But I guess the joke was on Frank. I didn't know I was setting him up for years of anguish. So, I call him and ask him if he wants to start a side project with Sturgeon and he was into it. It was a totally different scene than what he was into. He wasn't familiar with the squats and Leftover Crack scene. I thought it would be cool to get the Degenerics into this scene.

Frank Piegaro: I already knew who Sturgeon was because I saw Choking Victim in the early nineties. I wasn't familiar with Leftover Crack until Bill made me hip to them. I went to C-Squat—this was old-school C-Squat—to see Sturgeon. I met him when he just got off tour and he really seemed like he was in a bad way. But the one thing about Sturgeon is that he's one of the most driven people that I ever met. He'll crawl to fuckin' get there, but he'll get there no matter what. Tenacious to a fault. That's why he has sustained himself.

Bill Cashman: Later, Frank came over to C-Squat. I remember when Ara, Sturgeon, and Frank got together. They jammed on some songs that Sturgeon had. Some of the songs ended up going on the Leftover Crack split for *Deadline*. "Life Causes Cancer," "Baby Punchers," and one other song. Some other songs made it to the first Star Fucking Hipsters album.

When Sturgeon first jammed with Frank, he wanted Frank to be the bassist. But Frank excels at being a guitarist. Sturgeon was like, "I want Frank to be the bassist!" I was like, "Why would you do that? Why wouldn't you want him to be second guitarist?" Sturgeon was like, "Well, he's too good. I can't replace him." I was like, "Fuck!" So Frank started playing bass.

Then, Frank was playing bass for a couple Choking Victim gigs in New York because Sasha didn't want to play bass. So, that version of Choking Victim was John Dolan, Sturgeon, and Frank. So, Frank was on bass and played. Even before Star Fucking Hipsters was a serious thing, Frank was playing in some weird version of Choking Victim.

So, Star Fucking Hipsters was coming together and it was mostly Sturgeon, Frank, and Ara. It was Sturgeon putting the pieces together. It still didn't have a name. He was like, "I might call it Star Fucking Hipsters again." I was like, "Oh, God, please don't, it's a terrible name." He just liked it. It was weird to me because he *already* had a band called Star Fucking Hipsters. It just meant something to him—I just don't know what.

Sturgeon: At that point, I didn't understand branding. I didn't understand how much of a brand Leftover Crack was. Like, shit, I could have taken Star Fucking Hipsters and called it Leftover Crack and we could have done really well. But it wouldn't be the same. But if you took Leftover Crack and called it Star Fucking Hipsters, it would have done just as badly. If you come out with a new band, everyone expects it to be bad—but it wasn't! There are hardly any good side projects, but I feel like Star Fucking Hipsters is a good side project. I wouldn't even call it a side project.

31

The Deadline Split

Sturgeon: Around this time there was a lot of third-party manipulation. Maybe, say just for example, Alec wanted to do some shows. So Alec would tell me that he had talked to Brad because he knew that Brad and I weren't talking that much, and nobody was communicating really. Alec would invoke someone's name that didn't necessarily agree with him, or Ron, our booking agent, would do it. Or Ron would say, "Alec said this," but he knew Alec and I weren't talking so he would get things over on us. Everyone would play this weird game of manipulating everyone else by invoking everyone's name. I would see through it but would be like, "Fine, whatever."

Brad Logan: Communication at that point was almost non-existent. There were all these resentments, misunderstandings, and people really fucked up on drugs. Never a good combo. To me it was a ship without direction, a waste of a good thing, and a waste of time.

Bill Cashman: Sturgeon, Ara, and Frank Piegaro demoed the songs that would wind up on *Deadline*. Then he invited Frank to the studio in Brooklyn to come play on *Deadline*. I know Ezra got there and he was feeling butt hurt.

Brad Logan: The way that Frank was introduced to us was so odd. We were being told this guy we didn't even know was going to be playing on the record, and we didn't have a choice. So, I guess at that point it felt like we were all being treated as employees. It made the sessions feel awkward and weird.

Bill Cashman: Brad, Alec, Ezra...they all looked at Frank as someone that was replacing their job. I was hoping that they would love him because Brad played shows with the Degenerics when he was in F-Minus.

Brad Logan: I knew Frank had no idea what he was walking into. It was an emotional minefield and I thought it was a dick move bringing him into the middle of it.

Bill Cashman: Frank did not end up being on *Deadline* at all, in part, due to the friction. But Frank did end up playing in some version of Leftover Crack in Australia. So Frank was in some bastardized version of Choking Victim, some bastardized version of Leftover Crack, and he was in Star Fucking Hipsters. We were on tour one time and Frank was like, "When the book is written about this band, I'll be the little-known eighth guitarist guy that nobody knows or remembers." And I want everyone to know that he was the best musician out of all of them.

Sturgeon: I wanted to put the Deadline split out on BYO, but I had sent BYO a letter years before when Choking Victim signed to Hellcat. So, I figured it's worth apologizing because I didn't know what I was talking about when I was twenty. Back then, I wrote a letter to BYO—at that point Bouncing Souls and Hepcat were having trouble communicating with BYO. I think BYO was having trouble at that time. I wrote them a letter for no reason except that I was hanging out with Mike Trujillo, and I think he was going to the first Punk Rock Bowling—it wasn't even a festival yet. Epitaph and Fat and BYO would just go bowling.

The letter said I was glad I didn't sign to BYO because they fuck their bands over. I didn't know what I was talking about. The Bouncing Souls guys hadn't told me that they were being fucked over—I think they were just unhappy at the moment. I don't even think my communication breakdown with BYO was their fault. I think it was my fault because I didn't have a good way to contact them. They *wanted* to sign Choking Victim. I sent them a cassette copy of our demo, which probably sounded terrible.

I gave a letter to Mike Trujillo and he took it to Vegas and that letter was shown to every single person that would listen. I guess for years to come people talked about it. I was just writing because I was in a new world because "I can write a letter to those guys?!" I was being reckless just because I could communicate with people

So, *Deadline* was split with Fat Records and Alternative Tentacles. Fat did the CD and A.T. did the vinyl. But that's only because Jello guilted Fat Mike. I had told Mike he could have the whole thing. I also told Mike that I mentioned it to Jello, but wasn't calling him back. Jello straight up went to Mike and guilted him into letting A.T. put out the vinyl. That's, like, not my fault. That was weak-minded of Mike. He let Jello talk him out of the vinyl. Whatever.

Fat Mike (Co-owner/Founder—Fat Wreck Chords; Vocals/Bass—NOFX): I had already done a live Subhumans record. I've known Dick and the Subhumans forever. I was pretty interested in that. I'm pretty sure Leftover Crack brought the idea to us and wanted to do a split with Subhumans or Citizen Fish. I'm a huge Subhumans fan… or I should say I'm a huge fan of Dick. That was interesting to me.

Jesse Luscious: Dave Adelson was the head of A.T. at the time, so I didn't get all of the details. I'm pretty sure Sturgeon wanted A.T.

involved. He went to Fat and said he wanted A.T. involved. I was stoked to have something with Citizen Fish, which eventually lead to us doing a Citizen Fish record and a Culture Shock record. As far as I know, Sturgeon went to Fat Mike and said, "I want this release to split between two labels."

Ara Babajian: I know that Sturgeon had been wanting to get in with Fat Mike and so maybe the split was his way to do that. He was looking to trade up.

Sturgeon: I met Mike through Brad and Christina White Trash. It's funny because both Fat Mike and Jello Biafra took a lot of convincing to become fans of Leftover Crack and then they became rabid fans. It's weird. It shouldn't have taken that much convincing for Fat Mike to like our band! I think he wasn't ready to take a chance on a weird band like us, considering our reputations and politics. In fact, I feel like I'm still trying to convince Fat Mike that we're good. But see, the thing is, he needs to convince me that NOFX is good. I don't need to do anything to him.

JP Otto: We were playing at Bottom of the Hill before any of the Fat Wreck Chords stuff and Fat Mike came on down. Mike got squirted in the face with breast milk by one of Sturgeon's friends. She just whipped out her tit and squirted him in the face with breast milk! I think it takes a bit to shock that guy and he was shocked.

After the show, Sturgeon and Mike are in the merch area and they are in there having a pretty loud discussion about Leftover Crack and putting a record out on Fat. It's *just* after the show is over and all these kids are still standing around and these guys are talking label stuff and Sturgeon looks at Mike and says, "If we put out a record on your label, we're gonna make your label legit! We're gonna make Fat Wreck Chords legit and that's what's gonna happen if we put out a record on your label!"

I'm thinking to myself, that's pretty ballsy, and then I'm like, "You know, he's right!" And you know what, it did! Can you imagine in '94 or '95 a crusty punk wearing a Fat Wreck shirt? No way. But now you see that all the time. It's kind of one of those things with Sturgeon, when he's right, he's right, and he's right a lot of the time.

Fat Mike: I learned about Choking Victim because their history preceded them—living under a bridge and just being crusty punks. Someone at Fat Wreck Chords made me listen to *Mediocre Generica* and I was like, "Holy shit, this is good!" I was a fan immediately. We've always done political bands at Fat Wreck Chords and Leftover Crack are political. The *Fuck World Trade* cover is just amazing. What attracted me to them was the musical interludes between songs and the organ and the different instruments. It's really rough music to listen to, especially vocally, but it sounded so eclectic to my ear. It was like nothing I had heard before.

Sturgeon: I'm more a fan of NOFX than Fat Mike has ever been of my bands, but that's not saying much. I'm not a fan, I like some of their songs...I think NOFX has too much content. I think NOFX doesn't need to have the eleven records they have right now. They could just have four or five records from those eleven and have way better records. But when they spread all the way across 150 fucking songs, it's hard for me to give a shit. My attention span is almost less than Mike's. That's cool your songs are two minutes, but you have too many of them.

I think it's bad to put out too much content. It's hard to get into a band if there's too much content. Even if you like it, it feels like you're just in shallow water. Maybe I don't have time to get into NOFX, really. I feel like I'm better off with a band that has two records—not being so established that you have fans that don't give a shit about the things that *you* give a shit about...like political things. I feel like Mike has given a really easy out to his fans to not be political at all. But then he started being political later. But then he had already made it okay to not be political.

Ara Babajian: As far as our side of that split, I thought it was artistically a low point for the band, fun material to play but kind of silly. "Baby Punchers"?

That's where the funny might have become a little silly. I like the music for a lot of the stuff there, but I think we could have done better. I think at that point, Sturgeon was saving his best material for Star Fucking Hipsters and Ezra was saving his for Morning Glory. And there was really not much of a future for that particular lineup of Leftover Crack. But the process of making that split? It was kind of a druggy mess.

Sturgeon: We were recording *Deadline* in Brooklyn, and it's the same day that we're going to fly to England to do Rebellion and I think we were going to tour Europe a little bit. It's me, Brad, Alec, and Ezra and we're meeting our drummer Candee. Somehow Ezra came in really early—usually I called the shots, you come in here or there, but Ezra would go around me a lot.

He went in at like nine a.m. and recorded all his guitar parts and they sound perfect—the only evidence that I have that he wasn't all there was when I went in to put in the lyrics for "Life Causes Cancer" and I'm going through his vocals, he is fucking pilled out of his skull, he can barely talk. He's slurring and must be blacked out. I'm trying to decipher his lyrics. I get to the solo vocals. I'm asking him, "What are your lyrics?" and he says, "I have no idea."

We're in the studio and Ezra is in Brooklyn. He's in touch with Alec and he called from under a bridge and he doesn't know where he is. He has like a $2,000 plane ticket and we have some really big shows coming up and he doesn't know where he is.

Brad Logan: Ezra calls and says, "I don't know where I'm at!" Alec goes, "Well, what's around you?" Ezra says, "I don't know! I'm under a bridge!"

Sturgeon: And we're just trying to get him on the plane. We don't get him on a plane. He comes in two days later and I'm playing guitar in Sheffield, England, and during our set he comes onstage and plays the last few songs with us.

Our next show is Rebellion. We drive up to Blackpool and we go in and we line check right before we play. We're all standing there and Ezra disappears. So, he flew out to Europe and played maybe six songs in Sheffield. We're in Blackpool with maybe 5,000 kids waiting for us to play and Ezra disappears after he just line checked five minutes earlier!

Then, the next day Ezra is in the hotel room and he's sick, and I'm like, "Fuck!" I take his guitar and pedals and I'm like, "I guess you're not coming on tour with us." I guess I didn't have to kick him out of the band right then, but I was mad. If it happened now, I feel like I would put him in the van because I don't want to play guitar. But I don't think I knew enough or was sensitve enough to know what it all entailed.

Ezra had a deal with Hellcat and booked time with Steve Albini and I guess Roy from Nausea was coming to play drums and he went into rehab instead of doing what any sensible musician would do, which was buy a ton of heroin and record in Chicago and *then* go to detox.

Alec had this way of rehiring Ezra behind my back. I think he thought he was in danger of getting fired if Ezra was fired first. He might be next in line. I asked him, and Alec would always be like, "I dunno," or, "I don't remember." Ezra would just be back. He was just back and Alec knew that I was too "nice" to keep him fired.

Brad Logan: Alec kept bringing Ezra back because he was the best musician in the band and is an amazing songwriter. Plus, we all liked him.

Dave Dictor (Vocals—MDC): I'm on the intro for the Leftover Crack/Citizen Fish split. Sturgeon wrote it and gave me some money and we met up in San Francisco at Fat Mike's studio. On it, Sturgeon says, *"Hey, Dictor!"* and I said something back. For years, everywhere I'd go, people would yell out, *"Hey, Dictor!"*

We played England together. We have a little bit of an older following and they have this younger following. Everywhere we went, people thought I was Sturgeon's father.

Some security guy held me at the door until someone had to explain that I was Dave from MDC, and not *just* Sturgeon's father.

Sturgeon: We played with Citizen Fish somewhere and I was quite aware that they were putting out lots and lots of records, and fewer and fewer people were listening to them and watching their shows when they were coming around. I knew how much of an influence they were on us. I knew that we were getting more popular than ever, and there was no reason why our fans wouldn't be fans of theirs and vice versa. I also knew I never had good credibility with the political punk scene for some reason—probably because I was a heroin addict for so long. Maybe because Brad was a heroin addict for so long. Maybe because Alec was a heroin addict for so long. That *will* do it. It shouldn't do it. In these times, that's the final frontier of civil rights—the war on drugs.

I talked Citizen Fish into it. I used to be very convincing, I used to be able to do pep talks to get people to do stuff with our band that didn't want to do stuff with us. Give me twenty minutes, I'll get them to do it.

Dick Lucas (Singer—Citizen Fish, Subhumans, Culture Shock): When I first met Sturgeon, it was at Rebellion Festival and I was rushing about with fifty-eight things to do at once. Apparently, he thinks I was quite abrupt in speaking to him…which I probably was. This guy, with a tattooed face, comes up to me, "Hey, you don't know me, you're Dick, right?" I'm like, "Yeah, hi, mate, right, have a nice one. Sorry, I've just got to do this……"

Years later, he said I was really standoffish and rockstar-ish to him, which I was quite embarrassed about… That I didn't find out about until one night he says it on stage, "Hey, look, there's Jasper, he's alright. He's great. Dick, he just ignored me the first time I met him!" What the fuck! Like, can we have a chat about this before you slag me off in public? So the first time I met Sturgeon, I didn't know who he was. Just this strange-looking American young chap.

Ara Babajian: We'd been touring with Citizen Fish for a couple years in the States. Sturgeon had always been a big fan of theirs and had always admired Dick and Jasper. We all got along famously. They were such humble guys and such a great band to deal with on a nightly basis that it probably kept us together being around a bunch of veterans for a couple of years who slept on floors every night, practiced what they preached, and sort of held a mirror up to our worst excesses.

Jesse Luscious: Citizen Fish are old friends of mine from the Gr'ups. We toured with them in 1993. I went to see them in Chicago, and they were talking about whether they should do the split with Leftover Crack. I was like, "Well…it will definitely introduce you to a similar, but much younger, crowd. As to whether you'll get along or not," I was like…"Uhhh…I'm a little dubious." I was dubious about the whole thing, but it worked out!

Dick Lucas: The *Deadline* record was a drawn-out process. We didn't actually meet Leftover Crack in the process. There was a lot of debate by email about what we should actually call it because

Sturgeon really hated one-word album titles. But I guess I talked him 'round that *Deadline* was a good one, and then it was.

This painting I did ended up on the cover and there was a dead body in the foreground and everything was in ruins, and it just sounded like a good title for the picture. Thinking up albums titles is the worst part of making a record! What are we going to call it?! The title is the penultimate thing. The last thing is getting the artwork worked out.

Sturgeon: *Deadline* is alright. It got fucked up in mastering. We sent in the masters and when we got that back, they sounded distorted and weird.

For that record, there were certain songs I presented to Brad, Alec, and Ara, and said, "Which songs would you rather record?" I definitely offered a few of the better Star Fucking Hipsters songs, and I also offered "Life Causes Cancer" and another song that was easier, but wasn't as good. "Life Causes Cancer" is one of the least interesting and least good Leftover Crack songs. It's kind of generic, there's not too much to it that sets it apart with a lot of songs with similar chords.

Frank definitely mentioned that during that record, there was a sense that people were not nice to him because he felt people were trying to take his job.

It's funny because what I ended up doing was withdrawing music from Leftover Crack and ended up using it with Star Fucking Hipsters. That attitude is not okay with me. It's the opposite of okay. If people are going to act like that, that they have some ownership of the things I make up on my free time and they're going to act like it's their right to record some song I made, they can fend for themselves. I don't need people getting jealous or acting like they are entitled for whatever reason they may rationalize.

I was like, "Fine." I never really protested because I knew I had enough songs for another band anyway. What happens is starting new bands becomes a subtle revenge in a way when I feel mistreated or if I feel like people are acting like I'm their property or my intellectual property is their property, or whatever. My way of dealing with it is to do something different with different people.

Ara Babajian: I think *Deadline*, which Leftover Crack would record not too long after Star Fucking Hipsters formed, could have been better, because I heard all the songs when they were Star Fucking Hipsters songs and they were awesome. So, if you could imagine the Star Fucking Hipsters songs as Leftover Crack Songs, you could have imagined what the next Leftover Crack record would have sounded like.

Dick Lucas: On *Deadline*, we covered Leftover Crack's "Clear Channel (Fuck Off!)." The song was very true. At the time, things were being bought out and capitalism was seeping into a scene that didn't want it at all. And if you're a band and you've moved out of the basements, and then you've moved to the small clubs, and then you've moved to the medium clubs, and all of a sudden, all the medium-sized ones are owned by these corporate fuckwits—if you're not very aware of what's going on, it turns out the place that was very cool to the locals a few years ago is now a shithole to the locals because it has been bought out by LiveNation or whatever. If you're not aware of that, it's like, "Why is everyone down on this place all of a sudden?" And then you find out. They seep into every place in the music industry they can just to make a fuckload of money. Music and money are idealistically so far apart.

We didn't include Rancid from that list of bands being attacked at the beginning of the song. After the album came out, we get to read a complaint from Sturgeon about us skipping Rancid in the liner notes. You could have mentioned this a *loooong* time ago instead of sticking it in the artwork? It's weird. It's true, we did miss out Rancid and we did fail to mention someone else, but it really didn't matter. It was like, okay, we missed out Rancid because we sort of knew people in Rancid a little from before they got all huge and we didn't want to be seen as slagging off Rancid as Citizen Fish. It was just a thing left out and Sturgeon made it a bigger thing than it needed to be because he put it in the liner notes. But, hey ho.

32

Golden Showers

Brad Logan: After *Deadline* came out, we were playing in Florida. In the middle of our set our merch person came up to us. She said, "The promoter told me that he had to leave and to give you this." It was envelope with money in it. I was like, "I'm onstage... You're supposed to settle up after the show, count up the money, and he takes a cut and we take a cut." I was literally in the middle of a gig, so I stuffed the envelope in my pocket.

After the set, we open the envelope and it is short...very short. To us, that wasn't cool. We had an agreement. DIY style. No contracts, no corporate anything, a handshake. I was the "booking agent" at the time, and if he had just talked to me first anything could have been worked out. So, after the show me and somebody from one of the bands go to a nearby bar and ask around. We let it be known that he shorted us and we're looking for him. We just wanted to have a chat, and see if we could get a few bucks back. After all, he wasn't just shorting us, he was shorting all the bands on the tour.

We find out that the promoter hangs out at another bar. We go there. We ask around there and no one knows him. But, as we are leaving, a kid comes up to us, and gives us his home address. Then, the kid actually drives us to his address. The promoter's apartment is upstairs and the lights are on. We had deduced that he had a problem with cocaine and that he probably "borrowed" some of the money out of the envelope to score. Also that he had been dodging us all over town, and he didn't give a fuck about having a "chat" with us. Fair enough. I might have done the same thing in his position. But that's not what we agreed to.

We pulled up to the house and someone got out and hurled a brick through his window. Then we drove off, satisfied that we had settled up the value for the amount we were shorted. It was a drive-by bricking.

Dick Lucas: The tour was Leftover Crack, Citizen Fish, and Witch Hunt. It was a neat combo of bands. It was unity there—a good class of old and new bands. I love Witch Hunt. They're wonderful people. The twins are gorgeous and they're a good laugh. And they've got that accent. And I can never quite tell them apart... well, I can, but I can never remember which name fits with which face. But then, I'm shit with names.

These kids were going completely apeshit over Leftover Crack in a way they don't go apeshit for us—we were more dancey, more skanky, and all that. Leftover Crack goes all out, some ska, some hardcore, in all directions, so there was an edge to the crowd, which was refreshing. It makes you a bit nervous, which is good.

The tour was really significant for me. Talk about the decades of influence of punk being passed down by one generation of punks to another. There we were, playing with Leftover Crack and Sturgeon's first gig at Gilman was Citizen Fish! The kids there at Leftover Crack gigs, they are completely insane and they know all the words. They buy thousands of their records. I thought, "Bloody hell, this is awesome." Where it came from is sort of important, but the fact that it carries on forward is way *more* important.

In our heads, we were getting old. We were doing it for thirty-odd years or whatever. In my diary I put, "We are leeching on their youth and they are leeching on our experience!"

A New York show was sold out and the cops knew the Leftover Crack crowd could be trouble, so they canceled the gig. There had been trouble at Leftover Crack shows before. People would get into fights or urge fights to happen. There was a sort of spark in the air that something might kick off. And sometimes it did. I mean, how much status does a band get by the cops canceling their gig in New York? Dude! So, we did a gig in Asbury Lanes that replaced one that had been canceled, thereby reducing our status by about twelve points.

Denise Vertucci: On that tour, we all were comfortable because we were touring together. In Cleveland, the show was sold out and a lot of kids couldn't get in. Sturgeon took Erik's acoustic guitar and went outside and played for the kids that couldn't get in. That was a really wonderful moment.

Later, we were at a hotel because we didn't know anyone in Cleveland, and it turned out that Mischief Brew was staying in the same hotel as Leftover Crack. In the morning, Erik took the dogs out and I was packing up to go out to the van. On that tour, we had our pugs Lola and Fritz with us. Erik was rushing to get the dogs out of the hotel because we had to pay extra to keep dogs there. Erik texts me and was like, "You gotta go out into the hallway because Fritz took a shit and you gotta clean it up." When I went out to the hallway, I saw a footprint—someone had stepped in the shit.

Later, Erik is in the lobby checking out and Alec comes storming into the lobby and yells at the guy in the counter, "*THIS* is fucking *GROSS*! I walked out of my room and I stepped in *shit!*"

Erik is like, "Dude, come here for a second…dude, I am really sorry. My dog is old and he had to go!"

That was our first real introduction to Alec and he was like, "You have *your dogs* with you?"

Brad Logan: One night we played a show in Detroit. Detroit is one of my favorite places to play always—rowdy, enthusiastic, over-the-top audiences. Total crowd participation. After the show, the band split up and went their separate ways. Ezra went to a party with a couple of carloads of kids from the show where he proceeded to get hammered.

Then, at some point he walked into the middle of a bonfire that the kids were having at this outdoor warehouse party. He went up like a human torch. He caught on fire and just stood in the middle of it until some kids pulled him out of it.

Subsequently, he was taken to the emergency room of the local hospital where he almost lost his leg because of the degree of burns received on it. He showed up the next day like nothing happened. And then we went on to play another show like it was just another day. I know he still has scars on his leg to this day.

Denise Vertucci: In Champaign, Illinois, Erik was like, "When they do 'Born to Die' or 'Infested' we'll jump up there." So, I just happened to be standing there in the front...and...well...

Brad Logan: Sturgeon peed into a bottle. Right there, on stage. It was a small club and it was extremely packed. It was a no-backstage kind of thing. I could see him pissing in a bottle while facing the drummer, with his back to the stage so people couldn't see him, which, to be fair, I've seen many times. "I'm in the middle of a set, I have to piss, I'm gonna do it right here." I can dig that.

Denise Vertucci: We were all like, "That is not pee." But Sturgeon kept saying it was and he convinced someone to come up to the front and like drink some of it and the person took some of it. *Ugh.*

Brad Logan: Then, he gets on the riser and starts shaking it all over the audience and anyone in splashing range. I caught a huge-ass *GULP* of it, straight to the face. It wasn't intentional, but I got nailed right in the face, a fuckin' mouthful. That's one thing that *would* make me leave the stage. "Yeah, you know what, have a great set, I'm fuckin' out of here." Golden showers are where I draw the line.

I packed up my shit. I walked out of the side door straight to my room, shedding my clothes along the way, and went straight into the shower. I couldn't get clean enough.

The band kept playing. They didn't even notice I left. Which was good. I preferred it that way. The show must go on.

Chris Mann (Guitar—Intro5pect): Never in my life have I seen a man wanting to explode so badly. I felt so bad. Brad stormed out and I went to go see if he was alright. He was just washing his eyes in the sink and he was in no place to be consoled. He was just, *"What am I doing with my life?!"* I went back inside and Dave, our singer, asked if he was alright and I said, "Man, I would hate to be on that band!" Little did I know that years later I'd be *in* that band…

Dick Lucas: There was a guy somewhere at a gig in the West Coast tour, and he wanted a lift with Leftover Crack back to the East Coast, and he was playing a keyboard, and Leftover Crack has a tune that has a bit of Pachelbel's Canon at the front of it, and Sturgeon said bring the keyboard up on stage and you can do this at the start of the gig. That's quite a bit of organization when the band will be onstage in about a quarter of an hour. And the guy did it and played it really well. It was that spirit-of-the moment positive help-the-guy organization—whether he got a lift I don't know—but he certainly got out and played when he didn't expect to. The spirit-of-the-moment kindness and positivity. There was a lot of that about.

I've kept a journal for years and I wrote in it a lot on this tour.

"Tales from Brad of going to a donut store last night and Sturgeon doing a striptease in there. Locals weren't at all impressed. How does he stay alive? Insane. He didn't remember it and normally hates donuts."

That was on his thirty-first birthday in Baltimore. His voice came back that day. He was smoking PCP earlier and he offered me some and I said no. I said, "I know where my head is at," and he said, "I wish I knew that." Robert, who was driving us about, made me write "do not smoke PCP" in marker pen on my arm.

Later, I wrote in my journal, "Ara, Sturgeon, and Amy went off to someone else's house as did Witch Hunt. I sat up on piss beer— Budweiser. I was told an acronym for it is 'because you deserve what every individual should enjoy regularly.' So I got busy: 'Basically ugly drunk white enthusiastic idiots shall eventually retch.'"

Right now, my relationship with Sturgeon is where it always has been. Deal with him as he is, in the mood he's in, when I meet him next. It could be anywhere from drunk to ecstatic happy sad thoughtful unthinking, but he'll never shy away from a conversation no matter what mood he's in. He's a good fellow. I've got a feeling that he's been through a lot of rough stuff, including being beaten up by several types of people, and it hasn't really put him off carrying on. It hasn't subdued his spirit. Far from it. I think some people in the crowd get riled up by his outspokenness; his thoughts spill out no matter how offensive they may be, and that spontaneity is a large attraction in seeing Leftover Crack live.

Sturgeon's heart is in the right place and his mind is in several places. He puts it all together and represents individuality in a remarkable punk band.

33

Ezra Quits

Ara Babajian: Ezra quit sometime after *Deadline*. Sturgeon and Ezra are both strong-willed, crazy geniuses. That's the long and the short of it. At one point, they might have been kind of close, but maybe not. They were always sort wary of each other. Each wanted to make sure that they weren't subsumed by the other's guy vision.

There was a power conflict. It was Sturgeon's band. However, Ezra arguably wrote one of the more popular songs around that time, "Gang Control." Ezra, kind of with his little finger, can just create this great art. Ezra just has this natural ability to do shit like that while we all have to work a little harder.

So, the combination is that you're talking about one guy who is the leader of the band and the other who is a "star" in his own right and they're in the same band.

I think it was one of those situations where the tour came up and Ezra said he didn't want to do it anymore. I don't think there was a big blow-up. I think it was, "Fuck it, I'm not showing up." Around that time, I came to the same conclusion. I tried to make it work, but it didn't seem worth it to me at the time. It didn't seem right.

Those were the end days. Sturgeon couldn't make another Leftover Crack record until Ezra was out of the picture. He didn't want to entangle himself any further with Ezra. It was good while it lasted, but things have to change eventually. And for Leftover Crack, it was a good thing that Ezra left, that I left, and so on. Bands get new life when these things happen and creativity is regenerated.

JP Otto: There was some tension between Ezra and Sturgeon. I think it was mainly ego driven. At some show, they played the Leftover Crack version of "Gang Control" and the Morning Glory version of "Gang Control" *back-to-back* and they were asking the crowd, "Which one did you like better?" It's like you made everybody in the band go through and learn each version just so you could sword fight?! It's totally bananas.

Sturgeon: The thing is, JP played in Morning Glory. So everybody already knew both versions. Anyway, Ezra ended up leaving the band because he got signed to Fat Wreck Chords somehow. The people that helped him with that, I don't know who they are. He was putting out the new Morning Glory record. But we also had a Leftover Crack tour coming up. He said he couldn't make it. I was like, "Well, I'm in three bands. I'm in Leftover Crack, Star Fucking Hipsters, and Choking Victim. I have time for all of those. You are saying that you don't have time for Leftover Crack because of Morning Glory? If I have to train another guitar player, then I might not need you to come back." He said, "That's fine."

JP Otto: I think Ezra really wanted Morning Glory to have the same trajectory as Leftover Crack, but I don't think it ever really did. It was a lot of ego and jealously.

Sturgeon: Morning Glory was great, but I think the scope got thinner and thinner as the band wore on. As they got on Fat, I think the self-importance that Ezra felt for the band is reflected in the lyrics and the art and the fun of the songs. They used to be more fun but they lost a sense of humor. I don't really like that in music, especially in punk music. If there's no sense of humor, it's hard to pull that off and if they do pull it off, I still think it's kind of silly, like the Clash. You're pulling off this thing that you're the most serious punk band, but you're not. You're getting away with it and it's fine and I still love the Clash, but it's still a little ridiculous, being so pretentious.

So, I feel like I'll always have the advantage over a band like that even though we'll never be respected over the Clash. At least I've never taken Leftover Crack that seriously. We're not important. We're important to some kids and that's awesome, but it's not like something to look down on anybody about. That defeats the purpose of being important to those marginalized kids. It would make no sense at all and be completely hypocritical and completely devalue what that band stands for.

Dick Lucas: It was amazing that the band kept reserving each blow that they were dealing out for themselves. But Brad and Alec, being sources of sense and organization, could deal with Ezra being spaced out on heavy drugs for a portion of his life and Sturgeon's idealistic, frenetic keenness to get everything done at once. You have a solid base there to keep it together. They had a different number of drummers they could use. Sometimes they'd get Miguel in on trumpet. Or sometimes there's a keyboard. It's solid enough to tour off of. Which is a great way to do it. A fluid exchange of members if necessary, but with a basic backbone of core members for a length of time.

Ezra once said to me, "Don't the Subhumans ever argue?" We sort of don't. We sort of grin and bear it if someone's being an idiot and we try to not have two people being an idiot at once.

Leftover Crack would sometimes rage at a level most other bands would consider reason enough to call it a day. But they thrived on edginess, bluntness, and hyper-sensitivity, more than occasionally soaked in booze, so arguments were common enough not to matter as much as to people who rarely argue.

Ezra would drive off to one hotel and leave the band to stay in another. There would be times when Sturgeon would be punching his way around the stage and Brad would say, "Fuck this!" and just drop his gear and get off, "That's it. Fuck this. I'm off."

Live stuff is all chaos. I think a slight part of their attraction is the chaos at a live show. The idea that it might all go wrong and there's a magic when it goes exactly right. You can't argue with it in that sense. It's dynamic and chaotic at the same time.

The negativity as to Leftover Crack was actually all contained within the band. It didn't spill out onto the stage, not too much. But they weren't negative toward the crowd. Well, they could be. But that's because when you're in Nashville, apparently what you gotta do is insult all the people in Nashville by saying their mothers are their sisters and have three fingers and all that. That was another time I was amazed that Sturgeon didn't get beaten up.

34

The Donut Social

Chickenman (fan): The donut social event happened in September 2008. I had seen Leftover Crack play at Tompkins Square Park in August. At the August show, the band or the promoters were given a summons of some sort for playing too loud.

So, Leftover Crack ended up doing a show in front of the Ninth Precinct on Fifth Street and Second Avenue sometime in September. It was called "The Donut Social." I believe the name was created by the organizers. My good bud Bill Cashman was one of the organizers.

I showed up and was trying to stay on my best behavior. It was a different version of Leftover Crack. Adam was playing at the time. Eric from Planned Collapse was playing in that version. The drummer was someone else. It was absolutely terrific. There were a few songs that were played and the set got cut short because the police did not like it.

Chris Ryan: Sturgeon did the standards you'd expect—"One Dead Cop" and anything that called out "fuck the police." The police weren't happy. But they just stood there. Then, someone gave Sturgeon a box of donuts. I guess it was already called the "donut social." Sturgeon started whipping donuts at the cops and he was pretty effective with his aim. He was hitting cops with donuts at a distance. You'd see him whip a donut and it would have some curve and you'd think the cop was safe and it would hook around and hit him. It was a new level for the cops. They were used to being shouted at. I think they thought they were showing restraint, but they were getting hit with donuts. There was a white shirt, which is a highest-ranking officer, and he got hit with a donut. He had red in his eyes and Sturgeon in his eyes and they wanted that little donut-throwing freak. So, that was the end of the show and the police advanced.

There's nowhere to hide, but Sturgeon, like, ducks and hides between two amps. I think he changed his clothes. There might have been a kid standing there with a hoodie or something. And everyone looks almost the same—everyone has on the same dark clothes. Eventually he ended up in a *Big Lebowski* mohair sweater. He looks like a Jedi in a robe. He looks more like Ewan McGregor than Squatter Sturgeon.

It actually worked and he was able to weave through the army of cops coming at him. He bends around the corner. I stuck with him. Now, we're on the streets of New York and cruisers are coming and they are all looking for Sturgeon. It was the only time I can think of Sturgeon showing genuine regret for something he has done in life—face tattoos. I don't think he regretted the donut throwing, but the face tattoos. It was like a *Warriors* moment—we have to escape to C-Squat and one of the biggest gangs from New York is out to get us! It was, "Dude, I got tattoos on my face. We're fucked!"

I was like, "Let's just pull the drawstring as tight as we can and try to not look like punks and try to get back to Alphabet city." We get through Tompkins and for once there are no cops in Tompkins. We're going through the park and there are all these kids camped out there and they all go, "Stza! Stza! Hey, Stza!" and they have an acoustic guitar and he just can't resist.

So he goes over to them and starts campfire singing "One Dead Cop" and all the kids are singing. The priority went from "let's get underground" to "all the teens screaming one dead co-o-o-op!" Some rogue cop must have spotted it and calls it in and the cops start appearing around the circle.

The police come and I think Sturgeon tried to make a run for it and I think some of the kids tried to cover. But these were big cops—beefy, bulging guys—and these were skinny travelers and the cops grab Sturgeon and threw him in a cop car. It was climatic. He was like the Teflon Don. All these years, they tried to catch him but never did…but they *finally* got him!

But the kids decided to try to break Sturgeon out of the police car. The kids are shaking the car and banging on the hood, and dumping garbage on it, in some misguided "save Stza" mission. The cops are like half-confused. One of the more crusty traveler guys was like, "Maybe we'll fight a cop," and the cop shoved a guy and the guy turns back and shoves the cop and the cop is like, "Oh, this is real."

Cop tactics are to go after the main instigator. And here, the main instigator was Chickenman.

Chickenman: I jumped on top of the cop car. But it started to move with me on it. I was like, "This is going to end pretty badly." Then, I hit the ground and lay there because I didn't want to get the shit kicked out of me. About five cops came and they picked me up and they put me in the police car next to Sturgeon.

So, me and Sturgeon were in the police car together. There was one more pit stop that the police made. There was a girl named Arianna and she got arrested. They went out to go stop her and they left Sturgeon and myself in the police car alone. I tried to convince Sturgeon that we should get out and just run away. But he wasn't digging it. I was like, "Here's our chance to get out of here."

And he was like, "How are going to take the handcuffs off?" I'm like, "I don't know? Get an axe?"

It was too late and they ended up coming back in and someone took a photo of Sturgeon and myself in the police car. It was a photo shoot and I did not want to have that happen. We went to the Ninth Precinct. Sturgeon and myself and Arianna, we were in the holding cell. They split us up. I was in the holding cell with Sturgeon.

Chris Ryan: The kids are all amped up and they go back to the Ninth Precinct. I don't know how this happened, but they almost immediately had signs. There's "shoot cops, not deer," "free the Stza." These were GOOD signs—not just like magic marker on pizza boxes. I have no idea where they got these signs. They were almost of professional quality.

Chickenman: My dad came down. He's an attorney. When he saw what was going on, he turned around and left without saying a word. He wasn't very happy. I had been having a lot of problems with arrests and was told to stay out of trouble. I thought I was going to have a lot of problem with this.

We ran into Ed and Mad Dog, and we all went down to Central Booking. It was pretty frustrating to be down there again. I vaguely remember that there was a point where some of the guys in Central Booking were very fascinated with Sturgeon's "Kill Cops" tattoo.

People in the cell tried to get Sturgeon to turn the cell into, like, a rap war. Some of the guys were spitting rhymes back and forth at each other and they wanted Sturgeon to be involved. He did not do that great, but he gave it a shot. He'll probably deny it and say it did not happen but I remember it very, very well. He tried to give it a shot. The corrections office was not digging it.

We spent about twelve hours in there and then were released. I ended up going to community service and going to anger management, or I could face another alternative. I did do the community service and the anger management. The guy there knew I was going to just get a piece of paper signed. I went back to court and got cut loose pretty easily. I'm still angry all the time.

35

Star Fucking Hipsters Solidifies...and Dissolves

Frank Piegaro: At first, Star Fucking Hipsters was myself, Ara, and Sturgeon. Sturgeon was friends with Nico. We had recorded half of the first album before Nico came into it. Then we had a rotating cast of characters. Yula came into it after a little while.

Sturgeon: Nico lived next door. I had seen her sing in other bands and she seemed to take to it and do a good job. Just having Frank and Ara at the core made it very easy, because they are both professional musicians. Frank and I would switch between bass and guitar. And getting Nico in to sing half the time was pretty simple.

Nico de Gaillo (Singer—Star Fucking Hipsters, Casa de Chihuahua): I knew Sturgeon from C-Squat. I lived in C-Squat a few years, then I moved down to Brooklyn and then I moved back to C-Squat and we became next-door neighbors. Sturgeon's a hell of a musical talent. But I hated him when I first met him. I fuckin' hated him. He said something very insulting to me at *Holidays in the Sun.*

But two months later, when I got an apology from him, I was told that it was the first apology he made to anyone in quite a long time. He told me that he was doing a music project and he was looking for a female secondary singer. He asked me to try out for it. At that point, I was messing with drugs already, but I started not long before the band.

The first practice I went to was the first time I met Ara. I liked the music. I came in and tried out. I mortified Sturgeon. I was strung out and he told me to never come to practice looking like that. I was skin and bones.

Bill Cashman: Star Fucking Hipsters was important because Sturgeon was so burnt out on Leftover Crack. Sturgeon didn't want it to be a Leftover Crack copy. He wanted it to be more hardcore, and he only wanted to play benefits. He wanted a band that would play more DIY shows and be more connected to the community. He felt everyone in Leftover Crack was greedy and only in it for the money.

Nico de Gaillo: Sturgeon made it very clear that this was a money project for him. He wanted to have a successful pop-punk band.

Bill Cashman: So, Sturgeon asked me to manage Star Fucking Hipsters. I had never done that before. Really, he manages all of his bands—I was just Sturgeon's friend and would help him get shows. Sturgeon wanted me to help him plan all of this stuff and I moved into C-Squat as his guest. Around that time, the building saw me organizing things, so they saw me as someone that had a little bit of a head on his shoulders. So, they offered me an apartment in exchange for helping them legalize the building. So, Star Fucking Hipsters changed the course of my life. Even though I was only around the band for a little while, I'm still in C-Squat.

Frank Piegaro: Musically, Star Fucking Hipsters was something different for me. I grew up in the New Jersey hardcore scene. While I like that, I like other things, too. Sturg, while he can be gravelly, sometimes it's just a pop song. Nico has amazing harmonies. Ara is just the best drummer. I'm proud of all three of the records. I have issues with each of them. But I love them all.

Bill Cashman: When the record went to Fat, Sturgeon got Nico to sing. I think everything had been recorded. Nico was living in C–Squat. She was in band called Casa de Chihuahua, and played washboard. She was living in the apartment next to Sturgeon.

Sturgeon asked Nico to sing. He knew she wasn't really a singer, but he thought he could coach her. She's cool, she's rad, and she's an incredible artist…and she had an attitude and she's Ezra's ex-girlfriend. Sturgeon thought that was an extra dig. That wasn't the main thing.

Sturgeon: In no way, shape, or form did I want Nico to be in Star Fucking Hipsters because of Ezra. As far as I knew, they were still friends. It's beyond my capacity to even imagine why someone would befriend someone or hire someone to make somebody else upset. It's not a thing that makes any sense at all.

Nico de Gaillo: I don't think there was much of a contention about Sturgeon and Ezra and myself—at least not on my end or Sturgeon's end. But there was a bone of contention between me and Ezra regarding that. When I first joined the band, we were all on good terms. Sturgeon made it clear that he didn't want to be out front all the time, that he was sick of dealing with people, and that he wanted some of that weight taken off. So, that was a good reason to have a secondary person helping with the singing.

Fat Mike: Sturgeon asked me to produce the first Star Fucking Hipsters record, but in a funny way. "Yeah, I want you to produce my record, but I don't want you to tell me anything…but I want you to produce it." I do have a way of producing things. I produced that record at Motor Studio, which is my studio, and it was a lot of fun. They all flew in and I went over songs with Sturgeon. Nico was there.

Nico de Gaillo: The first recording session was tough. The first time I went to record it, I was dope sick, horrendously dope sick. It didn't work. So, I straightened out and tried it again and it turned out to be alright.

Fat Mike: Nico was really fun to work with. Frank was really fun to work with. Sturgeon was very focused for that record. He knew what he wanted it to sound like and I did my best to keep all the metal off the record because I'm not a fan of metal, or crust-metal, or any kind of metal at all. I wanted to make it more of a punk record and more melodic, so that's what I focused on.

Sturgeon and I weren't pals, but we became pals during the recording of the first SFH record. When he moved to Oakland, that's when we became pals. And what I mean by that is we would ride our bikes together twice a week. We're both in bands, so when we are not on tour, we'd go to lunch, we'd go to the movies—we went to the movies a lot. We just did stuff that dudes do. We didn't go to shows together. We just did stuff during the day because we don't have normal lifestyles.

We also spent time picking up dirty needles for the needle exchange. That's how we found Sam Sadowski—that's Closet Fiends, the street kid that I put out a record for. We found this street musician and we put her in the studio that night and that's her album.

We were brought up in the same kind of situation. We had single mothers who didn't see us very often and we were kind of like loners that found punk rock and punk rock saved our lives. Our stories are very, very similar. Jewish mothers that were single, and that's how we grew up, abandoned by our parents.

Bill Cashman: Then, that summer I was on tour with Leftover Crack. Sturgeon said, "I need a bassist." He realized Frank was too good to be on bass. So, I called Yula from World/Inferno Friendship Society to be in the band. I think Yula might have been some kind of pop star in Israel. I don't know the whole details, and no one seems to really know.

Really, Yula is not on the record. She's on some interludes between the songs. She learned the songs and did a tour. She also did a couple shows around town.

The "first" show that we booked was at Mehanata bar with A-Truth and Triangle Fire. It's the Bulgarian bar and it used to be the home base for Gogol Bordello. It was Sturgeon, Frank on bass, Ara on drums, and Nico singing. It was packed.

That was going to be a big show, so before that show I thought the band needed another warm-up. So, I booked them last minute a night before at an anarchist house in Brooklyn.

Frank Piegaro: We went from the frying pan into the fire. We didn't know each other and we just had to learn on the fly. Our first few shows were awful, just awful. It wasn't until maybe six months of touring that we became really strong. We worked for it.

Bill Cashman: Yula ended up doing a tour with the band and then she expressed that she wouldn't be able to do more tours. So, Sturgeon asked me who I could find. I found this guy Chris Pothier, and then Ara couldn't tour, so Sturgeon found another drummer named Alex. The first real touring lineup was Alex on drums, Sturgeon, Frank on guitar, Chris on bass, and Nico singing.

At first Nico was very shy. She was very soft...too soft for a front person. Sturgeon would talk between songs. He wanted her to be the lead, but it wasn't going to happen because it was Sturgeon's band.

Ara Babajian: With Star Fucking Hipsters, I just got too busy and I wanted to have more time at home because my son had just been born. It wasn't a personality thing. Star Fucking Hipsters wanted to do hard touring and wanted to sleep on floors and tour for six or seven weeks. I didn't want to do that at that point in time.

Frank Piegaro: Ara didn't do any of the tours. He just kind of did the record. We had this drummer Alex for a while. Chris Pothia came in after Yula to play bass.

Bill Cashman: The band was sounding great. Everything was cool. We get down to Florida and we played a show at a DIY space, and we got asked to play a house party. By then, some cracks were starting to appear.

In Gainesville, we played Fest and that was great. Then, we played a house show. In front of the house, Alex, the drummer, was walking around and he tripped and his eyeball went into the top of a chain link fence. When he pulled up, his eyelid got ripped in half.

At Fest, you're walking around and there are drunk punks stumbling around a suburban town like a zombie film. I see this one zombie I knew from New Jersey, Jay Zombie. Jay stumbles up and sees three beautiful punk rock girls consoling Alex. The first thing Jay says is, "If I knew that beautiful punk rock women would hang around me all night, I would poke myself in the eye!" Things started falling apart.

I took Alex to the emergency room. I stayed with Alex all night. It was going to become apparent that he needed to stay in the hospital for a day or two. So the band decided not to cancel the St. Petersburg show. They got P-nut from the Degenerics to play drums, who was touring with the band. I booked a practice space and P-nut learned half the set. P-nut played all the songs that he knew and then Sturgeon was going to play drums on a song or two since Nico and him traded vocals.

During the show, Nico was smoking and she put the mic in Sturgeon's face because he was drumming. But he got really mad that there was smoke in his face and he didn't want to get burned.

Nico de Gaillo: At that show, I got two of my fingers broken. Sturgeon got drunk and decided to get on the drums. He asked me to hold the microphone so he could sing and drum at the same time. But I had a cigarette in my hand and the smoke got in his face. He attempted to slash the cigarette with his drumstick, but he missed and broke two of my fingers in the process. I was a tattoo artist full-time at the time, so it was a problem.

Sturgeon: I was drumming on the song "Only Sleep." The song was both Nico and I singing, but not at the same time. We're going along fine. She sings and then holds me the mic for me to sing. I'm already having trouble breathing because I'm out of shape and drumming. Singing and drumming are the two most labor-intensive activites in a band.

When it gets to my vocal part on the third verse, Nico puts the mic by my face to sing, but there is a cigarette, and I can't breathe, sing, and drum. I'm trying to catch Nico's attention, shaking my head as in, "No, please, put out the cigarette!"

In a super wrong-headed attempt to keep everything going, I tried to "swat" the cigarette from her hand. In my head this makes sense in that I tried to lightly tap the easy target out of the situation so we could keep going. I don't remember if we finished the song or if I was even aware that I hurt Nico. I might have known I accidentally hit her hand, but it never occurred to me that it was anything serious.

My grandfather had just died after I visited him on our way to our Miami show and on the way back from the Fest we stopped at this place where my family was meeting. I was closer to him than anyone else in the family. This might be one of the reasons that I was oblivious to Nico's injury. I remember not even being told that I broke two of her fingers for at least three or four days.

Bill Cashman: I knew that wasn't on purpose, but everyone was super pissed at him. Like I said, I knew it wasn't on purpose, but he still couldn't bring himself to apologize. When you bump into somebody on the street, you don't mean it, but that doesn't mean you can't say that you're sorry. Everyone was shunning him.

Nico de Gaillo: I was tempted to quit then, but I didn't. I figured it was just a drunken stupid moment on his part. I got a half-assed apology for it. Also, I loved the music. We were playing good music. It was fun to do, so I didn't quit.

Bill Cashman: Afterward, Sturgeon and I were on the beach talking. He said to me, "I'm happy that you haven't abandoned me, too." I was like, "Well, I think I'm going to finish out the shows that I helped you book this fall and winter." We got into a fight because I wanted to take money out of the band fund to pay for Nico's house dues the next month. She was a tattoo artist and with broken fingers she was going to lose her way to make money.

We got into a fight. At that point I was like, "This is kind of fucked." So I said I was going to stop working for the band.

Sturgeon: The argument that Bill claims we had might have had everything to do with the fact that I didn't know that Nico had broken fingers, but he's asking the band to pay her house dues. I don't think I was given the chance to process what had happened. I think that I felt a bit betrayed that no one felt they needed to inform me of my recklessness.

Bill Cashman: The next night was worse. It was the night that Obama got elected. It was in Georgia. Barely anybody showed up. The bartender was talking about how Obama was the antichrist. So, then Sturgeon goes on stage and is really funny and making fun of the guy. At the end of the night, the guy hands six dollars, six more dollars, and then six more dollars to Sturgeon. "That's all you get! Six and six and six!"

Sturgeon wanted to throw a rock through the window of the club, but I wouldn't let him do it. So, he started screaming at me.

He wasn't calling me Bill. He was calling me "BradAlecAraEzra" in one long run-on sentence. I don't know what he meant by that.

When he was doing Star Fucking Hipsters, Sturgeon seemed happier. It seemed like he was making a positive change. I was his friend and I was like, "I'm helping him do this!" It was like a fresh clean slate. But when we got home from tour, I gave Nico the money from the band bank account. It was like 300 bucks. Sturgeon flipped out. He said, "If you don't pay the band back, if you don't get that money, I'm going to tell everyone you're a poser-squatter." I was like, "What grade is this dude in?" First off, I never said I was a squatter. Second, what the *fuck* is he talking about? It was some kind of childish threat.

Sturgeon: Bill has a tendency to make matter-of-fact statements that are completely fabricated in his head, especially when it comes to quoting people. Why the fuck would I tell anyone Bill was a poser-squatter? Who would I tell it to anyway...?

Frank Piegaro: We played 924 Gilman. A friend of mine now, who was not a friend of mine then, Cole Gates, he collected a bag of vomit from his friends. He's kind of a prankster and very funny, but this was bordering on gross. He ended up collecting a bunch of vomit from his friends. The Gilman gig was with La Plebe and maybe Citizen Fish. Cole ended up in the middle of the stage during "Two Cups of Tea." He hurled the bag of vomit.

Sturgeon: A bag of vomit got thrown on me, but it didn't get thrown on anyone else. We were playing "Two Cups of Tea," and this plastic bag that ended up being several plastic bags is lobbed at me and it breaks on my chest and guitar and it's just full of liquids.

I had been drinking and I can't really place it. It's a very familiar smell and taste in my mouth. I looked over to Nico and was like, "What...what is this?" She was like, "That's *vomit.*" It dawned on me that it was in my mouth and my eyes and I started to throw up and we are still playing the song. I heard afterward that a lot of people started to throw up after I threw up. It was kind of like the scene in Stephen King's *Stand By Me* with the pie contest. A bunch of people who heard me say it was vomit, and saw me throwing up, also started throwing up. It was a total barf-o-rama.

Kate Coysh (Vocals—, Leftover Crack, Reivers): It was a horrible, disgusting, awesome display. Mostly I just remember getting bounced around in the crowd and trying to avoid getting puke on me.

Frank Piegaro: After P-nut left, then Mikey Erg came in. It kind of solidified after Sturgeon, myself, Nico, and Chris and Mikey Erg at the end. That was the core of it for a while.

Mikey Erg: I was in Penn Station on the way down to Jersey for band practice. I got a call from Frank Piegaro. He was like, "Would you…be into joining…Star Fucking Hispters…if that came up?" And I was like, "Yeah, fuck yeah!" I was a fan of Sturgeon's music anyway and I'm not opposed to playing music that I love and I was very stoked on the idea.

I always thought of myself as being into a ton of different stuff. I definitely understand that I'm known for being in pop-punk bands, so people may see it as crazy that I was in Star Fucking Hipsters. But it didn't seem that weird to me.

But I feel like a few months went by after that call and I thought it wasn't happening, and then I got a phone call, "Here's three songs that we're going to jam on Thursday." I was familiar with the songs and then I became very familiar with them and then we practiced. I guess it was an audition, but it felt more like a practice.

We went through the three songs fairly quickly. Sturgeon, at one point, just brought up They Might Be Giants and he wanted to do "Ana Ng." I was like, "I love that song!" I believe we worked it out at that practice and I believe I floated the idea of doing the verses as a ska part. In any case, even if that's not true, most of my tryout for Star Fucking Hipsters was us working out that arrangement of that song. We liked it so much that we had to do it on the record.

We recorded the third album and then toured. We did a bunch of practice jamming—pretty much just me, Frank, and Sturgeon. We'd recorded a bunch of jamming on a digital recorder and then eventually got the band together and finished the songs. It felt like a whirlwind. Within a couple of months we were on a plane out to San Francisco to record the record.

Fat Mike produced the record, quote, unquote. We did some preproduction with him. We would play him the songs acoustically in the back room of Motor Studios in our little apartment space. He would play the production role of, like, "This verse doesn't need to be as long as it is," or, "Maybe put the bridge here instead of here," and do some rearranging. But when we were in the studio, it was mostly Jamie the engineer whom we dealt with most. Fat Mike produced the record technically, but I didn't see him as much as I thought that I would see him.

Boots Riley (Singer/Emcee—the Coup): My friend Roberto Miguel, he does these crazy old-timey songs. I met him and we recorded some mashups with Coup songs and old-timey stuff. He had me come out to a show and I met Sturgeon and he hit me up and asked me to be on the album so I did it. I don't even really remember what my lyrics are. The day I recorded them, I went to a coffee shop, wrote some stuff, and then went and laid them down, really quickly. I'm interested to hear what I said.

Mikey Erg: During the recording, I knew Boots Riley was going to be on a song. I was so excited that that was happening and I was there! He was about to come to the studio. So, I was like, I'll go get a bite to eat and be back for the session because I wanted to watch him spit. As I was walking back to the studio from whatever restaurant I was at, he walked past me. Apparently he had gotten to the studio in like five minutes, just did his thing, just did it perfectly, and then split. I was so bummed!

So, during recording, we were out in San Francisco for like a week or a week and a half and then we all kind of remembered that we had a show at the Parkside on the Sunday we finished the record.

We were so wrapped up in making the record that we kind of forgot that we had a show and we had never played as a band before! Like, literally, certainly none of the old songs. Basically the new songs we kind of just fucked around and jammed on. We really polished them in the studio. We kind of spent the Saturday before the show on Sunday just woodshedding our back catalogue and then we played our first show ever as that lineup in the Parkside in San Francisco.

But the show was mind-blowing. We played fucking surprisingly well for never having been a band before. It was great. Jello Biafra was there. I was walking into the men's room when Jello was walking out. It was like, he said something to the effect of, "I'm a huge fan of your drumming," as he was walking out and I said, "I'm a huge...fan...of...you," and those were the only words that were exchanged. Apparently he was very excited about my drumming. Later on, Frank was like, "Jello Biafra was backstage and all he was talking about was how good we sounded with you and he thinks you're the *best drummer the band has had!*" I was very excited about that, obviously.

When you get into punk rock, one of the first things you find out about is the Dead Kennedys and how great they are. They're an entry point. It's almost like when you see him out in the wild... Am I actually seeing him or am I dreaming?

Sturgeon: Right before Nico left the band, it was like pushing a square peg through a round hole. It made it really hard to get her into practicing or writing new material because she just got way too much into drugs. It was too hard to keep the band going with her lack of interest. Then, she left the band and it became harder to make the band enthusiastic and be enthusiastic for everybody. Eventually, I was like, "I'm done. I can't just keep putting new members in that don't give a shit, members that don't want to sing."

Frank Piegaro: I've seen Sturgeon and Nico bicker at different times on stage. Some things I only knew about later on. They both can give as good as they can get. They've known each other a long time. You really couldn't, as a member of the band, intervene. They had a certain bubble where they existed and fought. I feel like sometimes there was this big thing where people were like, "Poor Nico!" Dude, Nico is strong as fuck. Like, don't pity her. She's nobody's fool. "Oh, poor Nico." You don't know Nico, man. She can fuckin' hold her own, man.

So, I was like, to myself, "you just gotta keep on keeping on for better or for worse. It's not just a band survival thing. It's a YOU survival thing. Because YOU have to survive with this band for another five weeks."

Nico de Gaillo: Frank had a lot of stress, having to be neutral. It made him have a rough time of it, I think. I think everyone felt they were caught between me and Sturgeon all the time.

Mikey Erg: The Star Fucking Hipsters tour was one of the first tours I did after the Ergs broke up. I was just excited to be on the road again. Maybe surprisingly, my time touring with them *wasn't* crazy. There was nothing like, "Oh, my God, this is *insane*." We'd play the show and then go to the place we stayed that night.

I will say, at that point, everybody was trying to stay kind of clean. That was the thing about those tours. We would show up late and leave as soon as we were done. At that point, we didn't want interactions with the kind of people that we didn't want to interact with. Sturgeon was definitely trying to be cool. In that case, it was pretty much like every other tour—let's *not* go to the all-night party. That was fine with me. I was fine with going to sleep.

Nico de Gaillo: I don't think most of the band was doing drugs on tour. Though, at one point, Sturgeon had too many Xanax and drank too much booze and he cracked his head open and we thought he killed himself.

Bill Cashman: Star Fucking Hipsters had morphed into something being just like Choking Victim and Leftover Crack. "Yeah, this is what it's like for the first record, but the second record will be totally different." But it just ended up being an extension of Leftover Crack. It's the same kind of sound.

Nico de Gaillo: I think what it was, as time went on, the audience wasn't calling out as much of the Leftover Crack songs as they were earlier. Sturgeon wasn't getting as much of the attention as he had been. I think it started to trouble him. I think that really fuckin' bothered him.

Sturgeon: I definitely wasn't bothered by not getting attention. I definitely did not want to be the front person in the band.

Nico de Gaillo: In the beginning, at times, it seemed like it was okay. But it became like I was a scapegoat for Sturgeon. Whenever there was a problem, it was my fault. He and I were the most familiar out of the people we were playing with and it seemed like I caught a lot of bullshit.

I started noticing things weren't going so well. Sturgeon noticed that if he accused me of being on drugs on tour, it really got under my skin. But I never took drugs on tour. I always made sure to take my Suboxone. In fact, I was supplying Sturgeon with Suboxone.

On tour in Colorado, Sturgeon was in a particularly foul mood and he accused me of taking his Leatherman. Then he found it. I asked *when* he found it, and he said something nasty. I made a bad joke and we got into a fight. So, I said, "Fuck it, I'm out," and walked off the tour. If Sturgeon had just called on the phone and talked to me, I would have gone back on the tour. But instead of a phone call, I was told to fuck off.

Frank Piegaro: Everyone bowed out in dips and drabs. I was there after Nico left the Denver show. We kept going and we did all the States and we did Australia. But things had fallen so flat. Sturgeon wanted to keep doing it because he was so driven. But for me, we put so much work into it, five years of touring and recording and, "Oh, we're about to hit the fucking next level with this thing," that it was just too much for me to want to pick up the pieces. We had gotten to a tier, it crumbled, and we were back at square one. It was just too much for me.

The third record had come out in, I think, October. We did the record release show in Brooklyn, at Europa, and that was my last show. Sturgeon, I think, kept it going a little while longer. I think they went to Europe with a completely different band. Chris was still in the band but I think he just wanted to go to Europe to meet with friends. I don't think he was too jazzed about the band.

Mikey Erg: So, in my opinion, I never quit Star Fucking Hipsters. We just kind of didn't do anything for a while. Then, there was a tour of Europe that they were doing. Frank quit and the bass player quit and it just seemed like it fell apart. I got asked to do a tour of Europe, or maybe just the UK, with them. But I had joined Off with Their Heads, and they were doing the same circuit, the same festival thing, and so it was the same time, so I was already committed to the Off with Their Heads thing. So, as far I know, they got another drummer. I never said, "I'm not gonna be in this band anymore." That's my understanding of it.

Bill Cashman: Despite everything, I think the time period of Star Fucking Hipsters *was* an important time for Sturgeon. Leftover Crack stopped playing often. Morning Glory started playing more. Brad started some bands, like Pagan Icons and Rats in the Wall. These people that were really burnt out on each other got to have this other creative outlet for a little bit. They didn't get the success that they got from their former band and went back to those bands with a fresh voice. It's a period where maybe the band had to take a break to come back and to do another. Maybe *Constructs of the State* never would have happened if they didn't go out and see other people.

Mikey Erg: I haven't spoken to Sturgeon in a while. No real reason. We just haven't been in the same room. Some of my favorite times were at the recording sessions for the third album—at nine or ten o'clock and we would pass around a bottle of Johnnie Walker and just talk for hours. Having music conversations with him was a fun or rewarding thing to do. I would think we're cool with each other.

Nico de Gaillo: If it didn't mean a night in jail, I'd probably kick Sturgeon's ass. But I hate the tombs.

Bill Cashman: Man. That band ruined so many people's lives, didn't it?

Frank Piegaro: Sturgeon and I had a really great partnership. We did all these amazing things. Playing behind him—that's what I wanted to do is let someone be the mastermind, the front person, and me do my thing behind it. It was the greatest of times and the not-so-greatest of times.

Sturgeon: I've never worked so hard and had so little to show for something in my whole life.

36

Leaving A.T.

Jesse Luscious: Eventually, Leftover Crack left A.T. So here's the thing… Earlier in my life, I worked at Lookout Records and was also simultaneously in a band on Lookout Records. I saw firsthand how an independent label shouldn't deal with bands when it comes to royalties and things. That's the shortest way I can tell the Lookout story.

When I went to Alternative Tentacles and became the general manager, I was very clear that I wanted to use Lookout as a model for how *not* to do things, even though we had money problems at Alternative Tentacles. That's not a secret. This is a time when physical sales were being slaughtered by the advent of digital sales. Jello is a person who doesn't want bands to misunderstand things. I said I would be as proactive as I can with a staff of four people… down to one or two people later on…in terms of royalties about letting bands know what they're owed even if we can't pay them at the time, and having honest conversations about when we can pay them and not just blowing them off and not just not responding and really trying.

With a label like Alternative Tentacles or Fat Records or Epitaph, or any label that has put out hundreds of releases, or dozens and dozens and dozens of bands, some things just won't get accounted for, or some bands will disappear. I was always very aware of how I had been dealt with as a band member by labels in the past. I was really open about my history. When I talked to bands while at A.T., I said, "Look, I've been in a band, I've been ripped off by labels, I've been paid, I've written contracts, I've signed contracts. The whole gamut. I'm representing the label, but I'm gonna do my best to be up front with you about what's possible. I'm not going to tell you what you *want* to hear, because one thing that I would critique Lookout on is they would tell us what we *wanted* to hear instead of what was *reality*.

When I went through the royalties of all the bands, Leftover Crack was earning a lot of money. We paid a fair amount. We didn't pay all of it. We did say things like, "We can do this much this month, and that much that month and we'll pay the mechanicals here and the artistic royalties there," in email to the whole band. We paid everybody separately so everybody got separate checks or PayPals.

Alec is an accountant, so he was, like, really always on top of stuff. He was always like, "Oh, so I was looking at the details of this statement and…um…so…uh…I have a question about this detail…" And I was happy to do that. I wish bands would look at their royalty statements. "Oh, there's a check? Great, I'll cash it." I wish they would look at what pay period is being paid or what record is this for or does the pay period come after the last pay period? When was the last time they got paid? Most band members, it's not in their wheelhouse.

For me, Alec was kind of refreshing even though he would bust my balls. He's an accountant! That's what he did, which I think is hilarious, with the basis of a band like Leftover Crack, and the things they sing about, to have a financial professional in the band!

I would talk to him, like, "This is the situation, we can't do that, we can do this."

For many, many, many years, Sturgeon actually kept the rest of the band off A.T.'s back. They were selling records and we did owe them royalties. We couldn't keep up the royalties on a regular basis and we would report to them and say, "This is how much you're owed." Jello would put in his own money to help pay bands. We were always knocking it down but they were always making money, which is great, which is how the record industry is supposed to work...making money, not *not* paying bands.

At a certain point, Sturgeon is playing some solo shows. At this point, he's been my primary contact with the band in terms of money, but I'm always emailing the others at the same time— "A check is coming to you all." Sturgeon is the only one who communicated a lot. He was always very friendly. "Hey, we know things are tough, but we want to do this recording or go on this tour," so that would be an impetus to find some money and they would come to us and sometimes we could help. Sturgeon was doing a solo tour and he saw that Jello and the Guantanamo School of Medicine was doing a tour in Ireland.

Sturgeon got on the bill. It was Jello's show, so they were like, "We're gonna add this band," so they got them on the bill with a promise of some pay and some food. So basically it was a totally bro-deal from Jello to Sturgeon. Sturgeon turns around and gets totally fucked up—which isn't weird. It's Sturgeon, it's a show, the odds are is that it's going to happen. But what happened was he got in a conflict with Robert Dietrich, who is one of Jello's dearest friends. Robert is from Germany and is a tour manager and honestly a really good person. He's German and he's been anti-racist since he came up in the German punk scene in the eighties. Like here, people beat up Nazis. It's not a fucking joke. Sturgeon goes off the rails and starts saying that Robert is a Nazi just because he has a German accent or some shit like that. I'm pretty sure Robert decked him—I think he punched him or had to be pulled away. Sturgeon started this shit and got called on it. Robert was very upset and Jello and his whole band were upset.

Jello was like, "Well, we got you on the show and this is how you repay us? By getting drunk and insulting this guy for having a place you can play?" It's fucked up and wrong. I think Sturgeon has a lot of these stories in his history. But Sturgeon hit back with an attack, saying, "You're all lying, you're after me," you're this, you're that. Jello wanted Sturgeon to apologize to Robert and the band, but Sturgeon wouldn't and that's where it went south, really far south.

While I've had conversations with Sturgeon about this—he is 100 percent sure that his perception of how it happened is how it happened, but I've also spoken with Jello and everyone on the other side, and their stories all match together—that's like five or six people and they weren't black-out drunk or fucked up or on whatever he was on, so I have my suspicions, you know?

Jello wanted a couple of apologies and Sturgeon wanted an apology and they are both very strong-headed, stubborn people sometimes. At that point, I think Sturgeon didn't see a point in protecting A.T. from the rest of the band when people wanted money—and he wanted money. So, basically, he came back with, "I'm pulling all of my records." At A.T., if you do that, you're not coming back—ever. Unfortunately, I've had the experience of bands leaving Alterative Tentacles a couple of times. And, I've had to explain, there's no coming back from that. You're 86'd. Period. It doesn't matter if you guys later get along with Jello. It does not matter. So be really, really sure you want to do that.

Obviously, Sturgeon is one of the main players in both Leftover Crack and Star Fucking Hipsters. But he did this without consulting the rest of the band members. So, I'm pretty sure they were like, "Well…this doesn't really help us get our money…but we weren't getting paid as quickly as we thought we should have…so maybe we get paid somewhere else." My impression is that it was because of the amount owed under royalties, but it all happened after this blowup in Ireland.

Sturgeon says, "We're moving all the Leftover Crack and Star Fucking Hipsters records over to Fat Wreck Chords, so call Chad and work it out with him." I was like, "Okay." Chad was basically General Manager at Fat for like seventeen years.

So, I called Chad and was like, "So, Chad, I hear you are taking Leftover Crack off Alternative Tentacles' hands…" It was NOT what he wanted to hear. Sturgeon had already worked his magic at alienating people over at Fat Wreck Chords at that point.

People ask me, "Was that sad to do?" to lose Leftover Crack. I'm like, "Absolutely not." We got *Fuck World Trade* for 40,000 physical copies over a ten-year period. That's awesome. We got that record for the major part of its life in terms of sales. It was a landmark release, kids love it, and it will always be a part of the Alternative Tentacles history, even if we're not putting it out anymore. We got that record for the best ten years of its life, basically.

Sturgeon: There are so many inaccuracies in Jesse's third-hand retelling of this that I'm not sure that I have the energy to tell the actual story and set it straight.

37

There's No Place Like Home

Kristen Ferrell: In late 2001 or 2002, I had just gotten through a very, very nasty divorce. I had married very young, had a baby very young, and divorced very young. I wanted nothing to do with guys. "Sorry, I'm going to be the cat lady forever, fuck you, I'm done."

I was working at a record store in Lawrence, Kansas. This guy came into the record store and saw me and kept trying to get my attention, but I was a dick to him over and over. He went outside and called his friend Jen Johnson from F-Minus and he said, "I just met the girl I'm going to marry. I don't know how, but I'm going to marry her." That guy was Brad Logan.

I later learned that he was on tour as a guitar tech for Pete Yorn. He kept trying to come back to the record store just to talk to me, but I wasn't working until the last night. Just as we were closing, he saw me leaving. He stopped right in front of me and was staring at me and I remember passing by him being like, "Who's this fucking creep?"

He ran to the venue, the Granada, and he talked to a mutual friend. He knew my friend because he had been through Kansas before. He was running around the Granada asking, "Who's the girl with the long black dreadlocks at the record store?!"

He wrote this really cute note on a piece of cardboard and lodged it through the door of the record store for me to find. It has his email on it. The next morning I get a call from my friends at the record store like *"Hey, there's a note for youuuuu, you better come get this…"*

And normally, I throw that shit away. I don't know why, but for some reason, I didn't, which is so out of character for me. The internet was in its baby phases. The girls at the store had done as much online investigate that they could to learn about Brad and F-Minus.

I waited a few days, and then I email him, like, "What the fuck? Why are you leaving girls notes at the record store? Are you a creep?" He was like, "No, no! I'm not a creep, I swear!" We emailed each other for a while and then eventually I gave him my phone number and let him call me, and after a long while, I let him come visit me, but he had to stay at my friend's house because he still could have been a creepy rapist, so fuck him.

We just kept that long distance relationship going for a while and then we got married and we've been together for eighteen years. Eventually, we moved to LA.

Brad Logan: At that time, I was touring and when I wasn't playing, I was road crew for bigger bands and that was my job nine months a year. But Kristen's not particularly a fan of California—it's quite different than the Midwest.

Kristen Ferrell: When I knew Brad and I were getting married, I grabbed my kiddo and took off to California. I was in the same town as my ex-husband and he was just not getting past the fact that we were divorced. So, instead of Brad coming to Kansas, we just went out there to settle down. It was so expensive and the struggle just got so hard. Brad was on tour for nine months and I was like, "Why am I paying so much in rent and I'm always working, so I never get to see my kid, so why are we working so hard for this existence when Brad is not even here?"

So, Brad was on tour in Germany and I sent him an email: "in fifteen moves I can be back in my parents house in Kansas. I'll meet you there." So, like, fuck you. Poor Brad, he never had a choice in the matter.

Brad Logan: We moved into her old house that she was living in before she moved out to California and we bought that and moved into it. Our mortgage was like $600 a month, if that tells you anything about the cost of living out there. Honestly, I was ready to go from California.

Kristen Ferrell: Brad lost his mind in Kansas. Poor baby. I remember it was after he was done with tour—we had been there for a couple months but he had only been living in Kansas for maybe a few weeks. I had a gallery show in Seattle, so I flew out to Seattle for that show. Brad calls me up in literal hysterics, just freaking out. He was like, "So, I have decided that I wanted to explore the town more so I was gonna see what was out past the Walmart by the interstate. You know what's out there? Cows! Just fuckin' cows! There's just fuckin' *cows* out there! And you keep driving and there's just *cows*! *Walmart and cows*! That's all there is! *Walmart and cows*! What the fuck am I gonna do!"

That's Kansas, honey.

Brad Logan: There would be times where it was just abject terror. At night, sometimes there would just be quiet. You can look up and see the stars. There are streets with no streetlights. You can stare in one direction and see nothing but cornfields for miles. That would fill me with terror sometimes. And sometimes it would be an absolute breath of fresh air.

Kristen Ferrell: The biggest thing that came along with being in a relationship with me was that I had a kid. "I have a kid and my kid is more important than you, Brad, and you're going to have to deal with that." And he did. He never wanted kids and never had been around kids. Really, that was the most interesting evolution of Brad as being a father figure.

Brad Logan: Being a parent is something I never wanted to be, but it came with the territory. I loved my wife so I learned how to do it. No parent knows what the fuck they are doing, they just learn how to do it. I think that, at least, little kids want to have someone to tell them what to do. It helps them to feel secure and safe. Parenting someone and telling them what to do doesn't mean being an asshole or not listening to them or not allowing them to develop their own likes and dislikes and personality. There are times to discuss things and there are times to just say, "Well, no, this is how it's going to be."

Kristen Ferrell: Brad also had it really easy. We were able to do good cop/bad cop because I'm the mom and I'm always the bad cop and because he's stepdad, he gets to be the good cop. With parents, it's usually shared, but I was like, "I'm always going to have to be bad cop." Whenever I threw out, "No, you're in a timeout and you're going to stay there until you can speak with kindness," Brad would sidle in and be like, "Hey, buddy, you know you got this? Fist bump!"

Brad Logan: I heard things come out of my mouth that I couldn't believe! I said things that when my parents would say them, I'd say, "I'll never say that when I grow up!" And then, decades later, I hear myself saying, "These are the rules of the house and if you don't like them, you can move into your own place!" Oh, my God. I can't believe I just said that.

Sullivan Beck (Son of Kristen Ferrell): I may have said, "You're not my real dad!" like once.

Brad Logan: Yeah, I shot that down real fuckin' quick. No, I'm not your real dad, but I'm the other adult that lives here and you're the kid!

Kristen Ferrell: Brad never came into it with expectations. He never expected Sully to see him as a dad. "No, I'm not your dad, I'm your *Brad*." That means he's his buddy dad. He's here to help out and just kind of be around.

He was just another adult that cares for Sully, the same way a grandparent or an uncle would. That's Brad's way of coming in but not demanding a role. "Yeah, I'm here, what's up?" It works really well when you don't try to alpha shit, which he doesn't.

It blew everybody's mind when he was dating someone, and then married to someone, who had a kid. He really stepped up to it in a way that I think shocked everybody. But it didn't shock me because I didn't know the Brad that everyone else knew. I only knew the one that I met. And he had to step up and he did. He still has to figure out things sometime. "I don't know what the fuck I'm doing!" Well, no parent does.

Brad Logan: You figure that as your kid grows up, "Am I going to enforce this or let it go?" Pick your battles is the theme. It's not a good idea to let your kid eat nothing but candy all day. But letting your kid believe in whatever religion or God or not that they want and listen to any music they want or adopt any political ideology, that's up to them. You'll always hope they'll be influenced by you and your likes and dislikes, but if they don't, you love them anyways because you are you and they are them.

But I didn't know what the fuck I was doing the whole time… and I still don't.

Interlude
Mental Health

Nicole Enriquez (Guitar/Vocals—Witch Hunt; School Social Worker):
Think about your left brain hemisphere versus your right brain
hemisphere. Your right brain is the emotional brain and the left brain
is the logic and rationale. In order to tap into deep suffering, and in
order to face it and acknowledge it, you really do need to go into
your unconscious mind. Music, art, and other techniques heal people
because these things affect the left and the right brain. The left brain
is talk therapy, so you talk through it and articulate it—but some
people aren't even there yet, so the right brain can approach these
issues when a person can't articulate the issue.

Janine St. Clair (Bass/Vocals—Witch Hunt; School Social Worker):
Music really can be a huge source of healing when it comes to
mental health and mental illness. Playing music and creating
music is such a powerful a form of expression. For people that
are just listening, it can be very positive coping skill. A lot of us
lean on music to get through really hard times. When people are
struggling and need to heal emotionally, music often is a tool that
aids that process.

Nicole Enriquez: Art and music are possibly the most healing
forms of expression and I think that's why people who are

suffering mentally are drawn to music. Just talking is not enough sometimes. Personally from playing music, there is no experience that can even come close to that feeling. It's the most mindful sensory experience. As someone that is always thinking, analyzing, and planning, I don't think when I'm playing music. You are just being. You just are.

Because of that, I don't think it's a coincidence that people who make music that is especially moving often have mental health issues. I think some of the greatest artists are suffering or have known suffering—the stereotypical "mad artist." Look at Van Gogh. He spoke about how he put his heart and his soul into his work and as a result, he lost his mind. Some of his paintings were done while he was suffering. He would make these beautiful paintings like *Starry Night*, which is what it looked like outside the asylum that he lived in.

I think about Frida Kahlo. She had that accident with the bus and a metal pole almost ripped her in half. It went through her body, in the front and out the back, and she was in immense pain for the rest of her life—and her most famous paintings are paintings of her suffering and dealing with that pain. She actually felt physical pain from the act of painting itself.

Janine St. Clair: Look at Nick Blinko of Rudimentary Peni. He had to go off his medication to do art, and his art is so intricate and fine. I read that he didn't have the same motor skills and dreams when he was on medication, so he made the ultimate sacrifice and he went off his medication to produce his art.

Though it is important to add that psychotropic medications don't negatively affect creativity for everyone and the benefits for psychotropic medication for people that require it can be immense. I know many people on psychotropic medications who are stable and extremely creative.

Nicole Enriquez: Punk is so political. It's verbal. It's intellectualizing, and the music is the healing emotional part of it. For many of us, it is the perfect intervention in many circumstances, and I think that's why there is a deep connection between people who are suffering and who are brilliant artists.

Alice Hour (Education Safeguarding and Welfare Officer; Vocals— In Evil Hour): Mental illness is prevalent in the punk scene, but it's also prevalent in society. It may be more prevalent in punk than other walks of life because punk might be more likely to have people that can't live in a nine-to-five world, so they might be drawn into a world that allows for alternatives. Punk attracts extreme personalities and in extreme personalities you find a lot of mental illness.

Janine St. Clair: Feelings of hopelessness, social isolation, depression—I think a lot of musicians and a lot punks experience this. That may very well be the reason that many of us got into the scene. And that raises the issue, what do we do when music espouses a negative message, or a message that suggests self-destructive behaviors?

I do think these lyrics like that can be a positive experience. It's a feeling that "I'm not alone and there are others that I can connect with." It can be a part of having this sense of belonging, it could save someone's life at the same time.

Denise Vertucci (Educator; Head of Fistolo Records; Mischief Brew contributor): For some kids, they are finding something relatable. A kid looking at somebody and being like, "I've felt this way myself"—it can be cathartic and helpful. If people are able to take it with a grain of salt, it's useful. A lot of the lyrical content is not something I condone, but I definitely think some kids can benefit from hearing that someone feels like they do. You do hope that the glorifying of stuff takes a back seat and it's not gonna influence anybody to say, "This band sings about this and I'm gonna do it too!"

I'm sure that has happened, but I see the value on the other end of it. Music has such an influence of being healing and most likely for every one kid that was like, "Cool! I'm going to do drugs!" there was a handful of kids who were influenced along the lines of, "This person feels like me, but they're an adult now and they are still alive."

Alice Hour: Leftover Crack take that uncomfortable subject head-on and talk about it in a very personal way. I think most bands would not be able to do that without being maudlin or exploitative. But at the same time, Sturgeon is singing about those things in a band called Leftover Crack. So, it's not all meant to be taken in a totally serious manner. In the back of your mind obviously, there is a self-destructive element to the band, but also one that deals with those topics in a way that maybe they *can be* approached, even before you get to the topics about suicide.

Nicole Enriquez: I could easily argue that messages about wanting to commit suicide or doing drugs are harmful for listeners. But I also strongly believe that music and writing is such an outlet that censorship is really dangerous to both the writer and the listener. To inhibit creativity or messages can be really stifling. Artists should feel empowered to write about whatever they want to write about. They don't need to hold the entire responsibility of how a listener will interpret the message because you can't control how they will interpret that message.

I do think that youth listening to messages about suicide and drug use *can* be very harmful. Punks who are anti-establishment might not have a secure attachment with their parents, maybe they are feeling isolated, hating the world—punks are not looking to idolize celebrities and I think that it's the musicians who can speak to them in a way others can't.

I will add, the human brain doesn't fully develop until you are age twenty-five. The front of your brain, the prefrontal cortex, is responsible for higher levels of thinking, impulse control, and analysis. So, a kid that is feeling super isolated or depressed and they hear a song like "Suicide (A Better Way)"—I think that some kids without the ability to project into the future, maybe a kid could go through with some of those maladaptive behaviors. So, I think it's important for the artist to think about these things.

Janine St. Clair: And that brings up the issue of what we do when artists we like or admire, or even our friends, say things that aren't good or if they behave erratically. It may be the social worker in me, but I feel compelled to offer support to others if I see somebody behaving erratically or if their behavior shifts in a way that doesn't seem right, whether it's offensive or just bizarre.

I do understand both sides. I do feel that punk should be a safer space—there's no place that's totally safe, so a *safer* space—from the threats that we might normally face in the external world.

So when I see those behaviors, it's a red flag to me. There must be a reason why they are behaving the way they are. But I do feel conflicted over the "you're no longer invited here" mindset.

Alice Hour: It's a difficult question and not something you have a blanket answer for. It depends on the art and it depends on the artist. William Burroughs wrote some of the finest American literature, but he also spent a large portion of his life fucking prepubescent boys in Tangier. We don't burn all of our William Burroughs books, do we?

I wouldn't say you *must* separate the art from the artist, because if the artist has done something that is offensive to the core of you, it will color your view of the works and I can't make that decision for you.

Denise Vertucci: You call people on their shit. I think about this issue a lot. I often think of it in the context if Erik were still here. Erik didn't necessarily like confrontation, but he didn't want to be associated with people who had shitty views.

I also understand, now that I work with a more diverse group of people, sometimes people go off on a weird tangent when they are upset about something and they can't quite express themselves. But if you can have an open dialogue and not just shut them out, you can get a different understanding and see why they are doing what they are doing.

Nicole Enriquez: When we see red flags, it could be a sign that someone is really suffering or they are in the middle of a process that they haven't recovered from. I don't expect perfect behavior in the punk scene…or in anywhere. When you shun someone from a scene, they will go to a new area and they will continue the cycle of committing the same thing in another community.

I don't think being a good person or a bad person is a binary. I think in the punk scene, many of us, because we feel so isolated, we come with baggage, with mental health issues. So, being a good person is a practice or it's mindfully, intentionally really looking at your imperfections, really acknowledging them, and educating yourself and trying to make yourself a better person.

If all of us looked at it on a spectrum of "I am working on my imperfections and working toward being a better person," I think we could hopefully accept more people in this regard. We could help them make changes instead of shunning them and forcing them into another place of shame, which will only make maladaptive behaviors worse.

Denise Vertucci: Many people that have mental issues and self-medicate, they're going to be more erratic and behave certain ways. But if you know the person well enough and you know deep down they have a good heart, you can kind of understand where they are coming from.

Janine St. Clair: People in our lives have died from self-inflicted injuries—suicide, self-inflicted drug abuse, drug overdose—and I really believe a lot of these people needed one person to reach out and accept their imperfections.

I have seen people show genuine remorse and work toward change. I think about rejecting people from a scene and thinking about what could happen to them, what has happened to them, what has contributed to the behaviors that they have, and what they need. So it makes me sad.

I do think we all need to be accountable for our actions. Words are not enough, and I don't think we can just blindly forgive. It takes a lot of work, it takes a lot of action, and I think everyone deserves a second chance.

38

Constructing Constructs

Sturgeon: I didn't really have an intention to do another Leftover Crack record by the time Star Fucking Hipsters had started. Any song that I would have used in Leftover Crack, I would have used in Star Fucking Hipsters.

But after the third Star Fucking Hipsters record in like three or four years, the band fell apart. I was really depressed. We put out a record and didn't even really play any shows for it. I kind of didn't know what to do. After a month or two, I realized like, "Oh, wait, I guess we could do another Leftover Crack record," even though I didn't really want to do another.

I didn't want to put out a shitty record. It's a fact every record has a couple of songs that are cuttable. Also, we're a punk band. We're not going to play more than an hour. So, that's one reason why on *Constructs*, the songs are shorter. People's attention spans are getting shorter. With shorter songs, you can play more songs in a set and people are happier when you play more songs.

Fat Mike: Sturgeon knew *Constructs had* to be good. He spent months and months writing this album. You knew it *would* be good because of how much time he put into it.

This system locks you up for life, They'll throw away the keys for spite /
They search your insides and they darken any light, You end up empty,
broken, tortured, day and night / They search for questioners of lies,
And mental health is their disguise / But best believe they're full of hate,
They will mislead us to control our shining lives / They are corrupt
ambitious constructs of the state

—Excerpt from "Vicious Constructs"

Sturgeon: "Vicious Constructs" is influenced by Penny Rimbaud's book *Shibboleth*. It's the book about what lead up to Crass, how Penny and Gee Vaucher went from hippies and became militant. It's about his friend, Wally Hope, that was committed against his will in mental institutions in England. They drugged and shocked him so much that he was a shell, and when he got out, he killed himself. Penny and Gee decided that the hippy peace and love thing wasn't what it's about. They turned their eyes toward the state, which ground up their friend and took the spark out of his life…

Penny Rimbaud (Drummer/Lyricist/Cofounder—Crass): There's no information on the subject of Wally and his death that isn't in *Shibboleth*, really. It's all there. I'm always really pleased if people pick up my stuff and use it. That's what it's for.

Sturgeon: You have a story that is similar to *One Flew Over the Cuckoo's Nest*. Somebody that is not crazy but is put in the institution for people called "crazy" by the state and they are turned into a husk of their former selves. That was influential on my life.

I grew up a block from Bellevue Hospital. I was born in '76, and my neighborhood was filled with homeless people that talked to themselves. I realized that it was because Ronald Reagan cut funding from mental institutions, so they just released them onto the street. Over the years, with Olivia from No Commercial Value, we'd visit her friends that were locked up. I was taking acid and was really thinking about shit. The thing that kept causing fear for me was the police.

What that portal led to was being in buildings that were shoeboxes...we were in a sixteen-floor building and I think it went from A to M, so there were at least fifteen to twenty apartments on each floor. It's a lot of people stuck in one building and on acid you really think about shit like that, being in this fucked-up shoebox situation. If you go outside of your shoebox, and if you act "crazy," you might end up locked up, and not just in jail, but in a mental institution. And that's more believable if you live a block from it.

To this day, I still have a fear of being locked up—waking up and being in a mental institution against my will and not being able to leave because I'm at the mercy of psychiatrists and people that don't want to understand me, and don't understand me, and don't like me, and want to keep me there. I think that's to be feared more than death.

So, I wrote "Vicious Constructs" about that. Sascha from Choking Victim was locked up a lot when he was younger. He had manic episodes and I've had manic episodes. The stuff he has told me is terrifying. When I see evidence of a manic episode rising in my head, I try to get away from whatever is causing me to be unbalanced.

Penny Rimbaud: I've been told that the record is influenced by my work, Gee's work, and Crass. When a band or artist repurposes my art or material, it's never annoying. Sometimes it's not very good. I know Gee, who is responsible for most of the imagery we used in the day, used to get tired of what were sort of bad pastiches of her work, which didn't actually have much to say. But I mean, if we've influenced, if Crass inspired I don't know how many people to form bands, and some of them were good, and some were absolutely awful—but the fact that people got up and did stuff because people were inspired by what we were doing, that has always pleased me. It's what we wanted to do. We want to get rid of elitist rock and roll heroes and all that shit and get down to doing it ourselves and amusing ourselves. It wasn't to become some rock and roll star or some big money geezer. It was so we could share things. It was about sharing our energy and our skills. And if sharing is people going off doing bad versions of Crass songs or anything else, that's fair enough. I don't mind. At least they're not sitting on their arses. Our response to that was always it's nice to see people do things.

Sturgeon: Fly is friends with Penny, and I played the song for Fly and she liked it and played it for Penny, and he really liked it and wanted to be in touch. But I was still working on the record and I asked if he could possibly collaborate with me. He gave me the spoken word section and he actually gave me a song—it was his and Gee Vaucher's noise project. It was a CD that was like seventy minutes and it had like 100 tracks.

Penny Rimbaud: I don't think they ever spoke to me directly. I don't really recall ever passing them along any information. I don't do stuff to get a name or to get money. I do it to inspire people to do things and if that involves bits and pieces of my material, I'm always very pleased that they've done it. That means it's working, doesn't it? It's better than sitting on a bookshelf. I don't think I've ever heard the album.

Sturgeon: Penny wanted me to use one track and I couldn't find it because it got misplaced in a former partner's car. I almost feel like it was misplaced on purpose out of malice. So, I just used samples that I found instead of the music, which I still, to this day, regret. I'm sure it was great and it would have been cool to say that they played these instruments on this record.

Penny and I were in touch a lot. We went back and forth at least a dozen times talking about the record. After a while, contact became sparse. Eventually, when I mentioned that we were going to be on tour in England, I asked if we could stop by Dial House, and I stopped hearing from him…

Penny Rimbaud: I've been told that I am credited with "Badassery" on the record. As I understand, in America, "Badass" is sort of like not being afraid to express your own opinion even if it goes right against convention. A badass is someone that's out for it. So, I don't mind being a badass if it means getting up people's noses, which is an English expression. You're sort of winding them up, getting them to think, making them question their own stupidity… or wisdom.

39

Constructs of the State

Donny Morris (Drummer—Leftover Crack): Recording *Constructs* was weird. It was mostly recorded at Fat Mike's studio, Motor Studios. Josh the engineer was there. We recorded all the songs separately over the span of a couple of years. We would have the skeletons of like six songs and we would record the skeleton and I'd do it to a click track so we could mess with the structure. For the most part, I hadn't even heard the song and I was recording it!

Chris Mann (Guitar—Leftover Crack): *Constructs* was already well along by the time I joined the band. I felt like the dog that had been adopted just to keep mom and dad together. It felt like I was in the eye of the storm and everyone was just…decompressing against each other, I guess.

Kate Coysh: I came in just to do some crowd vocals for what became *Constructs of the State*. Sturgeon said, "See if you can do this one thing," and then it was, "Well, that sounded good," and then it was, "How about this?" and, "How about this," and I just recorded more and more things. I just chewed up whatever he gave me and I really liked it. And then I was asked to join up and tour with them.

I know this sounds corny, but Sturgeon writes like a true composer. He sees the big picture before anyone does and he has a very clear vision of what he wants it to sound like. He is relentless in that pursuit.

Chris Mann: Sturgeon was just so laid-back the entire time during recording. Usually there's a guy breathing down your neck the entire time. But Sturgeon was just chilling out in the other room while Donny and I recorded. I don't know if Sturgeon knew this, but it gave Donny and I the freedom to be creative.

I remember looking around the room at Motor Studios and you see the instruments of musicians that you idolized when you grew up and you hope that you can contribute to the legacy and do that legacy justice.

I was able to contribute to about eight songs. Two are unreleased—"Brad Sabbath" and "Watership Down." The problem was that I really had no idea what these songs were like. I just showed up to the studio and that's every musician's worst nightmare. I had really good support from Donny and we were kind of each other's rocks through the recording of that album.

Donny Morris: During the recording, Brad and I got into it for a little bit. We were sleeping at Motor to record there. I had taken the isolated guitar booth that was all plugged in and ready to go. There was nobody to disturb me or to wake me up to tell me that shit was going to start. One day, I just woke up to a blaring G-chord. It scared the living fucking life out of me. I came out so angry. There was half of me that knew that no one knew that I was in there, but I wouldn't allow myself to acknowledge that. I was so fucking angry that I was ready to fight. I was in fight-or-flight mode.

Brad Logan: In one of the rooms of the recording studio was all of Mike's BDSM gear. It was in the community lounge and kitchen area—racks, bondage furniture—which you didn't really want to touch or sit on.

Kate Coysh: At that time, there were a lot of different personal things going on in the band. It seemed like a lot of transitions for people—lifestyle changes and location of living changes. Even though the band was facing their own personal turmoil, when it came time to get together to practice, they were like a well-oiled machine.

Chris Mann: Donny and I rehearsed at a grueling regimen over the course of months, sometimes until four o'clock in the morning. I memorized their entire catalogue and kept a notebook of every note and every lyric. My first show with them was at the Observatory, and it was two sold-out nights. To say I was a little shaken by this prospect was...*true*. Before the show, we were practicing "One Dead Cop" and there's a part where we all jump in the air. Alec laughed that I had the fact that we jumped in the air in my notebook.

After the final practice, Sturgeon told me, "Congratulations, it doesn't sound like *total* shit," with emphasis on the "total." The whole show I only looked at my shoes and my hands because I didn't want to mess up any notes. I only looked up to dodge projectiles thrown at me—this trashcan kept following me all over the stage the entire show. That trashcan was gunning for me.

You always know that you are doing a good job because after the show they don't say anything to you. If you mess up, you know you'll hear it, so the highest compliment is if they don't say anything at all.

There was a guy, was from this band / Secretly Canadian / His ego kept him sad and blue / Dissatisfied, his sickness grew / He traded his guitar for drugs / And ended up with body bugs /

He took so many Xanax sticks / He lost his humour and his wit / An empty, confused, sober shell / Suboxone led him straight to hell

—Excerpt from "Bedbugs and Beyond"

Kate Coysh: The song "Bedbugs and Beyond" referenced Ezra and I sang on the track. For me, I can always take the easy route and say I didn't write any of the lyrics. So, I was kind of coming in as a hired gun. The song was definitely provocative. They knew what they were doing. It was kind of a response to what their friendship, Sturgeon's and Ezra's, was at the time, if you could call it that. They are divisive and reactionary people in all of the best of ways and you're gonna feel it.

Chris Mann: I realized I was stepping in for Ezra. That weighed on my mind. But the last thing you want to do is fill someone else's shoes. You have to fill your own. Everyone wants the guy before you, but what they get is the guy in front of them. So, I did my damnedest to make sure that I left it all on the stage.

I braced myself for it before playing. I was *ready* to get heckled. But maybe there was one or two times out of the entire time I played where some guy chanted, "Where's Ezra?!" and did three slow claps. So, I just got on the mic and said, "I don't know, you can ask him." It's one of those things that I didn't have any skin in the game regarding the drama before I got there. I was asked to be here and if I can give whatever form of energy asked by the crowd or required for the record, that's literally what I live for. It's your own way of saying, "Fuck you! *This* is what *I* got."

Ezra Kire (Guitar/Vocals—Leftover Crack, Morning Glory, INDK): From the time I was born, it was very clear to me what my purpose in life was. I was convinced that my purpose in life was to help people. I've always wanted to help people. Because of the circumstances of my life, music was the first platform through which I was able to help people. When that finally ended, and the torch had to be passed to the next generation of songwriters, I had to change my platform to continue my purpose. Music was just kind of a means to an end for me. But no one can be a conduit forever. I had to fill that emptiness with something else. Now, I continue through other means doing that thing. I feel like if I didn't find that thing, I probably wouldn't have a good reason to live and continue on with my purpose.

Sturgeon: I really do love that record a lot. The only thing that bugs me about the record is that when I wrote a lot of the stuff, especially the vocals and the lyrics, I didn't take into account my personal vocal range. In the past, pretty much up to *Deadline*, every song was practiced and played and I had rehearsed it to some extent, because we were always waiting for money to record, as opposed to being ready to record and having money for it. So, what happened, several songs on *Constructs* are out of my vocal range and they are some of the more popular songs on that record, and we don't play them because I'll lose my voice.

That's my main regret with that record. I should have tried to rehearse more. As I get older, it's harder to rehearse. I get really self-conscious about lyrics and vocals. It's weird. I can't just write song gibberish...I can, and on occasion still do, but I don't like to rely on that. Therefore, I don't really end up rehearsing, because I get too shy about vocals and I don't have lyrics to it.

Brad Logan: I think *Constructs* is a really good record—in fact, I think it's my favorite Leftover Crack release. Well, maybe second favorite. The songs are shorter and to the point and the people that performed on it did a such great job. Kate really fuckin' nailed it on her vocals. Prior to hearing the record I had never even met her. Then, when I was listening to songs she recorded I was like, "Who the fuck is *this*?!!"

40

ﬀeaturing...

Sturgeon: *Constructs* is definitely influenced by hip hop in a lot of ways. The most obvious way I think is having guests on the record. You want to make it more of a community record instead of a competition.

Jesse Michaels: They asked me to do a guest spot for "System Fucked" and they also asked me to do a video. Usually when people ask me to do a guest track, it's because they have a ska or reggae song and they don't know what to do with it and they figure I can spice it up. Here it was one of the better songs on the record, so I appreciated that. So I went down there and did it.

On a general level, I can relate to Leftover Crack. They are into much more of a crust punk aesthetic where there's more "fuck you, I wanna kill you and worship Satan!" That's not really my vibe. But I do relate to the general feeling of rebellion and dissatisfaction, so I was down to sing with them. And the whole "I don't wanna go to war, fuck you!" That's a classic trope of all the bands I grew up listening to—Gang Green, the Fix, Toxic Reasons, the FUs, Reagan Youth, Government Issue. They all had songs about not wanting to get drafted, which is funny because I don't think any of them were ever in the slightest danger of actually being drafted.

Sturgeon told me jokingly that they let me direct the video just because they wanted to play with me live. There may be some truth to that...and it's okay if there is. It's funny either way.

Sturgeon: I hoped deep down that having Jesse direct our video would put us in a live music situation that would enable us to back him on a couple of Op Ivy songs. But I would have chosen him to direct the video regardless. He's just one of those people that can try anything artistic and immediately excel. If I didn't appreciate him and love all of his art so much, it would probably be infuriating. But we're all better off for having his influence on all of our bands and our lives. There's that film where they imagine a world where the Beatles never existed. I shudder to think of the world and my life in particular if Op Ivy never existed.

Years before, I had seen and heard Rancid since they were playing house shows in Oakland. The only song that I liked seemed to be "Hyena." It bothered me for years. Why didn't I like Rancid but loved Operation Ivy? The mystery was solved when I met Jesse Michaels years later. He's an extraordinary talent and a smart, funny, caring person...with as many mental hangups as I have... easily. There's a heart in Op Ivy that takes the band to a whole other level that Rancid never seemed to reach.

I've had a handful of moments in my life that I consider unequivocal achievements and at the very top sits out set with Jesse at Bridgetown DIY in LA and just how good Leftover Crack sounds playing "Sound System" and "Unity" with Jesse. I love Jesse for so many reasons. I really can't think of any reason not to love him.

Brad Logan: The first time I met Jesse was when we were rehearsing "System Fucked." I didn't know what to expect. Actually, I was a little intimidated. He was quiet and reserved, but he quickly warmed up. I found Jesse to be a pretty funny and likeable guy.

The night of the show, it was at Bridgetown DIY—a place in a strip mall in El Monte, California—and it was pissing rain. There were only about forty people there and all of them were losing their shit.

Sturgeon: Supposedly we were banned from playing Phoenix due to the riot. We might still be banned from Phoenix. Since we couldn't play Phoenix, we started playing malls and bars outside of Phoenix. I don't mean an indoor shopping mall. I mean like strip malls.

So, *Constructs* had "Amanecer de los Muertos" on it. That's pretty much Alec's song. To be fair, the original lyrics were "we're *going* to the mall, we're *going* to the mall!" I don't really have anything to say about going *to* the mall. But we have played *at* malls, and we probably will again.

Having Joe Jack talking with me in the beginning of the song really ties a lot of other musical and cultural influences together for me. The song title translates as "Dawn of the Dead" in English. The Romero film was shot at the King of Prussia mall in Pennsylvania. The Dead Milkmen reference the mall and film in "Punk Rock Girl," kind of in the video definitely. Having Joe Jack doing an almost "Bitchin' Camero" intro makes it an extremely rewarding, multi-reference song about Leftover Crack playing in a strip mall behind disgusting, homophobic Chick-fil-A.

Erik Petersen of Mischief Brew is also from Philly and on that song. That was another exciting bonus. I met Erik twenty-something years earlier. When I was recording *Fuck World Trade*, Leftover Crack were playing a lot of benefits around the RNC in NYC. Things like legal aid for the arrested protestors. At that time, a friend of mine gave me a tape with the new Against Me!, Erik Petersen, and some other stuff. I was listening to it and saying, "This new Against Me! is amazing!" It sounded like they had somehow topped the *Axl Rose* stuff, but it turns out what I thought was Against Me! was my first time hearing Defiance, Ohio. Then, I heard the Erik Petersen stuff and loved that, too. I didn't know why I hadn't heard it yet, since I was told he was from Philly.

I kept hearing Erik's name and I liked his music. Leftover Crack played a legal benefit for RNC Protestors at the First Unitarian Church. After the show, everybody went to Clark Park. Everyone was like, "Erik Petersen is playing Clark Park." There were like 300 kids watching Erik Petersen and I was like, "It's Erik and Denise!" I had known Erik for like ten years at least because Erik and Denise were the first people that came to more than one Choking Victim show. One of the few times I didn't ride back to New York with Choking Victim, I stayed at their place in West Philly.

They are like the only people that just let me stay at their place back in the day without being with the band. They were really friendly, hospitable, and trusting while the rest of the world was awkwardly "nice" to our faces while talking shit behind our backs.

I didn't even know that Erik played guitar! He never mentioned it in like ten years. It says something about his personality that he was like, shy but proud, but there's a type of humility that is really admirable when a person has so much talent. In retrospect he was probably sitting on his hands and biting his tongue so as to not show off his songs. That's a special type of person that can do that.

Once he realized that I was a fan, he asked me to be on the Mischief Brew album *Smash the Windows* with "10,000 Fleas." When I did that song, I wasn't that crazy about it. I'm still not crazy about it. It seemed to me to be kind of like a filler song. A bit Tom Waits-y, which I had started to get sick of from people playing his stuff out in the squats and traveling. It's not going to ruin the record, but maybe it's not the best song on the record.

I feel like Erik put me on that song because he felt it was lacking something. He may have felt like I helped save that song. But, when

I was walking out of the studio, he put on "Nomad's Revolt." I was putting my winter coat on and was like, "Hey, can I sing on that?! Can I do backing vocals on the chorus?" Right away I knew it was a great song. I just wanted to be a part of it. But he was like, "Oh, no, I already have a lot of people on this song" and all of the songs. So, I think he had the same thing like Leftover Crack and our community efforts, where he wanted people he respected or his friends on his songs. So, as it were, that song was earmarked for other people. So, I was walking away and felt I was shrinking like a flea...in ego and influence... "Okay..." I'll just scuttle out onto another dog, hopefully it'll still keep me as warm as that other new song sounds...

Denise Vertucci: When Erik would write songs, there were certain songs where he had someone in mind. When he wrote "10,000 Fleas," he said, "I can see Sturgeon singing that." Sturgeon wanted to sing on "Nomad's Revolt." Sturgeon was like, "I wanna sing kill off Columbus!" Erik was like, *"No."* Erik could say that. They had a mutual artistic respect. I know Erik was stoked to sing on *Constructs*. He had to go to into the studio, but we all went to the brewery so I could have a Hell or High Water. We were like, "Ha ha ha! You have to be a grown-up and sing and we're going to the brewery!" But I know Erik was excited to do it.

Sturgeon: I was surprised when Erik died. During the *Constructs* sessions, we did another song with Erik, written by Stu Daly from Chewing on Tinfoil called "The Dead." It's not completely done. I didn't want to release it to make it seem like I was capitalizing on his death. I want to give it a proper release.

Alec Baillie: *Constructs* had some older songs that had been reworked on it as well.

Sturgeon: I've been reworking old No Commercial Value songs since No Commercial Value stopped playing. There are songs in

Choking Victim, Leftover Crack, and Star Fucking Hipsters that were No Commercial Value songs. It's awesome to do because I was worried about having good material for the record and then you realize that there are all these old songs that never got properly recorded. No Commercial Value recorded a demo at NYU in like a day. We never really sold it. Alec and I wrote the stuff.

Olivia and I were the singers in No Commercial Value. On *Constructs*, we were getting into territory for songs that she originally sang. I tracked her down and asked her if she wanted to be on the record. She said no, but she said we could use any of her lyrics that we wanted. I knew she would probably say no, and she's just not interested in performing. She doesn't even listen to punk rock anymore as far as I can tell, even though she's the person that got me into punk.

Joe Jack Talcum: I had known Sturgeon a while, so I wasn't surprised when he asked me to be on his record. I've always liked playing with him.

Sturgeon: The first band that I got into of my own accord that my parents didn't have a copy of or my brother, who is a year and a half older than me, didn't have was Dead Milkmen. The first time I actually went and bought some records of my own accord was after Al-TV, which was when Weird Al Yankovic would take over MTV and play his own videos and a lot of other weird videos—not just alternative bands, but bands that were more whimsical or wacky, or that were clever in more of a nerdy way than a narcissistic way, like They Might Be Giants and Dead Milkmen.

I found *Metaphysical Graffiti* in the bargain bin of a CD store on Christopher Street in the West Village. I got it for like $3.99 and to this day, I feel that it is the Dead Milkmen's best record—even better than the almost perfect *Beelzebubba*. On "Rock the 40 Oz.," the first line of the second verse is taken from "Dollar Signs in Her

Eyes" from that album. It's a really beautiful ballad that is probably the Milkmen's most political song.

It's interesting looking back at the Dead Milkmen catalogue. What I noticed is that Rodney Anonymous sings most of the songs, but, once or twice an album, Joe Jack Talcum sings a song that he wrote. I think he does that because he writes really catchy, almost "pop" songs. And when you write a really catchy song like that, it's hard to give it up to another singer. It's the same instinct that has us singing in the shower or in the car or signing up for karaoke. Look at "Punk Rock Girl." Joe Jack sings it. He could have let Rodney sing it, but I think he didn't want to let it go.

He can be kind of flat and unemotional when you are talking to him or watching him perform. I don't think it's a façade, but that's what he often projects. I don't think he is that, but that's what he likes to put out there. My guess is that it's a defense mechanism. Joe Jack, and I'm not trying to put him down because I love him, he could be typecast as the stereotypical wimp—he's skinny, he's shy, not tall, he doesn't project an alpha personality, necessarily. He's someone that very likely got picked on in high school or junior high and probably got into punk and rock music because of that, and probably found the other Dead Milkmen because they got picked on, so they leaned toward each others for support...this is all wild speculation, my favorite kind, but I think there's some truth in there.

I'm the same. I come from a similar background. I had low self-esteem and very few friends. I avoided fights at all costs and I always felt abysmally alone. I definitely turned to music and art as a defense mechanism. I certainly had the time to practice playing drums and then guitar since I would rarely have any place to go on the weekends. It didn't help that I had a pretty strict, early curfew when I could hang out with other kids. It made me look like what

I was—an overprotected latchkey nerd. None of the other kids seemed to have parents that cared about where they were or what they did.

I've covered Dead Milkmen songs a bunch. Ten years prior, I connected with him through mutual friends to do a benefit show in Brooklyn. He was really surprised that I was influenced by his band.

I think it was early 2000, we were playing Philly at the Pontiac Grill and we had an upside-down American flag, and that got us banned from playing there when they realized that we were *THAT* band, so they canceled our show last-minute. There were gonna be a lot of disappointed people, including us, but we were fortunate enough to play the house of the Low Budgets. It was called the Pleasure Bungalow or something like that.

By the time of *Constructs*, I had already worked with Joe Jack a lot. I didn't realize that the Dead Milkmen were coming around on tour and playing at Slims the very night that I found out. I tried to see what his schedule was gonna be like between sound check and the show, and it seemed like there was no time for him to come to the studio, so I asked him if I wrote a sketch, would he be on it. And he was fine with it. Having Joe Jack in our liner notes and on our record, it's like up there with that Jesse Michaels credit.

Joe Jack Talcum: We were on tour and I didn't have much free time, so I recorded the script Sturgeon gave me into an iPhone. I was happy to be a part of his record.

Sturgeon: On *Constructs of the State*, I really got most of the people that I could think of that I had never worked with yet that I was influenced by and that would actually be involved if I asked them. There's plenty of people that if I asked they wouldn't be on someone else's record in a million years, especially a punk record. But this is kind of like tying up the loose ends of things that I haven't achieved in my life, you know? I feel like once I document that,

I don't have to name-drop. The list that I have of contributors and collaborators is really impressive, for me, at least. In my own taste of music, I've gotten pretty much everybody that I could access and get a message to.

There is only one person that said no. They didn't even say no. They, like, deferred to someone else, and then that person sent me a really shitty Facebook or Myspace message that didn't make any sense. They were, like, clowning me or some shit. It was a pretty cheap shot and, of course, humiliating.

That was Blake from Jawbreaker. He's the only person that responded negatively to me asking if I could get him to contribute to one of my records. I get it, he's "misunderstood." But I feel like he might turn that into ammunition and use that as a way to put people down.

It's funny, because that really affected my relationship with the band Jawbreaker. They were always a huge inspiration for me. I saw the documentary about Jawbreaker, and his band and him are practicing, and his bandmates are playing parts of their old songs and he's just refusing to play. In the past, I would have been like, "Oh, he's just shy…" No, actually, he might just be a dick.

I met him through a friend of mine who was dating the bass player in one of his bands. Things got weird. I had spoken to him on several occasions throughout my teenage and adult life and he seemed like a nice enough person. Later, I was living in Austin for a little while and I saw Blake do a solo thing with a laptop—some weird beat-driven things and a few acoustic Jawbreaker songs. I saw him and was like, "Hey, Blake, it's Sturgeon…from New York…" But I had glasses on, so maybe I looked different? He took me by the shoulders and put his face level to mine and looked me in the eyes, and then looked away, then he let go, and he walked away without saying anything… It was really weird.

It's funny because, out of every band that I've been influenced by, I've probably stolen the most things from Blake and Jawbreaker than anyone else—musical things, and vocal inflections. There's "one dead co-a-a-a-a-ap"—extending that vowel is from Jawbreaker. I don't necessarily sound like any other punk singer. I have a few different voices that you'll hear on a record. There are not too many other bands that sound like Leftover Crack. I feel like I have a unique voice and I feel like so does Blake, and I feel like if there's one person that I stole the most from it is Blake.

41

Deconstruction

Kate Coysh: After the album came out, we had a show at the Metro in Oakland, but I was working the bar at the Elbo Room before the show. Out of nowhere, wearing one of the best fucking suits I've ever seen in my life, Sturgeon rolls in…on roller skates, singing some dumb eighties song! The image of him rolling into the door on roller skates still makes me crack up. What's with the roller skates, man? But he fills the suit out. He looks good!

Aaron Carnes (Writer): After *Constructs of the State* came out, I set the interview up with Sturgeon over email. I was working on a book about the history of ska. Sturgeon was playing the Holy Diver in Sacramento. When I got there, he was MIA. I found the tour manager. He told me that Sturgeon had roller skated over to Rite-Aid. He managed to get Sturgeon on the phone and Sturgeon told him that I should drive over to Rite-Aid and pick him up.

Keep in mind, I'd never met him. We'd just spoken via email. In the Rite-Aid, I see him in line with a handful of stuff and wearing his roller skates. I introduced myself and we head over to my car. As we're driving back to the venue, he tells me he wants to go to a grocery store to get something to eat. We go to a place that is like a Whole Foods. We look around and talk about the book; he then orders a juice at the juice bar and pays for it. Then we go around the self-serve food stations and he casually puts a bunch of food into a container as we chat. He looks around and sees that no one is looking, then he says to me, "I know this isn't very ska," and then he roller skates out the front without paying for the food.

Greg Daly: At *Stoked for the Summer*, that's a festival thrown by the Bouncing Souls, we were done, and we were just chilling. The Bosstones were going up and everyone is having a good time and I get a text message from the Bouncing Souls manager. He says, "Come right now and meet me in the production office trailer!" We already got paid, so I'm like, "What's could this be?"

I go in and they are like, "This is so-and-so and he's the general manager and this is so-and-so and *he's* the head of security." I'm like, "Hey, guys…what's up…?"

So they said, "So…uh…a couple of your band guys got in a fight out in the street, outside of the dressing room." I was like, "For real?" "Yeah, they were fighting and then rolling around on the ground and one guy was trying to smash a whisky bottle over the other guy's head. Needless to say we can't have this. You gotta get your guys under control!"

I was like, "No problem, I'll take care of it." They go, "You know if they're fighting in here it's our problem, but if they are out on the street it alerts the attention of the local police and we can't have this shit here, blah blah blah blah." I was like, *"Alright! Alright! I'll handle it!"*

Then, the manager of the Bouncing Souls was like, "Yeah, I saw Donny trying to smash Brad's head with a bottle of Johnnie Walker!" and I was like, *"WHAT?!* Wait a minute…" I look around the office, "This isn't about Sturgeon?!" They were all serious, saying like, "No…" I just started laughing and they all start looking at me like I'm insane. "This is very serious," they say.

I was like, "You mean to tell me there's a problem and it's not Sturgeon causing it? You also mean to tell me that *Donny* is trying to fight…*Brad*?!"

Pete Steinkopf: We were all like…*Brad* was involved in a fight? *Brad*?!

Greg Daly: The next morning, Brad and Donny just happened to be on the same flight, sitting next to each other all the way to California. You see, it's not always Sturgeon. He gets a bad rap. No one's hands are completely clean in this band.

Kate Coysh: My time in Leftover Crack was between other projects. My schedule is pretty fuckin' strict and I don't mess around. I wanted them to have freedom to tour with other people so I phased myself out. There was never, ever, ever any drop of ill will from any of the band members or myself and it was just a natural progression and growth for all of us.

I wouldn't trade my time with them for the world. I'll talk about it with pride for the rest of my life. Who else gets to tour with their favorite childhood punk band and tour all over the world? I'm a lucky motherfucker.

Chris Mann: Eventually, I had to leave the band. There were external things in my life and as much as you want to be where you are, you have to go where you are needed. My exit was amicable and I told the guys I was leaving before the summer tour. It's always bittersweet to leave something that you worked so hard for and earned your keep. It's definitely something that I can be proud of.

Alice Hour (Vocals—Leftover Crack, In Evil Hour): I joined Leftover Crack after Kate Coysh left. I was the second singer…well, *a* backing singer—I dunno. I don't want to be grandstanding and say, "I was second vocals!" I definitely did back-up vocals.

I had been introduced to Sturgeon for the first time at *Rebellion* 2012, but I can't say it was a conversation. It was more like, "Oh, my God, that's Sturgeon!" Their bass player and drummer couldn't get into the UK, so they used the guy that was driving with them for drums. It was an absolute car crash of a show.

Sturgeon and Brad have always sought out to work with female artists and have always made it a point to include women in projects. They do that not in a tokenistic sense but in a sense of wanting to broaden their output and have people from different backgrounds add their own individual things.

I always loved the band. The bottom line is that it was good songs and had some death metal vocals. I think the big thing that draws a lot of people is the offense, the exaggerated imagery, which, when done right, can make good points in complex topics. Despite the offense, there is an intelligence behind the complexity. You can start a conversation very quickly by the *Fuck World Trade* T-shirt, but there's truth behind that T-shirt as well. It doesn't answer any questions. But, as we look further into the lyric and the subject behind the songs, we realize that the points are quite meaty.

It's cliché to say, but it was amazing. Basically, one of my favorite bands of all time asked me to perform with them. It was a privilege and it was affirming in the sense that I must be doing something right for this band to ask me to perform with them.

And let's be honest. I was basically just another person standing on the stage—everyone is there to see Sturgeon and Brad, but the fans were really enthusiastic. There were a couple of times that things did go negative. There was one show where we were playing "Gang Control" and Sturgeon walked offstage.

Brad started playing and I thought Sturgeon was going to come back, but he didn't! So, I sang the whole thing and the fans were into it. Their fists were in the air and they were hugging me afterward. It was a really positive experience out of something that could have been really bad. The fans were so cool about it!

On the last night I was on tour, Sturgeon got onstage and I want to say he was *uncomplimentary* about the soundman, but he was more pointed than that. Halfway through the show, the venue started to give back refunds. So, don't insult the soundman. The whole venue turned against him almost immediately. He left and went backstage. That was literally the only time I had people climb over the barrier, get in my face, and yell, "You go back and get him!" So I'm like, *"You* go back and get him!"

The driver had to sneak him out of the venue with half the audience chasing them down the street.

To be fair, the venue was trying to wind him up. The backstage was about the size of a large refrigerator and the staff was like, "You need to go out there and apologize." If you tell Sturgeon to do something, he'll do the opposite. And that's what happened.

That's kind of the beauty of Leftover Crack, isn't it? Half the people go and want to see a car crash and then, when there is a car crash, they start bitching about it after. And also, everybody wants a Leftover Crack story to tell afterward or bait Sturgeon to get a rise out of him, and when they get one, everyone kind of acts surprised about it.

Brad Logan: I was hanging out at this club one night in Long Beach and this guy comes up to me and puts his hand out to shake mine. I didn't know who it was and I was in the middle of a conversation with somebody. So, I shook his hand and said, "Hi." The guy looked vaguely familiar, but I went back to the conversation that I was having. Then a voice said, "Brad, it's Tim."

I did a double take and realized that it was Tim Armstrong. I didn't recognize him because of his beanie and the long beard that was down to the middle of his chest. I was blown away. It had been about fifteen years since we had seen each other. I gave him a bear hug and we had a laugh. We talked for a few minutes about how cool it was to see each other so unexpectedly. I told him I missed him. And I did.

Because the meeting was spontaneous, I didn't have time to think about any of the past conflicts or struggle that we had been in regarding Leftover Crack. All that anxiety, all that worry, I didn't feel any of that in that moment—I didn't even think of it. I was just glad to see my friend and I think maybe he felt the same way.

I felt as comfortable around him as I did all those years of touring together. We just clicked, as old friends do. He was with somebody else and was leaving. We agreed that someday we should get together and catch up on things and that was it. I haven't seen him since then, but I'd really like to.

42

The Death of Alec

Brad Logan: I talked to Alec early in the evening the night before he died. He was in a pretty bad spot. He was very sad. I tried to talk him down and tried to remind him of all the great things he had going on in his life and how much everybody loved him. By the end of our conversation, he seemed to be in a reasonable state of mind. I texted him later and didn't get a response. I figured he was busy and out and about.

The next morning, I woke up to a deluge of texts and missed phone calls and I just knew he was gone. I talked to Al and Sturgeon. I think we were all in shock. We had been through this before, but it didn't make it any easier. Grief never truly disappears.

I was shocked, but I wouldn't say I was totally surprised when I found out Alec had died. As is the case with most of my friends. The way we live and the groups of people we run around with— it's always expected or at least a possibility. The end is always near. A lot of us lived our lives like we had a death wish for years and years. But it's sad and it bums me out because I loved him and I'm gonna miss him. There's a profound void in my life, and in the band where he used to be. I just took it for granted that he would always be there. I'm gonna miss the guy. I'm really gonna miss the guy.

I would hope that he has found some peace and if he has, then I'm happy for him.

Ezra Kire: I wasn't surprised when I heard Alec had died. Nothing surprises me anymore. I ran into him a couple of times after I left the band. He moved back to NY and he lived in my neighborhood. It was always nice to bump into him.

Alec was a lovable rascal. I liked him just because of that. Confucius said that goodie goodies are the thieves of virtue and by virtue, he meant wisdom. Essentially what he meant is that people that are all good are the thieves of wisdom, because wisdom is comprised of both the good and the bad. You must know both sides of everything. Alec was a dichotomous character that was well aware of the polarized world that we live in and I fuckin' loved him for it. You always knew what you were going to get from him but you had to go through the stages. He was a rapscallion. You knew what you were going to get because the empathetic side always won out in the end but you had to go through all the steps to get it.

I think Leftover Crack was Alec's lifeblood. He loved it. It's the one thing he did really well and it was consistent throughout his life. He met Sturgeon when was he was very young and they played together for a long-ass time.

Ara Babajian: I was surprised when I found out that Alec had passed away. He was the last one out of our band that I thought would die. I mean, he'd just gotten a dog and a vasectomy…so, it seemed like he was planning for the future. The emotions I felt at first were like a factual acceptance of the matter. Then, as the hours and days went by it became total heartbreak and heaviness. I wound up back in therapy trying to deal with the loss. It's been a really deep and horrible loss for me, perhaps the worst death I've ever experienced. Those feelings just continue. They're merely absorbed and I'm learning how to live with them. I'm sad that I can no longer bullshit with my friend, can no longer look forward to playing music together, having dinner, calling each other on the phone and figuring out life.

There's extra emotional resonance for me because the drummer and bass player relationship is such a huge thing. We had an extremely soulful musical connection, bordering on ESP. That's something you look for all your musical life. Most people never find it. Also, he'd been with me from the start of my musical career in New York, which was Agent 99. Then, for the next thirty years, we'd essentially grown up together. We went through all of life's stages together and all of our career stages together, reinforcing each other at every turn. I can't emphasize enough how horrible and haunting it is to lose someone you are that close to. He was the first musician I met in New York with whom I really clicked. And when that happens, it certainly makes you feel a lot less alone in the world.

Ezra Kire: When I went to Alec's wake, somebody asked me if I wanted to speak. I wasn't planning on speaking, but I figured, "why not," ya know? I told this story at his wake because it sums him up. One day Alec came to me, and we had just finished a show and he had finished paying everybody out. And he said, "Well, we won't be working with that guy anymore." And I said, "What do you mean?" He said, "He failed the honesty test." I said, "What's the honesty test," ya know? Well, every time Alec would pay someone, he would pay them one dollar too much, and if they counted the money and kept it, it means they failed the honesty test. I thought that was amazing. Then I thought, "I wonder if he was doing that to me?" But I never counted the money.

Some of us there played some songs. I played with Sturgeon for the first time in many years. Playing music with Sturgeon at the wake was an odd feeling. It was simultaneously the most comfortable and most empty that I had felt in a long time. I played those songs on stage for so long that it was second nature to be up there. It really felt good.

I had already put an endcap on music a long time ago. I did that in honor of Alec, his life, and contributions to the world. I've had differences with the band for a long time, but for just a moment, I wanted to forget about that and just focus on Alec.

Ara Babajian: Alec brought solidity both musical and managerial. He was sober throughout my tenure and managed the band's finances with a mercenary intelligence. He took pride in the band and it really showed in the consistency of his playing and in the way he would look out for us on a personal level. He booked all the hotels, always made sure each of us got all the dumb little things we needed on tour, always made sure we got paid, never bitched about anything, even when personalities in the band became truly difficult. He just kept his focus and thus we kept ours. He stayed strong and dependable, which enabled us to either fuck off or stay strong accordingly.

Alec is irreplaceable. The relationship, the chemistry between he and Sturgeon was one of the main engines of Leftover Crack and Choking Victim. Those bands will definitely be able to carry on, Sturgeon will always find sidemen willing to play those songs, but the spirit of the band will never be the same.

43

The End...?

Sturgeon: In general, I am proud of Leftover Crack. There's very little that I'm not proud of when it comes to the band. The band has stayed true to what I wanted to do. I'm proud that I've been able to keep us out of the snares and pitfalls that a lot of bands get caught up in. I've never been shortsighted about our music and politics. I do think other people in our band have been. I've been strong enough to argue my point to steer the band in the direction I wanted to steer it in.

I do feel jaded by the many people that have betrayed me or turned on me for apparently no reason. But if the same thing repeatedly happens, sometimes maybe you have to think, "Maybe it's me?"

Here's what bothers me. I've become a victim of so much gossip that it's out of control. Honestly, like, I feel drowned in people's mistaken opinion of me and people's lies. I've never felt so slighted and so drowned and so bullied. That's how I feel.

I'm not rich. I don't have money to insulate me from this stuff. I don't have a million friends to stand up for me. I spend most of my time alone. I've spent most of my life alone because I always have had trouble making friends. All my friends are dead. The people that would stand up for me are mostly dead. There are good people out there that will stand up for me, but it's not lost on me that people are taking advantage of the fact that my friends are dead and that I am nice and that I won't call the cops and that I'm not violent. There's not really a lot of…if you fuck with me, there's not a lot you're gonna have to deal with. There's not some shitstorm that's going to come down on you.

So, I have no idea what the future of Leftover Crack will be. I'd like to say that I have a lot of songs, but I have a lot of music—I don't have lyrics. I can always write music, but I don't have concrete ideas of songs that I want to write about, or themes or subjects that I haven't already made songs about. What do I want to tackle? What can I tackle in a clever way that nobody else has? It's not stuff that is very easy for me to figure out.

To varying degrees, I've faced writer's block before. Lately, for the last few records, I've been writing the music. It's easy for me to write the music. The hard part is what the song is about. I don't know. I can't tell if it's because I'm uninspired or if I'm unhealthy, or it's just because I've sung a lot of different songs. Maybe if I wasn't as self-conscious about revisiting things as I am it would be easier. I think I have at least 100 songs out there between three bands. When does it become an exercise in futility to keep going because of money? Because we need a new record to tour on? Those are not very good motivators for me.

Because we've been, maybe, "spoiled" by having people pay attention to our stuff, it is easy to fall into the trap of thinking what you do is precious. Just because someone will pay money for something doesn't mean it's worth something. It doesn't mean it shouldn't be free.

Brad Logan: Sturgeon and I have been friends for a long time. We have an unspoken understanding. I know he has problems. I have problems, too. We don't always need to talk about our problems with each other. Is it my business to solve his problems? Is it his business to solve my problems? What does that have to do with us being in a band and making music?

Sturgeon is a very sensitive and intelligent guy underneath it all. His behavior, perhaps sometimes, seems to be contrary of that, but I know that's not true. I met him before he was "the Stza." I met him when he was twenty and I thought he was one of the funniest humans I ever met. He still is.

I do think Leftover Crack has been a success on a lot of levels. To me as a fan, I always felt the band were pushing some very important agendas lyrically—gender equality, anti-fascism, anti-homophobia, anti-transphobia—topics that matter and wrapping them in some really interesting ideas musically.

There doesn't need to be any credit assigned or credit due. That's not what it was about.

When people were attacking us physically because of the lyrical content of some of these songs, I knew that we were doing the right thing. Whatever happens now isn't even important. If the band implodes or fades away, that doesn't matter.

It seems the price to pay for what we achieved was for the members to sacrifice themselves and to become the architects of their own destruction. Was it worth it? I'm not sure.

Afterword
by Regina Dentata

I was not a crust punk, nor even a punk by some definitions. I was one of the "earnest, deadly serious hardcore" kids Brad mentions early in the book. Straight-edge spoke to me in those days. A child of a drug-addicted mother and alcoholic grandparents, having seen my sister, aunts, and cousins fall one-by-one into the grip of meth or heroin or alcohol or all of the above, I felt an internal imperative to keep myself under the strictest control. However, my family and friends were never far from my mind or heart. I didn't feel the kind of contempt for my fellows that so many of the smugger OC straight-edgers seemed to feel.

Too, as I entered college, I became radicalized. I read Ms. magazine, I quit wearing makeup, I buzzed my hair. The personal became political. *I joined a Coven!* I had become...a feminist. OC hardcore did not quite yet know how to deal with feminists in those days. Fugazi provided some direction, but straight-edgers weren't sure how to deal with them either at that point. From the ashes of Minor Threat arose this new band that no one knew how to categorize. Were they straight-edge? Ian Mackaye was cagey. Guidance on homosexuals was lacking as well. Should we be okay with them? Uh...maybe if they're not all flamboyant. Are we vegetarians or not? You're not truly straight edge if you eat meat.

Or fuck that. We're into health and fitness. Protein is a part of that. Abortion? Well, how does that align with Shelter's newfound Hare Krishna faith? Even the guitarist of Inside Out, one of my favorite bands at the time, fell under the Hare Krishna spell. Never could figure that one out.

The resulting mishmash of ill-conceived opinions and practices further alienated me. Once again, I found I didn't fit in completely. Some shows didn't allow moshing because women might find the aggression off-putting. I respected the sentiment but hated the application; I loved to mosh and stage-dive with the occasional boost from the fellows in Infest (Hi, Joe and Matt!). In a subculture where I was the minority, I got completely drowned out. As it happened, I left Southern California for graduate school on the Central Coast. I attended a few shows—Downcast, Green Day, and Born Against at the Red Barn—but soon I abandoned "the scene" for academia.

It seems like no coincidence that Brad and I met each other now. Aside from mere geography (I moved back to SoCal sometime after graduate school), I think what brought us together is a shared belief. It seems to me that what unifies crust punks, squatters, musicians, scenesters, hardcore fans, straight-edgers, activists, vegans, and, dare I say, feminists, is this resounding "NO." No, we shouldn't treat people and other living beings as commodities. No, we won't participate in our own exploitation. No, we won't tell others how to live. And, no, we won't withhold the necessities of life, food, shelter, medicine, autonomy, or love from those who refuse to become useful or even acceptable.

Janine St. Clair captures this sentiment in the interlude on mental health:

"And that brings up the issue of what we do when artists we like or admire, or even our friends, say things that aren't good or if they behave erratically. It may be the social worker in me, but I feel compelled to offer support to others if I see somebody behaving erratically or if their behavior shifts in a way that doesn't seem right, whether it's offensive or just bizarre…When I see those behaviors, it's a red flag to me. There must be a reason why they are behaving the way they are. But I do feel conflicted over the 'you're no longer invited here' mindset."

She attributes her urge to reach out to her career as a social worker, but I would suggest the opposite. This urge, while not all-pervasive, is prevalent in counterculture communities. Perhaps her instinct to offer support is an outgrowth of that same resounding NO that led her to punk in the first place. It seems to me that Brad's ability to wrangle the banged up, beat up, strung out, burned out, and down and out without moralizing or ultimatums is an implicit example of this shared belief in action throughout the book. In a poignant moment, Brad uses humor and clear-eyed practicality to cut through the maelstrom of addiction that churned around him and the band, "Hey, Darby Crash! Wipe the heroin off your shoulder and get in the fucking van!"

I am writing this afterword on the night of Hexennacht, a Satanist holiday, in remembrance of those who died as a result of persecution. It's a somber day of reflection, and in that way perfectly reflects my mood upon finishing the book. I mentioned that it seems like no coincidence that Brad and I met now. The shared circles we run in today still involve artists and free-thinkers, but they're gatherings in support of secular charities that provide relief to the suffering. Without moralizing, without judgement, without demands. Just a shared understanding of the various ways in which we scream our NO in an indifferent world.

Regina Dentata, Minister of Satan
May 2021

Timeline

1992   Choking Victim forms

1994   Choking Victim releases *Crack Rock Steady* 7-inch (Self-Released)

1996   Choking Victim releases *Squatta's Paradise* 7-inch (Self-Released)

1997   F-Minus forms

1998   F-Minus releases *Failed Society* 7-inch (Hellcat)

1998   Choking Victim releases *Victim Comes Alive* 7-inch (Hellcat)

1998   F-Minus releases *Won't Bleed Me* 7-inch (Pelado)

1998   Choking Victim breaks up

1999   Choking Victim releases *No Gods/No Managers* (Hellcat)

1999   F-Minus releases *F-Minus* (Hellcat)

1999   Leftover Crack forms

1999   Leftover Crack plays first show at Headline Records, Hollywood

2000   Leftover Crack releases *Rock the 40 oz.* 7-inch (Bankshot)

2001   F-Minus releases *Suburban Blight* (Hellcat)

2001   Leftover Crack releases *Mediocre Generica* (Hellcat) on 9/11

2001   Ara quits Leftover Crack

2001   Morning Glory releases *This is No Time Ta Sleep* (Self-Released)

2001   Crack Rock Steady 7 / F-Minus split released (Hell-Bent)

2002   INDK releases *Kill Whitey!* (Go-Kart)

2003	F-Minus releases *Wake Up Screaming* (Hellcat)
2003	Morning Glory releases *The Whole World is Watching* EP (Blacknoise)
2004	Leftover Crack releases *Fuck World Trade* (Alternative Tentacles)
2004	Phoenix Riot
2004	Brandon Chevalier-Kolling RIP
2004	F-Minus breaks up
2004	Brad Logan moves to Kansas
2007	Star Fucking Hipsters forms
2007	Leftover Crack and Citizen Fish release *Deadline* (Fat/Alternative Tentacles)
2007	Nick Phillips RIP
2008	Star Fucking Hipsters releases *Untill We're Dead* (Fat)
2009	Star Fucking Hipsters releases *Never Rest in Peace* (Alternative Tentacles)
2009	Ezra quits Leftover Crack
2011	Star Fucking Hipsters releases *From the Dumpster to the Grave* (Fat)
2012	Star Fucking Hipsters breaks up
2012	Morning Glory releases *Poets Were My Heroes* (Fat)
2014	Morning Glory releases *War Psalms* (Fat)
2015	Leftover Crack releases *Constructs of the State* (Fat)
2018	Leftover Crack releases *The E-Sides and F-Sides* (Fat)
2020	Alec RIP
2021	*Architects of Self-Destruction* released (Rare Bird)

Who's Who

Adam Zuckert: Drums—F-Minus, Final Conflict

Alec Baillie: Bassist—No Commercial Value, Choking Victim, Leftover Crack, Agent 99

Alice Hour: Vocals—In Evil Hour, Leftover Crack

Amery Smith a.k.a. AWOL: Drummer—F-Minus, Leftover Crack, Suicidal Tendencies, Beastie Boys, BS2000

Ara Babajian: Drummer—Leftover Crack, Star Fucking Hipsters, the Slackers, Agent 99

Bill Cashman: First Leftover Crack Fan; Manager—Star Fucking Hipsters, World/Inferno Friendship Society

Boots Riley: Vocals/Emcee—the Coup; Filmmaker

Brad Logan: Guitar/Bass/Vocals—F-Minus, Leftover Crack, the Adolescents; Hellcat Records Employee

Brandon Chevalier-Kolling: Drummer—Leftover Crack, X-Possibles

Buju Banton: Famous Jamaican dancehall singer

Caroline Bowden: Resident—C-Squat, Serenity

Charlie Ackerman: Hellcat Records Employee

Chickenman: Man about town

Chris Mann: Guitar—Intro5pect, Leftover Crack

Chris Ryan: Guitar/Vocals—Team Spider; Filmmaker

Christina White: Epitaph Records Radio and Publicity Department

Coach: Drummer—Two Man Advantage, The Bullies, Leftover Crack

Dale Tomlinson: UK Van Driver/Tour Manager—Leftover Crack

Dave Dictor: Vocals—MDC aka Millions of Dead Cops

Denise Vertucci: Head—Fistolo Records; Contributing member of Mischief Brew

Dick Lucas: Vocals—Subhumans (UK), Culture Shock, Citizen Fish

Donny Morris: Drums—Leftover Crack, Intro5pect

Eden Brower: Former Resident—C-Squat, Fetus; Vocals—Eden and John's East River String Band

Erica Daking: Vocals/Guitar—F-Minus

Erik Petersen: Vocals/Guitar—Mischief Brew, The Orphans, Kettle Rebellion

Ezra Kire: Guitar/Vocals—Leftover Crack, Morning Glory, Choking Victim, INDK

Fat Mike: Bass/Vocals—NOFX; Founder—Fat Wreck Chords

Frank Piegaro: Guitar—Star Fucking Hipsters, The Degenerics

Greg Daly: Tour manager—Leftover Crack, Choking Victim, Napalm Death, Subhumans, too many others to name; Employee—R5 Productions

Jack Terricloth: Vocals—World/Inferno Friendship Society

Janine St. Clair: Bass/Vocals—Witch Hunt, The Brood

Jello Biafra: Vocals—Dead Kennedys, Guantanamo School of Medicine, Head: Alternative Tentacles Records

Jen Johnson: Bass/Vocals—F-Minus

Jesse Cannon: Engineer/producer

Jesse Michaels: Vocals—Operation Ivy, Common Rider, Classics of Love; visual artist and filmmaker

Jesse Townley: Vocals—Blatz, The Criminals, Pathogens; General Manager—Alternative Tentacles Records, Lookout! Records

Joe Jack Talcum: Guitar/Vocals/Keyboard—The Dead Milkmen, The Low Budgets, The Town Managers

Joe Porter: US Van Driver/Merch Person—Leftover Crack

John John Jesse: Bass—Nausea; Guitar—Morning Glory

Josiah Steinbrick: Bass—F-Minus

JP Otto: Drummer—Leftover Crack, Morning Glory, The Stockyard Stoics

Kate Coysh: Vocals—Leftover Crack, Reivers

Kristen Ferrell: Artist

Lars Frederiksen: Guitar/Vocals—Rancid, Lars Frederiksen and the Bastards

Mike Trujillo: Producer; Guitar—Leftover Crack

Mikey Erg: Drummer—The Ergs!, Star Fucking Hipsters, Direct Hit!, way too many other bands to list here

Nico de Gaillo: Vocals—Star Fucking Hipsters, Casa de Chihuahua

Nicole Enriquez: Guitar/Vocals—Witch Hunt

Penny Rimbaud: Drummer/Lyricist/Producer—Crass

Pete Steinkopf: Guitar—Bouncing Souls; Producer

Pezent Shayne: Bassist—Choking Victim; C-Squat Resident

Renee Louise: Vocals—Skarp

Ron Martinez: Booking Agent—Leftover Crack, too many other bands to list

Scott Sturgeon a.k.a. The Stza a.k.a. Crack Daddy Cane: Vocals/Guitar—No Commercial Value, Choking Vicitm, Leftover Crack, Star Fucking Hipsters

Seth Olenick: Hellcat Records Intern; Photographer

Skwert: Drummer—Choking Victim, INDK; Former C-Squat Resident

Steve Albini: Audio Engineer—Electrical Audio Studios; Guitar/Vocals—Big Black, Shellac

Sullivan Beck: Son of Kristen Ferrell, stepson of Brad Logan

The Wix: Hellcat Records Employee

Tim Armstrong: Vocals/Guitar—Rancid, Operation Ivy; Founder—Hellcat Records

Acknowledgments

Thank You:

Adam Zuckert, Alec Baillie, Alice Hour, Alternative Tentacles, Amery Smith, Angela Baillie, Ara Babajian, Bill Cashman, Boots Riley, Brian Santostefano, Brody Dalle, Caroline Bowden, Charlie Ackerman, Chickenman, Chris Boarts Larson, Chris Mann, Chris Ryan, Cris Qualiana, Christina White, Dale Tomlinson, Dan O'Mahony, Dave Dictor, Denise Vertucci, Dick Lucas, Donny Morris, Eden Brower, Erica Daking, Ezra Kire, Fat Wreck Chords, Frank Piegaro, Greg Daly, Hellcat Records, Jack Terricloth, Janine St. Clair, Jello Biafra, Jen Johnson, Jesse Cannon, Jesse Fisher, Jesse Michaels, Jesse Townley, Joe Jack Talcum, Joe Porter, John John Jesse, Josiah Steinbrick, JP Otto, Kate Koysh, Konstantin Sergeyev, Lars Fredriksen, Mike Burkett, Mike Trujillo, Mikey Erg, Nick Phillips, Nico de Gaillo, Nicole Enriquez, Penny Rimbaud, Pete Steinkopf, Pezent Shayne, Renne Berol, Renee Louise, Ron Martinez, Seth Olenick, Skwert, Steve Albini, Sullivan Beck, Tim Armstrong, Travis Keller, and all the fans.

Brad Thanks:

Kristen Ferrell, John Gentile, Bill Ward, Scott Sturgeon, Taylor Hamby, Nate Jackson, Tyson Cornell, Hailie Johnson, Damian Abraham, Regina Dentata, and Nick Gomez.

John Thanks:

Cathy and Joe Gentile, Brad Logan, Tyson Cornell, Hailie Johnson, Damian Abraham, Mike Ayers, Jackie Ford, Tony Rotondo, Victoria Croul, Mac Reynolds, and the Posse. Overseen by C.A.G.

Keeping Faith

BOOKS BY FENTON JOHNSON

Crossing the River: A Novel

Scissors, Paper, Rock

Geography of the Heart: A Memoir

Keeping Faith: A Skeptic's Journey

Keeping
FAITH

A SKEPTIC'S JOURNEY

FENTON JOHNSON

HOUGHTON MIFFLIN COMPANY

BOSTON   NEW YORK   2003

For information about permission to reproduce selections from
this book, write to Permissions, Houghton Mifflin Company,
215 Park Avenue South, New York, New York 10003.

Visit our Web site: www.houghtonmifflinbooks.com.

More information can be found at www.fentonjohnson.com.

Library of Congress Cataloging-in-Publication Data

Johnson, Fenton, date.
   Keeping faith : a skeptic's journey / Fenton Johnson.
      p. cm.
   ISBN 0-618-00442-4
   1. Johnson, Fenton.   2. Spiritual biography — United States.   I. Title.
      BL73.J644 A3   2003
      291.4′092—dc21
      [B]   2002032708

Book design by Anne Chalmers
Typefaces: Minion, Scala Sans

Printed in the United States of America

QUM 10 9 8 7 6 5 4 3 2 1

To Shirley Abbott
and
Barbara Kingsolver

and to those who choose the monk's path,
inside and outside the enclosure

Facing west from California's shores,
Inquiring, tireless, seeking what is yet unfound,
I, a child, very old, over waves, toward the house of maternity,
    the land of migrations, look afar,
Look off the shores of my Western sea, the circle almost circled,
For starting westward from Hindustan, from the vales of Kashmir,
From Asia, from the north, from the God, the sage, and the hero,
From the south, from the flowery peninsulas and the spice islands,
Long having wander'd since, round the earth having wander'd,
Now I face home again, very pleas'd and joyous,
(But where is what I started for so long ago?
And why is it yet unfound?)

— "FACING WEST FROM CALIFORNIA'S SHORES,"
WALT WHITMAN (1860)

CONTENTS

x   Contents

READER'S NOTE

IN THE COURSE of my research I interviewed several hundred monks (Christian and Buddhist), priests, theologians, rabbis, lay contemplatives, and scholars; I spoke with many of them several times. I have infrequently used pseudonyms, always identified as such, to honor the requests of those Roman Catholic monks who for a variety of reasons wished to remain anonymous. Quotations are transcribed from those conversations. The points of view contained in the accompanying analysis are mine and should not be ascribed to the monks and contemplatives I interviewed.

Common usage assumes the term *monk* to imply masculine, *nun* to imply feminine, but many sisters with whom I spoke perceive *nun* as carrying an implied acceptance of the persistent worldwide relegation of women contemplatives to second-class status. Accordingly, I have chosen to use *monk,* inclusive of both men and women, and to restrict the use of *nun* to those instances in which using *monk* would risk confusion. *Monk* implies not a gender but a way of life. American contemplatives, Christian and Buddhist, increasingly employ *monk* as a gender-neutral word, by way of acknowledging the historical contributions of women to contemplative practice.

For those unfamiliar with monastic life, possibly the greatest confusion arises over the relationship between the terms *monk* and *priest.* Monks have taken vows, the precise nature of which varies from one religious order to another. They usually choose a particular order because they perceive its vows to be most in keeping with their individual character and spiritual search. Priests also take vows but generally pursue a more rigorous education in the philosophy or theology of their tradition. Unlike monks, they are invested with the power to perform certain rites. In a Christian monastery such as Gethsemani, all priests are monks, but many of the monks have chosen not to become priests, sometimes because they lack the interest or skills for intensive study, sometimes because they reject the hierarchy implied in the creation of a priestly caste. Buddhism maintains similar though less formal distinctions.

Like all disciplines, religious practice has a specific vocabulary that includes terms not commonly encountered in daily conversation. I define those words as they appear, but for those unfamiliar with monastic practice or Buddhist terminology, the glossary at the back of the book may be helpful.

Because I write of religious and philosophical systems that are non-Western and non-Christian, I use the secular B.C.E. (before the common era) and C.E. (common era) in place of the Western custom of B.C. (before Christ) and A.D. (anno Domini, that is, in the year of the Lord). I have chosen to use the term *Hebrew Bible* rather than *Old Testament,* to avoid the implication of hierarchy or supersession implied by the latter. When abbreviating *Roman Catholic Church,* I have preferred *Roman Church* to the more common *Catholic Church,* since several Christian churches employ the adjective *Catholic* as part of their official names.

Given recent controversies surrounding the writing of nonfiction, I feel compelled to note that the events I describe happened as I describe them, as precisely as I am able to report within the limitations of time and space. Where the privacy of the individuals involved required fabrication or rearrangement of events, I indicate as much.

PART
ONE

1

IN SEARCH OF
THE UNFOUND

ON THIS PLEASANT EVENING of July 1996, the long, narrow chapter room at the rural Kentucky abbey of Our Lady of Gethsemani was filled with monks. Along the right wall, under an image of the risen Christ, stood our Trappist hosts, the "white monks," dressed in white robes covered with black hooded scapulars and cinched at their waists with broad leather belts. Next to them, wearing black robes, stood the Benedictines, the "black monks," the more publicly engaged, apostolic of the Roman Catholic contemplative orders. Among these monks were scattered a few women, most dressed in the white blouse and below-the-knee gray skirt favored by many post–Vatican II sisters. Along the left wall, under a batik banner of the seated Buddha, stood the Buddhist monks, some wearing maroon trimmed with saffron, others wearing saffron trimmed with maroon. A single Japanese monk wore dove-gray robes trimmed in black and white; a single Taiwanese nun wore saffron, peach fuzz sprouting from her newly shaven head. Among these Asians mingled the American Buddhists — some wearing black Zen robes, some wearing street clothes. Some of the Asians were Americans, naturalized priests and monks whose Buddhist congregations include American Jews and Roman Catholics and Protestants. The Christians and the American Buddhists were almost all Caucasian; the Asians ranged from Japanese ivory to Sri Lankan browned butter. Timothy Kelly, abbot of Gethsemani, and the exiled Dalai Lama of Tibet stood at front center, focal point for this international convocation of Buddhist and Christian monks and lay contemplatives.

The assembly presented a picture postcard of institutionalized religion, East and West: a few men on the stage ran the show, while the women — a clear majority of those present — looked on. But one does not expect

3

an embrace of gender equality from religious institutions, and I settled into the territory with a familiar interior sigh. I had been invited as a writer, which is to say as a kind of anthropologist whose job is to reserve judgment and simply observe. A significant aspect of that observation is to learn and follow local customs, and so when the time came to perform the first Buddhist bows, I followed the example of my neighbor and bent — although not too deeply; I saw myself as a skeptic and an American, inheritor and expression of centuries of Enlightenment rationalism. *All people are created equal; liberty, equality, fraternity* — this was my creed and my mantra, and I was not much given to bowing to anyone, whether to the pope or the Dalai Lama. But the writer does what he must do for the sake of the story, and so when the Dalai Lama passed I imitated my neighbor, ducking my head and joining my palms.

Then Abbot Kelly took the microphone and called upon us to pray, opening with the sign of the cross. Here I had no need to look to a neighbor; I have known this script since before memory — the fingers to the forehead, the heart, the left then the right shoulder, a simple gesture I once inhabited as easily as lifting my hand to wave goodbye . . . and I could not do it. All around me Roman Catholics made the sign of the cross, but my right hand remained at my side. The abbot's prayer was brief; before long he closed it by repeating the gesture. Again my hands hung stubbornly at my sides, dead weight. Even for the sake of the story, the body refused to go where the mind willed.

Here among the believers, seated at the foot of the bloody Christ for longer than any time since the Lenten vigils of my childhood, I was stunned by the anger that simmered up from some repressed place. I was possessed by anger — the pit in the gut, the quickening pulse; I recognized the signs. I was angry at the institution of the church, any church; angry at myself for letting it get to me *(all that therapy for nothing)*; angry at being so alone in my anger.

Or so I thought. Then across the following six days of this convocation of Christians and Buddhists from North America, Asia, and Europe, most of whom had dedicated their lives to contemplation, I discovered one word that arose so often that finally conferees agreed to a moratorium on the subject, and still it returned: anger.

Evidently I was not as alone as I had thought.

What was the source of this anger? The ready and obvious answer would be sexual repression or its aftereffects, but I am suspicious of ready and obvious answers. Desire in all its manifestations lies at the heart of what it means to be human — I know this from experience, and I would shortly learn that Buddhism posits as much in its first, foundational principle. But desire assumes many guises. Again and again the convocation participants returned to the subject of anger, but they were discussing a symptom, not a cause; the cause might be more accurately described as *longing*, with anger the result of its frustration.

But what were we longing for, and why was it yet unfound? I could not then address that question, but thanks to those hands, rigid at my sides, I understood this much: anger had taken up residence in my house, where it had dwelt long enough to take control. And — child of Western psychology — I understood that I must engage that anger if I was to find peace.

❧

This particular leg of my journey began a few months earlier in my Kentucky hometown at the Sherwood Inn, the hotel-tavern acquired by my great-grandfather Thomas Hardin Johnson in the mid-1870s and run by my family in the century-plus since. On a bright spring afternoon in March 1996 I was visiting for the celebration of my mother's eightieth birthday and standing on the Sherwood porch when my aunt poked her head out the door to tell me there was a knock at the back door.

At the Sherwood "a knock at the back door" usually means one thing, so I cut through the bar, grabbed a couple of beers, and went out back to greet one of the monks from the nearby Trappist monastery, Our Lady of Gethsemani, a crow's mile across the Kentucky hills. Brother Paul Quenon, tall, ascetically thin, and slightly grizzled as befits a poet-monk, had hiked over the steep hills that the locals call "the Knobs" to let me know that in the approaching summer Gethsemani would host an international convocation of Buddhist and Christian monks and lay contemplatives, with the Dalai Lama of Tibet in attendance. Almost thirty years in its ripening, the Gethsemani Encounter was the fruit of a 1968 meeting between the Dalai Lama and Thomas Merton, author of *The Seven Storey Mountain*, the bestselling autobiography of Merton's journey toward joining the Gethsemani community as a Trappist monk.

I did not know Brother Paul well. We first met because someone recommended his poetry to me and I was curious — what would it be like to be a poet inside the enclosure? He'd joined Gethsemani in the early 1960s, had Merton for his novicemaster, and taken solemn vows in 1968. But Paul was among the more private monks, not one who came to town to buy hammers or nails and who occasionally visited community families. On that particular spring day he wasn't delivering pressing news — a thunderstorm or a wrong turn on the path and I'd never have received it. I'd have been back in San Francisco, struggling with my next book, which I was certain would be a novel.

I accepted Brother Paul's invitation to attend the Gethsemani Encounter partly as a means of dodging the looming terror of beginning that novel. I'd been considering creating a Buddhist doctor and a Trappist monk as its principal characters, but I knew little about Buddhism and not much more about monastic practice. What better way to learn about these, I told myself, than to spend a few months researching an article about the contemplative life?

Years later I see with the crystalline vision of hindsight that my decision to attend the Encounter was not a casual detour but another step in an unfolding path. After all, my fate is so common the French assign it a name — *le donné*, the youngest child who is given to the church. Until recent times the progression among sons was clear and unyielding: the oldest male inherited the property; the second went to the military; the third went to the government; the fourth went to the church. Ninth of nine children, fourth of four boys, bookish, homosexual, I had "religious orders" all but engraved on my forehead; I was destined for the church.

But I also came of age in the 1960s, those tumultuous years in which all traditions were open for questioning and in many cases dismissal. For reasons this journey will bring me to reconsider, I determined early on never to set foot in a church except to please my mother — and sometimes not then.

A visit with American Christian and Buddhist monks would provide a quick look at the road not taken — that was how I justified my decision to attend the Encounter. I would go as a tourist, someone who rents a car, checks into a hotel, spends a day or two driving around, and returns home filled with tales about the quaint and charming ways "they" do things. I'll learn Buddhism in a few months, I thought, pick up a few stories from the monks, and combine these for a quick article. Then I'll get back to the novel and my comfortable life in my beloved San Francisco, city of self-satisfaction.

But one embarks on an interior journey at peril of one's whole way of being. What I'd planned as a quick week's visit turned into a cross-country journey through the briars and thistles of faith and (its traveling companion) desire, with no compass save for an inquiring but ignorant heart. What follows is a chronicle of a skeptic's journey into the wilderness, a casual excursion that transformed itself into a search for what it means to have and to keep faith.

2

THE GETHSEMANI
ENCOUNTER

I ARRIVED for the Gethsemani Encounter in a thunderstorm, the sky flashing and grousing and grumbling. I had arranged to spend evenings at the house where I grew up, and I stopped there to visit with my mother before heading to the monastery. Before the grass was dry she took up one of her riffs, a theme of her conversations these days — the materialism of contemporary kids, the way they expect as a given everything TV dangles in front of them. Meanwhile, the neighbors were planning pilgrimages to places where the Virgin Mary has been sighted — on Christian cable they followed the news from Medjugorje, the Balkan village where thousands had gathered in hopes of witnessing her latest apparition. Another neighbor had told my mother of apocalyptic apparitions of automobiles falling from the heavens.

Mother, for fifty-plus years a devout Catholic, deadpanned a squint at the clearing sky. "Cars falling from the clouds," she said. "Must be a bad year for the Ford dealer."

You see where I come from, the American place: faith and skepticism, the odd couple, uneasy partners under a single roof.

❧

The Encounter's opening press conference took place in a small, windowless basement room. Television cameras took up a third of the space, and their floodlights raised the room temperature to something worse than stifling. By the time the conference began, audience and panelists gleamed with a patina of sweat, but here in the late twentieth century television must be accommodated, and so under the blinding lights we squeezed into our chairs.

The Dalai Lama, smiling from behind the familiar industrial-black spectacles, opened with a short statement:

If science and technology could eliminate all our problems, we would need to question, Why have religion? Especially as religion sometimes sows more hatred than the contrary. But material development alone cannot solve our problems, and so we need a religious tradition. But if a restaurant served one kind of food at all meals and at all times it would soon have no customers. The mind needs the variety of religious traditions. Our task is to reduce conflicts between the traditions which already exist.

In answer to a question about the growing number of American Buddhists, the Dalai Lama demonstrated the calm, rational approach to religious belief that has made him so popular among Americans. "It is better for people from Christian countries to follow their own religious traditions," he said. "Some individuals will have an inclination toward the Eastern or Buddhist path. In such cases it's very important to consider the change slowly and carefully. Then if you become convinced that the Eastern path is more effective, you can adopt it." A reporter from the county newspaper asked after his stand on abortion, a charged issue in this rural, Roman Catholic corner of the world. "All human life is precious, but because of severe overcrowding we need nonviolent birth control," he said. "The best route is to become a monk — we are making a real contribution." The audience — mostly reporters — chuckled, and the Dalai Lama chuckled, but with this difference: we were laughing at what we took to be a joke; he was smiling at our refusal to take him seriously.

෴

The next morning Timothy Kelly, abbot of Gethsemani since 1973, welcomed the assembled participants. "How one lives one's life is the only true reference to the validity of one's search," he said.

Yes, indeed, I thought. And yet asked to name the message of the institutionalized church in all its forms, I would begin by listing a host of doctrines and dogmas, few of which have any direct relevance to how I live my life. *Who is this abbot,* I wondered, *and how has he made a place for himself in this authoritarian church?*

A scholar stood to set forth the Christian understanding of the universe. "Christians have a personal notion of God," he said. "We understand all creation as inherently good. Evil is a distortion of inherent goodness, caused by a fundamental misdirection of our free will." In other words, human beings introduced evil to the world, as mythologized — or narrated, if you wish — in the opening pages of the Bible, where Eve and then Adam choose to eat the fruit of the Tree of the Knowledge of Good and Evil and are cast from the Garden of Eden. The Christian speaker indicated that he would be unable to embrace a design for the universe that did not include a personal God.

The moderator handed the wireless mike to a Sri Lankan monk, who looked at it as if it were a device imported from another planet, then held it at arm's length. "The Buddha tells us that we are wasting time in discussing questions that have no answers," he said,

> and in our tradition wasting time is what you perceive as a sin. The question of whether the world was created at a single moment, or whether God exists — these questions have no answers. And there's no possibility of a meeting of Buddhist and Christian ways there. So let us instead look at the nature and causes of suffering, which issue is common to both religions. The Buddha teaches that we are born to *dukkha,* which is usually translated as "suffering" but is better translated as "dissatisfaction." And we can liberate ourselves from that dissatisfaction by cultivating the mind.

Another Buddhist speaker pointed out that in the Buddhist tradition the mind is primary and precedes every phenomenon. Everything, including one's own salvation, originates in the mind, with meditation as the key to its discipline. "'Meditation,'" he said, "is not the proper translation for the act central to Buddhism. A better word would be 'development,' because the point of the act is to develop the mind's self-awareness and through that its awareness of its interdependence with all the rest of the universe."

A Japanese Zen priest took the mike to explain the Zen Buddhist conception of human potential. "In our tradition enlightenment is inherent in us," he said. "It's as if this room has been dark, then I light a candle and bring light, so that the darkness is gone. The darkness has not gone anywhere, it's just that the darkness has been transformed into light. The potential for light was always there." In this way of seeing the world, good and evil are ever-present and interdependent: just as light implies dark, good implies evil — each contains both the implication and the contradiction of the other; each is necessary for the other's definition; each has been present throughout existence, which has no beginning or end but is round and recycling.

Norman Fischer, co-abbot of the San Francisco Zen Center, opened his comments by pulling out a portable gong, to "guide us through a few moments of meditation." *The Roman Catholics boss us around,* I groaned to myself, *and the New Agers pull out personal gongs.* Fischer spoke of "finding the monk in each of us," of the shift in the contemplative tradition from collective experience inside an institution such as a monastery to the individual meditating in a private, personal space. He ended by thanking us before describing the place of sitting meditation (zazen) in Zen Buddhism. "In zazen we practice meditation with a strong sense of the purposelessness of practice," he said. "Then we get up and resume our life just being as aware as we can be. Because sitting is supremely useless it allows us confidence in ourselves."

Fischer pointed at the crucifix that hung to one side of the chapter room. "Brother David [Steindl-Rast, one of the co-moderators] converted me to the power of the Christian message years ago, but I find the body on the cross quite sad. I ask of the Christians here: how do you work with that image which is so omnipresent in this place?"

A Korean Buddhist seconded the question. "In Mexico the cross is everywhere," he said, "and always so much bloodier than here in the United States."

I shared Fischer's objections to the image of Jesus contorted in agony — I had been raised with the crucifix only then to leave it behind, or so I'd thought until I'd been unable to make the sign of the cross. But now I was touched by the Korean monk's question. Was the image of the suffering Jesus omnipresent in Mexico because the Roman Church forced it on the poor and uneducated? Or did they find some solace in it that was beyond the comprehension of the prosperous and skeptical?

༄

The midday memorial mass for Thomas Merton, who had devoted the latter years of his life to bringing together West and East, opened with the public announcement that only Roman Catholics would be permitted to receive communion. Not even Protestants would be allowed to participate.

In the sixth century, Benedict of Nursia composed the regulations, prohibitions, and wisdom that came to be called the Rule of Benedict; it continues to be the template for most contemporary Christian monasteries. In it he places the utmost importance on how one treats a guest — beside the door to the Gethsemani reception area an engraved plaque quotes from his rule: "Let all guests that come be received like Christ." Raised in a tradition of hospitality, I took personal offense at what I considered an embarrassing violation of manners. Let us imagine: Jesus has multiplied the loaves and fishes to feed the poor and hungry, but then he posts a disciple at each pile of food to quiz the guests and to turn away any who don't meet *his* particular interpretation of dogma.

Why am I here, writing about this calcified, violence-mongering, dogmatic institution? I wrote in my notebook. *Why bother?*

Communion began. Some people, presumably Roman Catholics, processed to the priests. I stayed in my seat.

☙

During the morning sessions I came to realize that though almost all the Christians present would characterize themselves as liberals, the Buddhists spanned the range of the political spectrum — to grasp the difference between the combative Sri Lankan and, say, Abbot Norman Fischer of the San Francisco Zen Center, imagine the Reverend Jerry Falwell and Father Daniel Berrigan jointly representing Christianity. I began to realize the magnitude of my ignorance — I had thought of the term *Buddhism* as indicating a single, unified religion when in fact it encompasses denominational differences as great, perhaps greater, than those in Christianity. And yet here were Buddhist monks from conservative and liberal traditions uneasily but willingly sitting cheek by jowl — because they had been invited by outsiders, Christians who were largely ignorant of the fine points of Buddhist doctrine and so could blithely assemble such disparate elements. *What the Christians need,* I thought, *is for the Buddhists to get them together under one roof.*

☙

Among the official participants at the Gethsemani Encounter, men greatly outnumbered women; among the observers — sitting in the rear but not allowed to participate — women significantly outnumbered men. At one point in the morning's session the Sri Lankan Buddhist took the microphone. "To be sure I understand," he said. "In your tradition, women are considered inferior to men." A Trappist priest responded by illustrating the relationship: hands extended, one high at his shoulder, the other down at his waist.

A remarkable point about this exchange: as world religious traditions go, Christianity, even in its more conservative forms, is relatively enlightened in its attitudes toward women. In many traditional Asian Buddhist communities, for example, women are still considered untouchable when they are menstruating. The exchange between the Sri Lankan and the Trappist brought me to wonder at the historical roots of religious institutions' denigration of women, especially in Christianity, where Jesus was notable for his open and embracing attitude toward all outcasts, including women.

Then Dr. Yifa charged to the front of the room for her presentation and we straightened our backs and paid attention, partly because of her role as the only Asian woman present, partly because of her youth, and partly because Taiwanese Buddhism has no centralized institutions poised to punish and so, unlike the Christian women, she spoke relatively unfettered by obligation or fear.

Yifa began her Buddhist studies in her native Taiwan. "I went to the temple and told them I wanted to become a Buddhist nun," she said. "But I looked carefully to see if they treated men and women equally. When I saw that they did, then I shaved my head." Several times she referred to her recently granted doctorate in Buddhist studies from Yale University. "My master realized we have to understand American culture if we are to function in the world, and so he sent me to Yale for my studies," she said. From Yale she went to California, and she spoke now with a mix of Chinese-accented English and Valley-speak.

The microphone was passed to the Japanese Zen monk. "In Japan the number of monks and nuns is decreasing," he said. "Why is it that the number of nuns in Taiwan is so great? Please tell me your secret. Or if you can't tell me, please export some of your monks and nuns to us!"

Amid laughter Yifa rose. "If you offer women equal positions we will come," she said. "Because my temple provides equal opportunity it attracts intelligent people."

Later I buttonholed Yifa for a conversation under a massive ginkgo in the monastery's meditation garden — appropriately enough, since ginkgos, like Buddhism, were imported to America from Asia. "I joined the *sangha* [the community of monks] to make it richer and more attractive to others," she said. "A pond is dead water unless it has a stream of new water coming in." Her comment brought to mind the diminished and aging monastic communities of the West, even as she pointed out how coming to America changed her way of seeing herself:

I've become more critical as a result of coming to America. We have a rule that even older nuns have to bow to the young male monks. The rule isn't often followed, but since studying in America I'm filled with the confidence to challenge that. I don't think of all the truths as ultimate but judge them against their historical background.

The Buddha didn't write but only spoke his *dharma* — his teachings. The oldest disciple of the Buddha — who organized the first major council after the Buddha's death — was much against women, and he oversaw that first discussion of the various memories of the Buddha's precepts. Later precepts were added by men, never by women, and there was always a fear of women. The men were afraid of their own weakness — for them women were a challenge.

She suggested that if Christianity is to be accepted by educated people, its teachers should not talk so much about God. "If I were a Christian priest, I'd preach about loving-kindness, compassion, and wisdom, but not about God." Our conversation reminded me of how ignorant I was of the history of the institution that as much as any had shaped who I am. I knew that Jesus embraced outcasts, but I knew little about the history that bridged his life and teachings to the churches that preach exclusion and misogyny as directives from God.

&

As the afternoon session was about to begin, a young priest sat next to me. "Catholic, I assume?" he said with a smile — a conversation-opening pleasantry. *"No!"* I responded, and I saw my vehemence reflected in his startled eyes. My heart beat faster and I found myself speaking with more force than I thought myself capable of feeling about a subject I thought I'd resolved long ago. "Well, I was raised a Catholic," I said, "but I'm a gay man and the Catholic Church has made clear it has no place for me."

Where had this anger come from? Shall I detail its sources? I grew up in a sexually repressive culture, an agony hardly limited to gay men or to Roman Catholics but especially acute in a small Southern town removed from cosmopolitan influences that might have intimated a wider variety of ways of being in the world. In the 1950s and early 1960s, the combination of unchallenged priestly authority and repression of any mention of sex and sexuality created an ideal environment for childhood abuse — emotional, physical, and sexual. In the rural Catholic schools of my childhood I witnessed the first two types; the third would remain outside the pale of language for another forty years, only then to reveal itself, to my sorrow, to be as much an aspect of that authoritarian system as the more public forms of abuse. As I came of age I found most churches to be emphatic supporters of the war in Vietnam long after it could be defended as a righteous response to injustice or essential to national defense. Some churches supported the civil rights struggles of African Americans, but more stayed on the sidelines, while some actively preached discrimination and intolerance. Meanwhile, Roman Catholicism betrayed its explicit mission as a sacramental church, preserving the power of a dwindling population of aging priests rather than returning to its historical roots by allowing priests to marry or women to perform sacramental functions.

Throughout the 1980s and 1990s I helped some of the most virtuous men of my acquaintance as they died of HIV, when silence was the best the dying and their caretakers could hope for from institutionalized churches. Many priests and ministers suggested the sufferers deserved their fate, and almost all helped spread the disease by blocking or criticizing frank discussion of sex and sexuality. When my HIV-positive lover, a Jew and the only son of Holocaust survivors, began to grapple with his mortality, I asked if he might find some comfort in attending temple or synagogue. He shrugged off the suggestion. After his death, in a desperation of grief I considered returning to the church of my childhood — what was religion for but to offer solace at such dark moments? But crashing a party to which I had been so explicitly disinvited seemed a fool's invitation to more pain. I kept my distance.

A reasonable observer might comfortably characterize the history of the institutionalized church as a series of greater and lesser blunders, and yet its priests and ministers and bishops still claim the authority to judge the realities of our lives. Excepting its size, my family is typical: among my siblings I have a divorced brother and two divorced sisters, all of whom have remarried outside the Roman Church, as well as another sister married in a Protestant church because the Roman Church would not sanctify her marriage to a previously divorced man — and then I am the gay son. Of eight children who lived to adulthood, the Roman Church rejected five, in each case for reasons connected to the most courageous and difficult decisions of our lives. A woman frees herself from an ugly marriage, a woman marries a man she loves, a man decides he cannot lie to himself or others, and the Church responds by naming us outcasts.

The young priest's question ("Catholic, I assume?") hardly deserved my retort, and as the afternoon session began I felt the familiar gnaw of guilt. At the same time, another familiar voice suggested that the extraordinary fact lay not in my snapping back but in my very presence here in the chapter room. Others had grown up with similarly unpleasant memories of their childhood churches, only at some point simply to cut bait and walk away. Why couldn't I?

As if in response to my thoughts, a Buddhist speaker rose. "Anger is a bad thing. Under no circumstances can it be accepted as a good thing, because when it is present love cannot be."

Throughout the afternoon speakers addressed the subject. Father James Wiseman, a theologian from Catholic University, pointed out that "in Christian traditions some authors say all anger is wrong, to be done away with, gotten rid of. But others, chief among them Thomas Aquinas, say anger is a proper response to injustice, and the fight against injustice arises from that anger." In a later, private conversation Blanche Hartman, co-abbess of the San Francisco Zen Center, challenged that concept. "I found this question of righteous anger and injustice coming mostly from the Catholics, who have a notion in their tradition of a just war," she said.

> I supported World War II but now I don't feel as if war solves any problems — or at least that it makes more problems than it solves. My internal experience of righteous anger is one of duality, separation — "I'm right, you're wrong." That doesn't mean I don't grieve over injustice but I can't fix it by being right and making someone else wrong. That's power against power. . . . This is our challenge: how to be in the presence of anger without being caught up in it, a center of peace in the presence of turmoil.

Her comments articulated one aspect of the longing so palpably present in the room. *That* was what I and the Encounter participants wanted: to be able to remain calm in the presence of anger; to feel our emotions fully but not to be their slaves.

✍

Midway through the Encounter I made an appointment with Brother Paul Quenon, who had extended the invitation to attend. The weather was gloriously cool and we sat outside, away from the comings and goings of the chapter room.

I asked Paul if he thought there was a connection between the urgency with which the Encounter dialogue returned to the discussion of anger and the absence of the mention of desire among a convocation of people many of whom had taken vows of celibacy. "Monastic life is a search for purity of heart," Paul said.

> For the fathers of the church, the two basic passions were desire and anger, but today we're more comfortable talking about anger than talking about desire. It's interesting that while everyone at the Encounter speaks of anger, no one has brought up the issue of celibacy — but anger is the other side of desire. We desire something or someone, then we don't get what we want and we get angry. Or we do get what we want, only to discover it doesn't fulfill our desires, and *then* we get angry. . . . When you get together a group of people who have devoted their lives to serenity, it's not surprising that anger would come up again and again.

❧

Short, stocky, bald, with bushy black eyebrows like brush strokes angled across a rice paper complexion, the Japanese Zen priest opened his presentation with a parable — across the week I came to think of him as the storyteller in our midst. "To understand this story," he began, "you must understand that in Japanese *tori* means 'bird,' and *satori* is the state of enlightenment that other Buddhist traditions call nirvana.

"A monk was walking in a forest, seeking firewood, when a bird *(tori)* flew down in front of him and sang, 'Catch me!' He began to run after the bird but never caught it, so he gave up. At that point, fortunately or otherwise, a branch fell on the bird — on *satori* — and killed it. The bird," he said, "might be called Zen meditation." The story illustrates the importance of refusing to be attached to achievement:

> Zen cannot start without doubt. Each Zen master starts his life with great doubt, not a simple or objective or conscious question such as "What is it?" but instead a greater, all-encompassing doubt. . . . So the Zen monk always teaches the importance of "doubtness." If a man climbs to the top of a high ladder he not only has nothing to do, he'll also have pride in what he's accomplished. The Zen student must get there and then forget everything, all the struggle. We say, "Soup that tastes of miso is not good miso soup" — meaning that you have to lose the essence in order to succeed. Thus here at Gethsemani we should

not search for a common territory — a place where we're not alien — that would be an illusion, because we *are* alien to each other. The only way is deep and full respect for the other as we are.

Once I had expected that religion would explain the world, then I rejected it when its explanations failed the test of logic. But as I listened to the Japanese monk I considered that perhaps the error lay not in religion's faulty explanations but in my faulty expectations. Perhaps religion might serve some purpose other than to satisfy reason's demand to know why.

⁂

In 1953, warned by followers of impending imprisonment, perhaps death, at the hands of the Chinese Communists, the Dalai Lama, then eighteen years old, fled the Tibetan capital of Lhasa for a tortuous journey across the Himalayas to Dharamsala, India, where he continues to live in exile, removed from his native land and the Tibetans whom he had vowed to lead until death.

In 1996, seven Trappist monks of the community of Atlas, Algeria, were warned by local Christians that their lives were in danger from Islamic extremists. Following procedures set forth in their governing Rule of Benedict, the monks convened to establish consensus as to their course of action. On the first secret ballot they voted to flee, even though the Trappists take a vow of stability which binds them until death to their communities and to the places where those communities are established. After passing the night in prayer and contemplation, they took a second secret ballot, in which they voted unanimously to honor their vows by remaining in Algeria. Within weeks they were found with their throats cut.

The abbot of the Algerian community had written a "spiritual testament," distributed to the Encounter participants. "If it should happen one day," he wrote, "that I become a victim of the terrorism which now seems ready to encompass all the foreigners living in Algeria, I would like my community, my church, my family to remember that my life was *donné* [given] to God and to this country . . . I have lived long enough to know that I share in the evil which seems, alas, to prevail in the world." He refers to the assassin whose visit he anticipates as "you, my last minute friend, who would not have understood what you were doing." "Yes, for you too I say this *thank you*," he wrote, "and this *A-Dieu*, 'to God' — to commend you to the God in whose face I see yours."

The monks' murders were fresh in the memory of the Trappist who presented their stories, and he described their deaths as any devout Catholic would see them: the culmination of the spiritual ideal in martyrdom, in imitation of Jesus. And yet what is the worth of a life? For the sake of a vow, for the sake of one's word, does one preserve life or give it up? An American Buddhist rose to point out that a Buddhist might say that the Trappists, in deciding to stay and face almost certain death, had not helped anyone and had in fact brought more evil into the world by provoking their assailants into violence.

For a shocked moment the Catholics looked blankly at one another, uncertain how to address this questioning of martyrdom, the supreme Christian gesture. A Trappist abbot rose to note that those most distressed by the story of the Algerian Trappists' decision to choose martyrdom were Buddhists, and he turned to the Venerable Ghosananda, a Cambodian monk known internationally for his work among the refugee camps at the Vietnamese and Thai borders during the worst years of the massacres under the Khmer Rouge regime. "Speak to us from your experience," the Trappist asked Ghosananda, "from those years in Cambodia — compare the place of the monks murdered in Cambodia to the Trappists who chose death in Algeria."

For the first time since the Encounter's opening, Ghosananda took the microphone. He was a tiny man, wizened and spotted with age and possessed of a tranquility born of suffering. During the reign of the Khmer Rouge, some fifty thousand of his fellow monks had been murdered, along with countless countrymen. In Vietnamese refugee camps Ghosananda had ministered to thousands of Cambodians fleeing for their lives.

Now he took the microphone from the Trappist abbot and spoke in soft, barely audible, heavily accented English. "In Cambodia we say, If you know suffering, then you understand the dharma."

A long silence followed. In his comment I considered how, among my relatives and friends, those with the most complex relationship to spirituality, whether manifested as religious devotion or vehement atheism, were so often those who had suffered in some profound and particular way: a painful divorce, a dead lover or child, a difficult marriage, growing up gay, or perhaps simply possessing an especially sensitive heart.

❧

Somewhere in that last week in July a day arrived when, below conscious perception, my body realized summer was ending. For two months now the sun had beaten down, brutal at midday, and then the moment arrived when I felt the promise of autumn in the slanting light that signals summer's end.

Across the highway from the monastery drive, the land slopes upward to a low hill crowned by a statue of St. Joseph. The hill is not steep or particularly high but it sits alone. Its top offers views for miles in all directions, to the wooded ridges that define and enclose the bowl of this wide valley. In the golden dying light a line of black-robed Benedictines were climbing the hill, and I pulled my car to the roadside to watch. The sun slipped from the sky, trailing the spectrum from fiery red through orange and yellow and into the indigo of night encroaching from the east. From my vantage point the Benedictine monks were silhouettes in black against the rainbow sky. In their procession I felt some connection to something that had come before and would be here long after I am gone, long after the monastery is gone.

The next day I was up at dawn to drive to the monastery for lauds, the second of the canonical offices (that is, ritual prayers), held in praise of the Creator of the rising sun. Mist steamed from the fields and clung to the trees, where it caught and held the gathering light. As I turned into the monastery drive, the sun broke through the rising mist like a koan. Now a line of Buddhist monks dressed in saffron robes were ascending the hill to the statue of St. Joseph. From below I saw them illuminated by the blinding ball of the rising sun and it was as if nothing had changed in ten hours except, magically, the color of the robes.

The abbot of St. John's Monastery, a Benedictine abbey in Minnesota, opened Friday afternoon's last full session. "The first word of the Rule of Benedict is *Listen.* My own church has been arrogant in telling God where God can speak and God will not abide that — and so I have come to understand the importance of listening."

As if to underscore the tensions in the Roman Church, the abbot's comments were followed by the Encounter's only presentation by a member of the Roman Church's governing hierarchy. After a week in which the liberal Christians had bent over backward to accommodate their Asian guests, Joseph Gerry, bishop of Portland, Maine, and consultor to the Vatican's Pontifical Council on Interreligious Dialogue, rose to speak. "There are no self-made saints," he said, harking back to the teachings of Augustine of Hippo, the fourth-century architect of Western Christianity generally acknowledged as the chief promoter of the doctrine that without the help of God's grace no person may achieve salvation.

In contrast, as the Buddhist speakers had pointed out, Buddhism posits that everything springs from the mind, that meditation is a means of disciplining the mind, and that reliance on help from outside — specifically, from God, or the gods — is no more than a crutch that absolves us of confronting the terrible, liberating truth that we are what we do, no less but no more. As I listened to Bishop Gerry I considered whether Buddhism, with its emphasis on self-reliance, is more spiritually in tune with American-style democracy than Christianity, which is hierarchical from its very positing of God as the power enthroned above us all.

Bishop Gerry offered a reality check for those who wanted to believe that the differences between the two religions were merely superficial. In his talk he told us what we must believe if we are to call ourselves Christian — and, by extension, exactly what we must believe if we are to be saved. He concluded his talk by focusing on what we will become after our deaths, in marked contrast to the emphasis of the Buddhists on how we spend our lives. His choice of verbs pointed up the difference — he spoke of "being saved," a phrase that shifts responsibility away from the individual to invoke a beneficent outside force (in Christian theology, grace). Meanwhile Buddhists spoke of "achieving nirvana," with the phrase implying that each of us is the actor in determining his or her fate.

Not that Buddhists were immune to either/or thinking: the truculent Sri Lankan rose to accuse Bishop Gerry of "building castles in the air" in his frequent invocation of God and supernatural powers. Their tart exchange manifested the energy that uses religious belief as a means to the end of defining and then declaring war on the Other.

❧

That Friday afternoon I sat with the Japanese Buddhist priest, whose cheerful parables had provided an accent of humor in a conference that at times veered dangerously close to lugubrious. Like many monks of his generation, he described his arrival at a monastery as less a matter of choice than as the result of economic straits and tradition.

I've been a monk since two years old, but I feel it was my fate to become a monk. I'm the youngest of ten. Temple masters have no families — so some devout parents will give their children to the temple — they believe that if they donate a child, boy or girl, to the temple the next seven generations of the family will go to heaven. I was earning money from chanting at ten years old. My friends teased me — maybe their teasing was the beginning of my consciousness of being a monk.

He had never before been to America or even in a Catholic monastery, but he recognized the essence of Gethsemani as monastic and felt very much at home. "The number of monks is decreasing everywhere in the world, but there are still people who seek the truth," he said. "The more the world becomes secular, the more important this kind of place becomes."

Leaving my conversation with the Japanese monk, I thought ruefully of my childhood: *youngest of nine children, a loner in childhood, teased by my classmates . . . maybe that was the beginning of my consciousness of being a monk.* But then what does it mean to be a monk? My storytelling monk had supplied as good a starting place as I could imagine: "People who seek the truth."

❧

The schedule listed an evening "Fire Ritual," but before I could ask for the details a portly Benedictine moved among us like a border collie among sheep, separating us into Buddhist and Christian camps. The Buddhists were to carry burning incense, the Christians lighted candles, as we ascended the hill double file to the foot of the statue of St. Joseph, where the *schola* — the monastic choir — was to sing a program of medieval music.

By now many of the Buddhists had departed, and the Benedictine choirmaster was much distressed at our ragged lineup. "Too many Christians!" he wailed. He ducked inside the abbey and rounded up a few straggling Buddhists, then agreed in the interests of symmetry to allow a crossover by some of the more ecumenically minded Christians. He explained each line's role twice — "complex as a football play," my notes read. Veteran of too many protest marches, I foresaw fighting the wind to keep the candle lit, only to have my pants spattered with wax.

But the evening turned out serene and uncharacteristically calm — it was almost possible to keep a candle lit while climbing the hill. The sun wrapped itself in a cloak of apricot and old rose while the landscape of my childhood gradually unfolded at my feet. My evening and morning visions merged: the Benedictines in their black robes, the Trappists in their white robes, the Asians in saffron and maroon to match the deepening sunset, unfurling up the emerald hillside in two lines, the medieval harmonies punctuated by the trills of redwing blackbirds. Across the highway an elderly couple was picnicking, and as we filed to the statue with our candles and incense, the wife took a photograph, its flash a small, brilliant diamond in the dusk.

I sat my internal skeptic on the dunce chair and told him sternly, *You see: a little bit of discipline and your Benedictine monk has done what portly drama queens do — created this beautiful moment, a fitting end to a rich week.* I considered this fact: "seeking the truth" requires only an open mind and an open heart. *Perhaps,* I thought, *some time with the monks might challenge me to find more of both.*

⌘

Over breakfast on my last morning I sat with the Venerable Ghosananda. He had lost eyebrows as well as his hair to age, and now in the cool morning air he wore a bright yellow polyester Cincinnati Bengals watchcap — on loan, I suspected, from one of the Trappists — perched atop his bald head.

I asked him why he thought a gathering of people devoted to contemplation focused so frequently on anger. Like so many of the Buddhists, he responded in metaphor, comparing anger to the cobra, sleeping in the house until awakened to bite; greediness to the lusty rooster; and ignorance to the pig, always seeking, knowing nothing. He elaborated on his analogy:

> If we see an ugly thing we are unpleased; that gives birth to anger. When we see a friendly form we want it, and that gives birth to greediness. If we don't notice at all, if we pay no attention — this is where Buddhism focuses — that's a neutral feeling, which gives birth to ignorance. . . . Anger is more dangerous than desire, but easier to uproot; desire — attachment — is less dangerous but harder to uproot. Anger cannot be rooted out with anger — therefore it must be contained. We have discussed anger more than greediness or ignorance because it's visible and we can see it, but the others rest inside.
>
> Always it comes. Not only we but the whole world is destroyed by anger. In Cambodia, we had this anger, this sleeping cobra which woke up and bit us. Therefore we do not blame any people. We only ask, What is the cause, what is the condition that destroyed us? The cause, the condition that destroyed Cambodia was anger.

⌘

I had better confess up front: despite their history of abuse and oppression, I have faith in the two great collective human endeavors, the church and the government. I believe that they can be instruments of justice and peace. The church shelters child abusers and the government protects the wealthy, but in the face of such corruption — which is always with us — there arises someone like Dorothy Day, the devout Catholic who devoted her life to using the power and the money of the Roman Church to benefit the poor of New York, or Dietrich Bonhoeffer, the Lutheran theologian who defied Hitler and the Nazis and who was imprisoned and shot. These people give lie to apathy; their lives are arguments for faith that I have never heard refuted by the most eloquent skeptic. Their examples haunt me when I think about the institutions of religion; they force me to question how much of my cynicism is based in reality and how much is a convenient justification for lazy self-righteousness.

In listening to and watching Ghosananda, I understood dimly how some part of my anger had its roots in envy. Though I have been given much, how dissatisfied and grasping I am, how little peace I have found! Born healthy and white and male, an English-speaking citizen of the American Empire — these great advantages I owe entirely to fate but take for granted, even as they surely outweigh the challenges of being born working-class and gay. Now I was listening to a man whose life had been one long confrontation with violence and death, and yet his simple presence projected peace into the room. He offered an education complete and whole. Watching him speak, I felt some intimation of the power of faith — how it defines its world; how skepticism vanishes in the forthright, unflinching embrace of all that is, joy and suffering; how faith is the proper human response to the awe plus terror plus beauty plus agony that together make up the mystery of what it means to be alive.

With Ghosananda I felt I was listening to a man of great faith, who seemed free from the anger about which he spoke with such eloquence and which had so readily seized me. In that moment I resolved to seek to understand what teachings had brought him to this place. I resolved to learn more about Buddhism and about meditation. I recalled Timothy Kelly's welcoming words: "How one lives one's life is the only true reference to the validity of one's search." In a different era history and custom would have destined me for the church; as it was, I probably understood less about the church than any of the institutions that had shaped my way of seeing and being in the world. How had it evolved from the teachings of Jesus, whom I thought of as a wandering proto-hippie preacher of love and virtue, into a place where outsiders have to fight to be allowed to participate? And where in this long history was the place of that foundational impulse to bow down and adore? As I left the abbey on that last Saturday evening, I resolved not merely to accept the reality of the church as a given but to ask a skeptic's questions: Where did it come from? How did it come to be an institution of power and exclusion? And where in this long, bloody history was the place of the contemplative life?

3

CROSSING THE RIVER

BEFORE UNDERTAKING any journey of consequence, travelers do well to take stock of their baggage. In my case that entails unpacking my peculiar blend of rural Roman Catholicism with what passes for liberal Protestantism in the South. After I left my tiny hometown, I came gradually to realize that my internalized cultural conflict was a very American battleground: Roman Catholics form the nation's largest single denomination, but our country's political heritage, power structure, and governing ethic are indubitably Protestant. To this mongrel inheritance, then, I owe my mixed allegiances to belief and skepticism, to the bloody crucifix and the empty cross.

ॐ

"Catholics are like muskrats," my father once said. "They're never found far from water." Throughout Catholic grade school, my classmates and I received maps, distributed by the Louisville archdiocese, illustrating my father's premise. Entitled "No-Priest Land USA," the maps colored in black those American counties lacking a single Roman Catholic priest. The South was, of course, a sea of black, penetrated by peninsular strips of white, where true to my father's observation, Catholics had settled along the rivers. Much later I would realize that farmers, often Protestants, frequently came by land, over Ohio's National Road or through the Cumberland Gap, whereas urban-dwelling Catholics and Jews more often came by water, down the Ohio or up the Mississippi. Throughout the South, farm families were overwhelmingly Protestant, while Catholics and Jews clustered in the cities, drawn there by their interest in commerce, industry, and flat-out self-preservation — they found safety in numbers.

Which begins to explain the ornery character of the Roman Catholic counties where I grew up. We were rural Catholics, something of an oxymoron in the South, descendants of English and Scots-Irish farmers who fled religious persecution in their native lands. Sometime in the eighteenth century my paternal ancestors entered America, probably via the Catholic city of Baltimore, probably intending to farm the hill country of western Maryland. There they encountered more hostility, this time from already-established, mostly Protestant farmers. My immigrant forebears did what every adventuring soul did in those days — they continued west until they reached Kentucky, the California of the eighteenth century, where late in that century they founded Roman Catholic communities. They built the first Roman Catholic churches west of the Appalachians and north of New Orleans and engaged the services of the first Catholic priest ordained in America. Later they procured an energetic French bishop, Joseph Flaget, who set about promoting his wilderness parish of Bardstown, which in 1808 would be named (along with Boston, Philadelphia, and New York) to join Baltimore as America's first Roman Catholic dioceses.

The maps of No-Priest Land didn't identify specific towns or parishes, but it was easy to locate my home parish: St. Catherine's Church in New Haven, Kentucky, one thousand solidly papist souls. We were a headland in white, surrounded on three sides by dark Protestant hordes. Right on the county line, we were separated from No-Priest Land by the Rolling Fork River — the width, in summer, of a basketball court.

We did see Protestants, mostly Baptists, in New Haven. Their own counties were dry (they had outlawed the sale of alcohol), and they kept us Catholics in the business of quenching their thirsts — my family's Sherwood Inn depended on their business. Otherwise, the two religions barely acknowledged each other. Our county oriented itself to the north, to Louisville and the Catholic counties strung (with the muskrats) along the Ohio River. Across the Rolling Fork, LaRue County looked toward its Protestant theological kin farther to the south in Kentucky and Tennessee. No physical barrier existed; there was only the force of social custom. We knew our place, the Protestants knew theirs. "The red fox has his territory, the gray fox has his territory, and they don't mix," my father said. We were the reds, they were the grays, almost nobody crossed the line.

Nobody, that is, except my mother. Seventh of eleven children, born on the Protestant side of the Rolling Fork, she grew up wild, partly because her own mother died young. She rode motorcycles, smoked cigarettes, and flirted (dangerously, as it turned out) with the Catholics across the river.

Then she went away to the city, to Lexington, Kentucky, where she attended college, the only one of her sisters to seek education beyond high school. After classes she walked across town to work as a waitress in a boardinghouse. Each evening she passed a Catholic church, where she heard the choir and the organ and the hymns in Latin. Standing on the corner outside Sts. Peter and Paul, she said to herself: *I want that music.*

She dropped out after that first semester, to return to her hometown and wait tables until she met my father. They dated a few times — Mother told him she didn't believe in long courtships. To marry she had to convert — in those days a woman had little choice — but I suspect that my father was the surface onto whom my mother could project her longings for a more richly layered spiritual landscape. Three months later my mother was baptized, said her first confession, received her first communion, and spoke her marriage vows in a 6:00 A.M. ceremony attended by almost no one from either family. My father's aunt, a nun, wrung her hands and told my mother *she* thought my father ought to have become a monk. "Well, if he hasn't made his mind up by now it's time somebody made it up for him," my mother snapped.

Like all the Catholics among whom I lived, I grew up knowing that I lived on the edge of a sea of Protestants even as I knew almost nothing about them. We visited our non-Catholic relatives rarely, never entering their churches. When my Protestant grandfather died, we were expected to obtain special permission from the parish priest to attend his funeral. "To hell with that," my father growled, and packed us into the station wagon for the ten-mile journey south.

Decades later, the New South has made inroads into this particular frontier of No-Priest Land, but the contrast can still catch the eye of the observant traveler along the old Jackson Highway, U.S. 31E. North of the Rolling Fork, the countryside is sprinkled with convents and monasteries, the Abbey of Gethsemani among them. Catholic homes in New Haven display the range of papist paraphernalia, inside and out: crucifixes featuring Christ in agony; holy water fonts; blessed palms hung to protect the house from fire, tornadoes, disease; statues of the Virgin protected from the elements by upright bathtubs half-buried in the earth and painted blue. I think of two nineteenth-century wood mosaics of the Sacred Hearts of Mary and Jesus that hang in my family's home — dark walnut hearts, one pierced with seven swords of blond maple (Mary), the other crowned with thorns fashioned of golden chestnut (Jesus), both dripping rich cherry blood.

This is civilized voodoo, with no analogue in the spare Protestant homes a few miles to the south. Decorated with Norman Rockwell reproductions and sometimes a plain wooden cross, these living rooms offer little evidence of the darker side of religion. Years have passed and still this contrast sticks in my mind: my father's people kneel to chant Latin with a golden-robed priest as clouds of incense rise to an Old World Jesus, writhing in agony on a gleaming brass crucifix enshrined on a marble altar, at the same time that across the Rolling Fork, a few miles to the south, my mother's people sit on plain oak pews before a black-suited preacher, who shouts and thumps his Bible beneath a cross as vacant as the tomb of his distinctly New World Christ.

*

"No history of Gethsemani would be complete without a history of the Johnsons' kitchen," one of the Trappists told me. No one remembers exactly how the family relationship with the monks began, though its deepest roots probably lie in my father's character — "I'd have been a monk," I overheard him say, "except I can't stand religion." The monks of Gethsemani brought into our house some experience of a larger world where conversation might venture to subjects other than crops, cars, and genealogy. Many had arrived at the monastery in the 1940s and early 1950s, unwilling to go to war (a religious vocation was one way out) or shell-shocked from it.

Brother Clement, among the closest of our Trappist friends, described how he first met my father.

> I was looking for better fittings for the monastery boiler, and I went to him because I heard he had a scrap pile. He told me to look through what he had, and if I didn't find it to come back the next day. And I didn't find it, so I came back the next day and there it was, sitting right on top. He looked at me and winked. "We got to get Uncle Joe [Joseph Seagram, owner of the distillery for which my father worked] into heaven somehow."

And so my father befriended the Gethsemani monks and they began to visit, first at the rented house near the distillery, later at the house they helped us build a few miles down the road from the abbey.

Then came children, many children, though with nine kids my family was more or less on par with most of our neighbors. After their eighth child my parents ran out of names, so they gave me over to the monks for naming. By now — the early 1950s — they had become regulars at our dining table. Through various subterfuges they slipped from the abbey to make their way to our house, managing to arrive just before supper. *They* got pork chops, *we* got fried baloney, but still as children we adored their company. For the most part they were educated men, Yankees from impossibly exotic places (Ohio, New Jersey) who stayed late into the evening, drinking beer, smoking cigarettes, watching football on television, and talking, talking, talking.

The monks after whom I am named are pictured in a photograph that I still have. One year old, I am sitting on the table in front of Brother Clement. Mother balked at naming me Clement ("over my dead body"), and so she asked after his birth name, which had been John. Next to Clement stands Brother Fintan Dwyer, the monastery's baker. More familiar with Hollywood movies than with ninth-century Celtic saints, my mother spelled his name in the manner of a character actor of the day, and so I became John Fenton.

One brother was fond of a grass skirt someone had sent my mother from Hawaii. When the moon was right and the whiskey flowing he donned the skirt and some hot pink plastic leis, then hoisted my mother to the tabletop and climbed up after. There she sang "Hard-Hearted Hannah" ("the vamp of Savannah, G-A!"), while her partner swayed his hips and waved his hands in mock hula. Later he launched into Broadway tunes, warbling in falsetto with his arms thrown around one or more of his brother monks.

Brother Fintan made elaborate cakes for each of my birthdays until I was five. Then he left the monastery, for reasons I would not discover for many years.

*

Because we were so Catholic, because the roads were bad, because we were a land of small farms and towns, because of the fierce loyalty of Southerners for keeping things unchanged — for all these reasons we were decades behind our times. In the early 1960s the parishes of Nelson County still assembled every year for Corpus Christi, in a great procession to worship the body of Christ as made manifest in its monstrance, a tall, golden cross holding at the intersection of its arms a round glass window displaying the sacred host.

Corpus Christi falls in early summer, well into high heat in the upper South. We assembled in two columns outside the walls of the Abbey of Gethsemani, segregated not by race but by gender. Women in their A-line dresses stood to the left; to the right men sweated it out in their dark Sunday suits. Only the polyester betrayed the passage of almost a thousand years — a medieval man or a woman from twelfth-century Chartres or Canterbury, set down in our midst, might take up the chorus ("Tantum Ergo," "Pange Lingua Gloriosi") without missing a beat.

I walked between my father and brothers and stared at the wall — nubbled, whitewashed cement block, seven feet high — that separated us from the Gethsemani enclosure. WOMEN NOT PERMITTED UNDER PAIN OF EXCOMMUNICATION, the sign said. Barely old enough to read, I understood "excommunication" to involve electrocution, or maybe hanging. On the other side of the wall, I thought, lay all that was mysterious, profound, unknown in my crushingly dull life.

Twenty years later, most of this would be gone, victim not (as many would have us believe) of the Second Vatican Council — no amount of Latin and incense could have slowed the onslaught of consumer culture, which brought prosperity and big-city skepticism to the remote corners of America. But I remember those gatherings not as assembled yet disparate individuals but as the communion of many souls, massing like bees in a hive — impossible to think of any one of us apart from the whole.

I am a veteran of the authentic small-town experience, and I do not romanticize it. The community held its nonconformists in thrall to public opinion, which was swift to condemn and ostracize. Women married young and had children, or they left — the single woman who stayed was regarded with pity and suspicion. The elderly were wholly dependent on the generosity of their families, who sometimes came through and sometimes did not. Black people were treated at best as children, at worst as animals. The church, Roman and Protestant, oversaw and endorsed the whole complacent racist, misogynist, homophobic structure.

But those collective celebrations of faith were a powerful, binding magic: to have known them in the flesh means never to leave them entirely behind. A talisman or touchstone, they connect me to a world in which, for better and worse, the individual is less significant than the enduring community — to an ancient world, that is, where survival depended on clan and tribe.

⁂

A few days after one of those Corpus Christi processions I stood behind Gethsemani's wall when Father (impossible to think of him as "Dad") took me along on one of his visits. We stopped first at the Sherwood, to pick up a fifth of Antique, the bourbon made at the distillery where he worked. Then we were back in the fire-engine-red Country Squire, driving the winding three miles to the monastery.

As shotgun rider I knew my task — I got out and tried the latch on the gate. "Locked," I announced with some satisfaction. I was nervous about entering the enclosure, never mind that I was gender qualified; I equated it with looking under a nun's habit. From deep in his multipocketed overalls Father produced a key — somehow, faced with a locked door, the man always had the key. A few minutes later we were sitting in Brother Martin's plumbing shop, where a crucifix reigned over the jumbled pipes.

Across the next half hour monks trickled in. First to arrive were what years later one of the monks would call "the upper-bracket party circuit." Brother Fintan had already gone "over the wall," the phrase used by both monks and convicts to describe a brother who has made the break for the outside world, but Marcellus, Christopher, and Alban were there, along with Clement, ringleader of my father's friends. These were the "lay monks," the blue-collar monks who labored with their hands in the fields and barns and shops, with whom my father, himself a laborer, was most comfortable.

I remember hands, callused and swollen from work; Father's Knights of Columbus ring, chipped red glass in false gold, bent and knicked from the times it got in the way of some hammer or wrench, until the day when it nearly carried his hand into a planer and he left off wearing it for good. Father was in his element: among the pipes and the tools and the grease, telling stories, with a bottle of whiskey making the rounds.

The summer day lengthened into dusk, the whiskey bottle emptied. The monks traded stories of their own, stories set in places with elevators and sidewalks and pay telephones. I was bored beyond imagination's reach, but I absorbed at least the exotic flavor of these distant Yankee cities, the beginnings of my resolve to get away, to see the world, to leave this sleepy town outside of time and become instead a creature of ambition and desire. "It's almost suppertime," I whined at some point, to receive from my father a look of irritation and contempt that made clear I'd not be accompanying him back anytime soon. Long after dark we drove home, to a cold plate my mother had left sitting on the table.

⁂

Those born into pre–Vatican II Roman Catholicism must accept that few other North Americans can grasp its sensuality, its insistence on the omnipresence of mystery. The rasp of the newly starched surplice against the skin, the deep, flat drawers smelling of naphtha from which I pulled the priests' vestments of the season or the feast, the little brass spoon and boat reserved for incense, the particular smell of that particular incense, the special words reserved for holy functions — *surplice, sacristy, monstrance, chasuble* — these words are engraved on my tongue, along with the altar-boy Latin that I mumbled without knowing the meaning of the words. The effect was to enter an imagined world, a fantastical world — the world, in fact, of theater, where everything stood for something else and everything was or had the potential to be sacred.

To attend Easter midnight mass as a child was to experience mystery rendered palpable, the Theater of Faith. We approached St. Catherine's Church guided by the light of a few votive candles, illuminating the stained-glass windows from within. Inside, in near-pitch darkness, we groped our way up the aisle, to sit beneath statues shrouded in mourning robes of purple satin. The service began on the church steps, with the blessing of oil and fire; that same fire spread through the congregation via beeswax tapers passed from priest to communicant, accompanied by Latin at once foreign and as familiar as our native tongue — *Lumen Christi, flectamus genua, levate* — these words speak to me across time, arousing now as then a keen sense of the mystery of the word and the world.

Then the litanies, interminable, repetitious chantings: first the Litany of the Saints, the unabridged version, honoring hundreds of saints (St. Lucy, *ora pro nobis;* all you holy virgins and widows, *miserere nobis);* then the Litany of the Blessed Virgin Mary (House of gold, *ora pro nobis;* Mystical Rose, *miserere nobis).*

And then the dramatic climax: long after midnight, the pipe organ, silent since Holy Thursday, pulls all stops for the Gloria. The church lights come up, the priest sheds his white robe and black stole for shimmering gold, incense rises in clouds, with a tug of thread mourning cloths drop from statues, banks of flowers and lit candelabras appear on the altars, and over all tower bells recklessly peal, their deep-throated voices palely echoed in the high-pitched clamor of the altar chimes.

For a small child, at once half-asleep and charged with the thrill of staying up far later than on any other night, this was powerful stuff — though not necessarily more powerful than the Bible-thumping revivals of fundamentalist Protestants or the mystery rites of the Mormons. That I found the experience so moving and formative is an indication less of the

power of particular beliefs than a testimonial to the power of the instinc-
tive impulse toward spiritual expression, which transcends doctrine and
dogma.

⁂

At what moment did I lose touch with that impulse? Somewhere around
fourth grade — let us call it May, the Virgin's month. Memory conjures up
the town cemetery, where I was walking home from school with my cousin.
We were in the same grade but he was born in January, I in October; he was
nearly a year older than I was at an age when a year seemed a decade, a lifetime, an eternity. On this particular afternoon, for possibly the first time in
my life I raised a troubling theological question with a peer. "About this
Virgin birth," I said.

My cousin was ten years old, a buck, a heterosexual. He lobbed a rock
at the wings of the stone angel who mourned over the grave of a rich Johnson who we pretended was our ancestor but wasn't. "Babies come from
girls' holes," he said flatly.

"Well, sure," I said, though this was news to me, and it would be another year and more before I would accept this miracle, that something so
large as a newborn baby — I had a vast family, I'd seen and held newborn
babies — might emerge from this tunnel, this canal not much bigger than
. . . The logistics boggled the imagination as they still do, but I was stuck on
theology and so I returned to more familiar territory. "How could that happen?" I asked. "I mean, for a woman to have a baby without —"

My cousin drew up short to regard me with the fourth grader's eloquent expression of contempt. "You don't really believe all that stuff, do
you?"

In fact until that moment I had believed every word. I'd read it in a
book, after all, I'd been to church countless times where all the adults I
knew solemnly swore they believed. But I quickly picked up on his tone of
voice and was as enthusiastic as the apostle Peter in my denials.

Before that afternoon I'd never considered the option that I might
choose not to believe. Walking home through this same cemetery, I
scanned the skies for apparitions of the Virgin. If she'd appeared in Mexico,
in Canada, in France, why not Kentucky? And in each case she'd appeared
not to the rich and powerful but to children of the working classes, children
like me. Under hills snowy with blossoming dogwood I considered this,
that I lived in a Catholic *county* if not *country,* that surely the difference of

an *r* was not of such great consequence to the Virgin. I prayed and hoped and half expected that she would appear above the knobs and that I, a well-behaved student, might be the first to see her when she revealed her glory. But when no voices and visions came, I decided this was because I dwelt among heathen.

Or maybe I lost my faith in the seventh grade, as a result of my single hour of sex education. Aged Father Gettelfinger, the silver-haired German Catholic tyrant who ran my town for close to forty years, spent most of the hour refining the precise definition of "too far" — the point at which the sinner crossed the line from the moral misdemeanor of venial sin to the felony condemnation of mortal sin. The hand on a girl's knee was venial; any higher was a ticket to hell.

Amid this lecture on garden-variety ways to hell, a classmate got in a zinger of a question. "Is jacking off a mortal sin?" he asked. Father Gettelfinger blanched and nodded and ended the session, but his nod was enough to confirm a suspicion I'd been dodging for years: anything that felt this good must be really, really bad.

That afternoon I climbed a tall knob and wrestled with my conscience. Each time I masturbated I was committing a mortal sin. Each time I went to communion without having confessed that I had masturbated counted as another mortal sin. Each time I went to confession without acknowledging my guilt was yet another mortal sin. And confession — sheesh. The thought of telling Father Gettelfinger, who knew the identity attached to the voice on the other side of the grille, that not only had I done the deed but that I had done it hundreds of times, at every opportunity, that I had been doing it since my earliest consciousness, that even now I was devising ways to prolong and intensify it — this was as impossible as giving it up. Was I prepared (as the terms of a good confession require) to give it up? "No way," I spoke these words aloud, not defiantly but in weary recognition of my fallible flesh. This was a contradiction I could not sustain, between the frank sensuality of this most voluptuous of Western Christian traditions and its niggardly attitudes toward the body's rich and varied landscapes. Instinctively I knew that something was seriously amiss in this separation of body from soul, flesh from spirit, though I was unable to express this duality in words. I never went to confession again.

From my discovery of the outright lie of the Virgin birth — for that was how I saw it then — I began to learn that appearances are not necessarily the same as realities, that a gap of variable dimensions lies between what we profess and how we manifest that profession in our lives. This important lesson holds the key to both duplicity and art, but as a rebellious teenager and later as a skeptical adult I saw only the deception. I came to associate religion with hypocrisy, a connection strengthened by the dawning realization of the omnipresence of desire and the ways that institutionalized religion manipulates it to terrorize and oppress.

In 1968 my ecumenical horizons suddenly broadened. Partly because of rising tuition and decaying facilities, partly because my parents grew tired of battling Father Gettelfinger over the behavior of their free-thinking children, they transferred their last three children from Roman Catholic schools to the public high school in my mother's native Protestant county. Each morning my brother, sister, and I walked the half-mile through town, past the curious eyes of our grade-school friends (now bound for the parish high school) and down to the bridge over the Rolling Fork, where we boarded the school bus for a circuitous ride to Protestant Hodgenville, birthplace of that notable Protestant Abraham Lincoln.

I was fourteen. Repercussions from rock-and-roll, Vietnam, race riots in nearby Louisville were reaching my hometown. Inheritor of my mother's nonconformist blood, possessed by the inflexible logic of adolescence, I rejected the Roman Church with the same fervor with which I'd once believed.

I considered atheism, but this was too far beyond the pale. Besides, at some subconscious place I understood that I had been fated (donné) for faith and that faith required a discipline that atheism was not likely to provide. I resolved instead to shop the religion market, which I understood to mean the bewildering variety of Protestant sects. I designed for myself an ecclesiastical survey course, consisting of Sunday visits to the Protestant churches of my high school classmates.

I remember vividly the plainness of those religions, contrasted with St. Catherine's gaudy mysticism. Statues, monstrances, marble inlaid with gold leaf, stained glass — St. Catherine's had all these to excess. The interior walls were covered with murals painted by Italians imported for the job: angels trailing banners ("Gloria in excelsis Deo"), whole walls covered with patterns of interlocking acronyms (BVM, IHS), crucifixes festooned with lilies, pelicans tearing open their breasts to feed their blood to their young — a metaphor for Mother Church. Entering the stark wood-and-plaster whiteness of the Hodgenville Baptist Church, I grasped in a dim way how different the act of seeing must be for those who came to faith in a room so empty of things to look at.

As an American, schooled in political principles rooted in Protestantism, I was attracted by the Protestants' easy alliance between democracy and theology. Most Protestant congregations elected and, when they deemed necessary, rejected their preachers. Services were led by deacons — mere mortals, my classmates' fathers, who had been sanctified by no order other than the respect and votes of their fellow worshipers. These men had *sex*, for God's sake; my classmates were indisputable proof of the fact. The preacher characterized humanity's relationship with God as downright personal, incorporating a respect for the process of questioning that had no equivalent among Roman Catholics, to whom the inquiring mind was evidence of the devil's presence. I was pleased by the Protestant notion that the route to God involved individual reflection and modification.

All this seemed so rational, so sensible, so *American*, demanding nothing like Catholicism's rigid adherence to doctrine and dogma. How impressively different from the arcane theology and inflexible orthodoxy of my church — *the* Church, as it styled itself, with an upper-case *C*. I was sure that I had found what I had been searching for: religion based on logic and intellectual consistency.

And yet I left those Protestant services dissatisfied. I had been raised to believe that religion served as humanity's collective acknowledgment of mystery; in these Protestant churches I found little that was mysterious. These services bore the imprint of hands of remembered generations, whereas the services of my childhood church had been shaped by hands outside of memory, embracing and incorporating the ancient rites along with their gods and goddesses of mountains and plains, skies and seas. It was the shaping of those hands reaching forward from prehistoric time that my Catholic side found to be the sine qua non of an authentic religious service. Lacking it, Protestant worship seemed to my inexperienced heart uncomfortably like social exercise.

✦

Caught between equally problematic manifestations of belief, Roman and Protestant, I stopped going to church altogether, along with many of my peers. For a while, among my Protestant friends, I was afraid that I had been alone in longing for religious expression that was both unreservedly ecumenical and emotionally profound. Then I left Kentucky and discovered others who shared my dilemma, in kind if not in degree, people who had come to faith in churches of one denomination or another only to find each one's exclusive claim to truth unacceptable and, in fact, oppressive. At the same time, we valued tradition and wanted to participate in carrying it forward.

The Roman Church does not encourage the bending and cutting of its precepts to individual conscience, but the same might be said of Orthodox Judaism or fundamentalist Protestantism. We are handed an identity before having a say in the matter, and we spend our lives running from it, pretending we have left it behind, or grappling with it as Jacob wrestled with his angel.

In thinking of the churches of our childhoods, what comes first to my mind is their uncompromising demand that we accept them on their own terms. It is exactly because they demand our love so wholly and unconditionally that they draw us back in spite of ourselves, that we find them so hard to leave behind.

⚘

I first encountered Asian philosophies in my twenties, in San Francisco, through a close friend who had a master's degree in Japanese art. One evening when I was grappling with a difficult decision she asked if I'd consulted the I Ching, the ancient Chinese Book of Changes. When I scoffed at her suggestion, she asked, "So what are you afraid of? If you're a skeptic, you ought to be willing to give it a try and form your own opinion. The worst that will happen is that you'll find it useless."

I have returned to her argument again and again as a means of expanding my limitations and boundaries. In fact I found the I Ching to be fascinating as a historical document and useful indeed as a compilation of wisdom on how to live, but the most significant aspect of that encounter was its challenge to what had become my easy, familiar knee-jerk skepticism.

In the months following the Gethsemani Encounter I was stumbling in the dark, but this much I understood: the price of serenity is a forthright, constructive engagement with anger. How I might accomplish that I did not know, but I recalled a parable related at the Encounter by the storytelling Japanese Zen priest: "How does one find one's way forward in the dark?" he asked. "By reaching out and feeling for the way, one step at a time." With this parable in mind, I decided to reach out.

I considered, then rejected the idea of traveling around the nation to sample various spiritual traditions. Most religious and philosophical traditions observe some kind of contemplative practice, but learning a tradition thoroughly enough to write about it with authority requires years of study. From respect for the richness of those traditions I decided to restrict myself to those that had been present in the United States long enough to contribute to and be shaped by the American religious psyche: the Judeo-Christian tradition, migrating westward from Europe, and the Buddhist traditions, migrating eastward from Asia. By comparing these different traditions and their institutions, I might identify the characteristics they shared and tease out a common denominator I could then label "faith."

I wanted to consider faith apart from its often bloody history, in hopes of learning how to preserve and enhance it in my own nonsectarian life. I planned to search for it like any reporter or anthropologist, conducting research, interviewing persons whom I considered to be its exemplars, and then condensing this information into a coherent description. In this way I could isolate faith, then consider how it could be cultivated apart from doctrine and dogma. I decided, too, that I would learn the history of monasticism, this peculiar institution that had featured so prominently in my life and that was devoted to the cultivation and preservation of faith. Among Christian traditions that meant focusing on Roman Catholicism, though I would visit Episcopal monasteries to experience how monasticism manifests itself among Protestants.

But why seek out monks, when the life they choose seems at first glance such an anachronism, isolated from the modern world and sealed off from doubt? At first I knew only that I sought the antithesis of the world of ambition and desire I'd once so eagerly longed for. Growing up in community, I felt that visceral need to belong, to rest in the knowledge that I live as part of a continuing symphony that would be altered, however imperceptibly, by the silencing of my voice. At least in the ideal, these men and women had devoted their lives to the search for wisdom and had joined a monastic community in the way that a Greek of the classical era would have attended the Academy of Athens, the institution for the study of philosophy founded by Plato.

These logical reasons lay behind my decision to seek out the monks, but mystery was also involved: throughout my twenties and thirties I had sought always to figure things out, to compare all the choices and make the "right" decision. Now in my forties I had begun to think instead of trusting the path, of concerning myself less with shaping and directing it and more with being receptive to what came my way. I'd grown up in the presence of Gethsemani; for most of my adult life I'd lived blocks from the San Francisco Zen Center. At the right moment in the right place Brother Paul had opened a door — was it not my responsibility to step through, if only to see what lay on the other side? I recalled again the admonishment of my old friend: "What are you afraid of?"

First grade, St. Catherine's Grade School, New Haven, Kentucky: we were almost sixty children with one nun, but discipline was not much of a problem; it was 1959, the 1960s were no more than a rumble on the horizon, and the nun's black habit and white wimple were enough to maintain order. Aged Father Gettelfinger entered for his weekly visit — the school yard still buzzed from the previous week, when he'd smacked to the ground an eighth grader he'd overheard cursing. That week's question was "What are the seven gifts of the Holy Ghost?" We were to recite them from memory, then to say which of the gifts we most wanted; for every gift omitted, the transgressor received a sharp rap across the palm with a yardstick. Father Gettelfinger rapped his way down the aisle. Some of my six-year-old classmates held their tongues — they preferred the assured raps to the terror of trying and failing.

Can I answer his question now, forty years later, standing at my computer? No cheating, no resorting to the Web: Fortitude, Knowledge, Piety, Fear of the Lord (which we understood as "Fear of Father Gettelfinger"), Counsel, Understanding, and finally, because I was a greedy, ambitious child and it struck me as incorporating all the others, the gift I told Father Gettelfinger I most wanted: Wisdom.

4

ORIGINS OF THE CONTEMPLATIVE
LIFE IN THE WEST

MONASTICISM is among the oldest of human archetypes; like the family, like marriage, like the complex rituals of desire, it predates recorded history. It is less a manifestation of any particular religious tradition than an outgrowth of the human imperative to ask why. It is the practice of the search for a state of integration with the whole of being that Buddhist monks call nirvana (or, in Japanese Zen Buddhism, *satori*) and that Christian monks call purity of heart.

Monasticism appeared at least as early as 1000 B.C.E. on the Indian subcontinent, hothouse for so much of human culture. Theologian Ewert Cousins speculates that monasticism arose almost simultaneously with the individuation of consciousness — as soon as humans perceived themselves as individuals apart from their communities, a few panicked at the notion of a fate distinct from that of their tribe or clan. They ran for the hills and the caves, to contemplate the mystery of being alive and alone.

That monasticism is so ancient complicates the terminology associated with it. Across history the word *monk* has been used to describe a wide range of individuals and practices. In the West, our words *monk* and *monastic* (derived from ancient Greek *monos*, "one alone") contain and express solitude, and in fact the earliest Christian monks were hermits who lived in solitude near or in the deserts of the Sinai peninsula.

In various forms and at various times some version of monasticism has manifested itself in all major contemporary religions, but it achieved its apotheosis in Buddhist and Christian practice. In both East and West, the practice evolved from being eremitic (from the same Latin root as *hermit*) to become primarily cenobitic (from Greek *koinos*, "common," that is, those who live in community).* In the East, Buddhist monks observe the precepts of the *vinaya*, their governing rule, with its roots in the earliest Buddhist teachings and oriented toward a collective life. In the West, the Benedictine orders (of which the Trappists, including those at Gethsemani, are a subset) abide by the Rule of Benedict, composed in the sixth century C.E. with a presumption of cenobitic life.

Buddhism evolved directly out of monasticism — Siddhartha Gautama, the sixth-century B.C.E. Hindu prince commonly referred to as the Buddha, began his interior exploration by joining one of the small bands of mendicant ascetics who roved (and continue to rove) the Indian subcontinent. From its origins in north central India, Buddhism spread rapidly in all directions, but it survives most notably to the south, east, and north. Buddhists to the east and south (including Sri Lanka, Burma, and Thailand) practice a more orthodox version of Buddhism called Theravadan (The Path of the Elders), which generally defines the goal of the practice as nirvana, the "extinction" or "peace" attained in the triumph over *samsara*, the endless cycle of desire and dissatisfaction that comprises this world of suffering. Northern or Mahayana Buddhism, sects of which are prominent in Tibet, China, Japan, Vietnam, and Korea, emphasizes compassion for all beings and teaches that the goal is not extinction but rather a purified rebirth as a bodhisattva, an enlightened being who returns to earth to help others until the entire world and all its creatures have been liberated from *samsara*.

In contrast, the Bible (Hebrew and Christian) contains no explicit references to monasticism. Contemporary Christian monks describe their life as an attempt at a literal imitation of the life of Christ, citing Acts 4:32, "Now the whole group of those who believed were of one heart and soul, and no one claimed private ownership of any possessions, but everything they held was in common" — though this description is more accurately applied to the first Christian communities than to the life of Jesus (about which we know so little) or to those first hermit monks of the Sinai deserts. These third- and fourth-century Christian eremites had as much in common with Hindu and Buddhist ascetics (or with early Greek or Jewish ascetic communities) as with the infant Christian hierarchy of Rome, geographically almost as distant from them as the Indian subcontinent.

---

* For ease of reference, the glossary at the book's end includes definitions of these and other specialized terms.

Christianity's earliest recorded monastic communities date from the early fourth century, when Pachomius, a Roman soldier turned Christian who probably brought his military training to bear in formulating his ideals for monastic life, founded monasteries for men (and eventually women) in the marshes and deserts west of the Nile Delta. These communities evolved over centuries to become the powerful abbeys that advanced the Roman Church's temporal ambitions and that in the Middle Ages were often synonymous with politics and intrigue. In the 1840s Anglican religious orders sprang up as part of the Oxford Movement, which sought to restore some pre-Reformation practices to Anglicanism. Still, in Western Christianity almost all monks are members of one or another of the wide variety of Roman Catholic orders. Of these orders, the Trappists are among the more strict in their profession of a life of asceticism, contemplation, and prayer. Though suppressed under Communism, monasticism has remained central in the various sects of Eastern Orthodoxy. There, as throughout the first millennium of Christianity, priests are generally allowed to marry, and only monks and bishops must vow to be celibate.

Considered (for the moment) in the ideal, monasteries have offered both West and East a model of a simple, contemplative life to inspire the larger secular world. They are communistic communities where property is shared, with the time freed by collective labor given to contemplation and prayer. They aspire to be exemplars of life lived not for the future but in the here and now, a life built on and lived by faith.

That function continues, but with some notable exceptions the practice of monasticism is in decline. As culture has become secularized in both East and West, monasteries have emptied. North American monastic populations peaked in the 1950s, as men fled the draft, or rebelled against World War II or the Korean War, or attempted to come to terms with their aftermath, and as women sought one of the few options available for those who did not want to marry and bear children. For many of those men and women, midlife questioning coincided with the 1960s, when they left the cloister in droves. A second wave left in the 1980s after the accession of John Paul II to the papacy, when the move toward a married priesthood and the ordination of women came to a halt. Gethsemani, one of the world's largest Trappist monasteries, had almost 250 monks in the early 1950s; now there are fewer than 70, with their median age nearing 65. In the rest of the world, monasteries are holding their own mostly where they are perceived as opposition to a repressive regime (as among Tibetans in exile) or where (as with Buddhist monasteries in Burma or Roman Catholic monasteries in the Philippines or in Africa) they offer a means of social advancement and financial security in desperately poor countries.

♨

Strongly influenced by Japanese art and by its underlying Buddhist principles, Van Gogh wrote in a letter to his protégé Emile Bernard, "The earth had been thought to be flat . . . science has proved that the earth is round . . . they persist nowadays in believing that life is flat and runs from birth to death. However, life, too, is probably round."

Despite mounting evidence that neighboring cultures have always influenced each other, thinking and scholarship in the history of religion strike me as anything but round. There are, of course, notable exceptions. The psychologist William James was the great pioneer; his *Varieties of Religious Experience* (1902) introduced the English-speaking West to the concept that the impulse to faith was universal and that systems of belief should be judged on the merit of their teachings and not from some preconceived notion that one (Christianity) was intrinsically superior. And James has noteworthy heirs — religious historians and theologians such as Mircea Eliade, Joseph Campbell, Elaine Pagels, and Karen Armstrong.

But for the most part Western religion assumes that a wall exists, snaking along the eastern boundary of modern-day Syria, that has long blocked commerce in ideas while permitting the exchange of goods, art, slaves, even armies. Despite literary and archeological evidence as well as common sense, the Christian churches and, until recently, secular universities have treated Christianity, our dominant religious tradition, as if it arose unadulterated from the pure springs of Judaism filtered through the consciousness of Jesus and set forth in the writings of the four evangelists and the apostle Paul to become the Roman Catholic Church, or the Southern Baptist Church, or the Orthodox Church — whatever church happens to be *my* church. The hierarchy has protected this illusion from simple ignorance as well as outright deception. Though the real story is both more interesting and more spiritually challenging, many church leaders choose to preserve the status quo.

If Christian monasticism — critical to the Roman Church's accumulation of power and wealth — has no biblical antecedent, and if we acknowledge that Antony (anglicized as "Anthony"), whom Christian historians once identified as "the first monk," learned the art of the ascetic life from those who came before him, where then lie its origins?

I like to think (with Van Gogh) that history is round, like the planet on which it takes place. I like to imagine the Athenian merchant of the fifth or fourth century before Jesus, delighted that his caravan of precious goods from Asia has arrived safely but just as excited at the prospect of a dinner party at which his friends will hear gossip from the travelers. For that night, anyway, his table will be the center of attention of Athens, by any modern standard a very small town.

Let us note that in the fifth- or fourth-century B.C.E. world of our Athenian merchant — the world of Socrates and Plato and Aristotle — civilization lay exclusively to the east and to the south, in Persia and India and China and Egypt. At the time of Socrates, his star student, Plato, and Plato's student Aristotle — the seminal "Western" thinkers — Rome was a gathering of huts on the wrong (that is, west-facing) shore of the Italian peninsula. The notion that it might someday surpass Athens in cultural sophistication was unthought of and unthinkable. Precious materials, crafts, military threats, ideas — all these lay to and came from the East, including tales of the wandering ascetics of India, men and some women who voluntarily abjured worldly pleasures, seeking wisdom through self-mortification. In this world lacking electronic diversions, in which the undertaking of any journey was risky, in which people memorized lengthy poems for recitation on demand, an exchange of goods and soldiers was surely accompanied by the exchange of ideas.

Consider two examples:

- Around 525 B.C.E. the Buddha proposed that the world of the senses is illusory, that the truth is to be sought and found through the mind. One hundred fifty years later, several thousand miles to the west, Plato proposed that the world of the senses is illusion, that truth lies in the world of Ideas.
- Until the conquest of northwest India in 326 B.C.E. by the Greek general Alexander, artists of the subcontinent represented the Buddha as a footprint or a tree. Alexander's cultural goal, however, was the fusion of Greek and Asian cultures, and with his armies came Greek sculptors skilled at literal renditions of the human form. Soon afterward we see the first figurative representations of the Buddha, portrayed not as the chubby philosopher that Chinese artists would later imagine but as a slim, muscular young man, in keeping with the governing principles of classical Greek art.

Is it possible that Plato and his contemporaries had no exposure to the philosophies of the lands with which Greece traded material goods and fought in battle? Did the sculptors who followed in the wake of Alexander's conquests trade only aesthetic sensibilities but not their underlying ideas? Linguists have long agreed that the major languages of western Europe share a common origin with Sanskrit, the classical tongue of the Indian subcontinent. Language is nothing if not a conduit of ideas — a word like *mother* surely cannot travel across a continent while leaving behind the ideas that shaped it. In fact, whole texts can travel — at a site on the border between Afghanistan and Russia, archeologists have uncovered a previously unknown treatise of Aristotle. Other examples of the cross-fertilization of ideas are easy to cite. As the foundation of Judaism, Christianity, and Islam, the Hebrew Bible is replete with examples of the Jews worshiping the gods of peoples whom they conquered and having their God assimilated in turn by their conquerors.

This syncretism reached a particularly rich expression in the first century c.e., when one of the greatest formulations of Buddhist doctrine took the form of an extended conversation (to embellish the point, a Socratic dialogue) between the Buddhist monk Nagasena and the Greek Bactrian king Milinda. Since the founding of Alexandria (332 b.c.e.), most cosmopolitan of Mediterranean cities, Hindus of the Indian subcontinent had maintained a trading outpost there. Around 200 c.e. Clement of Alexandria, one of the most influential of early Christian writers, named as his greatest teacher one Pantaenus, a convert from Greek philosophy who had been a missionary in India — where he discovered Christianity to be already established. Clement apparently shared his teacher's interest in Indian wisdom and is the first Christian writer to mention Buddhism.

An understanding of the roundness of history enables us to appreciate the debts Western and Eastern religions owe to each other. Religions absorbed and modified neighboring gods, goddesses, doctrines, and rituals not from some idealistic precursor to today's ecumenism but because polytheism assumed a diversity of deities and beliefs. Conquered peoples in particular had good reason to assimilate from their conquerors — since people believed the gods supervised and intervened in human affairs, a ruler's victory was a persuasive argument for the superiority of those deities and rituals.

The rise of monotheism in the West gradually ended that casual syncretism. The Buddha built his philosophy from Hindu elements, and the Jews borrowed ritual and doctrine from their Zoroastrian conquerors. But early Christians chose martyrdom rather than acknowledge the supremacy of the Roman emperor to their God. Christianity would build its churches with the stones of pagan temples and would appropriate pagan holidays and symbols, but always under cover of an elaborate mythology designed to conceal their pagan origins and to service the principle of a single omnipotent God.

This idea first occurred to me at the Gethsemani Encounter — that the same elemental questions provided the foundation for both Buddhism and the early Judeo-Christian monastic traditions. After their initial cross-fertilization, as a result of geography and politics, each pursued and refined its approach largely to the exclusion of the other; though each can stand complete on its own, the dedicated seeker finds that they complement each other as halves of a globe combine to make it whole.

☙

The Cistercian monastic order was founded in 1098 in France in a marshland known as Cîteaux (*Cistercium* in Latin; thus the order's name) by men who felt that Benedictine monks — at that particular moment in history the principal guardians of the contemplative tradition in Christianity — devoted themselves too readily to the affairs of the world. Though the Cistercians would produce formidable scholars and abbots as well as two popes, their emphasis would be on manual labor, as evidenced in the phrase they chose to characterize their undertaking, *Ora et Labora* (Prayer and Work). They adopted a strict rule of silence, with talking forbidden except at prayer or in emergency; today's sign languages have their roots in the hand signals developed by Cistercian monks. Among their first reforms was the refusal to accept children as candidates. The great Benedictine abbeys from which the Cistercians sprang had been populated in part by babies abandoned on the doorstep or in some cases conscripted from the local population, then raised by the monks, a practice that invited a range of abuses. In contrast, all candidates for the Cistercian order had to be at least twelve years old, an age at which the medieval boy was assuming the responsibilities of adulthood.

By the eleventh century much of Europe's fertile lands had reverted to woodland and marsh after the elaborate infrastructure of roads and aqueducts built during the Roman Empire had deteriorated. The Cistercians specialized in taking marginal lands and through hard labor transforming them into livestock pastures and arable fields — the pleasing aspect of large cultivated fields in present-day Europe is in part due to their labors. They developed grange farming, in which laborers were quartered far from a central abbey, enabling a monastery to control vast acreage. In contravention to their governing Rule of Benedict, which specifies that only virtue and seniority may be used as hierarchical standards, they adopted a two-tiered system of monastic life in which local serfs, often uneducated and illiterate, might join as "lay monks," with their duties confined to manual labor, while "choir monks," often ordained as priests, remained at the abbey to conduct administrative tasks and scholarship. Prior to this innovation, serfs had been considered little more than slaves by their feudal overlords. Working under the Cistercians meant that the value of their labor was supported by the authority of the Roman Church, now their economic ally against the nobility. Motivated in part by economic self-interest, serfs flocked to the newly established abbeys, and monastic populations exploded. In 1134 there were 19 Cistercian monasteries; by 1153 there were 343; by the end of the twelfth century there were 525, scattered from Ireland to Palestine.

To ascribe the rise of Cistercian monasticism to purely economic forces, however, would be an oversimplification. For the duration of the twelfth century, belief, politics, economics, and society were integrated in a way that, for better and worse, has never been duplicated. For perhaps a century Cistercian monasticism — in effect, belief-based communism — was the culminating expression of that integration, a disciplined life of prayer and work in community.

Women were caught up in the religious fervor of medieval times, though records of their undertakings usually come to us from the pens of celibate males, not the most judicious reporters. At the opening of the era, convents were frequently dumping grounds for unwanted daughters, widows, or married women who were infertile or had borne daughters and then had been abandoned by husbands in search of male offspring. As the centralized, celibate Church grew in power, abbesses were often relieved of what little power and independence they had previously held. Women's foundations had difficulty finding donors, since the wealthy supported monastic institutions primarily so that members of the order would pray for them. In the medieval era the Christian mass came increasingly to be understood as the apex of prayer — and since women could not say mass, they were inherently excluded from providing the service prospective benefactors sought. Women's foundations were often forced to share their income (donated or earned) with men's abbeys and often gave more than they received in return. They had no choice but to associate themselves with a men's foundation so as to receive the required clerical supervision and to have someone to celebrate mass and hear confessions, but men's foundations were often reluctant to take on this responsibility.

In this the Cistercians were no exception. Cistercian foundations for women blossomed along with men's, but the superiors of the order at first refused to supervise the women. Later, buckling to popular demand, the order briefly accommodated them, then finally removed itself altogether from associating with any new women's foundations. Women then turned to the Beguines,* a newly founded, less formally organized order that required no permanent vows but that entailed forswearing property and living a celibate and frugal life devoted to charity. Women flocked to *béguinages* — communities of Beguines — until in some parts of northern Europe these greatly outnumbered men's foundations. But these too were eventually forced to submit to clerical supervision and to confine their charitable activities within enclosure walls.

Before long the Cistercian men became major players in the medieval economy, cornering the wool market in England. That wealth led to corruption, which in turn sparked reform, followed by austerity, followed in turn by prosperity that led to corruption and new reform. Finally, in the seventeenth century, a French abbot instituted an especially strict observance at the monastery of La Trappe, France, from which today's Trappists derive their name.

The Trappists first arrived in Kentucky as political refugees. The American Constitution, ratified in 1788, and the French Revolution of 1792

---

* The word has a fascinating etymology, particularly in light of the intimate relationship I was coming to perceive between faith and desire. In French *béguin* is the word for the hood on a woman's cloak or cape, presumably worn by women who had no formal habit and who took only informal vows. But *béguin* lies at the root of the verb *s'embéguiner*, meaning to become infatuated with or to flirt — the "Béguine" of Cole Porter's song "Begin the Béguine" is a fast-paced erotic dance originating in the French Caribbean. Thus the Beguine might be said to be "flirting" with a religious vocation, or perhaps to be "infatuated" with God.

had brought about one of the greatest achievements of Enlightenment philosophy — the codification of the separation of church and state. For the
first time in history, religion at least theoretically ceased being intertwined
with government. America was already so religiously diverse and the nation
so young and unformed that it accommodated the first stages of that radical change relatively painlessly. In France, however, the Roman Church had
operated hand-in-glove with the monarchy for centuries, and both Church
and state had a long history of using the monastic orders for political intrigue and abuse of power. One of the first acts of the new government of
revolutionary France was to seize church property and to require that
clergy and monks sign oaths of allegiance to the expressly atheistic government. Those who refused were imprisoned, sentenced to hard labor, and
sometimes tortured and executed.

Some Trappists fled to Switzerland, from which in 1803 they sent a
delegation of twenty monks to America, where they eventually arrived
at the recently founded Roman Catholic communities of the Ohio Valley. They settled briefly on a site not far from the present-day Abbey of
Gethsemani. For complex reasons (among them the difficulty of life on the
frontier and the easing of restraints on French monasticism after Napo-
leon's defeat) remnants of this first band of Trappists ultimately returned to
France. Then the revolutions of 1848 once again endangered clergy and
monks, engendering another wave of immigrants to America. A second
band of French Trappists found its way back to Kentucky, to the same rural
Catholic counties in the center of the state. The Bardstown diocese had by
now moved to Louisville, but it was still led by the aged but indefatigable
Bishop Flaget, who was delighted to welcome the return of the French ex-
patriates. This time the foundation stuck.

By 1848, the time of their second flight to Kentucky and the founding
of the Abbey of Gethsemani, the French Trappists, chastised and impover-
ished by revolutions, were austere and reactionary. History had plunked
them down in the heart of the new empire, growing to rival any yet seen by
humankind. They had crossed an ocean and half a continent to wake on a
chilly, rainy December day, charged with founding a medieval institution in
the land of don't look back; a group of men living in medieval time, set
down in the nation of manifest destiny. They looked at the stony, thin soil,
the lumpy landscape, and then set out to do their job.

Gethsemani's current census of approximately seventy monks is in the range of its historical average — its monks are concerned less with declining numbers than with advancing age. "We have to get some new people here," one of the younger monks told me. "I can only push one wheelchair at a time." Admission to the community is challenging: applicants are told to return for several visits, then asked to visit other communities, then asked to undergo psychological testing before being admitted as a postulant. After six months the postulant is considered a novice and provided with a white robe. After another two years' service he is evaluated by the abbot's council, an elective body composed of "fully professed" monks, that is, those who have made their final, solemn vows. If approved, the "junior professed" monk serves another three years, petitioning each year for approval to renew his vows. At the end of those years — almost six years after his arrival — the candidate may petition to take solemn vows, a request voted on by the entire community.

Both men and women may make retreats at Gethsemani, with the year more or less evenly divided between them; the retreat house is booked well in advance, though the women's weeks fill long before those reserved for men. Visitors are discouraged from entering the enclosure, with women still forbidden behind the walls. Contemporary readers will perhaps be surprised to learn that the Trappists' governing Rule of Benedict does not specifically include the most famous disciplines of monastic life — poverty and chastity — as part of the monk's vow. The Rule commands communal ownership of property while forbidding the gratification of "the promptings of the flesh," but the interpretation of these general directives is left to the monk and his abbot.

The Rule *does* require vows of stability, conversion of manners, and obedience. In the vow of stability *(stabilitas)*, the monk swears to maintain lifelong allegiance to and residence at the monastery at which he professes his vows. From the time of final vows Benedictine monks know where they will likely spend the majority of their lives, where they will be cared for in their old age, and where they will be buried. Throughout the Middle Ages, in times of political, economic, and social upheaval this vow enabled the Benedictines to establish a network of stable administrative units through which they and the Roman Church could extend their influence.

Conversion of manners *(conversatio morum suorum)* is the most ambiguous and difficult to translate of the vows, though any Benedictine would find in it the source of Merton's concept of "total inner transformation." Benedict does not precisely delineate its intentions. These days it is understood to incorporate poverty and chastity as means to the end of the radical reconstruction of individual personality required by monastic life.

Finally, while the Rule is replete with advice and specific instructions to ensure that the abbot is a model leader, it leaves no doubt who is in charge. Obedience *(oboedientia)* is an exercise in developing and sustaining humility, that most important of monastic virtues, and monks are to obey their abbots even if they believe them to be wrong.

Of these vows, obedience is chief among equals. The Rule begins with a command — "Listen carefully, my son, to the master's instructions" — then, in case the listener misses the point, uses forms of the word three times in the first paragraph: "This is advice from a father who loves you; welcome it, and faithfully put it into practice. The labor of obedience will bring you back to him from whom you had drifted through the sloth of disobedience. This message of mine is for you, then, if you are ready to give up your will, once and for all, and armed with strong and noble weapons of obedience to do battle for the true King, Christ the Lord."

Disobedience was after all the first sin, as Eve, then Adam defied the command not to eat of the fruit of the Tree of the Knowledge of Good and Evil. Disobedience is a sin of self-consciousness — the individual perceives himself as apart from the communal whole, whether the clan or the tribe or the race, and decides to act in his or her interests rather than submit to tribal custom and authority. No worse sin existed in early consciousness, which saw survival as staked to collectivity so completely that the violator who struck out alone was often punished by death.

In keeping with the vow of obedience, the first virtue of monasticism is humility, which the Rule discusses in a lengthy section filled with language guaranteed to raise an American's hackles: "The first step of humility is unhesitating obedience, such people as these immediately put aside their own concerns, abandon their own will, and lay down whatever they have at hand, leaving it unfinished." The goal is to cultivate not servitude — that is, submission out of fear or hope of material gain — but that most un-American of virtues: humility, submission voluntarily undertaken to subdue the grasping ego.

Today a roaring six-lane interstate brings the visitor within twenty-five miles of Gethsemani, with the last miles accomplished over generally excellent highways; but in the 1950s to drive from Louisville to Gethsemani over slow, winding country roads was to descend through layers of a sort of living, functioning archeological dig. Louisville, Southern in character but Midwestern in its dependency on the industries of chemical processing and automobile manufacturing, was a real city, with some direct and at times influential connections to world politics and society. Bardstown, the county seat, focused in those days on the pursuit of Southern, gentlemanly occupations — the manufacture of bourbon and the farming and sale of tobacco. At Gethsemani, the dig's deepest and most culturally isolated layer, a small community of monks relied on horses and manual labor to eke a subsistence livelihood from the rocky earth. With rare exceptions they observed the Cistercian vow of silence. The monks mortified the flesh, sleeping on pallets in unheated rooms and fasting on not much more than bread and water throughout Lent and on all Fridays.

This was the remnant of the Middle Ages, three miles from my parents' home, that I came to know as a child.

❧

Buddhist practice was first established in North America among Asian immigrants, though its influences may be detected in some of our most seminal works of literature. The New England Transcendentalists, Ralph Waldo Emerson and Henry David Thoreau chief among them, were familiar with Buddhist principles if misinformed about their particulars, and they incorporated elements of Eastern philosophy in their writings. Thoreau published translations of Buddhist texts in *The Dial,* the Transcendentalist magazine, and waxed enthusiastic about its teachings. Emerson's study, now preserved in Concord, Massachusetts, as it was at the time of his death, features a substantial number of translations of Buddhist and Hindu texts.

Buddhist practice in America was largely limited to immigrant populations, however, until service in the Asian theater of World War II introduced millions of Americans to Asian philosophies and religions, chief among them Buddhism. These they brought back to America, most notably to California.

In 1959 the Japanese Buddhist Shunryu Suzuki arrived in San Francisco to serve as priest for Sokoji, the Buddhist temple (housed in a former synagogue) that served the city's Japanese American neighborhood. Two years earlier Jack Kerouac had published *On the Road,* manifesto for the beat generation and replete with references to Buddhist principles. Zen philosopher Alan Watts and Japanese writer D. T. Suzuki were popularizing

Buddhist thought in lectures at the American Academy of Asian Studies and at the San Francisco Art Institute, while on late-night radio Watts was broadcasting dharma talks in which he set forth basic Buddhist teachings. Zen was literally in the air.

Shortly after Suzuki Roshi's arrival (*roshi,* "venerable old teacher," is an honorific), the first Westerners began attending the Sunday services at Sokoji. They sought his teachings and leadership with all the enthusiasm and naiveté of converts; Suzuki responded to their eagerness and adulation. He introduced his students to traditional Zen practices, long abandoned in Japanese temples — among them extended meditation sessions (*sesshin*) and the chanting of Buddhist precepts (*sutras*). He was the motivating force behind the American practitioners' 1966 purchase of Tassajara Hot Springs, a remote and dilapidated resort in California's Coastal Range, to be developed as the first Zen monastery in America. Xerox magnate Chester Carlson provided the single largest donation toward the down payment.

Before long Suzuki was spending more time with his newcomers than with his Japanese American congregation, until in 1969 the Sokoji board of directors forced him to resign. A few months later, with Carlson again providing a substantial portion of the down payment, the American practitioners bought a former Jewish women's residence and renamed it the San Francisco Zen Center, or City Center, as it is familiarly known, with Suzuki Roshi as its priest. About the same time, George Wheelwright, cofounder of the laboratory that pioneered uses for polarized light, sold the Zen Center a parcel of his Marin County coastal ranch for a sum never disclosed but small enough to constitute a gift. On that land the Zen Center opened Green Gulch Farm, the third and last of its branches, which continues today to grow organic greens and vegetables and to serve as a model for living on the land in the context of a Zen Buddhist practice.

The San Francisco Zen Center runs its three facilities (City Center, Tassajara Zen Mountain Center, and Green Gulch Farm) on a yearly budget of around $3 million. At any given time some fifty persons are in residence at each site, though many of those are transient. Men and women retreatants are welcome on a space-available basis at all three locations, though Tassajara is closed to visitors for the intensive winter sessions. Visitors pay for room and board, though at each facility they may reduce their fees by working alongside the longer-term residents.

The Zen Center's roster of permanent residents is close to seventy, making it nearly identical in size, financial outlays, and income to Gethsemani. Gethsemani retains around $800,000 to support its monks, translating into an annual outlay of between $5,000 and $11,000 per monk. It divides the remainder among other, less financially stable Trappist monasteries, the Church, and a sizable budget (some $200,000 in one recent year) for local charitable donations. Zen Center members enter into charitable undertakings, but the Center does not maintain a charitable giving program as such. "In Zen, the practice of meditation is the offering," Zen Center co-abbot Norman Fischer told me. "Zen starts from the assumption that the fruits and power of one's contemplation are not only beneficial to oneself. We meditate and chant for the benefit of all beings."

New Zen Center members report to the practice committee, made up of older, more seasoned members; each new member has what Christians might call a "spiritual adviser," an older community member with whom to stay in close touch. The practice committee keeps tabs on students' overall commitment and meditation attendance and decides which of the applicants will be accepted for the intensive meditation sessions at Tassajara. To be considered for the Tassajara winter session, the applicant must first complete a multi-day, intensive sitting meditation called *tangaryo,* as well as *sesshins* at the other Zen Center branches or an equivalent center. Persons wishing to continue as members must spend at least one winter at Tassajara. At some point during this intensive meditation training, many complete *jukai,* a rite in which they publicly vow allegiance to the "Three Refuges" of Buddhist practice: the Buddha, the dharma, and the *sangha.*

Unlike the Trappists, however, individual members of the Zen Center take no vows of permanent stability. Though the goal of meditation practice is a radical transformation of character, practitioners take no vow equivalent to the Benedictine "conversion of manners." Nor is there an official commitment to obedience, though in traditional Buddhism the abbot or abbess is all-powerful as administrator. In recognition of the dangers inherent in such unfettered power and in response to scandals involving its abuse, the Zen Center limited the terms of its abbots and governing board members and developed thoroughgoing policy guidelines for dealing with internal disputes and grievances.

Fischer described the Zen Center's financial evolution and current status:

> Our commercial ventures have been successful — the retreats, the
> guest program at Tassajara — but we also started regular businesses in

the world . . . Now we have many more students but fewer in residence. At first the concept was if you wanted to study Zen, you moved to the center and took one of its jobs. Now the concept is you can have a career and study in addition to that, or you can live at the center for a few years while pursuing your practice.

We have a financial challenge ahead of us — we're trying to discipline ourselves to set aside money. There's a view that we shouldn't plan for tomorrow, that we shouldn't institutionalize. Another view is that to be responsible stewards we have to plan for the future. Trappists have a vow of stability — if you go through the system they assume the responsibility of caring for you. As we face the issue of some of the older monks needing care, we're having to deal with that. How do we decide who stays, who doesn't?

⟿

Sometime after the Gethsemani Encounter I picked up William James's *Varieties of Religious Experience,* a book I'd long postponed reading.

James's book calmly asserts that the many approaches to truth are as many friends, each ready to learn from and to teach the other if only we would let them. In our sound-bite culture, however, one passage has achieved the status of cliché. Some assiduous speechwriter, probably armed with an unabridged volume of familiar quotations, cadged from James to create a catchy reference to a "War on Poverty," and the phrasing has stuck with us, up to and including the "War on Drugs." The context of James's comment provides a vastly more profound message, ignored by the speechwriters perhaps because they knew that Americans did not want to hear it:

> . . . what we need now to discover in the social realm is the moral equivalent of war: something heroic that will speak to men as universally as war does, and yet will be as compatible with all their spiritual selves as war has proved itself to be incompatible. I have often thought that in the old monkish poverty-worship . . . there might be something like that moral equivalent of war for which we are seeking. May not voluntarily accepted poverty be "the strenuous life," without the need of crushing weaker peoples? . . . when one sees the way in which wealth-getting enters as an ideal into the very bone and marrow of our generation, one wonders whether a revival of the belief that poverty

is a worthy religious vocation may not be the "transformation of military courage," and the spiritual reform which our time stands most in need of.

Among English-speaking peoples especially do the praises of poverty need once more to be boldly sung. We have grown literally afraid to be poor. We despise anyone who elects to be poor in order to simplify and save his inner life.

... the desire to gain wealth and the fear to lose it are the chief breeders of cowardice and propagators of corruption. There are thousands of conjectures in which a wealth-bound man must be a slave, whilst a man for whom poverty holds no terrors becomes a freeman. Think of the strength which personal indifference to poverty would give us if we were devoted to unpopular causes ... while we lived, we would imperturbably bear witness to the spirit, and our example would help set free our generation.

James was a New England Protestant, not particularly well-schooled in the practice and variations of monasticism. Still, I read the paragraph with the kind of electric reaction one feels in the presence of truth. Why a monk? Why is it that these radically different cultures, East and West, have so universally and timelessly developed and sustained institutions where spiritual exploration may be undertaken unencumbered, insofar as possible, with material possessions and external commitments? What must a man or a woman give up to best preserve and cultivate virtue? And what relevance has the ascetic journey for those of us in the larger secular world?

James's words revealed to me what I had until then only dimly understood: I was seeking not so much a history of monasticism but rather access to purity of heart, its reason for existence. I wanted to understand what had been done to me — the cultural tattoo that, for better or worse, I had received in all those Corpus Christi processions and midnight masses, and later, in my adult, city life — but I was also seeking to understand and thereby validate the choice to live simply, to choose frugality over materialism, to find the courage to set out on the interior journey.

✧

At the time of the Gethsemani Encounter I was in my early forties. I had sat at the deathbed of my father, of too many friends during the earliest years of the AIDS epidemic; I had buried a lover, dead of AIDS. During those years my bitterness against institutionalized religion grew sharp — when

I most needed the wisdom and solace of my forebears, the institutions charged with preserving and offering it turned their backs.

A few weeks before the Gethsemani Encounter I learned that I had to move out of my San Francisco apartment. Thrown on the housing market in that most expensive of American cities, a writer in midlife, I decided I might as well leap into the void. For a writer New York is the factory; for this writer, I decided, it was time to spend some time in the factory. As I began my search for the nature and meaning of faith, I moved to New York.

5

A PROFOUND
SILENCE

IN A MANHATTAN LOFT, a former photography studio high in a nondescript Chelsea office building. Sunday morning. Raining. A cold day in late spring. Outside the windows, the rooftop water tanks so ubiquitous and unique to Manhattan, and looming in the near distance the Empire State Building.

After months of reading about Buddhism and talking to Buddhists, I have come to the New York Zen Center to sit zazen, a word composed of two roots: "sitting" *(za)* plus "meditation" *(zen)*. From college until moving to New York I'd lived in northern California, hotbed of Asian culture, and so I had friends who'd spoken to me of a whole range of Asian practices, among them meditation. A friend offered to pay for training if I wanted to take it; I'd politely declined. The whole idea struck me as so flaky — sitting cramped like a pretzel, waiting for enlightenment.

For most of my years in northern California, as a refugee from a relatively established culture (rural Kentucky) to the johnny-come-lately American West, I had been suspicious of the fondness for the new and faddish that I saw so often in San Francisco. Just like Americans, I told my friends, to pick up a tradition reaching back thousands of years and try to make it ours overnight. Just like Californians, I said, to seek spiritual growth on a cushion, instead of ministering to the sick and the poor. And then I was invited to the Gethsemani Encounter, and then I moved to New York, and then I found myself in this Manhattan loft.

My Roman Catholic–trained sensibilities had trouble embracing as sacred this gritty, industrial space, even though it might be furnished with a gold-painted Buddha and an altar. The priest demonstrated several positions for zazen — I ended up kneeling, my feet tucked under me, my buttocks supported on a cushion. It occurred to me that if I were back in St. Catherine's Church and the priest announced we were about to have a half-hour of silent prayer, I and the congregation would sneak a look at our watches with a collective suppressed groan. And here I was, volunteering to do what amounted to the same thing. *Why am I here?* I asked myself. Instead I could have been at home with French toast, maple syrup, and the *New York Times,* as good a ritual as I've devised for a bachelor's Sunday morning.

I arranged myself on my cushion, which I would learn to call a *zafu.* My knees cracked and popped.

The priest made multiple bows to the floor before a statue of Shakyamuni Buddha (*you'll never catch me doing that,* I muttered to myself), then led us in chanting a *sutra* — a litany or creed of belief. The ushers handed out chanting sheets for the newcomers, but I was impressed to see that most of the congregation already knew by heart this prayer, at least as complex and long as the Nicene Creed. What was this business with "form is emptiness, emptiness is form"? How can there be "no ignorance, and no extinction of it"? What was a bodhisattva, and what was the Prajna Paramita on which he or she was supposed to rely?

I fought back the urge to excuse myself to the restroom and head for the street. I was here as a writer; my job was to keep an open mind. I reminded myself that a non-Christian (as well as many Christians) encountering in the Nicene Creed the phrases "God from God, Light from Light" would be equally at sea, and for good reason. Still, I began that morning to understand that the study of Buddhism and of the ascetic life that I'd resolved to pursue would extend beyond reading a few books and having a few conversations.

A few months later I would come across a succinct description of meditation:

> Directions are given for our practice. In a place, which must be quiet, spread a thick cushion and sit yourself on it in an upright posture. Now first swell out the abdomen and put your strength there. Let the shoulders be in a straight line below the ears, and navel below the nose. Make the spine straight. The mouth should be shut, but you may have the eyes slightly opened. Making the breath flow gently will help to secure a correct posture. Then meditate on the text you have been given, or in

the case of beginners there is a method in which they count their breaths and so remove dull and distracted thoughts. . . .

— Sessan Amakuki, *On Hakuin's Zazen Wasan*

I was struck by the specificity of the instruction, and by its emphasis on the physical: do this with my hands, my spine, my breath.

Among those of us raised in a religious tradition, who can remember being taught to pray? Before memory I was taught to join my hands in the familiar pointed temple, and I was taught to memorize prayers and to respond to litanies. But no one paid much attention to the particulars, even as at some subliminal level we children understood their significance. Somewhere around the fifth grade, the boys abandoned the upward-pointing temple of the hands in favor of the carelessly linked fingers dangling at the belt buckle — a visible symbol of our rejection of reverence, which we were coming to understand as an attribute of the feminine and therefore of the weak.

Now, as I sat in Manhattan, the deep-throated gong sounded and all went quiet, and this interesting thing happened: it worked, sort of. I'd been instructed to notice my breathing, to count each breath in and out, to focus my mind on that interior place — and not just any vague, psychic inner space but a particular point midway between my navel and my back. When my attention wandered I was to notice where it wandered, whether to a sunny beach or a failing relationship; to remark on the place it had chosen to go; and then gently to pull it back to this particular place in my particular body in a real, particular world.

At the first period's end we rose, processed to the empty hall, where we walked in *kinhin*, in which we set each foot carefully and mindfully (another Buddhist term) in front of the other. Then we returned to the meditation room, where we sat for another forty minutes.

From the Ash Wednesday services of my childhood, the words welled up of their own accord: *"Remember, man, that thou art dust, and unto dust thou shalt return."*

This was the fact of things: I could not have done this in my twenties, when an hour was an enormous chunk of time. Now, in my forties, I have come to know suffering. I have held the hands of the dying. I have a more intimate relationship with time. I recalled the words of Ghosananda, speaking at the Gethsemani Encounter: "In Cambodia we say, If you know suffering, then you understand the dharma."

But here's the glitch: in these two forty-minute sittings during which the young Buddhist priest had told me to contemplate how life is emptiness and attachment, how I must let go of those illusions, I instead considered how strange and wonderful life is, how even in this plain cube of an industrial space in lower Manhattan an hour of conscious being is a delight, how the purpose of meditation seemed not to contemplate suffering and dissatisfaction but instead to honor the incomprehensibly vast gifts I've been given. I was supposed to be counting my breath, one, two, three, up to ten and back. Instead I found myself saying over and over, *I am grateful, I am grateful.*

At the period's end I felt calm, washed clean, my head clear, no more but no less than that. I walked home empty and dissatisfied, with no souvenir except the lingering soreness in my thighs.

At that Manhattan zendo, I'd encountered both a glimpse of the core of silence that must sustain a teacher like Ghosananda, and the vast distances that separated that tradition from the contemplative traditions of the West. My life had been intimately intertwined with one of the leading institutions of the contemplative life in the West and with its church, and yet I'd never sought any deep encounter with that life.

The writer and religious historian Joseph Campbell reports how when the knights of King Arthur's Round Table went in search of the Grail, each entered the forest at the darkest place of his own choosing — each knight knew that the greatest rewards lay hidden in the most fearful place. I could study the contemplative tradition in Western Christianity for as long as I wished, but this was no substitute for living it out. And so that rainy Manhattan afternoon I wrote Timothy Kelly, abbot of Gethsemani, asking if I might return to Gethsemani as a retreatant among the community of monks.

6

THE MOST FEARFUL PLACE: A GETHSEMANI RETREAT

TWO MONTHS after that first sitting at a Manhattan zendo, early on a hot July day, I arrived at Gethsemani as a retreatant. Along with some twenty or so other men, I stayed in the guest house, adjacent to but outside the monastic enclosure.

Mother dropped me at the entrance. In the nineteenth century the homesick French Trappists had modeled their abbey after those of their memories, down to a long allée lined with trees — distinctly North American sweet gums, not the most elegant choice, but these were French monks after all, who probably expected that the local flora would adapt to their cultural imperatives. In a major renovation the monastery shifted its formal entrance to the west, then a winter ice storm toppled several of the trees and decimated the crowns of those left standing. Today they bear the humble look of the newly tonsured postulant.

Mother pointed at the enclosure wall, where the sign that once forbade women under pain of excommunication has been replaced with a discreet MONASTIC AREA — DO NOT ENTER. The gate to the enclosure, however, remained closed and locked. She shook her head. "How many times have I driven through that gate with Father snoring in the passenger seat, to drop some monk off in time for 3:00 A.M. vigils. I wore a cap so anybody who saw me would think I was a man."

"Mother!" I recoiled in mock horror. "Under pain of excommunication!"

"It wouldn't have been the first time."

The wide, rolling valley that cradles the Abbey of Gethsemani was once the bottom of a vast sea whose billions of shellfish and mollusks left their shells to be compressed by the weight of water and mud into a fine white limestone. The earth rose, the waters disappeared — the great flood of Noah ended in the slowest of motions — and a river, the placid Rolling Fork of my childhood, formed its meandering course. Patches of denser, harder shale eroded more slowly than the surrounding limestone, creating steep, lumpy knobs, today heavily forested; their undulant serenity recalls Chinese landscape paintings. The knobs have had millions of years in which to mature, until today they embody the comfort of a grandmother's ample bosom.

This was the landscape that the young and impressionable Merton called "paradise." This is the landscape of memory.

∼

Gethsemani nicely illustrates the monastic penchant for architectural labyrinth, a metaphor for the Roman Church itself. Each new abbot is expected to leave a visible mark on a place, often by adding onto or tearing down his predecessor's projects. The result is a hodgepodge of buildings reflecting the architectural and liturgical obsessions of a given historical moment, fascinating to look at but impossible to navigate without a map and a compass. To enter Gethsemani's maze of cells, chapels, and living and work spaces is to step back in time, or maybe outside of time; eliminate electricity and the medieval monk would feel at home.

I entered the retreat house with trepidation and defiance. I was here with a purpose — to observe a peculiar institution of the past to learn what it might offer a more enlightened present and future. I had been raised in a family that partly because of our connections to the Trappists had managed to travel among people.wealthier and more cultured than our lot, until courtesy of a scholarship from Seagram Distillers I went away to Stanford University. I left behind the womb of family, or so I thought, to enter the exhilarating world of my independence.

As an entering Stanford student I'd given no thought to class and little to money. I took for granted that I would raise myself above the hand-to-mouth existence of my roots. That was, after all, the American way, an Enlightenment optimism regarding the limitless capacity of reason to decipher, name, and master every aspect of the universe. Each generation may presume itself superior to its predecessor in the irresistible progress toward growing prosperity and the perfection of humankind. The monastery whose doors I now entered represented a quaint remnant of a bygone world. From experience I knew that good men lived here, but I assumed they'd been trapped by forces of history and superstition that through hard work and native intelligence and good timing I had escaped. I knew that Dom James Fox, abbot throughout the 1960s, had earned an M.B.A. from Harvard before joining the community, but such aberrations did not undermine the overall progress of reason toward enlightenment. Christianity and especially the Roman Catholic Church were hotbeds of superstition that with time would be rooted out and enshrined in museums — as in fact they richly deserved — next to gorgeous medieval icons and illuminated manuscripts. We the enlightened would retain only the essence — the Sermon on the Mount and the frescoes of Giotto. Mythology would become, once and for all, the servant of reason, which would ultimately explain everything under the sun, as well as the sun itself.

Then life happened, and death — my lover and all those virtuous friends dead in their prime, the venality of the politics that surrounded their deaths, the evidence, growing daily, that technology, as the practical application of reason, may engender as many problems as it solves, with some of these problems (nuclear waste, global warming) lacking an apparent solution . . . and then I found myself standing at the monastery gatehouse, a kind of entryway to the past.

On my first day as a retreatant I arrived barely in time for terce, the mid-morning office. I settled into my stall to hear as the first reading of my journey the Letter to the Hebrews, possibly though not certainly from the hand of the apostle Paul: "Faith gives substance to our hopes and convinces us of realities we do not see."

I was bemused at the coincidence of these famous words on faith speaking to me across the centuries, but I was having none of it. Religion justified the oppression of the poor and the weak and exalted the rich and powerful: that was how I'd come to see it at the end of my high school survey of the Protestant churches of No-Priest Land, and that was how I saw it on the morning of the first day of my explorations at Gethsemani of what it means to have and keep faith.

Two conversations with monks — one who remained, one who left — revealed radically different perceptions of Gethsemani's entry into the contemporary world. John Dorsey, once Brother Clement, the abbey cellarer (the equivalent of its chief financial officer), summarized the changes he oversaw:

I entered in 1944, at twenty-six years old. The futility of war imposed itself on men looking for something real — I never doubted but the order was providing that.

When I went to Gethsemani it didn't have a money problem because
it was a subsistence operation. We made our own clothes and food —
in the autumn we'd take a trench and line it with straw, put in carrots
and Chinese cabbage and potatoes, then cover them with straw and soil
to last the winter. But for a higher standard of living you have to engage
with the outside world. How are you going to pay for health care? for
fuel? We had fuel in the forest — the bakery ovens were fired with
wood, and even the choir monks would spend time chopping and
stacking wood. We had a blacksmithy, a carpentry shop. But then —
led by Merton and lots of the younger men — the tendency became,
we didn't come here to work. So the hours were shortened, and there
was more leisure time. When I first came we had horses, then we had
one tractor, then we had a dozen. It wasn't planned but it happened by
increments.

I made so many changes and I hated them all — we were going in a
direction I didn't like. I loved the self-subsistence — but you can't pay
for the health care and the electricity and the other big items. Brother
Coleman said to me, "Of *ora et labora, labora* is heading south." So I
was having to get rid of the horses I loved.

Brother Simeon Malone arrived in the 1950s, not long after Brother
Clement, but he offered a different perspective on the transformation from
medieval to contemporary modes of being.

In the days when I first came, the monks processed from refectory to
church, reciting the Miserere in Latin. I had come for an exploratory
visit and I was up in the choir loft all by myself and I heard the monks
chanting, gradually building in volume — it was very moving. That
was my first exposure to the monks. I was to be interviewed that afternoon, and I was anxious, I was praying — "God, if you want me here
— give me the grace to say the right things during my interview." And I
guess I did, because here I am.

I entered as a lay brother. The life then was more ascetic, more devoted to manual labor and penance . . . We hadn't changed in nine
hundred years. In the early days asceticism was intended to help the
monk purify his life. By the twentieth century it had changed into a

means of keeping control. No one questioned things — that was the life, and it was hard. In the early 1960s I had sympathy with the blacks because like them we lay brothers were in the back of church as second-class citizens. The choir monks had the power to vote and we didn't, even though the Rule of Benedict says that the monastery's only hierarchy should be that of strict seniority.

We accepted dumb work, make-work, fasting. We had 250 men in the enclosure and were crammed elbow to elbow into the place with absolutely no privacy. We slept in a single large dorm room, got up, went to church, scriptorium, mass all together — there was never a time when we weren't elbow to elbow. We weren't allowed to cross the road to go in those beautiful woods — a vast wonderland of beauty across the road that we couldn't appreciate, even though silence and solitude were preached as desirable.

The main gate was locked, and if you had a key to get out, you had status. You might only have one key, but you'd put it on a big leather strap and the rest of them didn't have a key. You could leave money sitting around all day long, but put a screwdriver down and it would disappear in a moment.

Every change that has been made has been positive, needed, welcomed. Now we have private rooms. Now I can go to my room, take off my shoes. Now we all vote for the abbot or for a brother's entrance into vows. What we have now is much more wholesome and more conducive to prayer — closer to the Rule of Benedict than before the changes.

✿

Crusty, florid Father Matthew Kelty had been a priest for some years before entering Gethsemani in 1960. After Merton successfully reintegrated the eremitic tradition into cenobitic monasticism, Matthew spent many years living in New Guinea as a hermit before returning to Gethsemani to serve as counselor for retreatants.

Matthew presented the boundaries of a practiced therapist — he waited for me to raise the issues I wanted to discuss, even as I waited for him to offer a conversational opening that a man or woman enduring an emotional crisis might seize. I wanted to learn how he dealt with sexual issues — homosexuality, sexual abuse, marital infidelity — in an environment so hostile to discussing the realities of the flesh.

I asked about gay and lesbian retreatants. Father Kelty was amiable but not forthcoming. Our conversation continued, but I found my old anger welling up, and though I took copious notes, in the end I paid little attention. Only one note, made to myself, stands out: "I do not think that a man or a woman facing a sexual crisis, whatever its nature, could find much solace in this place, save what they might find in the silence of their hearts."

Among the monks of my childhood who had remained at Gethsemani, my father's best friend had been Brother Martin DeLoach, an African American of medium height who wears thick-lensed, black-rimmed glasses. As a retreatant I was technically not allowed in the enclosure, but I took advantage of my father's prerogatives and slipped inside to seek out Martin in his plumbing shop.

Radiant with good humor, Martin waved me into an old cracked leather chair — "Dom James's chair," he said. "You'd look good in it." On his cluttered desk he had photos of his brothers and sisters and their children, and an icon of an African American Virgin and child, Our Lady of the Streets. Though he must have been well into his sixties, he looked ageless, not a gray hair showing in his close-cropped hair.

He compared the monastery to the tribes of Africa. "I've never been there, but I understand that they elect their chiefs for life, and that's kind of like the abbot. I still think you'd make a good monk," he said. "You're a monk already. You stay at home alone with your work, writing, and that's beautiful, and I imagine there's a little suffering that comes with that. And that's what makes a monk, you know. Alone with God, and finally we're all monks, every one of us, because we can be as social as we want but when it gets to that last moment, we're all going to be alone."

I asked how he came to be a Catholic. He was raised a Baptist in the red dirt country of Alabama, north of Mobile, then his family moved into the city and he made friends with a Catholic boy. Martin got him to come to the Baptist church and he got Martin to come to the Catholic church in the African American community — a visit that changed his life:

> On that first visit the priest told me, "Good Baptists make good Catholics," and that's always stuck with me. I loved the gesture and ritual, the artistic side of it. So I converted and came to Kentucky for seminary, and I visited the monastery and I was drawn to that beauty, the rhythm

and grace of the priests' movements, the voices of the men chanting to-gether. I saw the monks in their habits in procession and I listened to the singing in Latin and I fell in love with the place.

He left the seminary and joined Gethsemani as a lay brother.

I asked him if he had experienced prejudice at the monastery. "Never," he said, "except what I felt in my heart. We're all here for the same purpose, which is to live more fully in Christ."

As he spoke I recalled an afternoon with my family, sometime in the early 1970s, when Martin and another monk stopped by for supper. My three-year-old nephew toddled up to Martin as he sat in one of the big Adirondack chairs my father had built from scrap lumber. "Can I pat your head?" my nephew asked. "Well, sure," Martin said. "But why do you want to do that?" "Because Grandfather told me if I wanted good luck to rub a nigger's head," my nephew said. In the dead silence that followed, my heart sang with vindication at the old man's being caught in his own bigotry.

Now Martin and I talked of how we struggled with difficult and com-plicated fathers. "I had a dream," Martin said, "in which I saw my father as a young man, and I walked up to him and kissed him, something I never did when he was alive. I woke with tears on my cheeks." I told him of my last conversation with my father, shortly before his death. He was sitting under the last leaves of autumn in one of the Adirondack chairs and I went to join him. He wanted to speak, but he was choked with emotion. I understood that he was trying to tell me something of great significance — that he loved me, perhaps, or that he was proud of me, or that he was afraid of dy-ing. My heart filled with anger at the memory of humiliations and beatings as a child, his contempt for me in my days of long hair and rebellion. *Twenty years too late, you old son of a bitch,* I thought as he struggled for words. I pointed across the road at a clearing on the hillside. "Must be a new house going in there," I said. A month later he was dead.

After a pause Martin spoke of walking in the woods with thoughts of envy and resentment of this or that fellow monk. "And then the Holy Spirit whispers in my ear what trash this is and I give it up. You can't go to com-munion with anger in your heart," he said. Walking back from Martin's plumbing shop, I considered how useful it might be to have a daily ritual that required pausing, evaluating, and accepting responsibility for my ac-tions.

⁑

That night's reading was from one of the desert fathers, leaders of the first Christian monastic communities founded in the Nile Delta in the fourth century. Those communities' leaders saw themselves as fathers to the younger monks. "Speak a word, *abba*," begins each of the hundreds of parables of the desert monks, a sentence that resonates with respect for the Word and for the abbot as the ideal father — *abba,* from which comes *abbot,* means "father" in Aramaic.

My attention wandered in the reading, until brought back to the present by a desert abbot's warning to his fellow monks to set a good example for their charges, for "there is no exception to this rule: as it goes with the father, so will it go with the son." I am my father's son, and I wondered what this implied for me — if I was bound to follow his difficult path.

⁂

Toward the end of my father's life many people who weren't relatives comfortably called him "Father," the way the monks of ancient times called their leader *abba.* He was generous to a fault with others, harshly critical of his children. I never saw him touch any person, including my mother, except to shake hands or in anger, which came upon him rarely but seized him wholly in its demon claws when it did; often, I suspect, when he had been drinking.

Shortly after that painful moment in the Adirondack chairs, he and I shared a tender, silent drive through the countryside he had never left and which he knew so well. I returned to my distant job and life the following day, then returned a month later to help him die. I entered his room moments before he slipped into a coma from which he never emerged. The last word he spoke, I write with humility and sorrow and quiet pride, was my name.

What forces would lead a man to beat, belittle, and terrorize a child? His own father's alcoholism, his own beatings and terror as a child — as good a demonstration of the Buddhist principle of karma as I've encountered. I learned from him to be judgmental, a fault I have spent a lifetime exorcising. I learned to touch no one from affection but only for sex — another challenge to overcome. But I also remember this, one of my most ordinary and vivid memories:

Summertime and he is painting windows, with their endless boundaries of wood and glass. He dips the brush, wipes it against the lip of the bucket, touches it to the inside of the wood strip that separates pane from pane. Soundlessly he takes a deep breath. He guides the brush down the strip of wood, exhaling as he goes. The brush is an extension not only of his hand but of his heart and mind. He reaches the bottom of the pane just as he exhausts his breath and the brush exhausts its paint. The wood is smoothly covered; the glass spotless. No one taught him what the Buddhists call "mindfulness practice" and yet there it is, he is his work and it is him, the dancer is his dance. Years later I write first drafts in longhand because the flow of the pen across the paper preserves the unbroken stream of words from the heart and mind through the body to the page. I will struggle to write sentences as my father painted windows, or planed wood, or laid bricks, or built furniture. I will struggle to be one with my work.

If I am to be brought to faith, it will be through the body.

*

A city boy now, I was unwilling to rise at 3:00 A.M. for vigils but professional compunction hauled my dead weight out of bed for lauds at 5:45 — from Latin *laud,* for "praise," but also related to the Old High German *liod,* for "song." Outside the church, birds were going wild with praise, singing of a wet summer finally turned hot and an abundance of creeping creatures to eat, in a chorus as crazy as anything by Charles Ives. Mellifluous meadowlarks, grating grackles, cooing doves, robins, chickadees, cardinals, and from some high point overlooking all, a mockingbird, singing mostly covers, it's true, but doing it in his own Sinatra way. In the long narrow church the voices of the monks echoed from the whitewashed brick walls, at times overwhelmed by the birdsong.

I listened to the day's reading in which the writer praises the diversity of gifts: some are given wisdom, some are given knowledge, some are given faith. The implication is that no one is given all gifts even as everyone is given some gift, and this is surely true: I had not been given faith in God or in myself. That morning for the first time I made the connection, though I did not yet know what to make of it.

*

I met with Brother Paul Quenon under the massive ginkgo that shades one corner of the meditation garden. Born and raised in the Ohio River towns of West Virginia ("Catholics and muskrats are never found far from water"), Paul is a man of dark eyes, fine bones, and an easy tan that contrasts nicely with his silver-and-pepper beard. He is one of the few monks who actively tends to his body (swimming in summer, running in winter) but he is also among the most serious in his engagement with ascetical practice. Even on the coldest nights he sleeps outdoors or in an unheated cell with the windows open, a practice that he insists contributes to his good health.

In our conversation he identified himself openly and comfortably as gay. Asked if he felt men and women have a different experience of spirituality, Paul considered a moment before replying.

> Men feel things at a different pace than women. . . . I think people who advocate mixing the genders in all ways will discover that we each have ways of communicating that don't happen when the genders are mixed. . . . I entered the monastery as a confirmation of my own masculinity — I needed to belong to a men's community. Whether I still need that [he cracked his knuckles loudly], I don't know. There's a different embodiment of the Spirit in women.

I pointed out that if we accept that sexual attraction arises between people of the same gender, we eliminate the most obvious rationale for same-gender communities — that is, that they ease the practice of celibacy. Paul agreed that same-gender monastic communities are being challenged to rethink their foundations. "That's another difference between women and men — women don't have as much investment in the hierarchy. They're willing to push the envelope, to experiment with structure. And women are so perceptive! They perceive things I don't necessarily want known long before men do."

Which makes women's exclusion from power all the easier to understand, I thought, as I returned to my room for an afternoon nap.

◦

I met for a long conversation with Brother Alfred McCartney, a cheerful informant who spoke with an undercurrent of rigorous intellectualism and skepticism and a genuine love for the institution. All these combined embolden him to criticize it, or perhaps he's just old enough not to care about the consequences:

> The reason [for Gethsemani's declining numbers] is that we project an image that all we have to offer is liturgy and work, when today people are seeking God through meditation. We have too much money. We have charitable commitments to and in the county, but we've become

the worst possible thing for men of faith: we're respectable men of substance, making a living — bourgeois.

Most [new vocations] who come here now have been born after Vatican II and fancy that if they can return to the world as it existed prior to that, all problems will be solved. This is a problem throughout the [Roman] Church — all our orders have it — we have as vocations fervent people who are emotionally immature, full of pious humbug, they don't know their theology.

In its beginnings the Church decided it was not going to be an elite church — it would be an egalitarian church. But that means you'll be divided against yourself. John Paul II is more concerned with politics, when we, the Church, ought properly to be concerned with loving one another.

Alfred, who identified himself as "a big fan" of my work, told me that he is gay, and I began to wonder whether I was drawn to speak with the gay monks because they were more forthcoming, or from some nonrational, intuitive fellowship, or whether there were in fact more gay monks than I'd supposed. Alfred estimated that twenty of Gethsemani's seventy monks are gay, but our conversations revealed that already I knew some of whom he was unaware.

That the monks do not proclaim their sexual orientations does not necessarily imply dissemblance. The monastic experience has traditionally been seen as a rebirth — people drop their pasts and talk little about them. Only in recent years have any of the monks troubled to include their last names in an introduction. At the same time, the younger gay monks openly characterized the institution as "homophobic" — hardly a surprise, given the tenor of the church where it makes its home.

⁂

A medieval doctor would categorize Sister Maricela Garcia as fire — the life-giving heat, with all the joys and risks entailed in it. Born in Mexico to a poor family, she spent years in a teaching order before seeking out the Trappistines, the women's branch of the Trappists. Olive-skinned, dark-eyed, middle-aged, her cropped black hair just beginning to show salt, she is a García Lorca woman, shining with a passion that brought about her transfer from her Trappistine monastery in northern California to Gethsemani. When tensions in her community ran high, a mediation team sent her from there to Gethsemani for what the abbot called "a cooling-off period" of three months that have become three years. She has lived as the only woman among an enclosed, cloistered community of seventy men. Though her future place of residence is uncertain, she has remained, partly because tensions with her former community were unresolved, partly because of her affection for Gethsemani, partly because no one knows what to do with this outspoken, idealistic woman, and partly because (I suspect) the abbot appreciates her presence as a kind of living parable (or koan, as the Buddhists might have it) likely to instruct this cloistered community of men better than any lecture. Father Kelty remarked how, only a few years earlier, "a shock went through the community when the UPS driver drove to the shipping dock and turned out to be a woman. Now Sister Maricela is here. Twenty years ago her being here would have been unthinkable. When she came, the abbot made nothing of it, didn't preach to us — that being so, maybe the monks here are capable of making other changes. Or maybe not."

We met on the small lawn outside the reception room, where we spoke over the hum of the industrial-size air conditioner that cools the retreatants' wing (among Timothy's first acts as abbot was to have it turned off in the church). The words tumbled out of Maricela in an eloquent stream — she was passionate in her commitment to the order and to the church as well as to their reform.

Like so many in the contemplative orders, she came because she read Merton's *Seven Storey Mountain*. "He touched something that was Latin in me, that I couldn't put a finger on," she said. "My desire to find meaning in what one does — my desire for solitude and prayer." She began as a nun in a teaching order, but she left because "I couldn't find meaning in its practices — the rosary, the offices — these didn't touch my interior life." She joined the most radical of the Trappistine houses, where the focus was on achieving the kind of life transformation spoken of by the great mystical poets. She described their process of questioning the old ways:

> [At my monastery we] followed tradition at the same time that we asked, "Why are we saying these prayers? What's their significance in changing my life?" If I'm not changing the way I'm living, there's no purpose in these practices. I came here not just to hide myself but because I have a responsibility toward the community and the world, but especially myself. Because we emphasize that it's by developing oneself

that I can best achieve a realization of the means to respond to injustice and anger. Stop blaming the world and take responsibility — a very Buddhist concept. My sisters and I keep the tradition of reading aloud [*lectio divina*], but we evaluate the passage and if it's not appropriate we change it. We've read the Bhagavad Gita, the Upanishads, Merton. We don't say the cursing psalms, and we change the language of the Bible to make it inclusive.

I asked for her thoughts on why anger had been such a theme at the previous summer's Gethsemani Encounter.

It's a great gift to be poor. One's accepted as such. It's created in me a great respect — if I have a need, I have to decide whether I can meet it or not — because I was brought up in a poor family. In a materialistic society we ask, "If someone else has it, why can't I have it?" Or on the other side we say, "I have it. How can I keep anybody else from getting it?" And this creates dissatisfaction. Anger comes up because I don't have what I want — I feel the sense of injustice and therefore I get angry. Or because I have to spend all my time protecting what I've got.

I've reacted against psychologists because they encourage us to express our emotions — I saw how that only serves to create more anger. No matter what wrong is done to us we are responsible for our response to it. To turn the other cheek is not just to be passive but to take the responsibility for creating peace. I don't believe in righteous anger, because it will always give us an excuse to strike back.

At a visit of the abbot general, the leader of the Trappists, she rose to question directly the Trappists' self-satisfaction and complacency.

I asked: "What are we doing to awaken a questioning attitude in the people who come to us?" These practices are centuries old. Their essence can stay, but the expression needs to change. We wear a dress from the twelfth century that stands up because it's so dirty, but we can't take it off because we'll be naked. That's us not wanting to change, fearing change and not really understanding our own worth.

Our task is to question how we see Jesus — it will take a long time for the Catholic Church to realize what Christianity is all about. And I wonder about why so much emphasis on defending the doctrine instead of living it. My anger rises because I want to see change, I see the need of the people to be guided rather than all this stuff that doesn't help people grow spiritually.

To me the obvious issue is that we're dying out. Younger people are thirsting for a spiritual life — to me we're not doing our job.

We spoke for over an hour, and still there were more words, but the bells for the next office closed our conversation, which she ended, characteristically, on a note of appreciation of her hosts. "What strikes me about this community — their maturity in accepting me," she said. "They didn't do it out of politeness or charity — they've shared with me their life."

⁂

One of the monks pulled me aside to say some kind words about my writing. "I'm a big fan of your work," he said, a phrase I was beginning to understand as code for "I'm gay, I know you're gay, it's all right." Now in his fourth year at Gethsemani, he was one of its very few new arrivals, and his accent identified him as one of the few monks with Kentucky roots. "I was at the seminary and I was haunted by this place," he said. "I used to come over and ring the bell late at night and ask for a place to stay just to see if they'd give me one, and they always did. I entered on my fortieth birthday — I had wandered in the desert for forty years."

He readily identified himself as gay but asked that I not use his name.

I've transcended being categorized as gay. The need for an identity from sexuality is rather shallow — so get over it. You're gay and you've been ostracized by the church — but do you need to take your identity from that part of yourself? I've moved beyond that. It's not a question of denial or repression — that part of me is vital — but it doesn't dominate my identity no more than any single aspect of my personality dominates. It's interesting to me that somebody as old as you is stuck in such a place.

I asked him why, if he's transcended being categorized, he won't allow me to use his name.

I don't want to be identified by name because in novitiate I fell in love with one of the brothers. Ten years ago I wanted this more than anything. He left and begged me to leave with him, but I felt God wanted me to stay. He felt a strong need to live his life as a gay man — whereas I felt a need to live my life as a man, with no adjectives attached.

I've had a rough time here with resisting authority. But with obedi-
ence comes a great deal of freedom. By putting myself under obedience
I am free to be me. For the first time in my life I can look for teachers.
Before this, hell would freeze over before I'd ask anybody for help. Here
I have teachers in Timothy, Harold, Alfred, Gerlac. A lot of the older
brothers, they're not angry — you can look at them and tell.

Later Brother Alfred would ask if I'd spoken with this relatively young,
brash arrival. "He's our prophet," Alfred said. "He represents the wave of
the future," and so in my notes I named him Brother Isaiah, prophet for
Gethsemani.

✍

Father Timothy Kelly was elected abbot in 1973, third in a series of good
Irish administrator abbots. Unlike his predecessors, he does not use the abbot's honorific "Dom," derived from the Latin *dominus* (master). He is a
small, thin, elegantly featured man of a delicate handsomeness and high-
strung physicality. If in medieval terminology Maricela is fire, Timothy is
mostly air, inclined toward the intellect, the spirit, the world of ideas, almost to the exclusion of the material world.

We met in his spacious office, simply furnished with plain oak chairs
and a large, remarkably neat desk. Only a crucifix and an icon of the Virgin
occupied the exposed brick walls. He spoke with a cheerful, nervous intensity, born, perhaps, of his own audacity in inviting me here. I'm hardly the
first writer to stay at Gethsemani, but I am among the few to come as a
skeptic, and without a doubt the only writer to arrive as an insider, a member of the surrounding rural community of which Gethsemani is one facet.
In addition to which I am an openly gay man, visiting a community of the
Roman Church, whose paranoia around sexuality has reached inquisitorial
proportions.

Timothy himself is an outsider, a Canadian transported to the rural
South. He came to Gethsemani, he said, "because I was looking for meaning, and I thought, 'Why not spend one's life in the single-minded search?'"
His father disowned him, telling him he was running from his life. His
mother was hardly more supportive. "It's occurred to me," he said with a
wry smile, "that I became a monk to show her who was in charge — and
she never gave in. Even after I was elected abbot, when I went to see her she
said, 'Why are you going back to that place?' An Irish Catholic woman who

might have wanted me to become a diocesan priest — that way maybe she'd have retained control." Some months later I will read in Thomas Merton's journals, "In the natural order, perhaps solitaries are made by severe mothers."

With my conversation with Brother Paul in mind, I raised the subject of the vow of celibacy and the difficulty of honoring it. Timothy looked a little bemused. "I haven't thought about it a great deal of late," he said. "Monasticism comes from Greek *monos,* 'one alone' — someone who is single, unified in himself. Celibacy is a way to help us unify the heart — to take away dispersion."

"That may be true for the older monks," I said, "but what of the younger ones? And what about those of us who live in a culture obsessed with making money from everything, especially from sex?"

"The question is, How do we use and direct the energy that comes from sexuality in a way that deepens the heart?" Timothy said, and I was struck by how often the monks answer my questions with questions. "Perhaps the Buddhists have better traditions here. Christians are influenced by the late nineteenth century — mostly negative, as in, 'Don't do it.' The question is, How do we positively direct that energy? Here at Gethsemani we've not dealt with that — our tradition of hard manual labor provided a ready place to avoid those questions. But now with an easier life I wonder if we shouldn't reflect on how to make celibacy a positive force."

He told a desert father story: "Two monks are walking when they come to a stream, where there's a woman trying to cross. One of the monks helps her across the stream on his back. The monks walk on for an hour or so until finally the monk who had refrained from helping the woman says to his partner, 'I wouldn't have touched that woman.' And his companion says, 'Yes, but I left her behind an hour ago.'"

"Monks aren't the ideal Christians," Timothy said. "People come here because they want to be hooked up with the holy monks, when what *we* want to do is to learn from *you.* The Vatican wants to see us as ideal Christians, when the monks ourselves have a much humbler view of our positions."

Timothy had submitted his request to retire, but his superior had refused to accept it, and Timothy, obedient as his vows demand, remained in the traces. I asked him to evaluate his successes and difficulties in his long tenure.

I haven't found a new metaphor or a good metaphor for calling people to a disciplined life that ultimately leads to freedom that leads to God. As young people we were pushed too much to the image of Jesus on the cross [as the operant metaphor], but you get older and you find the relevance of that concept to the whole of life.

The whole difficulty of the Church now: Where does she get her authority to teach? How much of Gregorian chant was about being a community saying a mantra together? In switching to another form of music are we really aware of what we've done, how much music was a part of the culture?

As he spoke I thought of the retreatants' hymnals, how after only a few days as a retreatant I involuntarily flinched when I saw that the upcoming hymn dated from the twentieth century, because experience has taught me that the writing of a good hymn is a very particular art, that the art must grow organically from the culture, and that few twentieth-century composers have been able to pull it off. Music doesn't lie, and it's impossible to fake faith, and so the twentieth-century hymns sound false to the ear and the heart. *What does it say of our culture,* I wondered, *that we have lost the ability to sing praise?*

Timothy continued:

In the late 1960s we had a policy — we didn't accept anyone from broken homes. But now everyone is from a broken home. We don't feel we have the wherewithal to be a halfway house, but maybe we should be more willing to act in that regard. Younger people who come here are conservative, not really knowing where to go.

Of the monks here, one third or so are pre–Vatican II Catholics whose concerns center on having lost a sense of security and meaning as a result of all the changes that have come about. Another third are seeking something new that's an evolution from what they've known in the past. The other third are cynical — they've lost their faith. From them I would hope for some kind of breakthrough or enlightenment. Why else continue? I'd like to think it's not just inertia or fear, that there's something profound that they're looking for. Hopefully there are enough brothers working with something deep — I don't think it's just fear. There's a fraternity to it, wanting to be with people and to share a life.

I asked him about the incongruity and the challenges of a single woman — Maricela — living among a community so prominently and historically reserved for men.

> Sister Maricela's community was in transition and she came here for a retreat that got extended while her house went through some difficult times . . . she'll be going back to her home foundation in a few months. I offered the Gethsemani community the option of writing me anonymously about Sister Maricela and one wrote: "Women are sin." Can you believe it? Gender concerns are more difficult for this cloistered community than for a more active community. In this context there's not much opportunity for relief from infatuation. If you're more involved with the outside world, maybe that relief is more readily found.

We spoke of words of counsel that he might provide to his successor, if and when his superior accepts his application for retirement: "Trust other people; trust the community. There's a wisdom there — how to tap it is the question. People really do want to do the right thing, to live together in peace. We read aloud from the Rule of St. Benedict and we get to the place where he talks about what kind of person the abbot ought to be, and the reader always places the emphasis on 'ought' — what kind of person the abbot *ought* to be [he laughs]."

Timothy recalled the time in the early 1960s when Merton, taken to a Louisville hospital for back surgery, fell in love with his nurse and began a clandestine affair that, judging from his recently published correspondence, was consummated in spirit if not in fact.

> Benedict says a man who is suspicious should never be abbot. At the same time, you have to recognize the tip of the iceberg when you see it. When Merton was involved with a nurse, he was phoning her from the cellarer's office. Someone overheard his conversations and told Dom James. But rather than go to Merton, James went to the cellarer and asked him to speak to Merton about it — James had the wisdom of giving Merton a chance to come to him, rather than speaking from above.

The bells called us to sext, the midday office, and though our conversation was only beginning, in my many stays at Gethsemani across several years I will see Timothy miss an office only once. I followed him to the church, where the humid light of the southern summer filled the high white spaces. The bell echoed through the church as the monks took up the chant. I thought of Timothy's kindness in inviting me, and in appreciation I bowed with my fellow retreatants at the call to prayer.

⌘

Brother Fintan had long since left Gethsemani, among the first of those who went over the wall. Later Brother Clement left, took back his secular name, and married my aunt, who had been a nun, and thus he became my Uncle John years after I was named for him.

And so I sought out Brother Alban, once the fair-haired sidekick to the ruling trinity of Clement, Fintan, and Marcellus. Alban had been big and strapping, a giant to me when I was a child, though it's been so long since I or anyone has seen him stand that I can no longer tell his height. Now he is wheelchair-bound with multiple sclerosis, bloated from fluid retention and the inevitable weight gain that occurs when someone is unable to walk.

Like me, Brother Alban was the youngest of his large family. He had entered the monastery at fourteen years of age, child of a big Ohio Catholic family whose father had died young. Later he would tell my mother that he stayed put only through contemplating the stained-glass image of the Virgin (removed in the church renovation of the 1960s) squirting milk from her bare breast into the baby Jesus' mouth.

Over these years, as Alban has grown progressively more disabled, the community has found work for him that requires less mobility. Now he's assigned to the reception desk. Across the past week I've watched him handle multiple calls using the speaker phone or ignore the phone altogether when an old friend stopped by.

Earlier that week, Alban had entered the infirmary to be treated for pneumonia. I went looking for him there, to find that in the monastery infirmary (in contrast to its dormitories) there are almost no empty rooms. I encountered aged Brother Giles, another old friend of my father, deaf as a post, who shouted directions to the basement dining room, where Alban and an old friend were sharing a beer.

We were in the rural South, and so the three of us talked about the past. Alban told how he first met my family — his truck broke down in front of my family's house, the small rented house with a breezeway through the middle that sat across the road from the distillery where Father worked. Shy in his lay brother's brown robes, Alban had refused my mother's invitation to come in but had her phone the monastery for help while he stayed on the porch eating the pumpkin pie she'd offered. His recollection conjures up the afternoon: the clapboard house, rented from Seagram & Sons, its peeling paint grimy with the coal dust that rained from the distillery smokestack; the passel of kids, tumbling across the patchy yard, scattering the chickens; Alban, tall and muscular, all angles and grin. Decades of joy and sorrow, births and deaths, brothers joined and (mostly) brothers departed, a community transformed, a life circumscribed by disease, but the body will have its way: "Man," Alban said, sipping his beer and smacking his lips, "your mom made a *great* pumpkin pie." He drained the last of his beer just as the bell rang for compline, last office of the day — I was beginning to understand that no dancer has a better sense of timing than a monk. Alban motored his way back to the infirmary.

Walking to this, almost the last office of my retreat, I realized I was eager to return to my glittering city life even though the week had raised more questions than it had answered. What was the proper relationship between the body and what we call faith? And where did doctrine and dogma fit in all this? How did one properly mesh a commitment to an interior life with a commitment to service? What could lead an intelligent person to choose a life of service to God (a word I wrote with reluctance)?

At the end of compline visitors and retreatants formed two lines to be sprinkled with holy water by the abbot, in one of those medieval gestures I have resisted. I remembered the words of Brother Martin about the importance of ending the day with a pure heart . . . but I thought too of how all that superstition had been used as a weapon against the poor, the outsiders, women, homosexuals, nonbelievers. I stayed in my seat.

After compline I walked outside to clear my head. As dusk fell on this clear moonless night, the fireflies emerged with the stars, and soon they were about equal in number. A whippoorwill began its resonant call, two mournful notes followed by a rising note of hope. In looking over this pastoral landscape I thought of Alban, his indefatigable good humor in the face of the worst of fates — on a later visit Alban will inform me with cheerful relish that in the old Cistercian sign language the symbol for "boss" was a closed fist with the middle finger raised. I thought of the ways and means of teaching and wondered if I was big enough to accept the lesson Alban offered, or if I might become that big.

☙

While at Gethsemani I encountered Merton's last writings — a revelation, since they are so different from the starry-eyed naiveté of his earlier work. For the last decade of his twenty-seven years at the Abbey of Gethsemani, Merton had been studying and writing about Eastern philosophies and religions. Though within the monastic enclosure and often censored by church authorities, he had been enormously influential in introducing Western Christian thinkers to Eastern philosophies, particularly Zen Buddhism. On his only trip to Asia he met the Dalai Lama in Dharamsala, India, the Tibetan leader's capital-in-exile. Less than three weeks later Merton addressed a Bangkok convocation of Buddhist, Christian, and Hindu monks. A few minutes after he ended his speech (his concluding words were "and now I will disappear"), he died in his hotel room, apparently electrocuted by the faulty wiring in a fan.

"What is essential in the monastic life is not embedded in buildings, is not embedded in clothing, is not necessarily embedded even in a rule," Merton said in that last speech. "It is concerned with this business of total inner transformation. All other things serve that end. . . . I believe that by openness to Buddhism, to Hinduism, and to these great Asian traditions, we stand a wonderful chance of learning more about the potentiality of our own traditions."

Total inner transformation. No more revolutionary words could be spoken. They rest at the heart of the American dream, which, we like to tell ourselves, is the human dream. As the new millennium begins, what can they mean? For a skeptical Darwinist in the age of materialism, what does it mean to have and keep faith?

7

WAY-SEEKING MIND

A GRAVEL ROAD descends through a twisting, churning river of sandstone, down through chaparral redolent of sage and chamise to a tumbling stream lined with stately sycamores and oaks. The days are endlessly blue, with a pleasant breeze in the afternoon from the great ocean, an unseen but palpable presence over the peaks. The creek bed blossoms with yellow monkeyflower, scarlet penstemon, a dark blue, late-blooming Douglas iris. Heated by the earth's living core, steaming water seeps from the rocks to be captured in deep pools, their sulfurous stench cut by the sinus-clearing menthol of steel-blue eucalyptus. Nearby an organic garden puts forth corn and tomatoes and squash just coming ripe, edged by bright yellow evening primrose and sunflowers and magenta cosmos under blue-gray agave spiking from stony cliffs. At midday the glare blinds in both shade and light, but as the sun slides down the ecliptic, the coppery sandstone takes on contour and color until it glows as if lit from the furnace within.

Twilight. Kerosene lanterns light the paths. A swimming pool would appear too strange here in the heart of the Pacific coast wilderness, but there it is, with a scattering of toasted women in hot pink Lycra, portly parboiled men in Speedos floating in the steaming, earth-warmed water. Black-robed men and women move with languid steps along the raked and graveled paths, waving away mucus flies (even paradise must have its worms), making their ways to the Japanese-style zendo, where high-pitched clackings and a deep-throated gong call them to meditation.

California: if we hadn't invented it, it wouldn't exist.

❧

The architecture at Tassajara Zen Mountain Center is vaguely Japanese — white, wood-frame cottages with slanting roofs and doors so low they threaten the American head. Though the complex has survived earthquake, flood, and fire, like so much California architecture it imparts a sense of impermanence, a jerry-rigged human creation on the living, restless earth.

A succession of structures has come and gone since the Esselen Indians first built bowls of rocks to facilitate bathing, but across time the principle has remained the same: the pools gradually decrease in temperature, until the bather arrives at the chilly, rushing waters of the creek, which has hollowed holes deep enough for immersion. The odor of sulfur, present throughout the Tassajara ravine, is especially strong here. The bather feels at once exhilarated and humbled by the forces of nascent being — somewhere close at hand, to judge by the heat and the smell, the first act of creation is still in process.

To support itself, Tassajara takes in paying guests in the summer months, making enough money to funnel a surplus to the San Francisco Zen Center's other branches: City Center, located in the heart of San Francisco, and Green Gulch, the Zen Center's organic farm, located across the Golden Gate Bridge. The summer guests may or may not be interested in sitting meditation or Buddhism — thus the bikini-clad loungers by the pool. But in the winter months the landscape, external and internal, changes dramatically, as the rustic resort atmosphere gives way to an ascetic community whose only residents are long-time Zen Center members and others who have applied and been admitted through a process that requires demonstrating serious commitment to Zen practice.

I first visited in midsummer, enrolled as a "guest practitioner," a status that required me to work in the mornings but left my afternoons free. To reach Tassajara I took a winding two-lane road from the rocky Pacific beaches of Carmel, past the resorts and ranches of wealthy retirees and Silicon Valley executives, until I was thirty and more miles inland, into the Santa Lucias (Holy Lucy, Sacred Light). There a narrow gravel road leads up and over a four-thousand-foot mountain to a deep crevasse, not really a canyon, not enough flat ground to earn the name. Gethsemani walls itself off from its placid landscape with mortar and stone; at Tassajara the steep-sided mountains form a natural barrier between the Zen Mountain Center and what we call civilization.

I came to San Francisco as a college freshman in 1971, ignorant of most everything except that I had seen hippies on television and I wanted to go where I thought they were. By then most were beginning the decompression that would ultimately lead to families, graduate degrees, suburban homes, all the responsibilities Plato would ascribe to the realm of the exterior, tangible world of the senses, and yet I was shaped by that hiccup in history, the 1960s, when for a few brief years the nation halted the business of expansion to look inward. Across the next two decades I would acquire the rudiments of Eastern philosophy via cultural osmosis — transmogrified, modified-and-adapted, turned-on-its-head Buddhism, but Buddhism all the same. *Be here now. That's so Zen.* These phrases fall from my mouth without thought, but it was left to the workings of serendipity (the Trappists might say "the Holy Spirit") to bring me to a place where I could talk to the men and women whose ideas and ideals were already lodging under my roof.

As I searched out a cart to convey my bag to my sleeping quarters, I considered that only a city person could stay here for months at a stretch; someone raised in the country would demand less drama and more companionship from the landscape. Tassajara Creek chatters past low stone buildings and the newer zendo, built mortise-and-tenon, not a nail used in its construction. Benches along the creek are hewn from fallen sycamores, so that it's hard to tell where the sitting ends and the tree begins. Oaks and ghost pines cling to the parched mountainside. Here the collision of the great subterranean plates, Pacific to the west, North American to the east, has jammed earth's oldest and youngest rocks together and up to form impossibly steep crags. The heat generated in that collision gives birth to one of the most generous of North American hot springs.

In the mid–nineteenth century a man named Quilty purchased the property from its earliest white owners and set up a horse trail. He built the first bathhouse, the first cabins (some still standing), and the stone floor of the dining room, its sandstone blocks left over from the rock carved from cliffs to make the original road. Quilty's road cost ten thousand dollars, an enormous sum for the time, but after its completion the builder threw in the towel and sold the road to the county at cost. Soon thereafter the springs became a popular destination for the well-to-do of Salinas and Monterey.

The Indians knew Tassajara as a sacred place of rest and healing; the Spanish hung game and butchered cattle from the trees to dry in the relentless summer heat (the name, so sweet on the tongue, means "place for drying jerky"). But the trip from Monterey and Carmel is long, hot and dusty in summer, cold and slippery in winter, when rain, snow, and mud slides sometimes close the road. By the early 1960s Tassajara had become not the posh resort envisioned by its founder but a lowlife adventure, a drinking destination, a place to get high and party down, until the San Francisco Zen Center purchased it as the site of the first Zen monastery in America, under the leadership of the Japanese immigrant priest Shunryu Suzuki.

Suzuki (not to be confused with Japanese author and Zen advocate D. T. Suzuki) was born in Japan in 1904, oldest son of a Buddhist priest, and as such was expected to enter his father's profession and eventually assume control of his temple. According to his biographer, David Chadwick, he was not especially bright and was so mule-headed that in an effort to teach him humility, his teacher assigned him nine bows instead of the customary three. (Decades later, working from the same principle, Suzuki would require nine bows of his American students.) Like Merton, he had a checkered past. In the 1930s Merton apparently deserted an Englishwoman pregnant with his child; their fate is unknown, though a rumor continues to circulate (Merton's biographer gives it little credence) that they died in the German bombing of London. In those same years, Suzuki Roshi arranged to annul his first marriage after his wife developed tuberculosis. Neither man spoke or wrote about the women they had abandoned, though in a 1944 will composed on professing his final monastic vows, Merton made oblique reference to his lover's existence ("this second half [of my savings] to be paid . . . to the person mentioned . . . in my letters, if that person can be contacted").

With an eloquence that has moved millions, Merton writes in *Seven Storey Mountain* of his decision to give up his worldly ambitions to join the Trappists, but a close reading of Michael Mott's biography and conversations with those who knew Merton reveal a man less than assiduous at questioning his own motives, who along with many other men of the 1940s came to the Trappists in part to avoid being drafted. In those same years, Suzuki was reluctantly housing soldiers and Korean slave labor in his temple. He generally opposed the war effort but refrained from speaking publicly against it, instead choosing accommodation under duress. Merton devotees are fond of pointing to his pro–civil rights and anti-Vietnam stances as evidence of his breadth of vision, but it's of note that in a journal entry made in 1967, barely a year before his death, he disparages the "fairies" who inadvertently interrupted his outdoor romancing on an evening date before he became a monk. Suzuki Roshi was capable of betraying longtime associates and was famously thoughtless and intractable toward his second wife. Both Merton and Suzuki seemed driven in part by the need to expiate past sins, and both chose the New World as their place of starting over — Merton traveling west from Europe, Suzuki east from Asia.

"Aren't we fortunate our teachings come to us in flawed vessels," a Tibetan Buddhist priest told me. Perhaps one characteristic of genius is the ability to inhabit the present so fully as not to be crippled by the memories of past transgressions. In their later years both men went to painstaking lengths to emphasize their fallibility, but even so their devotees often speak of them as superhumans. There's something unseemly in that celebrity worship, that speaks of some deep-seated human need to believe in Oz, or Santa Claus, or heaven — a fantasyland where human beings are perfect, with *perfect* solipsistically defined as incorporating all we perceive ourselves to lack. A more appropriate lesson to draw from their stories might be that saints are far more common — and fallible — than we like to believe. We are surrounded by Mertons and Suzukis, whose very proximity renders them so ordinary to us that we take them for granted.

On this first visit to Tassajara, because I'd meditated infrequently since my first visit to the Manhattan zendo, I sought out the *ino* (temple caretaker) for a reorientation. He was in his midtwenties, tall, with buzzed roots beginning to sprout from a shaved head. He offered the simplest of guidelines, similar to those I'd received in New York. "If you can work your way toward sitting in full lotus, that's great, but it will take time to get that flexible," he said. "If you can only sit in a chair, then sit in a chair. It doesn't matter where you sit, it's in the act of paying attention to how you're sitting. The point is to still the mind." He spoke of focusing the attention on the act of breathing, counting each breath to ten, then back to one, then back to ten. "Notice how your body feels. Notice how you hold your hands." He demonstrated a *mudra*, one of several hand positions for meditation; at the San Francisco Zen Center, in the preferred *mudra* the left hand rests over the right — "the intuitive over the intellectual" — and the thumbs are allowed to touch lightly so as to form a circle, symbol of the roundness of being. "You'll get distracted, of course," he said. "Don't get upset at being distracted. Notice what you're thinking about, catalogue it if you want, maybe to revisit later on. Then return to noticing your breath and your body. Is your back straight? Are your ears over your shoulders? Have you let yourself slump?"

"What's the goal?" I asked.

"The goal is to have no goal," he answered. "The goal is to take a few minutes just to be."

The eminent scholar Etienne Gilson summed up the theological revolution proposed by Thomas Aquinas: "The most marvelous of all things a being can do is: to be." Aquinas, meet Suzuki Roshi.

The *ino* showed me to my sleeping quarters in a converted barn, where I occupied a cubicle along with ten or so mostly college-age students, working at Tassajara's summer guest session in hopes of being invited to return for the more rigorous winter sittings. He handed me a summer schedule, then left.

The beating of the *han* — the wooden plank struck to signal an imminent session of meditation — woke me at 5:30 A.M., groggy and grumpy less because of the hour than because my college-age bunkmates had returned at 3:00 A.M. from some expedition whose nature I assumed included the young women quartered at the opposite end of the camp. In that first period of zazen I stumbled around the zendo, sitting in the wrong place, confused and irritated by the strangeness of the ritual, and embarrassed by my clumsiness when all those about me apparently knew what they were doing and did it gracefully.

As part of the service that concluded zazen, the community chanted in what I took to be Japanese:

Kan ze on
Na mu Butsu
Yo Butsu u in
Yo Butsu u en
Bup po so en
Jo raku ga jo
Cho nen Kan se on
Bo nen Kan se on
Nen nen ju shin ki
Nen nen fu ri shin

The temple assistant sounded out the rhythm of the chant on the *mokugyo,* a fish-shaped drum whose steady rhythmic beat might have been the thrum of some large, collective heart. As we chanted, the beat quickened from a walk to a trot to a full-on run of syllables as foreign and musical as the church Latin of my childhood — the analogy leapt effortlessly to mind, sound without sense or practical application.

Kan ze on	Introibo ad altáre Dei.
Na mu Butsu . . .	Ad Deum qui laetíficat juventútam
	meam. . . .

An essential aspect of the sacred, it occurred to me in the midst of the Japanese chant, is that it cannot be bought or sold. Whether gesture or thought, almsgiving or prayer, the sacred act is done not for personal gain but for the sake of the doing. Ritual originates in the ordinary, necessary acts of survival (eating, drinking, rest) but transforms these into metaphor (communion, zazen). By distilling these ordinary acts to their essences, ritual invokes the world beneath and beyond their surfaces.

In the space of that thought my skeptic's hackles rose: *At best it's a bunch of aging hippies who have figured out how to support themselves on as little work as possible. At worst it's a cult, following the familiar pattern of offering wounded people shelter and hospitality in exchange for their labor and money and blind commitment. If we were asked to chant in Latin, the room would empty in seconds.*

But then I remembered my conversations with Brother Martin at Gethsemani and the words of the desert *abba* — "As it goes with the father, so will it go with the son." My father belittled all that was new and strange and different, not because he had considered it and found it wanting but because it made him feel insecure to venture into an unfamiliar world where he was not in control. *The old man wouldn't be caught dead doing this,* I thought. I took up the chant card.

Somewhere the great gong sounded, ending the chants, followed by nine bows to the floor. My every muscle, ligament, tendon, and bone resisted this gesture of self-abnegation. As a gay man I had struggled most of my life to establish self-respect; here I was being asked to give it up, in exchange for what? But I had moved forward with the participants rather than hang back with the visitors, so my choice was to stand like a lone tree amid a felled forest or join in. I gritted my teeth and knelt nine times, up and down, touching my forehead to the cool, unvarnished floor, then swayed in place while my neighbors chanted the closing prayer:

Great robe of liberation
Field far beyond form and emptiness

Wearing the Tatagatha's teachings
Saving all beings

On my first work morning I was assigned to housekeeping — a vital task for a resort. I am not a good housekeeper, a failing I made clear to the work leader. "An opportunity for practice," she said cheerfully, and though at first I thought she meant improving my skill at tucking hospital corners, in fact she was giving me an introduction to the Buddhist admonition to view adversity as opportunity: embrace the making of that bed.

I was placed in the charge of a nineteen-year-old college student, who looked visibly apprehensive when I told him I was forty-three. A refugee from a conservative Christian college, he was neither comfortable nor adept at criticizing the work of someone twenty-plus years older; I was not adept at accepting his awkward critique — an opportunity for practice indeed. While he was outside emptying trash, I flipped a quarter at the bed he'd just made — it bounced off. My beds wrinkled and sagged the moment I turned my back.

Fluffing pillows, scrubbing toilets, mopping floors, I thought of a job I'd taken after my second year of college. Broke after a semester of study in France, I hired on at Nationwide Uniforms — known in my Kentucky hometown as "the sewing factory" — turning out shirts, jackets, and pants for the nation's police and fire departments. Six men managed three hundred women, each woman seated at a sewing machine, each assigned daily output quotas pegged to her seniority. The longer a woman was on the job, the faster and cleaner she was required to produce. Bonuses were available for women who ratted on their fellow workers, turning in those who claimed sick pay but who were really caring for children or hungover or both. There was no union — or rather, there was a union that actively collaborated with management in keeping wages low and benefits nonexistent. As a man, sweeping floors in a job created by the friendly boss to help me pay for college expenses, I started at $1.85 per hour, thirty-five cents an hour higher than the rate for a skilled seamstress with a year's experience.

I lasted six weeks. I hated every minute of this most useful experience, across the course of which I had my eyes opened a bit wider to the magnitude of my good fortune. Like the women with whom I worked, I got through the day in anticipation of the ride home, where the woman who'd most recently played hooky brought the carload up to date on what was happening on the soaps. These lively, funny, blue-collar women would have quit or been fired before taking advantage of the stool-pigeon bonuses dangled before their noses.

Farmwork and housework are dull, repetitive, sometimes backbreaking, but they can be counted on to vary with the crops and seasons, the product is immediately tangible and useful, and there is always the fallow time of winter. At Nationwide, a seamstress might spend the better part of her life sewing seam after seam, sleeve after sleeve, year after year. How and where could she find or create meaning in such a life? These women stayed sane — those who did — through their loyalty to one another, their hopes for and stories of their children, their love of the soaps, and yes, I had to admit it, through something I would call faith.

"An opportunity for practice" sounded like nothing more than a variation on the mantra of my Catholic childhood — "offer it up to Jesus." And yet when I later returned to Gethsemani to live among the monks, one would tell me this story: "When I got out of the army I was depressed, disintegrated. Every day I would pick up my father after work and I'd think: *How can he do this, working every day at a menial job?* So finally I asked him and his answer was, 'Love for my family and faith in God, trusting in God.'"

Why had I set out on this search for faith? This sentence has cropped up in my imagination: I am a blue-collar boy thrust into the glittering city, attempting to understand the consequences of the choices I have made, the places where history has taken me. In my case that history is integrally intertwined with what was for fifteen hundred years the dominant spiritual, cultural, educational, and scientific institution of the West: the Roman Catholic Church. And then there was my mother, the convert — anyone who troubles to convert has been giving some serious thought to the big questions, and I inherited that from her.

Sometime in my twenties I began asking her, "How did you endure and keep so cheerful?" Twelve pregnancies, three miscarriages, nine births, her second child dead at two weeks, her eldest son dead in midlife, a grandson accidentally killed by his father, a severely alcoholic brother who always turned to her, and responsible for food on the table for ten people for two and three meals a day, seven days a week, for thirty-five years, life a constant struggle to make ends meet. And always she answered, "Because of my faith." Eventually I began to wonder, *What is this thing she calls faith? Why don't I have it, and is it possible, this late in the game, that I might acquire some?*

A friend to whom I related this story scoffed at it. "It was her faith that brought her all those kids," she said. Cleaning rooms at Tassajara, I thought, possibly for the first time, that we do a disservice to the virtue we call faith in confusing it with the complex structures of belief and doctrine that make up institutionalized religion. *Belief* told my mother not to use birth control, but *faith* sustained her through her life. As I tucked sheets and whacked pillows and chased dust balls out the door, I realized that I was searching not for confirmation of the structures of belief — doctrine and dogma — but for something less tangible and more important: the sustaining virtue we call faith.

❧

Maybe news of my dismal housekeeping skills had reached the work leader — whatever the case, the next day I was reassigned to the kitchen.

In the kitchen, the *tenzo* (chief cook) with the broad Southern accent knelt on the rubber mats. Preparing for a bow to the floor, he unrolled a straw tatami mat. A spider ran out. "A sentient being!" he exclaimed, then, in case we missed the point, "Don't step on him! He loves life as much as any of us." With the spider safely ushered out the door, the *tenzo* lit candles and incense at the little kitchen altar with its tiny sitting Buddha. We joined in chanting a verse from *Instructions to the Cook*: "A joyful spirit is one of gratefulness and buoyancy."

Then a fellow worker chose from a list of kitchen precepts; today it was "Label and Store Properly." The *tenzo* gave a little lecture on labeling leftovers and prepared items so they could easily be found. "A compassionate gesture," the *tenzo* explained, "because otherwise the guest cooks can't find what they need and they get angry. Very bad karma."

I was handed a bowl of garlic, with the instructions to peel and crush four cups. After the tenth or twelfth clove I discovered the power of the plant. My fingers burned, my eyes watered. I thought longingly back to those inert, inoffensive sheets and blankets. I turned to my neighbor, chopping onions, to strike up a conversation, but the work leader poked her head through the doorway. "Morning work is conducted in silence," she said sternly. The old familiar resentment rose in my throat. *It's bad enough to be condemned to peel and crush four cups of garlic. What would make the time pass better than pleasant, aimless conversation?*

Two hours and countless cloves of garlic later, my fingers blistered beyond sensation, I had accumulated close to four cups. The bell rang for lunch — I eyed the measuring cup. A few quick cloves and I'd have the job finished. I took up another clove, but the work leader poked her head out the door again. "Kitchen service is starting. Put away your apron. Be sure to wash and dry your knife."

"I only have a few cloves left," I said. "I'll finish in just a second."

"Somebody else will get it done," she said. "When the bell sounds, we stop working."

Pavlov's dog, I thought as I hung up my apron. *The bell rings and my job is to salivate.*

✍

Something happened at these early morning sittings at Tassajara. I began to compose myself carefully on sitting, to notice if my pants were pulling at my legs and if so to loosen them, to notice if I had a tickle in my throat, and if so to clear it before the gong sounded. I began learning, that is, to live in dialogue with my body rather than as its overlord. I lost myself in the silence, in the waking of the birds, the murmur of the creek, the occasional muffled cough. I lost my self and went to that place of no thought, the hypnagogic state somewhere between and outside of waking and sleep; a cat watching a mousehole, wholly present to the world and yet in some way apart from it. I sat in this way for the full forty minutes — beginner's luck, or, as Suzuki Roshi would have it, beginner's mind.

In the years since, I have had glimpses of that place, but now the ever-clever mind has figured out where I'm trying to go and (as my sitting instructor had predicted) is not to be denied, generating an endless series of distractions . . . I may never return to that place of beginner's mind, and yet on those first mornings of sitting I began to wake to this terrifying, liberating understanding: memory resides as much in the body as in the head. To understand the whole physical body as the seat of memory, to grasp how life is the accumulation of gesture, how I become what I do, how every moment contains and expresses the sum of my history as it contributes to shaping my future — this was for me the beginning of change.

✍

METTA SUTRA

This is what should be accomplished by one who is wise, who seeks the good and has obtained peace:

Let one be strenuous, upright, and sincere, without pride, easily contented and joyous. Let one not be submerged by the things of the world. Let one not take upon oneself the burden of riches. Let one's senses be controlled. Let one be wise but not puffed up; and let one not desire great possessions even for one's family. Let one do nothing that is mean or that the wise would reprove.

May all beings be happy,

May they be joyous and live in safety.

All living beings, whether weak or strong, in high or middle or low realms of existence, small or great, visible or invisible, near or far, born or to be born, may all beings be happy.

Let no one deceive another, nor despise any being in any state; let none by anger or hatred wish harm to another.

Even as a mother at the risk of her life watches over and protects her only child, so with a boundless mind should one cherish all living things, suffusing love over the entire world, above, below, and all around without limit; so let one cultivate an infinite good will toward the whole world.

Standing or walking, sitting or lying down, during all one's waking hours let one practice the way with gratitude.

Not holding to fixed views, endowed with insight, freed from sense appetites, one who achieves the way will be freed from the duality of birth and death.

⁂

Asked what brought them to sitting meditation, American Buddhists cited (in no particular order) Alan Watts, whose 1960s midnight radio talks guided a generation of 1960s hippies out of their stoned haze and into meditation; drugs, especially LSD; Thomas Merton, who at the time of his death was writing about his encounter with Asian spiritual traditions; and Ed Brown, author of *The Tassajara Bread Book,* whose recipes, accompanied by Buddhist insights, painlessly introduced thousands of Americans to the guiding principles of Zen practice. In the new millennium Watts and Merton are dead, drugs are demonized, but Ed Brown has just bought a house, published a new book, and received dharma transmission, in which the teacher recognizes that the student is adequately prepared to assume the responsibilities of teaching others to continue the Buddhist lineage.

We met outdoors in the dappled shade of a live oak, embraced by the dry summer heat. Graced with a cook's solid heft and cheerful mien, Brown emanates a kind of puppy-dog exuberance, and though he's every skeptic's caricature of the whacked-out Marin County hippie, I found it impossible not to be infected by his sheer good humor — midway through our con-versation I wrote, "Is it possible to have this much fun being a monk?"

As it turned out Brown was uncertain about the label. He puzzled over the definition of the term.

> I don't think of myself as conceptually inclined, so I don't know that I can say what a monk is, or isn't. I think about it more in Zen terminol-ogy — "way-seeking mind." Some part of people that is seeking — everybody is in some sense or at some level seeking. I don't identify on the surface with what constitutes a monk, but I identify with that part of people that's trying to find out what it means to be alive, to be hu-man. We say, If a layperson is whole-hearted, sincere, reverent, grateful, isn't that the same as being a priest or a monk?

He offered the example of jazz musician John Coltrane. "He's a musi-cian who puts his heart into every note — no single note is more impor-tant than another. I heard him talking on the radio — in every word you could hear reverence, gratitude, awe. He couldn't wait to get back to his stu-dio." Coltrane is an exemplar, according to Brown, of how we should all look upon our lives:

> To be in touch with the preciousness of your life — whether you call it God, or Buddha nature — people want that. It's mysterious how peo-ple find their lives — with some people it's more obvious than with others. I talked to a handwriting analyst who looked at how I wrote my F's. So I changed how I write my F's and within one year I got dharma transmission, bought a house, and finished my book. Is that coinci-dence or not?

"We tell people that when the lunch bell rings you stop working, even if you're in the middle of what you're doing," Brown said. "You lay your knife on the counter and take off your apron and leave. That rule, with its implication of nonattachment to accomplishment, seems generic to mon-asteries wherever they are." I thought about how my writing, which I had first undertaken out of the love of words and a desperate desire to save my-self, had become a job like any job. Could I return to it in the spirit of nonattachment?

As I write this now I take down my own batter-and-oil-stained copy of *The Tassajara Bread Book,* from which so many years ago I learned to bake bread. "Homage to the Perfection of Wisdom, the Infinite, the Holy," I read in Brown's introduction, and only now, well into my Buddhist studies, do I recognize the opening words of the Buddhist chant in homage to Prajna Paramita, goddess of wisdom. But that's the way of a life — in your impossibly unscarred twenties, when life is infinite and time is one long Saturday afternoon you buy a book to learn how to bake bread, and twenty years later you find yourself talking to its author under a spreading live oak in the wilderness of the coastal canyons of California, wounded but wiser for it.

*

THE FOUR NOBLE TRUTHS

I. Life is *dukkha* ("suffering" or "dissatisfaction"): we are born to want what we cannot have.
II. With diligence, the causes of this suffering can be discerned.
III. These causes may be addressed — there is, in fact, a cure for the disease.
IV. This is how it's done, the Eightfold Path:

THE EIGHTFOLD PATH

1. Right view — formulate an accurate vision of what's really happening.
2. Right intention — align yourself with that vision.
3. Right speech — take care to speak mindfully to yourself as well as others.
4. Right conduct — act toward others as you would have them act toward you.
5. Right livelihood — earn your living through means that are consistent with these principles.
6. Right effort — work diligently despite obstacles and discouragements.
7. Right mindfulness — keep focused always on these principles.
8. Right concentration — be present with the task or person at hand.

*

Seeking to be a conscientious scientist even in the slippery territories of the soul, William James considered religion biologically necessary, for it "enables rational man to accept and even embrace the vicissitudes of an uncaring universe on which he is finally dependent." James goes on to rank

Buddhism and Christianity as probably the best of the world's religious systems. In both religions a man or woman must die to the superficial, unreal life in order to be reborn to the real life; the highest state of being lies in the most complete renunciation of the transient, material world. Both teach that attachment to material goods is illusory; both teach nonviolence. But Buddhism, at least in its purest forms, gives no consideration to a divine creator and rejects the spiritual efficacy of external rites or sacraments. It emphasizes self-purification and self-discipline, achieved within the *sangha,* the contemplative community. Though both religions posit salvation as the appropriate human goal, their most significant difference might be generalized as the difference between salvation from without (Western Christianity) and salvation from within (Buddhism).

Buddhism posits self-reliance, turning us sometimes gently, sometimes firmly back to this stark principle: we have no strength but our own strength, no final source for understanding but that which we arrive at through the careful evaluation of our particular experiences. To quote the Buddha, "Know not by hearsay, nor by tradition . . . nor by indulgence in speculation . . . nor because you honor [the word of] an ascetic; but know for yourselves." If *atheist* is defined as "one who does not believe in God," Buddhism is not, as popularly supposed, an atheistic religion, although many of its American practitioners count themselves as atheists. Asked to comment on the gods, Shakyamuni Buddha kept a profound and respectful silence. The most apt modern rendition of his response might be "no comment," which communicates neither belief nor disbelief.

Whereas Western Christianity posits a companion, the guiding hand, trust in the Lord. Salvation comes about through grace, undeserved and sometimes unasked for. As noted in the Roman Catholic–Lutheran joint declaration on salvation, "All persons depend completely on the saving grace of God for their salvation . . . as sinners they stand under God's judgment and are incapable of turning by themselves to God to seek deliverance. . . . Justification takes place solely by God's grace."

Writing reveals the writer to himself: in recording an excerpt to express the essence of Buddhism, I cited the Buddha; in recording an excerpt to express the essence of Christianity, I cited an official church document. My choices revealed the measure in which, raised a Christian, I have come to conflate Christianity and its institutions. In this formulation, a Christian is not someone who follows the teachings of Jesus but someone who subscribes to one or another of the institutions that interpret those teachings, whether a country fundamentalist church or the Vatican.

At Tassajara I determined anew to see if I might make some sense of how and why Jesus' life and words could give rise to institutionalized Christianity in all its forms. By extension I might come to understand what it would mean to name oneself not Roman Catholic, or Baptist, or Presbyterian, but simply Christian.

Following Japanese monastic practice, Tassajara measures its schedule by dates rather than days — "four" and "nine" days (that is, dates containing the numeral 4 or 9) are holidays. On the next nine day, then, I packed a vegetarian's dream bag lunch — garlicky hummus spread on thick slices of rosemary bread, with fresh greens from the Tassajara garden, an organically grown orange, and freshly baked chocolate chip cookies that had crept from the guest tables to the resident dining hall.

I set out to explore the lower reaches of Tassajara Creek. Passing the *han* outside my sleeping quarters, I stopped to read its inscription:

WAKE UP!
Life is transient
swiftly passing
be aware
The great matter
don't waste time

I clambered through the boulder-strewn funnel called the Narrows. ("There's a rule that the summer practice people are supposed to stay away from the Narrows at midday," the young *ino* had told me, "because the hikers sunbathe nude and can, like, get out of hand, you know? But that's a rule everybody pretty much handles on their own.") Aloes and agaves and yuccas grew along the creek, with the remnants of their blossoming stalks still standing. Cottonwood and sycamore roots washed bare by spring floods presented fantastic sculptures, the trees tall and thick thanks to all that water, but come a wet winter to be felled by their beneficent creek. Hikers, naked as promised, slept on the house-size granite boulders.

I walked farther down the creek, leaving the sunbathers behind, until I reached a quiet pool where I puddled about on my own, naked in the crystalline water, an impossibly pleasant afternoon of time deliberately and mindfully wasted.

Amid lengthening shadows I climbed back up the creek, past the now-deserted Narrows, up through the camp to the Zen Center cemetery where a rough pillar marks the grave of Suzuki Roshi, whose ashes were buried here after his death in 1971. Around my ears, mucus flies droned their baritone buzz with mosquitoes in mezzo-soprano counterpoint. Someone had placed fresh flowers at the monument and raked the soil at its foot. To one side a rolled tatami mat awaited a meditator's use.

How does one man change the course of many lives? How does the mountain come to Mohammed? This small man, by most accounts unexceptional, combined personal discipline with a sharp perception of the forces of history and a willingness to submit to them.

The Buddha's last words were "Be mindful and vigilant." Vigilant against what? As the sun set I left the Suzuki Roshi memorial and set off down the path, letting my mind chase its endlessly digressing rabbits. *Might a little less garlic have improved the hummus? With no gas station nearby, how will I fill up the rental car? Which of my San Francisco friends will I visit next week?* — for already I am living a week hence rather than living where I am, already I'm among those old friends, even as I'm descending through dusk into the Tassajara camp. And when a week hence I *am* among them, I will be planning what I must do still later, still further into my life, still closer to my death.

I was walking in this way, living where I was not, when a high-pitched buzz — a sound I knew before knowing — startled me back to the here and now. A six-foot rattler prepared to strike — in my oblivion I'd almost set my boot on its head. I backed slowly away. We studied each other, but I'd been the careless one. The snake had been in full view, and though in the dying light it was camouflaged to near invisibility against the mottled tan and copper stones, had I been present to the trail I could not have missed seeing it. In a moment it vanished into the poison oak and chaparral.

I walked on, humbled by my stupidity. Days, now, of being told to pay attention, resisting every step of the way because *of course*, I've muttered under my breath a dozen times, *I'm a writer, I always pay attention, too much attention*, only to receive the most emphatic demonstration of exactly how oblivious I am. For any animal in the wild, vigilance is a given: a moment's inattention and it's something else's supper, for something else is always alert to the opportunity provided by another creature's inattention.

Now we have isolated ourselves from the need to pay attention. In our prosperous industrialized world, we live not by attention but by intention — we assume the immediate fulfillment of our every wish, whether it's for transportation *(get in the car, turn the key, go)* or strawberries in winter. Even as our intentions are fulfilled we are planning new ones. We are millennia into self-consciousness — but, as my considerate rattlesnake reminded me, a self-consciousness that devotes much of its time and energy to avoiding itself, dreaming instead of the never-present future.

And yet the imagination, our human gift, finds sustenance in daydreams. Edison imagined light at the fingertips before he invented the lightbulb; a team of nuclear scientists imagined a city's destruction before they invented the bomb. "In dreams begin responsibilities," wrote the poet Delmore Schwartz. Where is the middle path between the imperative to act and the imperative to be, to focus the senses in the fact of being, the balance point between the human ability to enact change and the need to refrain from doing something simply because we can?

In the valley's deepening dusk, the kerosene lanterns lit the paths — someone had provided me a way. I was returning from the wilderness to the human community, back to this small symphony of human endeavor. I thought back to the words of the storytelling Japanese monk of the Gethsemani Encounter: "Everyone enjoys midnight under the bright advertisements in town. Those people don't realize there's a light shining above, but you have to be a lamp in the deep mountain dark where sometimes a traveler will pass only once in months. For him the lamp is most important — no matter how seldom the traveler comes, you have to keep giving light in the deep mountains because the traveler is coming up the mountain at the risk of his life."

✸

"I had a friend who recommended Tassajara for the summer — I told her I couldn't go for that much time." Kathy Egan was speaking, a Florida-born, middle-aged woman with waist-length, blonde-into-silver hair and an affection for calling her conversational partner "honey." "So I came here for two weeks, then went back home and left my job and my husband and came back for the summer. I'd already been exposed to Buddhism through Alan Watts, listening to his tapes and his midnight radio show, stoned out of my mind. But by the end of that summer, when I bowed out of the circle I said, 'Now I know what it is to take refuge in the *sangha*.'"

Like many Zen Center members, she described herself as having strong faith as a child:

> The best Buddhist I ever knew was my grandfather, and he probably never heard the word. But he embodied the teachings — he was a gentle, compassionate, soft-spoken, generous person. . . . I had a great belief in the benevolent force — but the only one I knew was through the Baptist Church. And I was a dedicated member, until at some point I saw they got something wrong — maybe it was because of their support of the Vietnam War. That caused me to lose my notion of an all-powerful outside force.

When I asked her what she found most profound and necessary of the Buddhist teachings she had acquired, she named the lessons of the origins of suffering. "The great majority of people seek a spiritual practice because they have tragedy in their lives," she said. "Deep inside we know what we need to fully express ourselves — but to reach that place we have to sit down and get quiet." She was persuaded of the opportunities celibacy offered for deepening one's practice, even as she was realistic about her own ability to sustain it:

> Spiritual practice means something different to all of us whether you're a man or a woman. I've seen the same problems and joys come from men and women. For some people celibacy is a barrier to intimacy — but it can be taken on as a powerful practice to see how much desire runs our lives. I did it for three months, then took a Christmas break.
>
> Honey, I was married at seventeen — I was divorced for two or three years but certainly not celibate during that time. I finished high school but never went to college. Then I had a sixteen-year relationship — and so for three months from the time I was seventeen to when I was forty-two I was celibate. I consider making love just as important as making vows.
>
> It's wonderful to see people come here who are so wounded they can't express themselves except in hard ways. They start by being all jive — and then something happens, they get sincere. People get in touch with being grateful. This is a place they can go and feel safe, even if only for the summer.

꙳

"I read the Christian mystics and I wanted what they tasted." Jack Kōsho McCall spoke of his years as an Episcopal priest in Maine. A small man, bald by choice, with thick black eyebrows and a down-easter's reserve, McCall spoke passionately of the constraints he left behind when he left the priesthood. "Merton introduced me to Buddhism. From there I took some training in psychosynthesis. That gave me some taste of altered, intuitive consciousness — as did LSD in college, thank God." Buddhism attracted him because of its emphasis on practice and results. "If you go to a priest and ask about mysticism, he'll say, 'Go to church and read your prayer book.' If you go to the Buddhists, they'll say, 'Do this and that and then we'll talk.'" He described his years in Episcopal seminary as "socially and sexually amazing," but he found his experience as a parish priest disheartening, and only partly because, as a gay man, "like everybody else, I had to hide. At the Zen Center that's not even an issue." Here, he felt, he'd found the combination of tradition and openness to change for which he'd searched:

> Religion isn't about making sense of things, though that's nice. That's the icing on the cake. The cake for me is the ritual. I love to celebrate mass — a transcending of personal self. Zen practice is about transforming the self, not transcending it; though if you celebrate mass long enough until you learn the technique, you may be able to achieve a self-transformation.
>
> So I made a decision: I'm here now so why not just be here. Despite my great plans and ambitions my life has moved me here — being ordained a Buddhist priest was like finding shoes that fit. I felt that about being ordained an Episcopal priest, but where do you exercise it? With whom?

As an Episcopal priest, in addition to hiding his sexuality, McCall dealt daily with what he called "the God word":

> When Buddha was asked to tell us about the nature of the gods he smiled and said nothing. I thought that was terrific. I'd spent twenty years trying to explain the inexplicable. After so many years of bringing everything back to the G-O-D concept, here there's a great silence. We abuse both the name of Jesus and God by talking about them too much.
>
> Jesus paid no mind to the priest class — the ones who stood be-

tween — he saw no need for priests. Here in America the vipassana folks [teachers of meditation without ritual] are making inroads, just dealing with suffering and meditation. But I like Zen because of the ritual and the beauty — the bodily, physical expression of inner beauty.

As I left my conversations with Kōsho McCall, I remembered the comment of the Benedictine abbot at the Gethsemani Encounter: "My own church has been arrogant in telling God where God can speak and God will not abide that — and so I have come to understand the importance of listening."

On the morning of the last day of my stay I encountered Kathy Egan on the path, and she executed the *gassho,* the small bow with hands brought together that residents are supposed to perform at their every encounter. In summer, with the paths often occupied by paying visitors and with the residents under the pressure of serving the guests' needs, this formality is more often observed in the breach; still, the more attentive and relaxed of the long-term residents honor the protocol.

But I was not so quick to the draw, and so in my seconds-too-late bow I was left feeling awkward, maladroit, as if once again I'd overlooked or screwed up some essential ritual. As we fell into step I sighed. "So many rules! I've never encountered so many chances to screw up."

Kathy grinned, an enigmatic Cheshire cat smile. "Yes, but to so little consequence."

We walked down the path, and I told her of my struggle with bowing. "I'm not much given to getting down on the ground in front of another human being, much less a statue," I said.

"Honey, it's just a bow," she said. "What's the big deal?"

A passing observation, but in it I saw my large investment in self-importance and how that was a scrim for my insecurities — my lack of faith in myself. A man who was secure and confident would embrace making mistakes as the necessary and inevitable price of learning. How much of my anger arose from my knee-jerk determination to appear always in control? And how much of the world did I deny to myself as a consequence? On that day of my departure I began to think of the bows in a different light, not as a burden but as an opportunity to learn humility, set free from embarrassment or consequence. Practicing humility here might enable one to do so later (at a meeting, before the microphone, on a stage, or in a difference with a friend or a lover) with confidence and dignity and as an act of respect, for the person encountered as well as for oneself.

"A monk is a person of gratitude," Kōsho McCall had said. Years later and a continent removed from Tassajara I encountered these words in my notes, and I was struck by their simplicity. The notion that I might become a person of gratitude — I who have so much to be grateful for and yet still I devote myself assiduously to grousing. Somewhere in these hot Tassajara days I began to listen to how often I complained, how carping was my conversational mode, how much of my thoughts and life I gave over to regret, recrimination, or anticipation. And I began to grasp the implications of the verb *practice,* which can mean any disciplined undertaking (as an attorney is said to *practice* law) but which in a religious context means a never-ending striving toward perfection, as in *practicing* meditation. Then the process of striving — the *practicing* — turns out to be the thing itself.

✿

Autumn in New York: school begins, the smell of pencils freshly sharpened, no one has yet gotten a lousy grade, anything is possible. As an experienced writer, I face the class of expectant, ambitious, hungry faces and all I have to teach is doubt and humility.

Newly back from Tassajara, I decided to meditate at home. I began by setting my alarm to wake me fifteen minutes earlier than usual. After my breakfast but before my coffee, I chose a place in front of a large, north-facing window where the changing light would wash over my shoulder. I set the alarm for twenty minutes — from my experience at Tassajara I knew that without a mechanical reminder of the period's end, I'd sneak glances at my watch. I took off my watch. I found a straight-backed chair and sat on its edge.

I stood. Chaos wants form; I needed a way to begin. How did I know this? From writing. And, farther back than that, from the storytellers of my family and place and upbringing as well as the great narratives of the Roman Church. The readings from the Bible, the progression of the liturgical year, the plowing of the fields, the speaking tongues of scarlet Pentecost, the growing things, the long green season of ordinary time, the feasts and festivals that we have all but forgotten, the intersection of men's time (the linear, chronological progression of this never-to-be-repeated year) with the women's (the ever-returning, never-changing cycle of the seasons). From all these sources I learned that chaos wants form, which means embracing a discipline.

And so on that Manhattan morning I sought out a small portable gong from India that a friend had serendipitously given me. I found a candle. I lit the candle and struck the gong, and sat for twenty minutes of time on which I had imposed a form. A small creation. Life as art.

8

ANTONY, ATHANASIUS, AND THE RISE TO POWER OF WESTERN CHRISTIANITY

BECAUSE I have been raised in Western traditions, raised with Trappist monks, in my exploration of the historical roots of religion I gravitated to reading about Western monasticism. There I discovered quickly enough that to study its evolution is to study the evolution of Christianity.

By the time of its Roman occupation, the region we now call the Middle East had a long tradition of syncretism (from the Greek *syncretimos,* a federation of Cretan cities; thus, any synthesis of differing cultures or belief systems). The Judeo-Christian tradition has strong roots in the East. Christianity's doctrines of a single God presiding over heaven and hell, a resurrection of the dead, a last judgment that includes an individual evaluation with appropriate punishment or reward, our conception of angels and devils — all these, as well as the Jewish extension of strict rules of dress and diet ("keeping kosher") from priestly to daily life, the West owes in greater or lesser degree to the Zoroastrian religion that once dominated northwest India and Persia. Through the conquests of the great Persian leaders, these ideas came to influence the whole of the Middle East.

This is not the place to visit the rich, complex history of Zoroastrianism, largely lost to the West, except to note the depth and range of the trading and influence that existed between peoples in a world that we moderns often imagine to have been culturally, economically, and linguistically isolated. The prophet Ezra, traditionally attributed as the first to write down the canonical books of the Hebrew Bible, was appointed during the Jews' Babylonian captivity by the Persian (and Zoroastrian) emperor Cyrus to be their scribe. Isaiah the prophet (or prophets; most scholars believe his books to be the compilation of several contributors) praises Cyrus for permitting the exiled Jews to return from Babylon to Palestine. Scholars attribute the striking differences in the creation myths of the first and second chapters of Genesis to the influence of Zoroastrianism, absorbed by the Jews during their Babylonian exile: Genesis 1, with its emphasis on the power of the spoken word and the Spirit as mover and creator, shares remarkable similarities with older Zoroastrian myths; Genesis 2, the story of Adam and Eve, seems more particularly Hebrew in origin. And so the Fertile Crescent of Babylon acts, as a glance at the map strongly suggests, as a conduit of armies, trade, art, and ideas from East to West. The importation of monasticism from India via Persia and the Middle East, though conjectural, seems entirely likely, particularly given that nowhere in the Bible's vast scope is there a specific reference to monastic practice.

However monasticism arose, by the time of Jesus some version of communal ascetic life was well established if not especially common. Philo of Alexandria, a Jewish philosopher who lived at the time of Jesus, describes in detail the Jewish ascetic community near Alexandria called the Therapeutae. Probably a contemplative sect of the Essene Jews, the Therapeutae (Philo suggests that the name — "healers" — refers to the role of contemplation and asceticism in healing the soul) were men and women who lived communally, practicing moderation in all things and devoting themselves to prayer, contemplation, and the study of philosophy. Philo describes their daily lives, taking care to contrast their sober banquets with the ostentatious feasts of the Romans and the drunken revelry of Plato's *Symposium.*

We may never know whether Jesus spent time among the Essenes, though that might provide a credible accounting for some of the years between his infancy and his adult public ministry. We can observe without qualification that Jesus demands of his followers a simple, rigorous asceticism that fits hand-in-glove with the monastic life.

Jesus' followers were a ragtag lot, drawn to his preaching exactly because it validated their experience. All three of the synoptic Gospels (Matthew, Mark, and Luke) quote Jesus as saying some variation of "The last shall be first, and the first last." The earliest Christian communities counted the poor, the enslaved, and women on their rolls. With the foundation of the first Christian monastic communities in the fourth century, many of those poor joined because the collective environment provided a greater assurance of shelter and food (however humble) than they had ever known. They also received rudimentary training in reading and writing, skills heretofore reserved for the wealthy but considered by the early monastic communities as necessary for anyone seeking to follow a religion based in the Scriptures. These monasteries were very likely the first institutions to offer systematic instruction in literacy to candidates regardless of social or economic background, establishing a commitment to the study of the word that extends through the monasteries of the Middle Ages to the founding of the first great universities.

Those earliest Western monasteries functioned as one of many bridges between a world of oral history and a world in which minimal literacy is required for participation in culture. In these institutions, human consciousness discovered itself through the medium of the written word. In their merger of manual labor and scholarly study, those first Christian monasteries near the Nile Delta would abet this transformation from reliance on oral history to written documents as the primary means of preserving and passing on wisdom.

By the mid–fourth century, monastic settlements were well established on the fringes of the Egyptian communities of the Nile Delta. For the most part, they consisted of men — the desert was a man's world, less because of its harshness than because the solitary life was the antithesis of the feminine engagement with childbearing and the familial and social responsibilities it entails. All the same, some women ventured into the desert, where after years of fasting and self-mortification they took on the aspect of men.

Their transformation becomes more comprehensible when one considers that the ascetic life had always drawn upon athleticism for its most powerful and enduring metaphor. The writings and stories of these desert monks are replete with references to the struggle of the athlete, a discipline the early Greeks named *askesis,* source of our word *ascetic.* The desert women hermits were the fourth-century equivalent of the Olympic marathon runner, small-breasted, sinewy, tough, the body trained — or subjugated, if you prefer — to the demands of the will.

Monastic communities sprang up in the desert surrounding the Nile Delta like the utopian societies of America's mid-nineteenth century or the hippie communes of the 1960s. Like the leaders of those utopias and communes, their founders set out with rosy expectations, making no allowance for the realities of human nature, only to discover that in any such communal enterprise there's always somebody who won't wash his dishes.

Founded on the pleasant fantasy that all would contribute according to their ability and take according to their need, that first Christian community, founded by Pachomius, quickly dissolved in bickering. Chastened but undaunted, he began again, composing a rule — a set of governing principles — by which all the monks must abide.

The heyday of these Nile Delta monasteries lasted about a century. Through the example and works of traveling monks, their histories and simple rules spread throughout the eastern half of the Roman Empire; later their influence would penetrate to the West. They provided a catalyst for the explosion of interest in the ascetic life. Scholars offer varying opinions of the population of the monasteries of the eastern Mediterranean, but at their peak they counted at least a thousand monks, though some estimates range much higher. Sometimes they lived in mixed-gender communities; more often they were segregated by sex. At the same time their influence spread far beyond their walls — they became proving grounds for Christianity, places where on the largest scale yet seen in the West, men and women attempted to live collectively as lovers of wisdom.

Any study of early Christian monastic history must begin with a reading of Athanasius's *Vita Antonii* (Life of Antony), the biography of the desert hermit published in 356 C.E., a few years after Antony's death.

In the year 251 Antony was born to prosperous Christians of the Nile Delta, where the great pyramids, already two thousand years old, lay only a few miles upstream, monumental evidence of Antony's ancestors' engagement with the spirit world. As he reached his late teens, both of his parents died, leaving him in charge of their home and his younger sister.

At this impressionable moment, Antony heard in church the famous passage from Matthew 19:21: "If you would be perfect, go, sell what you possess and give to the poor, and you will have treasure in heaven." Immediately he sold his family's property and gave the income to the poor, keeping back a bit to support his sister.

Returning to church, Antony heard the instruction not to concern oneself with the future, to live in and for the moment. So he gave away even his few remaining possessions, placed his sister under the charge of respected virgins of a local convent, and set about learning the discipline of the monk. Across his long life — 106 years — he became the prototype of the desert holy man, whom Christian historians once traditionally identified as "the first monk."

The notion of Antony as the first monk is pure myth. In the opening pages of his biography Athanasius makes clear that the boy turned to other ascetics in his village to learn the discipline of monastic life, and makes reference as well to women's convents. Other sources offer considerable evidence of an ascetic tradition in Egypt extending to well before the arrival of Christianity. As a leading monastic historian told me, "Antony became the 'first monk' less because he was unique than because, in Athanasius, he had the first publicist."

As Antony's biographer, Athanasius was at least as interested in serving his own particular agenda as in promoting Antony's example. He composed *Life of Antony* as an exercise in aretalogy, in which the goal was to praise the deceased, with flaws and blemishes excised and virtues described in the context of miracles, so that the subject might serve as the best possible role model for the reader or the listener as well as the best possible means through which writers might advance their particular points of view.

As Athanasius tells the story, Antony made his first hermitage in the tombs of the village dead, the usual residence for the aspiring monk, since the tombs provided an ever-present reminder of the transience of the material world. Later, as an expression of his eagerness to grapple with his demons on their own turf, Antony moved by successive stages deeper into the desert, until finally reaching the "Inner Mountain," three days' and three nights' journey from the Nile, in the wildest and most inhospitable wastes of that most forbidding of deserts, the Sinai.

Like all the ancients, the Egyptians of Antony's time perceived the city as the abode of the gods. The wastelands beyond were the territory of the demons, a contrast that was especially significant in Egypt, where only the thin margin of irrigated lands along the Nile could support village life. With each move deeper into the wilderness, then, Antony was upping the stakes of his confrontation with the forces of darkness. Athanasius was eloquent in fantasizing that struggle, in a passage so vivid that for centuries it has been a favorite subject of Western painters:

So [Antony] was taken back [to the tombs] . . . and, as before, the door was closed. Again he was alone inside. Because of the blows [from the demons] he was not strong enough to stand, but he prayed while lying down. And after the prayer he yelled out, "Here I am — Antony! I do not run from your blows, for even if you give me more, nothing shall separate me from the love of Christ." . . . Now schemes for working evil come easily to the devil, so when it was nighttime they made such a crashing noise that the whole place seemed to be shaken by a quake. The demons, as if breaking through the building's four walls, and seeming to enter through them, were changed into the forms of beasts and reptiles. The place immediately was filled with the appearances of lions, bears, leopards, bulls, and serpents, asps, scorpions, and wolves, and each of these moved in accordance with its own form. The lion roared, wanting to spring at him; the bull seemed intent on goring; the creeping snake did not quite reach him; the onrushing wolf made straight for him — and altogether the sounds of all the creatures that appeared were terrible, and their ragings were fierce. Struck and wounded by them, Antony's body was subject to yet more pain. But unmoved and even more watchful in his soul as he lay there, he groaned because of the pain he felt in his body, but being in control of his thoughts and as if mocking them, he said, "If there were some power among you, it would have been enough for only one of you to come. But since the Lord has broken your strength, you attempt to terrify me by any means with the mob; it is a mark of your weakness that you mimic the shapes of irrational beasts." And again with boldness he said, "If you are able, and you did receive authority over me, don't hold back but attack. But if you are unable, why, when it is vain, do you disturb me? For faith in Our Lord is for us a seal and a wall of protection." So after trying many strategies, they gnashed their teeth because of him, for they made fools not of him but of themselves.

To contrast Athanasius's thrilling portrait of Antony's struggles with the experience of a contemporary hermit, on one of my later stays with the Trappists I walked an hour through the high muggy heat of August to the hermitage of Father Roman Ginn, who lives on the abbey's remote back acreage with his two donkeys, Hosanna and Hallelujah.

With his long, unkempt gray beard and unshorn hair Father Roman could pass for the original Antony. The monks have built the walls of his one-room hut from recycled scraps of particle board, and fashioned a roof from a patchwork of corrugated tin and translucent green plastic.

Roman invited me inside, to sit in an armchair bleeding stuffing from holes chewed by squirrels and mice. Bent from osteoporosis, he has an eponymous nose rendered all the more prominent by his thin face, but he read aloud without resorting to glasses, selecting a book by Cardinal Newman that had been set between the poetry of John of the Cross and *Mules and Donkeys: A Guide.* Then he lay down the book to speak of his particular experiences as a modern hermit.

> Being a hermit is not a pleasant way to live. You have to pray to keep going. There could be moments of ecstasy but I sure haven't run into them. Mostly it's a humdrum and down-to-earth life. I have the donkeys to take care of, especially in winter — they're creatures of the desert and don't like colder climates.
>
> The only pleasure I really get in it is reading and prayer. The rest is dog work. Cutting wood, feeding the donkeys. I haven't gotten the donkeys trained yet and they're all laughing at me up at the monastery. One's been really sweet since I got him, but the other has been a trouble. Every night I give them a lesson for a few minutes — my goal is to get them to ride me the mile and a half to the abbey and carry back the groceries.
>
> In a hermitage you just pray for the Church and wait to see what happens. I was glad to get away from the regular office [that is, prayers] — that was a drag. I practice my own version of *lectio divina.* All it is, is learning to pause while you're reading — using the book as an aid to meditation.
>
> St. Paul tells us that nobody is really free. You're bound to Christ, or your passions, or to habit or whatever. But I feel freedom here compared to what you have in the monastery.

He rose and walked barefoot outside, where Hosanna and Hallelujah were already coming to his snuffling call. I carried a pear in the pocket of my loose pants, but Hosanna, paying very close attention indeed, sniffed it out and had his nose in my crotch before I could push him away. We inspected the squash and tomatoes Roman grows amid the goldenrod and ironweed. He showed me the grate where he cooks over fires made of newspapers brought from the abbey.

Walking back to the abbey, I considered these questions: What exactly is the nature of freedom? Does it mean freedom to buy what one wants when one wants it? Or freedom from enslavement to all those raging creatures of desire?

⁂

Some historical background provides a context for interpreting Athanasius's reasons for his grandiloquent overwriting of Antony's story.

In the early fourth century, after a long period of relative tolerance, the Roman emperor Diocletian resumed Christian persecutions with unprecedented ferocity. During these persecutions, according to Athanasius, Antony was moved to leave his desert hermitage and visit Alexandria, seeking martyrdom, but his reputation was already such that the authorities feared the public outcry that would ensue on his death. Antony had to content himself with offering prayers for those condemned to die.

Enter the wily Constantine, one of Diocletian's four heirs apparent, a master politician and military strategist who through genius and luck defeated his three competitors to win control of the crumbling Roman Empire. A lover of pomp, wildly ambitious, Constantine set out to break with the politics of the past by consolidating his empire far to the east — a strategy that included shifting its capital from Rome to Byzantium, soon to be renamed Constantinople (eventually, under the Ottoman Turks, to become modern Istanbul). He needed a new religion that could fulfill the needs of the state as serviceably as the gods and goddesses had once served the Caesars of Rome.

As a Roman statesman and general, Constantine was well aware of the role of a shared, universally accepted religion in underpinning the unity of the state. Moving the tired, confusing panoply of ancient Roman gods and goddesses from their Roman temples and altars was out of the question; for starters, their presence in his new capital would imply the superiority of the city and culture he was vigorously supplanting. Christianity had advantages: its monotheism concentrated power in the hands of a single God — the analogy to an earthly emperor would not be lost on his citizens. And there was his personal experience — his Christian mother, Helen, best known for the legend of her discovery of the cross on which Jesus was crucified, surely influenced her son toward accepting the upstart religion. In addition, at a critical moment Constantine had invoked the Christian God, and the gamble had paid off. According to Christian chroniclers, on the night before the crucial battle of the Milvian bridge (312 C.E.), he had a vision instructing him to have his soldiers affix the intertwined Greek letters *chi* and *rho* (the first letters of the word *Christ*) to their shields. Constantine won the battle; the opposing commander fell from the bridge and drowned.

Most significant for Constantine's purposes (though in later centuries

Christian historians neglected, forgot, or disguised this historical reality), Christianity was a religion of the eastern Mediterranean. Its roots were in Palestine; the authors of its Gospels and most of its major early texts wrote from the same cultural milieu as Byzantium-Constantinople. Most wrote in Greek, the common language of the eastern Mediterranean, and spoke Greek, Aramaic (a derivative of Hebrew), or both. Many Christians lived closer to Constantinople than to Rome and were culturally, linguistically, and philosophically of the Middle East.

The new emperor knew opportunity when he saw it. In 313 C.E. Constantine issued the Edict of Milan, returning confiscated properties to Christians and reiterating the ban on persecutions that his predecessor had enacted. A master politician among the gods as among men, he continued to perform obeisance to the pagan sun god, but he took care to include Christian bishops in all official ceremonies. He did not declare Christianity the official state religion — he would leave that to a successor — but by being baptized he lent it the stamp of official approval, and before long the church had a central role in tactical and political decisions once considered the domain of statesmen and generals.

Hoping to end the divisive doctrinal wars that plagued the still-young religion, in 325 C.E. Constantine called the Council of Nicaea. This first convocation of all the bishops of Christendom was called not by a religious leader but by the emperor — an indication of what was to come. Most bishops were old enough to remember Diocletian's last great persecution. Now they were invited by the emperor himself, who worshiped their God and offered them a junket and an expense account. The council was dominated by bishops from the eastern Mediterranean — of the more than two hundred present, less than five were listed as being from the Latin-speaking West.

At Nicaea, knowingly or otherwise, Christian leaders faced a historical fork: either they would demand that Constantine emulate the revolutionary egalitarian culture that Jesus lived and preached and that had been key to Christianity's explosive growth, or they would conform to the prevailing patriarchal, hierarchical model of the state as long practiced by Rome and its ancestors, inherited and continued by Constantine. Was there any possibility that the bishops would reject such an invitation to power and stability? Constantine offered the recently beleaguered Christians his official embrace. Already he was constructing magnificent churches in his new capital.

In fact they had no real choice. From time to time Constantine visited the assembly he had called and financed, and though he took care to sit on his golden stool, theoretically the servant of the theologians, in fact he was not subtle in his agenda: he wanted a hierarchically imposed orthodoxy and he wanted it now, to serve as a glue to unify his new empire. Under Constantine's watchful eye the basic elements of Christian theology were hammered out and articulated in a profession of beliefs that has survived almost seventeen hundred years. The Nicene Creed, still chanted at many Christian services, for the first time definitively established who was "in," who was "out," what was orthodox, what was heresy in Christianity.

As important as the creed, though, was the role of Nicaea in grafting the new religion onto the Roman political model. To this day the Roman Church embodies the governmental structure of the Caesars, expressed in a hierarchy that culminates in an all-powerful, infallible emperor-pope.

The impact of institutionalization on what had been a fledgling, marginalized sect was swift and profound. Where the grandparents had gone to the circuses to watch Christians tossed to the beasts, the grandchildren flocked to Christian congregations to be baptized, in a rite that was rapidly becoming a minimum requirement for social and political advancement in the new, increasingly Christian empire.

And yet the rank-and-file Christians of the fourth century were a contentious and fractious lot, many of them outcasts who had never known power, members of the lower classes to whom Jesus had first preached. Many responded to the official embrace with outrage, perceiving it as a betrayal of basic Christian principles. Many of the outraged became monks. Before the Edict of Milan many Christians had understood martyrdom as the best possible imitation of Jesus. Now that literal martyrdom was no longer possible, the "living martyrdom" of the ascetic life came to be seen as a substitute. In the century following Nicaea, monasteries blossomed as Christians sought places where they might live out the teachings of the Gospels in communities modeled directly on Jesus' life rather than grafted onto the political and governmental structure of the empire.

And all, perhaps, because of a woman. We do not know the influence that Constantine's Christian mother, Helen, exerted on her son, though it appears to have been substantial. We do know that Constantine, master politician and military genius, as important as the church fathers Augustine, Jerome, and Aquinas in constructing modern Christianity but responsible to an empire that included the widest range of competing sects and philosophies, worshiped both the Christian God and the competition until his death. Then, ironically, the emperor who arguably did more than any single person to advance the Christian cause was, in the tradition of the Roman state religion he had supplanted, declared a pagan god.

✢

In light of this historical context, Athanasius's *Life of Antony* takes on an additional resonance.

Published barely twenty years after the Council of Nicaea, *Life of Antony* became the fourth-century equivalent of an international bestseller, translated into multiple languages, required reading for the educated Christian or pagan, and frequently read aloud to the illiterate — a prominent Antony scholar compares the effect of his text on the Christian world of late antiquity to the impact of twelve-step programs on America.

As portrayed by Athanasius, Antony represents a significant step in the emergence of individual consciousness and conscience. Like Jesus, Antony undertook the mythical journey to hell and back, with the difference that no one suggested that Antony was other than a mortal, whose choices were immediately relevant to those of other mortal men and women. His interior journey takes place in the desert, but it is a very real desert, a place that could be visited (and was) by many during his life. He became a Christian version of Theseus's challenge to the Minotaur or Beowulf's battle with the monster Grendel. Contemporary psychologists interpret the demons Athanasius describes with such relish as metaphors for the mental illnesses that threaten us all, though the desert fathers understood lust as a minor temptation compared to avarice or what they called *accidie*, the failure of will we identify as chronic depression and treat with Prozac.

In Athanasius's vision, however, Antony is never alone even when he is ostensibly alone. He is always supported and sustained by the invincible companionship of the invisible Jesus — or, more accurately, by his faith in Jesus. It's an important distinction, given the politics of the era and especially those of Athanasius. The great theological struggle of the early church often centered on a question that remains central today to both Buddhists and Christians: to what extent do we transform ourselves, and to what extent must we rely on grace? During Antony's time, the great heresy — ultimately to be rejected, though never completely quashed, at Nicaea — was the contention of the priest Arius and his followers that Jesus was divine like God but in lesser measure than God. As a young man Athanasius had attended the Council of Nicaea and witnessed its vision of a vast, unified church. He undertook to write *Life of Antony* both to advance the cause of orthodoxy (which is to say, allegiance to the principles set forth at Nicaea) and to crush the opposition (those who questioned the full divinity of Jesus). In his description of Antony's life he takes pains to show how at every spiritual crisis Antony, though possessed of superhuman resolve, must call on Jesus to win final victory; when it comes he invariably attributes it to Jesus' intervention.

Throughout the third century, as the legal and political authority of the Roman Empire weakened, individual hermits could and did assume great power locally. Many holy men and a few women of the eastern Mediterranean became arbiters of community disputes, dispensers of counseling, and interpreters of the Scriptures. As hermits they were impossible to police and control from afar. Ensconced in monastic communities, however, their edges would be smoothed by obeying a rule and an abbot responsible to a centralized, institutionalized church.

Athanasius's promotion of external intervention in the form of divine grace served to promote the growth of centralized monasticism, for it taught the individual that he or she must always turn outward (and presumably upward) for spiritual direction and assistance. This principle — shortly afterward to be refined by Augustine, who offers Antony's biography as the cause of his conversion to Christianity — did not immediately or intrinsically require the individual to be baptized, married, shriven, and blessed at death by institutionally certified priests. But propounding the necessity of external help was the first step toward requiring that sacraments be administered at the parish church, by the church's authorized representatives. Thus the doctrine of grace, which favors outside assistance over independent effort, supported the Christian church's gathering of power.

Life of Antony promoted church-centered orthodoxy as the foundation for monastic practice. Historians argue over the complex causes of the shift in monastic practice from eremitic to cenobitic — that is, from solitary to communal — but *Life of Antony* surely contributed to a trend that would intensify in the centuries to come, as the secular authority of the Roman emperor disintegrated and the Roman papacy stepped into the void.

On the hot, dusty walk back from Father Roman's hermitage, I realized that the Roman Church of my childhood was not the church of Jesus (a wandering Jew who had no church) or of the hermit Antony, but the church of Constantine and Athanasius — the strong, centralized institution that had become less a vehicle for spirituality than a political, economic, and (until relatively recently) military power, geared toward using doctrine and dogma as a means to achieve and enforce conformity.

❧

Athanasius describes Antony's death in a pattern standard in biographies at least as far back as Plato's description of the death of Socrates: Antony foresees the moment of his death, gathers his closest disciples, admonishes them not to grieve, cheerfully instructs them to bury him in an obscure place where his corpse cannot be dug up for veneration, fires one last volley at those whom he (or more likely, Athanasius) perceives as heretics, and expires. In an odd and revelatory coda, Athanasius offers Antony's fame as proof of his virtue, since God would grant such fame only to the most holy man. It's not the first time in the book that fame is linked with virtue — another clue, perhaps, to Athanasius's agenda of using the holy monk's story to push his own Nicaean version of orthodoxy. In this he was merely following the aretalogist's prescribed form, in which biography does not render factual history but offers a moral and political example.

Ah, the poor holy men and women who stumble into fame! "We're not anti-Merton but we're not great Merton fans, either," a Gethsemani monk told me. So many people form idealized notions of the monks' lives from reading *The Seven Storey Mountain,* the impassioned work of a young, idealistic convert who later took some pains to distance himself from its naiveté. Antony's story offers an example: despite Antony's explicit instructions to his disciples, he failed to rescue his reputation or his corpse from exploitation. Athanasius used Antony's story to promote a centralized orthodoxy as removed as one can imagine from the real Antony's solitary retreat, while the monks who today occupy the site of his desert hermitage will (for a small fee) show the visitor what they claim is his tomb.

9

GOD ALONE

ON AN UNSEASONABLY WARM, overcast New Year's Day my mother drove me to Gethsemani, where I was to stay not as a retreatant but to live with the monastic community. I wanted to return to this place, so central to my childhood, to deepen my search for what it means to have and keep faith. At some buried, half-acknowledged place, I wanted to subject my skepticism and anger to the most intensive scrutiny.

In my childhood the visitor swung open a studded wooden door to gain admittance to a small, dark gift shop that was then one of the monastery's principal sources of cash. At night the door was barred (shades of the Middle Ages), but a small square peephole covered with a grate allowed the night porter to inspect the after-hours caller. From the rear of the shop another wooden door opened into the monastery enclosure. It was a kind of air lock, a waiting room where the women might be sifted from the men, then the men resifted for those who had some purpose for admission behind the wall. The aspiring monk entered here — some did so conventionally, with an advance appointment and a chance to look the place over, but many, inspired in part by Merton, showed up as he had: knocking at the little barred window, sometimes in the middle of the night.

But change is inevitable — the old gatehouse could never have handled today's steady stream of tourists and retreatants. And yet the new reception area has the charm and functionality of a discount-chain hotel lobby, when the soul in its dark night seeks the mystery and metaphor of that little barred peephole.

At the reception desk Brother Alfred greeted me with big ears and a broad grin. "You're a brave man!" he said as he assigned me my room, and though he was jovial I felt comforted to have my apprehensions affirmed.

120

Why apprehensive? Is it because I who already lead the life of a monk — alone, days in silence engaged in writing, the contemplative's art — feared I might get sucked in? Or was it fear of the prospect of confronting my contemporary versions of Antony's demons?

Alfred directed me "through God alone, to the top of the stairs." I stepped outside, where I got his pun: a carved stone lintel reading GOD ALONE spans the doorway to the enclosure courtyard. Alone to God? Alone with God? For God Alone? To God Alone? God Is Alone? Through God Alone? I swung back the gate and stepped through.

My cell: about twelve feet by twelve feet. A cot, a pillow, a sink, a small mirror, a wardrobe or chiffarobe, a crucifix as the sole wall ornament. Heat. A small desk. A floor lamp. A hard chair. A view into the enclosure courtyard. A wooden stool of a pattern often duplicated by my father, Shaker-like in its simplicity and practicality.

I was here to do the real thing — very well, I would comply: to bed that night at 9:30 P.M., then up at 3:00 A.M. for vigils, first of the canonical hours.

Who would have thought that the aptly named vigils, accomplished in the dead of night, would be the most elaborate of the offices? Though considered in the context of religion as art, and art as the cry of being, this makes sense: what service would be more elaborate than that held at the moment of the greatest crisis of being — farthest from sunset, with dawn no more than a promise?

This night was a "special vigil," meaning that once we were seated in our stalls, the lights would be extinguished and the service accomplished in the dark. One by one the white-robed monks processed to the lectern to read, by penlight, passages from the letters of Paul and the writings of Bernard, the Cistercians' best-known saint, who wrote moving sermons on the Canticle of Canticles (also called the Song of Solomon) and at the same time preached the Second Crusade, that exercise in pillage and rapacity. The readings speak across time of joy and sorrow and delight and fear of life and death and, for those who know Bernard's story, of the capacity of our noblest intentions to result in terrible unforeseen consequences. Between the readings: silence profound as darkness.

Something touched me, seated in the dark amid these men praying to a woman — for Mary dominates the Cistercians' liturgy, created for the most part at the height of the Middle Ages, when the old pattern of worshiping God the Father yielded to the adoration of the Mother and the Son. Men glorify Mary as a virgin, and the ideal of sexual abstinence as necessary for perfection has been used for centuries to demonize women. And yet this fact remains: on this morning, for the first of many times I am a man among men and together we lay down our power, humbling ourselves before a goddess who, like Jesus, achieved her holiness as a living human being.

The greatest power lies not in the use of force but in its voluntary restraint — "the power/not to use power," the poet Stephen Dunn writes. Mercy is the deliberate restraint of power; compassion is the coupling of mercy with the understanding of our shared fate, the powerful and the weak bound together by our humanness and the whole round interconnectedness of being.

What was I witnessing and participating in but a ritual celebrating, protecting, preserving an evolution of the human understanding of our relationship with the divine? Once the approach to the gods demanded blood sacrifice — less than five hundred years ago the Aztecs built an elegant and sophisticated culture around it; the Hebrew Bible is strewn with animal and human sacrifice. Now we men bowed to celebrate the merger of mercy with compassion to become love. It's possible to see our understanding of ourselves and our place in the universe as evolving from those first hermit monks in the wilderness, contemplating in terror and wonder their separate and particular fates, to philosophers (for example, Plato, building on the labor of Socrates and, before him, nameless other teachers) who posit consciously sought reunion with wholeness and oneness as the soul's longing and goal. We long to return from whence we came; we long to sustain our individual identities but without such acute self-consciousness, which first separates us from community by making us aware of our aloneness, then seeks for ways to repair the breach. We need to believe in the particularity of our individual identities, even as none of us can exist for long without community — not even Antony.

What was I doing, sitting in the dark among the monks, but seeking to repair the breach between myself and my experience of the divine? I considered how I had wounded myself: I had left my family and my community in search of money, sex, and power, and I found more than my share of each, enough to learn both that the longing for them is insatiable (see Buddhism's First Noble Truth, page 97) and that they create their own burdens.

Merton wrote to the English novelist Evelyn Waugh, "Talented people tend to trust in themselves — and when their own resources fail they will prefer despair to reliance on anyone else, even on God . . ." He refers to "the servitude of doing things for your own satisfaction . . . slavery to our own desires is a terrific burden."

This is my particular struggle: arrogance, an insistence on going it alone, a refusal to ask for help. How do I address that wound? Might monks, living out their community consciousness in this frenetically individualistic age, offer a model for healing?

On some white night to come, I will remember and take heart in the knowledge that in some monastery somewhere in the world, a group of people have collectively risen at the darkest hour with the purpose of holding God to his promises.

On this first morning I was assigned to the cheese factory, where the Trappists use a recipe adapted from their Norman heritage. Orders for cheese have been dropping, partly because of a bad rap from the cholesterol counters, though the sales of bourbon-laced fudge that the Trappists took up making only a few years back are booming, evidence of America's twin obsessions with staying thin and eating fat. Still, the monks keep making cheese, the only one of their products preserving some connection to Gethsemani's farm days and beyond to their earlier agricultural roots.

I took up the task under the supervision of Brother Conrad, now in his sixties, another of my father's old pals. In contrast to Father Gettelfinger, Conrad represents the bright side of German Catholicism, at once cheerful and fearless and completely engaged with the work at hand. Following him through the cheese barns, past the gleaming stainless steel vats and giant mixers, I wondered how productive I might become if I managed to acquire his focus on the moment.

My job was to work with the crew who were turning and "massaging" the cheese — Brother Norbert, Brother Gaetan, Brother Placid (who matches his name, despite Norbert's jokes to the contrary). Working in clammy refrigerated vaults, Placid and I wrestled each rack of cheese from its shelf, gently pried each wheel from the board, dipped it in a vat of salted water, scrubbed it lightly ("it needs massaging," Norbert said, "or so the book tells us"), dipped it in the water runoff to reinforce its culture and give it a slight rind, then returned it to the rack. The racks were awkward and heavy — each held ten or more wheels of cheese, each weighing a couple of pounds and arranged along the ten-foot plank. Soon my body was too cold to work with ease or grace. More than once I was saved from dumping a rack of cheeses on the floor only by the quick action of a fellow worker. The room reeked of whey, my hair reeked of whey, and though I wore rubber gloves, for days afterward my hands reeked of whey. "Cheeses for Jesus!" someone chortled, an old jibe coined by Merton and popular around here. "Gethsemani — 'get-some-money,'" another joked.

The next day I was shifted to photocopying Merton's book contracts, make-work I gratefully accepted.

❦

Brother Columban Weber (he asked that I call him "Colombo") wore a Kentucky blue cap from a local tavern that perched on his oversized head — at well over six feet he towers over most of his brethren. He had been assigned to the Trappist monastery in Rome — located just outside the Vatican, its proximity a sign of the order's favor in the eyes of the papal hierarchy — but problems with his health had compelled him to return. Words spilled out of him; he couldn't say enough fast enough:

> Those guys who went over to your parents' house — I wasn't a part of that upper-bracket party circuit. But I really admired your father. He had a real dignity about him — he prided himself in what he did. He didn't say it but when he met me he thought, "This guy doesn't know how to drink, doesn't know how to smoke, and I'm going to help him grow up." And he was right. I was wet behind the ears. Alban and those guys were like doctoral students and I was the new kid.
>
> I was born in 1946, second-oldest of a huge Michigan family — twelve kids. I was attracted to the externals of religious life and joining the monastery was a way to get out, and so I came at eighteen.
>
> We're a bunch of benign bachelors, but there's a whole system that takes a lot out of a person. What makes a person want to do that? Low self-esteem, insanity? It's not on the level of spirituality. There are other things going on.
>
> Can we get away from guilt? Can we get away from the notion that the God figure is about to destroy us? Who can believe in that? I can't believe in anything but love. Faith has to be a human experience, with family or friends or whoever, it's not going to happen through ritual. Transcendence comes through love. There's nothing a person can't do

or won't do when in love. What is that force? Why can't we define it? What would make a person give a whole life to a monastery? What would drive Mother Teresa? After a while you just can't talk about it, you come to a point of silence. Sometimes all these motions are totally meaningless — Merton was a symbol for a lot of us because he was looking for a different form.

Faith is all a symbol of something — when you associate it with the body you incarnate it, you make it real. The sign of the cross is just another way of doing that. In some way our life is very symbolic — the walls of the enclosure and so forth — but does it really mean anything? Most of us go through routines most of the time. Part of me says, "The structure is killing me, it's taking everything out of me." The trick is to work out a relationship with that. We tend to glorify a lifestyle we don't know. I expect people glorify the life of a monk; I glorify the life of a writer.

After a while you have to look for more freedom. After a while you realize time is running out and you don't have a lot more options. I try to approach each day as if it's new — where there's life there's hope. Many of the older monks have regrets about not having lived more fully, but you can't get energy out of that. The good energy comes out of love and engagement.

࿔

In the early 1960s, flush with manpower and, along with the surrounding countryside, reaping the wealth of the transition away from subsistence farming, Gethsemani undertook to renovate the abbey church. Not for the first time — every few decades someone had taken a stab at redecorating the church. The enclosure lawn had changed contours even more often, originating with precisely trimmed hedges embodying geometric French formality and evolving to today's Japanese-influenced meditation garden with its faux waterfall tumbling over carefully arranged boulders into a lotus-strewn pond, a transformation that constitutes a rather perfect metaphor for the shift in orientation in American spirituality from Europe to Asia.

In its initial expression architecture arises from and expresses some organic truth about a place. A limited budget, local materials, and ingenuity can result in plain, honest structures in which form follows function — Shaker buildings come immediately to mind, as well as the older parish churches scattered throughout Gethsemani's neighborhood. Renovations, on the other hand, often arise from an excess of disposable income, with idle hands becoming the playground of you-know-who. "When laypeople get bored they go bungee jumping or rock climbing. When monks get bored we redecorate," Father Kelty told me. The plans reflect a combination of institutional politics, committees, and inertia, with results ranging from horrifying to merely mediocre.

The abbey church, originally faux-Gothic imported from France, fit well enough with the pastoral landscape — squinting hard enough, viewers could imagine themselves in Normandy, the Cistercians' home base, and the glimpse of its silver-painted spire through the trees was among the more thrilling sights of my very dull youth.

> Then suddenly I saw a steeple that shone like silver in the moonlight, growing into sight from behind a rounded knoll. The tires sang on the empty road, and, breathless, I looked at the monastery that was revealed to me as we came over the rise. At the end of an avenue of trees was a big rectangular block of buildings, all dark, with a church crowned by a tower and a steeple and a cross: and the steeple was as bright as platinum and the whole place was as quiet as midnight and lost in the all-absorbing silence and solitude of the fields. Behind the monastery was a dark curtain of woods . . . and beyond that a rampart of wooded hills, a barrier and a defense against the world.
>
> — Thomas Merton, *The Seven Storey Mountain*

Every word of this lovely passage speaks of the convert's naiveté and enthusiasm, not least his perception of the hills as "a barrier . . . against the world." But as Merton would learn and acknowledge (at least in his journals, where he wrote without fear of censorship), the world is ever with us, and the silence and seclusion of a monastery, as anyone who troubles to go on retreat rapidly discovers, are not an escape from trial but an entry into its distillation, all the more intense because voluntarily undertaken.

By the 1960s the steeple of my childhood (and metaphorically, Merton's) was rotting, and change, fueled by Merton's later writings, was in the air. The monastery had money in its pocket and a restlessness that reflected that of the nation and the world. The stained-glass windows, with their portraits of saints and virgins, were replaced with mullioned abstract pastels. The walls were stripped to bare brick and whitewashed. The arched, ogival ceilings were eliminated and the crossbeam timbers revealed. Eight massive steel columns — simple I-beams — support the ceiling of the apse and the weight of the bell tower; these were exposed to form a semicircle around the altar. The smaller side chapels, provided so that the many priests could say daily mass, were abandoned in favor of concelebrated masses with all priests present. Today the abbey church gives the impression of a Gothic zendo — the long sight lines and soaring height are unmistakably Western, but the spare simplicity strongly invokes Zen Buddhism. Only the platinum-painted steeple suffered in the process — removed to the nearby woods, it has rusted and rotted beyond recognition; its square stub of a base remains, rising from the abbey roofline like a finger amputated at the joint. Some of the monks saved chunks of the old architectural features, which they carted to the woods, where retreatants may encounter a grinning gargoyle or the single word *Pax* carved in stone.

The renovation offers a rich metaphor for what was hoped, what was realized, and what was lost in the heady post–Vatican II days. The nineteenth-century, pseudo-Gothic church was beautiful in its way, derived from the last wholly original statement in Western architecture until the rise of modernism — a statement in stone and wood of an Old World religion grounded in belief. In a stained-glass window removed in the renovation but unearthed and preserved by the current cellarer, Cistercian founder Robert Molesme kneels at the feet of the Virgin and Child, who are handing him a building symbolizing the monastic order, while overhead hovers the familiar dove of the Holy Spirit.

The notion is charming but beyond the capacity of many Americans to view as anything more than a symbol; like it or not, most of us have been infected, or blessed, with a measure of skepticism. The frankly penitential rituals of Gethsemani's strictest periods have given way to an emphasis on contemplation, a change embodied in the shift to an architecture evoking Asian principles. Outsiders — I among them — may bemoan the loss of the farm, but for a group of aging men, perhaps it is better to have the austerity expressed more in the architecture and less in the practice.

⌘

I found Brother Martin surrounded by pipes, Y joints, grease traps, snakes, and the other paraphernalia of his plumbing shop. In winter he closes his door, and so this time I saw on its outside a larger-than-life takeoff on Mondrian (bright squares of white, yellow, red, blue) painted by a fellow monk. I'd brought nothing to drink and I apologized for arriving empty-handed, but Martin brushed away my apologies. "I don't drink much anymore," he said. "It stopped agreeing with me." He offered me again Dom James's old, cracked leather chair, facing a massive canvas painted by Brother Lavrans, the monastery's best-known visual artist, who left in the 1970s to join a gay commune in Georgia and died in the 1980s of AIDS. Taller than a tall man and wide as my reach, the painting is an abstract starburst of sunset colors, not the brilliant sunsets of the American West but the colors of winter sunset here in Kentucky, pastel blues and lavenders merging into gray.

As the short winter afternoon slid into dusk, I took up the conversation that Martin and I had left off six months before. What could Martin have meant in telling me that the only racism he'd known was in his own heart? He answered my question with a question. "We're all racist in our own ways, don't you think?" Then he offered examples of what most would consider not racism but jealousy and envy, leading me to consider that perhaps skin color only provides an excuse to unleash these timeless vices.

Soon enough, lack of whiskey notwithstanding, Martin and I returned to the subject of my father. "He was deep," Martin said. "He was a religious man, really. He felt things deep. He was a deep thinker." A vision of the old man came to mind: snoring gently through the 6:00 A.M. mass, while I tried vainly to wake him for communion.

Talk of fathers led easily to speculation about the abbot — once again Timothy had put in his request to retire and this time it would likely be granted. "After so many years I don't know what we'll do without him. You should be here to take his place," Martin said, and though I laughed out loud he held his ground. "I could see you as a monk," he said. "I could see you talking to the pope. I know at least one monk who's very much edified that you're here, and praying like mad for you. You'd be the first local boy to come back and run the place."

"Why a monk?" I asked. "I mean, why become a monk?"

Martin paused and knitted his hands. Behind his black, thick-rimmed glasses his forehead furrowed. "A monk is a monk," he said. I asked him what he meant. "You tell a monk to do one thing, he's just as likely to do the opposite."

"Well, on that point I qualify."

"We live in community, in which we're bound to each other but in which we're encouraged to become eccentrics. We're a community of eccentrics," he said, and told the story of the abbot banishing an elderly liturgist to a hermitage because the liturgist — whose job is to select and coordinate hymns, ritual, and music — couldn't tolerate his successor. "You know the difference between a terrorist and a liturgist?" he asked, the lead-in to a joke I will hear repeated several times. "A terrorist can be persuaded to negotiate."

Later that day, sitting under the bare-limbed ginkgo — warm enough, in late January, to sit outside with only a light jacket — I considered how some need more structure than others. Some slip easily into the typical patterns of living in this world — high school, maybe college, first job, marriage, children, retirement. Others, maybe most others, take on these forms reluctantly. Some never take them on at all. The lucky and smart of these become superstar entrepreneurs or successful artists or small farmers, occupations outside the forms. The less lucky become the poor and outcast. With something of a shock I understood that my father had been among the reluctant. However he loved working with his hands and roaming the woods, raising a family required that he submit his free spirit to the demands of a blue-collar job, working for the man, bound to the wheel. His struggle was now mine, except that I had no family, I had no master except myself.

Thanks to zazen and the Buddhists, I was beginning to realize that I was engaged in a battle with demons, that writing is my particular battleground but that each of us chooses his or her own, and that the prize in the struggle is nothing more or less than life, which is to say love, which is to say God. I understood that the search for the father is the search for the Father — not an especially original observation, but one that I was surprised and humbled to see flow from my pen.

In one of the readings I'd heard the name of John Cassian, fourth-century monk, and after one of my first middle-of-the-night vigils I took up his voluminous *Conferences* to read: "Prayer is not perfect when the monk is conscious."

Buzzed on Maxwell House Instant and waiting for dawn, I was taken by Cassian's simple, forthright, eloquent expression of what it means to live with? for? by? through? GOD ALONE. Cassian writes that glimpses of God are brief, darting, sudden shafts of light, but this strikes me as a romantic's point of view. The greater challenge is the creation, maintenance, and sustenance across time of a wholly integrated life, of which monasticism is one type and model.

The people I most admire achieve that integration. "No duality," as the Buddhists have it; mind and body, heart and soul, individual and community realized and integrated into a single whole, the great unity, the One of ancient Greek philosophy, achieved by being lived out moment by moment.

Drawing their metaphor from what they perceived as the greatest art, the Greeks saw philosophy as the means of sculpting one's own life: just as the sculptor removes the excess rock to reveal the statue hidden within, so philosophers' discipline enables them to carve away petty obsessions and concerns so as to allow their true selves to emerge. The goal: to be unconscious while sustaining full consciousness; to be fully aware (in the Buddhist sense of the word) without being aware; to merge spirit and flesh, mind and body, so that life becomes a prayer, an ongoing sculpture, art. "Prayer is not perfect when the monk is conscious."

At 5:00 A.M., still no hint of midwinter dawn on the horizon. Merton writes that he was at Gethsemani for two years before he realized that the hours between vigils and lauds were to be used for reading and contemplation rather than for an extended nap. If Merton took two years, I thought, I can take two weeks, and so I lay down. As I fell asleep a sharp wind rose from the south to rattle the aged windows.

※

On this day we celebrated the Epiphany, the feast of the visit of the famous Magi to the infant Jesus. The lector read the first verse of the Gospel of John: "In the beginning was the Word, and the Word was God." There it is. A = A. God = the Word, the Word = God, the foundation of culture: words, beautiful words, the breath of life transformed into our means of making community, making communion, the Spirit become tangible, the Word made flesh.

Surely this is something to aspire to, the prima facie refutation of my skepticism: the ease and lack of self-consciousness with which the novice-master Brother Gerlac, an older man of considerable standing in this community, drops to his knees. I am so lacking in humility! Even now, a year and a half into my intermittent life among the monks, I kneel grudgingly if at all. If, as the wise men and women of the desert assure us, humility is the key to virtue, what does this mean to me, a cocky and insecure American?

And then the service ended with Timothy's sprinkling us with holy water, brothers and lay congregation, and on this evening, member of the community, I fell in step and bowed, to feel the drops strike my forehead like tears.

⁂

On an overcast afternoon I met Brother Paul for a long hike into the Forty Acre Knobs, the forested hills that define Gethsemani's western boundaries. Nearing his sixtieth birthday, wiry as a terrier, thinner than a rail, Paul leapt up the almost-vertical hillsides with the agility and grace of a deer; more than a decade younger, I huffed and puffed in his wake. He'd just led a discussion of celibacy with the "junior professed" — monks in preparation for taking their final vows — and now as I struggled to keep pace I asked him to summarize the conversation.

"The purpose of celibacy is to heighten love, not to frustrate it," Paul said, and though I understood that he was distinguishing between agape (love as friendship) and eros (erotic love), nonetheless, eros remains, capricious, problematic, universal. Most mammals have estrous cycles, I pointed out — a kind of built-in governor of sexual desire; they give sex their undivided attention for a few days or weeks and then it's over, at least until the next burst of hormones. Humans have as among our great evolutionary achievements the potential for having sex twenty-four hours each day, seven days each week. "Maybe that's why we've been given reason," I mused aloud as I struggled down a slippery slope that Paul negotiated with ease. "So we can have some means of controlling our sexual drives. Healthy celibate people remind those who are sexually active that restraint is a choice."

"That's not to say sex is a bad thing," Paul said.

"Not at all," I replied. "It's a good thing we have sex. To start with, if we're paying any attention at all, it's what keeps us humble, by reminding us that finally we're just another creature."

Which is why, I thought later, I abuse it so, using it as a weapon — against others, against myself. How poorly I know myself, how often my lack of self-knowledge plays itself out in sex — how it becomes the stage on which I play out my anger, insecurity, doubt, all nicely disguised behind the scrim of desire. I thought of the celibates I knew, how the most fully realized among them (Martin, Paul, Maricela) struck me as having used celibacy as a means to self-realization. By refraining from giving themselves to one, they had taught themselves to give to all. And at the same time, I thought of the many celibates for whom the discipline became a source of bitterness, a constant, physiological reminder of inadequacy and weakness, failure and guilt — which, like me at my worst, they projected onto others.

$\approx$

That evening as I sat in the reception area, a woman entered to speak to the monk at the front desk. They greeted each other as old friends; after some small talk she broached the subject: could the monks help her out with some money? The monk on duty asked, What had she done with the money she'd received a month earlier? Her husband, whom she'd kicked out three months before, drank it up. Was there some way to keep the money out of his hands? He came and stole it from her. If she fought him he threatened to sue for custody of their children. Some more questions and the monk gave her a slip of paper. "You phone this number and tell them I sent you," he said.

Later I learned that this same monk is locally famous for wanting to give away all, including the barn; the local poor know when he's scheduled to sit at the reception desk and show up when he's there. ("A few years back he gave away the toilet out of the wood shop," one of the monks told me. "But the monk in the wood shop pouted and so the abbot made him go and get it back.") Once the monastery routinely handed out alms, but some twenty years ago they discontinued the practice. "We were creating a scene," one told me, "where a whole group of people showed up at once and we had to judge among them who was most needy and deserving." Now the monastery quietly pays the salary of several local caseworkers, to whom they send the poor for guided assistance in negotiating complex federal, state, and local welfare agencies, as well as the private charities to which the monastery gives donations.

The system is neater and cleaner, but what's lost with the removal of the poor from the monastery landscape? When one recalls that the primary ecclesial justification for Christian monasticism is that it represents a collective attempt to follow as closely as possible the example set by Jesus, the irony becomes evident.

Here as elsewhere, the monastery epitomizes the culture in which it lives. I want the poor removed from my life, to any neighborhood but mine. I want to help them, but I don't want to touch them or have to look at them or deal with the messy, awful quandary of choosing between the paraplegic and the schizophrenic for my pocket change. The poor have gone the way of the barnyard animals, their smells and trouble and unending demands packed off to an institution, or a factory farm, or a ghetto, or a foreign country, allowing me to meditate in peace and quiet.

⁂

At the next morning's mass, I find myself asking, *Can I really believe that I'm consuming the body and blood of a man who died two thousand years ago?* The moment for communion arrived. I stayed in my seat.

In front of me sat a trim, compactly built woman with thick, short black hair. As I watched she joined the communion line and reached its head, the last person to receive. The priest paused, and for a lengthening moment he paused, and from someplace outside of rational thought, above and beyond conscious choice, I understood that I was supposed to witness this moment. In contravention of all church teaching the priest was refusing to give her communion. The woman was refusing to stand aside. We waited. We waited. After long waiting (she was not budging, the other priests had all finished with their communicants and were back at the altar; the show must go on), the priest gave her the host.

The woman (I learned later) had written to the papal nuncio, complaining that this particular priest had been too intimate with another woman retreatant. The nuncio (whom I imagine ensconced in an overstuffed armchair; somehow I can't divest him of a pince-nez) was the duck on the proverbial June bug, promptly ordering the priest to cease and desist. And then the letter writer returns, to seek him out to receive communion.

⁂

> We're beset by groups of hangers-on, camp followers, who are problematic and who wheedle their ways in. They're often women, often in a difficult relationship with their husbands, lonely. They come to a community of gentle men and they claim to be simple souls, but they invest their hopes in the community and are outraged when we don't measure up to their expectations.
>
> — Gethsemani monk

⁂

I encountered the gay monk I call Isaiah in the meditation garden. He waved me over to a bench. "How many years did it take to build up the anger that would keep you from joining the monastery?" he asked. And I thought, *There it is, that word again.*

"Why don't you just give in and join the community?" he asked, grinning.

"That would require a long answer," I said.

He slapped my back. "Sex ain't all they make it out to be."

"That's only *part* of the answer," I said.

Timothy may question his ability to lead the monks spiritually, but he has the capacity to offer a one-sentence homily that has more impact than a fifteen-minute diatribe. As we sat for the second of our conversations, I recalled his opening statement at the Gethsemani Encounter: "How one lives one's life is the only true reference to the validity of one's search."

We spoke of the role of ritual in monastic spirituality. "I think the Buddhists chant mostly to create an atmosphere conducive to contemplation," he said. "This is true of Gregorian chant as well, but as time went on we loaded it with intellectual weight. The office can't be backed with emotion-rousing music, and on that front Gregorian chant qualifies. But that means there's always a struggle between the desire to keep the music austere and the desire to have it be more emotional."

We talked about the use of gender-neutral language in the translations of the Scriptures and the text of the rites: "There's a big struggle over that these days. Can you alter the word of God? Can you use more inclusive language, and what's the impact of that? Our previous liturgist found intimations of Jesus in the Psalms. If we take away the masculine pronouns, are we removing or weakening their prophetic qualities?" The struggle is not limited, however, to theological or spiritual questions.

The New Revised Standard edition [of the Bible] that just came out translates Paul as writing "Brothers and Sisters" instead of just "Brothers." The Canadian bishops sensed a fight and so they just printed the books and started using them before there was any official agreement with the Vatican — which came down on them, but the books were already in distribution and they largely got what they wanted. The U.S. bishops are cowed and so we're using a new translation that's just awful. The complicating factor is that the Holy See wants us all to use a single text — that's especially important in America, because the market is so large. If we use their single, approved translation, then they get all the royalties. This battle over who controls the translation has been going on for years. Here we're using the Revised Standard Edition — it's not explicitly feminist but it's quite good. But when a new lectionary comes down later this year, we'll have to use that.

At a chapter meeting earlier that week Timothy had instituted one of the monks as a lector, giving him the right and responsibility to read at office and at mass. Though the regulations require that the abbot, in full abbatial regalia, perform the service in the church, Timothy held the service in the chapter room and wore only his simple Cistercian habit, in keeping with his low-key style. In his remarks he described how, historically, the lector was among what were once called "minor orders," since they were designed as stepping-stones for "holy orders," the sacrament of priestly ordination. "This poses a problem for the Church," he said, "because these minor orders were once viewed as steps to ordination as a priest. But now women are allowed to be lectors but are not allowed to be priests." He left the contradiction to us to resolve.

In such ways is change accomplished: *sub rosa, sotto voce,* brick by brick, until Martin Luther, or Martin Luther King, Jr., stands atop the accumulated pile of bricks and proclaims the new order.

The bells rang, signaling the midday office. I followed Timothy to the church, where gray light penetrated the high, wintry gloom. Outside rain was falling. The bell echoed through the church as the monks took up plainchant. "The cleft in the wall where the dove can hide, where water is found," we said together.

Maybe this is a place we must all find our ways to, I thought as I bowed, *if not in fact then in our hearts.*

❧

Sister Maricela and I spoke again later in my stay, this time as she was nearing the end of a busy afternoon at the front desk, greeting visitors. Timothy had assigned her a once-a-week slot on this job, the monastery's most public position, where the visitors and retreatants could hardly avoid acknowledging her presence as a woman in this men's community. Encountering her at the reception desk, I was struck by Timothy's courage in placing and protecting her here as well as her courage in living out the assignment.

She greeted me, smiling but with a rueful sigh. "I know every person who comes in the door is a manifestation of Christ," she said. "I just wish that sometimes he would stay home."

The air had turned cool, and though we tried to sit outdoors the chill drove us into the small conference rooms reserved for private conversations. I asked Maricela to talk of her experiences with greeting guests in her Trappistine habit, as the official representative and (often) first impression of this all-male institution.

> More conservative men come here and they see me and think, *What are you doing here?* Whereas women think, *Why can she be there and not me?* For some of the men their vow of monastic life is in reference to gender. But all the monks here have been mature enough to live with a woman around — none feel inhibited or awkward. They relate to me like older and younger brothers — that's very beautiful to see.
>
> I'm not an obstacle except for those who have the idea that they've joined a male community. They gain their identity by who they live with. It's like I'm ruining the spot — to address that requires spiritual growth. Why would any human being be in our way to living with God? If someone sees another human being as an obstacle, then I question their inner growth. If you don't grow to become what you're supposed to be, why are you here? Society at large is changing and seeing women less as sex objects and more as human beings. Suppose you come here and you're attracted to men? It's not sexuality but how we use it.
>
> You know who lives a Christian life? The Buddhists. Because they live it out. We say, Jesus preached to include the outcasts, but as soon as we encounter the prostitute or the gay man we say — oooh, we don't want that. If anyone here is afraid to see legs and breasts I question their vocation. [The Indian-born philosopher] Krishnamurti tells us that as soon as we define ourselves as belonging to some religion then necessarily everyone else is outside. I think that as soon as you find what you're looking for, you should drop religion. All the great mystics find their ways to this point.

She spoke of her hopes that the community would vote on accepting her on a longer-term basis — though one of the monks has told me privately that if such a vote were taken she'd be asked to leave.

On my last day Brother Paul took me to Merton's hermitage.

DECEMBER 12, 1960.

Real solitude [at the newly occupied hermitage]. Peace. Getting acclimated to the surroundings. The valley in front. The tall, separated pines to the west, the heavy, close-set, denser pine wood to the northeast, the sweep of pasture and the line of bare oaks to the east, various clumps of pine and poplar between east and south, bright sky through bare trunks of ash, elm, and oak to the southwest, where a shoulder of hill hides the abbey. A great dance of sky overhead. A fire murmuring in the fireplace. Room smells faintly of pine smoke. Silent. . . . After having thought for ten years of building a hermitage, and thought of the ten places where one might be built, now *having built* one in the best place, I cannot believe it.

It is nevertheless real — if anything is real. In it everything becomes unreal. Just silence, sky, trees.

— *The Journals of Thomas Merton*

Merton's hermitage is still used — the monastery occasionally loans it to visitors. The ceiling leaks — not surprising for a flat-roofed building not constructed for durability. He built it from plain yet functional materials, nondescript whitewashed cinderblock and limestone taken from the nearby creeks and hills, though the fluorescent tubes of Merton's era have been replaced by incandescent fixtures. Limestone blocks form a cross over the fireplace. In a small side room stands the simplest of altars. From the porch, broad enough for sitting on a summer evening, Paul and I looked across the shallow valley to the distant wooded line of Muldraugh's Hill, and gazing over the forest, I was reminded anew of how blessed I was to come to adulthood in a place that pleased and pleases the eye.

೨೭

Compline: last of the day's services, accomplished in near darkness on this the last night of my visit — here in midwinter the sun has long set. Timothy sat in the abbot's stall, the first seat on the altar's right, his place marked by his abbot's crozier, a simple staff of wood. Maricela sat to his right, as I sat on the novicemaster's right. Seated next to our guides, I saw the aptness of the metaphor: the shepherd with his flock.

The office opened with reading from John Cassian. Brother Lavrans's tall Nativity banner, still hanging in this post-Christmas season, dominated the apse: St. Joseph, the Virgin Mary and Child, the Magi, and the animals scattered playfully up the tall, high, green field, their rounded forms muted beneath the folds of their robes but expressing rejoicing all the same. I offered a silent prayer for the artist.

And what is it, after all, but a bow? Among the Buddhists I had brought myself — or, more accurately, my commitment to the discipline of writing had brought me to lower my middle-aged knees and touch my forehead to the floor, nine times, no less. The sign of the cross was as loaded as ever, but I had come to understand my resistance less as a protest against the blindness and injustice of institutional religion than as a manifestation of my own need to believe in a clutch of demons outside so as to avoid looking at those within. Now the sign of the cross seemed to me a gesture of community in suffering, a sign that I had taken my place among those who know the dharma. "Faith is all a symbol of something," Colombo had said. "When you associate it with the body you incarnate it, you make it real. The sign of the cross is just another way of doing that." On this my last evening of this stay among the monks, I signed myself a Christian.

(How hard it is for me even now, years later, to write those words.)

The service closed with lights out, as Isaiah, the monk most recently arrived, lit two candles before the icon of the Virgin and child.

> Grant us restful sleep
> And a peaceful death

In darkness seventy men's voices took up the Salve Regina, my favorite childhood prayer, sung in plainsong that reverberated through the long, high, brick-walled cloister:

> Hail holy queen, mother of mercy, hail our life, our sweetness and
>   our hope
> To you we cry, poor banished children of Eve
> To you we send up our sighs, mourning and weeping in this vale of
>   tears.
> Turn then, most gracious advocate, thine eyes of mercy upon us,
>   and after this our exile
> Show us the fruit of thy womb, Jesus. O clement, O precious, O
>   sweet Virgin Mary.

The great bell tolled three times three, then shifted to a peal as we processed in darkness to our sleep.

⌇

I phoned my mother to pick me up — it was time to go to California, to a second visit to Tassajara, now in its midwinter role as America's first Zen Buddhist monastery. Brother Martin happened by the guest house as my mother pulled in the drive. The three of us stood chatting for a moment. "Martin, you haven't aged a bit in twenty years," Mother said. "You don't have a gray hair on your head."

"Clean living and a pure heart," I volunteered.

Martin looked a little sheepish. "Don't tell a soul," he said, "but it's Grecian Formula."

And then the drive home, during which Mother had the last word. "I never set that much store by authority," she said, revealing the Protestant American part of her soul. "I told Father Gettelfinger that the Catholics put so much emphasis on authority that they forget the real truth that lies underneath. I guess the theologians feel sorry for us peons, but one of the monks told me he thought I had everything pretty well figured out, and that made me feel pretty good, coming from a monk, you know." And so this most loyal and devout of Catholics who has spent a lifetime in the Altar Society, the Sacred Heart Sodality, making cakes for the church fundraisers and flower arrangements for the services, teaching catechism to her children — at eighty-three years old she says, "I never set that much store by authority," and I think, *So much for the pope.*

10

Being in Doing

A FRIEND who shared a cab to the airport in New York ridiculed sitting meditation — "self-centered navel-gazing," she called it.

I looked out the window at the crumbling warehouses and bare-limbed trees of Brooklyn. "If we can teach kids that a piece of bread can be transformed into the body and blood of Jesus, we can teach them to appreciate their bodies," I said, then sat back, bemused at the readiness and passion of my response.

☙

Up at 4:00 A.M. to drive four hours south from San Francisco to Tassajara through a furious El Niño storm. Inland from Carmel the skies cleared as I drove into the oak and manzanita of the California coastal mountains. Now, in January, under fragrant bay laurel, chamise, sage, and madrone, the grass was turning the electric green of a wet year. As I parked, a covey of California quail dashed across the gravel, their quivering top-knots distinguishing them from their cousins in the eastern United States — here at the edge of Western civilization we're all permitted to be a little wacky.

The cheerful contractor who was remodeling the Tassajara dining hall drove me up and over the mountain — in winter only four-wheel-drive vehicles are allowed to make the trip. "Women are taking over the world," he remarked as we crested the ridge separating Tassajara from the comforts of technoculture. "The president of the Zen Center board, the co-abbess of City Center, and the director of Tassajara are all women." As we pulled up to the Tassajara dining room a woman strolled out, wearing a T-shirt celebrating women's conquest of Annapurna. The contractor pointed and waved. "The head of my crew," he said.

"How do you think men will respond?" I asked. "To being asked to share power, that is."

"*Forced* to share power." He gave the parking brake an amiable tug. "We'll learn to live with it."

The next morning I awoke before the scrub jays, to an oppressively heavy rain. I pulled on my clothes and stumbled along the lantern-lit paths.

For its winter months Tassajara had accomplished the transition from rustic resort to monastery — I was the only outsider present, and rituals were observed with greater particularity and at greater length. Day and night a greater sobriety and focus permeated the small valley.

In winter session all members of the *sangha* must wear robes to zazen, and so Kathy Egan sorted through a closet to find me a used robe. As I tugged it over my head I asked myself, *What is this thing with the material world? It's only a piece of black cloth.* And yet as I struggled into it, I felt descending over me a level of seriousness — or maybe I felt only the atmosphere of wintertime at Tassajara, when all present have made a significant commitment of time and resources, when the rain emphasized the fact that to be here now, at the bottom of this damp, dark, winter-wet canyon, was hardly a vacation. The robe represented seriousness of intention incarnate, a symbol of the transformation of an idea into a lived reality.

But what's to distinguish this from play-acting? A few months later a conservative Catholic, overhearing my stories of zazen at Tassajara, will scoff. "I don't doubt the sincerity of the undertaking, but they're not monks," he said. "They go for three or six months and feel virtuous about living in the woods, and then they drive their expensive cars back to luxurious houses." Crudely put, perhaps, but a fair objection, duly registered. But at this particular moment — up well before dawn, struggling into a damp, clammy robe, to spend the next several hours sitting zazen — what I remembered was a comment, made by a seasoned visitor in my previous, balmy, summer visit. "Wintertime at Tassajara makes the Trappists look like Boy Scouts," she said. I was about to discover what she meant.

Robe in place, I removed my shoes, then joined the procession to my *zafu.* I bowed to the room (to the community), turned around to bow to my seat (to myself), turned again and lowered myself to sit on my cushion, then turned clockwise to face the wall, tucking the zafu under my buttocks for support and arranging the robes to cover my legs and feet. The wooden clapper sounded, flat and harsh. The abbot responded from his cottage, three knocks on the clapper that hangs outside his window — *get your act together, I'm coming.* The lanterns flickered, my shadow danced against the wall — he must have entered the room. He made a circuit of the zendo, checking to see that his charges were in order — here as at Gethsemani, the abbot is the guardian of the flock. As he passed behind our backs, one by one we bowed to the wall. He took his seat, the deep-toned gong sounded, and in its vibrating hum we descended into stillness . . . but then my desire to get back to *doing* something asserted itself, and before long I was cranky and tired.

The good part of these hours-long sessions of zazen: water from the hot springs is piped under the zendo floor, warming it on the chilliest mornings — a great incentive to sit. Across hours of sitting I listened to the pattern of the rain, first soft, then increasing until it drowned out the rushing stream, then gradually slackening until the voice of the stream reemerged, reinforced. A kind of dialogue or counterpoint of water music, with the drippings from the trees on the roof acting as random punctuation. How often in this busy, complicated, overcrowded, difficult world do I make the time to sit and listen to its changing rhythms? Instead of counting my breaths, I found a kind of mantra presented itself with each inhale and exhale: *Here. Now.*

The bad, or at least the tough part: intensive zazen is not an undertaking for the faint of heart or weak of knee. The practice reveals my self to myself, and though this is why one takes on challenges, what I learn is not always what I'd like to know. In my case I was finding first and foremost that I worry too much about the future at the expense of the present. I was learning, to my dismay, just how very little faith I possess.

∽

The morning meditation with bows before the altar, the lighting of incense, the chanting of the *sutras* — across my days at Tassajara I gradually became familiar with the rituals, until by the last day my mind began to let go as my body began to perform the motions from its own internalized memory. Perform an act often enough, and the pattern engraves itself on the body as surely as wrinkles on the forehead: the body remembers.

The French philosopher Blaise Pascal (1623–1662) spent his life wrestling with questions of belief versus doubt. In his famous wager, he concluded that one might as well believe in God, since the rewards of belief may be great while the penalties of choosing belief are paltry. How, then, is the skeptic to subdue his skepticism?

> You want to find faith and you do not know the road. You want to be cured of unbelief and you do not know the remedy; learn from those who were once bound like you and who now wager all they have . . . follow the way by which they began. They behaved just as if they did believe, taking holy water, having masses said, and so on. That will make you believe quite naturally . . . Custom is our nature. Anyone who grows accustomed to faith believes it . . .
>
> — *Pensées*

Faith, then, begins not in the mind but in the body, in gesture and action.

Since I'd been a teenager, I'd been so angry with institutionalized religion that I'd refused to participate in its rituals. As a result my need to venerate had no outlet; my body had no explicit means of connecting with my soul, though at times I found in activities as varied as sex, or drugs, or hiking a means to the same end. I sought these out because they were (usually) fun, but I sought as well an outlet for my need to engage the sacred, to be reverent, to venerate. *Venerate:* the word has its root in *Venus*, the goddess of love. In one sense, then, to be unable to venerate is to be unable to love.

Pent-up emotions — unacknowledged or ignored — take the form of their opposites. Insecurity becomes arrogance; fear becomes bluster; the tender heart, given no outlet for its love or compressed into inflexible institutional forms, turns cynical and bitter. I recall the Gethsemani Encounter, how its monks, Buddhist and Christian, Asian and American and European, turned and returned to speaking of anger.

And so what had become of my anger?

Plato divided existence into the material world and the world of Ideas. The material world is the tangible, physical world of our daily lives, the world of rock music and littered tabletops and migraine headaches and Vermeer paintings. The world of Ideas is intangible: Faith, Hope, Beauty. Beauty, the principal Idea toward which we should strive, consisted in the absolute, unchanging ideals of philosophy. All corporeal matter was relative — with time it aged and decayed; the Vermeer painting yellows and fades. Only the ideal could endure generation after generation, across the rise and fall of empires. A contemporary eighth grader might easily make the same distinction between the world of the body and the world of the brain; a Christian theologian might distinguish between the world of the flesh and the world of the soul — in each case the former is transient, the latter enduring.

We in the West have inherited Plato's division between body and spirit; it is deeply embedded in our conscious and subconscious mind, and yet a close look reveals some serious weaknesses at its heart. Exactly how is the mind, or the soul, separate and distinct from the physical world, from the body? Zen philosopher Alan Watts asked, "Why do we say 'I think' but not 'I am beating my heart'?" Both are functions of the body, and not thinking is almost as great a challenge as willing one's heart to stop.

Plato established for the West a duality between mind and body, spirit and flesh, that was taken up by almost all the competing sects of late antiquity, among them Christianity. That duality, much contaminated with various cult philosophies, has colored all Western thinking.

Plato may have borrowed the idea of the duality of flesh and spirit from the Zoroastrians, who were flourishing to the east in Persia, or he may have come up with the idea on his own. Either way, his eloquent treatises on this notion set Western thought, ultimately including Christianity, on a path markedly different from that of the East.

For the Buddha had long since proclaimed that no such distinction exists. "Form is emptiness, emptiness is form," the contemporary Buddhist still chants, though a Westerner might better understand the point if it were rephrased: "Body is Soul, Soul is Body." No duality exists; the universe (from Latin *uni-*, "one, single," and *versus*, "turning") is a single interdependent whole in which practice must not be separated from theory; in which the relative (that is, the ever-changing material world of our Vermeer painting) cannot, should not, must not be separated from the absolute (that is, the constant, unchanging truths of the world of Ideas). To illustrate with a specific example: Plato distinguishes between the transient beauty of a particular youth and the enduring Idea of Beauty. The former vanishes with age, while the latter is eternal. The distinction is critical, Plato argues, because people need enduring standards of virtue — facing the ever-changing vicissitudes of daily life, we need absolute values to which we can turn in determining right and wrong. In contrast, the Buddha argues that everything, including the formulation of moral values, resides in the mind, that we are each responsible for testing all assumptions against our particular and individual experiences, and that though universal truths exist they are not independent of human experience but are formulated in response to that experience.

It's impossible to overstate what a very different way this is of seeing and living in the world. Heinrich Zimmer, the great German scholar who together with his Indian colleague A. R. Coomaraswamy introduced Indian art and history to the West in the twentieth century, understood India as well as any Westerner, and yet he wrote, "It would not do to seek to constrain the Oriental conceptions into the delimiting frames familiar to the West. Their profound strangeness must be permitted to expose to us the unconscious limitations of our own approach to the enigmas of existence and of man." Well into his studies of Eastern philosophies, Merton wrote, "As religions, Zen and Catholicism don't mix any better than oil & water . . . [Persons from each] would return having attained just enough understanding to recognize themselves as utterly alien to one another."

And yet especially for the American, situated by history and geography between Europe and Asia, West and East, Christianity and Buddhism are less radically opposed than they at first seem. The Spirit dwells in Action, Action expresses the Spirit; Emptiness is Form, Form is Emptiness; God is Love, Love is God. Each depends on the other to achieve meaning. In the absence of the other, each is impossible to conceive. The Christian who believes in God but does not transform that belief into love — that is, into action — is no Christian. The Buddhist who seeks material rewards in the absence of a commitment to virtue is no Buddhist.

Maybe this is the most important role of ritual, as collectively evolved, sanctioned, and celebrated theater through which a community learns and teaches how virtue must be acted out through the body if it is to be worthy of the name. Ritual is the formalized acting out of Plato's Ideas, the place where the Spirit becomes incarnate, expressed through the body in real-life gestures such as zazen . . . or the sign of the cross. Thanks to zazen — thanks to making my mind calm down, enabling me to dwell quietly and wordlessly in my body — I was beginning to grasp the meaning and significance of the central principle and metaphor of Christianity, the Incarnation: the transformation of thought into gesture, Idea into action, the timeless ideal into the here and now, the Word into flesh.

*

According to Japanese Zen practice, a young man seeking admission to a monastery must sit outside the gate in supplication; only after the passage of sufficient time to demonstrate the seriousness of his commitment is he allowed to enter. That period of waiting has become *tangaryo*, five days of zazen in which the newcomer does not leave the zendo except to bathe. At Tassajara each three-month session, autumn and winter, opens with *tangaryo* for newcomers, a kind of Zen boot camp (I heard the phrase from Zen Center members) I was unwilling to endure.

The price, though, is that I ate alone, separated from the community. These were the terms of the deal, established in advance, and appropriate; I was an outsider, an intruder, not a member of the community.

Sitting alone over my supper of soba noodles, I thought back to my anger at the Gethsemani Encounter, when the Buddhists were barred from communion, the essential Christian meal. The Roman Catholic exclusion is founded in belief: non–Roman Catholics are denied communion because they have not officially professed acceptance of Roman Church doctrine, which in this particular case translates into an acceptance of the authority of the pope. In contrast, my rejection at Tassajara had more the feel of being denied membership in a club because I'd not endured a hazing. Still, exclusion is exclusion, and eating alone in the dim, cold dining room I felt its power and its wound.

In an afternoon work session at Tassajara, the leader assigned me to run a chain saw. "But I've never run a chain saw," I protested.

"That's okay, there'll be somebody around to show you. It doesn't *matter*," she said, "that you're no good at it. That's not the *point*."

From my chain-saw-wielding brothers I had learned, if not to run a chain saw, at least to respect it. I dug in my heels and refused. I ended up being assigned to split kindling with a hatchet, as great a threat to my health as a chain saw, perhaps, but at least wielded with only muscle power behind the blade. Later David Basile, the overseer of facility operations, told me casually, "Lack of continuity is a big problem here. We train people, but then they go away and then we have a whole new group. We haven't had many casualties, though in the last practice period two people lopped off the tips of fingers."

For someone such as I, so geared to goals and achievement, to sit at Tassajara was like traveling in a foreign land where I was determined to get some grasp of the local culture but lacked the language or the cultural understanding. Everything was strange, the days seemed like one mishap after another. At the end of the day I hid in my cubicle, grateful for the familiar words inside my head, if nowhere else.

*

Winter residents observe far more conscientiously than their summer counterparts the practice of exchanging bows with every person whom they meet, and I was not much better at remembering the custom than on my first visit. The camp is long and narrow, traversed by a single path, but at what point must one bow? If someone is ten feet away, chatting with a neighbor or gazing at the moon, should one stop and bow? It's another of those Zen Center rules that provide a skeptic's field day, but as the writer I was obliged to go along — or to try; more often than not I forgot, only to flush with irritation *(these stupid rules!)* while arresting myself midstride to execute a graceless bow in response to someone else's greeting.

With the passage of days, though, I came to understand the cultivation of the habit as enforcing presence in the here and now. I had to make space in my too-busy mind for the person who stood before me, rather than planning for tonight or tomorrow or next week. The incessant bowing worked as an internally imposed speed limit — the bow *felt* as if it slowed me down considerably, though in fact it required only a second or two. I noticed my resistance to putting on the brakes, any brakes, for fear that the demons might catch up with me — the mind's fear of its own solitude; my fear of occupying the present moment, from terror of what I might find. Extend that analogy to a whole culture and one gets some sense of just how great the impact of the embrace of Buddhism might be on the Western emphasis on external realities; how great the transformation when we forgo, even for a moment, the world of flash and dazzle for the world of pause and think.

*

That afternoon my work companion spoke of her impending dharma transmission — roughly the equivalent of the Christian rite of ordination, except that in Buddhism, lineage is all important. Through their teachers, at least in theory, all transmission recipients can trace their lineages back to the Buddha himself.

The printed word allows information to be more widely distributed (for example, through books) than does oral history, which operates within the limits of what an individual or community is able to remember. But trusting solely in the printed word means that a single war or cataclysm can wipe out generations of learning — the ancient Greek understanding of a heliocentric solar system disappeared from the West for almost a thousand years before reemerging, by way of Islamic astronomers, in the work of Copernicus and Galileo. Less spectacularly, the printed word gives us permission to be lazy, license to forget (or never to learn) our hard-won lessons, since we can just look them up in a book.

How shall we convey learning and wisdom to the next generation? The question is essential and contains at heart an important distinction between the Judeo-Christian tradition of the Word and the Buddhist tradition of silent meditation. Jews and Christians transmit their traditions through the spoken and written word. Though in fact priests, ministers, and rabbis learn ritual from their elders as part of their training, in theory a person could become a priest or a minister or a rabbi by entering a library and spending long enough studying the right texts, so long as he or she could find an authority to perform the rites of certification. Zen Buddhism usually requires similar intellectual training of its priests and teachers, but the heart of the teachings is passed on in the living examples of the teachers to whom the students attach themselves. Zen practice is thus (at least in its ideal) closer not to the seminary-trained priests and ministers and rabbis of the West but to the ancient Greeks, where one earned the title "philosopher" by living out the principles he or she espoused.

The process is difficult for the word-centered West to comprehend, especially given the inadequacy of the translation of the terms. Yet despite this sense of foreignness, across my days at Tassajara I felt growing inside me something like that calm core. For the first time in my life, when confronted with powerful emotions, I found myself stopping to ask, *What is the real source of my anger? Does it lie with the person in front of me, or am I using him as a foil for avoiding my own demons? Who am I, apart from those stormy emotions? And how do I find my way safely through the gales?*

For study period we met in the yurt, an unheated, circular canvas tent full of scholars wearing mackintoshes and down parkas and watch caps and scarves, their breath faintly visible above their Buddhist texts. Norman Fischer entered and the students collectively spoke a welcoming chant in Japanese. As we settled into our seats, I wondered again, *Are we being seduced simply by Buddhism's foreignness, which is to say the ease of taking on a philosophy removed from our heart of hearts?* One way to avoid the self is to migrate to another tradition altogether, since its doctrine and rituals lack the visceral impact of those we were introduced to as children and that surround us, in all their corrupted forms, in our adulthood. The new teachings seem so wise, and dismissing the unwanted parts is so easy! And yet in those very unwanted parts — the uneaten broccoli on the child's plate — can lie the challenges whose engagement provides the key to growth.

At Tassajara I noted what was being taught, over and over — the emphasis seldom on doctrine, almost always on how to live a virtuous life, how to sustain loving-kindness in the face of anger and suffering. How exhausting to be present all the time! "Relax into it," Fischer said. "Practice being present in your room. Be aware of the obstacles — which are clinging to self, which usually takes the form of judgment" *(that's me he's talking about)* "or daydreaming" *(me again)*. "When our practice becomes the way that we live, we've achieved a kind of maturity."

Fischer is describing what the Roman Catholic writer Flannery O'Connor, paraphrasing the theologian Jacques Maritain, called "the habit of art": using discipline as a means of shaping the self toward good habits — in this case, the habit of being present to the moment, invested in the task at hand rather than its outcome. As Fischer told the crowded room:

> All work is a meditation on impermanence; building a building that will eventually fall down. Failure is the great teacher. We all have huge aspirations in practice — "sentient beings are numberless; I vow to save them." You'll be in sorry shape if you depend on success for happiness, because ultimately everything fails. Only failure counts. Why do something you have a high likelihood of success at? What's the interest of that? All this taken together amounts to this: we can love ourselves and love others.

✍

At twenty-four years, David Basile directs Tassajara's physical plant — the maintenance shop, the plumbing, the electricity — "anything that's not human," he told me cheerfully. With prominent cheekbones and ruddy cheeks, as tall as and thinner than air, he has the fine bones, Roman nose, and sensual lips of an Edwardian dandy, accompanied by the weathered hands of a man who works outdoors and with tools. Like many of his generation, he grew up rootless. His parents were Peace Corps volunteers, and he lived in various overseas countries until going to college in California, where he began reading Buddhist texts — *Zen Flesh, Zen Bones* and *Dropping Ashes onto the Buddha* were his favorites. Tassajara was the first place where he put down roots.

Basile described the geology and natural features of the Tassajara Canyon. "There are a total of around twenty hot springs here or nearby, each of which has a different mineral content and temperature. The ones we use have an especially high content of lithium."

"So that's why everyone's so cheerful," I said.

He grinned. "I wish I could say you were the first person to make that joke." He described the man who trained him for the job in terms that made him sound like my father: his mentor did not allow him to work at first, jerking the saw from his hand, but gradually let him do a little more, then a little more beyond that. "I had to learn by sitting and watching," Basile said. "Which of course was the point."

> I never worked a day in my life until I came to the Zen Center. Then I discovered work and how I had a love for physical exertion. In the summer I'd do head work in the office, but in the winter I'd go to the shop. . . . The training is good — very focused. When we work together we don't talk about other things — the physical plant is a patchwork of many people's minds put together and I have to sit in silence a long time to figure out why and how it got that way.

I recalled my father, how he could do anything with his hands. There was a brilliance to that — the discipline and patience to take an unfamiliar machine, manufactured a generation earlier with parts now long outmoded and out of stock, and dismantle it, examining each nut and bolt and screw with an eye to deciphering the logic of its original designer, then discovering the break or the flaw and inventing an acceptable substitute from salvage, then reassembling the whole without plans or diagrams but only from the design memorized at the time of disassembly.

Basile continued his thoughts:

> All through zazen, again and again I practice letting go thinking about work. And that carries forth into the day. So that encountering a challenge at work is an opportunity to be absorbed, concentrated. There's a certain *samadhi* [focused concentration] in work that's not different from practice in the zendo.
>
> We have both a sense of doing and a sense of being. Zazen is not re-

ally doing anything but just getting the opportunity to be; whereas work practice is doing things and not having much chance to be. Buddhist practice allows me to find the being in doing. When the bell rings to end work practice you let go. That's why we make new people observe the rule of stopping at the bell, no matter what.

Finding the being in doing — what is this but merging Plato's world of Ideas with his material world?

We walked to the higher parking lot in search of sun, a common winter pastime at Tassajara, where the mountains to the south cast their shadows over most of the buildings, but our patch of sun was soon swallowed by thickening clouds, harbingers of the next storm to sweep through. With the memory of those warm summer days still vivid, though, I asked Basile to offer a young man's perspective on the place of infatuation and sex in a Buddhist practice.

Sexual energy is an overwhelmingly powerful force that does demand to be studied. Especially in the summer it comes up, where it's handled skillfully and unskillfully — mostly the latter by people new to the practice. But venerable elders have been known to yield. The level of trust and intimacy here — it's hard for people not to confuse that with sexual energy — ideally we feel it and don't repress it but don't express it.

I fell in love two summers ago — I was present through most of it, but a certain amount of the time I was . . . [he laughs]. Our relationship was supported by the community. With her I have an everyday intimacy that I don't have with the rest of the community.

Many of us are new to Buddhism, new to monastic practice. And so few elders are here that it would be good to have some clarity about the whole thing. We have a tradition that supports relationships. Suzuki Roshi said, "Having sex is like brushing your teeth — you don't want to do it too often, but you don't want to forget about it, either." All the teachers here are coupled — it would be harder to be celibate. Those who want to practice celibacy are frowned upon, as if they're sexually repressed.

꧁

The next morning, as I walked to zazen at 4:00 A.M., the full moon was setting but still high over the mountain. The moonlight cast shadows of branches on the palette of wet leaves as the monks in their black robes hurried past. After the last zazen I forgot to take my cushion to the aisles. There we lined up for a service that included another half-hour of sitting — in my case, with no cushion. Then we stood and immediately made nine bows to the floor, but my aging knees refused to unbend. Nine times — and I was counting — I weaved and faltered and nearly fell, entangled in my robes, looking, no doubt, like an overgrown crow.

At that morning's zazen, all my anger came back. It didn't roar back, but it was there — the anger at injustice and wrong, at the oppression and lies among which I live, the conspiracy of silence fostered by the men (and sometimes women) of the religious hierarchy, my cowardice in confronting all these, my complicity and collusion. But as I sat I came to understand this: *The anger is the easy part, and venting it, once I get over the social taboos, even easier. It's figuring out what to do with it that's hard.*

※

Zazen is about being where your anger comes from — it comes from a wound. You have to sit still enough to let the wound show itself — so that the wounded part can trust you. Sitting is the only vehicle I have to face myself — left to myself I'd eat popcorn and watch TV and run away.

— *Kōsho McCall*

※

And still there is much anger. First and foremost, anger at my loneliness, which is to say unresolved anger at my lover's death. To be in love, in San Francisco, in Paris . . . I was brash and young and only dimly aware of my great good fortune, until his death taught me the measure of my blindness and arrogance. Which was the greater gift: his love while he was alive, or his death and the awakening it brought? Shortly after returning to New York I would interview a wise gay Jesuit who will read what I have written about that love, that life, that death. "When something happens that's so profound," he will tell me, "the holiness of it closes the door on your ability to receive it soon again."

And yes, anger at being gay, being deprived of the world of not questioning, being deprived of and excluded from the world of power. No matter that almost all good that has happened to me (including my lover) has grown from that exclusion, human nature will want what it cannot have (Buddhism's First Noble Truth, page 97), and what I want is the comfortable sense that the world "belongs" to me, even as in my heart I know the idea is preposterous. The poor and oppressed do not have to labor for the gift of understanding that the world does not "belong" to them; that is the nature of their reality. To the extent that being gay has given me access to that wisdom, I am blessed.

Which, as my anger makes abundantly clear, is not to say that I accept and embrace that wisdom.

JE

This morning I received four corrections:

1. Standing shod an inch past the line beyond which one is not to wear shoes.
2. Standing in the wrong place in the zendo.
3. Talking during work practice.
4. Hands folded incorrectly during kinhin (walking meditation).

Kathy Egan delivered this last correction, kindly enough and in the typical Californian way — "You know, honey, I don't know that it matters but when we're doing kinhin you don't hold your hands in a *mudra*, but just interlock them."

My old resentment rose *(Don't tell me what to do)*, but even with it lodged in my throat I understood: *I am learning to listen, I am learning to let go. What is at stake, after all? What is at the root of this pointless anger?*

JE

As I entered Abbot Norman Fischer's cottage he was instructing his assistant in the art of building a fire in his small stove. Once alone, Fischer and I seated ourselves on the tatami mats and discussed the wide-ranging world of faith and monastic practice.

According to Fischer, at the time of Eihei Dōgen (1200–1253), the teacher who popularized Zen practice in Japan, Buddhism "emphasized magical, esoteric ceremonies conducted by priests for the upper classes, and veneration of nature spirits and Buddha and bodhisattva figures. Dōgen responded by encouraging active, personal experience of the practice of Buddhist truths through zazen and community life." Fischer's description might be applied to the Roman Catholicism of my childhood, where Vatican II was an effort to shift the Roman Church from "magical, esoteric ceremonies" to an active, personal experience of Christian truths.

The Zen Center is running out of room, Fischer told me, turning away qualified people who would like to live at one of its three facilities. "We never had a concept of a cloister or enclosure or a vow of stability — both are key differences between Zen and Catholic traditions. The Zen monastery was always a place to train, not to stay," he said. And yet as people have entered the community and established themselves, the center has found that maintaining enough turnover to accommodate newcomers, especially in San Francisco, with its exorbitant housing costs, has become increasingly problematic.

From Fischer's translations of the Buddha's instructions to the monks: "As long as they do not authorize what has not been authorized already and do not abolish what has been authorized by rules of training . . . they may be expected to prosper and not decline." The passage struck me as a prescription for death, precisely contradicting Suzuki Roshi's succinct summation of the essence of Zen: "Everything changes." Institutions that endure are those that successfully balance the imperative to preserve with the inevitability and necessity of change. But what do we preserve and what do we reject or modify? In a conversation held later in the week Fischer told me, "It's an idealistic fiction that there's any tradition preserved as it was."

> If we tried our best to do everything as the Japanese did it, it would still be different. To me the question is not, Do you preserve tradition or change it? Instead the question is, How conscious do you want to be of the change and how does it happen? In the monastic tradition you have to make change with trepidation. Religion is inherently conservative — that's one of its positive aspects. You don't say, "The numbers are down so let's have some girlie shows!" You have to change slowly and with fear and trepidation — but you have to have confidence that you can manage the change.

The Zen Center has moved aggressively to adapt the Buddhist precepts governing the treatment of women to contemporary North American sensibilities. "We know that the Buddha initially opposed ordination of women," Fischer told me,

> but that he eventually relented, and that there was a *sangha* of women in his lifetime. But there's a strongly misogynistic streak in early Buddhism, that was embodied in the Scriptures when they were eventually written down. . . . A few years ago, at my insistence and against some opposition, the Zen Center drew up a list of women ancestors — we

took the names from the *Therigata: The First Buddhist Women,* translated by Susan Murcott. Now we alternate chanting those names with the traditional list of male ancestors.

∞

For my last evening service I violated protocol by turning around to watch Fischer as he made his bows before the altar. The zendo was dim, lit only by kerosene lamps, as he removed a square of cloth from the ample sleeves of his robe. With military precision he spread the cloth on the floor, then smoothed its wrinkles flat before kneeling on it to prostrate himself before the altar. He bowed full length to the floor three times — in every culture and nation always and everywhere the magic number. Then he walked to his cushion and sat facing the wall. The room dropped into a stillness focused on his androgynous assistant, seated at the altar's side, the shaven head gleaming in the amber light, rising like a lamp from the robe's black folds.

I left in midafternoon of the next day, catching a ride with the weekly grocery delivery van before the next deluge threatened to close the road. My last glimpse, over my shoulder and out the back window, was of Norman Fischer, dressed in workboots and jeans, hefting a box of bleach to his shoulder to carry to the storage room.

The next morning I woke promptly at 3:50 A.M., the hour for first zazen. As I snuggled back into sleep I thought, *Gee, I miss those folks, that life.*

11

A Marriage Made in Heaven: The Coupling of Jewish Ritual and Greek Philosophy

At the gethsemani encounter, though its Christian participants were of a decidedly liberal bent, more than one Christian speaker asserted that because Buddhism does not have God or gods at its center, it's not a *religion* but a *philosophy*, with a clear implication of hierarchy in the comparison. And yet William James defines Buddhism as a religion because it engages "the feelings, acts, and experiences of individual men in their solitude, so far as they apprehend themselves to stand in relation to whatever they may consider the divine" (a generous definition that, interestingly enough, takes solitude rather than the communal experience as its starting point).

As I grew more familiar with the intimate relationship between early Christianity and Greek philosophy, I recast the question. Rather than ask whether Buddhism's focus on what the West calls philosophy renders it incapable of being a religion, ask instead, How did Western Christianity come to emphasize doctrine and dogma over the example of the life of Jesus as portrayed in the Gospels? How did it come to value obsession with the letter of the law over obedience to its spirit?

≈

In its earliest manifestations, religion existed primarily to propitiate gods and goddesses, to keep them on our side so that they would send plentiful game and, after we developed agriculture, the right amount of rain at the right time, ensuring a bountiful harvest. To serve this end men and women devised elaborate rituals to celebrate and remind us of our place in the great cycle of birth, death, regeneration, and rebirth. Religion arose side by side with the structures of community governance, which served in part to guarantee a continual stream of sacrifices and libations so that no deity would feel neglected and retaliate.

Religious expression in these prehistoric times was quite different from contemporary practice. At a time when the connection between sex and procreation was poorly understood, women were most likely seen as sole progenitors of life, and goddess worship and fertility cults prevailed. Possibly as a result of conquests by northern nomadic tribes, however, female deities and fertility rites were gradually suppressed — the Hebrew Bible is replete with examples of their sometimes violent overthrow. The celebration of fertility yielded to the adoration of omnipotent, awe-inspiring, masculine gods.

But remnants of those female deities persisted. The principle of wisdom is consistently personified as feminine, notably in ancient Greece, where philosophers (from Greek *philo,* "love of," and *sophia,* "wisdom") were "lovers of Sophia" and thus "lovers of wisdom." In contrast to the practice of rites undertaken to ensure fertility or appease deities, philosophers proposed the study and practice of virtue undertaken for its own sake.

In 387 B.C.E. Plato founded the Academy, the first Western institution devoted to the study of philosophy. Often considered the prototype and predecessor of the modern university, it might as accurately be labeled a proto-monastery, whose "monks" sought inner perfection through education, discipline, and submission to the search for wisdom. For the next nine centuries the Academy served as the hotbed of philosophical discourse.

In those first four centuries after Jesus' crucifixion, almost all Christians lived under Roman rule; Roman culture was in many ways a reinterpretation of Greek culture, adapted to Roman purposes. The Romans were pragmatists, wildly successful as conquerors and at the engineering wizardry that makes for a comfortable life — gorgeous aqueducts to bring water to cities, handsome coinage, excellent roads to facilitate travel and communications, a sophisticated legal system for the processing of lawsuits and the prosecution of criminals. But their art, their gods, and their ideas they stole from the cultures they defeated, chief among these the Greeks. Throughout these centuries, though Athens was now subject to Rome, Greek and its variants were common tongues throughout the eastern Mediterranean, where all literate people had at least passing familiarity with

Greek philosophical traditions. As English is the language of contemporary Western intellectual and philosophical discourse (supplanting French, which reigned in the seventeenth and eighteenth centuries), so after the first century C.E. Greek was the language of philosophy and culture for the Roman Empire, with Latin serving as the tongue of everyday Roman conversation.

By contrast, the Jews were at various points in their history a wandering, persecuted people who might well have passed into oblivion but for their devotion to a single, omnipotent God and to the Word as the instrument of God's direct communication with them. The Jewish commitment to monotheism and to the sacred Word (first as an oral history, then as a portable document) endured as a touchstone across geography, exile, and time itself. Belief in God, embodied in the first of the Ten Commandments, was the cornerstone of Judaism, but all remaining nine commandments deal with behavior rather than doctrine. To this day Judaism emphasizes ritual and regulation of behavior over particulars of dogma or fine points of theology.

Greek philosophy was based on deductive logic, with its followers obliged to act on their conclusions. Philosophers were defined in the doing, by how they acted toward themselves and their world — pressed to clarify his definition of justice, Socrates answered, "If I don't define justice in my words, I do so by my conduct." The Greeks expected the philosopher to be an eccentric, someone driven by his or her love of wisdom to sacrifice all for it. If others were influenced by that ideal so much the better, but Socrates would never have claimed to teach, at least not in the sense of telling others how to lead their lives. Rather, in the method we still call "Socratic," he asked questions of his listeners, hoping to help them uncover the wisdom they intuitively understood but were unable or unwilling to acknowledge or engage, intending to provoke them into becoming philosophers, "lovers of wisdom." The key to all wisdom, in the phrase attributed to Socrates and inscribed over the doorway to the oracle at Delphi, was KNOW THYSELF — the implication being that wisdom could arise only from within, from seizing responsibility for knowing and acting from one's particular place in the world. Visitors seeking to know their futures were thus directed to know their present selves, for to fully understand the present would be to know the future.

Philosophers participated in religious rituals honoring the deities because these were part of a good citizen's duty, but with rare exceptions the stories of the Greek gods were not intended to offer guidance for moral behavior (think of Zeus abducting, raping, then abandoning all those boys and girls). The Greek religion — that is, the myths of the gods — served more often to remind us of the capriciousness of Fate, herself a goddess: remember how little we control, how all mortals are subject to the whims of the universe, fate, the gods, God.

The Greek philosophers undertook to identify and live out what we *can* control. They specialized in identifying eternal, unchanging truths, then living by them as closely as possible. They showed how in the face of the worst that fate can offer (consider Socrates, unjustly condemned to death), a man or a woman could respond with courage and so retain dignity. As creatures at the mercy of the forces of nature, we are unable to control fortune, but as human beings we may use reason to control our response to it. In doing so we become masters of our destiny, we become larger than life, we become, in fact, divine.

The Greeks conceived of philosophy as a design for life, a path into and through the forest of experience. But the design was largely limited to a subset of society — the citizens, almost exclusively male property owners who constituted perhaps 10 percent of the total population of Athens; noncitizens — women, children, slaves, and resident aliens — made up the great majority of inhabitants. There had been occasional experiments in egalitarian living — Pythagoras, a fifth-century B.C.E. predecessor of Socrates, founded a community for men and women that emphasized equality — but these attempts were notably short-lived. Such communities positioned themselves against a social order in which free males occupied the highest rung and monopolized the rights of citizenship. Socrates and his successors proposed principles that they perceived as universally applicable, but they seldom questioned the social hierarchy that placed male citizens alone at the top.

Yet society was somewhat more fluid than the history books may imply. For example, a number of pagans converted to Judaism because they admired its combination of ritual observance and fealty to the principles of the law; also, Greek slaves were occasionally elevated to citizenship in recognition of their intellectual brilliance. Still, the Jew was almost always *born* to Judaism; the Greek *chose* to be a philosopher. A Jew might be rich or poor, well educated or illiterate; a Greek philosopher was almost assuredly born, or at least elevated, into citizenry. To render the point more concretely: Judaism posits monotheism, a particular belief system not empirically demonstrable (despite generations of effort, the most brilliant minds of Judaism and its descendants have yet to produce indisputable proof of the existence of God). Judaism thus proceeds from a statement of belief constructed on an accident of genealogy. In contrast, Greek philosophy proceeded from principles of reason constructed on an accident of geography. When Socrates tells his audience that "any desire for goodness and happiness is love — and it is a powerful and unpredictable force," he assumes that the principle is open to discussion and modification by reasoned argument. The Jewish commandment descends from the model of religion as a means of honoring and propitiating the gods; the principles of Plato derive from the model of philosophy as a means of identifying and living by wisdom.

⸎

Early Christian leaders were well aware of the contrast between the Jewish religious and the Greek philosophical traditions. Eager to demonstrate that Christianity, this new kid on the block, was the legitimate inheritor of both the Jews and the Greeks, they devoted much of their writing and preaching to the synthesis of Plato's writings with the Law of Moses.

In undertaking this syncretism they drew most notably on the example of Philo, a thoroughly Hellenized Jew who lived in Alexandria from around 25 B.C.E. to 50 C.E., the approximate historical moment of Jesus. Fluent in Greek but barely knowledgeable in Hebrew, Philo laid the groundwork for early Christian writers by taking as his life's great task the synthesis of Jewish Scripture and Greek philosophy.

As an adept of Plato, Philo hasn't much use for the body, which he sees as unavoidable baggage that the soul must carry for a while as the price of the journey to God. Philo also recalls the Jewish concept of God as unknowable and nameless — when Moses asks the Lord for a name, he receives in response the tetragrammaton, Y H W H, not really a word but probably drawn from the Hebrew verb *hayah*, "to be," usually rendered as *Yahweh*, I AM WHAT IS. Philo sees this conception of God, central to Judaism, as dovetailing nicely with Plato's understanding of God as the ineffable One. Philo was a mystic for whom man's goal and bliss lay in a vision of God, achieved in a series of steps familiar to anyone who has undertaken the contemplative life in any tradition, in which the seeker abandons sense perception to become absorbed in prayer that is wordless and unencumbered by petition. According to Philo, since reason depends on the unreliable perceptions of day-to-day reality, it can provide only indirect evidence for the existence of God, whose true essence can be embraced only through intuition, by venturing into the wordless state of Moses' encounter with the burning bush: "Do we see the . . . sun by anything other than that sun, or the stars by any other than the stars, and . . . is light not seen by light? Similarly, God too is his own splendor, and is seen through himself alone . . . The pursuers of truth are they who form an image of God through God, light through light." Three hundred years later, Philo's phrase will find its echo in the Nicene Creed: "God from God, Light from Light."

All the same, Philo is Greek-trained and a speaker of Greek. As a dedicated admirer of reason, he makes clear that he has little use for ostentatious displays of ecstatic belief; ritual without inner devotion is valueless. Drawing on Moses' farewell address to the Jews ("Now you must circumcise your hearts" — Deuteronomy 10:16), he writes that the circumcision that matters is that which leads to what a Benedictine monk would call a "conversion of manners" — a radical commitment to virtue. But Philo was too traditional to abandon the rite of circumcision; it would be Jesus, the radical reformer, who would suggest that the time had come to leave behind the letter of the law in favor of its spirit — a teaching that the apostle Paul would interpret as justification for abandoning the requirement of circumcision altogether.

Philo saw Scripture as revealed truth that completed the partial, reason-based truths of the Greeks. At the same time, he borrowed from the Greeks the concept of virtue established only through action, not by birthright. His goal was to live in and abide with paradox — in this case, a mysticism cloaked in the rich robes of reason, the product of Moses' conversations with God overlaid with Socrates' conversations with his students.

Philo's writings were so influential that the early Christian historian Eusebius assumed him to be a Christian, reporting that he met Peter on a journey to Rome, where (according to Eusebius) Philo offered Peter instruction in the doctrine of the Trinity. Jerome, translator of the Hebrew Bible into Latin and one of the leading early Christian theologians, includes Philo on a list of church fathers. The Christian debt to Philo becomes still more apparent in the influential theologian Gregory of Nyssa's crowning work, *The Life of Moses* (probably written in the early 390s), whose title and structure Gregory flatly steals from Philo's great work of the same name. Gregory takes the idea (long-standing in Jewish theology and central to Philo) of Moses as the embodiment of Judaic wisdom and shows how Jesus is the culminating expression of both pagan (that is, Greek) philosophy and the Jewish Scriptures. Gregory adopts and embellishes Philo's allegorical interpretation of Exodus, drawing a parallel between Moses' ascent to encounter God on Mount Sinai with the Christian ascent to God through the practice of virtue and prayer.

What becomes clear on reading Gregory or any of his contemporaries is how comfortably they saw themselves as the merger of and successor to these two ancient traditions, Jewish and Greek, one based on culture and ritual and an elaborate tribal narrative, the other founded on reason. They assumed that the ideas and ideals of Socrates and especially his student Plato manifested themselves in the very real actions and example of Jesus, who in his parables and sermons drew upon the prophecies and principles of the Hebrew Bible while remaking them in his own vision. As a Jew, Jesus would most likely have seen himself as a prophet, but the evangelists who convey his story to us, schooled in the traditions of the Greeks, present him as a philosopher, a "lover of wisdom," who set out to teach not by writing but through the example of his life (like the Buddha and Socrates, Jesus never wrote — except, tellingly enough, in the sand). Like Socrates, Jesus spoke in parables that required his audiences to puzzle out the truth for themselves. Like Socrates, he chose death, even as both men were given the option to flee.

The greatest philosophers so completely and seamlessly inhabited their lives that death was of no consequence, since to betray one's principles would be to betray oneself, a living suicide worse than death from the poisoned cup or on the cross. The four evangelists are to Jesus' life as Plato is to Socrates, as the later monks are to the Buddha, as Athanasius is to Antony. They are scribes who (like Athanasius) understood themselves as aretalogists — their role was not to record an objectively accurate portrait (they would have found the modern concept of objectivity strange in the extreme) but to render the life of Jesus as role model and inspiration.

Like Athanasius and Augustine, the Gospel writers knew the Hebrew Scriptures backward and forward, could quote them better than any contemporary television evangelist, and included multiple references to them in their writings. We should hardly be surprised to find Jesus' birth, life, and death "predicted" in the Hebrew Bible when the evidence abounds that the Gospel writers deliberately echoed the earlier prophets in writing Jesus' story. Athanasius would later do the same in writing Antony's story; Augustine would follow suit in writing his memoir, the *Confessions*. A prominent theologian has advanced the argument that the evangelists deliberately modeled the death of Jesus on the death of Socrates as described by Plato, knowing that the more sophisticated, influential members of their audiences would get the message that the former had superseded the latter. In this sense the apostle Paul may be described as the "inventor" of Christianity as Athanasius is the "inventor" of Christian monasticism and Augustine the "inventor" of the powerful, centralized church; they extrapolated corporate policy from what Jesus offered only as individual example.

Am I less touched by Jesus' example when I realize that Isaiah's eerie ability to predict Jesus' coming exists because Luke knew the book of Isaiah thoroughly and borrowed from it accordingly? On the contrary, I'm moved more deeply than ever by the human capacity to recognize wisdom when we encounter it and to record it in a way that best ensures its survival — by incorporating it into a story; by making it a myth; by repeating it with variations on the theme. Moments after a traffic accident we begin constructing its story in a way that allows us later to recall not the precise sequence of events that led to the smashed fender, but a myth that unerringly reflects not the facts but the truth — our particular, individual truth, including our need to justify and explain and exaggerate so as to capture the emotive and psychological impact of the events. This is the truth of the storyteller, it is the truth of the Gospels, and it is a truth that eclipses mere fact. My study of the history of the Gospels was leading me to perceive them as living miracles indeed — miraculous in that they endure almost two thousand years later because those inspired writers did their work so well.

Philo and Jesus are hardly likely to have met, but I see them as very different spokespersons of the same historical moment. Philo articulated a synthesis of Jewish ritual and Greek philosophy for the educated elite. Through the example of his life and through his teachings, Jesus offered that same synthesis to the common man and woman. Christianity ultimately triumphed because, in Jesus' life, death, and resurrection, it mythologized the most profound cultural encounter of the day, that of religion and philosophy, the Jews and the Greeks, in a simple, moving story that could be memorized by common people of all ages.

And so the challenge of the Christian — he or she who would be worthy of the name — becomes to live as Jesus lived, to live as a philosopher, a lover of wisdom. KNOW THYSELF. Before my stays at Gethsemani and Tassajara, I might have argued that a religion *evolves* to become a philosophy, that with time and enlightenment it sheds more and more of its rituals and doctrines and becomes pure teaching. But across those weeks I was learning exactly how a religion and its philosophy exist not in the abstract but in and through the flesh, how the ideas engendered in the mind must fulfill themselves through the body. Through participation in ritual I was coming to see that the evolution is the merging of religion and philosophy, ritual and idea. The festivals, ceremonies, and rites of religion remind us of the principles of its underlying philosophy: Yom Kippur and Easter mark historical anniversaries, but more important, they remind us of our moral commitments and responsibilities as members of a community of faith.

❧

In Jesus' teachings these ideas, born of the intersection of multiple cultures, geography, and the opportune historical moment, coalesce and emerge as the understanding that whatever one's economic or social class, people are equal before the great democracy of birth and time and death and the challenge of living a life of virtue. For a century or so this movement toward a more egalitarian view of the human condition achieved its most notable expression in the golden era of Christian monasticism. In these early monastic communities the rituals of religion and the principles of philosophy coexisted in a symbiotic and creative tension, in the short span of time when Christianity was free from persecution but before it had been co-opted by worldly power.

The historical roots of monasticism lie not only in the ascetic practices of the prophets of Jewish Scripture but also in the similar asceticism of Greek philosophers and in practices and rituals imported from Asia. The monk is a philosopher, a seeker of wisdom, who is taking Jesus as his or her role model in the way that a student at the Academy of Athens might have chosen to follow Plato or Aristotle. The monastery is thus the remnant, carried forward even into contemporary times, of a community of people committed to the search for wisdom. Perhaps that, above and apart from the particulars of the vows, is its defining characteristic and the key to both its importance and its persistence across diverse and often hostile times and cultures. That was its essence; that was what drew me back.

PART TWO

12

SOLITUDE

MOST OF THE MANHATTAN mom-and-pop stores have street bins displaying the goods of the season, and I found it rich to watch them change. At the end of the previous summer I'd returned to sunflowers and Long Island tomatoes, then watched the progression to mums and statice mixed with acorn squash and pumpkins. Now I returned from my winter stays at Gethsemani and Tassajara to piles of citrus, an orange and yellow wash behind the plastic sheets the proprietors lower to protect the produce from the cold, until the coldest days of winter, when everything retreated inside except the firewood. The shelves were bare and forlorn, the image of want.

A Wednesday morning in this den of capitalism, and I set out to light a candle in memory of the dead. I stopped in St. Joseph's in the Village, the oldest standing Roman Catholic church in Manhattan. As a result of the city's penchant for profiteering by means of tearing down and building higher, the church is not so very old — it was completed in 1835, a small Greek Revival jewel of a building. The contrast between its Doric pillars and spare, elegant lines and the exuberant, frilly towers and gargoyles of St. Patrick's Cathedral or the Cathedral Church of St. John the Divine offers a visual metaphor for the wide range, even within a single religion, of moods and modes of perception.

The sun through the large south-facing windows, arched and mullioned with clear glass, filled the space with light. Though St. Joseph's sits on busy Sixth Avenue, the church held exactly eight people, including the priest and the lector. I was the only person under sixty. At one point or another all five of my fellow congregants inspected me as if I had arrived from Mars.

The priest launched into the mass, and I decided to stay. At Gethsemani I had been reminded of how as a child I had enjoyed the readings, the voices speaking to me across centuries. The lector, a woman, stood to read the Epistle, which was Paul's famous letter to Titus; among other instructions the apostle urges wives to be, in the words of today's reading, "submissive to their husbands."

In his sermon the priest acknowledged that though the letter to Titus is assigned to Paul, he sided with recent archeological discoveries that ascribe it to another, later author. Still, he assured the tiny congregation, this is of no consequence; it is the message that matters. As for that message, it's true, he said, that it flies in the face of much contemporary understanding of a proper relationship between man and wife. Still, we must understand it in the context of the times in which it was written and see that though our perceptions change, the letter still contains valuable truths about the necessity of submission between partners who love each other.

I appreciated his smooth segue from assigning submission to women, as specified in the text, to ascribing it to both partners.

The mass took longer than I'd anticipated, and rather than be late for an appointment, as the priest finished his sermon I rose quietly to leave. A glass-enclosed vestibule has been added at the rear of the church. On the other side of its large doors a middle-aged woman stood alone. We nodded at each other, and something about her open expression caused me to stick out my hand and introduce myself.

I told her I was writing about faith, and I asked if she had thoughts on the subject. Oh, yes, she said, I think of myself as among the faithful, but I'm divorced and I'm not permitted to receive communion. But you can still sit inside the church, I said. I know that, she said, but I feel unworthy.

I stepped into the busy brightness of Sixth Avenue, but all day I thought of this submissive woman, whose virtue is too pure to permit her to violate the rules enforced by the celibate, single, male priestly caste.

On my next visit to Kentucky, I received a call from a local woman asking me to meet her for a drink. We met in a tavern in the nearby county seat — I wondered at the choice of locations, as we might just as easily have met in my hometown.

The bar was quiet in midafternoon but still she insisted that we take our drinks to a small anteroom. "Somebody told me you're writing about the monks," she said. I nodded cheerfully. "There's something I want to tell you," she said. "There's something I want you to know."

As this woman unfolded her story, I knew that what she told me was true, must be true. The details — as much as she told me — had the ring of authenticity; her anxiety and evident suffering did not allow for any possibility of pretense.

She told me as much as she could bring herself to tell, not much but enough that I could guess at the remainder. I struggled to find the right question. "When did he first . . ." You see the power of the word — I could not make myself name the act because that would bring it into the world, would give it breath and life.

"When I was ten."

Ah. Ten years old. "And how long did this go on?"

"Until I was fourteen. Then he left the monastery, promising to come back and take me away with him. The next time he visited he was married."

I wanted to ask for the whole story, because from my experience as a gay man I had learned this about secrets, how bringing them to light divests them of their mystique and allure, how speaking them aloud is the first step toward letting them go.

I wanted to ask; I did not ask. I was an adult in midlife, a realist (or so I had told myself) about the widest range of human behaviors, and still I was overwhelmed by bitterness and anger mixed with resistance to accepting what I knew to be true. I did not have the courage to ask about the particulars of a story she had carried most of her life.

13

DESIRE

IN THE COURSE of the following year I visited Kentucky again and made
an appointment with Timothy Kelly, intending to speak to him about the
story I'd been told. The sexual violation the local woman had described had
happened before Timothy had been elected abbot, and the perpetrating
monk had long ago left the monastery. Still, I wanted Timothy's response
— had the Trappists known that this had happened, and if they had
known, what steps had they taken to deal with it?

Timothy and I chatted informally — the Trappists were celebrating
the 150th anniversary of the founding of Gethsemani, the 900th anniversary of the founding of the order, his calendar was crowded, he hadn't
much time. I sought a way to bring up the subject, but I could not bring
myself to speak the words, to make the story real. I looked at my watch.
Timothy had generously invited me into his home, his community. I was
the guest; I did not want to violate his trust. On top of which I had not
thought to seek this woman's permission to reveal her story. Sitting with
Timothy, I realized that to tell her story without first obtaining her permission would be to betray her confidence — a different kind of abuse.

The bells rang, signaling the next office. Timothy rose to attend. I
thanked him for his time and left.

Back in my hometown, on my last evening before leaving, another local friend stopped by. We chatted for a while with my mother, then I saw
him to his car. As we stood in the driveway he said, "I understand you're
writing about the monks."

"Yes, that's true," I said, less cheerfully than I might have. By now I had
a foreboding of what was to follow.

"I assume you know that there are people living here who the monks

170

had sex with when those people were kids. The monastery has paid them off so as to keep them quiet."

"I've heard something along those lines," I said.

We talked quietly of the matter for several minutes. In the end I promised to contact him if I thought he could be of help.

Much later I would realize that these people who have lived so long in silence wanted their stories told, even as they were not able to own them publicly. I was receiving a lesson in the reality of childhood sexual abuse: the abused cannot lay claim to their most valuable possessions — their only true possessions, which are their own stories. From fear, from shame, from a desire to protect others — often their abusers — they hold their tongues. And in that silence their stories gather all the power of fantasy until finally the familiar internalized demons become preferable to the world of ordinary suffering.

From that Kentucky visit I went to San Francisco, where I stayed with a friend while interviewing Buddhist scholars. More time had passed since I'd first heard the Kentucky woman's story and I'd told no one, wanting to wait until I had the chance to ask her permission. But stories demand to be told and now far from Kentucky I spoke it aloud, to a woman for whom I have great respect, a writer who volunteers at a center for poor and pregnant teens. "And so this woman and a monk had an affair —" I said.

My friend interrupted. "How old was she when this started?"

"Ten."

"That wasn't an affair," my friend said with indignation. "That was abuse."

And of course she was right. I had been unwilling to speak the word, to name the act for what it was. Such an ugly word, *abuse,* and in refusing to name it, I had committed the most common of sins, living in my own fantasy world, the world as I would have it be rather than confronting and accepting the world as it is. Some deeply ingrained part of me wanted to believe in a perfect place where holy men led flawless lives . . . set down in writing, the words reveal their own naiveté, and yet if life inside a monastery is no different from life outside, what is its point?

My San Francisco friend asked after details of that conversation, now months past, but I could not provide them. I could remember the setting, the small-town tavern's particular smell (cigarette smoke and food ingrained over a century), the murmur of a television in the adjoining kitchen, and the intermittent cries of the men watching a basketball game in a neighboring room, but I could not remember what we'd said — that's what memory does, as instinctively as the hand recoils from the flame. A moment of suffering is too great and so the mind misplaces the words, leaving the memory to be stored in the body. In this most emphatic way I was learning how the body and the spirit are one: a secret of this kind is a deep wound. A scab may form on the outside, but inside the wound suppurates until opened to air and light.

*

On the recommendation of Brother Paul, Gethsemani's poet-monk, early the following summer I rented a car and drove to Baltimore to speak to a Carmelite monk about the experience of women in the contemplative orders of the Roman Church.

By chance I arrived on the day of an open house, the one day each year when the sisters open the enclosure to their neighbors and friends. Browsing through the schedule, I noticed a presentation by Father Ray Chase, a diocesan priest who works with abused children under the auspices of St. Vincent's Center of Catholic Charities. The subject of his presentation: the artwork of Justin Wilke, a teenager with whom Chase had worked, who had been sexually abused by one of his camp counselors from age eleven to age fourteen and who had committed suicide at nineteen years of age.

I stayed around until midafternoon to attend Father Chase's talk. I expected, I suppose, that Father Chase would give a sermon accompanied by the pious moralizing typical of the institutional church's stonewalling and denial, but I wanted to see the paintings of this boy — barely a man — whose work had captured the Carmelites' imagination.

Like all genuine art, Wilke's work transcends description in prose. Two of the five paintings draw on images, reminiscent of the gay artist Keith Haring, of a man being torn apart by four hands. In the first, Wilke paints himself as a woman in black, fearful and grieving. His fourth painting he executed directly on his bedsheet, using his fingers instead of a brush.

On the facing wall, the Carmelites had posted a poem by the mystic and poet, patron of their order, John of the Cross:

> Let us rejoice, Beloved
> And let us go forth and behold
> ourselves in your beauty

to the mountain and to the hill
to where the pure water flows
And from there, deep into the thicket . . .

I decided to stay an extra day to seek out Father Chase.

I spoke with Sister Constance FitzGerald, a lovely woman with silvered hair and brilliant, penetrating blue eyes and a leading scholar of Carmelite contemplative life and the Carmelite mystical poet John of the Cross.

> Men are free to move in and out of the monastery, but what's called the "papal enclosure" — the strict confinement of cloistered women — is very important to Rome. There's an association between the place of women in society, the confinement of women contemplatives, and the whole dismissal of the feminine tradition of wisdom.
>
> We know Father Ray because he comes to offer mass here — after all, we can't do that for ourselves; we're not ordained. Because abuse has become such an issue, we felt showing Justin Wilke's artwork was an appropriate way to offer people something that would challenge them and call them to a new level of awareness, to face the things that need to be faced.

Father Ray Chase was a handsome man, dark-haired and with a plain gold band on his left ring finger. Though he looked younger, he was nearing fifty and had served as a priest for over twenty years.

According to Chase, Wilke's abuser was a teacher and camp counselor who "used art as a means to cross the boundary between play and sex." Like many abused children, Wilke found it difficult to break free even after the older man was apprehended. On Wilke's nineteenth birthday his abuser, having fled abroad, sent him a twenty-three-page letter and a video containing child pornography. Shortly afterward, Wilke asphyxiated himself by parking in an enclosed garage with the car motor running. With the video as evidence, his abuser was brought back to America, where he was convicted for transporting child pornography across international borders. He is now in prison, where like many abusers he continues to deny wrongdoing.

Our conversation turned to the relationship between faith and the body, where Chase spoke with eloquent if carefully chosen words.

People who have experienced assault come to a church that has a history of ambivalence about the nature of the body. The statements of the church regarding sexuality have most often focused on behavior the church identifies as problematic or sinful, and so the individual comes to believe that the church's stance on sexuality is negative, and so sees a chasm between her or his experience of body and the teachings of the church.

Chase shifted to speaking about the role masculine, patriarchal power structures play in the church's response to sexual issues.

We use exclusively male language to refer to God and yet households increasingly have no experience of a father. We project onto God many of our difficulties relating to males and fathers, rather than looking at Jesus' description of God as Father and using that as our paradigm. The way we genderize boys and girls has an impact — we teach boys not to ask for help, but then teach them to call on God. When a person is physically or sexually abused by a man, that can also deeply affect her or his understanding of God.

I asked Chase to address the relationship between the vow of celibacy and the realities of desire.

Among those who enter a celibate clergy there may be a belief that to become celibate will solve the problem [of their struggles with sexual issues and sexual identity], but eventually they realize that becoming a celibate is not going to make those problems go away. A great number of people in the helping professions, including the clergy, have a life history more complicated than those in other fields, and that history often includes abuse. Those who resolve those issues successfully are often able to use that experience in helping others. Those who don't resolve those issues have the potential of negatively impacting their work. We have not been successful at reaching out to clergy who have histories of physical or sexual abuse, partly because of those men's fear of discovery.

Finally we turned to discussing the relationship between faith and innocence — with *innocence* defined as "the capacity to place trust in another."

In his art Justin used the body to represent what's been done to the soul. Justin was trying to convey the importance and validity of innocence and the loss of innocence when that is not of one's own choice. . . . I see a fundamental connection between faith and innocence.

Faith is always uniquely personal — if we're to help someone it's critical that we know the nature of their faith . . . But I don't use words like *faith*. Instead I talk about it through the eyes of their own experiences. Justin's brother [abused by the same man, and also a suicide] didn't believe in God. I asked him, "What if we throw out the language and you tell me of your most meaningful and profound experiences?" And then he described a reality that was nothing less than a description of God's presence, but he needed to disconnect it from religious language because he associated that language with the world of adults that had been such a failure for him. He couldn't articulate those experiences in traditional language. A spiritual journey for him would have been finding a way to nurture those experiences so they became the substance of his life rather than moments of relief from it.

⁂

Later in the summer, back at my Manhattan desk, I looked back at my notes from that Baltimore trip to see what they and the work of Justin Wilke might teach me about the relationship between faith and desire. They provoked me to ask again why I had quailed before asking Timothy Kelly about the monastery's experience with abusers, why I could not ask the abused to tell their stories when I have learned from my own experience that stories spoken aloud can be more easily borne. For all these reasons I knew I should find these people and offer them at least the chance to tell their stories. *How did this happen . . . ? How did you feel . . . ?* Perhaps they would not want to talk — fine; I would have offered them the chance. I wanted to ask; I could not bring myself to ask.

Until this particular point in my journey I'd thought of history as a rock on which I might build something called faith. With knowledge about the history of the Judeo-Christian tradition, I could point to the flaws and fissures in the rock. I would know at what point Christians, once outsiders, began in turn to persecute and oppress others.

I wanted to *know*, I wanted to understand, I wanted history to make sense. If I understood those shaping forces maybe I could understand how a man, a monk publicly committed to kindness, could abuse someone and name it love; how the words and life of Jesus, this radical reforming philosopher, could come to form the superstructure for the Inquisition, the Crusades, the burning of dissidents, the lynch mobs of the South, the pope's silence in the face of the Holocaust, the oppression of women and gay men . . . in a phrase, the superstructure that passes for Christianity. I had set out to force my way, through the power of reason and knowledge, to faith . . . but the neighboring woman's story of abuse and betrayal overwhelmed reason and knowledge.

The story of the Kentucky woman and the artwork of Justin Wilke were teaching me that history was not an absolute rock but a construction of human hands and minds that must draw its integrity from somewhere else, some deeper and more enduring truth. What that might be I could not yet know or name, but on my journey into the contemplative life my Kentucky friend's revelation had tripped me up. I had stumbled backward into a much greater mystery than I'd bargained for, something as big as the sorrow of the race, the wellspring of our darkness.

And along with that darkness I had encountered something that keeps people going in the face of reason to the contrary, the virtue that sustained my Kentucky friend through her dark years during and after her abuse. Father Chase had connected faith with innocence, but innocence was not the same as ignorance. Those who grow up (as opposed to merely growing older) must leave behind the child's naiveté to *choose* innocence: to be fully aware of and present to the range of horrors humankind perpetrates and still to have faith.

The easy route would be cynicism. What, after all, had I expected? Every institution spawns its failures; every organization has bad members on the books. Sensitive men and women who are afraid of sex (and perhaps most of us should be a little more afraid — or rather, a little more respectful — than we are) or who sense desires that they believe are destructive are attracted to the monastic life as an escape. Of those men and women, many will honor their vows. Some will do so reluctantly and in bitterness, though some will find in the discipline of monastic life a way to open their hearts to love. Some will get sexually involved with adult women or men; many of these will leave — the history of Gethsemani in the 1960s offers ample testimony to the fact. And some will seduce or molest children. These should be expelled from the order and handed over to law enforcement officials for prosecution. This last course of action almost never happened until recently, when laypeople began to demand it; it is still the exception to the rule.

But it is not simply the circling of the wagons of the various churches to protect their own that is troublesome. These acts of abuse, and the institutional silence surrounding them, call into question the very profession of being a holy person, of dedicating one's life to the search for purity of heart. That was the chief source of my reluctance to confront the realities of abuse: I hesitated to invade others' painful and private memories, yes, but I was also avoiding confronting my comfortable illusions about what it means to be a person of faith, inside or outside the monastic enclosure. I wanted to believe that the holy man or woman is intrinsically different from you or me because so long as I perceive holiness as some exotic and extraordinary quality, I am absolved of the responsibility of cultivating it; I am absolved of the challenge of defining, then keeping, faith. But through the gift of this woman's story and Justin Wilke's art, I had been brought up against my own elaborate scrim of myths and illusions surrounding what it means to be holy.

And so I sought them out, the women and men who had been sexually abused by adults in whom they had placed their faith — by monks or (in one case) a priest or (in another) a teacher. What follows are not their individual stories — every woman or man with whom I spoke wanted to remain anonymous — but amalgams, collages of the details I was told.

Imagine, for example, that you have grown up on a farm, that you are twelve years old and there are no jobs. Twenty years from now tourism and better roads will bring ways to earn minimal wages, fast-food joints and lube shops and the like, but for now there is only farmwork and not much of that. Most of your neighbors have big families, plenty of hands for fewer and fewer jobs. Your father, who is a friend of one of the monks, asks him if the monastery might take you on and the monk obliges. Eager for money to buy cigarettes and presents for the girl on the bus, you jump at the chance. Your father is pleased — an extra dollar in this house goes a long way, and he's a little concerned about you anyway — you spend half your time with the rough crowd at the pool hall (*I know who you're hanging out with, don't lie to me, I've got eyes*) and the other half mooning over the girl on the bus.

And so you start by hauling boxes and sweeping floors, but pretty soon your father's friend asks you to work at the cow barn and you're happy about that; you like animals and being outside, and anything is better than hauling cardboard and sweeping floors. In the cow barn they have milking machines; the monk in charge has to show you how to fit one to the cow's udder, and he hunches over your shoulder and takes your hands in his to show you how it's done. You've milked cows by hand and anyway you're a quick study; you figure it out the first time around, but he insists that you don't have it right and so he shows you another time, and this time he leans into your back and keeps his hand on your shoulder. You don't like it, but he's a monk, he's the boss, what are you supposed to say? You keep your mouth shut, and every day he shows up at the same time, and now he puts his arm around your shoulder and his other hand in his work pants while you keep your eyes on what you're doing, anywhere but on him, and you pretend it's not happening, even when his hands reach around your shoulders to feel your back and arms and chest, though when he tries to go lower, you shift your body to block him — you have your limits — and he does not insist but takes back his hand, and no word is spoken, no word is ever spoken.

At home your parents ask how things are going, and your mother praises the monk who gave you the job and asks if you remember to thank him every once in a while, and you tell her you do but you don't. An evening comes when they have him to dinner, and your mother makes you come in from the yard and sit next to him at the table, and after he leaves she asks you sharply, "Where are your manners, lump-on-a-log?"

This goes on for a year or two; you try not to think about how long but long enough that you stop pestering the girl on the bus — you're afraid that she'll see the lie you feel like you're carrying on your sleeve, that anybody with any eyes could see, and you start drinking with the guys at the pool hall because when you're drunk you can forget about what's going on. Your grades go down and your mother says with worry and anger in her voice, "Well, at least you have a job at the monastery, you can always fall back on that, I guess." And then one day another monk walks into the cow barn when the monk who's your father's friend has his arm around your shoulder and the next day a new monk, a monk you've never met, is in charge of the cow barn, and you never see your father's friend again, which is just fine by you. Not long after, the cows are sold and you are let go. The new monk in charge of the barn gives you a ten-dollar bill and the first thing you do is to go to the bootlegger's and buy yourself some beer.

Or imagine this: for many years one of the monks has visited your family's house. He tosses you in the air and you shriek with delight; your brother paws at his thick monk's belt, but the monk laughs and says boys are too heavy for his back and he turns his attention back to you, already climbing atop a stool, your arms reaching out. You are seven years old.

And a few years pass until one summer day the monk invites you to take a ride with him in the big monastery truck. You go out with him, and he skids around corners and over dusty roads and at some point asks if you'd like to learn to drive. Of course you'd like to learn to drive, and so he sits you in his lap and puts your hands on the steering wheel and you go very slowly down an old gravel road that you've never seen before, and then he looks at the lengthening shadows and says it must be time to get back home and you beg and plead to stay out longer; this is so much more fun than anything that goes on at home, and you make him promise, *promise* that he will take you out again.

And he does take you out again, and this time you climb into his lap before he asks and put your hands on the wheel, and he puts his hands over yours, but he can't let you take complete control because your feet don't reach the pedals.

And you go on driving like this until the day comes — now you are ten — when he steers you into a wide spot alongside the road and he stops the truck there but holds you in his lap and runs his hand through your hair and tells you how much he loves you; he knows it's wrong and bad but he can't help himself. And you tell him it's not wrong and bad, that you love him too.

And so he arranges to meet you after school, to pick you up around the corner where no one will see, and you sneak away from your friends because you know at some place before knowing that this is wrong, but he makes you feel special; no girl in your group has a man who says what he says to you along those gravel roads arched with honeysuckle and wild grape and sumac and poison ivy.

To complete the picture, we must imagine a third person as well:

You have been raised in a devoutly religious family — the denomination could be any, but for the sake of consistency let us call it Roman Catholic. While you are still a boy, your immigrant family attains a small prosperity, probably for the first time in anyone's memory, until what matters above all else is maintaining the appearance that the family is like every other family — comfortable, prosperous, secure.

And on the surface your family *is* like every other family except that since your earliest memories your father has used you for sex. He would not see it this way. He always tells you he loves you — it is the only time he tells you he loves you — as you grow older he weeps when he tells you but still he takes you for long rides to an abandoned boathouse, or asks you to help him in the garage when your mother has taken the younger kids to a relative's. You are powerless before his power. He is your father whom you love, and you hate yourself for this love for without it maybe you could break free. This continues until the day you announce that you have earned a scholarship to a boarding school and you are leaving. From boarding school you join the military, from the military you join the monastery, or the seminary, because you want to make a better life for younger people than the life you had known. In all these testosterone-pumping years you touch yourself rarely and then with loathing and an avalanche of guilt, and you weep as you come. It is the only time you weep.

And then you are a holy man, welcomed into generous households where you are treated with a respect and deference you have never felt for yourself, until in one particular household you meet a girl who adores you with the kind of innocence and openness you once reserved for God — to that child you *are* God. In her eyes you see yourself as you might once have been, a self your father took from you before you were aware that such a self existed. Your longing for that lost self, your self, is a dam across the river of desire that this child breaches with her innocence and trust.

You are lost before the flood. Nothing in your life has had meaning until now. You construct elaborate fantasies of your future with this child in which you use your age and experience (that is, your power) to take her to some richer, bigger place. You know these are fantasies, but you have no one to tell them to but her, and her eager listening makes them seem even more possible. You understand, or think you understand, the magnitude of your betrayal and cruelty and selfishness, but each time you see her, you box those up and set them aside because, you tell yourself, at the bottom what you feel for her is love. You who have never known love have no standard against which to measure this overwhelming desire, and if it is not in fact love, you are not interested in calling it by any other name. Besides, after each time, in your guilt you convince yourself that this is the last time, that you will seize control of yourself and do what you have to do — flee the place, kill the child, kill yourself. But then days pass and you return to the familiar, comfortable lies. All the world is corrupt; if you need proof of this, you need only look to your church, where you know of men who are worse than you and everyone looks the other way, so what you're doing is not so bad after all. Then the opportunity presents itself again, and overcome by despair and self-loathing and desire, you seek comfort in your familiar wound, you return to abuse the child and yourself.

The parents must know, you object. Mothers always know, if they let themselves, and this world is so small.

Very well — let us imagine that these parents suspect or learn what is happening. What would you have them do? In this pious culture, which so many tout with nostalgia and to which they would have us return, these would have been their choices: to declare their suspicions *(to whom?)* and risk having them mocked — their word against the church, their word against the holy man's. You would have them confront the perpetrator, have him defrocked, brought to justice, a course of action that makes eminent sense in the bright light of the secular world but that in rural Catholic towns or suburban fundamentalist congregations or urban black communities would have led to disgrace for the family, agony for the child. With a boy, the story would have been hushed up — this behavior is beyond the pale of language. With a girl, there would be whispering: "Imagine. The little bitch. Twelve years old — or is she even that? — and chasing a monk." The parents would be considered people against the church, at a time and in a place where no one has fought such a battle. They and their children must live with the consequences; running away is not an option, especially if the church has helped provide what little prosperity they have. Publicly accused, the offending priest or minister or monk would suffer no consequences other than embarrassment and removal to some distant congregation or community.

And so for the powerless the only options would be subterfuge and manipulation, the power of the powerless. We can imagine, for example, a sunny afternoon when the mother contrives to corner the monk alone in the kitchen, and there she tells him in a hard, bright voice that allows for no response that she has heard tales, stories that sicken and disgust her, of priests and monks who pursue children. The message will be conveyed. A month later the monk will be gone.

Or more likely he will remain, untouched. It is the prerogative of power to take its ways of being for granted. Power defines itself in its setting of the terms of the encounter.

At twenty the farm boy we have imagined tried to hang himself. Now he is killing himself with alcohol, a slower suicide. The girl of our imagination carries everywhere a hard, dark edge surrounding a bitter longing. Her abuser phones, he tries to visit, he implores in his low deep voice that he still loves her, he has always loved her. He has children now, almost grown, good Catholics; he is a good Catholic, the Church set him free from his monk's vows so that he could marry and he did marry, but he has only one permanent thing in his heart and that is this obsession he calls love, which he carries for this girl, this child whom he abused when she was ten and eleven and twelve and thirteen and fourteen years old.

14

UNION

MOTHER SUPERIOR: Difficult trials await you, my daughter.
BLANCHE: Why fear them if God will give me strength?
MOTHER SUPERIOR: What God desires to test is not your strength
but your weakness.

— FRANÇOIS POULENC, *Dialogues of the Carmelites*

LET US BEGIN by describing the world as it is, rather than as we might
want it to be.

Pick seventy men from any discipline — doctors, farmers, auto workers, lawyers, soldiers, teachers, Protestant ministers, writers, Roman Catholic priests, Buddhist monks — and you will find that a substantial number
will have sexually abused children. Quantifying "a substantial number" is
almost impossible — organizations in charge of such matters have an ax to
grind, and no aspect of human behavior could be more difficult to measure. Still, more conservative estimates suggest that between 15 percent and
20 percent of people are marked by this experience, with girls significantly
more likely to suffer abuse than boys. Because many perpetrators are repeat
offenders, their numbers are harder to estimate, but this much is true: the
perpetrator is usually a man and is almost always someone close to the
abused child — a relative, a favorite teacher, a neighbor, the village priest.
The perpetrators were themselves most likely abused as children.

But let us also complicate our understanding of the subject. I will
name the act for what it is — abuse — even as I know men who have told
me how their first sexual encounter came about because, at twelve or
thirteen or fourteen, they approached a reluctant older man (twenty-five,
thirty, forty years old). And of the abusers I have known I must in truth
write this: they are not men whom I can easily name as evil. One was a considerate husband who provided well for his family; another was among the
best teachers at my high school, the man who first introduced me to the extraordinary notion that I might become a writer. These men were seized by

obsessions they carried to their graves — and, like Justin Wilke's abuser, when confronted they admitted the act but refused to acknowledge that they had done anything wrong. They who excelled in so many quarters clung to this obsession *because they could.*

And this is where the demons may be caught out, may be seen for what they are, and equally important, for what they are not.

҂

The evil lies not in desire, but to understand the nature of the evil I must grapple with the nature of desire. Abuse — and the secrecy that surrounds it — are symptoms, the visible aspect of a long, troubled, dishonest relationship between institutionalized religion and the reality of desire and its intrinsic connection to the experience and expression of the virtue we call faith.

Scientists have long agreed on the biological advantages conferred by sexual desire. Sexual reproduction involving two creatures, whether beetles or human beings, has a great advantage over asexual cloning, in which a creature duplicates itself (the reproductive mode of many plants and all bacteria). Sexual reproduction drawing on two gene pools yields vastly more genetic diversity, on which natural selection acts to render rapid evolutionary change. Life on earth was asexual — and virtually unchanged — for over three billion years, until the evolutionary innovation of sexual recombination arose, allowing life to evolve in a relatively short time from bacteria to the staggering variety of forms we know today. Sexual desire (the more, the better) has the advantage of maximizing the dispersal of genes into the next generation.

These facts diminish not a bit the profundity of the act, any more than they console the abused child or raped woman. A sexual relationship between an adult and a child almost always involves an abuse of power because the child is so inherently powerless. The adult who pursues sex with a child, or responds to a child's advance, abdicates responsibility in favor of the seductions of virtually limitless power. Such a relationship is founded not on love but on obsession, not on respect for the beloved but on a profound lack of respect for oneself.

҂

The historical roots of the tendency within the church to vilify desire in order to gain power reside in the period when Christianity was emerging from the creative encounter between Judaism and Greek philosophy. In one of those moments of serendipity for which the writer lives, I happened to be reading Philo of Alexandria on my journey to Baltimore, where the paintings of Justin Wilke provoked me into thinking more deeply about the symbiosis of faith and desire. Camped out in a comfortable recliner of the Metroliner, I encountered this passage in the midst of an anthology of Philo's writings, presented under the subtitle "Wisdom, the Daughter of God, Is in Reality Masculine":

> [H]ow can Wisdom, the daughter of God, be rightly said to be a father? Is it because, though Wisdom's name is feminine, her nature is masculine? Indeed all the virtues have women's designations, but powers and activities of truly perfect men. For [wisdom] which comes after God, even if it were the most venerable of all other things, holds second place, and was called feminine in contrast to the Creator of the universe, who is masculine . . . For the feminine always falls short and is inferior to the masculine, which has priority.
>
> Let us then pay no attention to the discrepancy in terms, and say that the daughter of God, Wisdom, is both masculine and the father, inseminating and engendering in souls a desire to learn discipline, knowledge, practical insight, noble and laudable actions.

In describing virtue as the exclusive province of men, Philo is only echoing the common understanding of his age. His innovation comes in the fierceness with which he insists that Wisdom is a man, however he may dress (like the cardinals and popes of Roman Catholicism) in woman's clothing. When in Plato's *Symposium* Diotima appears to deliver her discourse on the nature of love, Plato (hardly a feminist) makes no implication that underneath her robes she's a man. She is what she is, and what she is is a woman, handmaiden of Athena, goddess of Wisdom, patroness of Athens.

The personification of Wisdom as feminine and the presence of Athena as the city's patroness did not improve in any historically notable way the status of women of Plato's Athens. And yet the culture ascribed to womanhood its highest ideal. The fulfillment of that ideal demanded virginity — the historical connection between the virginity of Plato's Wisdom and the exalted place of virginity in Christendom is resonant and clear. The sanctification of virginity grew from a host of superstitions and customs founded on reason's perception of desire as the enemy and the "tainted" (that is, sexually experienced) woman as the personification of that enemy.

Still, in personifying Wisdom as a woman, the philosophers who sought Her aspired to transform themselves into outsiders — to learn to be the Other. Through diligent and devoted ascetical practices, they sought to understand what it was like to be an outsider — to observe from a critical distance both society and the individual human life they might otherwise have taken for granted.

⁂

The evolution in thinking that stretched from Plato's writing to that of the Christian theologians of late antiquity celebrated the powers of the mind. This emphasis on the cerebral was accompanied by a longing to be free of the aging, mortal, earthbound body. And so we have Plato quoting Socrates as saying that the most virtuous souls will rise to a place where they become pure thought ("those . . . who have properly purified themselves by philosophy live henceforth altogether without the body . . .").

The Christian doctrine of the Incarnation places a reality check on this dismissal of the body by accepting that consciousness, however invisible and intangible, is of the body as surely as the heart's beat. And in fact early Christians would eventually propose that, in contrast to Plato's heaven of disembodied philosophers, the body will rise at the Last Judgment to join the soul for eternity, whether suffering in hell or joyous in heaven.

This revolutionary idea originated in the eastern Mediterranean and was born of the merger of the Jews' engagement with the body (through ritual) and the Greeks' engagement with the mind (through philosophy) — a merger personified and exemplified in the life and teachings of Jesus. But the seamless nature of body and spirit could not be endorsed without qualification, since among all the great Western thinkers almost none could figure out how the needs of the body could peacefully coexist with those of the mind and the soul. The Jews had long since developed a philosophy of affirmed yet disciplined sexuality, but by the time of the Council of Nicaea, almost three hundred years after Jesus, the dispersion of the Jews in the diaspora placed Judaism in no position to influence Christian thought — even in the unlikely event that the Christians had been willing to listen. For their part the Christians, eager to ingratiate themselves with the dominant Roman culture and already Greek-influenced, looked to Greek philosophy for their models. And so Christianity gradually merged Plato's conception of the inferiority of the body with the extreme dualistic ideas prevalent in the declining empire to arrive at an outright split between body and spirit.

Those Christians who proposed more moderate approaches to this age-old conundrum were ignored or condemned. Where the desert fathers understood lust as only one among many challenges in the spiritual life, Augustine, the hot-tempered, Latin-speaking African, placed it first among trials. One of the most influential thinkers of the early church, Augustine became Christianity's chief proponent of the Roman idea that sex is a sign of weakness and that reason must construct an impregnable wall against the chaos of sexual appetite.

Thus did philosophers and theologians facilitate the rise of sexual repression as a tool for centralizing power in a male-dominated church. Seeking to glorify pure reason, Plato places it above and apart from the body. Philo elevates reason still more, while insisting on the masculine nature of Wisdom. Paul, who probably had formal training in Greek philosophy, draws on Plato's dualistic hierarchy of mind and body, spirit and flesh. Augustine, seeking to create an enduring institution amid a disintegrating empire, fuses Paul's message with an acute mistrust of desire, founded in the fear of loss of power and control as experienced in sex. Sixteen hundred successive years of church history produce a clergy trained to teach disdain for the body in order to sustain and augment the power of a male ecclesial hierarchy, which both epitomizes and reinforces a social structure built on the power of men over women and children.

Did the position of women in late antiquity worsen because, as the empire slid toward dissolution, as the barbarians invaded, men sought power and security where they could be found? That explanation, implied by religion scholar Karen Armstrong in her impressive *History of God,* strikes me as too abstract. Addressing the same phenomenon, the eminent historian Peter Brown theorizes that as the public sector grew more corrupt and chaotic, life retreated into the home, where men, already patriarchs, consolidated their power.

For my part, I think that as the West grew ever more self-conscious (Augustine's *Confessions* was a watershed document in this process), men became aware not only of the delights and rewards of such intense self-awareness but also of its fragility in the face of desire, perceived by both Christians and pagans as the beast in the jungle. Sexual desire was a constant reminder of the power of the body; its unpredictability and challenge to reason meant that it must be demonized. In the knees, in the heart, in the head, sex renders us weak — the wisest and strongest among us understand what it means to be a fool for desire — and to be weak is to be comically, tragically, poignantly human. And to be human is to be one with the material world rather than dominant over it.

Women were the obvious target for this demonization, since women are so intrinsically connected to the flesh through menstruation and birth, and since for most men, women are the source and object of desire. But any person engaged first and foremost with the body was a target — in his biography of Augustine, Peter Brown reports the first burning of homosexual prostitutes, routed from their Rome brothels in 390 C.E., an act he characterizes as founded in repugnance at the notion that men would betray their power by assuming the posture of a woman. In 415 C.E., with Rome recently overrun by the Visigoths, Augustine was in the midst of writing *City of God,* his monumental defense of Christianity against assertions that it had undermined the empire by bringing down the wrath of the pagan gods. In that same year a Christian mob, probably acting with the encouragement of their bishop, Cyril, attacked and murdered Hypatia, the first renowned woman mathematician, leader of the Neoplatonic school of philosophy of Alexandria and widely viewed as the symbol of pagan learning. Following her death, many scholars fled the city, beginning its decline from being Rome's rival as a center of culture and learning.

I do not wish to imply that the oppression of women and the demonization of sexuality were carried out with a fully conscious understanding of underlying motives and future repercussions. Teasing out from the complex tapestry of history the causes and contexts affecting one issue is difficult, especially when the issue continues to be controversial. Then as now attitudes toward sex and gender were bound up with every aspect of the culture; to consider them separately is like studying an organism apart from its environment. Still, given the apparently active hand of the newly powerful Christian church in Hypatia's death, one may see it and the brutal murder of the Roman male prostitutes as signposts on the route from the theoretical misogyny of Philo to the vituperative condemnations of the church father Jerome, who vilified women even as he was housed in a monastery built by Paula, the wealthy Christian patroness who supported him while he translated the Hebrew Bible into Latin.

And so from reason's fear of its own fragility, an elaborate mythology evolved concerning the insatiable sexual appetites of the powerless (women, slaves, homosexuals), which served to excuse the momentary weakness of the men who yielded to temptation. Meanwhile, Christian practice (and ultimately Christian monasteries) largely abandoned the relative egalitarianism characteristic of early centuries in favor of a hierarchical religion ruled by an imperial papacy and promoting a monotheism committed to worship of a single male God.

The concept of a single preeminent deity had been an aspect of philosophical discourse for centuries, but always as chief among equals, or as predecessor and progenitor of a panoply of lesser gods and goddesses. Even the forcefully monotheistic Jewish people made occasional accommodations with rival deities, including both gods and goddesses. With the rise of Christianity, however, the entire civilized Western world came under the doctrine of the single omnipotent God presumed to be male, to the exclusion of all other powers. Some denominations have made significant progress toward changing this model — the ordination of women is a major step — but by and large mainstream Western Christianity remains a hierarchy designed and implemented by and for men, in contravention of Jesus' teachings and of early Christian practice but very much in keeping with its administrative role model: the late Roman Empire, whose language, ideas, and power structure it inherited, from its contempt for the body to its long-standing practice of emperor worship, eventually transferred to the figure of the pope.

⁂

How does one find and hew to a middle path between puritanism and obsessive desire? Addressing the question requires considering the relationship between discipline and desire, but institutionalized religion has so demonized desire that any frank discussion of the subject easily dissolves into smoke and mirrors. But an examination of clerical and religious attitudes toward sex and sexual expression suggests the problems with the church's teachings surrounding desire.

A. W. Richard Sipe, a former Roman Catholic priest and now psychotherapist, published an exhaustive study of fifteen hundred people, all of whom have firsthand experience with celibacy and celibates — more than a third were priests in therapy, with the remainder composed of colleagues, lovers, the abused, or others. In A Secret World Sipe lists the many popes who fathered children, some of whom succeeded their fathers to the papacy; Julius II, more often remembered as Michelangelo's patron, found time to father three daughters. Sipe considers the deepest roots of the adoption of priestly celibacy to lie in men's fear of women's power, which led to the vilification and criminalization of sex. "If political power and economic questions had been absent," Sipe writes, "I doubt that celibate practice would have been legislated beyond monastic walls. . . . in the history of the pope's celibacy, we see that the shift was from the essentially horizontal power of the gospel . . . to one of male dominance over property and women" — a shift begun at the Council of Nicaea and accelerated by the Christian church's assumption of the mantle of power vacated by the Caesars.*

The heavy hand of Rome and the much-publicized prosecutions of gay or gay-sympathetic Protestant ministers have (predictably) driven self-aware gay men and noncelibate heterosexuals farther into hiding. Meanwhile the churches encourage those men (and, in some Protestant denominations, women) to become priests or ministers who have so successfully repressed their experience of desire that they're able to speak with conviction about its evils.

Among American Buddhists I commonly encountered the fiction that this situation is somehow better in Asia. Zen Center abbot Norman Fischer remarked, "In Asia the history is the same — always concubines or acolyte boys they fool around with."

In his later book *Sex, Priests, and Power*, Sipe writes, "No Christian church has developed an adequate theology of sexuality . . . no one has worked out an overarching, comprehensive, and integrative understanding of the nature and place of sexuality within the scheme of salvation . . ." Institutionalized religion demonizes desire because it is the most basic and universal of human instincts and so presents the greatest opportunity for power. In the twelfth century, the Vatican enforced celibacy (previously limited to monks) on its priests largely to centralize property and power in Rome, since priests who lacked legitimate children could not compete for

---

* Sipe acknowledges that his survey is unscientific — lacking control groups, for example. Still, given the sheer number of religious with whom he spoke, the seriousness of his purpose, and his own clerical experience, his figures merit attention. He estimates that "about 20% of priests vowed to celibacy are at any one time involved in a more or less stable relationship with a woman or with sequential women in an identifiable pattern of behavior. An additional 8–10% are involved in heterosexual experimentation that often involves incidental sexual contacts . . . 18–22% of clergy show some evidence of homosexual inclinations/behavior, though later estimates rise to 38–42%, with some given as high as 50%." Experience inclines me to lend credence to the latter figures, meaning that somewhere around half of those vowed to celibacy are either sexually active or gay or both.

the disposition of church properties. In the thirteenth century the Vatican declared marriage a sacrament, invalid unless performed by a priest. In doing so it reserved to itself the power to declare which children were legitimate and which were not. Thus it became arbiter of who could inherit property and titles and who was excluded, as well as which close relatives might be married and which inconvenient marriages could be annulled. In nineteenth-century Japan, the requirement of celibacy produced similar accumulations of wealth in Buddhist temples. To break their power, the emperor forced priests to marry, under the assumption that marriage would lead them to integrate more fully into their communities while depriving them of the mystique of celibacy. In all these cases, religious institutions justified mandatory celibacy with elaborate explanations and theologies, but in the end the effect was the accumulation and exercise of power — men's power.

The most common explanation for the high incidence of sexual abuse among religious orders is that the vow of celibacy required of all Roman Catholic clergy and of most monks in both Western and Asian traditions creates a population whose unaddressed sexual appetites cause them to resort to the nearest and most vulnerable victims — the young girls and boys who, as neighbors, family, or students, are in their company. But many experts believe married clergy are no less likely than their celibate counterparts to engage in abusive behavior. Some believe that both groups are more likely to be perpetrators than the population as a whole, though others feel that clerical abuse is only the most visible manifestation of behavior that is far more widespread than anyone cares to acknowledge or believe.

That point of view suggests that the phenomenon of abuse has its roots not in the vow of celibacy but in more profound issues of the relationship between the strong and the weak, the powerful and the powerless, men and women, adults and children, abuse and self-control, desire and spirituality. Abusers are drawn to counseling and religious professions because they who so vividly recall being powerless seek power — the power to do good, perhaps, but power all the same. But then they are drawn to children from their internalized lack of self-respect, a self-hatred which propels them toward those unable to assert themselves or to object. The situation is further complicated because both abuser and abused so often conflate the experience with love, because both want desperately to believe it *is* love. To name it love absolves abusers of responsibility for their choices, while allowing the abused children the illusion of being partners in a situation in which they actually have no voice or control.

This is self-deception on a grand scale and it is a corruption of love, which is by definition grounded in mutual respect. The relationship between abused and abuser is based not in respect but in power, and this is why the institutions of religion, for which power is more important than virtue, have collaborated in creating and sustaining this secret world.

❦

Augustine saw orgasm as a manifestation of evil because for that brief moment we are lost to reason, which to Augustine was no different from being lost to God, since (drawing upon the Romans, who drew in turn on the Greeks) he saw reason as the human manifestation of the divine. But that presumes that as humans we must think of ourselves as superior to nature rather than as part of it, and reason as distinct from the body rather than integral to it.

Why not perceive orgasm as a moment of entry into the divine, our window on transcendence? Most of us, most of the time, have sex not to make babies but to assuage desire — not just physical desire but the desire to love and be loved, the desire for union with the whole, for an end to the aloneness inherent in being alive. During sex, to invoke a Christian metaphor, we die to ourselves, however briefly; to invoke a Buddhist principle, we have a moment of surcease from *samsara*. We are one with ourselves, with another, with *the* Other; we triumph over solitude, even over death. And then it's finished, and we're alone, and dissatisfaction returns. But for the moment of orgasm, sex is the act of union, the model for all other unities, most especially for that final unity with all being that we call death. Our "little deaths," as we so resonantly label them (in French, *petites morts*) are, or can be, the integration of human desire and desire for God.

Why should we consider the pleasures of the body, however fleeting, as illusory? What person who has dwelt in his or her body in the experience of penetration, of being inside the other, or having the other inside oneself, can doubt that this is or has the potential to be some version of the authentic mystical experience? Why do we dismiss and denigrate it when experienced in the body, but glorify and sanctify it when experienced in the soul?

❦

Beside me, on the left hand, appeared an angel in bodily form . . . he was not tall but short, and very beautiful; and his face was so aflame that he appeared to be one of the very highest rank of angels, who seem to be all on fire. . . . In his hands I saw a great golden spear, and at the iron tip there appeared to be a point of fire. This he plunged into my heart several times so that it penetrated to my entrails. When he pulled it out, I felt he took them with it, and left me utterly consumed by the great love of God. The pain was so severe that it made me utter several moans. The sweetness caused by this intense pain is so extreme that one cannot possibly wish it to cease, nor is one's soul then content with anything but God. This is not a physical, but a spiritual pain, though the body has some share in it — even a considerable share. So gentle is this wooing which takes place between God and the soul that if anyone thinks I am lying, I pray God, in his goodness, to grant him some experience of it.

Throughout the days this lasted I went about in a kind of stupor. I had no wish to look or speak, only to embrace my pain, which was a greater bliss than all created things could give. . . . when this pain of which I am now speaking begins, the Lord seems to transport the soul and throw it into a kind of ecstasy.

— *The Life of St. Teresa of Avila by Herself* (1565)

ॐ

Teresa of Avila, doctor of the church (the highest title the Roman Church confers), was famously brilliant — to read her letters is to enter the mind of a woman bent on reforming and revitalizing her religious order, even as she was constantly one step ahead of the Inquisition and was well aware of the consequences should she fall its victim. She had no knowledge of Freud, of course, but she grew up in an era where she had certainly seen animals in the act of sex; it is difficult for me to believe that she was unaware of the eroticism underlying her mystical experiences.

ॐ

Sexuality is a sensual experience that goes right to the roots. A monastery wants to do the same thing. Poverty, chastity, and obedience — those set the boundaries of freeing the will. You have to get behind those things which are key to understanding the self and are at the heart of existence, the key to being alone with the Alone. Your sexuality has to be challenged in some way — I don't want to say it's quintessential to monasticism, but if you penetrate to any kind of depth you'll find your sexuality challenged. Once you've tasted the experience of God/ultimate reality/Zen nothing, it's hard to take sexuality lightly.

There's absolutely a connection between spirituality and sexuality but it can't be spoken about analytically. The point of sex is bringing life into existence, and that's our deepest desire, but we get caught up in the biological life and discount the spiritual life. People see religious ecstasy as sublimated sexuality — they see religious ecstasy as a form of sexual desire — when I think that the reverse is true, that sexual desire is a form of religious ecstasy.

— Brother Benedict Rust

If we consider simple procreation to be the principal significance of sex (as for centuries Roman Catholicism has claimed, drawing not from Judaism or from the Gospels but from Greek philosophy and various cults of late antiquity), we could accomplish the act with the investment of not much more than a few minutes of crazy lust. But in fact, in it we feel most acutely the paradox of our condition: as completely in union with another as we might ever hope physically to be, even as we remain locked in our profound aloneness, and only love can bridge the gap. *Post coitum omne animal tristis est.*

Kōsho McCall listed the dimensions of desire: "First, the biological urge to make the species continue; second, the physical urge for nurturing; and third, the spiritual longing for unity. We think we're so separate — but we're not, really. If we don't investigate that, we'll settle for what doesn't work, putting all the onus on a relationship. The entry into a relationship, the search for meaning are all part of the same drive for life and for oneness." Science focuses on the biological urge, McCall said, because of the three dimensions, it lends itself best to measurement and analysis. Psychology concentrates on the urge to nurture, again because it's so immediately obvious.

And yet in my experience, the longing for unity forms the deepest core of sex and sexuality — the desire to accomplish the impossible, to be one with another, with the Other, to be round and whole and complete. Far easier to compartmentalize sex as the scratching of some animal itch than to understand it as the physical manifestation of our spiritual longing to be whole and round and one.

And so what must it mean to embrace desire as the life force that sets in motion our search for union, whether union with another, with the Other, or with God?

I spent my teenage summers putting up hay for neighboring farmers. Each day I rose and walked the half mile to the bank steps, where I sat with five or ten other guys and waited for a farmer to drive by looking for labor. He chose a crew from among us, a delicate exercise in manners — how to choose a crew of five from among ten or twelve? Skilled at husbandry, farmers usually stuck by the genes — the guys from the families with reputations for endurance and discipline got picked first. After the first week a good worker would get called and picked up at home and have some assurance of a job as long as the hay held out.

The pay was low, $1 an hour from the cheapskates, $1.50 an hour from the generous. Each bale weighed between sixty and one hundred pounds, depending on the type of hay and the moisture it carried. The farmhand grasped the bale by the binder twine that held it together and heaved it onto the wagon, where another man stacked it in neat ricks until it was six or seven ricks high. I could heft a bale to the third or, as the summer wore on, fourth rick, but after that I had to get a hand from the man on the wagon, who seized the bale and pulled from the top. The best balers used physics to do the job — my boss picked up a bale with bare hands (gloves were for pansies like me) and swung it around him in a 360-degree circle, then used centrifugal force to heft it to the top rick — some twenty feet above the ground.

Dust from the hay clogged our noses and pores and eyes. We began work early, to take advantage of the cool morning, but in July in Kentucky "cool" is a state of the imagination, and we worked until the heat made us giddy and the sweat ran in glistening rivulets down our dust-covered bodies. At noon we broke for the farmhouse, where the housewife and her daughters set out what we called dinner, the day's main meal, a spread of ham, pork chops, roast beef, fried chicken, potatoes (mashed, fried, and sweet), baked apples, corn on the cob, fresh tomatoes, pickled cucumbers, iced tea, chess pie, and jam cake. Afterward we dozed under a tree until the worst of the midday heat had passed, then worked until the light failed.

A day came when we had a river bottom to clear and a storm threatening in the west — rain would ruin the hay. We worked from six in the morning until nine that night, breaking only for a sandwich, while the storm massed and boiled but held off. The first bolt of lightning broke from the sky just as the last wagon headed for the barn. I stumbled to the nearest water and fell in fully clothed. Lying in the mud, drops pelting and hogs snuffling around me, I stared up at the sky and swore, Scarlett O'Hara

of the pig pond, that with God as my witness I would never put up hay
again.

And I have kept my word, but now in midlife I am grateful to know in
my body the pureness of exhaustion that comes from hard work; the flush
of accomplishment of seeing the field emptied, the bales safely stacked and
awaiting winter, the fellowship among a crew of men who staked our collective strength against the massing forces of the gods and won, the elemental connection of flesh and blood to life and death that no desk job, not
even writing, can provide.

But I was a town boy; for all my time on the farm I lived within walking distance of the caution light, and so I was naive in a way that no farm
boy could be. One day after dinner my crew boss asked if I'd seen horses
fuck. "Oh, sure," I lied. He smirked and pulled me along.

In the merciless July heat we hooked our feet over the lower rail of the
fence around the breeding ring. We were men, watching. Someone released
the mare — barely more than a filly — "Her first time," the crew boss said.
She stood in the center of the breeding ring; we hung on the rails. Trem-
bling in the hot white midday glare, she pawed the earth and snorted. From
inside the barn the stud answered in a high-pitched scream, kicking at his
stall. Spared the burden of self-consciousness, the mare knew in her genes
exactly what to do; she spread her legs and urinated, a great cleansing yellow stream. At the sound and smell the stud's neighing grew frantic. He
pounded the doors of his stall with his hooves — no man would risk his
life to get near such focused power. The boss used a plank to lift the barn
door latch, and the stud charged out.

Later I remembered that I was supposed to look cool and nonchalant,
but at the sight of the stud's magnificent cock my jaw dropped. A mare's
uterus lies deep in her long body, and the stud's cock is designed accordingly — it grows to three feet and more, a skinny, eminently functional
plow.

The mare squatted, spreading her haunches. The stud climbed up her
back, seizing between his teeth the tuft of hair at the base of her mane and
pulling himself up. I watched slack-jawed as he guided himself into her and
she took him in as if she had been born to no other task. My own body
stirred. The rich yellow smell of the mare's urine, the stud's screams, the
brutal glaring heat — in a few minutes it was over. The stud dropped from
her back. The mare shook herself out and walked with slow, delicate steps

around the ring. The electricity drained from the air and I was left still agape, still hard.

A moment later the crew boss would punch my shoulder and make some comment about Saturday night in the back seat, but in this last moment of white-hot silence I understood many things at once. I understood that I was an animal, that I shared this powerful yearning with other animals, that the yearning was both bigger than I was and connected to every part of me, to the part that read books and scribbled words and sought out opportunities for daily masturbation and went to mass and sassed my father. I understood that sex joined me to the animals and to the vast ongoing energy of what lay beyond and that this was good, that the universe was round and whole and that I was round and whole with it. I saw that moment when the stud came and came and came, I saw the flexing muscles of his haunches and his eyes roll back until only the whites showed, and I understood both why civilized people held the act in such awe and fear and that this was the way it was done, to lose oneself in the other, to the Other, to lose oneself to a kind of death, that sex was or could be a little death. I who had never had sex with another person and would not for some years, — perched on that breeding ring fence, I took that stud as my mentor. I understood that when the opportunity presented itself, I would combine lust with human intelligence and I would have the gift of God in both.

And then the time arrived for me to have sex, and I felt neither lust nor intelligence but anger and shame. Throughout my teens, well aware that I was attracted to men, I recoiled at physical contact with anyone of either gender. On the morning after I first had sex — a few months after my twenty-first birthday — the man with whom I'd gone to bed put his hand on my arm. I shook it off. "Touch me again," I said, "and I'll break your neck."

*

Shortly after I turned sixteen, my namesake Brother Fintan returned to visit my family as well as his old friends at Gethsemani. We received him and his handsome companion with the usual hospitality. Monks came over — there was dancing on the table; we trotted out the grass skirt and plastic leis for my mother's dancing partner, now in need of a stool to climb to the tabletop but otherwise as sinuous and campy as ever.

Afterward I listened for the customary post-party gossip. Had Fintan arrived with a woman, the household would have been abuzz ("Who is she?

Might they get married?"). Had he brought a mere friend, there would have been idle chatter ("Nice man. Needs a haircut."). But: nothing. Fintan and his companion might never have sat at our table.

In my small town, among garrulous Southerners only one subject invoked a silence so vast and deliberate. That night I went to bed understanding that the man for whom I'd been named and his companion were lovers. Which meant that I was perhaps not the freak of nature I had until then believed myself to be; I was not alone.

Each of us must find for himself or herself the wellspring of faith. To judge from their devotion to Mary, many women find that place through their gender. My journey among the monks (and, as a result of it, among the abused) was bringing me to understand that for me the wellspring of faith resides in the source of my otherness, my homosexuality — the condition that led me, or rather *forced* me, to seize my destiny and determine my own values, even as it taught me to respect the given, those aspects of life over which I had little or no control.

※

If creative endeavor is to achieve fulfillment, it must evolve from its origins in the limitless, intangible imagination to achieve its expression in the explicitly limited realm of the body, the here and now, the present moment.

This is the genius of zazen, of sitting meditation: its insistence that the wordless state of prayer to which all seekers in every tradition aspire must be expressed in and through the body. The mind slips effortlessly around in time, yesterday and tomorrow and a century in the future or the past; I visit them all in my capacious and capricious thoughts, but my body lives only in the present. The body is thus not the enemy of the mind, or even its inferior — as, from Plato onward, Western culture assumes; it's not even separate from the mind. They function, or at least can function, as an integrated union in which the body provides the means of imposing discipline on the mind's otherwise formless wanderings.

Through zazen, then, and the paintings of Justin Wilke and the stories of abused women and men, I have been brought to consider what we lost in the transformation, proposed by Philo, of the feminine Sophia into the masculine Wisdom — in the Christian tradition, the Holy Spirit. If we can return to thinking of the Holy Spirit as Sophia (that is, as feminine), then the doctrine of the Trinity, with its presumption of the Incarnation of the divine in the person of Jesus, takes on a profound archetypal resonance. Jesus becomes the child of the union of the masculine Father with the feminine Holy Spirit. As zazen serves to ground intangible thought in the tangible reality of the body, so the Trinity serves as a metaphor for the family, the essential unit of human survival and civilization, the means through which the intangible creative impulse (the masculine Creator) cultivated in and through action (in the form of the feminine Spirit) achieves its expression in the real, physical world — the means through which the Idea becomes real, the Word becomes flesh. Christianity thus lays claim to its rightful place as the child of the masculine God of the Jews and the feminine Sophia of Greek philosophy. This model proposes the union (so eagerly sought by the theologians of antiquity) between the Jewish conception of religion based in the law as handed down by God and the Greek conception of philosophy based in reason. Jesus is the love child of YHWH and Sophia, the offspring of the union of the Law of Moses with the philosophy of Socrates and Plato and Aristotle.

How do churches, as vehicles of faith, deal with what several Roman priests and Christian ministers have characterized as an epidemic of sexual abuse? A bishop of the English Roman Catholic Church declared its commitment to "rooting out" the pedophiles, rather spectacularly missing the larger, more important questions: How do we heal the division, so deeply embedded in Western culture, between body and soul, desire and faith? How may our spiritual institutions embrace desire in ways that serve not hierarchy and power but mutual respect and union?

Father Chase is right in asserting that the tragedy of sexual abuse lies in the loss of innocence, but "innocence" does not refer to ignorance about sex. Adults often romanticize this innocence of childhood, sometimes to avoid talking to children frankly about human biology, especially if such talk requires confronting our own sexual insecurities and darknesses. Children who have access to information about sex and sexuality can preserve their innocence — a sense of wonder and faith — because they have the means to make choices about when they want to become sexually active. I have helped raise many children, and those whom adults have entrusted with straightforward responses to their sexual questions and curiosities are happier, healthier, safer, wiser.

Many cultures have at various times approved of the sexual initiation of a younger child by an adult, and any adult with sexual experience and an open mind can imagine how that might be a saner way to instruct the young in this powerful mystery than "don't ask, don't tell." But those cultures are not our culture, and in our culture sexual encounters between an adult and a child give rise to the need to lie. The adult makes the child complicit in the lie, and like all lies it complicates itself and bears fruit. This is among the most tragic aspects of abuse: how it plunges a child into the shadow world of deceit and mistrust, in which the child becomes a tool of power and manipulation. Her or his faith is challenged at an age when the child has no resources to fight back. The "loss of innocence" is more accurately described as a loss of faith: faith in herself or himself (witness the suicide of Justin Wilke), faith in others, faith in the power of love to heal, faith in God — these are different labels for the same loss.

Let us keep these stories in perspective, you may say. *The abuse of a single child, however objectionable, does not constitute an evil of the magnitude of the Crusades, or the Inquisition, or the Holocaust, or the savagery of the Khmer Rouge in Cambodia.* And of course in one way this is true. The fate of any individual pales in comparison to the fates of whole cultures ravaged, sometimes destroyed.

And yet place yourself in that barn, or in that monastery truck, or with that mother in that kitchen confronting her child's abuser. You are that boy who cannot quit a job because no other job is available and because you will have no explanation to offer when one is demanded. You are that girl just coming to adulthood, who must stand and smile as the man in whom you have trusted — in whom you have placed your faith — betrays you, with all whom you know and love as witnesses and supporters, while you must endure, alone and in silence. You are that mother, forced to keep silent in the face of the power of the church. You are that monk, driven by self-contempt born of your own abuse to seek fulfillment among powerless children. Considered in this fashion, the difference in these evils is not of kind but of magnitude, a single tree in a dark forest but no less a tree for all that.

✍

Faith is the province of those who know suffering (I recall Ghosananda: *In Cambodia we say, If you know suffering, then you understand the dharma*). For the poor and the oppressed, every day demands an act of faith. For some this serves as an opiate, but for others — I have known them — it provides the strength to imagine and ultimately to achieve a better world. Because they have no choice but to cultivate the ability to see the world as others see it, because their survival requires that they learn and live by the rules set by the strong and rich, the poor and oppressed know most intimately the uses of the imagination. Like those philosophers who sought Wisdom through ascetic practice, we the privileged and prosperous come to faith only by figuring out how to jar ourselves from complacency — unless fate intervenes to jar us from it.

જ

In the passenger seat of our rinky-dink rental car my lover was dying. I had driven two hundred kilometers to Paris with the accelerator to the floor because he feared the treatment he might receive at the hands of the provincial doctors. Stuck in Paris traffic, I felt him slipping away. When finally I located the hospital I parked at its main entrance, the only door I could find. I dashed up the steps and into the reception room, to blurt out my plea. "My friend is very sick with AIDS *(gravement malade avec le SIDA)*." All of the women at the desk rose and scurried to a back room. Reduced to begging, I begged *("Madame, je vous en prie")*. With a great show of hesitation one of the women turned back. I checked him in, to have the doctors place him immediately in intensive care. The next morning the head nurse ordered me to leave his bedside — only spouses and close relatives were allowed in the intensive care unit. When I resisted she threatened to phone the police. A few hours later he died, as I watched from the hall outside his door.

For a white American male, raised to believe he just might someday be president (in America, anything is possible for a white male publicly perceived as heterosexual), this was a revelatory moment, the stripping away of self-delusion to reveal the vast construction underlying my complacencies. Only now — literally now, as the words flow onto the page, do I understand that my homosexuality provided my particular doorway to the place the Buddha called *samsara*, the place where Jesus hangs in agony on the cross, a place that as a middle-class white man in America I might otherwise have managed to avoid: the place of the outsider, the world of suffering.

This was a great gift, exactly as dear as the price of its ticket.

જ

The peculiar place of the white, masculine-identified gay man is that I can "pass," occupying which side of the fence I choose, straight or gay, powerful or powerless . . . until I'm in that hospital hallway, seeking to be allowed to sit at my dying lover's bedside. Until that moment I thought I had accepted my outsiderness, the gift of my homosexuality, but I required his death to wake me to my own reality.

And now these stories of the abuse of children at the hands of men in whom they had placed their faith were continuing my education, bringing me to see how men live in power as fish live in water. Exceptions to this rule do not lessen its general truth. In its presence I was beginning to see how my power as a white male citizen of the empire made it so very difficult for me to come to faith; how most of the institutions of my culture, including those of religion, worked to sanctify and reinforce that power; and how my particular access to faith might grow from the place of my powerlessness, the place where I am manifestly not in control.

But people of both genders abuse children, and women sometimes abuse women. For this reason women are to men — as men can be to women — a koan, a mystery not to be solved but to be addressed with the faith that persistent and disciplined attention will lead, not to an answer, but to an embrace — to enlightenment. To write that women are a koan for men is only a subset of the larger truth, which is that the outsider is a koan for the privileged, the poor a koan for the rich, the weak a koan for the strong, the lover a koan for the beloved: an opportunity to examine the uses and responsibilities of power. My journey toward faith was teaching me that those drawn to God are so often those who have suffered, and the consolations of the mind, though they are great, cannot console the heart, which speaks in tongues without words.

※

This is perhaps the most necessary and profound of social realities: the vastness of the gap between what we say and what we do; the chasm between the life we pretend to and profess and the life we actually live. As I grow older and deeper into an exploration of faith, I feel that all significant truth resides in the judicious narrowing of that chasm, that a life of virtue consists of integrating the life that I profess and the life I actually live. Power resides in concealment; honesty represents a yielding of power, an effort to be transparent to oneself and to others, a gesture of respect to those among whom I live. The greatest act of betrayal by institutionalized religions lies in making the discipline of honesty more difficult ("don't ask, don't tell" prevailed in the churches long before it was adopted by the military) rather than providing support for living it out.

Bound by all the trappings of power, the powerful must pass through the proverbial needle's eye if they are to realize the fullness of life and love. But the outsider's perspective — a precondition of wisdom — is inherently available to the powerless, the excluded, the oppressed, the abused. Jesus, the quintessential outsider, understood this, which is why he continually points his listeners toward the powerless (children, repentant sinners, women, Samaritans) as the exemplars of wisdom.

Thus one source of the anger so omnipresent at the Gethsemani Encounter: the anger of the marginalized and oppressed; the anger of women and of men (many but by no means all of them gay) who have committed their lives to the pursuit of purity of heart, only to find that pursuit hobbled by the parent institution.

*

Western religion is in profound and prolonged crisis over the issue of no mediation between erotic and sacramental wholeness — the ambiguity and brokenness of most of Western Christianity.

The healing of the anti-erotic in Christianity is a great issue for me personally. The self-awareness of gay people and their struggle with the mysteries of the erotic make them a place where high voltage is flowing.

I try to be alive to the erotic dimension of all existence, seeking through prayer and meditation to be fully alive to the meeting place of divine and human desire. We need to move into and pray out of a space of erotic self-awareness. In some paradoxical way monks are the only people who can take the risk of doing this because of the domestication and bourgeois diversion of Christianity into forms that aren't open to the erotic and mystical experience.

— Rev. Martin Smith, Episcopal Monastery of St. John the Evangelist

*

What then is the relationship of desire to the quest for faith? Everything begins in desire, the life force, which is why religion has always had something to say on the matter. Religion springs from desire, and its agonies and conflicts often arise from its struggle against its foundational identity. We are of the animals, yes, but at the same time, in a way recognized by all the ancients, apart from them. And what is it that separates us from the animal world? One thing in human nature equates us with the divine, Aquinas writes: our infinite capacity for desire.

And so it is that we should expect and want our priests and ministers and rabbis and monks, celibate or coupled, to be men and women of great desire, particularly engaged with the ways and means of its expression and its discipline. I think of the all-embracing title of historian Jean Leclerq's comprehensive history of the Cistercian monks: *The Love of Learning and the Desire for God.* Love arises from desire, from which it follows that those who seek God, who is love (1 John 4:7), must integrate desire into their search.

God and desire are inextricable. At some intuitive level we know this, but then we get the connection wrong because we are afraid of our own power — fearful of the life force that rises within us, when it's so much easier and safer to be dead. And so we spin elaborate fantasies about life after death because we're so afraid of embracing life *before* death.

Subjecting desire to discipline (whether in the form of monogamy, or celibacy, or right conduct toward one's partners; whether in monasticism, or social activism, or meditation, or conscientious parenting) provides a way to union, with each other or with God — it hardly matters, since these are different names for the same end. Like any powerful force, desire must be channeled — in our case by reason, which is not its enemy but its soul mate. In a living relationship people engage its pleasures and challenges as a means of binding them more closely together. The monk (as *monos,* the root of the word, implies) uses it to bind him or her more closely to union with the whole of being that so many name as God. The monk or the priest is or can become a specialist in the disciplines of desire, one of many role models for all of us creatures of desire.

❧

John of the Cross, Francis of Assisi, Teresa of Avila, Dorothy Day, Thomas Merton — all were motivated by desire, all were at one point or another opposed by the institutionalized church, all have been vindicated.

If the institutionalized church is not to continue to facilitate a host of evils arising from the abuse of the power of desire, it must engage the fact that the women and men who seek God — as clergy, contemplatives, monks, or communicants — are motivated by desire. A healthy monasticism, as well as a healthy priesthood, ministry, rabbinate, or congregation, requires a forthright engagement with this most powerful life force, and the church in all its forms will not be healthy until it embraces this truth: desire coupled with reason is what brings us to God, who is love.

PART
THREE

15

AUGUSTINE OF HIPPO
AND JOHN CASSIAN:
GRACE OR WILL?

A GENIUS ARISES, born of the felicitous intersection of historical moment and individual character. He or she blazes through society, making waves and attracting disciples, but the originating genius is seldom capable of translating ideas into enduring practice. Sooner or later other, more pragmatic minds must institutionalize that energy or it will peter out. The eloquent rhetoric of Jefferson's Declaration of Independence achieves its fulfillment in the cautious compromises of the Constitution; the radical politics of Jesus take the form of the Christian church.

Two men, contemporaries and in their different ways monks, were critical in translating the message of Jesus into the doctrines and structures that form the foundation of Western Christianity and the contemplative life as practiced in Western monasteries. One was a passionate rationalist, driven by his need to know and to understand; the other was a contemplative mystic, content to dwell in the mystery of being alive. The first spoke Latin and was a preacher in the great rhetorical tradition of Rome; the second lived as a monk among the Greek-speaking monasteries of Egypt and Asia Minor. The Roman Church has conveyed upon the rationalist its highest honor, naming him doctor of the church; the mystic, once vilified, it has largely forgotten, except within its monastic communities, who revere his writings and his memory. They are Augustine of Hippo — St. Augustine — and John Cassian.

☙

Augustine was born in 354 C.E. in Hippo, in the remote provinces of north Africa, in the declining years of the Roman Empire. His parents were poor. His father, Patricius, illiterate, unfaithful, beat his wife, Monica, no less but no more than demanded by the custom of the times. She sought solace in religion with the intensity of an intelligent woman allowed no other outlet for her passion.

Patricius recognized his son's promise and made great sacrifices for his education, but his money intermittently gave out — Augustine criticizes his father for neglecting his moral training and writes of spending a year in idleness while waiting to receive the money to pay for his next year of schooling. (Perhaps one mark of genius is its assumption of entitlement. In writing of that idle year, Augustine shows no inclination to take responsibility for his own livelihood and in fact shows some impatience at the delay his father's poverty imposes on his ambitions. What would have been the effect on history, I wonder, had Patricius barked at his wastrel son, "Get a job!")

Augustine joined the Manichaeans, a cult founded by the Persian philosopher Mani that featured elements of Zoroastrianism (again the philosophical influences of the East extend westward). Manichaeism proposed that the universe is dualistic at its very core, divided between light and dark, spirit and flesh, good and evil.

The Manichaeans' uncompromising division of the world into opposing forces is the logical application of a duality in Western thinking that began with Plato and the enshrinement of reason. Their arcane doctrines and rituals originated in an attempt to use reason (as Plato would have them do) to answer how a benevolent God could allow the existence of evil. Convinced that evil could not possibly emanate from God, the Manichaeans proposed a dark, opposing force which takes its form in the material world, including the body, with all its appetites (for food, drink, sleep, sex among them). This cult, whose teachings Augustine followed for a decade, extended to an extreme Plato's division of the world into the material and the ideal, body and soul. To the Manichaeans, all that was of the spirit was good; all that was of the flesh was evil.

Smart and ambitious, Augustine set out to make the sow's ear of his upbringing into the silk purse demanded by the high society of the decaying empire. Whether because he perceived the Manichaeans' extremism or because he realized they were destined to be losers, he dropped out of the movement. Later he would attack them with the fervor of the reformed cultist, even as their obsessive division of the world into the clearly good and the clearly evil influenced his writing and work for the remainder of his life.

Twenty-eight years old, driven by ambition, Augustine decided to go to Rome. Monica learned of his plan and dogged his steps, until he resorted to lies to distract her long enough to slip away to a waiting ship.

In the capital of the empire he did as well as one might expect of a late arrival from the provinces. Within a year he was appointed a professor of rhetoric in Milan, Rome's rival as center of power for the young, rising Christian church. Not to be so easily shaken off, Monica followed her son across the Mediterranean. Shortly after her arrival she approved his marriage to a rich, socially well-connected Christian child, a girl barely out of her first decade, a common arrangement at a time when marriage was viewed as a business transaction best conducted independent of the disruptive influences of affection or desire.

Augustine dismissed his concubine, whom he had brought from Africa — a woman he never names. He had lived faithfully with her for many years, they had a son, by his own word he loved her greatly, but he was ready to trade up. He sent her back to Africa, much as fifteen hundred years later, in an odd historical coincidence, Merton and Suzuki Roshi would abandon women. Augustine's decision was entirely consistent with the pragmatic social customs of the Roman Empire; what's remarkable was not that he abandoned her but that in his later writings, unlike Merton or Suzuki, he publicly acknowledged remorse for doing so.

Augustine was baptized a Christian. Together with Monica he heard the preaching of the great bishop Ambrose, most powerful of Milan's Christian hierarchy, but he never penetrated Ambrose's inner circle. By now he was well into his thirties, a bright, sensitive, not-so-young-anymore rube seeking his fortune among the tired, inbred hierarchy of the decaying empire. For the sake of his career he had sacrificed love, family, homeland, and this was what he got in return: far from the familiar landscapes, he was giving lessons to bratty rich kids ("unscrupulous," he writes of them, "dishonest," "warped and crooked") who could have cared less about his heroes (Cicero, Jesus) and were instead absorbed by the conspicuous consumption characteristic of the times and in plots to avoid paying their teacher's fees.

Under the strain of the performance, he cracked. He contracted a lung illness that prevented him from teaching and had what Peter Brown (a biographer worthy of his subject) characterizes as a nervous breakdown. He read the Platonists, from whom he learned that "at the beginning the Word always was; and God had the Word abiding with him, and the Word was

God." Augustine found truth in their philosophy, but it was a truth lacking the birth, death, and resurrection of Jesus, the Incarnation of the divine.

At this critical moment he encountered a countryman from Africa who told him the story of Antony, the holy monk — undoubtedly learned from Athanasius's *Life of Antony*. "While he was speaking, O Lord," Augustine writes, "you were turning me to look at myself." After his countryman left, in the most famous scene in the *Confessions*, Augustine agonized for a day and a night in a garden adjacent to the house that he shared with Monica and his companions before yielding his fate to God. He renounced the world, including sex and his grand ambitions, and decided to return to Africa with his mother, to set up a monastic community and live a life modeled on that of Jesus and his apostles. Happy (Augustine writes) that her son had become the man she wanted him to be, Monica died en route.

Much of what we know of Augustine comes from his own hand, most particularly from his autobiographical *Confessions*, the West's first thorough exploration of an interior consciousness and as such the precursor of modern psychology, whether manifested in novels or movies or the therapist's office. Indulging in the psychological speculation Augustine pioneered, I wonder at the role of his remarkable mother in his remarkable life, and his equally remarkable characterization of her as a saint. Augustine tells us that her first concern was always his soul — even as he writes of her approving his engagement to a rich society girl. He tells us that she always wanted him to be a celibate Christian — but what of that arranged betrothal to a girl whom he later must have jilted?

It's a charming notion to think that the driving energy behind the man who constructed the template for much of contemporary consciousness was an unresolved Oedipal complex — the need of the good son to please his exacting mother, still another illustration of Merton's maxim that contemplatives are made by severe mothers. "Her life and mine had been as one," Augustine writes, referring not to his beloved concubine but to Monica. I find touchingly human this self-portrait of a man ambitious enough to leave the hinterlands for the capital, wily enough to prosper there, but too much the child of the provinces, too attached to his mother and to his roots to sever them and begin his life anew. And so he returns home, to become in this outpost of the Roman Empire the most influential of Western Christian writers.

Those for whom contemporary Christianity represents the epitome of conventionality must remember that for most of the first three centuries of its existence, it was a fringe cult frequently persecuted and almost always disdained. Men crazy or brave enough to label themselves Christians were likely to be unconventional if not downright anarchic; women became Christians in part because of its revolutionary promise of spiritual equality with men. These were independent, ornery folks, nonconformists and iconoclasts. Then the emperor Constantine embraced Christianity, and in not much more than a few decades people began joining the church not from conviction but from expediency. To advance their careers, to make the proper connections, to get the best jobs, increasingly one had to be a Christian, a fact the ambitious Augustine surely perceived.

In the fourth and fifth centuries, monasticism rose in popularity at least partly in reaction to this mainstreaming of Jesus' ideals. Monasteries became refuges for those original iconoclasts — places for the purists, as distinct from the Sunday society crowd. Augustine's monastic aspirations at least partly reflect the passionate convert's desire to escape the shallow, materialistic world epitomized by those social-climbing Christians. High irony, then, that Augustine, who returned to Africa to found a monastic community — to retreat from the hurly-burly, corrupt world of church and empire politics — should there be thrust into power and authority.

But this is the source of his fascination — his very public struggle to balance his competing aspirations: humility versus glory; the pure Christian ideal of simplicity and poverty versus his vision of a grand, powerful institution so well symbolized by the pomp of the later imperial papacy. One may see warring in Augustine the philosophical strands that have troubled Christianity at least since Nicaea and that would later be among the forces that divided it, first East from West, then Protestant from Roman Catholic.

Augustine's life is a textbook illustration of the questions about which he so brilliantly writes. What is the relationship between free will and destiny — or, as Augustine would surely name it, the workings of God's grace? When he returned to the provinces, Augustine could not have known that they would provide him an episcopacy, a safe, relatively stable base from which to write and preach. From Hippo he expanded his influence at a time when the great cities of the Roman Empire were besieged by invaders from the north.

Part of the modern writer's fascination with Augustine arises from trying to distinguish historical reality from his literary creation. Throughout the *Confessions* (Brown frankly categorizes them as fiction), Augustine juxtaposes studied innocence with literary calculation. To give one example among many: At his moment of spiritual crisis, Augustine endures his agony in the garden — a parallel, not likely to have been lost on his readers, to Jesus' agony in the garden of Gethsemani. Meanwhile he never tells us of the fate of the concubine he sent back to Africa or of the wealthy Christian child to whom he was betrothed. He had been trained as a rhetorician, after all, an expert in the arts of persuasion, and all evidence indicates he was superb at them. The *Confessions* must be read not only as a plea to God (though they are that) or as a chronicle of a personal spiritual journey (they are that, too), but as a long sermon designed to win the listener or the reader to Augustine's point of view on a whole range of issues, most of them involving the intersection between the ideal of peace and community proposed by Jesus and the pragmatism required to build a powerful centralized church.

For that was his undisguised goal. As a bishop he turned all his rhetorical genius to routing movement after movement that threatened to factionalize the strong, unified church to which he was devoted. He opposed the Donatist heretics largely because they did not share his vision of a universal, centralized church open to all. Eventually he authorized the use of force to suppress them, lending a precedent for the Crusades, the thirteenth-century slaughter of the Albigensians (a sect of unorthodox Christians centered at the southern French city of Albi), and the Inquisition. In each case the persecutors cited Augustine as they justified taking up arms not only against the infidel but also against fellow Christians.

If in fact Augustine bent and folded his life story to make better origami, does that lessen its literary and philosophical value? Not a bit. It is rather the transformation of a simple piece of paper into a complex work of art. The final measure of Augustine's writing is not its historical accuracy but the dimensions and artistry of the imaginative act and the shaping hand it exerted on who we are and aspire to be. He is enough of a rhetorician to understand that argument may be entertaining to the ears but seldom penetrates to the heart. Touching the hearts of men and women, so much more difficult to move than mountains — *that* requires a story line, a dramatic narrative, a human touch. Not least among Augustine's strokes of genius is the use of his personal history as material for his evangelistic cause, an understanding emulated, consciously and otherwise, by any number of writers since (among them Thomas Merton, whose *Seven Storey Mountain* is a twentieth-century *Confessions*).

In his letters to the various Christian congregations of the eastern Mediterranean, the apostle Paul provided the foundation for modern Christianity, but his letters are not much more than that — a spare, simple, concrete pad on which Christians might build spare, simple, autonomous congregations. Paul, whose Christian life began with a mystical conversion (knocked to the ground, struck blind, directly addressed by the voice of God), would be comfortable with the rocking, rolling, speaking-in-tongues testimonial services of some of today's fundamentalists. Augustine, the thoughtful rationalist, may have longed for such an unequivocal calling to the Godhead — "Say to my soul *I am your salvation,*" he demands of God in the opening pages of the *Confessions.* "Say it so I can hear it." But his story of his conversion is remarkable for its glancing mention of miracles, and Augustine, for all his rhetorical sleight-of-hand, is not about to make them up. In their stead he presents us with a struggle that could be *my* struggle, seeking to house under the same roof a fundamentalist's desire for the bedrock certainty of belief and the rationalist's airy skepticism.

In an era when books were most often read aloud, Augustine is writing a memoir, not an autobiography; a polemic, not a history. He is far less an autobiographer than an evangelist on a mission, which is no less than to set the story of Jesus' life, death, and resurrection in the context of a theology complex enough to address the great existential questions of Greek philosophy, yet simple enough to preach to the mass of people.

For all his talk of living in God, Augustine's ambition was the classical ambition, to live in memory: he devoted his last years to cataloguing and organizing his papers so that scholars might most effectively trace the evolution and nuance of his thinking. His preaching and writings accelerated the trend, begun at Nicaea, toward a church that would be a dominant political and military force for a thousand years: a role that survives in the Christian church mindset if not its reality. It's easy to say that Christianity muffed a chance to become a force for egalitarianism; a more reasonable analysis might be that the unstable times demanded a strong central church as a stand-in for the authority once exercised by the Roman Empire, and Augustine possessed the extraordinary passion, intellectual prowess, administrative skills, and dedication to bring that to pass.

✍

According to the Benedictine monk and monastic historian Father Columba Stewart (like Brown, a biographer worthy of his subject), John Cassian, Augustine's contemporary and counterpart, was born sometime in the 360s, possibly in what is now Romania, on the frontier between the Latin-speaking West and the Greek-speaking East.

As monk and mystic Cassian was as self-effacing in his writings as Augustine was effusive and self-revelatory. Cassian offers almost no biographical details except those that pertain directly to his larger spiritual and theological message. Augustine's anguished and passionate *Confessions* all but demand speculation about his personality; Cassian casts his two longest works, the *Institutes* and the *Conferences,* in the voices of the Egyptian monks who were his teachers, a technique that places him firmly in the background.

That Buddhist principles traveled across the trade routes to Plato's Greece seems intuitively true, but the evidence supporting the case is almost entirely circumstantial. In Cassian, however, we can pinpoint the principal means through which monastic life was transplanted from the Greek-speaking eastern Mediterranean to the Latin-speaking West. Traveling with his older friend Germanus, he went to Palestine in the 380s to become a monk. In a rare moment of self-revelation and in rich contrast to Augustine's relationship with Monica, Cassian writes of Germanus that they were "one heart and soul in two bodies."

Cassian and Germanus traveled together for the next twenty-five years. This experience has parallels to that of Augustine, whose lifelong friend Alypius — a man "ashamed of sexual intercourse," who found it "degrading" and "lived a life of utmost chastity" — followed him from Italy back to Hippo, where they ministered to neighboring congregations.

What is the contemporary reader to make of these enduring same-gender relationships? The most cursory study of the radically different sexual and social mores of late antiquity makes clear that modern categories (such as "gay") have little or no relevance, yet I'd be complicit in the great secret and ignoring my own experience if I overlooked the resonant bond that repeatedly arises from such pairings, male and female. Perhaps if we moderns were more open to experience, allowing it to speak to us rather than rushing to label and categorize and judge, we might rediscover the values of those same-gender bonds, defined apart from or in addition to the question of how we use our genitals.

After several years in Palestine, Cassian and Germanus traveled to the Egyptian monastic communities for what was supposed to be a brief visit. There they took up residence at Scetis, in the complex of monastic communities that under Pachomius, their founder, had originated Christianity's first monastic rule.

Cassian and Germanus lived for some ten to fifteen years among the Egyptian monks, until the theological controversies that dominated the late fourth century led to the destruction of the Nile Delta monasteries and the dispersion of their communities. The pair eventually made their way to Gaul, where Germanus is presumed to have died — Cassian gives us no clue. There Cassian took up his great work of transplanting the stricter, more regulated asceticism of the Egyptian desert fathers into the Latin-speaking West.

Essentially comprising modern France plus the Low Countries to the north, Gaul was fertile soil waiting for such a gardener. In the fourth and fifth centuries it was the Wild West to the long-established cities of the Italian peninsula, a New Age California to the staid burghers of New York. Inspired by rumors of Middle Eastern monastic life or simply by Jesus' example, monastic communities had sprung up in Gaul before Cassian's arrival, but they were poorly disciplined and tended toward fanaticism. Into this world of superstitious frontiersmen Cassian introduced an ascetic discipline focused on the pursuit of purity of heart, lived according to a rule embodying the ideals of poverty, chastity, and obedience, refined by more than a century of trial and error. Like Augustine, Cassian was not much interested in miracles, though he acknowledges them passingly. His focus was instead on laying the groundwork for the living of a virtuous life. True to his Greek roots, he emphasized the pursuit of religion in general and monasticism in particular as a philosophy, a way of life based in the cultivation of wisdom.

✍

In his *Conferences,* devoted to examining the moral challenges of the ascetic life, Cassian comes across as a gentle soul, more interested in virtue than in power. For this reason I find it not surprising that in a church that gradually became obsessed with temporal power, his star dimmed. As is the fate of many peacemakers, he was demonized by all sides, most particularly for his stance on the same question that preoccupied Augustine: the relationship between free will and destiny. How much do we choose, how much chooses us?

In writings that would eventually become official church doctrine, Augustine argues that we are fully and wholly dependent on grace — only

God can decide who among us will be elected for salvation. "I despise myself and consider myself as dust and ashes," Augustine writes. Only the power of God could draw up human beings, by nature so utterly debased. In a stance more congenial to contemporary sensibilities, Cassian argues that while the grace of God is essential to salvation, men and women can freely choose to accept or reject it. He compares our efforts to those of the farmer who tills the soil and plants the seed but who must rely on the rain, over which he has no control. In this formulation, "rain" is the grace of God, without which the farmer cannot produce a crop — but by the same token, without the labor of the farmer the rain alone yields only weeds and brambles. Cassian notes that Job could never have sustained the battle with his demons without God's help, even as he points out that the demons "had been conquered not by God's power but by Job's."

At a time of political chaos and the decline of the institutions of Rome, Augustine's argument, which placed power solely in the hands of God, was vastly better suited to the ends of a centralized institution, since it supported a vision of the world in which power, in the form of grace, radiates downward from a single, central source. The effect was to fortify and extend the role of the institutionalized church as an essential intermediary between the people and their God and to leave behind the ideals of shared property and equality in Christ Jesus that had been so central to the early church.

In a conversation with a priest who served a rural parish not far from Gethsemani, I asked how his parishioners were able to be both deeply religious and at that time the nation's largest suppliers of marijuana. "We've taught them to look to authority to address these questions," the priest said. "They come to the confessional and they ask, 'Father, is it a mortal sin to grow marijuana?' And I say, 'Well, it's against the law.' And they respond, 'Yes, Father, I know that, but what I want to know is, is it a mortal sin?'" The priest was pastor of a church called St. Augustine; in their preoccupation with the letter of church law over their own judgment, his parishioners were the theological children, in every sense of the phrase, of their patron.

To an unnerving extent we are shaped not by our wills but by our historical moment. Born into the disintegrating Roman Empire, Augustine the pessimist — or pragmatist, depending on your point of view — doubts any individual's ability to accomplish on his own any enduring good: "[F]rom my own experience I understood . . . that the impulses of nature

and the impulses of the spirit are at war with one another," he writes, cadg-
ing from Galatians 5:17. Veteran of the golden moment of eastern Mediterranean monasticism and the relatively stable Eastern Empire centered in
Constantinople, Cassian is more of an optimist or at least possesses greater
faith in the individual. In a gentle, indirect rejoinder he writes, "For it must
not be believed that God made the human being in such a way that he
could never will or be capable of the good. . . . there always remains in the
human free will that which can either neglect or love the grace of God." Augustine, the Latin speaker from the West, seeker of power in the socially
and politically stratified Roman Empire, argues that celibates are superior:
"though you [God] did not forbid me to marry, you counselled me to take
a better course." Cassian, the Greek-speaker from the East, shaped by the
democratic structure of the Egyptian monasteries, argues that though the
life of the monk was best suited for those seeking virtue, any ordinary
Christian could be the equal of a monk or a priest or a bishop: "The journey to God follows many routes. So let each person take to the end and
with no turning back the way he first chose, so that he may be perfect, no
matter what his profession might be." Augustine, the passionate Latin, is
preoccupied with eros, a Latin word usually if inadequately translated as
"passionate love." Cassian, the cool-headed Greek, preoccupies himself
with agape, a Greek word usually if inadequately translated as "friendship."
Augustine, who wrote and spoke Latin and does not seem to have learned
Greek, represented the Western-dominated future; Cassian was still of the
moment, with access to both tongues and traditions. The two men agreed
on most points, but their disagreement on the appropriate relationship between the individual and the institution — critical to Augustine's vision of
a strong, centralized church — was enough to cost Cassian his reputation.

As the means to transcendence, Plato posited reason, a quality he held
available to all men (if few women), a quality that men could cultivate. The
evidence of a life lived by reason was to be found in one's actions within the
community, the city, and the state. Plato's *Republic* — the title reveals the
author's intent — sets out to teach the art of being a good citizen in and
servant to our communities. Through that practice we fulfill our ideal destiny, which is to rise through virtuous deeds to become one with the greater
whole, which Plato defined as Beauty. That definition was very much to
influence the early Christian theologians' imagining of a God who (un-

like the vengeful, temperamental God of Moses, or the gods of Hinduism, whose characters encompass both good and evil) was all-good, all-benevolent.

For Augustine the acceptance of God's will complements and supersedes the discipline of reason as the foundation of the well-ordered life, but reason remains as the means. The *Confessions* — the title reveals the author's intent — chronicle Augustine's shift from his adolescent aspiration to understand all through reason (whether via astrology or philosophy or the weird logic of the Manichaeans) to his adult aspiration to understand all through the lens of his deeply personal relationship with God. But his aspiration remains the same — to understand all, to know for certain the answers to the great questions of being: *What, if anything, is the meaning of human suffering? What is the nature of happiness, and how may we secure it? What constitutes a virtuous life, and how does one best lead it?* In this Augustine anticipates the contemporary alienated seeker. As a metaphor for the answers to the great questions he offers not the Parthenon of Athens or the Roman Forum — symbols of the ordered city whose precise proportions their architects drew from ratios present in nature — but the lonely figure wandering the wilderness of the soul in search of his savior. Brown characterizes Augustine as "the first great Romantic," by which I take him to mean that Augustine was the first writer to articulate the journey toward transcendence as an individual search rather than as an undertaking that arises from and depends on one's actions in community.

In effect Augustine takes Athanasius's *Life of Antony* and rewrites it in the first person. His *Confessions* is no less polemical than the writings of Athanasius; his stroke of brilliance came with moving them from the realm of reportage to cast them instead as an extended address to his readers and to God. But he still relies on reason as the foundation of his theology. He returns to the question that preoccupied the Manicheans: *how could evil exist in a world created by a benevolent God?* Drawing on a skein of biblical evidence, Augustine elaborates the doctrine of original sin, an already-existing idea that had never received such detailed explication.

Rationalist that he is, if lacking the principles of scientific method, Augustine observes certain facts — how good parents can produce an evil child, how babies cry even in a mother's arms (an act he categorizes as evil), how physical and even temperamental characteristics clearly pass from parent to child. He considered, too, that orgasm required the loss of reason and that it could even occur (in the form of "night emissions") outside reason's control. Since, like Plato, he saw reason as the manifestation of the divine in humans, he saw in that loss of reason evidence that the act of sex must embody some essentially evil principle. Using deductive reasoning based on these observations, he concluded that the stain of the original sin of Adam and Eve must somehow be passed, like the color of the eyes, from one generation to the next. Since the only act of life that all humans share is our conception through orgasm, the transmission of the stain must take place during sex.

With today's sophisticated knowledge of genetics and human nature, we may find the idea absurd, but given the evidence and the tools of analysis available to Augustine, it made sense. And in fact as I grow older, the concept sneaks back into my life. In a classroom discussion a nineteen-year-old student asked, "Why is it that everything human beings turn our attention to seems to go wrong?" "Maybe there's something to this notion of original sin," I answered — but he had no idea what I meant, and so the discussion ended.

Only a dualistic intellectual descendant of Plato and former Manichaean could so confidently distinguish between the body and the soul. All the same, compared with many of his contemporaries, Augustine was a moderate in his attitudes toward regulating sexual behavior. He sanctifies sex when its purpose is procreation, specifically repudiating the many cults of the day (the Manichaeans among them) who claimed that sex was in and of itself a barrier to sanctity.

Still, an insistence on rational explanation characterizes Augustine's theology and persists in the Western mind (theological and otherwise) through Thomas Aquinas to the present. Compare his passionate insistence on wanting an answer ("Say to my soul *I am your salvation*") with John Cassian's gentle olive branch, extended in the last sentence of the thirteenth of his *Conferences*, in which he presents his own views on grace and free will. Cassian concludes by humbling himself before our complete inability finally to know any sure answer to these questions: "For how God works all things in us on the one hand and how everything is ascribed to free will on the other cannot be fully grasped by human intelligence and reason." Cassian was surely aware of Augustine's views, and though he wrote no explicit attack he made clear his perspective on the subject: "When a thing is found to be congenital . . . how can we fail to believe that it was implanted by the will of the Lord, not to injure us but to help us?" Not surprisingly, Augustine, spiritual and psychological father to the West and lionized in Western Christianity, is a minor figure among more mystically oriented Orthodox Christians, who in their turn revere Cassian, all but unknown in the West.

⁂

In his shift in focus from individuals' relationships to their clan, tribe, or city to each person's particular relationship with God, Augustine is thus a key figure — perhaps *the* key figure in the transition in Western culture from an emphasis on community to an emphasis on individual achievement. The Greeks and Romans lionized individual achievement, but taken as a whole their literature tells stories in which the greatest heroism consists of sacrificing comfort, safety, and even life for the community good. Iphigenia begs to be martyred so that her countrymen may sail for Troy; Aeneas's adventures culminate in the founding of Rome. Even Odysseus, always careful to cultivate his own fortunes, has home and hearth as the goal of his journey.

Augustine offers a different hero's journey, toward a deeply personal, intimate, individual relationship with God. He seldom mentions responsibilities to the city, the state, one's neighbors, or even family. To the extent that Augustine concerns himself with community, he seeks the other-worldly community of the saints, whose earthly correspondent is the church. Throughout the *Confessions,* he implies that if one takes care of one's particular relationship with God through the medium of the church, all else will fall into place. His writings reveal the most modern of struggles: that of the individual coming to terms with the delights and burdens of self-consciousness. He is the father of individualism, and of all nations perhaps Americans are most identifiably his children.

And yet how can the father of individualism also be the father of institutional conformity? Part of the answer lies in Augustine's ability to sustain contradiction — essential to a writer working on the largest canvas imaginable, which is nothing less than the shaping of the consciousness of the human race. But Augustine always points toward the need to submit to God's will — monk that he is, he struggles on every page to embrace humility and repeatedly emphasizes its importance. The rise of Enlightenment skepticism loosened Western allegiance to Augustine's commitment to the community of saints and to the authority of God as a means to rein in the inevitable hubris of humankind. And so as a corruption of Augustine's passionate, particular engagement with God, we arrive at the cult of individual achievement — whether in the arts or business or politics — unbound by constraints of loyalty to family, community, church, or God.

৵

Augustine's time as bishop subjected the ideals of the *Confessions* to the tedious world of administrative reality. He spent much of his life mediating arguments, raising cash, tending to the minutiae of keeping a community solvent and at peace; he encountered firsthand the challenges of implementing an inherently radical and iconoclastic philosophy. In his thirties he provided the church with the *Confessions,* a populist potboiler designed to touch and arouse the hearts of men and women. As he aged he came to understand that a great and enduring institution must be founded on rhetoric and reason, and so in his maturity he wrote *City of God,* primer for the church's ascent to dominance in the West.

At this critical juncture, with the collapse of Rome imminent and no clear successor at hand, the power of Augustine's pen and sermons turned the Christian church toward a hierarchical, centralized structure, the city of God idealized in Augustine's title. What might have happened had some kind of secular political authority remained in place in the West is anyone's guess. As it was, soon enough monasticism became less a communal expression of the search for purity of heart and for God than a tool in the hands of an ambitious and growing church.

Though Cassian was attacked in his lifetime, his advocacy of the individual's role in engineering her or his salvation was never officially condemned. But a century later the Council of Orange, in a decision later affirmed by Rome, would condemn the suggestion of any human responsibility for our salvation. Over time, Cassian would become what Columba Stewart calls "doctrinally suspect." Despite what Stewart calls his "incalculable influence" on Western monasticism, he would be denied sainthood in the West and relegated to theological backwaters.

৵

What is grace, and how does one recognize it? In the midst of my monastic journeys, I heard Father Matthew Kelty, Gethsemani's silver-haired, silver-tongued counselor for the retreatants, exploiting with Irish theatrical flair the story of author Flannery O'Connor's peacocks — which, according to Kelty, she bequeathed to the Trappist monastery in Conyers, Georgia. "Peacocks are bound to show you their splendor," he said.

No, they're not, I thought. *They're an illustration of grace: when you want them to open their tails they won't, and then you put the camera away and go about your business and you turn around and suddenly you're dazzled.*

In every way the American experiment is the product of that philosophical tradition, first written down in Plato and extending through Augustine to Aquinas to the Enlightenment philosophers of the seventeenth and eighteenth centuries and to the founding fathers of the American Republic, which perceives reason as the highest faculty of humankind, placing us closer to God than to the animals; according to certain medieval philosophers, closer to God than even the angels. We attack religion on the grounds that it is irrational, with the implication that if only it would yield to the pursuit of reason, we might finally achieve a society freed from oppression and exploitation.

And yet the atomic bomb, the multinational corporation, the great state-sponsored pogroms (Hitler's Germany, Stalin's Russia) were products of secular movements purporting to ground themselves in reason. The point is not that reason is evil, but that its institutions, like those of religion, are founded in human nature. As the all-powerful medieval church engendered the Crusades, so the all-powerful secular state engenders the concentration camp and the all-powerful business conglomerate engenders global servitude and pollution.

In the end I seek the middle path, the tone of which permeates Cassian but is present only intermittently in Augustine. I seek to understand within the limits of reason — but finally, as great contemporary physicists acknowledge, even reason must bow to mystery.

16

CULTIVATING THE HEART

TRAVELING ALONE, living alone can be a kind of continuing meditation. I return to my empty apartment, where courtesy of technology I can choose to fill the silence with any number of electronic machines, images, and voices to keep me living in intention, living for that new car or the coming vacation, living for retirement. Only when I arrive at the glittering future I discover that, as Buddhism so accurately predicts, I'm still dissatisfied. Or I can embrace and enter the silence, to see where it takes me over the months and years. Driving my rented car across the Golden Gate Bridge to Green Gulch, the Zen Center's organic farm, I reached to turn on the radio . . . then I returned my hand to the wheel, to drive in silence over the bridge, up and over the Marin Headlands.

I negotiated the potholes of the Green Gulch drive, passing a sign — SLOW: CHILDREN AT PLAY — and pulled into the parking lot, shaded by towering eucalyptus and filled with battered trucks and faded Honda Civics. Through the trees I saw a ragtag mix of old trailers, aging wood-frame bungalows, and an occasional newer Japanese-style cottage. In their midst sat an abandoned 1964 Chevy BelAir, overgrown with wild fennel and nasturiums. A children's playground held bravely forth, an assemblage of molded plastic slides and mazes and ladders. The surrounding trees were filled with children, their raucous cries echoing from the nearby hillside. *It's not a monastery,* I thought as I carried my belongings to my small room. *It's another in the long, distinguished line of American utopian communities.* Almost none of which, I might have added, outlived their founders.

That first afternoon I attended a dharma discussion, a fundamentalist Christian's nightmare of a scriptural study group, held in a tiny room overgrown with angelwing begonias and potted philodendrons. The angelic blonde with the halo of ringlets, the earnest young woman on crutches with a pierced lower lip, her wisecracking tattooed boyfriend, the middle-aged woman who was still searching — at four years she'd been here the longest of these students. Several of the younger attendees were summer interns working the organic farm.

American Buddhists can claim to be drawn to the practice because (as so many had told me) "it makes so much sense," but the Mahayana texts the group was reading describe miracles ("putting the king of mountains into a mustard seed," "pouring all the waters of the seas into a single pore without injury to any living beings") to equal any mentioned in the Bible. The workshop leader posed questions: "The heart of the matter is, how do you get free of suffering? But have you ever met anyone who's free of suffering? Finally we don't know why we're here."

The woman in charge of the organic farm raised her hand and spoke as much to herself as to the younger students. "If you can do anything else — surf, play guitar — then do it. But if you're driven to zazen, then pursue it."

✍

Before that evening's zazen I spoke with Dr. David Levy, a researcher at Xerox Park in Palo Alto who's developing workshops in "mainstreaming the dharma" — integrating Buddhist principles into the corporate world, beginning with the Eightfold Path, the foundation for Buddhist living. "I'm discouraged," Levy said frankly of his efforts. "As my own [Buddhist] practice has developed and matured, it gets harder to be a part of this corporate world that's so off track. . . . We've had no real impact — what can you do in the face of these institutions that are so omnipresent and yet so intractable? I just try to keep the faith."

After our conversation I headed toward the zendo, a handsome, low-roofed building surrounded by meticulously tended flowerbeds. I approached the first evening's zazen with the enthusiasm and butterflies that I might hold for a visit to the dentist. I dreaded returning — the old, familiar fear of the unfamiliar, of yielding control. Yet once on the cushion my body returned to sitting with remarkable ease. The peace, the smell of the kerosene lamps, the incense, the strange ritual with its chanting and bows and gongs and bells, the impetus to get it right. And I was discovering possibly the single strongest factor in drawing people to meditation or contemplative prayer: the power that resides in a room in which people have agreed not to talk; the power of collective silence. Here in yet another lovely setting I felt blessed. I settled onto my *zafu* (no robes here, where guests so frequently come and go) and recognized when Norman Fischer, now in residence as the Green Gulch abbot, passed behind my back, by the *shush-shush* of his too-long pants scraping the floor.

This is what I have discovered about the meticulous attention to the correct position of the fingers, the posture, the bows: the way it keeps me grounded in the here and now. Is my back straight? Are my ears above my shoulders? Are my thumbs barely touching? Paying attention to the body means constantly returning my mind to this moment, sitting on this *zafu*, in this room, amid these coastal mountains of California. Mistakes are in the past; worries are in the future; for the time of this meditation, anyway, I am concerned with neither. *Here, now.* Done often enough over time, that calm immediacy has a way of persisting through the day to become the habit of being.

❧

That afternoon, Norman Fischer gave a dharma talk, one of a series of lectures centered on Zen koans, nonsensical statements or questions (most famously, the sound of one hand clapping) intended to challenge the mind to free itself from rational thinking. He entered the conference room formally robed in dark gray and carrying the familiar hooked staff. The students took up a chant, the toneless Zen chant ending on the single descending note — if they'd wanted to make a more unpleasant sound they'd be hard pressed to find it, which was probably the intention of some Japanese Zen puritan. I found myself wistfully recalling the Trappist hymns and psalms, with their invocation of Aristotle's theory of the music of the spheres — the heavenly harmonies supposed to have been generated by the turnings of the marvelously ordered universe, imitated in the music of Gregorian chant.

Fischer sat at the center of a long couch between a young man on his left and a young woman on his right, each carefully perched in a sitting lotus on the overstuffed cushions. Behind Fischer, the windows framed a California hillside of Douglas fir and eucalyptus slowly engulfed by the encroaching ocean fog.

For the text of his dharma talk (a Christian would say, for the Scripture of his sermon) Fischer chose a koan questioning the reality of a painted rice cake. Which is more "real": the rice cake on the table or a painting of the rice cake on the table? "In seeking relief from suffering, you're already caught up in suffering," Fischer said.

> Awakening is about understanding that every experience, even that of suffering, can provide access to enlightenment. In every moment of our conduct the whole mystery of being arises, if only we would pay attention. The "real" rice cake embodies the world of our senses; the painted rice cake embodies the world of language and symbols. Dōgen [the medieval Japanese author of the koan] is telling us that the "real" rice cake and the painted rice cake are one and the same.
>
> The entire earth and universe is also in you. All the things of the world are in our eyes and tongue and ears and nose — we wear the earth. The Bible says we are made of dust. Good depends on bad; tall depends on short; East depends on West. The world of difference is all interdependent. We all think things are opposed, but it isn't so — nothing is in opposition but only in support. Mind and body aren't in opposition. . . . We must both know and eat the painted rice cake.

I recalled the Jewish conception of God as the unpronounceable, unknowable YHWH. Maybe zazen, I thought, could provide the means of distinguishing YHWH from the surrounding clutter of doctrine and dogma. Again I considered the distinction between dogma — the trappings of belief — and the virtue we call faith.

Afterward I waded through shrieking children to find Fischer in his office, where broken rattan furniture shared space with plastic baby Buddhas and bookshelves of contemporary Buddhist and Jewish writings, with a sprinkling of English and American classics, mostly Henry James.

Like Gethsemani's Timothy Kelly, Fischer had announced his intention to retire. Like Gethsemani, the Zen Center conducts its search for an abbot using unconventional standards. "We look for someone who's strong in faith in their practice, and who commands respect in the community," Fischer said. "Almost on purpose we don't search for job skills. We don't look for someone who gives a good lecture or who's a good administrator. These are good but the job is something other than those skills."

The issues surrounding dharma led to a question that had troubled me since my first serious consideration of Buddhism at the Gethsemani Encounter: Buddhists claim not to believe in a soul, and yet they believe in karma, the principle that our actions have consequences that manifest themselves in future lives, the nature and quality of which we shape in this current life. "If there is no soul," I asked, "why concern ourselves with consequences that endure beyond this life? What is the mechanism for passing karma from one life to the next? For that matter, what's the difference between karma and soul?"

Fischer began by questioning the definition of self, as contained and expressed in the idea of a soul. Buddhism posits the notion, terrifying to Christians, that we have no souls, at least not in the sense of an enduring essence distinct from any other aspect of our existence. Finally we are what we do, which is why our decisions about how to spend each moment are so important. What endures is not "the soul," with its implication of individual identity, but the cumulative consequences of all those minute-by-minute, day-by-day choices we've made; what endures is karma. Fischer cited analogies popular among Buddhists.

If you take away the windows and doors and walls and ceilings and floors, does a room remain? Christians would say yes — an essence remains, an ineffable essence they call "the soul." Buddhism says no — nothing remains but karma, the consequences of your actions. The flower is a combination of rain, wind, sun, earth, all the aggregate elements that comprise its existence; it's not possible to separate out some essence of flower apart from all these. Similarly, a Buddhist argues, each person is an accumulation of actions and influences, but no part of the person exists apart from those actions. Form is emptiness — there's really no person, in the sense of an enduring, particular personal identity. But at the same time, emptiness, in taking on all those aggregate qualities, is form — this "no person" appears as a person. The heart of Buddhism lies in its embrace of that paradox: we are both here *and* not here, in time *and* outside it, form *and* emptiness.

The problem with the conception of soul is the problem of attachment. If you perceive the soul as something that really and essentially exists, you become attached to it, and then it's just another cause of suffering — another way for us to hold on, to resist change. But we must have some mechanism for establishing the continuity of identity over time. Otherwise, since without identity there's no responsibility, what's to keep us from rape and pillage? In adapting the principle of karma — already ancient at the time of his birth — to his own teachings, the Buddha was trying to reduce attachment to the concept of a soul while at the same time establishing a foundation for continuity which establishes the basis for morality. There's no soul but karma still holds. Action has reaction; what we do has consequences.

If you plant an acorn and an oak tree grows, the oak is in the lineage of that acorn even though the acorn itself has vanished. But because it's causally linked to its progeny, they're strongly related. In the same way, future lives and past lives are related through time.

I liked this idea — karma as a kind of moral DNA, carrying forward the essential good and evil of our actions. As a method of reinforcing virtue the doctrine of karma may be superior to the Western conception of a soul, which for better and worse has only one try at salvation. In both cases, what matters is the sense of responsibility to continuity — the faith that our particular decisions and lives take place not independent of each other and the world, but as part of an intricately, mysteriously interconnected moral ecology, in which my decision to lie to a colleague or take dinner to a sick friend will have its effect, however imperceptible, on the quality of life for all human beings.

Using the discoveries of science, we have the capacity to establish that fact of continuity empirically — that is, to demonstrate its truths through scientific method. Indeed actions do have consequences, and our increasingly sophisticated understanding of ecology makes clear how actions reverberate in our lives in ways that we can only intuit: if I give over my life to the pursuit of comfort and security, when my mettle is tested I'm not likely to act with courage. The hard truth is that I build my character every day and every night, in my interactions with my friends and enemies, my family, the airline clerk, and the grocery boy. Karma, I decided, describes the accumulated character of those actions — brave or timid, generous or mean-spirited, and it extends into the future in ways independent of my personal identity. After I'm dead, no one will answer my e-mail, my particular strengths and weaknesses will end, even as the choices I have made across a life are my legacy to the world, the means through which I live on, for better and worse. The truth lies not in results but in process, in the day-to-day striving, in the reality of the never-present, ever-changing river of time. "Everything changes," Suzuki Roshi said, and embracing that reality should govern my ongoing choices.

Fischer and I turned to discussing the relationship between Eastern and Western philosophies and religions. We agreed that though no paper trail could establish their interdependence to the satisfaction of a scholar, to deny such mutual influences is no longer possible, given what we know of the military, economic, and cultural interactions of the ancient world.

Fischer speculated on the parallels between the evolution of the two traditions. As a cultural phenomenon, Judaism limited itself almost entirely to "the chosen people" — those born into the tribes of Israel. Simultaneously, a thousand miles to the east the earliest forms of Buddhism limited salvation (that is, the attainment of nirvana) to those who became monks. Around the time of Jesus, both traditions spun off descendants — Christianity in the West, Mahayana Buddhism in the East — which made their wisdom available not just to a select few but to all. In this context it is possible to view their evolution as part of the growing awareness of the dignity of each human being, part and parcel of developments that centuries later would lead to the Bill of Rights, the French Revolution, and the elimination of legally condoned slavery.

Both traditions, Christian and Buddhist, face the challenge of continuing to embrace and incorporate change if they're to remain viable. "It's impossible that all people who have spiritual hunger will be able to address that in monasteries," Fischer told me. "At one time neighborhoods centered around churches, and the church acted as an anchor for the neighborhood and a magnet for its spiritual seekers. What can we imagine to replace that model? What happens after you visit or live in one of the Zen Center communities? How do you take that experience home and offer it to others? These are the questions I want to engage."

The increasingly strident conservatism of Rome makes it an unlikely source for innovation any time soon, although, as one of the Christian monks told me, "We think of change in terms of centuries around here." "The Christian churches have many beautiful individuals," Fischer said, "who aren't small-minded but are having to pay lip service to rules they don't believe in. And that will lead to their dying away. And that's good" — here he grinned — "because they have all this real estate and we can buy it and turn it into Zen facilities."

I introduced the subject of celibacy and the interesting paradox that, as the Christian monastic orders struggle with their commitment to it, the American Buddhists are considering reintroducing it as an option. Fischer spoke to the recent interest in vows of celibacy among Buddhists at the San Francisco Zen Center:

> Some people take personal vows [of celibacy] that they share with their teacher. These vows are usually for short periods of time — a training period, or for a few years. I'd like to have more explicit vows of temporary celibacy — to honor it as a practice. Vows of temporary celibacy are quite different from lifetime vows, but for a time it can be very freeing — one gains a sense of oneself as a person, without reference to being a sexual object. If you're single you're constantly beset with the pain of getting together and breaking up. Celibacy allows you to focus on energy and spirit rather than on a present or potential partner.
>
> Living in community as a celibate can help you embrace the community as a whole. But no matter how you look at it, sexuality is a problem — you suffer if you're single and celibate; you suffer if you're single and not celibate, in and out of relationships. Even if you're in a relationship you have a lot to deal with in trying to relate to another person in the midst of an intense spiritual practice — and that can be suffering too.

Whether because of the presence of children at Green Gulch — with their evidence of at least procreative sex — or the absence of threat of repercussions from Rome, I felt comfortable in asking him directly about the appropriate place of sex in a religious practice. Fischer addressed the subject calmly and with disarming frankness.

> I think the significance of celibacy [as a religious practice] is overemphasized. After all, in a way we're all mostly celibate most of the time — most people most of the time aren't having sex. One way to look at being a monk is you don't have a mind of grabbiness. You can be celibate and be completely lascivious every minute. Celibacy does promote simplicity. That's its main aspect.
>
> I don't have the capacity for celibacy. But when I was young I found it impossible to have love affairs — it was so confusing and so difficult to practice right conduct. I don't think I was very good at it. I realized that if I wanted to continue practice I had to get married and so I resolved to find a wife. And I found Kathie and she found me and that was great.
>
> Before we married I had always prided myself on living simply — I could move my whole house in my car. And then we had twins and all

of a sudden I had a lot of stuff to cart around. Then one day I realized — it's all just one suitcase. One suitcase and then one suitcase and then one suitcase. It's all a state of mind. You make the effort to live simply, to be a simple person. It's the same with sexuality. If you want to be a religious person you have to be a celibate within a sexual relationship — it means you don't emphasize sex as the focus of your life.

Our sex life is simple, straightforward, not sensationalized. We enjoy our physical contact, it's important to us, but it's about our being together. It took us a while to figure out how to be sexual with each other — it's hard to be sexual with someone in a way that's good. It takes a great deal of honesty, warmth, and self-confidence. A good and normal sex life is rare in our oversexed world. All the advertising and titillation encourage us to feel bad about ourselves since none of us is doing it as often or as well as the people in the movies.

My wife and I emphasize friendship, mutual regard, and deemphasize passion in the sense of lust. At the same time, I know people who are eloquent on virtues of lust as a means of exploration. Look at [the poet] Allen Ginsberg — he was a wonderful person and a serious and devoted Buddhist practitioner — yet lust was an avenue of practice for him. The last things he wrote were about lust for young men. But he was an unusual person. For most of us I think that lust would interfere with the religious life.

*

When I was invited to attend a re-creation of an authentic Japanese tea ceremony in the small tea house that Green Gulch has built in imitation of those in Japan, I accepted with enthusiasm, recalling a description I'd read in Huston Smith's *The World's Religions*: "the celebrated tea ceremony, in which an austere but beautiful setting, a few fine pieces of old pottery, a slow, graceful ritual, and a spirit of utter tranquility combine to epitomize the harmony, respect, clarity, and calm that characterize Zen at its best."

"It's essential to show up on time," my hostess told me. "It shows disrespect for your host to be late." A Southern boy raised with manners, I arrived exactly at the appointed hour, only to wait for the other guests to straggle in.

The other guests: two middle-aged women, their long hair cut in twin mullets, dressed in jeans and lumberjack shirts and traveling outside the Tennessee mountains for the first time in their lives. Four buzz-cut men, early civil service retirees up from San Francisco, one sporting a pinky ring, another wearing a black leather vest over a muscle-T and trailing a bundle of keys on a long chain that dangled to his knees before looping back to his rear pocket.

For the occasion, the hostess had shaved her head. Only her thick dark eyebrows gave a clue as to the color and texture of her hair. She greeted us wearing a richly patterned kimono. We entered the tea house and sat on tatami mats — as the first guest to arrive, I was given the place of honor closest to the hostess and her assistant, a portly, ruddy man with green eyes and thick silver hair (*Mel Brooks wearing a kimono after a few martinis*, I thought). The other guests arranged themselves on their mats. The leather-vested buzz cut's looping keychain clanked against the polished hardwood floor.

"The guest traditionally compliments the host on the elegance of the setting and asks questions about the particular items being used," my hostess said. "As first guest, you get to ask the first question."

"You have a lovely room here," I said. "Maybe you could tell me a bit about the history of the ceremony."

My hostess brightened — she had lived in Japan, was knowledgeable on the subject, and began an animated description of its origins. I interjected an occasional question to clarify some points. As she talked her assistant became visibly agitated. Somewhere around the Middle Ages she paused for breath. Her assistant glared at her and jumped in. "You're not asking the right questions," he said to me. "I mean, I don't mean this as a cri*tique*, but you're not supposed to ask about *history*. You're supposed to ask about the *items in the room*."

Silence.

"Maybe you can tell me about the items in the room?"

The assistant smiled and settled back. "The wall hangings are done in the style of the southern provinces, late eighteenth century —"

"*Not* eighteenth century," the hostess said. "Nineteenth."

The assistant scowled. "Eighteenth."

"Nineteenth." She pointed at the teapot. "You may prepare the water." Silence.

From deep in his sleeve the assistant pulled out a purple handkerchief, which he unfolded in the most complex fashion — cloth origami. He built a small fire under the pot, boiled the water, handed it to our hostess. This, I could tell, was nirvana for the anal retentive.

With elaborately precise gestures and a mannered politeness the hostess passed me the tea. Crushed and powdered with only the smallest quantity of water added, it defined both its color — jade — and its taste — a superbly elegant bitterness. I poured awkwardly for my neighbor, the buzz cut with the loopy chains.

He took a taste. "Cool."

He poured for his neighbor, one of the lumberjack women. She peered into her cup as if it held a cockroach. "*I* don't *think* so."

I recalled the comment of a British professor of Far Eastern studies with whom I'd spoken that morning. "In Japan ritual is a way of life," he said. "In England, we do it but we don't take it seriously. In America, it's embarrassing."

Thinking back to that tea ceremony, I find in it the American dilemma — the immigrant dilemma. After all, the Catholic mass is no more native to this continent than the dharma talk or the tea ceremony. Having obliterated or confined our Native cultures with an efficiency that the Chinese in Tibet can only admire and emulate, Americans were left with what we wanted — tabula rasa, the blank slate of a continent on which to write whatever we wished. Freed from tradition and culture, we responded like the child in the candy store: manifest destiny is our motto, raze and exploit our method.

I left the tea ceremony, wondering if the American challenge consists of creating an American faith — an amalgam of all these traditions, West and East and our Native cultures, into something that no traditionalist would recognize but that would be the authentic American expression of spirituality, having arisen from the place where history has brought us.

჻

Two periods of morning zazen, then breakfast in silence, punctuated by the clink of spoon against bowl and the suck of nine-grain cereal ladled from the vat, until someone knocked together a pair of wooden clackers, signal for the end of what the Trappists would call the Great Silence. Tongues untied, we broke instantly into the chatter of children released for recess, each of us eager to add his or her voice to the great ongoing symphony.

Temporary vocations: the idea sounds great in principle — come to live the monastic life for a month, or six months, or even a year. And in principle this is how the Zen Center works. In practice, though, an institution with compassion and loving-kindness as its mission statement has difficulty asking people to leave. As a result, the Zen Center population is top-heavy, too many queen bees and not enough workers. Long-term residents grumble at having to explain to an endless stream of newcomers matters as simple as recycling routines or as complex as the thirty-year financial history of a collective enterprise with three locations. Newer arrivals grumble at the paucity of opportunity, as the hierarchy tends to be occupied by the most senior residents.

The following day, after first zazen, the community filed to the fields for its twice-weekly hour of collective work. Silence, except for the chucking of hoes against the soil, the clattering of the birds, and the nearby thrum of the Pacific; no thought but the pleasure of watching the brightening sky, the mist rising from a rill, and the satisfaction of decapitating dicots. This was very different from the farmwork I had performed as a teenager — partly because at Green Gulch I knew that if the deer ate the lettuce, someone would go to the local produce market to buy more. But the collaborative effort of raising food brings a satisfaction, a sense of community, that may be the real fulfillment for contemporary seekers.

✿

"I was looking for a community of any kind. I didn't care what it was, it could have been a nudist colony, just some place where everyone was together on principle." Over breakfast I spoke with Bryan Hopping, a regular in the fields, a tall, thin, rangy guy in his early twenties. "Logically it would have made sense to look at Christian monasticism," he said in response to my question, "but I'm a gay man and so I never seriously considered it" — a response with significant ramifications for Christian monastic vocations, judging from the numbers of gay men and lesbians I have encountered in the cloistered orders.

Hopping felt that his year at the Zen Center had been valuable, but he was concerned that he might fall into the structure and not be able to hoist himself out. When I told him that Gethsemani requires psychological testing of its candidates, he laughed. "Nobody here would get in!" As a college student he'd studied classics and thought about becoming a professor, but after working on the Green Gulch Farm he thought about going into a trade — something where he uses his body.

"We're requested to talk about sexual relationships with the practice committee leader," Hopping said,

> but what I do outside the Zen Center — sex, drugs, whatever — is pretty much my business. Most of us have strong longings for intimacy, connectedness. Most of us see sex as the means to those ends. Society

says that marriage equals intimacy, but we know that's not true. I don't
know what intimacy means — it's a word I use — I don't know that it's
possible to get it from sex. One of the amazing things that I've found
about being here — I ask myself, "Can I bring my experiences to practice? Does Buddhism have something to say to this?" And it almost always does. I always feel listened to — not judged — whatever subject I
raise.

I've put on ten pounds since spring farming season began — all
muscle. It's great to be tired like that, to feel my body — it's life.

Without exception the young men and women whom I met at the Zen
Center impressed me with their intelligence, sincerity, and passion. At the
same time, I left my conversation with Bryan Hopping wondering how my
generation had, in our turn and in our way, failed our successors. In questioning whether intimacy is possible in marriage or sex, Hopping was
speaking for all wounded veterans of sexual liberation . . . but if intimacy
isn't possible in sex or marriage, where may it be found? In the sexual revolution, have I lost some important aspect of being? If the sexual revolution
has brought me to this, ought I search to see if I tossed out a baby with the
bathwater?

*

The Green Gulch residents were preparing for a momentous event: as part
of a project to transcribe and publish the original tapes of Suzuki Roshi's
talks, the Zen Center organized a fundraiser featuring many of its founding members, a number of whom have gone on to be spiritual teachers.
Each member was to speak briefly about his or her memories of the center's founder. Among the speakers would be Richard Baker Roshi, Suzuki
Roshi's chosen successor whom the board had asked to resign in 1983,
twelve years after Suzuki Roshi's death, in a widely publicized scandal that
nearly destroyed the institution. His appearance, however brief, carried
symbolic weight — in the fifteen years since his forced departure, it was the
first time he'd been officially invited to return.

Even today longtime Zen Center members disagree on the causes of
Baker Roshi's ousting, though the wounds were sufficiently deep that the
decision to invite him to return required a four-hour meeting to air fears
and objections. Most often cited was Baker Roshi's abuse of power. Baker
had the fundraiser's golden touch in bringing well-heeled donors to the
Zen Center and was significantly responsible for the donations or arrange-

ments that enabled the acquisition of all three Zen Center facilities. At the
same time, he was hanging out with then–California governor Jerry Brown
as well as a raft of Hollywood celebrities, he appeared regularly in the newspaper and on television, and he took to driving a BMW to his many appointments, a car that he argued helped in his fundraising efforts but that
as a symbol of power sat poorly with a community dedicated to sharing.
Though married, Baker Roshi was revealed to be having an affair with a
student, and though the affair was by all accounts consensual among the affected parties, including his wife, the injection of sex into an already vola-
tile situation tipped the balance. After stormy board meetings, Baker Roshi
was ejected.

Wendy Johnson, a twenty-five-year Zen Center practitioner and gardener, summarized the fallout.

> The 1983 difficulty with Baker Roshi was a watershed event in our com-
> munity, a real crisis of faith. Baker Roshi was a renegade in many ways,
> but he was also the primary teacher at Zen Center through those years.
> It's wise to keep your renegades close, but somehow this wasn't possi-
> ble. From the Baker Roshi crisis we learned to be more forthright and
> less dependent on a single teacher, as well as to be more questioning
> and more open about previously unspoken topics, like dharma trans-
> mission. At the same time I felt we developed a kind of cynicism and
> sarcasm in our practice and that as an organization we became more
> conservative and institutionalized.
>
> A core question in Buddhist practice is how to find inspiration and
> satisfaction in your daily practice. For me this search is always con-
> nected to the plight of the world, to staying in touch with what is going
> on around us. The Baker Roshi troubles did not destroy my faith, but
> they did cause me to question my community and my practice more
> deeply.

Johnson, who with her husband has raised two children in the community, saw the presence of the children as among the Zen Center's greatest
achievements. She told me how the Green Gulch children rigged up a pole
with a pink banner raised to remind them to be quiet during zazen. "Each
drew on the banner an interpretation of what zazen meant to them," she
said. "Norm and Kathie's son drew a ferocious monk leaning over a kid and
saying, 'Sssh!'" And yet, as she also pointed out, children bring discipline to

adults; they keep us grounded. Their simple and unadorned perception of the truth confronts us with the layers of self-deception we have constructed to avoid it. "They often saved us from the threat of shallow piety," she said.

> Children brought us back to the real, lived life, again and again. Their sincerity and honesty popped any pretensions. We had to be real or they'd zip right over us. I count as our great success the fact that we have a center where we practice organic farming, work with children, and where we teach meditation in a rather worldly way. We offer one of the few places where young people can afford to come to learn those disciplines. How does commerce connect with meditation? I'm glad we're asking this question and dealing with it.
>
> It's an ongoing challenge to really understand the role and practice of lay and monastic students. We've blurred lines because we don't want to be too strict — I love that we're loose enough to have monks and lay people practicing shoulder to shoulder and questioning how our lives and practice intersect.

჻

Grandson of a tailor, Norman Fischer sat cross-legged on a cushion in the low-ceilinged room where he meets visitors and students, with needle and thread at hand. He was repairing a tear in an *okesa*, the ceremonial robe worn by Buddhist priests — a teacher indicates to the student that she or he is ready for ordination by announcing that it's "time for you to sew your *okesa*." Traditionally the student pieced together the *okesa* from scraps of material, signifying that the monk owned not even enough cloth to make a small garment, or, more metaphorically, that students have formed their particular wisdom from the patchwork of truths inherited from all their predecessors.

As a child Fischer lived over his grandparents' tailor shop in Pittston, Pennsylvania, a small city whose very small Jewish community clung together for mutual support, presenting a united front against prejudice.

> We had a wonderful rabbi, [the comedian] Jackie Mason's brother — Mason himself is a rabbi, part of that aristocracy of learning. It was that insulated Jewish world, where the Jews stuck together. Our rabbi was a smart, spiritual guy who was quite lonely. Most people weren't educated and he had no one to talk to so he talked to me. We met all

the time to study Jewish stuff. He was Orthodox but modern — interested in science. I went with him to the synagogue almost every day.

Fischer was interested in spiritual matters from his earliest memories,
leading us to joke about the existence of a gene for spirituality.

Despite my good relationship with my rabbi, Judaism didn't appear to
me as a spiritual path, a vehicle for truth — it was a cultural identity, it
was what I was. Plus I left home feeling dissatisfied with small-town
conventional life. I still identify Judaism with a conventional life. I
didn't want to get married, didn't want to get a job but I still assumed I
would be conventional — I remember one day thinking, "Gee, I never
applied to law school, how did that happen?"

My mother never liked the Zen Center. She kept trying to make me
feel guilty, so I became immune to guilt. My father didn't mind that I
was here, but she was upset because she couldn't tell her friends what
her son was doing. My father said, "What difference does it make what
you do if you feed your family?" My mother came in the winter to
Green Gulch and her point of view was: "You went to college and
you're living in mud."

As he said this I concealed a smile — I saw the haranguing Jewish
mother and her nice son who is torn between duty and rebellion, until he
addresses the challenge by breaking free and going to (where else?) northern California. And I recalled yet again Merton's comment about the relationship between severe mothers and contemplatives.

From challenges of parenthood Fischer and I segued easily into a discussion of the challenges of passing along wisdom in a culture where traditional community bonds have all but disappeared. "The idea of lineage is
essential to Zen — without lineage there is no Zen," Fischer said, "but the
sense of lineage we've inherited is unworkable in America. The teachers
who have had problems are those who have tried to take the Asian model
and put it here," an implied reference to the problems the Zen Center faced
with Richard Baker Roshi, whose style, learned from a Japanese roshi and
refined in stays in Japanese monasteries, many found imperious and dicta-
torial.

In Zen there's not a body of knowledge or even experience that you're
passing on — it's a way of being. You pick that up by hanging out with

each other. One can study Zen and study it well without an intimate relationship with a teacher but it does depend on a mystical, mysterious, ineffable feel for life, and that does, I think, come from lineage. This feeling for life — you don't get that by going to the seminary. That's the essence of Zen.

I asked him to define faith — the challenge that set in motion my own search.

The word translated as "faith" in Buddhism comes from the Sanskrit word *shradha,* also translated as "confidence," and is one of the necessary ingredients for enlightenment. Within the range of the various Zen traditions, the Zen Center practice is faith-based because we don't emphasize the experience of instantaneous enlightenment. Instead we emphasize faith — faith in practice, which is faith in the self, in the Buddha, in the universe, in your teachers.

Christianity is a revealed religion, in which faith dawns on you slowly and is considered to be counterintuitive, counterlogical. In Zen you develop faith in the course of practicing — little by little it ripens in you. But that's very similar in all traditions. Our style of meditation practice is not so different from prayer.

Thanks to my time among the Buddhists, I was beginning to grasp all the resonances of the word *practice* — as in "a practicing Christian." I had always assumed Christianity as the given — I had never before considered it or any philosophical ideal as something at which I might have to work, slowly and steadily over time, or that "achieving" it, like writing the perfect book or raising the perfect child, was by definition impossible. One could only *practice,* knowing perfection could never be achieved; one could only seek virtue, knowing that it cannot be found but only lived out; one can only address the great questions, knowing they have no answers.

❧

Linda Ruth Cutts was the first woman to be chosen *tanto,* or director of spiritual practice, for the Zen Center community. Shortly after I left Green Gulch, she would succeed Norman Fischer to become co-abbess with Blanche Hartman. She and I sat on a bench on the patch of manicured lawn outside the zendo.

Born and raised in a Jewish family in St. Paul, Minnesota, Cutts came west at a time of great pain in her life — "the practice of sitting still met me where I was with my pain." Throughout the 1970s, many residents of the Zen Center were living hand-to-mouth, using food stamps and getting free health care from visiting doctors, but as the members aged that became less feasible. "Now we pay our staff modestly — and part of that package is a three-week vacation and a week-long *sesshin* [intensive meditation practice]. We see the sitting as an integral part of the life." Cutts spoke of the "three Western religions" that Buddhism must adapt to in America — "democracy, feminism, and psychology" (I noted the absence of Christianity and capitalism). Like Fischer, she saw one of the challenges of Buddhism in America to be figuring out how to honor and celebrate the tradition while throwing out what's male-centered. "The Buddha says the dharma is neither male nor female — but there are other places where he says that women will cause monks to violate their vows."

She acknowledged that people who have suffered greatly are drawn to religious expression in general and Buddhism in particular.

> The internalized devaluing of self that affects women, gays, people of color breaks people's hearts. The pain and suffering one experiences — and the struggle to alleviate that suffering — if you're lucky enough, you find spiritual teachings that meet you there and tell you you're okay as you are. We've given zazen instructions to thousands of people, but the zendos are not overflowing — those who take it up are those who have suffered deeply. That experience of suffering is an important thread that runs through this group of people whom you might never otherwise have chosen to live with.

We discussed the difficulties that arise in both traditions around issues of sexuality. "From reading the ancient texts on monastic disciplines we know that issues of sexuality have been with us since earliest times," Cutts said. "People come together to practice — women and men, men and men, women and women — and chemistry is chemistry, especially when you're engaged in this intense practice."

As *tanto* she had to advise incoming students, many of them young men and women, about the "six-month rule," which prohibits sexual relationships for the first six months of residential practice.

> We establish this rule not because we want to curtail the activities of adults but because we want people to be left profoundly alone — just

like in AA they ask you not to start a relationship in the first year you're sober because you're lonely and unhappy. It's so unusual for young people to have anyone say anything to them about this aspect of their lives. For them to be asked to get to know someone before they jump into bed with them is extraordinary. People learn an enormous amount from that — that they've been seeking to assuage their suffering through another person, that they've been addicted to sleeping around as a way of taking care of their pain. We ask them to work in a new way with that — how about sitting still? They come up against how they've been living — women who have found a way to be accepted by sleeping around — that all comes up in zazen. And then the challenge becomes not turning away from the pain that comes up in zazen, not turning away from suffering.

Why are certain people drawn to spiritual practice? Because they have suffered. (In Cambodia we say, If you understand suffering, then you understand the dharma.) Spiritual practice, whatever its nature, is a means first to accommodate, later — with maturity — to embrace suffering. A visual artist might embody this truth in the form of a photograph of an Alabama sharecropper's wife holding her child, or a girl running from a burning, bombed city . . . or a man condemned to death and hanging from a cross.

We spoke of the elemental connections that transcend specific religious identities, and how, like so many Jews and Christians, she's found that her experiences as a Buddhist brought her to a new perspective on her own traditions.

When the four and nine days came along [Zen Center maintains a relaxed schedule on dates including a 4 or 9] I understood: this is like a Sabbath. My son was just bar mitzvahed here — as a family we're combining traditions but I think of them as family, lineage, tribal, cultural events rather than religious holidays. When my family came for the bar mitzvah the rabbi, who'd had Zen training, included a chanting of the Sh'ma, the Jewish watchword of the faith, as if it were a mantra. I'd never experienced being opened at that level to prayer practice and to God.

Like many Zen Center Buddhists she was puzzled when I asked her to define faith. She gave the matter some thought. "Faith — coming from a Jewish background, that word's not so familiar to me. For me the ultimate faith is to realize my true self. That there's nothing I can add to that. Faith is my living a seamless life, where one's practice is one's life in the kitchen is one's life in the zendo. I've lived within the sound of the *han* for twenty-five years — it's nothing special, that seamlessness in the life of faith."

❧

Driving back into San Francisco, I got involved in a fender bender with a foreign tourist who insisted on ascribing fault, though he had backed his car into mine and in any case his rental car insurance would cover all costs. As I faced my livid counterpart, the body repeated without the mind's volition, *Here, Now.* To my astonishment I found that though my pulse raced and my face flushed, I was not drawn into the vortex. When finally we achieved a resolution of some sort, I wished him a good time on the remainder of his vacation, and in the glimpse of comprehension that flickered across his features I saw that he heard my sincerity and was somehow touched.

Back on the road, I expected the queasy willies that follow on all that unused adrenalin. Instead I felt relief, that I could complete this particular day, at least, knowing that I had acted, in complete contradiction to my upbringing, my gender, and my nationality, as a maker of peace.

All well and good when dealing with bent fenders. But what about when dealing with lifelong patterns of racism, sexism, homophobia, religious and class prejudices — all the biases that have always infected human interactions?

17

BEYOND BELIEF

AFTER MY STAY at Green Gulch, I made the transition back across the Golden Gate to the Zen Center's urban headquarters, which members refer to as City Center. There a long-term resident recalled "those pre–Baker Roshi days, how wild City Center was, everybody fucking everybody else." I was inclined to believe his report, though in that free-sex-and-food-stamp era, his description might have been applied to almost any inner-city neighborhood of San Francisco. But "pre–Baker Roshi days" defines a small window in time — Suzuki Roshi died in 1971, only two years after the acquisition of City Center, and Baker Roshi almost immediately took charge.

Today's City Center has about it a seriousness of purpose, though of the Zen Center's three facilities it is (not surprisingly, given its inner city location) the most worldly. Residents conduct entrepreneurial businesses from their rooms (freelance writing, independent film production), and while no one appears to be getting rich, at times the place has the feel of an inner-city commune loosely organized around a Buddhist practice conducted for the benefit of visitors and a core of senior practitioners.

Over my first lunch the *tenzo* and I entered into discussion, in which he quoted the essential Buddhist teaching "form is emptiness, emptiness is form." "Identity is an illusion, all is a part of everything and everything is a part of the oneness of being. I can get my mind around that," he said, "in a way I never found possible with all that Christian doctrine."

I pointed out that, as he had reduced Buddhism to three words ("form is emptiness"), I might reduce Christianity to "God is love." "Expressed so simply, Christianity makes a lot of sense, too," I said. "Westerners have a hard time seeing it that way because we're immersed in it. My guess is that Asians find it equally hard to shed the historical burdens of Buddhism."

What were the sources of my newfound defense of Christianity? Why shouldn't each of us pick and choose (the Protestant side of my mother is speaking here) among the various wisdoms, when our lives and needs are so diverse? The question begs the old struggle between the individual and the community. A community relies upon a set of shared assumptions. If every member of the community defines those differently, soon enough there's no community. But if the community demands inflexible orthodoxy, it soon grows stagnant.

For the space of that afternoon at City Center I considered these matters — the gift of the understanding that God is love, how such a gift was worth the price of the ticket, even when the price tag included crazy Father Gettelfinger and eight years at St. Catherine's Grade School. Then I was brought up short by an encounter at that night's dinner, where I sat next to a visiting Protestant minister, a gay man appointed as chaplain at a Catholic university. The dean of students at his university had made a great public fuss over the ecumenism represented by the appointment of a Protestant, but after the press releases and the public introductions, the dean took the new chaplain aside to warn him against speaking to students about his sexual orientation. "There's nothing to be gained for anyone from that," he'd said. Because he needed the job and because the institution has a high profile, the chaplain complied.

☙

At Green Gulch, the chirping of the birds signaled the sun's rising: first the sparrows in the eaves, awakened by the arrival of the humans, a nice reversal of the usual order. Then closer and farther I heard the birds of the fields and forest and coastal chaparral, the towhees and redwinged blackbirds and quail — these last, emboldened by their contact with people, strolled the Green Gulch paths like miniature chickens, their young trailing behind.

Now, in the first morning's zazen at City Center, I traced the progress of the morning by the sound of scattered engines starting, as neighbors emerged from their homes to drive to work. Then the garbage truck ground its gears as it climbed the hill outside the meditation hall windows, its backup alarm beeping as it shifted briefly into reverse. Next came the liquid shush of the street cleaner, then the rumble of the first morning bus and more cars starting, until all merged into the big city's smooth and continuous background roar.

At that first morning's sitting, the chaplain's story of his coercion into silence brought to mind all my anger, a background roar to my consciousness. Once I would have yielded to its insistence; now I stopped to consider its sources. Was I angry at the institutions of Christianity, including but hardly limited to the Roman Church? *(Yes.)* Or at those who had the means but not the courage to stand up to them? *(A more qualified yes.)* Was I angry at Jesus' teachings or the example he and his disciples offered? *(No.)*

Sitting with my anger, I considered that rejecting the institution provides a suspiciously easy way to reject the hard truths posed by the teachings. The institution had introduced me to the root truth: "God is love." Why not let that truth speak to me, and let the anger go?

Discipline defines itself in the choosing of the more difficult path.

That morning I recalled a day, a few years earlier, on which I drove a relative on a journey fraught with emotional turmoil — her husband had died a few years before, and she was meeting a college flame who'd recently divorced. It was, to choose that most layered of words, a *date*, her first in more than twenty-five years.

On that drive she and I spoke of religion — she is a devout Christian and deeply uncomfortable, or so I'd assumed, with my sexuality. In fact our conversation revealed how for her Christianity is a religion of the goddess, specifically, the Virgin Mary. The guy gods (Jesus and his Father) provided the doctrinal foundation, and she paid them their appropriate homage, but she focused her passion and practice on Mary, not as virgin but as mother. "The Holy Mother," she named her, never "the Virgin Mary," a nice bit of linguistic subversion I'd never noticed. Compassion, understanding, forgiveness — these were Mary's virtues and the pursuit of them lay at the heart of my relative's faith, allowing no prejudice toward any human being — my sexual identity, it turned out, was immaterial. Out of my own fear and shame and anger, I had projected prejudice onto her, then taken refuge in the easy silence it permitted. The shame had been projected onto me by institutions such as the Christian churches, but I had chosen to cling to and even amplify it, from some intuition that an identity based in shame and anger is better than no identity at all.

What would be required of me to form an identity from some place other than my wounds? This was the scary, liberating question rising from zazen.

※

The familiar community work meeting opened the Zen Center day. We assembled in the dining room for our assignments. Again I worked with the kitchen crew, with mornings passed in silence, though in the afternoons we were allowed to speak. As at Tassajara, the *tenzo* opened each days' work with a small ceremony at the kitchen altar. At the lunch bell we left our tasks and gathered again. Now the *tenzo* took a pinch of food from each of the dishes we'd prepared, assembled these on the tiniest of plates, which he placed before a miniature Buddha. We chanted a *sutra* honoring the morning's work, then broke for the midday meal.

∽

"There is suffering in everyone's life, but those people whose compassion is deepest and broadest have known immense suffering." Zen Center co-abbess Blanche Hartman and I spoke in her City Center apartment, a roomy one-bedroom she shares with her husband — the same rooms where Suzuki Roshi once lived. "You don't go out looking for suffering, but you don't protect yourself from suffering that comes your way. Try to get close to it and be with it — try to be still and close." As she spoke the image, imprinted in childhood, of Jesus crucified rose involuntarily to mind and I thought, *What is the crucifixion, finally, if not a visual metaphor for Buddhism's First Noble Truth?*

Hartman is a quiet, strong-jawed powerhouse of a woman, a walking declaration of every human's right to live in peace. She crops her salt-and-pepper hair into a tight Zen helmet, emphasizing her outsized ears and thick eyebrows. Raised Jewish, the child of a University of Alabama professor, she was sent to Catholic elementary schools in 1932, when her public school closed for lack of funds. "The nuns there made a deep impression," she said. "These were women of deep devotion — there was something about them that stayed with me over the years. I have come to recognize that my first exposure to these profound questions came from these nuns." Her father, a Marxist, undertook civil rights work in the 1930s, in the course of which he was beaten, guns were fired at his house, and a cross burned on his lawn — experiences that deeply affected Hartman. When she was fifteen he left to join the army to fight in World War II. She finished high school and found employment as an aircraft mechanic — "I'd have been happy to keep doing that forever" — but the end of the war brought the return of the men and the end of such "male" work for women. She became an activist while pursuing a degree in chemistry.

In the 1960s, while her oldest son was a freshman at San Francisco State Teachers College, she had a confrontation that transformed her life. Her son was arrested while supporting a black students' strike that escalated into a violent confrontation between police and demonstrators. In response to a call from a black community leader for support from the wider community, Hartman went to the campus.

> I noticed that some pickets were pushing and jostling — and I was watching and thinking, *Where's my side?* Since Hiroshima I had become more devoted to nonviolent action, but my thoughts and opinions weren't necessarily nonviolent. After this particular day, I came to realize that I was *fighting* for peace.
>
> Things built up to the pre-planned confrontation, and the riot squad emerged. There was only one row of students between me and the police so I interposed myself without thinking — I made eye contact with the policeman and had an overpowering experience of identity with him, for which I'd had no previous experience. I was a statistician and a chemist, I'd done no reading at all in this area, but this was an experience not about concept, it was totally real and beyond discussion and outside the realm of understanding, but the fact of identity was incontrovertible and much more real than any conceptual ideas I had about life. . . . That evening, I was elected chair of the Parents' Committee in support of the strike, but in fact my political life had ended that moment I came face-to-face with the riot squad policeman. I began going to the Zen Center and met Suzuki Roshi, and I thought, *He understands what this is about* — maybe because he looked at me and saw no separation between us.
>
> I saw in Suzuki Roshi the ability to see virtue in everyone — to see the Buddha in everyone. Imagine being able to see virtue in everyone. Imagine being able to see every being as Buddha — even yourself.

Hartman became completely committed to the Zen Center after she passed out stipends at Green Gulch and saw how each person was paid according to need. "That's what attracted me to the *sangha* — the notion of a 'comrade' — it very much carried that meaning. A group of people who would live together and die together — there's tremendous strength in that." But she noted how the ideal had to receive its come-uppance. "Greed, hate, delusion are ongoing. They'll undermine every institution human beings can create, no matter how idealistic."

She noted that Zen monastic practice is not designed as a retreat from the world.

Even those who live in the monastery interact with the guests. The goal is a life devoted to spiritual pursuits above and beyond other considerations.

Let me tell a little story: When I walk leaning forward my mind is already at my destination — it's not here. When you find yourself in that moment of rushing to your destination, take one or two moments to take a breath, in and out. Notice that, then go on, present in your body. We get separated from ourselves when we're always aiming for a goal and not being where we are. Dogen said, "To expound the dharma with this body is foremost."

Many people want access to questions of how to live compassionately and are willing to give up a great deal to study this, but most are unable to give up their lives for months or years, even as they might be able to study for an intensive week or month in any given year, and then return home to live out what they learn. If you think of that as monasticism, there are lots of people practicing now. If you require of a monk that she be celibate and take a vow of stability, then there are few practicing. The numbers depend on your definition of terms.

Given the frustration women encounter in entering the patriarchal world of institutionalized religion, I asked, what does Hartman suggest that women do? "This is a matter of patience," she said. "Already we can see the patriarchy weakening in our lifetime. What's interesting is that in both Buddhist and Christian traditions wisdom is depicted as feminine."

⁂

The benefit to raise funds for the Suzuki Roshi archive took place the following Sunday afternoon. Richard Baker Roshi's return appearance was anticlimactic. In his allotted five minutes, Baker Roshi talked not about his deceased mentor but about our resistance to dwelling in the body. He offered as an example our habit to use one hand to perform most gestures. Passing the salt, shaking hands — consider, he suggested, how much more meaningful these gestures become when done with two hands instead of one. "With two hands, one passes oneself as well as the salt," he said. This is no less than an attempt to remake custom, to radically reconceptualize the relationship of the person to the surroundings, a transformation that can be accomplished only in the doing.

Paul Discoe, the benefit's most provocative speaker, denounced the whole project as wrong-headed. "If you asked Suzuki Roshi," Discoe said, "he'd say, 'Burn the tapes.' Buddhism is not an intellectual practice but something one must experience firsthand, so I'm not an endorser of this project to transcribe and print the tapes. I encourage you to find teachers and work directly with them."

Discoe's comments harked back to the Greek model of a philosopher, someone for whom writing and teaching were secondary (if pursued at all) to process, to living a life by and for principle. I thought of the monks of Gethsemani, how in their 150-year history only a small minority published books, how for most the life was an effort at achieving union, an integration of mind, spirit, and flesh, and in that unity becoming a living embodiment of the original creative force, what Plato called Beauty or the Good, what we in the contemporary West call God.

18

THE RULE OF BENEDICT AND
THE RISE OF COMPASSION

To the citizen of imperial Rome, the history of the world culminated in the empire, just as a nineteenth-century Englishman might have seen it culminating in London, or a twentieth-century American might have seen it culminating in New York, self-styled "Capital of the World." But in 410 C.E. "eternal" Rome fell before Alaric and the Goths, whose three-day pillage provoked horrified responses from the far reaches of the empire. From the safety of Palestine, the church father Jerome was not alone in seeing in the fall of Rome a prefiguring of the end of the world. "If Rome can perish," he wrote, "what can be safe?"

The invasions heightened the appeal of a refuge in the midst of a deteriorating culture and lent authority to voices that proclaimed religion not a means of living with uncertainty but a secure, stable point of reference. Thus in the centuries following the deposing of the last Roman emperor in 476 we find two contradictory forces at work. On one hand we witness the continuing establishment of monasteries where, following the model of the Greek schools of philosophy and of the original apostles, men and women established a wide variety of communities that emphasized imitating Jesus. At the same time the Christian church began vesting authority in a strong, centralized institution.

By the sixth century Rome would be in disrepair, its population plagued by disease, urban decay, and the almost constant threat of invasion. Across the previous century it had been repeatedly sacked by "barbarians," some of whom had already converted to Christianity, albeit unorthodox strains. Imagine living in such a city, surrounded by palaces, monuments, and temples so grand that their ruins will survive two thousand years, even as your neighbors are prying up paving stones to use in stopgap repairs and every year brings rumors of another wave of invaders. Such an environment provided fertile soil for superstitions, cults, and apocalyptic visions.

As the Roman Empire declined, so did the collective commitment to reason. The leaders of the factions competing for power, having witnessed the fall of this mightiest of human endeavors, had good cause to look to God, or the gods, to explain history. In Augustine's lifetime Christians would turn increasingly to the worship of holy relics and testimonies of miracles. Where in 390 he could declare that the miracles reported in the Gospels and in the Acts of the Apostles were no longer possible, by the end of his life Augustine was meticulously cataloguing their occurrence, partly because he was persuaded that in fact the times had changed, partly because as an old man he saw their importance in drawing pagans to his beloved church. With the decline of Rome, the cementing of the foundation of Christianity became even more paramount. For Augustine, committed to the sanctity and divinity of reason, if miracles were necessary, they might as well be documented in an intellectually respectable way.

The accommodation to and desire for power was only one of many forces that thrust Christianity into politics and eventually made it the predominant moral and political arbiter of Western civilization. The decay in Rome's secular authority left a power vacuum in the West; Christianity was present to fill it, especially once Constantine's legitimizing edict allowed it to draw the period's best and brightest minds.

Barely a hundred years after the Council of Nicaea, the Roman Church would require celibacy of its bishops as a means of concentrating their authority and focusing their power and property away from family and community and into the institution. Under Pope Leo I (440–461 C.E.), the papacy would begin to rival and eventually assume the roles of emperor and state.

In one of those profoundly resonant historical coincidences, the Byzantine emperor Justinian closed Plato's Academy, silencing Greek philosophy as an alternative to Christianity in 529 C.E., the year in which Benedict of Nursia is traditionally said to have founded his monastery at Monte Cassino, in the Italian mountains not far from Rome. There Benedict compiled the collection of directives, principles, and admonitions that would form the Rule of Benedict, the template for the expansion of Western monasticism that continues in use today. Though the Monte Cassino community would endure only some sixty years before its destruction at the hands of the invading Lombards, it produced Gregory I, styled Gregory the Great, the first monk to become pope.

By 590 C.E. political, social, and ecclesiastical conditions in Rome had deteriorated so thoroughly that no one was willing to assume the papacy. Only considerable pressure from his community and colleagues convinced Gregory to accept the office. A devoted ascetic whose austerities weakened his already tenuous health, Gregory turned to dogma to shore up the crumbling foundations of the culture.

Ruling at a time of near chaos and convinced that the end of the world was at hand, Gregory concerned himself with establishing a framework for beliefs that would be readily accessible to common folk. He composed a series of dialogues between an innocent newcomer and his experienced spiritual guide to convey Christian teachings to generations not as literate or well-trained in philosophy as their predecessors. The second of these dialogues presents a biography of Benedict of Nursia, founder of Gregory's monastery at Monte Cassino.

In a style that recalls Athanasius, Gregory's "biography" is a polemic, a treatise that fictionalizes Benedict's life to advance the rhetorical goals of the author. Drawing on classical models of art, architecture, and writing, Gregory structures Benedict's story with a symmetry that a geometer might envy, at the same time describing the miracles Benedict accomplished as a manifestation of his devotion to virtue: As a child Benedict rejoins the halves of a broken tray by praying over them. As a monk, tempted by the memory of a woman, he tears his clothes from his body and rolls in "sharp thorns and stinging nettles." Commanded by Benedict to rescue a drowning boy, a monk runs across water, in an echo of Jesus' miracle at Galilee. In the dead of night Benedict beholds the whole world gathered up into a single ray of light, formed for the purpose of carrying a holy bishop's soul to heaven.

The miracles Gregory reports in his biographies are no more astounding than those Athanasius described in his *Life of Antony*. What had changed was the context of the world in which they were reported. However Augustine creatively manipulated his personal history, his *Confessions* are notable for their lack of miracles. Augustine's conversion is dramatic, but it is occasioned by the most ordinary events (Antony's story related by a friend, a child's chanting a verse). Even where Augustine presents a remarkable coincidence, he makes clear that he is interpreting events rather than attributing them to personal, divine, miraculous intervention.

In contrast, in his biography of Benedict, Gregory established a papal precedent for belief in miracles as a foundation for faith. Though Gregory takes care to note that performing miracles is not a requirement for sainthood, his emphasis on the miraculous aspects of saints' lives set in motion the idea that true believers must accept miracles as factually valid — both Augustine and John Cassian, who admired logic and reason, would surely have disapproved of this requirement. Whether because of the erosion of Greek and Roman rationalism or because of their desire to manipulate the poor and ignorant, later church authorities would cite Gregory's detailed reports of miracles as they transformed the church from teacher and conduit of philosophy into promulgator of dogma and, in its name, violence.

Considered more generously, Gregory turned the church away from the often arcane speculations of the Neoplatonist Greeks and promoted narrative — the story of Jesus — to engage the mass of people. Illiterate peasants might not be able to read or grasp the theology of Augustine or other church fathers, but in their cradles they could and did learn the story of Jesus.

Some historians perceive the increasing engagement of the church with secular issues as a deliberate power grab. A more judicious view is that Christianity, one of the few stable institutions to survive the collapse of Rome, was the only available barrier against political and social chaos. Gregory redirected the church from using philosophy to using Jesus' story as its primary teaching tool. This shift was critical in the evolution of Christianity into the universal religion of the West. It prepared the way for the mixture of reason-based doctrine (three persons in one Trinity, original sin) and mythologized narrative (the three wise men, the Immaculate Conception of Mary) that would become the mainstay of the omnipotent church of the Middle Ages. Doctrine and the demand for orthodoxy would later provide the Inquisition its raison d'être, at the same time that storytelling elaboration on the Gospels' slim details of the lives of Jesus, Mary, and Joseph became the vehicle that kept alive and disseminated Jesus' radical message of equality, forgiveness, compassion, and love.

჻

Shortly after Benedict's death in or around 547 c.e., the Lombards destroyed all the monasteries of Italy, including his own Monte Cassino. Tradition has it that Benedict's monks made their way to Rome with a copy of his Rule; in any case, in 750 Pope Zachary was able to send a copy back to the newly rebuilt Monte Cassino community.

As with Constantine's support of the writing of the Nicene Creed, the widespread promulgation of the Rule of Benedict required the intervention of secular authority. In the course of his long reign (768–814 C.E.), the emperor Charlemagne, like Constantine, set about using religion as a tool for imposing orthodoxy and consistency of law throughout his diverse and fractious territories. His goal was to unite the Germanic and Roman peoples under one throne and to restore the empire of the Caesars, now to be named both "Holy" (because sanctified by the spiritual authority of the pope) *and* "Roman" (laying claim to the secular tradition and glory of the emperors of classical Rome). One means to that end was the dissemination and imposition of the Rule of Benedict.

Charlemagne's grand ambition disintegrated in territorial struggles among his grandsons, but not before the Rule was decisively established as the organizing tool for Western monasticism. As such it formed the template not only for the ascetic, contemplative life but for much of the social, political, and economic activity of western Europe for the next thousand years.

In discussing the evolution of cultural attitudes toward labor, the historian Arnold Toynbee pointed out that as human societies fractured into class divisions, the upper classes came to hold work in contempt — for both Greek and Roman cultures, the gentleman of leisure represented the highest social ideal. Benedictine monasticism, however, restored a sense of the sacred to daily work, a concept Benedict codified in his Rule. Summarizing Benedict's directives, Toynbee writes that the monk was "making work, once again, part of the practice of religion, as it had been, long ago, for pre-Christian tillers of the soil, and, before these, for Paleolithic cavemen. He is putting Christianity into practice by putting man's work back into its original and natural spiritual setting." This emphasis on the sanctity of work brought meaning to the most menial tasks because they were undertaken for the glory of God — though when I seek a contemporary equivalent I think less of the assembly-line cheese making at Gethsemani than of the miniature plate of food the Zen Center staff so carefully prepared and offered to the kitchen Buddha.

A sense that life has meaning is essential to human contentment. People seek money, sex, and power as a source of meaning as much as for their own sake. Men flocked to medieval monasteries for economic security, certainly, but they also were attracted to the possibility of a meaningful life. Since women's monasteries were required to attach themselves to a men's foundation, they had fewer options to amass wealth and so depended more on the wealth their members brought with them. Communities of Beguines — informal alliances of women who sought to do charitable work and to pray collectively — arose in part to address the longing of those women not of the nobility to participate in spiritual life.

The impact of Benedict's Rule cannot be overstated. As Toynbee points out, "Through Saint Benedict's Rule, agrarian life was restored to health first in Italy and then in the rest of the derelict domain of the Roman Empire in Western Europe . . . It is no exaggeration to say that the whole of the extraordinary economic development of our modern Western society . . . can be traced back to Saint Benedict's initiative." The Rule of Benedict is one of the landmark documents of human civilization — of our collective efforts to discipline and govern human behavior.

What aspects of the Rule have enabled it to survive wars and persecutions, to cross oceans and win acceptance in different cultures? To begin with, its author did not pretend that the Rule was a wholly original document. Like many great documents of civilization, it arose as an amalgam of collective wisdom. Benedict lifted whole portions from a longer predecessor — the Rule of the Master, so called because its author is anonymous — that had relied in turn on practices and examples John Cassian had imported from the monasteries of the Nile Delta and detailed in his *Institutes* and *Conferences*. Benedict drew as well on the example of Augustine, who had composed a simple rule for his community at Hippo. Though Benedict did not incorporate specifics of Augustine's rule, Augustine exerted a profound influence in his preference for communal life and monastic fraternity over the solitary, eremitic tradition exemplified by Antony. Forming his community at a time when the larger social order was crumbling and the streets were filled with cults and seers, Augustine mistrusted the hermit's life, however he might personify and individualize his own relationship to God. Instead he preferred the conformity — or civilizing influence, if you prefer — imposed by community life.

In promoting that life, Benedict had come a long way from the days of Antony's solitary wrestling with demons. Together with his fellow hermits Antony understood the hermit's life as a revolutionary undertaking through which the individual sought union with God in solitude. In undertaking his journey into the wilderness Antony represents something close to the "lover of wisdom" in the mode of Socrates — whereas the monks under Benedict's Rule gradually came to see themselves as something closer to a spiritual army of the Lord.

Benedict proposes nothing less than faith-based communism. Though in our time, communism as practiced by the state has largely vanished from the political map, the Rule of Benedict endures, for reasons that become apparent with the first reading. At every turn the Rule favors moderation over excess, the middle path over the extremes. Its Prologue concludes, "Therefore we intend to establish a school for the Lord's service. In drawing up its regulations, we hope to set down nothing harsh, nothing burdensome." It abandons the strict fasting and penitential rites of the desert monks in favor of an accommodation of human realities, among them, frailty. It favors flexibility over dogmatism, restraint and forgiveness over punishment:

> For the daily meals . . . it is enough . . . to provide all tables with two kinds of cooked food . . . in this way, the person who may not be able to eat one kind of food may partake of the other . . . let everyone, except the sick . . . abstain entirely from eating the meat of four-footed animals. . . . We read that monks should not drink wine at all, but since the monks of our day cannot be convinced of this, let us at least agree to drink moderately . . .

The Rule is suffused with love, the product of centuries of wisdom and experience in living the ascetic life. In our current age, with its glorification of individual genius, to read the Rule is to be reminded that humanity counts among its greatest achievements works that have been shaped by anonymous hands working collectively over time. In fact the Rule appeals to our deep-seated desire to do good — capitalist mythology notwithstanding, a desire as deeply rooted in the psyche as greed and selfishness.

The near-disappearance of the utopian communities of the nineteenth century, the hippie communes of the 1960s, and even the powerful Communist government of the Soviet Union underscores the brilliance of the Rule as a means of organizing enduring communities of men and women. Benedict's monasteries have accumulated centuries of experience in collective living. One must turn to so-called primitive cultures or to close-knit religious communities such as the Amish to find parallels. What seems clear is that the survival and prosperity of such communal undertakings require a commitment to some kind of collective expression of spirituality. However powerful it may be, altruism alone inevitably loses out to greed, envy, avarice, *accidie* — all the sins about which the desert fathers wrote with such eloquence. Benedictine monasticism has suffered its share of these evils, but still the institution has endured. The monks with whom I spoke universally attributed that endurance to their foundation in Christian spirituality.

The Rule is the legislative embodiment of the phrase Brother Martin used to describe Gethsemani — "a community of eccentrics." It preserves as paramount the well-being of the whole while recognizing the need to accommodate individual personalities and exceptions. As such it represents a compromise between the institutional demands for conformity and the individual demand for freedom of choice. It centralizes power in the abbot or abbess (even an abbot as self-effacing as Gethsemani's Timothy Kelly was often quoted as saying "an abbey is not a democracy") but limits that power with explicit prescriptions that temper justice with compassion. It names virtue, date of entry, and the abbot's judgment as the only standards for establishing hierarchy. Under its governance, at least in theory, an ex-slave might outrank a prince, and priests are instructed to maintain humility in submitting to the collective order. As such the Rule may be regarded as significant to the development of two concepts: the equal and inalienable rights of humankind and the dignity of the individual.

What does this model imply for a world suffocating under the environmental and social costs of corporate capitalism, which requires for its sustenance that each of us give first priority to our individual desires? "I live here because it makes so much sense," a Benedictine monk told me. Though I cannot imagine the mass of people flocking to monasteries now any more than in the fourth century, I believe, with William James, that "the old monkish poverty-worship" offers one enduring model of successful, collective human endeavor. Through reflection and action based on the Rule and other time-tested guides, we may come to see ourselves not as conquerors of nature and competitors with our neighbors but as creatures capable of living in harmony — which was, after all, the great metaphor of the medieval monk, enshrined in musical and architectural principles which we still use today.

*

In the centuries preceding Gregory I, Christians assumed that laypeople held the same sanctity as monks, a principle that survives in Eastern Orthodoxy. Women were far from social or economic equals, but at least in its infancy Christianity generally took seriously the admonition of Paul that all — including women and slaves — were equal in Christ Jesus. "In this style of piety which assumed literacy and leisure," Peter Brown writes, "women were not only the equal of men. They were, if anything, the unspoken model of male behavior." Writing from prison in 525 C.E., the great Christian philosopher Boethius, drawing on his extensive knowledge of Plato and his successors, could compose his eloquent *Consolation of Philosophy* in praise of "Lady Philosophy" without once mentioning Jesus.

But the closing of Plato's Academy and the rise of monotheistic Christianity eliminated feminine figures from the Western literary and religious imagination; Mary, though acknowledged as the mother of Jesus, was a minor figure in a theology preoccupied with the Trinity. By the time of the *Song of Roland,* composed in the tenth century to celebrate a battle that had occurred two centuries earlier, women had all but ceased to exist in the cultural landscape. No woman appears in the *Song*'s four-thousand-plus lines except Bramimonda, queen of the Moorish infidels, who visits one page long enough to be shackled and forced to convert to Christianity. Monasticism would continue to offer women the rare opportunity to become a powerful abbess or at least a chance to escape from their conventional role as vassal to a man. But as monastic life became the dominant church institution, men's monasteries were increasingly drawn into church politics, while women's monasteries became institutions where wealthy families deposited unwanted daughters, who were expected to arrive with a "dowry" sufficient to enrich the abbey besides covering the daughter's living expenses.

The egalitarian model of those early Christian communities and monasteries, emphasizing cooperation over competition, gradually yielded to the hurly-burly politics and militarism of a male-dominated church, bent on establishing itself as the single embodiment of religious, social, political, and military authority. On Christmas Day of 800, Pope Leo III justified his intervention into secular affairs — in the form of crowning Charlemagne emperor of both West and East — on the grounds that since the East was ruled by a woman (Irene, legitimate empress of the Byzantine Empire) the Eastern throne was in reality vacant and available for usurpation. That intervention was among the most significant of the many actions that deepened the involvement of the papacy and the Christian church in the world of secular power.

The Rule of Benedict, however, contained at its heart principles that countermanded Rome's push to power. As monasteries grew in prosperity they afforded their monks more privacy and more time for scholarship and contemplation. These in turn gave birth to an increased interest in the study of friendship — Aelred of Rievaulx (1109–1167), the Cistercians' great English writer, devoted himself to the subject. Of the many books of the Bible, the Canticle of Canticles (with its origins in pagan fertility rites and frank celebration of sexual desire) became the focus of monastic attention. The highly stylized icon of Byzantine painting, explicitly intended to invoke in the viewer a sense of awe and distance from the unknowable heaven of the saints, softens into the very human Virgin of the Renaissance, whose draped gowns reveal the curves of her knees and breasts. The infant Jesus, portrayed for centuries as a tiny adult, robed and crowned in gold and holding a scepter, is transformed into a laughing child sometimes shown suckling at his mother's breast. The scenes of his death on the cross begin to show features contorted in very human agony.

Women begin to appear on the public stage as figures of some considerable power, both political and spiritual. This is the era of Eleanor of Aquitaine, Joan of Arc, Hildegaard of Bingen, Julian of Norwich. Barely two centuries after the all-male *Song of Roland*, the troubadour poets of the twelfth century would celebrate the love of women, and though that love is idealized, nonetheless real, living women are restored to the public imagination. The most powerful monasteries, though all male, were manifestly communal institutions. Increasingly they concerned themselves with adoration of the Virgin Mary and the human aspects of her divine son, until the veneration of Mary as Virgin Queen challenged the very superiority of the male, triune God. Bernard's sermons on the Canticle of Canticles provided a religious correlative to the troubadour romances. Both emphasized the significance of particular, personal emotion, whether love of God or of another human being.

This emergence of the individual and the increase in visibility of women are as complex phenomena as any in history and are intertwined with the resurgence of a new version of Manichaeism, the cult to which Augustine adhered in his formative years. As medieval Manichaeans, the Cathars of southern France held two shockingly unorthodox beliefs: First, the body constituted a pollution of the spirit. Women shared the burden equally with men but (through ascetic practices including celibacy) were equally capable of shedding its burdens to be counted among the "Perfect," meaning those who had transcended the evils of the material world. Second, all bodily appetites were equally evil. If anything, intentionally procreative sex was more evil than sodomy or adultery, since pregnancy and birth only perpetuated human bondage to the flesh.

Coincident with the rise of Catharism, the courts of southern France allowed women to inherit property and to retain their titles even after the deaths of their husbands or the annulments of their marriages. Under this system adultery took on a high gloss of illicit allure, imbuing certain women with great power, since only they could know for certain the patrimony of the children to whom they gave birth. The court of Eleanor of Aquitaine was among the most famous in its celebration of what came to be known as courtly love — flirtation and sex subject to the discipline of a highly ritualized *courtoisie* (thus our word *courtesy*). Women remained vassals of men, but with the cooperation of genealogy and circumstance a few could and did exert enormous power that contributed to a revolution in attitudes toward sexual desire and its attendant emotions.

At the same time, the First Crusade (1095–1099) reopened western Europe to the Byzantine Empire. There the cult of the Virgin was flourishing, and women had not been so emphatically excluded from the public realm as had been the case following the collapse of the Roman Empire in the West. That this First Crusade was led by the Provençal count Raymond of Toulouse was surely an important factor in the introduction of the Virgin cult to southern France.

These historical forces brought about an explosive growth in the cult of the Virgin, of which the Cistercians were the chief monastic flowering. They dedicated themselves to her, wore white in honor of her purity, named their abbeys after her various honorifics (for example, Our Lady of Gethsemani), and took the Salve Regina as their signature hymn.

⁂

A hundred or two hundred people who agree to join in collective labor, yielding all profit to a common cause, are a powerful force. Multiply that by the whole of Europe and one begins to grasp how powerful monasteries were in shaping medieval life. Benedictine monasticism became the cornerstone on which medieval civilization was built. The Rule governed vast enterprises of learning, labor, and worship, each of which might include several hundred monks, boys instructed in the monastery school, a town dependent on the monastery, and large tracts of land worked by serfs. Their ascendancy shows that it is possible to motivate people to sacrifice almost all for the sake of an ideal, even as the same history gives ample evidence of corruption and greed on a vast scale. Because these monasteries were conceived as organs of the Christian state, in almost all cases the state reserved the right to appoint abbots, with appointments given to youngest sons of the nobility or to reward allies. Often the appointee was not a monk. The injection of state politics into religious life led to predictable results, in which the abbeys became pawns, generating wealth for their feudal overlords and for the coffers of Rome.

In 910 C.E., possibly the greatest of the medieval Benedictine monasteries was founded at Cluny in Burgundy. Along with other smaller centers, Cluny gave shape to the Benedictine model that persists today, characterized by close attention to ritual, an emphasis on study and learning, charitable undertakings, a commitment to the contemplative life, and quiet accommodation made for the occasional hermit.

The next several centuries saw the rise and fall of several monastic reform movements, all of which shared at their heart the intention of restoring the purity and simplicity of Benedict's Rule. The struggle was often between those who sought sumptuous palaces for the worship of the Lord and those who saw such extravagances as contrary to Jesus' message and an invitation to corruption. Even as the Benedictine houses were at the height of their influence, a movement arose that sought an even simpler and more austere practice. It gave birth to a number of orders still in existence, but its great expression came about in the Cistercian reform, founded in 1098. It emphasized solitude, poverty, manual labor, and alignment of the power of the church with the serfs against their feudal overlords. The Cistercian movement swept Europe, under the leadership of the charismatic preacher Bernard.

The ascendancy of Bernard's monasticism lasted perhaps a century, with medieval monasticism in general and Cistercian monasticism in particular reaching their peaks around 1200. In the character of Bernard one sees the contradictions that undermine any sweeping generalizations, bad

or good, about the history of the medieval church. He was the chief proponent of the Second Crusade, and though he was often reasonable, relative
to other warmongers of the day, he was also famously eloquent and bears
significant responsibility for fanning enthusiasm for that disastrous undertaking. At the same time he preached repeatedly on the Canticle of Canticles, that sensual tribute to love. His blending of asceticism, piety, and intellectual rigor with the passionate tenor of the age was key to developing
what monastic historian Richard Southern describes as "that union of
learning and high spirituality with popular forms and impulses that meets
us everywhere in the eleventh and twelfth centuries."

As the medieval Church grew in power it could not afford to ignore the
Cathars of southern France, especially as they dwelt in the very heart of
Western Christendom and controlled some of its most desirable properties.
At the beginning of the thirteenth century Pope Innocent III authorized
the Albigensian Crusade, the first organized, church-sponsored campaign
against heretics. The crusade against the Albigensians employed the especially brutal violence that seems to characterize religious wars; tens of
thousands of inhabitants of the Provençal city of Albi and its surrounding
countryside were murdered. The Inquisition arose in the aftermath of this
internal crusade, as the Roman Church sought to root out any remaining
heretics and to terrorize the general population. The traveler in southern France can today tour the astonishing Cathedral of Ste. Cécile in Albi,
less a church than a fortress constructed as an enduring reminder to the
Albigensians of the power of the church and the bloody fate of religious
dissidents.

In the end the Virgin cult survived, shorn of the frank sensuality that
had characterized the first flowering of troubadour lyrics. As had been the
case with the hermit monks of the fourth century, monastic institutions
served as a vehicle to defuse unruly and iconoclastic rebels, as Benedictine
and Cistercian monasteries preserved and enhanced the Virgin cult while
emphasizing her qualities of chastity, submission, and humility. Thus this
most powerful of female images was enlisted to support the medieval patriarchy, but not before she firmly and irrevocably established the place of
women in the spiritual imagination. The threads of her veneration would
be woven into human consciousness, eventually to provide a background
for the emergence of women as equals of men in the design and execution
of the great human tapestry.

It would be centuries before women achieved a modicum of parity with their male counterparts, but in this medieval ascendancy of the Virgin their station began a slow improvement which has continued, albeit in fits and starts, to the present. Richard Southern attributes no small part of this transformation to the Cistercians, ancestors of the Gethsemani Trappists, who along with the Benedictines emphasized veneration of the Virgin. "It was the Cistercians," Southern writes, "who were the chief agents in turning the thin stream of compassion and tenderness which comes from the eleventh century into the flood which . . . obliterated the traces of an older severity and reticence."

*

As a critical aspect of the Roman Church's accumulation of power, a series of medieval church councils gradually codified and institutionalized the sacraments. Rites that had once been performed in houses or on the steps of the church by the congregants themselves were moved inside and declared invalid unless executed by the Vatican's representative, in the form of the regional bishop or the village priest.

At a time when the kings and queens of Europe were often blood relatives and legitimate children preferred as the inheritors of power and property, the Roman Church became the sole authority for granting or withholding permission for cousins to marry, for legitimizing bastards, and for annulling barren or politically inconvenient couplings. Finally in 1139 the Second Lateran Council declared all marriages of priests null and void, thereby eliminating any possibility of inheritors' claims against church properties. The authority of Rome stood triumphant and unchallenged. Not until the Reformation, more than three hundred years later, would the clergy seriously entertain arguments for a married priesthood or bishops not subject to Rome.

The wealth generated by monasteries and the imposition of celibacy on the priesthood brought power and prosperity to the medieval church on a scale not seen since the glory days of the Roman Empire. At the same time, the celibacy requirement encouraged a knowing contempt for the institution and its culture of hypocrisy, which cast a shadow in which lies could be concealed. Across the following centuries Rome would become obsessed with temporal power, achieving its zenith in the courts of the high Renaissance, of which the grandeur of St. Peter's is an entirely adequate symbol.

Monasteries participated in this secularization of spirituality, to the point where they became symbols of church intrigue, power, and corruption. Many followed a cycle with stages of fervor, austerity, prosperity, corruption, and reform — Gethsemani's Trappists are descendants of the last great reform, instituted in the seventeenth century. But by the time of the French Revolution monasteries would be targets of the fury of the oppressed. Where once serfs had flocked to monasteries as their allies against the nobility, now they sacked and burned institutions they perceived as having been built on their backs.

The mystery of the workings of God, or Time, or History: yes, the French Revolution slaughtered all those monks, but who can doubt that the Terror (and, earlier in England, the seizure of monastic properties under Henry VIII) did Western monasticism the greatest possible favor, by removing it from the realm of secular politics? And once removed from power, monks lost favor in the sight of the Vatican as well, so that now they exist in an ecclesiastical backwater, free to explore an authentically Christian life.

⁂

Does the seeker focus on the role of the Cistercians in restoring to cultivation vast areas of western Europe that with the decay of the Roman Empire had reverted to forest and marsh, or should we concentrate on their greedy monopoly on the medieval market in wool? Do we emphasize the great Cistercian abbot Bernard's sermons on the Canticle of Canticles, in praise of love, or emphasize his preaching of the disastrous Second Crusade? Should we remember that in those years of political, social, and economic turmoil that followed the collapse of Rome, the institution of the church, whatever its foibles, preserved and promulgated Jesus' philosophy, or should we focus on the brutality of the Roman Church in suppressing the Albigensians and instituting the Inquisition? The seeker of corruption and greed will have no trouble unearthing it in monastic history, even as the pious will find stories of saints. For the purposes of my journey I was more interested in the implications of the Rule itself, in the discipline and promise of what in his last words Merton called "total inner transformation." *Stabilitas, conversatio morum suorum, oboedientia* — what could they mean, to me, to us?

19

A Member of the Community: Abbey of Gethsemani

BACK IN KENTUCKY, preparing for another stay at Gethsemani, I sat with my mother on the family patio, a jigsaw puzzle of flagstones Father had hauled from the creek, with the help of us kids and the monks. That August Sunday morning I asked if we were going to church. Mother considered a moment, then said, "I think I'm too pooped. I cleaned the altars — that was my church." Raised by Southern women, I understood the subtext of her response: at eighty-three, she would not have many more such mornings with her children; she was making her choices.

And so we sat, I in the Adirondack chair, she in the swing, wearing her coffee-stained nightgown, lime-green mules dangling from her feet. "Once Father Gettelfinger asked me, 'If you believed in reincarnation, what would you want to come back as?' And I told him, 'A cardinal in a tree!'"

"The Buddhists would say that's a lower form of life," I said.

She considered this a moment. "Well, that's okay with me. We all believe we're something special but we're just dots on the earth. If I have a heaven, it's on this earth. I see so many beautiful things, like the flowers and the birds and the good in people. If that's not heaven I don't know what is. And hell is some of the people I have to deal with . . ." She laughed. "I don't guess I'll be rated among the theologians and popes and all that. Father said, 'When you're dead, you're dead. That's it.' But he was fickle. . . . One of the monks said to me, 'When I saw how your family lived, to me that was true Christianity.' The monks coming around influenced the knowledge and thinking of our kids because it was so different from what the rest of the kids around here heard."

And I was the beneficiary of those visits, even as with bitterness I thought of another truth, that of the abused men and women and their pressing need to enter history, to have their stories told.

⁂

In the months since my last visit I'd heard that Sister Maricela had been sent abroad to a Trappistine monastery, but then I encountered her at Gethsemani's front desk, wearing her habit, greeting retreatants. But over the next several days I saw that she no longer attended the offices. One monk told me the community had asked her to refrain from participating; another said she'd chosen to stay away because she felt uncomfortable attending. I was reluctant to speak to her — I would have to ask why she had returned, and yet I couldn't imagine any answer she could comfortably give to me, an outsider.

⁂

Once again I was assigned to the cheese room, where I spent the morning standing at a hot machine, shrink-wrapping each individual wedge of cheese in plastic. My job was to place the wedges in the machine, then inspect them after the operation to ensure they were properly sealed. Some joking and conversation — the middle-aged novice across from me declared he was going to change his name from Robert to . . . another monk interjected, "Bob!" Robert shook his head. "Too hard to spell." A lay worker turned off a noisy fan. "Now you can hear yourself think," he said. Another monk chimed in, "Not much to listen to." "Send those boxes over to Brother Fenton," someone called, followed by a moment of rich silence as the caller realized his mistake and the older men present remembered the first Brother Fintan, long dead. I wondered at the easy invocation of both the name and the honorific.

My partner in shrink-wrapping was a layperson, hired to help at busy seasons, who was much interested in my reasons for being at the monastery, in my writing, in telling me the stories of both of his wives and his several children, in asking if I would read his poetry . . . all that time with the Buddhists was having its effect: I found myself longing for the luxury of silence, which, in the face of the repetitive work, seemed more a blessing than a burden.

Despite its enclosure wall, the monastery was not separated from the world but a microcosm of it. A population explosion in the 1950s, the replacement of small farming with a more lucrative mail-order business that centered on mind-numbing assembly-line work, chaos in the 1960s leading to disillusionment and flight, housecleaning in the 1970s followed by the prosperity of the 1980s and 1990s, leading to financial security but also a crisis of faith — the monastery history might as easily describe the history of the nation, or of the developed world.

But what do we do with the leisure time brought to us, courtesy of financial security? Watch television, jet-ski, pollute, pray, drink, meditate, sleep? When I asked Brother Alfred how the monks used their afternoons, he shrugged. "Who knows?" At some point during those mornings of shrink-wrapping cheese, I remembered the holy and tender little services in the kitchens of the Zen Center, in which we presented doll-size portions of the morning's work to the Buddha. As we straggled away from our minia-ture assembly line, I thought of the irony of the evolution of Benedict's concept of the sacredness of work into a culture that mechanizes labor for efficiency and hates it all the while.

*

This morning's reading: from an encyclical of Pope John XXIII that cau-tions against "a dangerous activism" and extols a life of prayer. What, then, is prayer? What power words have! As much as I once felt resistance to making the sign of the cross, I still felt resistance to that word, antithesis of rational thought and discourse.

What would it have meant to Augustine, dedicated rationalist, cham-pion rhetorician, to pray — to silence his brilliant reason and yield himself to the discipline of intuition, to the Spirit, to God?

Outside in the chilly morning: the moon, a perfect half pie floating in the dark.

*

If you don't believe in the efficacy of vicarious prayer, it's absurd to be here. But I believe in the reality of the mystical body — the unity of all people in Christ. And some people of that body are called to a life of prayer. Monks are specialists in prayer — I hate the phrase "power-house of prayer," but maybe it's just the phrase I dislike.

— Father Alan Gilmore

*

Many of those who pray do so for the most elemental reasons: in exchange for our mumbled supplications we want something in return (food on the table, say, or peace of mind). It's useless to approach human institu-tions (whether governmental or corporate) and so we turn to superstition: maybe if I light candles to the Virgin, I'll find a job, and in any case it can't hurt.

But taken by itself this is a reductive and simplistic understanding of the impulse that motivates people to pray. Though all that wanting does exist, so vividly in evidence at the healing shrine of Lourdes or on *The 700 Club* — quid pro quo, prayers in exchange for some material improvement — most people who pray are also motivated by that same urge that has taken me walking in the California foothills in April: we are touched by the beauty of the world, and the sense that we are part of some larger ineffable, inexpressible, incomprehensible mystery.

Truth resides in paradox, and I hold this one close to the heart: being is at once comprehensible in the elegant formulas of science and philosophy and at the same time incomprehensible in its conception, creation, and execution. And so we have art, in this case expressed in ritual — perhaps in the form of a procession to the Virgin, perhaps as a bow before a statue of the Buddha. The common people may not have the words to express this motivation, but we witness and participate anyway for a whole panoply of reasons. Among these are peer pressure and the expectation of a good party to follow, yes, but also the desire to feel awe, to participate in a public ceremony that acknowledges and respects (and in many cases, physically incorporates) the impulse to bow down and adore, whether the vehicle for this adoration is a cheaply rendered icon or a marvelously branching tree. I am arrogant if I perceive myself as superior to or in sole possession of these emotions and responsibilities.

☙

The countryside was in drought, and Father Matthew scheduled a mass to pray for rain. He raced through it with efficiency and dispatch. The Gospel reading told the story of the miracle at Cana, where Jesus performs his first miracle to please his mother — although, good Jewish mother that she is, she doesn't really offer him a choice.

☙

A prominent American Buddhist editor offered the opinion that celibacy is the defining characteristic of a true monastery, but in our consumer culture I consider the commitment to poverty at least as dramatic. The vow to dispense with individual property transforms the monk into (depending on how you look at it) a true member or a true ward of the community. At the time of solemn vows Benedictine monks must dispense with all their property; they are specifically prohibited from giving it to the monastery, though they may donate it to the church or to a relative with instructions that it be given to the church. Courts have upheld the legality of the vow, meaning that a monk who changes his or her mind may not retrieve the lost funds. The internal courts of the Roman Church have held that monasteries have an obligation to help members who decide to return to the outside world, meaning that in voting to accept a candidate for final vows, the community takes on a lifelong obligation.

"Slavery to our own desires is a terrific burden." The words of Merton's letter are much present to me, on this my third Gethsemani stay. I am a citizen of a nation of servants to our individual desires, subject to an economics that energetically promotes the notion that the best of all possible worlds will emerge from everyone, everywhere, being a servant to her or his own desires. Set against this capitalist utopia is the concept of the vow, which implies the submission of one's desires to a larger ideal, whether it be monasticism, marriage, right conduct toward one's partners and friends, the completion of a book, or the raising of a child.

Contemporary society has solved this contradiction neatly enough — we have made it easy to break vows, as well we ought. Why should I turn to an institution to hold me to my promises?

Because over time I am not strong enough to keep them without help.

But in the absence of the iron hand of orthodoxy, how and where do I find the strength to keep faith with my vows?

In my background I never saw a vow work — in my family the pain of watching two people try to make it work when one of them wasn't honoring it was terrible. The test in my book now is tinnitis — I hear ringing in my ears in a way that is all but unbearable. I loved choir but I had to leave because of it, and it was very painful because you don't tell people about your business here and so you're judged by those who see you're not in choir but have no idea why. My vows are really being tested now because I'm completely isolated.

— Brother Joshua Brands

I consider the vows all myths. The vow of stability is not a vow to a place as much as to a way of life. A vow of poverty — are you kidding? I'm as poor as a church mouse but I'm living on a 2,500-acre estate.

— Brother Columban Weber

Retreatants who come here are looking for an island of stability that
they don't have on the outside and that they think the church has lost. I
hear retreatants talking about temporary vocations. I never bought
that. We take a vow of conversion of manners, stability — we're rooted
here — you can't take a vow of stability for only a few weeks. It's incon-
sistent with a God who doesn't change that he would give you a temporary vocation and anyway, how do you know how long is temporary?
All we know is that God calls and we answer — in faith we accept.

— Brother Simeon Malone

Brother Paul and I took an afternoon walk to Basil's Lake, named for Basil
Higdon, the monk whose heart had been broken, or so I'd been told, by the
arrival of mechanization. At the lake we stood neck-deep in pent-up spring
water and talked church politics and matters of faith, while minnows nib-
bled at my privates and horseflies buzzed around my head.

I asked him if the community discussed, collectively or individually,
the broader issues implied by Maricela's uncertain status or the Roman
Church's stance on gays and lesbians. "Not really," he replied. "Ten years
ago when we'd get together for a party, we'd discuss liturgy. Now we talk
about computer software." (Once again the monastery acts as microcosm:
ten years ago when I gathered with friends, we spoke of culture and ideas;
now we talk about computer software.)

The move to the right in the Roman Church disturbs him, Paul said,
but in facing it he focuses on the subject of today's Gospel reading: the
Transfiguration, in which Jesus appeared to his apostles as divine, convers-
ing with Moses and Elijah. "That's where faith lies," he said. "That's where I
place my faith. Asian religions talk about nonduality, but that's how I see
the Incarnation — no separation between flesh and soul."

"But Christianity has at its heart the understanding of body and soul
as divided and distinct," I said. "That all started with Plato, proposing that
the body is an impediment to the soul's search for beauty."

"Well, that's what it's been brought to," he said. "But for me the heart
of Christianity is the union of the spirit and the flesh in the example of
Jesus."

He called the Sermon on the Mount "the canon within the canon,"
since it gives us the signposts for the path to virtue. "That's the only way I
know to affect the world, to be as good a Catholic as I can be and hope that

this feeds into some slow change." He glanced at the sun. "Time to head back. Vespers at 5:15."

And then we were back at the monastery, a mile walk at a pace Paul had calculated, with a monk's unerring sense of timing, to bring us to the door just as the last bells were ringing. He disappeared into the enclosure, to reemerge moments later wearing his robes.

જ

The canon within the canon:

> Blessed are the poor in spirit; the kingdom of heaven is theirs.
> Blessed are the sorrowful; they shall find consolation.
> Blessed are the gentle; they shall have the earth for their possession.
> Blessed are those who hunger and thirst to see right prevail; they
>   shall be satisfied.
> Blessed are those who show mercy; mercy shall be shown to them.
> Blessed are those whose hearts are pure; they shall see God.
> Blessed are the peacemakers; they shall be called God's children.
> Blessed are those who are persecuted in the cause of right; the
>   kingdom of heaven is theirs.

જ

The monk I call Brother Isaiah was in my face again, once more asking what would keep me from throwing in my lot with a monastic community. Though he began by focusing on celibacy, he shifted soon enough to talking about obedience, the heart of the matter.

> People don't talk about sex here because we're celibate and it's so easy to stir up passion, that vital life force. It's not a question of repressing or denying it — it's maybe wisdom. I don't hang out in bars because I'm an alcoholic. And I don't sit around pondering sex because it doesn't make my journey any easier.
>
> I think you're right when you say that our fear comes from our lack of faith. People are near to being animals — and you corner any animal where they are afraid and they'll attack. I wonder if we're in control of anything — that's the fearful thing. We like the idea of being in control, but that's one of the hard things about being a monk — you have to give up control of your life.
>
> A couple of brothers here, I wonder why they're allowed to breathe

oxygen and exhale poisonous carbon dioxide. You tell me that celibacy is a power play — I say it's just the opposite. It makes you the most vulnerable person on the face of the earth. To try to be aware of the needs of humanity — to try to be compassionate — that's a power play?

The things I cherished most — my independence and freedom — that's what I had to give up. I never cared about power or wealth, but when my independence was taken away from me I had nothing, and so I was the loneliest man on the face of the earth. But as I've stayed I've found the community to be very life-giving. This community is very accepting of individuals — they give you space to discover who you are. I know more about myself now than I knew before coming to the monastery, and the loneliness has dissipated because I've been accepted into the community, where I've been given the joy of discovering who I am.

You become free when you become convinced of the overwhelming love God has for you — that you are the most precious thing in all creation — more precious and loved than life itself. That allows you to begin to let go of your fear. If you're so precious and loved by your Creator there's no need to fear failure, not being good enough, not having a big enough dick, whatever. You don't have to fight against your brokenness and woundedness, you can accept them because God is going to take care of you.

⁂

For the last time Brother Martin, my plumber friend, courteously seated me in Dom James's old leather office chair. "Maybe I'll get some wisdom from this," I said.

"You've already got wisdom," Martin said.

Our talk circled back again to my father, how much he meant to Martin. "He helped me get my plumber's license. He started out teaching me the basics, got me to enroll in a class at the community college. Then he got me some on-the-job training. That's what made it possible for me to stay in the monastery. The life was really hard, but the brothers helped, and your father helped me find my niche."

Why didn't he do that with me? I wondered, but I knew the answers. As a white man he could be the ideal father to an African American man in a way that he could never manage with his blood son. I think he was scared of me, with my book learning and my heading into the big world, and I know I was scared of him, with his big and sometimes violent hands and big voice and quick anger. I learned from him how to drink a great deal and still appear sober, and an intolerance of hypocrisy — important lessons, though contradictory; the first rendered me suitable for society, the second made me largely unfit. Only now, years after his death and as a result of my conversations with Martin, did I understand that I learned so little from Father because, like him, I was mule-headed and impatient, when he could teach only in the presence of the student's most essential qualities — Martin's qualities, the monk's qualities — of humility and respect. I could never have learned from him just to sit and pay attention; that I had to learn from an outsider, from the Buddhists.

"I haven't ruled out the possibility that I might become a monk," I said. "I'd have to be somewhere where I had the chance of venting some of my party boy side."

"Maricela wants to be here because we have something here and she senses that," Martin said. "My Baptist brother and his wife come here and they sense it too, they love the place."

"And what is that?"

"Somebody stays here long enough and I can always see the good in them, don't you think that's true?" and for a moment he could be Blanche Hartman, urging me to seek and acknowledge each person's Buddha nature — even my father's, even my own; and I understood that these conversations with Brother Martin, these weeks at the monastery were healing old wounds, maybe the oldest wounds: between parent and child; between the institution's need to impose discipline and the individual's need to seek and live out a particular fate.

*

Another special vigil. Impossible not to be touched at some atavistic place, sitting in darkness while men sing Gregorian chant, in intercession to the goddess. "Despise not our petition, O glorious Virgin."

The readings this morning, one after the other, of stories about how the people of Israel betrayed their God, how he punished them for it, how they repented and he had mercy and vanquished their foes through miracles, how they celebrated and then betrayed him again. And so it goes, until the last reading, from the writings of Cardinal Newman: "Change must happen from within. We wait season after season for some extraordinary external event or force to change our lives, but grace, the force of change, comes about only when we open our hearts to it."

And so even grace, so often touted as the force from without, comes about only when we choose to open our hearts to it; we can't see the peacock's tail explode in shimmering color unless we've made the time to place ourselves in his presence. Newman sounds suspiciously like not Augustine but John Cassian; and in his words, grace, one of the defining aspects of Western Christianity, begins to sound Buddhist.

⁂

It was Father Kelty's week to offer petitions, which are not collectively formulated but composed each evening by the monk who offers them. Father Kelty, the thaumaturgy of the Irish coursing in his veins, lingered dramatically on his *s*'s and *l*'s ("praissssse," "llllead"). He knew the weird acoustics of the abbey church and used them to effect.

And then he startled us all by coming out with, "That the filthy rich may realize their filth."

⁂

On this visit I asked Father Kelty directly about his impressions of the relationship between homosexuality and the contemplative life, and he was forthright in his response.

> My guess is that gays always dominated the religious life because it was a viable way of living. I would think that in the Middle Ages most were gay. They didn't call it that, of course. Look at the monasteries of the Middle Ages, which were centers of art, culture, peace — I always took it for granted that most of the monks were gay.
>
> What is at issue is not sex but love. Sex can be an expression of that. We have sex everywhere now and love nowhere. When love is answered you can control the sex appetite, no problem. I'm gay and I think it's a marvelous place to be. I'm probably the only one to write it publicly — no one has suggested anything to me, it's not an issue.

Instead of *gay*, a speaker younger than Father Kelty might use the word *queer* — persons who may be homosexual or heterosexual but who define themselves as outsiders, who dwell on the margins of power. People who lack power cannot assume that the world will meet their needs and desires and so must confront and engage the tension between working to change the world even as they embrace and live within it as it is given to them.

Not all those who live at the margins of power are sexual outlaws, of course. But both Old and New Testament repeatedly make the point that outsiders have special access to faith.

> The stone that the builders rejected
> Has become the cornerstone
>
> — *Psalm 118:22*

This verse recurs with minor variations at Matthew 21:42, Mark 12:10–11, Luke 20:17, Acts 4:11, and 1 Peter 2:7. In his letter to the Ephesians (2:20–22) Paul elaborates the metaphor, naming the whole pack of outsiders, prophets and apostles, as the foundation of the church, with Jesus as the cornerstone. In the Hebrew Bible, prophets lay down the law (in every sense of that resonant phrase) to their leaders and kings; in Sophocles and Shakespeare, the seer or the fool performs the role, acting as a check on the hubris that inevitably accompanies power. The early church fathers — among them Augustine — mistrusted monastic hermits for their tendency to act as contradictions to and consciences of those in power. Those fathers advocated instead the cenobitic monasticism that came to define the contemplative practice in the West in part because communities were easier to centralize and regulate than isolated, free-thinking, free-speaking hermits.

My conversation with Father Kelty catalyzed the idea, building across my times of sitting meditation and mass, of an integral and necessary relationship between desire and faith. Desire is to love as belief is to faith: each is a means to an end; each is so easily mistaken for the end. If I seek many bed partners to make me whole, I miss the point that wholeness is only possible through love — through the complete integration of the self, until it's no longer possible even to say "I love myself." Freed from a sense of a dual self, I can then accomplish the leap to an understanding of no separation between others and me. Not coincidentally, that revelation could be seen as the crowning wisdom of contemporary biology or physics as much as religion, since they both teach that we are no more (but no less!) than sentient bundles of energy moving through the universe. I seek faith through belief, wanting that it be found in a rule or a book or doctrine, whether in religion or in science or art, when belief can only prepare the way, light the path. Faith is found in the doing, the keeping of the lamp against all odds for the traveler who comes up the mountain in the dark.

I have noticed that monks have a talent for locating the materials they need to complete the most implausible tasks. God may provide by way of a rich Catholic widow or maybe just a neighboring farmer who doesn't know what to do with all that junk in the barn. But on this particular hot August day, Paul showed up with a length of wrist-thick rope in the back of the truck and invited me to help him hang it from a limb over Basil's Lake, so that at nearly sixty years of age he can swing out and do cannonballs into the water.

We never got around to hanging the rope, but we did locate the ideal tree and then went skinny-dipping again, this time with four guys who had trooped down from Ohio to camp near the abbey, attending offices between side trips to drink beer at the Sherwood Inn as well as seeking the company and counsel of Brother Paul, whom they'd each met long before on separate retreats. After our swim they invited us to the campsite for a cookout. We talked and drank and drank and talked. They told us how growing up they'd thought of people from Kentucky as barefoot hicks with hookworm and a ready hand on the trigger. I told them how we thought of people from Ohio as effete snobs who spent all their time working and had their priorities screwed up. I resisted the impulse to point out where they'd chosen to go on vacation, whereas I still harbored childhood prejudices of Ohio as a place to get across on the way to someplace else.

We drank until late and spoke of many things — of God, and life, and death, of their difficulty in being married, my difficulty in being gay, the difficulty of the human condition, *samsara*. Why be a Christian, and what was the proper relationship between Christianity and other ways of being in the world? Somewhere in the midst of these discussions I thought of the desert fathers and yes, some mothers — how after many years, not through worldly ambition but from their devotion to the search, they acquired a reputation for wisdom. In the last century of the Roman Empire, as its far-flung web of law and order weakened, villagers turned to the local holy men (and, rarely but occasionally, women) to resolve disputes, to unburden their sorrows, to seek counsel: "Speak a word, *abba*." Looking about at this circle of men who have been brought together, I saw how our brother Paul was continuing the tradition. And if we were only five, not fifty or five hundred, this was of no consequence — virtue spreads in mysterious ways.

And yet this community bears the burdens of stoicism that one would expect of a group of men. Monks suffer in silence and — though they live in community — they often suffer alone, until their only choices seem to be leaving in sorrow or staying in bitterness.

◈

Monastic life really forces you to face yourself. I came with the purest intentions — now I'm questioning everything, my motives, my life, my reasons for being here, my faith. . . . Is this environment helping my struggle with faith? No — it must be me — but as for the community, I don't think we build. We tear down rather than help.

— Brother Joshua Brands

◈

In this our last conversation Sister Maricela and I met outside, under the vast and ancient ginkgo. While we spoke I noted how she has made a practice of avoiding pronouns in referring to God — thereby avoiding labeling God with a gender.

My image of God has changed so much that now it's a problem because it's hard for me to fit anywhere. That's a problem but at the same time it's freedom. No one can constrain me in the interior — I feel an inner freedom, which is why I'm here.

Growing up I had an image of God as judge — that's how I understood God when I entered the religious life, a God of favoritism and of course a man, and the only way to know God was through studies and through reason. And I said no, that can't be. Now I realize God is boundless, we can't define God because as soon as we define God, God is diminished.

The mystery is always, "Why am I here, and not another place?" For me that means, "Why don't I feel any attraction to a woman's community?" Will I have to leave just because I'm a woman? People at the reception desk — especially women — question why I'm there and tell me I'm going to have to go. It's like they're saying, "How come you're here and I'm not?" And I hear people saying monastic life isn't what it used to be, because a woman is around.

I said to somebody, "I see you're disturbed about my being here — that's your problem. You see me as a sex object, not as a human being." "If this is men's week, what is a sister doing here?" they ask. "For celibates, when we go on retreat, we can't deal with women around." And I say to them, "That's a problem for you, not me. How can you be free? Did you hear the Gospel about the Samaritan woman?" And this particular priest said, "Jesus didn't know what he was doing sometimes." I answered, "Jesus didn't see women as sex objects, he saw them as people with dignity."

But there are some women who say, "How nice to see you here," and I know it's from a sincere heart. These are people who see me as a human being, not as a woman in a man's monastery.

The monks here relate to me more freely now, like brothers and sisters at home, than at first. I feel that's been very positive for both me and them. I see that I'm growing, that I've moved. They see women wearing next to nothing in magazines and newspapers, and I see them looking at these, so they have these thoughts anyway. Jesus didn't say we have to live in a monastic life — it's something we've chosen. If I were around and I were offering myself, trying to be noticed, to get them to feel that I'm attractive, I could see why I should leave. But I asked them, "Has my behavior enticed you or moved you away from yourself in any way?"

I don't fully understand what the problem is other than that I am a woman. As for my future — I shall know what to be when I get there, I shall know where to go when that time comes.

♨

Maricela's continued presence at Gethsemani provided a starting place for a conversation with Timothy about the place of women and outsiders in the Roman Church. Her situation was becoming more precarious because after twenty-six years as abbot Timothy had received permission to resign and had set the date of his stepping down. I asked him about his thoughts on the future of the Roman Church as a spiritual guide.

The Church as teacher is in difficult straits. The Church has been around for two thousand years — doesn't she have some positive way of speaking to gays and lesbians? Or take medical ethics — how can we dictate norms when we don't understand the technical issues? Or birth control?

There's a movement in Latin America to form "base communities" — groups of believers who share faith with one another. Why couldn't you just choose one of these people to be your leader or priest for a few years? Rome would go bonkers at such an idea. A few months ago Rome came out with a strong document on episcopal conferences, where bishops meet and take initiatives. American bishops did a document that questioned capitalism, another on peace and war, and they're good documents. But Rome has now forbidden the bishops to speak unless what they're going to say is previously approved. These are people afraid of losing power, authority.

Since the word emerged in his comments, I seized upon the excuse to ask, "How would you define faith?"

My own thought is that the faith life is enkindled through a small group of people. I think of faith as a horizon that you're called to — that the reality of who you are is the God — how you share in the life of God himself.

Ultimately our faith life is a lot simpler than what the hierarchy is interested in. Facing questions of life and death, I don't find faith gives much consolation. The question remains: what is this life about? You do receive an encouragement from those who have gone before, but I can't say that reading the latest Vatican document on extreme unction is consoling.

One point of difficulty is the church's unwillingness to acknowledge its past history. It's always felt it has this special role. In my boyhood we were taught that the church had all the answers:

> Catholic, Catholic, ring the bell,
> Protestant, Protestant, go to hell.

I don't abide by that any more. But the power in American Catholicism is with the money, and the money is conservative and willing to throw its weight around to achieve what it wants, to push the church in the direction of their choosing.

The time had come, in this my last conversation with Timothy as abbot, to raise the most difficult of questions. I told him of the conversation I'd had at the nearby tavern, where the neighboring woman had told me of her abuse by one of the monks. "You don't have to respond," I said. "But I'd rather offer you the chance to confront the story instead of being blindsided by reading about it." A look of pain crossed his face, but he took up the question.

Over the years we've had four cases of people claiming to be molested. In three cases the perpetrator was dead and so we had no legal respon-

sibility, but we settled with the claimant from a sense of moral responsibility. The fourth case was a man who has a history of being troubled.
I encouraged him to find an attorney and prosecute and get it done
with, but he's refused to do that. He doesn't live locally, but the monastery has supported his family, not to pay him off but as an act of charity. He came here once with a gun intending to kill someone and pulled
it out in my office, but I took it away from him.

The last bells for midday office rang. Timothy continued his response.

In my dealings with nuns I'd heard this story so often that I'd roll my
eyes and think, "Oh, no, here it goes again." So finally I was in the
kitchen one day and encountered a local woman who works here, a
good, solid Kentucky woman, and I said, "Don't you think all this talk
of sexual abuse is being blown out of proportion?" And she blew up,
told me the history of her own family, and I realized just how much of
this there is.

I know of a prominent priest, very visible, who's always seen with a
younger man. And I didn't want to leap to any conclusions, but now
he's about to be prosecuted. What is it about the most successful
priests, ministers, psychotherapists, that this happens? [Teaching or-
ders] have an especially high incidence of it — some have had to pay a
great deal to claimants.

By now midday office was well underway. I recalled a monk at the
Gethsemani Encounter, telling me she'd never seen Timothy miss an office.
Soon he would be called upon to preside over the midday meal. I excused
myself and left.

⁂

On the morning of my last day as a member of the Gethsemani community, I took a nap after vigils and woke barely in time to make lauds — the
day's second office — and the mass that followed it. I considered sleeping
through, but (as Pascal had promised in his *Pensées*) the power of habit
drove me to pull on my clothes and descend the stairs.

I entered by the rear doors so as not to disrupt the service, sitting with
the visitors instead of among the brothers. I looked at the Midwestern
Catholics who surrounded me and thought about how these people don't
think of themselves as prejudiced or homophobic; they're just busy in their
lives, as is good and right, busy with kids and careers and keeping the pan-

try stocked with peanut butter, and they look to their leaders to provide guidance because they haven't the time to consider every moral or political issue that arises. And on this matter, the matter of my humanity, my right to participate in what the church acknowledges are among the most meaningful of human gestures — worship and sexual intercourse — their leaders tell them that God made me the way that I am, but if I act according to my nature I am (to quote the official Roman Church statement) "intrinsically evil," "morally disordered."

Well, to hell with that.

Which is not to deny the issues at the heart of the matter. East or West, we have yet to construct a morality that deals responsibly with the body; we have yet to figure out how to have pleasure responsibly; we have yet to figure out how to substitute for the discipline once imposed by nature a working discipline of our own human making, a courtesy *(courtoisie)* to govern sexual intercourse. Above all, we have yet to create a balanced and sustainable relationship between insider and outsider, the rich and the poor, men and women, those with power and those without.

In its creation of an insular community presided over by an all-powerful abbot, is monasticism a retreat from adulthood? One of the wiser women of my acquaintance drew attention to the ways in which community has historically been used to reward compliant women as well as to oppress and ostracize those who deviate from its norms. The avalanche of accusations of sexual abuse reinforces the idea of religious life as an extended childhood: men (and some women) with sexual dysfunctions retreat into the arms of the church, which then protects them and gives them implicit permission to use their power in whatever ways they wish without fear of reprisal. For my friend — a woman whose life had often been constrained by community responsibilities and traditional roles — the declaration of the primacy of individual identity represents maturity, a declaration of selfhood, the seizing of one's destiny apart from the confining restrictions of family, church, and society.

My time among the monks led me to a different conclusion. I came to see the declaration of the primacy of individual identity not as an indicator of psychological maturity but as a kind of late adolescence, through which one must pass en route to true adulthood. Each of us must first realize the significance of our individual destinies — but then we must move on, to graduate to a recognition of the importance of our various communities.

We must define our needs and desires apart from community — but then return to live as fully realized women and men within the cooperative whole. The community then faces the challenge of how to embrace dissenters in ways that respect and utilize their differences. The message of Jesus, at least in part, is that the disdained, the poor, and the oppressed are vital to the health of the whole community. The most insulated among us encounters daily evidence of ways in which culture and society are enriched by these outsiders' perspectives; it is no exaggeration to say that the greatness of the American empire owes itself to the repeated introduction of unconventional ways of seeing and being in the world, and its willingness to embrace and assimilate those iconoclastic cultures and subcultures.

This is the great American challenge: to grow up, to preserve our commitment to individual rights and freedoms while recognizing that these exist within a framework of responsibilities to the whole. In this the Christian churches in general and monastic communities in particular ought and could provide models of maturity; instead they too often remain resolutely stuck in psychological, sexual, and emotional adolescence.

As a latecomer I entered from the back of the abbey church. *Why am I doing this? Why am I here?* — the questions well up now as ever. I thought back to the words of the Japanese Zen priest: "Zen cannot start without doubt. Each Zen master starts his life with great doubt, not a simple or objective or conscious question such as 'What is it?' but instead a greater, all-encompassing doubt. . . . So the Zen monk always teaches the importance of 'doubtness.'"

As the Gethsemani mass proceeded, I recalled Brother Paul's words: "That's how I see the Incarnation — no separation between flesh and soul . . . for me the heart of Christianity is the union of the spirit and the flesh in the example of Jesus."

And words of Norman Fischer: "A fully developed imagination enables us to live in a world that's ennobling without dwelling in some fantasyland. For a Buddhist, enlightenment is the development of the faculty of the imaginative vision that enables us to see the world in a transfigured way. That's what the Catholic mass is about, right?"

In that moment, courtesy of a Japanese Zen priest, a Trappist monk, and a Jewish American Zen abbot, all those hours in my parish church presented themselves to me in a new and brilliant light, as my first encounter with the power and necessity and purposelessness of art.

The mass: I enter the Gethsemani abbey church, high and long and narrow, whitewashed brick, plain as an empty hand whose lines direct my eyes forward to the dais, on which sit two vertical blocks of black granite topped by a horizontal black slab, lit from above by a single spotlight. Behind this altar stands the starkest of thrones: six flat planes (a back, a seat, two arms, two armrests) of polished oak. To either side: ranks of monks, robed and cowled.

I have entered the theater of faith. The setting prepares me for blood sacrifice; what I get is art. It is 1,998 years into the Christian era, thousands of years into the era of self-consciousness, and we are here to bear witness to the triumph of the imagination, the great human achievement: the acting out of mystery in metaphor instead of in fact. Transubstantiation: the bread becomes flesh, the wine becomes blood, we eat the flesh and drink the blood and so reenact the violent heart of the mystery of being.

To teach literal transubstantiation as the focal point of this genuine miracle is to take the narrowest point of view on the greatest work of ongoing performance art Western civilization has conceived. It is to collude with secularism in assigning the miraculous to the past, when in fact the spark of the divine resides in the present imagination, in the leap of faith required to conceive and achieve science, art, the Christian mass. That facility and faculty of imagination are the genuine and continuing miracle, which organized religion so often quashes as antithetical to the ends of institutional power. That leap of imagination leads to compassion, the understanding of our common gift and our common fate, and evil thrives in its absence. Like all great theater, the mass transports the audience to a time outside of time, to the place where time is open to eternity, to the authentic experience of God, who is no great gray-bearded guy in the sky but who rests in my heart and must be sought there in silence and stillness and solitude.

On my last morning at Gethsemani I accomplished an imaginative leap, to see consciousness as evolving from those first monks hiding out in the hills and caves of India through Plato, who understood unity with the whole of being as the soul's aspiration and goal. We move from the era of prophets who ascribe the mystery of being to external agents (gods and demons) to prophets (Buddha, Jesus) who direct us to the sacred place within. We move from an era when the acknowledgment of mystery demanded blood sacrifice to an era in which we are clever enough to substitute bread and wine and understand it as the real thing. The quality we draw upon to accomplish this extraordinary imaginative leap — this act of confidence in our human right and responsibility to shape the terms of our encounter with the divine, as well as confidence in the greater order in which our search takes place — we give the name of faith.

Standing in the Gethsemani church, here and now I was witnessing a miracle, in whose presence I had once searched my heart and found only anger. As I asked myself the old question, *How do I lay this anger down?*, I heard Brother Martin speaking at my ear: "And then the Holy Spirit whispers in my ear what trash this is and I give it up. You can't go to communion with anger in your heart."

If I am to be brought to faith, it will be through the body.

I stood and joined the line of sleepy retreatants filing forward. I did not understand how or why; instead I submitted to impulse, to intuition, to the desire to expound the dharma in this body, if only for the time it took to cup my hands and receive the host and place it on my tongue and swallow.

The Word becomes flesh, and dwells among us.

20

FACING EAST FROM CALIFORNIA'S SHORES

What we have to be is what we are.

— THOMAS MERTON, Calcutta, India, October 1968

BEGINNING WITH the later prophets, in a remarkable transformation mapped out in the books of religious historian Mircea Eliade, the Jews began to see history not as round but as linear. Previous peoples, including the Jews, had understood time as circular or round, in the way still characteristic of Eastern religions and philosophies. In this "round" interpretation, history is an endless recycling of birth, life, death, and rebirth, the unending loop that Buddhists label *samsara*.

In contrast, the later Jewish prophets began to perceive history as leading to an end point. A messiah comes to deliver the chosen people from their suffering; shortly afterward, the world ends in apocalypse. The damned are damned, the chosen people are saved, end of story, end of history. Time ceases to exist for everyone and everything, the good and the bad, the birds as well as the humans as well as the microbes. History became not a circle but an arrow, and the Jews (and by process of inheritance, Christians and Muslims) saw themselves at its tip.

Who can say why those later prophets came to this revolutionary belief? Perhaps it was the outcome of the Jewish defeat, enslavement, and exile in Babylon, circumstances so desperate that they gave birth to the messianic vision . . . but circular or linear, time and the flesh are all we can know with certainty, and the monastic schedule is a means of sanctifying the second by organizing the first.

Daily Schedule, Abbey of Gethsemani

3:15 A.M. vigils
4:15 breakfast available

5:45 (6:45 Sunday) lauds
7:15 Sundays: chapter meeting
7:30 terce (the "third hour"; 10:20 Sunday)
12:15 P.M. sext ("sixth hour")
12:30 dinner
2:15 none ("ninth hour")
5:30 vespers
6:00 supper
7:30 (Sunday includes benediction) compline

Winter Schedule, Tassajara Zen Mountain Center

3:50 A.M. wake-up bell
4:20 zazen (sitting meditation)
4:55 kinhin (walking meditation)
5:05 zazen
5:40 long kinhin
6:00 zazen
6:30 kinhin
6:40 zazen
7:10 service
7:40 breakfast
9:10 study
10:45 break
11:10 zazen
11:50 service
noon: lunch
1:40 P.M. work meeting, work assignments
4:15 baths, exercise
5:50 evening service
6:00 dinner
7:30 zazen
8:10 kinhin
8:20 zazen
8:50 chanting of refuges
9:30 firewatch/lights out

After only a few days of living these schedules, I began to understand how they transform day and night into a kind of lived meditation. Time loses its longer-term significance — Wednesday, Saturday, Tuesday become indistinguishable — and submits instead to a larger order. "Strike the evening *han* at the time when the lines on one's hand are no longer visible when the hand is held at arm's length," reads a command from Dōgen's instructions to his monks. After years of living by this discipline, the body constructs a cumulative memory that predates clocks, taking its authority from the sun and moon and stars — that is, from creation, or (the name this journey has brought me to embrace) God.

How is it possible to triumph over time? Even the durable arts, with the printed word among the most enduring, are ephemera when confronted with the reality of geologic, much less interstellar, time. "In the face of time, life is always at stake," writes Eudora Welty, a truth that we spend most of our time avoiding, when, courtesy of the contemplatives, Christian and Buddhist, I understand now that the real, liberating freedom lies in its embrace. Only those who do not fear death are free.

ॐ

This is the attraction and utility of monasticism, Eastern or Western — it is like art — in a very real sense it *is* art, the hours of life shaped to an ideal, never achieved but always present as a place to which to aspire. Like art it must be an end unto itself; its beauty and its truth arise from the impulse to create, that is, to declare our participation in the Godhead, for — if we are to believe the opening pages of Genesis — it is through the act of creation that God is made known. Monasticism is about making time sacred, removing from it any possibility of a price. And this is because monasticism and monastic time trace themselves not to the linear time of the later prophets and the book of Revelation but to the round time that came before. Monastic time is feminine time — the monastic space is an essentially feminine space — anyone who troubles to spend even a weekend at a monastery will perceive this at some subconscious place, though at Christian monasteries more tangible evidence abounds in the current and historical predominance of images of the Virgin — or, as the women of my family have taught me to name her, the Holy Mother. As institutions dedicated to a round, feminine culture, monasteries give the community priority over the individual.

In contrast, Protestantism asserted its commitment to masculine, linear time — our concept of the primacy of individual rights and individual achievement owes much to Protestant cultures. Tellingly, Protestantism does not comfortably accommodate monasticism, with the exception of those Anglican monasteries explicitly seeking to restore some of the values and institutions rejected at the time of the Reformation. In our individual-oriented culture, many of us now live removed from the passage of time in nature, conducting our lives in interior spaces where we gauge the passage of time by the watch and the clock — it's no accident that with the industrial revolution, clocks replaced crosses as the crowning ornaments of our tallest buildings.

Surrounded these days by evidence that neither the planet nor the human race can support six-billion-plus assertions of individual priorities, we feel the ancient tug toward community. Monasteries are overflowing with retreatants, if not vocations, because they offer a refuge from the cultural obsession with masculine, linear time, in which individual achievement takes precedence over all other considerations and in which everything, most particularly time itself, is quantified and measured, usually for the purposes of being bought and sold.

At a panel discussing the explosion of Buddhist references in popular culture, a prominent New York graphic designer posed this question: "In a culture where every image or idea can and will be used for commerce, how can anything remain sacred?" And if nothing sacred remains, why not lie and steal? When we're barraged with messages equating personal worth with material wealth, when the poorest poor can buy a gun, what I find astonishing is not that America has so much violence but that it has so little — testimony both to some elemental longing for virtue and to our willingness to fund a police state as the price of prosperity. Meanwhile, fundamentalist movements grow here and abroad, as people seek to find or restore value to lives that corporate capitalism perceives as another resource to be exploited, exhausted, and trashed. How can we, the prosperous and educated, abandon our involvement with those institutions that provide the great majority of the poor and uneducated with their primary community experience of beauty and meaning?

I left the place where history had put me because I understood my life as a line, or rather an arrow, launched into a future over which I had control. I would go to college, where I would learn to make the right decisions at the right times, say the right things at the right moments, work my way up the ladder of success (another linear progression). And now in midlife I see how life can be yielding as much as struggling, that the love and companionship found at hand is as rich as that found afar, and that the limits of family and creed against which I have rebelled can be foundations, beginnings as well as ends. This I learned from the monks.

"What is the theme of practice?" Norman Fischer asks the unheated Tassajara yurt packed with scholars. "Everyday suchness." And what is this "suchness"? "Things are just as they are, each thing has its own integrity free of self. There is no self, no judgment. Whether we see a cloud, listen to the stream, have a thought or sit zazen, the goal is to be present to that moment, to pay attention to what a miracle it is to be in the body."

And so how did we come to leave that present place behind, to enter instead the complex world of digital watches and cell phones and video cameras recording our every moment? The answer is as complex as memory and surely involves the intersection between consciousness and the technologies it developed — clocks and watches, along with elaborate means of recording history: writing instruments, surfaces on which to write, and means of distributing the written word. Today we devise ever more complex ways of "capturing" the moment, though we know that no moment can be fixed. *Everything changes.*

Even so, as I came to understand Buddhism and Christianity more fully, I began to perceive a brilliance and an evolution in the Judeo-Christian conception of linear time. As acknowledged by Buddhists from Asia and America, from the Dalai Lama to Norman Fischer, the great gift of the West lies in its coupling of action with ritual and doctrine. The notion of linear time leading to the Last Judgment developed hand in hand with the growing conception of a religion based on personal responsibility as defined in law and containing an element of conscious commitment to the community of humanity, not just to clan and tribe but also to strangers. These concepts of social activism and responsibility to strangers are all but absent from traditional Buddhism.

> There's a new Christian mysticism growing, born of contact with Asia, that gives new importance to the body. This is the wisdom of the East. Our bodies have a way of knowing far beyond our minds. This is our problem in the West: how can we know with our whole being? In the body you find spirituality. From the time of the Enlightenment we've had only reason — Western theology was divorced from mysticism, with the result that the divine has been kept separate from us, when in

fact it has to be totally incarnated — it has to be realized in the body. If you don't find it in your own incarnation, you don't find it. We manifest our spirituality through our bodies, the human form. Zazen, centering prayer — call it what you wish, it's a way to awaken to that which cannot be named, to awaken to our own inner mystery. It's prayer with the whole body, incorporating going beyond the mental to knowing with the whole body.

What the West has to offer: social concern, social outreach. The East can be concerned only with the interior and not realize the call to manifest that in the human community. Contemplation has to be manifested in service. The essence of all is the development of compassionate awareness. If you develop that, you have true service. Your spiritual practice is always for all beings, never just for yourself. When you no longer have any fixed self and are completely open to everything, that is when you're transformed to an awareness of spontaneous compassion.

— Brother Anthony Distefano

Christianity merged stories and rituals from the Jews with the philosophical ideals of the Greeks and expressed them all through the astonishing metaphor of the Incarnation. The Creator chooses the most humiliating of deaths so as to convince us of the reality that the divine lives within each of us, that death really is an illusion, that time is meaningless in the face of a forthright embrace of the reality of life, *this* life, enduring and eternal. "*Samsara* truly is nirvana — this world of suffering is in fact the world of paradise. *Samsara* is nirvana misunderstood, if we could only see it," Norman Fischer said. "The point of meditation practice is to let go of our deception." My mother expressed the same idea in more ordinary words: "If I have a heaven it's on this earth."

Can I disengage from the great masculine adventure of linear time, with its emphasis on individual achievement, to explore a rounder, more feminine understanding of time? Can I retain the cultural commitment to individual responsibility while subsuming my particular ambitions — my desire for money, sex, power — to the needs of the larger human community? I know only that I ask these questions as a result of my time spent in monasteries, the repositories of circular time. Monastic practice presents itself as a kind of antipode to capitalism. Where capitalism concerns itself with money, monasticism offers frugality; where capitalism concerns itself with sex, monasticism offers restraint; where capitalism concerns itself with power, monasticism offers obedience. Capitalism thrives on excess; monasticism offers discipline.

This is the great contradiction between our economics and our political and spiritual aspirations: capitalism excels in offering choice, but liberty fulfills itself not in choice but in discipline. Life is like water — it takes the shape of the vessel into which it's poured; remove the vessel and it's lost. We are seeking vessels into which to pour the chaos of life; we are seeking models of discipline.

Not that contemporary culture offers no such models. Corporate capitalism offers the considerable discipline of making money, and the discipline of military life is still available to young people (excluding homosexuals unwilling to lie). But both corporate and military disciplines rely on what William James called "the need of crushing weaker peoples," whether they are the assemblers of silicon chips in the Philippines or the strawberry pickers of California or the leftists of Grenada.

In his award-winning book *Guns, Germs, and Steel*, UCLA physiologist Jared Diamond has convincingly argued that diseases brought by European explorers (for example, smallpox) preceded them into the interior of the continent. Spread by pigs and other mammals, these wiped out native populations before they saw a single white person. Encountering this largely emptied continent, Europeans and their descendants pursued a mission — authorized, after all, in the Bible — to subdue and exploit. Now we have subdued and exploited the New World to its edges, but still we stand responsible to the great, ringing truth of our Declaration of Independence, a truth with its roots in the Judeo-Christian tradition and its first widespread expression in those early Christian monastic communities: that all men and women are created equal. We can seek new frontiers to exploit — the planets and the stars — or we can turn and undertake the perilous journey within, seeking the courage to name ourselves Americans and in doing so live out the responsibilities that come with the place where history has put us.

Why not fulfill our geographic and historical promise? Rather than reject the Judeo-Christian tradition or dismiss Buddhism as "a *philosophy,* not a *religion,*" let us forge our particular national character by grafting mystery onto logic, Christian mysticism onto Buddhist philosophy, the dis-

cipline of social responsibility onto the discipline of submission and acceptance, West onto East.

Let us preserve our religious institutions but mold them to that vision
in which the body is properly celebrated as integral to the expression of
faith, in which properly disciplined desire is one of many paths to that end,
in which we accord intuition its proper place as inextricable from reason as
a means of knowing and being in the world. Let us have an American
Christianity as well as an American Buddhism, each embracing elements of
the other, existing amiably with their Old World ancestors but mindfully
seeking a path founded in the egalitarian principles that gave birth to the
nation.

৯৶

In the course of my journey I have learned how the contemplative life in
the West shares roots with Buddhism, and how through the medium of
Greek philosophy that life was integrated into the fabric of the early Christian church. I learned how the impulse toward frugality and communal living espoused by those first Christians gave rise to the first Christian monasteries, which in turn evolved into the economic engine of the church and
through it, much of Europe. I learned how the monastic communities' subsequent wealth led to corruption but how they served as the primary institutional means of reintroducing the feminine into western Europe's
understanding of humanity and God. Knowing this history inspires me to
ask if we might turn back to the motivating impulse of those first philoso-
pher-monks, undertaking what William James called "the old monkish
poverty-worship," in which frugality serves as the means to discipline desire.

The Russian Orthodox scholar Paul Evdomikov sought to introduce
the spirit of monasticism into daily life. For Evdomikov, the monk was not
necessarily one who took vows and joined a monastic community, but one
who, in the words of scholar Cho Phan, "goes in search of his true identity,
of authenticity and integrity . . ." When I understand that all is holy, then I
will be a monk — not only understand but interiorize that all is holy, so
that I infuse every gesture and word with this understanding, as surely as
my life is infused with the food and water that I eat and drink. Each time
any one of us forgoes immediate gratification for some higher aspiration,
we are living, for the duration of that commitment, as a kind of monk.

Do I possess the courage to choose a frugal life? I have seen it done:
the wise ones who live a life of nonattachment, who are too busy inhabiting

today to worry about tomorrow. How does one find the courage to make that choice? The answer, surely, is through faith.

I began as a skeptic; I have been humbled by my own hubris.

*

The First Noble Truth of Buddhism is that life is suffering; at the heart of Christianity, Jesus hangs in agony on the cross. That suffering forms the central concern of our wisdom traditions should lead us not to despair but to faith — in their various ways, so different and yet so similar, the Buddha and Jesus taught that faith is the means to embrace and so to transcend suffering.

Courtesy of the Buddhists, I came to realize that faith is not at all the same as belief. Zen philosopher Alan Watts explains the difference: "Belief . . . is the insistence that the truth is what one would . . . wish it to be. . . . Faith . . . is an unreserved opening of the mind to the truth, whatever it may turn out to be. Faith has no preconceptions; it is a plunge into the unknown. Belief clings, but faith lets go . . . faith is the essential virtue of science, and likewise of any religion that is not self-deception."

Skeptic that he was, Watts contended that belief in God is antithetical to faith, because God, conceived as omnipotent power, necessarily stands between ourselves and complete letting go. But in revisiting my childhood beliefs I became aware of the role belief plays as a means to the end of faith. Usually expressed in metaphor (the burning bush, the resurrected Christ, the reincarnated essence of being), belief challenges the imagination to conceive and embrace a universe larger than what we immediately perceive. It engages a people in a collective imaginative act, one of the most powerful ways of binding us into a true community.

Which is where the trouble begins. When communities understand belief not as a means to faith but as a means to establish identity, sooner or later the guns appear. Catholic, Jew, Protestant, Sikh, Buddhist, Hindu, Muslim — these are powerful labels, easily used to identify and take up arms against the Other.

This is the challenge facing contemporary institutionalized religions if they are to be vehicles for peace rather than for dissension and violence: the teaching of belief as the map to faith, a means to the end but not to be mistaken for the real thing.

*

Once I understood the distinction between faith and belief, I assumed my challenge was to figure out how to maintain faith in the absence of belief —

to toss all that surface doctrine and retain only the faith that set it in motion. Would he be a wise man, the Buddha asks, who, having crossed a river on a raft, took up the raft and carried it with him? The wise man leaves the raft for someone else to use and continues on unencumbered. So it is with doctrine and dogma.

The problem with this formulation is that like love, faith withers in the abstract. I cannot love an idea; I cannot have faith in nothingness. Seekers may abandon the raft, as the Buddha wisely suggests; still, at some point we must turn back to the river, the source of life, which is always particular — a place, a time, a person, a community, a doctrine, a philosophy, a religion. Faith, it turns out, is built on belief (the Virgin birth, reincarnation, Aristotle's cosmology, or Galileo's, or Einstein's) and then preserved and cultivated through action. Doctrine and dogma can serve as means to faith — they introduced me to a world larger than my own perceptions and needs — but to mistake them for faith is to confuse the map with the journey. At the same time, to believe in nothing but the literal evidence of the senses is to be faithless, to lapse into the cynicism so prevalent in contemporary America. To accept this truth — that generosity undertaken with no apparent reward ultimately benefits the generous — requires the greatest act of faith, that must be sustained by some system of belief, whether religious, scientific, philosophical, artistic, or some combination of these.

And so my challenge becomes this: find the courage to live in doubt; find the courage to believe.

As it turns out, I have an advantage: I was handed the burden of belief before I had any choice in the matter; I lived among people of faith. That was a decidedly mixed blessing, and yet to know from before consciousness the silence that lives on the other side of "why?" — this is no mean gift. It is easier, surely, to find one's way back to the landscape of memory than to search for a place one has never known. Many people come of age and live in a secularized world in which they are mercifully freed of the baggage of belief — and yet in which they have never had access to religious custom or practice. For them I recall the words of Dogen ("To expound the dharma with this body is foremost") and Pascal ("Custom is our nature. Anyone who grows accustomed to faith believes it"). The mind follows the body; it has no choice because it is not apart from the body but one aspect of it. Find the ritual (Jewish? Christian? Muslim? Buddhist? Hindu?) and live it out. Or, barring that, make your own ritual, in humility and with the understanding that you are reinventing the wheel — but know that faith must be incarnate to be real.

☙

The first purpose of ritual, gesture, meditation, and prayer is to interiorize holiness — wholeness — through discipline, by calming the busy mind through a physical gesture, whether zazen or kneeling or merely closing one's eyes in a moment of contemplation. The second purpose is to engage the body in an imaginative act, to provide the vehicle through which the Idea becomes the deed, the Word becomes flesh. Through the imagination, subject to the discipline imposed by the limitations of body, we become larger than ourselves; we lose our solitude and enter into the wholeness of being; we become, in fact, divine.

Imagination lies at the heart of faith because to imagine anything better than the given is to make an effort where none is required and no immediate payoff presents itself — to imagine, for example, a world with less violence and more love. To the extent that this statement strikes my twenty-first-century ear as naive, my reaction results from my conception of history as a linear narrative. Instead, history must serve to help me formulate my own truth and live inside it — the ultimate imaginative act.

I can experience sacredness only if I create and cultivate it. The sacred and the holy are not confined to a place (a monastery) or a group (priests, monks) but inside each of us, waiting to be called forth, then acted out in faith, the name we give to the process of finding (as Norman Fischer had urged so long ago at the Gethsemani Encounter) the monk within.

☙

You may not be surprised to learn that the people from my hometown who approached me with their stories of abuse were my sisters and brothers. This is true exactly in the measure in which you acknowledge and embrace them as *your* sisters, *your* brothers — everyone's sisters, everyone's brothers, you. Which means that the genial monks who abused them are your brothers, your fathers, your husbands, your sons, your uncles, you, me. If you feel betrayal, rage, helplessness, or sorrow at this truth, then you are getting it, then you are understanding the message. You are a follower of Jesus, whether or not you name yourself Christian.

The goal of the man or woman of faith is to imagine the community of human individuals as interconnected and interdependent in a great, unified whole that transcends our apparent aloneness. Eastern religions incarnate this imaginative act in the joining of the left and right hands into a unified *gassho* or *pronam,* a gesture as central to Buddhism as the sign of the cross is to certain Christian denominations. No duality, no separation between left and right hands, between you and me, between each of us and the poor, the oppressed, the abused.

A great silence must surround this truth, hardest and most necessary to embrace.

❧

You must know really in your gut that the fact of your prayer and contemplative life engages the whole world. That's why we have the story of the abused boy in the chapel — to show that everything and everyone are connected, the way the mystics talk about the experience of the interconnectedness of everything.

— Sister Constance FitzGerald

❧

How does one keep faith in the face of evil? How does one forgive the unforgivable? Anybody can forgive the forgivable and feel virtuous about it. Whether we like it or not, the message Jesus proposes, if we take him at his word, is that we forgive the unforgivable — that we forgive those people whom we despise, those who have made us suffer unjustly, those who have profited by our suffering and yet are ignorant (or worse still, willfully blind) to the suffering they have caused.

How is anger resolved? Through forgiveness, which begins in the body. To approach the priest and take communion, in full knowledge of those centuries of abuse and torture and rejection, when reason and experience would demand that I turn my back . . . forgiveness begins in the gesture made contrary to reason, the decision to choose love when anger is so readily at hand.

❧

Faith, hope, and charity — the old catechisms named their translation into action the "corporal works of mercy," corporal (from Latin *corporalis,* "of the body") because these acts of virtue dwell in the flesh and blood, the living gesture, the here and now. Forgiveness is a discipline, a vessel in which the vinegar of anger is transformed into the wine that gladdens the heart. Practiced long enough, forgiveness defines the holy person — this is the quality that we sense that they have and for which we long: the capacity to be in the presence of anger and not get caught up in it, to be a catalyst for peace.

Before all else we must define ourselves in some place other than our wounds — to find the courage to define ourselves rather than let our wounds define us. This is the great challenge and forgiveness the means through which it is accomplished. Faith incarnates itself not in beliefs but in acts; not in what I believe about God but in the moment-to-moment decisions I make in choosing how to live this day, how to be one with myself and to love and respect and forgive myself and my neighbor. In this it is a necessary condition for wisdom.

ᔑᔑ

— *John Fenton. Can you name the seven gifts of the Holy Ghost?*

— *Yes, Father Gettelfinger. Fortitude, Knowledge, Piety, Fear of the Lord, Counsel, Understanding, Wisdom.*

— *And which do you seek above all others?*

— *Wisdom, Father.*

Wisdom, I have learned, courtesy of the monks, is not a pearl to be found after constant searching but rather the search itself. It begins in an act of faith. Like faith, it is a process, not a product.

Cassian tells us that monasticism cannot be learned from a book but only through living it out; the Benedictine commitment to *stabilitas, oboedientia, conversatio morum suorum* can be a means to that end. A commitment to stability does not mean that I must live forever in the place where I was born, but that I take the trouble to learn and respect the particular characteristics and needs of the place where history has put me. A commitment to obedience does not mean blind adherence to the pronouncements of authority but devoting time and effort to cultivating, then heeding my conscience, that interior and intuitive guide that I so often ignore. A commitment to conversion of manners does not require me to sell all and retire to the desert or to refrain from sex. It requires rather that I accord the spiritual equal weight with the material, that I practice not poverty but frugality, that I recognize the power of intimacy — the power of the body — and that I inhabit that power responsibly.

A product of a sex-, money-, and power-obsessed culture, I expected that the early monastic texts would focus on celibacy as the most challenging aspect of the monastic discipline; instead they focus on the endurance of being alone. Properly understood and practiced, celibacy is less about sexuality than about entering and embracing a condition of radical loneliness. Aloneness is the first *askesis,* the foundational exercise, the entryway to the understanding of the aloneness of the soul before its fate and in that overriding fact the brotherhood and sisterhood of humankind, through God alone.

~

Can I forgive the Paris nurse who ordered me to leave my dying lover's room? Can I forgive the bishops and priests and sisters and monks and ministers of Christianity who have so often been oppressed by its institutions, and who provided me a foundation for faith constructed of guilt, recrimination, and abuse?

"If you fill your life with anger against the church, you'll waste your life," a wise priest told me. "People find it very hard to live without enemies — we have a tremendous need for enemies." Do I have the courage to live without enemies, to look within for the sources of my anger? Can I open myself to the immigrant, to the homeless, to the poor, to whom — for all my highfalutin talk — I am so cold and distant? Can I forgo wealth that has been made by abusing the poor and despoiling the land? Like the abused boy counseled by Father Chase, I have been unable to use traditional language to describe my experiences of the sublime because I associated that language with a world that had failed me. But the fault lies not in the words but in the institutions that abused them. My task — the task of all seekers — is to find a way to reclaim the language of the spiritual life.

Do I have the courage to name myself a Christian — to define and then inhabit that word? And can I find the humility to listen and learn from those who have gone before? Rendered in such particular questions, faith reveals itself as the most exacting of disciplines, which may be why women and men in search of faith have so frequently sought it in the desert, the most challenging of environments.

~

I write now from Arizona, from the deserts of the Southwest, a place where the grandeur and tragedy of the American experiment seem more immediately present than elsewhere in the nation. To write about faith I left the bustling, civilized streets of Manhattan, inspired by some intuition that has always drawn people to the desert as the searcher's landscape. Perhaps it is the juxtaposition of beauty and indifference, the ever-present evidence of the provisional nature of all things human — to go out hatless on a summer day provides an instant reminder of the frailty of human endeavor before the power of nature. There is little gentleness here — no rounded contours or leafy vales. The interior forces of the planet stand unconcealed by vegetation. Here I am in the presence of the shaping hand of God with nothing to mediate the experience. Creation presents itself as the work-in-progress that it is, amid a landscape where I am so insignificant as to be unnoticeable. When I walk these canyons with a companion, only a few miles from civilization, I speak with a hushed voice because I understand that we are in church, wrapped in the living silence of God.

⁂

At the San Francisco Zen Center, Blanche Hartman continues (with Linda Ruth Cutts) as co-abbess. Norman Fischer has retired as abbot to write and to found the Everyday Zen Foundation, devoted to bringing Zen principles into the world in a variety of private and public settings. Kōsho McCall is serving in various administrative positions at City Center, where David Basile is also on staff. Kathy Egan continues as a Zen Center member, frequently spending time in the winter sessions at Tassajara.

At the Abbey of Our Lady of Gethsemani, the monk I have called Brother Isaiah submitted his request to make his final vows and so to be permanently accepted into the Gethsemani community; he was rejected. He has returned to a secular life in a nearby city. Timothy Kelly retired as abbot to be appointed as cellarer, a position from which the abbey council removed him a few months later. After a year or so working in the dairy, he was elected procurator general, a title probably inherited from the bureaucracy of the Caesars that designates someone who resides in Rome and acts as liaison between those who are asking (in this case, the Trappists worldwide) and those who dispense (in this case, the Vatican). Maricela returned to the Trappistine community from which she had come. Brothers Joshua Brands and Anthony Distefano have left the community. Alban's health continues to be fragile, but he can still be found at the switchboard, always irreverent, always good-humored. Columbo is in residence at Gethsemani, where he seldom attends the offices. Roman lives as a hermit in the fields, where Hosanna and Hallelujah show no inclination to cooperate in carrying groceries. Matthew continues to give nightly homilies to retreatants, though his voice is weakening and he sits instead of stands. Paul is active as the poet, ascetic, and desert father of the Kentucky knobs, though the new abbot has forbidden skinny-dipping, alone or with others. Simeon remains as a cheerful stalwart of the community, turning out handsome ceramics. Alfred continues as archivist and resident critic, the theologian who knows his history. Martin has begun to show a little gray at the temples.

⁂

In my last afternoon at Green Gulch, I walked from the farm to the beach, a quick half-mile hike past the neat rows of lettuce and beans and peppers and beets, past two horses waiting patiently near the gate for the passerby stocked with a carrot *(sorry, friends),* past the clink-and-clatter of cutlery against plate at the Pelican Inn, at whose outdoor tables I've shared pitchers of good brown ale with post-hike friends. A week of teetotaling and I could taste that ale in the air, but in my time at the Zen Center branches I'd lost the habit of carrying a wallet — I had a grand total of thirty-seven cents in my pocket. I considered, then rejected the notion of wheedling the bartender into spotting me a brew.

At the beach, named for John Muir, lover of the wisdom of the trail, the sun was lowering itself into a dull gray pillow of fog. A line of steel-blue pelicans soared a foot above the water, rising with each wave, sinking into each trough, at one with the sea.

This is the seeker's longing and goal: to be as one, to be one with the One. Turn, now, and look into my heart, and know that this is true. I have sought it in sex, in the pleasure and power of penetration I have sought to be inside the Other, to have the Other inside me. I have sought it in drugs, the yielding of the "I" into the great undifferentiated whole, my body's gases and metals, base and noble, transported in the illusion that for a few hours the joy and terror of being alive and alone are replaced by the even stillness of union with the whole. I have sought it in prayer and in meditation, this being inside the Other, the Other inside me. One word names it, and that is death; not for nothing did the writers of an earlier, more thoughtful age name our orgasms little deaths; the pervasive central metaphor of Christianity and yes, Buddhism, is *dying, to be reborn.*

We are drawn toward death as surely as the rain that falls on the mountain is drawn to the sea, and this is right and just, for union in oblivion is our common destiny as citizens of the great democracy of time. But while we are alive our lot is to choose life, to reaffirm daily that human endeavor has the capacity for good and to seek to augment it, to make each day an act of faith.

✍

Walt Whitman poses the American question:

> Facing west from California's shores,
> Inquiring, tireless, seeking what is yet unfound,

I, a child, very old, over waves, toward the house of maternity, the
    land of migrations, look afar . . .
Long having wander'd since, round the earth having wander'd,
Now I face home again, very pleas'd and joyous,
(But where is what I started for so long ago?
And why is it yet unfound?)

Like all questions of any consequence, the couplet that concludes Whitman's poem cannot be answered but only addressed, and then in the quieting of the busy mind so as to listen to the stillness of the heart.

Whitman and Ralph Waldo Emerson were the prophets of the nation's infancy, enabling us to learn self-respect and (in Emerson's famous wording) self-reliance. Now we are in need of a prophet to teach us how to merge self-reliance with an understanding of our connectedness to each other, to the rest of the world, and to what the monks, Christian and Buddhist, have taught me to name as God.

Heinrich Zimmer, the German who in the first decades of the twentieth century introduced the art and culture of India to the West, describes the place to which Westerners might aspire in addressing the question Whitman poses. Zimmer relates the Jewish theologian Martin Buber's retelling of the story of Rabbi Eisek, son of Rabbi Jekel, who lived in the ghetto in Cracow, "unbroken in his faith through years of tribulation, a pious servant of the Lord."

> One night, he had a dream; the dream enjoined him to proceed afar to the Bohemian capital Prague, where he should discover a hidden treasure buried beneath the principal bridge leading to the castle of the Bohemian kings. The rabbi was surprised, and put off his going. But the dream recurred twice. After the third call, the rabbi bravely girded his loins and set forth on the quest.
>
> Arriving at the city of his destiny, Rabbi Eisik discovered sentries at the bridge, and these guarded it day and night; so that he did not venture to dig. He only returned every morning and loitered around until dusk, looking at the bridge, watching the sentries, studying unostentatiously the masonry and the soil. At length the captain of the guards, struck by the old man's persistence, approached, and gently inquired whether he had lost something or perhaps was waiting for someone to arrive. Rabbi Eisik recounted, simply and confidently, the dream that he'd had, and the officer stood back and laughed.

"Really, you poor fellow," the captain said. "Have you worn out your shoes wandering all this way only because of a dream? What sensible person would trust a dream? Why look, if I had been one to go trusting dreams, I should this very minute be doing just the opposite. I should have made just such a pilgrimage as this silly one of yours, only in the opposite direction, but no doubt with the same result. Let me tell you my dream."

He was a sympathetic officer, for all his fierce mustache, and the rabbi felt his heart warm to him. "I dreamt of a voice," said the Bohemian, Christian officer of the guard, "and it spoke to me of Cracow, commanding me to go thither and to search there for a great treasure in the house of a Jewish rabbi whose name would be Eisik son of Jekel. The treasure was to have been discovered buried in the dirty corner behind the stove. Eisik son of Jekel!" the captain laughed again, with brilliant eyes. "Fancy going to Cracow and pulling down the walls of every house in the ghetto, where half of the men are called Eisik and the other half Jekel. Eisik son of Jekel, indeed!" And he laughed and laughed again at the wonderful joke.

The unostentatious rabbi listened eagerly, and then, having bowed deeply and thanked his stranger-friend, he hurried straightway back to his distant home, dug in the neglected corner of his house, and discovered the treasure, which put an end to all his misery. With a portion of the money he erected a prayerhouse that bears his name to this day.

Now the real treasure, to end our misery and trials, is never far away; it is not to be sought in any distant region; it lies buried in the innermost recess of our own home, that is to say, our own being. And it lies behind the stove, the life-and-warmth-giving center of the structure of our existence, our heart of hearts — if we could only dig. But there is the odd and persistent fact that it is only after a faithful journey to a distant region, a foreign country, a strange land, that the meaning of the inner voice that is to guide our quest can be revealed to us. And together with this odd and persistent fact there goes another, namely, that the one who reveals to us the meaning of our cryptic inner message must be a stranger, of another creed and a foreign race.

Perhaps I have always been a man of faith, though I required a journey to a distant region and encounters with strangers of another creed to open my eyes to the fact.

Back at Muir Beach, the fog had swallowed the sun. The chill wind off the Pacific sent me scurrying back up the path to Green Gulch; I'd forgotten not only my wallet but also my sweatshirt — I had been away from northern California too long. But once away from the beach the blue sky still held the sun's last light, and the Green Gulch creek throbbed with peepers, toads, an occasional owl hoot.

In the dying light I walked past the Green Gulch organic farm, in whose meticulously patterned fields I saw a twentieth-century equivalent to the gorgeously illuminated manuscripts of the medieval monasteries: the incarnation of love. Long after I left I was cheered by the memory of those fields and the young people who told me how the farm drew them to Buddhism before they knew anything of its practice or philosophy. Perhaps the encounter with the East via the Americanization of Buddhist principles might free us from our obsession with the great gray-bearded sky God and move us toward an understanding of God as revealed in our doing — in our acts.

As I walked up the path, the small valley fell silent. When I paused I heard behind me the dull roar and thump of the surf and in the nearer distance the creatures of the creek bed, resuming their calls.

Facing east from California's shores, I considered this fact: what power I have! My simple presence makes creatures of the world fall silent. As I walked I created for myself a circle of silence, a kind of little death, that returned to life only when I disciplined myself to stillness. In that spoor of silence I understood my power as a human being, power immediately and intuitively acknowledged by the animal world, and with that power its companion and helpmate: responsibility. Perhaps it is only by exercising that which makes us human, that which most makes us what we are — that is, our power to choose restraint, discipline, and responsibility — that we can achieve union with our world and so become truly wise.

Years into my monastic journeys, I was beginning to discover the purpose and challenge of faith: to steer me away from dogmatism (at one end of the spiritual spectrum) and cynicism (at the other) and toward an embrace of the enduring truths. Form is emptiness. God is love.

*

What would it mean to yield oneself to God's work? *Slavery to our own desires is a terrific burden.* From Christian monks I am trying to learn that the greatest force for change is simply to bear witness by living out a life of virtue as best I can, moment by moment, by little and by little. From Buddhist contemplatives I am trying to learn to accept and embrace the given, the *donné*, the place where history has put me.

I have lived divided between the hustle of the cities of the plain and the solitude of mountain vales. In my youth I longed after the model offered by Augustine — strong-willed, ambitious, self-conscious empire-builder; in my middle age I long after that offered by Cassian — gentle, self-effacing progenitor of the contemplative tradition. A case in point: to begin my research for this book, I moved to New York, as Augustine had once moved to Milan; to begin its writing I moved to the Sonoran desert of Arizona, much as Cassian retreated to Gaul.

I offer this observation by way of marveling at the mystery of one life, which accommodates such contradictory ways of being in the world. The interior journey demands only that I have faith that virtue and knowledge are their own, entirely adequate rewards and need not justify themselves as a means to money, sex, or power. Similarly, my search need not have a destination or a goal other than to live vigilantly in the place where history has put me.

In my experience that is the greatest of challenges: to subsume individual ambition to the labor of nurturing the peace-loving heart. And so in midlife I turned to meditation; and so I sought to learn to pray.

⁂

These days I meditate regularly — *religiously*, I might say with some wryness. I rise to a shower, followed by the morning kibble and, during basketball season, a quick glance at the sports page (the Kentucky heritage lives). Then I light a candle — the Virgin of Guadalupe, available for ninety-nine cents at my local supermarket, is the current favorite — and set a small alarm for twenty minutes. I perform three formal bows to the rising sun, then sit on a hard-bottomed, straight-backed chair. I keep my spine straight, my shoulders below my ears, my hands cupped at my navel, my eyes lowered but not closed, my tongue against the roof of my mouth — this last feels both natural and necessary. The Tassajara *ino* told me it helps to shut down the saliva glands, keeping the meditator from drooling on his shirt, but I imagine a more complex reason having to do with bedding down the tongue, if only for a few minutes. My mind wanders a good deal, and my body is usually the first to let me know — I notice that I've slumped or that my hands are resting in my lap, then I realize that this is because I'm thinking of how to get the kitchen mopped before the guests

arrive for dinner instead of concentrating on where I am and what I'm doing. And so I straighten my back and square my shoulders and come back
again to the breath, to the moment. I still resort to counting my breaths up
to ten and back, though often a simple word mantra presents itself: "Here /
Now," with each word corresponding to a breath in, a breath out; or, at
times of great trouble, "Strength / Courage." I have never had nor do I seek
moments of great revelation or enlightenment, but the discipline of sitting
— its *askesis* — has created over time a reservoir of calmness, a pool of
equanimity that I deplete through the day and that each morning's sitting
replenishes.

To balance the religion of silence I end the day with fifteen minutes of
reading from the religion of the Word, usually from the Bible, an exercise I
recommend if only to gain an understanding of the self-serving nature of
most of the flapdoodle that passes under the name of Christianity, how little it has to do with the Word that is its foundation. To read the Bible from
beginning to end is to witness a great labor of one human clan giving birth
to self-consciousness, as it seeks the ideals of compassion and love. The
persnickety, gossipy, vengeful God of the earliest encounters becomes the
majestic, ineffable Spirit whose praises Isaiah sings and whom the New Testament evangelist John equates with love.

And yes, I go to mass, because in it I am returned, however briefly, to
feminine time, monastic time.

> God doesn't live in time — God lives now; and during the mass for a
> few moments we step out of time into the now of God.
> — Father Matthew Kelty

Usually I receive communion. I receive in part because so few gestures
remain that bind me to the stranger, that declare that our common fate,
which is to be human, transcends distinctions of race or gender or sexuality
or economic and social class. I receive because Brother Martin said to me,
"You can't go to communion with anger in your heart," and so the act provides me with a once-a-week exercise in housecleaning, in which I am required to wrestle with my anger at the institution under whose roof I stand,
whatever its affiliation, to wrestle anew each week and be humbled by the
reality that its flaws are my flaws, its faults my faults.

But these are rational reasons to participate — reasons that might be

accepted over white wine in the academy. Really and finally I receive because I accept that a miracle transpires on the stage of each church that
makes a space for it to happen. For this is what I learned from the Buddhists: belief is the superstructure of faith, the means to the end of teaching
and disciplining the grabby self-consciousness, a means of forcing the rational mind to bow down to the fact that it is not the be-all and end-all but
resides in an order so vast that only the imagination can contain it. Belief
asked me to imagine a Virgin birth and from there to imagine the transubstantiation of bread into flesh, wine into blood, the essence of life. From
there it was only a short step to embracing the slow-motion miracle evidenced in the transubstantiation of rain on soil and sun on leaf into the
grape and then, through fermenting microbes and the cleverness of human
ingenuity, into wine.

"What to believe in, exactly, may never turn out to be half as important as the daring act of belief," writes Barbara Kingsolver. I believe because
the act requires that I become again like a child, like my nieces and neph-
ews who clamored to be read fairy tales long after they understood that
Cinderella was not going to pull up in her pumpkin coach, Rapunzel was
not going to let down her hair. Jesus tells us not to *be* little children but to
become like little children — that is, to grow up and leave behind childhood, then in our maturity to choose to return to its innocent faith in human endeavor. I believe because in doing so I accept that reality exists
beneath the surface, in the realm of the sacred. I act out that belief in Christian churches and Buddhist zendos because, flawed as these may be, they
are what is at hand; their flaws are my flaws, their virtues potentially my
virtues — if I will only dig. Everything changes, and I may influence that
change for the better — this we know to be true; ask almost any woman,
gay man, or person of color in America. I believe because doing so helps me
to strive for a deeper understanding of the wholeness of being and my part
in it. I bow before the mystery of the Incarnation because to do so is to bow
before the mystery of the vigilant imagination, that understands our common lot in all its pathos and glory and that arrives at the metaphor to contain and express both. I believe because all that is graceful and good in the
human condition arises from the disciplined imagination, including the
capacity to embrace and share our suffering and still to have faith.

I believe because, thanks to the Buddhists, I have come to understand
belief as *askesis,* a form for and discipline of the imagination that preserves
and promotes faith.

Must rationalism obviate faith? "Science without religion is lame," wrote Einstein. "Religion without science is blind." Contemporary physics is arriving at the realization that mystical, often monastic writers repeatedly present as the culminating fact of the contemplative life: the understanding that both science and art lead to mystery. Finally we can only glimpse the great unity, with an understanding increasingly supported by scientific evidence but finally sustained by a leap of faith. Immersed in and part of this great river of energy, we live every instant the precise analogue of the moment of transubstantiation in the Catholic mass, in which the divine order is at once revealed and concealed. Seen in this light, faith does not divide but unifies body and spirit, perception and miracle, science and spirituality.

The miracle of the imagination contained in and expressed through the body is so great that it can only be comprehended through metaphor. Throughout much of Western Christianity that metaphor is the act of communion: the bread stands in for the flesh, the wine stands in for the blood. Throughout much of Buddhism the metaphor is the act of sitting in silence. The Christian metaphor works primarily through the mind — although the metaphor is corporeal: I eat the bread and drink the wine. The Buddhist metaphor works primarily through the body — although the mind is what I set out to discipline. And so West and East, the unconscious miraculously creates metaphor capable of encompassing the miraculous. The Incarnation is the mystery of doing, of the Word made flesh, the Spirit become action, God is love, *philosophia*, love of wisdom. Zazen is the mystery of being, emptiness as form, form as emptiness, *philosophia*, love of wisdom.

Faith is first among the theological virtues because all virtue proceeds from it, including and especially love. Faith is the leap into the unknown, the entering into an action or a person knowing only that I will emerge changed, with no preconceptions of what that change will be. Its antonym is cynicism, born of fear. Prosperous America is a fear-filled society (consider our obsession with security, whether national or international, or in our financial, professional, emotional, and spiritual lives) because we are a faithless society. Without faith, without that willingness to embrace life, including its uncertainty and pain and mortality and mystery, the soul becomes stagnant. In choosing cynicism the soul may be the only aspect of the universe that can resist change and thus the only aspect of the universe that can really die.

Faith posits that, though we have brought ourselves to this troubled place — the world overpopulated, polluted, increasingly divided between rich and poor — we can find a way out. At the same time faith accepts that we cannot know everything, that we must humble ourselves before the great mystery and miracle of our lives. If we can bring that acceptance to science — if we can recognize science as existing on a continuum with art, if we can embrace both not as means to the accumulation of money, sex, and power but done for the sake of the love of knowledge, which is to say the love of beauty, which is to say the love of truth — we will have reason to hope.

ACKNOWLEDGMENTS

GLOSSARY

BIBLIOGRAPHY

ACKNOWLEDGMENTS

A MAN OR A WOMAN has no more precious possession than his or her story. A writer is the steward of stories, whose great responsibility is to do them justice. I am grateful to the monks and contemplatives at all the institutions I visited and to all who gave generously of their time and entrusted me with their stories. Most particularly I am grateful to the monks and contemplatives at the Trappist Abbey of Gethsemani in Kentucky and the San Francisco Zen Center, those named in this book as well as dozens of others who shared their stories and thoughts.

A host of friends and editors saved me from innumerable errors and helped with various production tasks. I offer special thanks to Shirley Abbott, Margaret Melanie Beene, Laurie Johnson Boone, Susan Brenneman, Jane Clayton, Martin Connell, Alison Hawthorne Deming, Nancy Johnson Derry, Colin Harrison, Kathryn Harrison, Elisabeth Horst, Pam Houston, Barbara Kingsolver, Karen Lamberton, Ken Lamberton, Suzanne Johnson Levonian, Jamie Marks, Roxanne Mountford, Peter Nye, Jayne Anne Phillips, David Schultenover, S.J., Kathy Seligman, Dr. Michael Steel, Columba Stewart, O.S.B., Pat Tamarin, Jason Thompson, Martha Johnson Young, and all the folks at the Institute for Ecumenical and Cultural Research but especially director Patrick Henry. I owe a particular debt of gratitude to my agent, Ellen Levine, and my editors, Eric Chinski and Pat Strachan. Much of what is good I owe to these, my faithful friends, readers, and editors; the flaws I claim as my own.

I am grateful to my colleagues and friends at the University of Arizona, whose faith became incarnate in the most tangible form: time off to write. Once again I am grateful to the staff of the MacDowell Colony, America's great monastery for artists.

My deepest thanks I reserve for my mother, Nancy Hubbard Johnson Head, the original seeker.

Portions of this book have appeared in different form in *Harper's Magazine,* the *New York Times Magazine,* and the *Virginia Quarterly Review.*

Homage to the Ancestors

I honor your spirits.
Help me find the wisdom to recognize the path and the courage to
follow it.
Help me find the courage to have faith.
Help me live within the great plan and fulfill it by leaving the world
better than it was given to me.
Thank you for making me possible.
Thank you for being my hosts.

— Composed in the kiva at Pecos Pueblo, New Mexico
November 12, 2001

Glossary

accidie (from Greek *akēdia,* "care, anxiety, grief"): Among the vices listed by the desert fathers as most dangerous to the hermit monk. Contemporary psychologists might identify it as chronic depression.

aretalogy (from Greek *aretē,* "excellence," "miracle"): A narrative of miracles performed by a god or semidivine hero, intended to offer moral example and instruction.

askesis (from Greek *askēsis,* "exercise"): In ancient Greece, the discipline of training and diet undertaken to prepare the athlete for competition or the soldier for battle; later adopted by early monks to describe their programs of fasting, prayer, and celibacy.

Benedictines: The most prominent order of Christian monks, tracing its roots to the abbey at Monte Cassino, Italy, founded by Benedict of Nursia in 529 C.E. There he implemented the Rule of Benedict, the compilation of rules, directives, principles, and admonitions that formed the foundation of Western Christian monasticism and that continue to be used to this day. Benedictines typically emphasize scholarship, study, and a careful attention to ritual.

bodhisattva (from Sanskrit, *budh,* "know" [as in *Buddha*] plus *sattva,* "reality"): In Mahayana Buddhism, an enlightened being — that is, one who has achieved nirvana — who chooses to be reborn so as to bring enlightenment to others.

cellarer: At a Christian monastery, the chief administrative officer in charge of the monastery's dealings with the secular world.

cenobitic (from Latin *coenobia,* "convent," with earlier roots in Greek *koinos,* "common," + *bios,* "life"): Describing monks who live in community, rather than as hermits.

chapter room: Each abbey is a chapter of its governing order; accordingly, its principal assembly hall is called its chapter room.

Cistercians: An offshoot of the Benedictines, founded at Cîteaux, France, in 1098 and devoted to labor (originally largely manual) and prayer.

choir monk (see *lay monk*).

desert fathers: A name generally applied to monks who lived in the deserts of

Egypt, the Sinai, Palestine, and Syria in the fourth century C.E. The name traces its roots to the *Apophthegmata Patrum* (Sayings of the Fathers), an oral tradition of pithy aphorisms and parables attributed to the best-known of these monks.

dharma (from Sanskrit *darmah,* "decree, custom"): An extraordinarily complex concept rooted in the understanding that every material object or person has a particular role or place in the scheme of existence. Harmony grows from the dutiful embrace of (rather than struggle against) that role. In Buddhism the word grew to signify the teachings and practice that collectively constitute the heart and meaning of the tradition.

dharma transmission: In Buddhism, the ceremony in which teachers recognize that their students are prepared and authorized to teach.

dukkha: The principle that humankind is born to suffering and dissatisfaction.

Eightfold Path: See page 97.

eremitic (from Greek *eremia,* "desert"): Describing the monk who lives in solitude; it shares its root with the English word *hermit.*

Four Noble Truths: See page 97.

gassho: In Zen Buddhism, the gesture of joining the hands, palms facing, while bowing the head.

han: In Zen Buddhism, a wooden plank struck to announce and mark periods of meditation.

ino: In Zen Buddhism, the temple caretaker.

karma (from Sanskrit *karman,* "action, fate"): The accumulated deeds of previous existences that collectively determine one's place in life, even as choices currently made are determining one's future.

kinhin: In Zen Buddhism, a meditation practice involving slow, deliberate walking.

koan (Japanese, *kō,* "public," + *an,* "matter, material for thought"): A paradoxical or superficially nonsensical statement employed in Zen Buddhism as a device to free the student from the constraints of rational thinking.

lay monk/choir monk: A hierarchical distinction, developed in Benedictine and Cistercian monasticism during medieval times. As Latin became the language of an educated minority, serfs (often illiterate) were taken on to perform the monastery's manual labor. Counter to the democratic principles of the Rule of Benedict — which specifies that only virtue and seniority may be used to determine hierarchy — a two-tier system gradually evolved in which as manual workers lay monks were subordinate to choir monks, who remained at the abbey and were often ordained priests. This division was officially terminated in the 1960s.

Mahayana Buddhism: An offshoot of orthodox Buddhism, developed in the first century C.E. and widespread in Asia (China, Tibet, Vietnam, Japan, Korea), which posits that a sufficiently virtuous individual may achieve nirvana in a single lifetime.

Manichaeism: A cult founded by the Persian philosopher Mani, centered on the proposition that the universe is dualist, divided between forces of light and dark, good and evil, and governed by an elect who practice esoteric rituals and claim access to secret knowledge.

mudra: Any one of a number of hand positions held during Buddhist or Hindu meditation and ritual.

nirvana: In Buddhism, a state of release from *samsara.*

office: In Christian liturgy, a prayer or series of prayers recited daily according to a prescribed schedule; also called the "hours."

okesa: In Zen Buddhism, a ceremonial robe worn by priests, sewn together from strips of cloth in a design based on ancient Buddhist robes.

rakusu: A miniature biblike *okesa* worn on the chest by Zen students to identify themselves as followers of the teachings of the Buddha.

roshi: In Zen Buddhism, an honorific meaning "venerable teacher."

samadhi (Sanskrit *samādhi,* "a placing together"): In Buddhism, the highest state of focused concentration achieved during or with the assistance of meditation.

samsara (from Sanskrit *sam,* "together," + *sarati,* "it flows"): In Buddhism and Hinduism, the eternal cycle of birth, suffering, death, and rebirth, which may be broken only through the achievement of nirvana.

sangha (Sanskrit *sam,* "together," + *han,* "to come into contact"): In Buddhism, a community (in Theravadan Buddhism, of monks) joined in collective study and practice of Buddhist principles.

satori: In Japanese Zen Buddhism, the state of transcendence sought through meditation practice; see also *nirvana.*

sesshin: Periods of extended sitting meditation, ranging in length from one day to a week.

sutras: Principles of Buddhism that as chants form the heart of ritual practice.

syncretism (Greek *syncretimos,* a federation of Cretan cities): Any synthesis of differing cultures or belief systems.

tangaryo: In Zen Buddhism, a period of sustained and intensive meditation, often lasting one week, required as a rite of passage before acceptance into a meditation community.

tanto: In a Zen Buddhist monastery, the director of spiritual practice.

tenzo: In a Zen Buddhist monastery, the chief cook.

Theravadan Buddhism: Orthodox Buddhism, in which nirvana is held to be reserved to monks and then only after many lifetimes of practice; primarily observed in southern Asia (Sri Lanka, Thailand, Burma, Cambodia).

Torah (Hebrew *tōrāh,* "direction, instruction, law"): The teachings of ancient Hebrew priests based in the first five books of the Bible (the Pentateuch) and presumed to be rooted in divine revelation.

Trappist (feminine: Trappistine): An especially strict reform of Cistercian monasticism (and therefore rooted in Benedictine monasticism) dedicated to prayer and self-mortification in the form of silence and fasting; founded at La Trappe, France, in 1664.

vinaya: The code of conduct governing Buddhist monastics.

vipassana (Pali *vipassanā,* "inward vision"): In Theravadan Buddhism, a style of meditation pioneered in Burma and Thailand and increasingly popular in the United States and Europe, in which ritual and doctrine are minimized and the emphasis is placed instead on meditation practice.

YHWH: The unspeakable, unpronounceable name of the Hebrew God. Today common usage usually adds vowels (Yahweh) to render it pronounceable.

zafu: In Zen Buddhism, the cushion on which a meditator sits.

zazen (Japanese *za,* "sitting," + *zen,* "meditation"): The practice of sitting meditation specifically intended to develop the faculties and awareness of the mind.

zendo: In Zen Buddhism, the room or temple where zazen is formally conducted.

BIBLIOGRAPHY

In the course of writing *Keeping Faith*, I read a wide variety of classical and contemporary works. I offer here a selection of those I found most valuable. "Source Readings" offer a selection of foundational works in each tradition. For those interested in situating these works and their personal search in a broader historical and philosophical context, I follow these foundational texts with a selection of scholarly works I found useful and influential. Finally, I offer a selection of readings that present an excellent general background for the reader interested in issues of philosophy or religion.

CHRISTIANITY

SOURCE READINGS
The titles published in the series *The Classics of Western Spirituality: A Library of the Great Spiritual Masters*, translated and edited by leading Judeo-Christian scholars and published by Paulist Press, provide an excellent introduction to the great works of the Western spiritual tradition. Each book includes helpful introductions and critical essays that place the work and its author in their historical context, as well as an extensive scholarly bibliography of use to those seeking to read more deeply.

The Bible: The King James translation is justifiably legendary for its musical language. For daily reading and consultation I use the more accessible Revised English Bible with the Apocrypha (Oxford University Press).

The Cistercian World: Monastic Writings of the Twelfth Century (translated and edited by Pauline Matarasso).

Concerning the City of God Against the Pagans, Augustine of Hippo (translated by Henry Bettenson): Augustine's monumental defense of Christianity against those Romans who felt that the empire had brought on its destruction by abandoning the old gods.

The Cloud of Unknowing, anonymous (edited by James Walsh, S.J.): This short work was among the most influential documents of medieval Christianity. It presents an eloquent testimonial to an apophatic understanding of God — that is, an understanding that assumes that God is beyond understanding and that any attempt to describe or label God only diminishes God's reality.

Conferences, John Cassian (selected and translated by Colm Luibheid); *The Conferences,* John Cassian (translated by Boniface Ramsey, O.P.).

Confessions, Augustine of Hippo (translated by R. S. Pine-Coffin): Required reading. The seminal document of Western self-consciousness; the original work of creative nonfiction.

The Consolations of Philosophy, Anicius Manlius Severinus Boethius: Another of the most influential premodern works. Boethius, a sixth-century nobleman unjustly imprisoned (and eventually executed), conducts a series of conversations with Lady Philosophy on the concepts of fairness, justice, and faith. Jesus is never mentioned, but the book is the classic example of the blend of Greek and Christian philosophy that provides the foundation for contemporary Western thought.

The Death of Socrates (translated by G. M. A. Grube); *Republic* (translated by Desmond Lee); *Symposium of Plato* (translated by Tom Griffith); *Thaetetus* (translated by Robin Anthony Herschel Waterfield); Plato: The British philosopher Alfred North Whitehead famously observed that after Plato all is footnote — perhaps an overstatement, but encountering Plato the observant reader comes quickly to the understanding that Christianity is Plato's philosophy overlaid with a veil of narrative and ritual. The Griffith translation of the *Symposium* deserves special praise — it revels in the frank sensuality of the original, providing a thoroughly engaging experience for any reader.

Hymns on Paradise, Ephrem the Syrian (translated by Sebastian Brock): Lovely, moving poetry by a fourth-century desert father that presumes an inherent link between material and spiritual worlds.

The Interior Castle, Teresa of Avila (translated by Kieran Kavanaugh, O.C.D., and Otilio Rodriguez, O.C.D.).

The Life of Antony and the Letter to Marcellinus, Athanasius (translated by Robert C. Gregg): The biography of a hermit monk that took the fourth-century literary world by storm and inspired Augustine to a radical transformation of his life.

The Life of the Blessed Syncletica, Pseudo-Athanasius (translated by Elizabeth Bryson Bongie): A rare portrait of a desert mother.

The Life of Moses, Gregory, Bishop of Nyssa (translated by Abraham Malherbe and Everett Ferguson).

The Life of Saint Macrina, Gregory, Bishop of Nyssa (translated by Kevin Corrigan): Working from the death of his beloved sister Macrina, Gregory transforms Plato's *Death of Socrates* into a Christian polemic.

The Life of Saint Teresa of Avila by Herself (translated by J. M. Cohen).

Meditations, Marcus Aurelius Antoninus (translated by A. S. L. Farquharson):

Among the greatest of Roman emperors, Marcus Aurelius was philosophically a Stoic. His short, judicious thoughts are superior, even in translation, to any contemporary self-help writing.

Meister Eckhart: Selected Writings (translated by Oliver Davies).

Pensées, Blaise Pascal (translated by A. J. Krailsheimer).

Philo of Alexandria: The Contemplative Life, The Giants, and Selections (translated by David Winston).

The Poems of Saint John of the Cross (Spanish and English text; translated by Kathleen Jones).

Pseudo-Dionysius: The Complete Works (translated by Colm Luibheid).

The Rule of Benedict: In Latin and English with Notes (Timothy Fry, O.S.B., editor): This work provides an indispensable, highly readable history of the rise of Benedictine monasticism along with the authoritative translation of the Rule on which it was based and commentary by leading scholars. For a thought-provoking contrast, read *The Rule of the Society of Saint John the Evangelist*, a contemporary adaptation of Benedict's Rule formulated by the brothers of the Episcopal monastery of St. John the Evangelist in Cambridge, Massachusetts. *Benedict's Dharma: Buddhists Reflect on the Rule of Saint Benedict*, edited by Patrick Henry, compiles the thoughts of four leading Buddhist scholars on Benedict's Rule.

Saint Augustine: The Trinity (translated by Stephen McKenna, C.SS.R.).

Saint Gregory the Great: Dialogues (translated by Odo John Zimmerman, O.S.B.).

Sayings of the Desert Fathers (translated by Benedicta Ward, S.L.G.).

Showings, Julian of Norwich (translated by Edmund Colledge, O.S.A., and James Walsh, S.J.): One of a number of medieval hermits who walled themselves into rooms that adjoined the town cathedral, Julian is among the most eloquent of medieval women writers.

The Wisdom of the Desert: Sayings from the Desert Fathers of the Fourth Century (translated by Thomas Merton, New Directions 1960).

HISTORY OF CHRISTIAN THOUGHT AND PRACTICE

Adam, Eve, and the Serpent, Elaine Pagels.

Alone of All Her Sex: The Myth and the Cult of the Virgin Mary, Marina Warner.

Cassian the Monk, Columba Stewart, O.S.B.: Authoritative and highly readable.

Christianity, Social Tolerance, and Homosexuality: Gay People in Western Europe from the Beginning, John Boswell.

Desire of the Everlasting Hills: The World Before and After Jesus, Thomas Cahill: An excellent, highly readable introduction to the historical landscape of Palestine at the time of Jesus.

Early Christian Thought and the Classical Tradition: Studies in Justin, Clement, and Origen, Henry Chadwick.

The Family, Sex, and Marriage in England, 1500–1800, Lawrence Stone.

The Gnostic Gospels, Elaine Pagels.

Guide to Thomas Aquinas, Josef Pieper.

Harlots of the Desert, Benedicta Ward: A useful survey of the women hermits who were contemporaries of Antony and who helped shape the eremitic tradition.

History and Thought of the Early Church, Henry Chadwick.

A History of God: The 4,000-Year Quest of Judaism, Christianity, and Islam, Karen Armstrong.

How the Irish Saved Civilization: The Untold Story of Ireland's Heroic Role from the Fall of Rome to the Rise of Medieval Europe, Thomas Cahill.

Love in the Western World, Denis de Rougemont: Dense, challenging, but unrivaled in its scholarly examination of the historical roots of the phenomenon we call romantic love.

The Love of Learning and the Desire for God: A Study of Monastic Culture, Jean Leclercq, O.S.B.

The Making of the Middle Ages, Richard Southern.

"Man at Work in the Light of History," Arnold Toynbee, from *Man at Work in God's World* (edited by G. E. DeMille).

Medieval Monasticism: Forms of Religious Life in Western Europe in the Middle Ages, C. H. Lawrence.

A Monument to Saint Jerome: Essays on Some Aspects of His Life, Works, and Influence, edited by Francis X. Murphy, C.SS.R.

The Origins of the Christian Mystical Tradition from Plato to Denys, Andrew Louth: A definitive, thorough examination. Challenging but indispensable.

The Perfect Heresy: The Revolutionary Life and Death of the Medieval Cathars, Stephen O'Shea.

Saint Augustine, Garry Wills: An easy introduction to the most fascinating of the fathers of the Roman Church.

Saint Thomas Aquinas, G. K. Chesterton.

The Story of Christianity (Volume I): The Early Church to the Dawn of the Reformation, Justo L. Gonzàlez: Provides the general reader with a comprehensive if somewhat dry overview of the history of the first millennium of Christianity.

Three Gospels, Reynolds Price: A contemporary novelist's translation and thoughtful commentary.

All the works of the great classical historian Peter Brown are strongly recommended for their presentation of impeccable scholarship in clear, readable prose. Chief among these:

Augustine of Hippo: A Biography: The definitive work.

The Body and Society: Men, Women, and Sexual Renunciation in Early Christianity: Essential for those seeking to understand Christianity's complicated relationship to the flesh.

MODERN CHRISTIANITY

The Abbey of Gethsemani: Place of Peace and Paradox; 150 Years in the Life of America's Oldest Trappist Monastery, Dianne Aprile: A well-researched history, appreciative of the institution's virtues while frankly acknowledging its flaws.

Amazing Grace, Kathleen Norris.

The American Religion: The Emergence of the Post-Christian Nation, Harold Bloom: A landmark book in detailing the evolution of the American religion from the Transcendentalists and fundamentalists of the nineteenth century to the more radical strains of the twentieth.

The Book of J, Harold Bloom.

The Brothers Karamazov, Fyodor Dostoyevsky (translated by Richard Pevear and Larissa Volokhonsky): The only novel on this list, and for good reason: the Grand Inquisitor's speech details and demolishes the duplicity of those who have used Jesus' message to acquire power and manipulate others.

By Little and By Little: The Selected Writings of Dorothy Day (edited by Robert Ellsberg): Inspirational, in the most pragmatic way; faith rendered incarnate.

The Catholic Church: A Short History, Hans Küng (translated by John Bowden): A short, readable history by one of the Roman Church's most renowned and most faithful dissidents.

The Cloister Walk, Kathleen Norris.

Dakota: A Spiritual Journey, Kathleen Norris.

De Profundis and Other Writings, Oscar Wilde: "From the depths" of the prison term that contributed to his early death, Wilde writes of the parallels between the life of Jesus and that of the artist.

The Gethsemani Encounter: A Dialogue on the Spiritual Life by Buddhist and Christian Monastics, edited by Donald W. Mitchell and James Wiseman, O.S.B.

Papal Sin, Garry Wills: The doctrine of papal infallibility demolished in an impressively persuasive book.

The Seven Mountains of Thomas Merton, Michael Mott: The authoritative biography of this Trappist thinker and writer.

Sex, Priests, and Power: Anatomy of a Crisis, Richard A. W. Sipe: A cogent and concerned analysis of the troubled relationship of the Roman Church to power and desire.

Virgin Time, Patricia Hampl. A lovely memoir of a faith journey in Italy.

Why I Am a Catholic, Garry Wills.

The works of the Trappist writer Thomas Merton deserve special mention. *The Seven Storey Mountain* is a remarkable achievement, a near-rival to Augustine's *Confessions* in its ambitious and romanticized portrayal of one man's spiritual journey. For a more hard-headed engagement with the trials and rewards of the life of the spirit, I recommend the later writings of Merton, composed when he was often in forthright conflict with Rome over its stance on issues as diverse as civil rights and the Vietnam War.

The Asian Journal of Thomas Merton.
Basic Principles of Monastic Spirituality.
The Intimate Merton (edited by Patrick Hart, O.C.S.O., and Jonathan Montaldo): Excerpts from Merton's writings chosen to reveal his psyche as much as his politics or theology.
Raids on the Unspeakable.
Seven Storey Mountain.
A Thomas Merton Reader (edited by Thomas P. McDonnell): An excellent overview of Merton's writing.
The Waters of Siloe: A history of the Cistercians by their best-known writer.
Zen and the Birds of Appetite.

BUDDHISM

SOURCE READINGS

A Buddhist Bible, edited by Dwight Goddard.
Buddhist Scriptures, selected and translated by Edward Conze.
The Narrow Road to the Deep North and Other Travel Sketches, Matsuo Bashō (translated by Noboyuki Yuasa).
Zen Flesh, Zen Bones: A Collection of Zen and Pre-Zen Writings, edited by Paul Reps.

HISTORICAL BUDDHISM

The Buddha, Michael Carrithers: A concise biography that includes a brief, clear introduction to basic Buddhist principles.
Christian and Oriental Philosophy of Art, A. K. Coomaraswamy.
How the Swans Came to the Lake: A Narrative History of Buddhism in America, Rick Fields: The authoritative history of the arrival and spread of Buddhism in the United States.
Myths and Symbols of Indian Art and Civilization, Heinrich Zimmer: A lifetime of field research and scholarship condensed into one dense but highly readable book. A superb introduction to the culture of the Indian subcontinent and thus to the historical roots of Buddhism.

CONTEMPORARY BUDDHISM

Buddhism in America, Richard Hughes Seager.
The Buddhism of Tibet, Tenzin Gyatso, the Dalai Lama XIV.
Buddhism Without Beliefs, Stephen Batchelor: A thought-provoking presentation of Buddhist principles shorn of dogma and doctrine.

Crooked Cucumber: The Life and Zen Teaching of Shunryu Suzuki, David Chadwick: The authoritative biography.

My Land and My People, Tenzin Gyatso, the Dalai Lama XIV.

The Path of the Buddha, Kenneth W. Morgan.

Shoes Outside the Door: Desire, Devotion, and Excess at San Francisco Zen Center, Michael Downing: A detailed history of the scandals surrounding the rise and fall of Richard Baker Roshi, Suzuki Roshi's successor as abbot at SFZC.

Spiritual Advice for Buddhists and Christians, Tenzin Gyatso, the Dalai Lama XIV (edited by Donald Mitchell).

Step by Step: Meditations on Wisdom and Compassion, Maha Ghosananda.

Tao: The Watercourse Way, Alan Watts: Watts is occasionally criticized for over-simplification, but his works provide possibly the most accessible and well-written introduction to Eastern thought.

Thoughts Without a Thinker, Mark Epstein.

The Three Pillars of Zen, Roshi Philip Kapleau: The classic introduction to Zen practice.

The Way of Zen, Alan Watts.

The Wisdom of Insecurity, Alan Watts.

Zen Buddhism: Selected Writings of D. T. Suzuki (edited by William Barrett).

Zen in America: Five Teachers and the Search for an American Buddhism, Helen Tworkov: An excellent profile of the personalities that shaped American Buddhism.

Zen Mind, Beginner's Mind, Shunryu Suzuki: The essential little book of Zen.

Thich Nhât Hanh: Essential Writings (edited by Robert Ellsberg).

Cultivating the Mind of Love: The Practice of Looking Deeply in the Mahayana Buddhist Tradition.

Going Home: Jesus and Buddha as Brothers.

OTHER TEXTS ON RELIGION AND SPIRITUALITY

The Chalice and the Blade: Our History, Our Future, Riane Eisler.

Encountering God, Diana Eck.

The Essential Writings of Ralph Waldo Emerson (edited by Brooks Atkinson): Emerson is *the* American preacher and prophet. To read him is to understand where we have come from and so, with close attention, to perceive where we are going.

Faith and Reason, edited by Paul Helm: A well-edited compilation of excerpts from works by the widest range of thinkers writing on possibly the oldest of dichotomies.

The Future of Religions, Paul Tillich.

Leaves of Grass, Walt Whitman: Along with Emerson, essential reading for a full understanding of the American religious and philosophical character.

The Myth of the Eternal Return, or Cosmos and History, Mircea Eliade: Together with *The Sacred and the Profane,* seminal works that establish the connection between contemporary, secular culture and prehistoric religious belief and ritual. Necessary and humbling.

The Passion of the Western Mind: Understanding the Ideas That Have Shaped Our World View, Richard Tarnas: A comprehensive, readable survey that provides a framework into which one may later fit more specialized readings.

Philosophy as a Way of Life, Philippe Hadot (edited by Arnold Davidson; translated by Michael Chase): A dense and life-changing book that demonstrates the direct connection between contemporary thought and Greek philosophy. Challenges the reader to live as a philosopher, a "lover of wisdom."

The Varieties of Religious Experience, William James: The book that introduced the English-speaking West to the notion that religious traditions should be evaluated solely on the basis of their philosophical merits as well as to the concept that humankind has an essential psychological need to have and keep faith.

When God Was a Woman, Merlin Stone.

The World's Religions, Huston Smith: The standard lay person's overview.

Zoroastrianism: Its Antiquity and Constant Vigour, Mary Boyce.

Zoroastrians: Their Religious Beliefs and Practices, Mary Boyce: An excellent overview of the religion that greatly influenced all Western religious traditions and that survives today among India's Parsi communities.